W9-BQK-409

DOSTOEVSKY

Other books by David Magarshack

Biography
STANISLAVSKY
CHEKHOV
TURGENEV
GOGOL

Criticism
CHEKHOV THE DRAMATIST
STANISLAVSKY ON THE ART OF THE STAGE

F. M. Dostoevsky. Portrait by V. Perov. 1872

DOSTOEVSKY

by DAVID MAGARSHACK

Harcourt, Brace & World, Inc. / New York

first American edition 1963

Library of Congress Catalog Card Number: 63-8102

Printed in the United States of America

All translations from the Russian have been made by David Magarshack

CONTENTS

LIST OF ILLUSTRATIONS

DOSTOEVSKY

[1]

THE GENESIS OF GENIUS

Dostoevsky has always remained an enigmatic figure to his biographers. This is partly due to his own reluctance to lift the veil from his life. But it is also to a large extent the direct result of his irreconcilable inner conflicts, for no great Russian writer has been so much at war with himself as he. This becomes particularly evident from two letters Dostoevsky wrote in reply to two women correspondents who both questioned him about the problem of a dichotomy in human nature. One of them, a painter, complained in her letter of "a dualism in her nature raised to the *n*th degree. This," she went on, "forces me to do something that I know perfectly well I should not do, and in a most compulsory way, too, as though all the circumstances conspired to make me do it. This shows itself particularly in small things. All these various feelings arising out of the dualism in my nature agitate and torment me and build such a maze round me that only the hand of an experienced psychologist like you could lead me out of it into the open. This is why I feel the need to make a full confession." Dostoevsky, who often complained of his own "insufferable" character was naturally aware of the problem and he even devised a remedy for it. "Why talk of dualism?" he wrote in his reply.[1] "It is the most ordinary trait of people's character, though not perhaps of quite ordinary people. It is something that is peculiar to human nature in general, but it is not by any means as pronounced in everyone's character as in yours. That is why I feel such a strong affinity to you; for this dualism of yours is exactly like mine, and I have had it all my life. It is a great torment, but at the same time also a great delight. It is a powerful consciousness of a great need to render an account of yourself, a consciousness of the presence in your nature of the need for a moral duty towards yourself and towards humanity at large. That is what this dualism means. If you were not so mature spiritually, if your mental development had been limited, you would not have suffered from this dualism. On the

[1] *Letters,* April 11, 1880.

contrary, it would have been replaced by great self-conceit. But this dualism is nevertheless a great torment."

Very characteristically Dostoevsky suggests two ways in which one might combat, though not wholly overcome, the disagreeable consequences of dualism. It is advice drawn from his own experience. "I know," he writes in the same letter, "that you are an artist, a painter. Let me give you a piece of advice from the heart: do not give up your art, but devote yourself more than ever to it. I know and I have heard that you are not very happy. Living in solitude and letting your memories prey on your mind, you are liable to make your life too somber. There is one refuge, one remedy: art and creative work." The second way throws an even greater light on one of the most puzzling aspects of Dostoevsky's character: the strange ambivalence of his religious beliefs, which he tried to overcome by an emotional surrender rather than a fearless analysis of its cause. "My dear Katerina Fyodorovna," he concludes his letter to the distracted artist, "do you believe in Christ and in His promises? If you do (or if you want very much to believe), then give yourself up to Him entirely and the torment of this dualism will be greatly alleviated and you will find a way out of your mental troubles, which is the main thing."

Dostoevsky's other correspondent was the wife of the principal of a secondary school in Moscow, whose private life seemed to have gone all awry. She wrote to ask him whether "an abnormal situation, an abnormal and painful relationship, can go on forever, year after year, without a way out of it. Does the way out of such a situation," she asked, "really depend entirely on the character of the people involved in it? Can a person split in two without ever wishing to make an effort to find a way out of a situation like this?"

Now Dostoevsky himself had been involved in exactly the same kind of situation with his first wife, and the answer he gave to this question illustrates to a large extent his own way of solving that kind of problem. "You have put a very difficult question to me," Dostoevsky wrote,[2] less than five months before his death. "It is a question which, alas, I can only answer in general terms. Is there a human being today who does not suffer from such a predicament? A man can, indeed, be split in two forever and, in doing so, he will, of course, suffer. If there is no hope of a solution, a good and all-reconciling solution, then one must as far as possible find it without hurting oneself or anyone else in some new and quite different activity capable of providing sustenance to the spirit and of quenching its thirst. I think that is best. Besides, your question is put in terms that are much too general. Do you realize, for instance, that I am least of all capable of answering such questions? This is because my position as a writer puts me in quite a special class as far as such questions are concerned. I always have at my disposal a ready-made activity as a writer, to which I give myself up with enthusiasm, to which I devote all

[2] *Letters*, August 16, 1880.

my efforts, all my hopes and all my joys, and I find my solution in this activity. Therefore whenever faced with such a problem I can always find a mental activity which at once transports me from painful reality into another world. Having such a solution ready at hand whenever any difficult and painful problem arises in my life, it is as though it is of no consequence, for I feel secure, and I can even afford to take a prejudiced attitude towards it, *just as I like*."

Dostoevsky does not offer the consolations of religion to his second correspondent, whom he had met in Moscow during the Pushkin celebrations in June 1880, for no doubt he knew that the religious aspect of escaping from the dilemma of dualism, which meant so much to him, would cut no ice with her.

If one turns to Dostoevsky's early childhood one cannot help being struck by the many opportunities which this fundamental trait of his character had for its development. There were, to begin with, his own attitude towards his father arising from the mystery of his father's origin, the feeling of inferiority arising from the fact that his father and his mother belonged to the two most despised classes of Russian society (the clergy and the merchant class), the difficult relationship between his father and his mother, the constant rows between his father and his mother's relations, and most of all his father's violent death at the hands of his peasants. Dostoevsky himself was perfectly well aware of the importance of the experience of childhood in the subsequent development of a man's character. Writing in 1877 in the July-August number of his *Writer's Diary* about the only visit he had paid to the estate that had once belonged to his parents and where he had spent some of the happiest years of his childhood, he declared that those years had left "a deep and strong impression" on his life. "No man," he wrote, "can live without the sacred and precious memories of his childhood. He may not think of them, but he preserves them unconsciously. Those memories may be bitter and painful, but even the suffering one has been through may afterwards turn into something sacred for the soul. Besides, man is of necessity prone to take notice of certain experiences of his past so as to be able later on to reorient himself. And the strongest and most influential memories are almost always those which are retained from one's childhood."

II

What were those "sacred and precious" memories of Dostoevsky's childhood? Unfortunately, Dostoevsky never revealed them. His reticence can perhaps be best explained by his own reluctance to throw any light on the dark recesses of his mind where so many secrets were tucked away. We have two reports of his attitude towards his childhood. The first is from Dr. Stepan Yanovsky, whom Dostoevsky had known in Petersburg in 1846. "After we had become close friends," Yanovsky records,

"Dostoevsky told me a great deal of the painful and cheerless conditions of his childhood, but always spoke with deep feeling of his mother, his sisters and his elder brother. He greatly disliked talking about his father and begged me not to ask any questions about him." The other comes from Dostoevsky's second wife. "Dostoevsky," she records, "gladly recalled his happy and tranquil childhood and spoke with warm feeling of his mother." The two statements only appear to contradict each other. In talking to Yanovsky, who obviously had heard of his father's violent death and was curious to find out what Dostoevsky would tell him about it, Dostoevsky was thinking of his father and "the painful and cheerless conditions of his childhood" for which he was responsible; in talking to his wife, Dostoevsky was thinking of his mother and "the happy and tranquil" times he had spent with her.

To Dostoevsky the memory of his father undoubtedly assumed nightmarish proportions, particularly in his later life. When he dreamed of his father, his second wife records, he knew that some misfortune was about to befall him. On January 28, 1870, while living in Dresden, Dostoevsky wrote down in his notebook the following dream he had of his father: "I saw my father (I have not dreamed of him for a long time). He pointed to my chest, under the right nipple, and said: 'There is nothing wrong with you anywhere, but here it is very bad.' I looked and indeed there seemed to be a tumor under the nipple. My father said: '*Don't strain your nerves*.' Then there was some kind of family festivity at my father's and his old mother, my grandmother, came in, and all his forebears. He was glad. From what he said to me I concluded that I was in a very bad way. I showed my chest to another doctor, who said: 'Yes, it is there. You haven't got long to live; *your days are numbered*.'

"N.B. On awakening in the morning, at twelve, I noticed on the very place on my chest which my father had pointed at a spot as large as a nut which was very painful when I touched it, just as though I had touched a bad bruise; never has anything like that happened to me before."

In the following year (on April 28, 1871) he wrote to his wife from Wiesbaden: "I dreamed of my father last night, but in so dreadful a state as he has only appeared to me twice in my life, predicting terrible misfortunes, and twice the dream has come true."

But what is interesting about the first dream is not only that his father appeared in it in his usual role as a prophet of doom, but that his father's mother, whom Dostoevsky had never known, and his "forebears," who were a figment rather than a reality, should have also appeared in it, and that his father "was glad" at their appearance. Here for the first and only time we get a glimpse into the mystery of Dostoevsky's father's origins, which must have greatly occupied his mind as a child. It was one of the agreeable delusions of the Dostoevsky family that it belonged, as Dostoevsky's younger brother Andrey declared in his reminiscences, "to one of the very ancient noble Lithuanian families which existed before 1600," but that "either because my father, having run away from his parents, had not taken with him all the documents about his origin, or for some other reasons, he had registered himself as a nobleman of the Moscow province only after having obtained the rank of Collegiate Assessor (which at that time conferred the right of hereditary nobleman). I remember," Andrey adds, "that whenever anyone asked my father why he never tried to provide legal proof of his ancient noble origin, he used to reply with a smile that he did not belong to the race of geese who saved Rome. But he did not try to obtain the necessary proofs because it would have cost too much."

More recent research into these reputedly "noble origins" merely reveals that at the beginning of the sixteenth century some descendant of a noble Tartar family was granted "part of the village of Dostoevo (near Pinsk) as a patrimony" and that his descendants assumed the family name of Dostoevsky. The name is mentioned in various official documents of the sixteenth and seventeenth centuries, some of them referring to robbers, highwaymen and murderers, but from 1655 no mention is found of any Dostoevskys. In the eighteenth century the name again crops up, but it no longer has any aristocratic connections: its bearers are priests, and, indeed, Dostoevsky's grandfather was a priest in the small town of Bratzlov in the province of Podolsk. Dostoevsky's father, Mikhail, born in 1789, was also destined for the church and, accordingly, sent to the Podolsk theological seminary.

The Russian seminaries were to become hotbeds of revolutionaries in the forties and fifties of the nineteenth century, and to Dostoevsky the word "seminarist" was to become synonymous with the most despicable kind of godless rebel; but, as his father's case shows, even at the beginning of the century the seminary bred rebellious spirits. Mikhail Dostoevsky was one of them. His son Andrey describes his rebellion in rather mild terms. "Not feeling any vocation for the priestly calling, my father left his father's house and, with the consent and blessing of his mother, joined the Moscow Medico-Surgical Academy." Mikhail joined the only medical school in Moscow at the age of twenty, on October 14, 1809. The break with his family had been so violent that he broke off all relationship with his parents and refused to discuss them with his children. In his dream Dostoevsky had tried to effect a reconciliation between Mikhail and his mother sixty years after the event—quite extraordinary evidence of how deeply he had felt this rift between his father and his father's family.

This was a strange and violent beginning to Mikhail Dostoevsky's career as a doctor, but it was entirely in agreement with his strange and violent nature. His children were terrified of his uncontrollable temper, in spite of the fact that he never beat them. This was undoubtedly the result of the inhuman flogging he himself had received at the seminary, where sparing the rod was considered an unforgivable sin. It was, indeed, so extraordinary at a time when corporal punishment was the rule not only in all State-run schools but in almost every Russian home that Dostoevsky put his father among "the progressives" of his age. "One day at the end of the seventies," Andrey records, "I happened to mention to him [*i.e.*, Dostoevsky] our childhood and our father. My brother at once grew excited and seizing my arm above the elbow (his usual habit when having a heart-to-heart talk) he said warmly: 'Why, do you realize that they were progressive people . . . and even today they would have been progressive. And how deeply attached they were to their children! Such parents we shall never be.'" And in a letter to Andrey on March 10, 1876, Dostoevsky noted another fact that made him feel well disposed towards his father. It was that "the idea of an absolute desire to make their children *better men* (in the literal and highest meaning of the word) was the fundamental idea of our father and mother, notwithstanding all sorts of deviations from it."

This was the best Dostoevsky could bring himself to say about his father at the end of his life. In 1848, towards the end of his first period as a writer, however, he felt much less inclined to say anything good about him. This is shown in the thinly disguised portrait of his father he drew in the unfinished novel *Netochka Nezvanova* in the person of Fyodor Ferapontovich (a passage he carefully expunged from the collected edition of his works). "He was not a bad man," Dostoevsky wrote, "but whether it was because someone had hurt his feelings, humiliated him and was his secret enemy or simply because he really was an excellent man, who, to his undoing, took this fact too much to heart, he was exceedingly fond of constantly expatiating to his wife and even to his little children, whom he kept in reverential awe of him, about what a good excellent man he was, what great services he had rendered to society, what enemies he had made and how little he had reaped—I am afraid I cannot remember what exactly he had reaped, but I am just expressing myself in his style. When he spoke in this fashion, he would even burst into tears and was sure to end with some highly effective pose, either throwing open his dressing gown and, holding his breast up to his unseen enemies, saying: 'Strike!' or, addressing his small children, asking them in a sternly reproachful voice what they had done to repay him for all the benefactions he had showered upon them; had they repaid him by a thorough study and the perfect pronunciation of the French language for all his sleepless nights, for all his labor, for all the blood he had shed for them, for everything, for everything? In a word, having shown off to his heart's content, Fyodor Ferapontovich proceeded to vent his spleen upon all the members of his family for the inexplicable indifference of men and society to his civic and family virtues, and every evening transformed his home into a little hell."

A more specific reference to his father and to his relationship with him occurs in Dostoevsky's letter to Baron Alexander Wrangel, his close friend in Siberia, from Semipalatinsk on March 9, 1857. Discussing Wrangel's relations with his father, Dostoevsky wrote: "I know extremely well (from experience) that unpleasantnesses of that kind are unbearable, particularly as both of you (I know that) love each other. There is a kind of everlasting misunderstanding on both sides, which the longer it lasts the more complicated it becomes. You just can't do anything about it. No explanations will restore agreement, and if they do, it will only be for a moment. There is only one remedy: separation. During the first days of separation he will grow fond of you again and he will be the first to say he was wrong about everything. Characters like your father's are a strange mixture of a most gloomy kind of suspiciousness, morbid sensitivity and generosity. Not knowing him personally, this is what I think of him, for I have known in my life exactly the same kind of relationship as yours with him."

Here are a few random extracts from the doctor's letters to his wife which may serve to illustrate the above characterization:

On July 9, 1833: "In Moscow I was met with troubles and worries. . . . Everyone is against me, no one takes any interest in me, but God will judge them for my afflictions. . . . You may have finished haymaking in Darovoye, but I am certain the hay will rot away and all because you would not listen to me. . . . Take care of yourself for my peace of mind and my happiness."

On August 6, 1833: ". . . Richter [the head doctor at the Marinsky Hospital] got the order of St. Stanislav, 2nd class, with a star, while we, of course, got nothing. That is why I did not write to you. However, this is how it always was and always will be: the sheep graze, but it is the shepherd who feeds them, shears them, and makes a profit. . . . Don't worry about me, my friend. I was expecting more, but I can wait for less!"

As for his grandiloquent posing, here is an example of it from the same letter: "I was about to exult, when the clouds gathered, there was a clap of thunder, and everything went to rack and ruin. Yes, my friend, thus our best intentions come to nothing. . . ."

The following description of the doctor was left by one of the peasants of his village of Darovoye: "He was a brute of a man. He had a black soul—that's what! One day he was walking in the garden and Fedot Petrov was plowing the field behind the garden. The master sees Fedot, but Fedot cannot see him behind the trees. 'Send Fedot to me!'—'Why didn't you take your cap off to me?' 'But I didn't see you, sir!'—He was flogged. Another peasant, Ivan the Broad, didn't see the master, neither. He was bringing in the corn from the fields in a cart. The master comes out from one side of the field, takes off his hat, says, 'Good morning, Ivan. You see, I'm the first to take my hat off to you, so—away with you to the stables!' And he too was flogged. In winter the peasants didn't know what to do: if you took your cap off to him, he started shouting: 'You're taking your caps off on purpose, you sons-of-bitches, you want to get a cold and stop working.' If you don't greet him—it's bad again. They say," the peasant concluded, "that his son, Fyodor Mikhailovich, had become a great man. I don't believe it, say what you like. It can't be that such a father should have a famous son. I don't believe it."

The doctor was murdered by his peasants in June 1839. There are several versions of how he came to be killed. Dostoevsky's daughter, Lyubov, disposes of it in a few lines: "One summer day," she writes in her reminiscences, "he drove off from Darovoye to Chermoshnya and never returned. He was later found halfway to Chermoshnya, suffocated with a cushion from his carriage. The driver disappeared together with the horses. A few more peasants disappeared at the same time. During the police investigation, the peasants testified that it was an act of vengeance."

Andrey Dostoevsky, a boy of fourteen, was at boarding school in Moscow at the time, and his account, written over forty years after the murder, contains a few additional facts. "Exasperated by something the peasants had been doing," he writes in his reminiscences, "my father lost his temper and began shouting at the peasants. One of them, more insolent than the rest, replied by shouting abuse at him, then, afraid of the consequences, cried, 'Come on, lads, let's do him in!' and at this call, all the peasants—there were about 15 of them—rushed at my father and, needless to say, killed him on the spot." Andrey hints that at the investigation the police were bribed by the peasants, though he does wonder where the peasants could have got the money from. After a post-mortem, he declares, the authorities seemed to have been satisfied that the doctor had died of a heart attack. The family, he adds, were reluctant to contest this verdict, because if the true state of affairs had been disclosed, almost the whole male population of Chermoshnya would have been sent to Siberia and his father's heirs would have faced ruin.

Dostoevsky seems to have been the first to have learned of the true circumstances of his father's death. It was he who informed his elder brother, Mikhail, about it, but, as Mikhail wrote to his Moscow relatives, "brother wrote to me vaguely about what has happened." Dostoevsky's letter has not been preserved, though it must have been more circumstantial than Mikhail suggests, for why else should Mikhail go on to express his horror at "the terrible death" of his father? "Two days in the fields," he writes. "There was perhaps rain, mud, the peasants heaping insults over his mortal remains! . . ." Dostoevsky must, therefore, have had all sorts of gruesome details of his father's death, details that caused him to have nightmares long after the event.

The full description of the doctor's murder was supplied many years later by Daniel Makarov and Andrey Savvushkin, two peasants of the village of Darovoye. "The Chermoshnya peasants," they stated, "decided to finish off the master, Mikhail Andreyevich. It was about St. Peter's Day, June 29. The master's coachman, David, agreed to help them. So they all got ready. On that day the peasants used to take the manure to the fields, but four peasants—this was what they had arranged beforehand—did not drive out into the fields. The sun was high in the sky and master asked the village headman if all the peasants had gone to work. 'No, sir,' the headman says, 'four Chermoshnya peasants have not gone to work.' 'Are they ill? Who are they?' Well, so the headman says, 'Yefimov, Mikhailov, Isayev, and Vassily Nikitin.' The master was carrying a big stick with him that day, so he pointed to it and said: 'All right, I shall cure them!' He then ordered his coachman to harness the horses to his open carriage. Well, the coachman could not hold out any more and so he said: 'Don't go, sir, something may happen to you there.' The master started shouting at him and stamping his feet: 'Don't you want me to treat them? Harness the horses at once!' So the master arrived in Chermoshnya. The peasants were standing about in the street. 'Why haven't you gone out to work?' 'We're ill, sir,' they said. 'Oh?' said the master. 'Well, in that case I'm going to cure you!' And he raised his stick. The peasants fled from him into the yard, but he ran after them. As soon as he ran into the yard, Vassily Nikitin, a tall, strong, healthy fellow, seized him from behind by the arms, but the others stood still, looking frightened. Vassily shouted to them: 'What are you standing there for? Forgotten what we'd planned to do, have you?' The peasants then rushed at the master, caught him by his private parts and twisted them. They did not beat him for fear of being heard. They unclenched the master's teeth, poured the entire contents of a bottle of spirits they had specially prepared down his throat and thrust a rag into his mouth. That's how the master got suffocated. His coachman took him away and threw him out under an oak tree—the tree is still standing there now—not far from Chermoshnya. Then, without going to Darovoye, he drove to Monagurovo for the priest. When the priest arrived, the master was still breathing, but he was already unconscious. The priest gave him absolution. He knew what had happened, of course, but kept it dark, didn't give the peasants away. Afterwards the examining magistrates from Kashira interrogated everybody, even tried to make the children talk by giving them sweets, but they failed to discover anything. Seemed to have died of a fit. He had had such fits before. . . ."

The doctor was a heavy drinker and he may have suffered from attacks of delirium tremens (dipsomania was a family weakness of the Dostoevskys—Fyodor's uncle and two brothers died of it), but the fits could also have been epileptic in origin and need not necessarily have been followed by the usual epileptic symptoms—the aura, loss of consciousness, muscular spasms, and the fugue—so graphically described by Dostoevsky in his novels. That would at least explain the hereditary epileptic taint in the Dostoevsky family. Dostoevsky's younger son, too, died of it at the age of three.

III

The doctor was thirty when he married Maria Nechaev, the eighteen-year-old daughter of a well-to-do Moscow merchant. By that time he had seen service in the army during the 1812 campaign and was still an army doctor at the time of his marriage. A year later, however, after the birth of his first son, Mikhail, on October 13, 1820, he was given a post on the staff of the Moscow Marinsky Hospital for the Poor and put in charge of the women's outpatients' department. A year later, on October 30, 1821, his second son, Fyodor, was born; after another year his eldest daughter, Varvara; two years after that, on March 15, 1825, his third son, Andrey, whose memoirs are the only firsthand evidence we have of the Dostoevsky ménage in Moscow; four years later twin daughters—Vera and Lyubov, the latter only living for a few days; two years after that, on December 13, 1831, his fourth son, Nikolai; and, finally, on July 25, 1835, his youngest daughter, Alexandra. Two years later Dostoevsky's mother died of tuberculosis.

While Dostoevsky certainly inherited some of the less amiable traits of his father's character, such as his uncontrollable temper, his quarrelsomeness, his gloomy self-absorption and his hypochondria, he owed his great sensibility as well as his sentimentality to his mother. Indeed, as has been observed by several of his biographers, his mother's letters (she spent the summers on their small estate, which she managed, and many of her letters to her husband have been preserved) abound in the same kind of diminutives and caressing terms as the letters of Makar Devushkin, the hero of Dostoevsky's first novel, *Poor People*. But it is, surely, a no less remarkable testimony to the close bond between Dostoevsky and his mother that the caressing terms she uses in her letters, such as "my angel," "my priceless treasure," "my divinity," "my eternal friend," "my life," "my incomparable darling," and such phrases as "I send you kisses without number," "I worship you more than my life," etc., are all to be found in Dostoevsky's letters too. His mother's strong influence in the shaping of Dostoevsky's character is also shown in his belief in all sorts of signs and omens, fortunetellers, saintly fools, pilgrims and holy men of one sort or another. She belonged to the most superstition-ridden class of the Russian population, was extremely religious, and was greatly upset at the slightest augury of bad luck. Andrey recounts one such incident in 1831. The doctor was about to buy the small estate of Darovoye, about a hundred miles from Moscow, and one summer day he had to go off to inspect it. "After having said good-by to mother and having kissed us all," Andrey writes, "father got into the carriage and was driven off, intending to stay away from home for almost a week. Two hours later, as we were sitting at table and having tea, we saw the small carriage drive up to our house again and father jump out of it. It seems he forgot his passport, without which he was not allowed to pass through the tollgate. . . . But on catching sight of father mother collapsed in a faint. . . . This episode," Andrey concludes, "that is, my father's sudden return, was often remembered in our house and regarded as a bad omen: that the estate we were going to buy would bring us no luck."

What was the relationship between the doctor and his wife? That it was far from ideal, we have the testimony of two peasants from their estate. Daniel Makarov declared that his master was a stern, "bad man," while his mistress was a "kindhearted woman." A peasant woman, Avdotya Spiridonovna, declared that "the old master wanted to flay our peasants alive, but she, poor darling, wept and wailed, imploring him in Christ's name not to punish them. He used to lock her up in the pantry—don't you dare to interfere with me!"[3]

The extravagant endearments with which the doctor's letters to his wife are larded were hardly expressive of genuine feeling for her. A single, quite innocuous-sounding sentence in one of his letters to her at the time of her last pregnancy brought a reply from her that disclosed the whole tragedy of their marriage, a tragedy that Dostoevsky, however young he was at the time, must have been aware of, as indeed becomes all too apparent in the relationships between husband and wife which he described at some length in his two last novels: that of Versilov and the peasant woman he eventually married and that of Fyodor Karamazov and his second wife, Alyosha's mother. "You write to me, my friend," the doctor wrote to his wife in the country on May 23, 1835, "that you are suffering from heartburn and that you are trying to get rid of it by eating sweets; God only knows why you get it, you never had it during your former pregnancies, and I advise you to send to Zaraisk for magnesia, it would help you best of all; I am sorry I sent you only a few sweets, I was afraid they might get spoiled if it rained."

Her reply is quite an astonishing revelation of the extent to which her husband's morbid suspiciousness could go. "In your last letter," she wrote, "you reproached me for my heartburn and said that I never suffered from it in my former pregnancies. My friend, on thinking it over, I can-

[3] The fact that the doctor should have refrained from flogging his children while having no scruples about flogging his peasants merely shows that he shared the prevailing view among Russian landowners, who regarded their peasants as chattels. Even his wife regarded the peasants' newborn children as she would a litter of pigs—for she could dispose of both by selling them. In a letter to her husband on May 3, 1835, Dostoevsky's mother felt the need of apologizing to her husband for distributing oats among the poor peasants of Chermoshnya. "I could not have left them without any nourishment, could I?" she wrote. The doctor's way of dealing with his peasants is best seen in the following two extracts from his letters to his wife. On May 26, 1835: "You write, incidentally, that our cow in Chermoshnya was unlucky in calving, but you don't mention the cause of it. If it was the dairy-maid's fault, you did wrong in reprimanding her a little and not flogging her as an example to the others." And on August 23, 1834: "I hear that Kharlashka, the good-for-nothing, is lazy. You must be more strict with him, and, if necessary, flog him."

not help wondering whether you are again tortured by the same unjust suspicions of my unfaithfulness which have been so disastrous to both of us. If I am not mistaken, then I swear to you, my friend, by God Himself, by heaven and earth, by my children, by all my happiness and my life, that I never was and never shall be guilty of breaking the solemn oath I gave you, my dear friend, my only one, before the holy altar on the day of our wedding! I further swear that my present pregnancy is the seventh strongest tie of our mutual love, on my part—a pure, sacred, sterling and passionate love, unchanged from the very first day of our marriage; I hope you too are satisfied with this oath, which I have never given you before, first, because I was ashamed to demean myself by an oath of my faithfulness to you after sixteen years of our union; secondly, because of your preconceived ideas you were little disposed to listen to me, let alone believe my oaths; but now I swear it, for I wish to spare your precious peace of mind. Besides, I suppose you are more likely to believe my oath now because of my present condition, for what woman would dare during her pregnancy to swear by the Lord, when any hour she might have to present herself before His terrible and just judgment? And so, whether you like to believe my oath or not, I shall put my trust in Providence which has always been my support and strengthened me in my grievous plight. Sooner or later the Lord in His mercy will hearken to my tearful prayers and comfort me in my grief, enlightening you with His sacred breath and revealing the whole unsullied purity of my soul to you. . . ."

In reply to his next letter, in which he begged her not to forget him in the "lacerated condition" of his soul, which he had never experienced before, she again referred to the fact that he had blighted her life by his fits of morbid jealousy. "You know," she wrote at the beginning of June 1835, "I have always been deeply grieved to see you in that state of great and unjustified distress, and I am particularly so now when I can imagine you looking sad and on the verge of despair, and for what reason?—because of a false idea which goodness only knows why it should have entered your head. . . . I do not doubt your love, yet, though I love you more and more with a pure and sacred trust, my love goes unseen, my feelings are not understood, I am regarded with low suspicion. . . . Meanwhile the years pass, my face grows sallow and is covered with wrinkles, the gaiety of my natural disposition is turned into mournful melancholy, and this is what I have been living for, this is the reward of my unsullied and passionate love; and if I had not been fortified by a clear conscience and the hope that I can trust in Providence, the end of my life would be lamentable indeed. . . ." And she concludes: "I do not curse you, I do not hate you, but I love and worship you and share with you, my only friend, everything I have in my heart. Forgive me, my dearest friend. I am writing on a little scrap of paper so that no one but you should read it, only I adjure you on my love not to be distressed or sorry on my account, for I have long ago submitted to my fate and got used to anything."

She had been married to him for sixteen years when she wrote that letter, time enough to sense the true tragedy of his life, the tragedy of a man who had begun life as a rebel against his environment and slowly and painfully realized that he was a failure, but who, instead of blaming himself, blamed everyone else, even her who was bearing him his last child and was already showing signs of succumbing to the illness which was to carry her off in another sixteen months. Dostoevsky, too, was beginning to sense his father's tragedy. Three years later, on October 31, 1838, he wrote to his elder brother from Petersburg. "I am sorry for poor father. What a strange character! Oh, how many misfortunes he has suffered! It is awful that there is nothing I can do to console him. But do you know? Father doesn't know the world at all: he has lived fifty years in it and has the same opinion of people he had thirty years ago. Blissful ignorance! But he is very disappointed in it—that seems to be our common destiny!"

When this letter was written the doctor had already retired and was carrying on a life of drink and debauchery on his estate. Life had indeed passed him by. And it is hardly a coincidence that even in his early works Dostoevsky deals mainly with the tragedy of people who, like his father and his uncle, sought forgetfulness in drink, people who were, or thought themselves to be, humiliated and insulted, people who put up a bold front to the world only to be crushed by its indifference and derision.

IV

Practically everything we know about Dostoevsky's early life comes from the reminiscences of his younger brother Andrey. More facts have been supplied by Dostoevsky's second wife and (less reliably) by his daughter, Lyubov. None of this material, however, is sufficient to give a picture of Dostoevsky's inner world, that is to say, of the development of his character, of the growth of his perceptive faculties, of the way he reacted as a child and as a boy to his environment and the people of that environment. We have, for instance, this graphic description by Andrey of the way the doctor gave Latin lessons to his two elder sons: "The difference between my father as a teacher and the teachers who came to our house was that with the latter the pupils sat down during the whole of the lesson, while with my father my brothers not only did not dare to sit down but did not dare even to lean on the table, although the Latin lesson often went on for a whole hour or longer. They just stood there like graven images, declining in turn: *mensa*, *mensae*, *mensae*, etc., or conjugating *amo*, *amas*, *amat*. My brothers were terribly afraid of those lessons, which always took place in the evenings, for father, for all his goodness, was extremely strict and impatient, and, above all, short-tempered. At the smallest mistake, he would get angry, lose his temper, and start shouting, calling my brothers lazy good-for-nothing blockheads. In extreme cases, which were not so frequent, however, he would even stalk out of the room without finishing the lesson, which was considered worse than any punishment."

Then there is this description by Andrey of the way his father used to take his forty winks after the midday meal. "Immediately after dinner father used to retire to the sitting room, the doors of the dining room were closed and he would lie down on the sofa for his after-dinner nap. This lasted for one and a half to two hours, and during that time absolute silence reigned in the dining room where all the family was sitting. We spoke little or in whispers, so as not to wake father. In summer, when flies were particularly numerous and fierce, my position during father's rest was even worse. Sitting on a chair beside the sofa on which he slept, I had to drive away the flies from father with a linden branch, broken off a tree in the garden every day. These one and a half or two hours were a real torment to me, for, isolated from the rest of the family, I had to spend the time in absolute silence, sitting in one place without moving. And I could expect no mercy, if, as sometimes happened, I missed a fly and let it bite the sleeper! . . ."

These after-dinner naps were not, of course, introduced for the benefit of Andrey. It can be reasonably assumed that Dostoevsky, too, had carried out this fly-swatting duty and, no doubt, he too had had to put up with his father's shouts of rage whenever he happened to fail in it.

What Dostoevsky's reactions to these outbursts of his father's were we can only guess from the advice he gave to a mother shortly before his death. "Be kind," he wrote to her on March 27, 1878, "and let your child understand that you are kind (by himself, without any prompting) and let him always remember that you have been kind to him. Then, believe me, you will have fulfilled your duty towards him all through his life, because *without wishing to influence him in any way* you have taught him that kindness is good. In that case he will remember you all his life with respect and even, perhaps, with a feeling of tenderness. And if you were ever guilty of any bad action, or at any rate any thoughtless, painful or even ridiculous action, he will *without a doubt* sooner or later forgive all your bad actions for the sake of the good ones, which he will remember. You can't do anything more for him. Besides, this is more than enough. For the memory of anything good so far as one's parents are concerned, that is, the memory of kindness, truth, honesty, compassion, the absence of a false feeling of shame and—as far as possible—of lies—all this will make a different man of him, sooner or later, be sure of that. . . ."

Dostoevsky was extremely sensitive about the suffering of children, as becomes quite obvious from the description of the maltreatment of children in *The Brothers Karamazov*. This sensitivity of his was undoubtedly the result of the *moral* suffering his father inflicted on him, the

Latin lessons being only one example of it. Dostoevsky certainly resented his father's autocratic ways more deeply than the rest of the family, for, as Andrey remarks, he was in all his actions "a real live wire," as his parents used to say. "My brother Fyodor," Andrey declares, "was very hotheaded and he used to stand up for his opinions energetically, and, generally, was rather sharp in his expressions. Whenever this happened, my father used to say, 'Oh, Fedya, learn to control yourself! Mark my words, you'll end up badly! You'll be wearing the red cap one day!'" The red cap was worn by privates, and in the reign of Nicholas I even noblemen could be pressed into the army as ordinary soldiers for the slightest misdemeanor.

"I am quoting my father's words not as a prophecy," Andrey hastens to explain, for, of course, they did come true in the case of Dostoevsky, "for a prophecy is the result of foresight, and my father could never have imagined that his children would be responsible for any misdemeanor. I quote them merely as proof of the impetuosity of my brother's character as a boy." Dostoevsky's mother's comment on his high spirits in a letter to his father was: "I am not surprised at Fedya's escapades, for we must always expect such things from him."

The cramped conditions under which they were all forced to live made the doctor's outbursts even more unbearable for his children. The apartment in which the Dostoevsky family and their servants lived was in a three-storied annex of the Marinsky Hospital and consisted of a long, dark passage and two rooms. A partition, which did not reach to the ceiling, cut off the back of the passage, which was made into a "nursery" for the two elder boys. In this dark, windowless cubbyhole Dostoevsky had to sleep with his elder brother, Mikhail, till at the age of thirteen he was sent to a boarding school. Of the two rooms of the apartment, one, known grandiloquently as the "ballroom," was quite large, with two windows looking out into the street and three windows into the courtyard. "This ballroom," Andrey records, "was our living room, where we did our lessons and had dinner and tea." The other one, the "sitting room," "our rest room," as Andrey describes it, had two windows, and, like the passage, was divided by a partition, behind which was the parents' bedroom. The kitchen was across the entrance hall. It had a huge Russian stove and bunks for the servants. Under the staircase, leading to the first-floor apartments, was a boxroom, used as a pantry. The passage and the "nursery" were painted a dark gray color, the "ballroom" a light yellow and the "sitting room" a dark blue. "Wallpapers," Andrey remarks, "had not yet come into use in those days." The apartment was heated by three large Dutch stoves with blue-edged tiles. The furniture in the "ballroom" consisted of two card tables, on which the children did their lessons, and a round dining table together with a half a dozen enormous birchwood chairs with horsehair cushions covered in green morocco. In the sitting room was an enormous sofa, a couple of easy chairs, a dining table, a chiffonier, and a bookcase. The "bedroom" had two beds and two huge chests, used as wardrobes. There were no curtains; the windows had white calico blinds.

There were no lamps in the house ("Father did not like them," Andrey remarks), and the rooms were lit by tallow candles (the more expensive wax candles were only used on solemn occasions), and late at night by the dim light of the icon lamps in the corners of the rooms. In winter the children had to spend the long evenings at home, and the flickering light of the guttering candles as well as the slanting rays of the sun as they came through the windows of the ground-floor apartment at sunset left a deep impression on Dostoevsky. Indeed, some of the most dramatic scenes in his great novels as well as in his early stories take place at sunset or in the light of a guttering candle. In *The Brothers Karamazov.* Alyosha remembers "an evening, a quiet summer evening, an open window, the slanting rays of the setting sun (it was the slanting rays that he remembered most of all), an icon in the corner of the room, a lighted lamp in front of it, and on her knees before the icon his mother . . ."—a picture that Dostoevsky himself must have seen many times. In one of his early stories, *Mr. Prokharchin,* it is a guttering tallow candle end that lights up the scene of the down-and-outs crowding round the bed of the dead miser in search of the gold hidden in his mattress; in his unfinished early novel *Netochka Nezvanova,* it is in the light of a guttering tallow candle that the panic-stricken girl watches her crazed father playing his violin over the dead body of her mother; it was in the flickering light of the candle in the lantern that Dostoevsky (as he relates in *The House of the Dead*) watched the faces of the sleeping convicts appearing and disappearing out of the darkness and bringing home to him with increasing force the sheer horror of his position; in *Notes from a Dark Cellar* it is in the light of a candle that the hero observes the effect of his tormenting speeches on the twisted face of the prostitute, who looks at him "with a half-mad, almost senseless smile"; in *Crime and Punishment* it is in the flickering light of a guttering candle that Raskolnikov first catches sight of the angry and flushed face of Mrs. Marmeladov, and it is in the same flickering light of a candle end that Sonia, the harlot, reads to Raskolnikov, the murderer, the Gospel story of the raising of Lazarus; and, again, it is in the flickering light of the candle that, in *The Devils,* Peter Verkhovensky watches the rigid and erect figure of Kirilov shortly before he shoots himself.

V

Fourteen people lived in the cramped quarters of the doctor's apartment. Dostoevsky's parents and their five children (their last two children were born after Dostoevsky and his elder brother had gone to a boarding school) and their seven servants. Dostoevsky's sister Varya usually slept on the sofa in the "sitting room," and his younger brother and sister, Andrey and Vera, slept in cots in their parents' bedroom. The nurse, Alyona Frolovna, the wet nurse (Dostoevsky's mother only breast-fed her first baby; for the rest wet nurses were engaged), and the maid slept in the dark, windowless boxroom next to the bedroom, and the four servants slept in the kitchen. The servants were: the coachman David Savelyev, who was to play such a sinister part in his master's murder, and his brother, Fyodor, caretaker and, on the rare occasions when Dostoevsky's mother had to pay a visit in town, footman (he donned a livery and a tricorn for those occasions), both of them Ukrainian serfs bought by the doctor before his marriage; the cook, Anna, also a serf acquired before the purchase of the Dostoevsky estate; and the laundrywoman, Vassilissa, a serf, who, as Andrey expressed it, "threw a shadow on the sort of life our serfs lived" by running away.

Alyona Frolovna deserves special mention not only because she was the most eccentric member of Dr. Dostoevsky's household, but also because she was the only one to stick to the family to the very end (she was living on the estate looking after the two youngest children, Nikolai and Alexandra, when the doctor was murdered). She was rather tall and very fat, "her belly hanging down almost to her knees," as Andrey writes. She was a "Moscow" citizen, as she proudly called herself, that is, a freeborn woman, and, being unmarried, was fond of describing herself as "Christ's bride." Her only weakness was snuff. Her wages were five rubles a month, but because she was never paid, the trustees of the doctor's estate had to pay her back her wages after the doctor's death. Sleeping in the cubbyhole with the wet nurse and maid, she nearly suffocated for lack of air and screamed in her sleep. "It was not really a scream," Andrey writes, "but a kind of frantic howl." When asked what had been the matter with her, she invariably replied that the house demon was strangling her. When advised by the doctor to eat less, she would reply: "I tried to, sir, but it's even worse—I dream of gypsies and I can't sleep all night." The doctor tried his sovereign remedy for all ills—bloodletting—but that did not seem to help.

Dostoevsky mentions Alyona Frolovna in an autobiographical passage in *Poor People* and he gave her name to Lisa Tushin's nurse in *The Devils*. In 1876,[4] he recalled the following incident of his childhood:

"I was only nine years old when on Easter Tuesday, about six o'clock in the afternoon, our whole family, my father and my mother, my brothers and my sisters, were sitting at the round table and, as it happened, were talking about the country and about how we would go there in the summer. Suddenly the door was flung open and in the doorway appeared our serf, Grigory Vassilyev, who had been entrusted with the management of the estate in the absence of his masters. Now, instead of

[4] *A Writer's Diary*, April.

the 'manager,' who always wore European dress and looked highly respectable, we saw a man in an old peasant coat and bast shoes. He had walked from our estate and, on entering the room, stood still without uttering a word.

" 'What's the matter?' my father cried in alarm. 'Look at him! What's the matter?'

" 'The estate's burned down, sir,' Grigory Vassilyev announced in a deep voice.

"I won't describe the scene that followed this announcement; my father and mother were not rich and had to work hard for their living—and that was the sort of Easter present they received! It turned out that everything had been burned to the ground—the peasants' cottages, the barn and the cattle sheds, even the spring seeds, some of the cattle and a peasant called Arkhip. At the first moment of panic we imagined that we were faced with complete ruin. We all fell on our knees and began to pray. My mother wept. Then suddenly our nurse, Alyona Frolovna, whom we paid a regular wage, for she was a freeborn woman, that is to say, the daughter of a Moscow artisan, went up to my mother. She had nursed and brought us all up. She was forty-five at the time, of a bright, cheerful disposition, and she used to tell us such lovely fairy tales. She had refused to take her wages for many years, saying that she did not need any money, and they were paid into the bank. By that time about five hundred rubles had accumulated there and she hoped to make use of them in her old age. And now suddenly she whispered to my mother:

" 'If you need any money, you'd better take mine. I don't mind. I don't want it.'

"My parents did not take her money. They managed somehow without it. . . ."

Dostoevsky recalled this incident of his early childhood to refute the arguments of his opponents who refused to accept his view of the Russian peasant as the sole repository of divine goodness and wisdom and, unwittingly no doubt, he distorted some of the facts. His parents bought the estate of Darovoye in the province of Tula in 1831. A year later they bought the adjoining smaller estate of Chermoshnya, becoming the owners of a total of over 1,300 acres of land and 100 serfs. The fire, which destroyed the village of Darovoye, occurred in 1833; Dostoevsky was, therefore, not nine, but twelve, at the time. According to Andrey, the village burned down because the peasant Arkhip took it into his head to roast a boar in his yard. There was a terrible wind at the time, and Arkhip's cottage caught fire. The fire spread quickly, and the whole village burned down. Arkhip, who rushed into his cottage to save his belongings, perished in the flames. Andrey, who must have read his brother's account, does not mention Alyona Frolovna's offer in his account of the fire. But even if Alyona Frolovna did offer to lend her wages, they could not possibly have amounted to 500 rubles, since she was with the family for another six years, and all that was owed to her at the end of that time was 600 rubles. As for Dostoevsky's parents managing "somehow," Andrey puts it more definitely: "It seems," he writes, "that in this misfortune my parents were also helped by Alexander Kumanin."

Alexander Kumanin was a rich Moscow merchant who married Alexandra Nechaev, the elder sister of Dostoevsky's mother. He used to visit the Dostoevskys regularly till the doctor picked a quarrel with him. They seemed to have made it up at their father-in-law's deathbed, but Kumanin never came to visit the Dostoevskys again while the doctor was at home. An even more violent quarrel occurred between the doctor and his wife's brother, Michael Nechaev. Michael, who was a draper's shop-assistant, used to visit the Dostoevskys every Sunday. "His arrival," Andrey records, "was a joyful occasion for us children, because it was usually accompanied by a concert. My mother played the guitar quite well and, as for my uncle, he played the guitar like a real virtuoso, and one of his guitars was always kept at our place. After dinner mother used to take up her guitar and my uncle his, and the concert began. At first they played serious things, then all sorts of mournful ditties, and, finally, gay folk songs, my uncle occasionally humming the words. [Dostoevsky copied out one of his uncle's songs and many years later used it in *The Brothers Karamazov*, Book V, Chapter 2, Smerdyakov's "Song with a Guitar."] It was fun, it was great fun!" Then Michael's visits were brought to an abrupt end because Michael had been making up to their young and pretty maid, Vera. "Mother," Andrey writes, "noticed that something was going on between them, and one day she saw her brother slip a note into Vera's hand. She snatched the note from Vera: it was a love assignation. My parents asked my uncle to follow them into the sitting room. There my mother accused her brother of trying to seduce her maid, and my uncle, without trying to defend himself, called her a fool. My father worked himself up into a passion and slapped my uncle's face. The doors of the sitting room were flung open and my uncle, looking red and excited, left our house never to return. . . . Our maid Vera was, of course, immediately given notice. . . ."

An interesting sidelight on the frequent storms in the doctor's household is thrown by the following question Dostoevsky asked himself in his *Writer's Diary*:[5] "Why is it that from my very early childhood and throughout the whole of my life, whenever I found myself among a festive crowd of Russians, I could not help feeling that they were merely pretending to be in a festive mood and that they would all of a sudden start a row *just as if they were at home?*"

Indeed, life at home would have been made absolutely intolerable for Dostoevsky (as it was later on made intolerable for his elder sister, Varvara) but for the fact that so long as his mother was alive his father's more violent passions were kept in check and the family preserved its

[5] January 1876.

unity. As Dostoevsky himself expressed it in one of the articles he contributed to *The Citizen* in 1876: "Ever since I can remember, I can recall the love of my parents for me. In our family," he goes on, "we knew the gospels almost from early childhood. I was only ten years old when I knew almost all the chief episodes of Russian history from Karamzin, which my father used to read to us aloud in the evenings. Every visit to the Kremlin and to the Moscow cathedrals was an event of great solemnity to me. Others may not have had the same kind of memories as I have."

VI

The readings usually took place in the sitting room in the evenings. They seem to have been a regular feature of the rigid daily routine observed by the doctor. "The days," records Andrey, "passed one after another very monotonously, according to the order introduced once and for all. We got up early in the morning, at six o'clock. At eight o'clock father had to go to the hospital or 'the wards,' as we used to say. At that time the rooms were tidied, the stoves heated in winter, and so on. At nine o'clock father returned from the hospital and drove off at once on his rounds, for he had quite a large private practice. In his absence we, the children, were doing our lessons. Father, as a rule, returned at twelve o'clock and soon afterwards we had dinner, after which father retired to the sitting room for his nap. At four o'clock we had tea, after which father went to the hospital for the second time. The evenings we spent in the sitting room which was lit by two tallow candles, and if father was not busy with his hospital case notes he read aloud to us. During holidays, especially at Christmas, we and our parents sometimes played cards in the sitting room, and Fyodor, owing to the liveliness of his character, took every opportunity to cheat, in which he was shown up several times. Punctually at nine o'clock the table was laid for supper, and after supper we, the children, knelt before the icon and, having said our prayers and bid our parents good night, went to bed."

One of Dostoevsky's earliest memories went back to the time when he was three. He remembered being brought by his nurse into the sitting room one afternoon and being made to kneel in front of the icon in the presence of visitors and recite the Prayer: "I put all my trust in thee, O Lord! Mother of God, keep and preserve me under thy wing!"—a prayer that he later taught his own children and that he was fond of repeating himself. In *The House of the Dead* Dostoevsky recalls the Lenten service in the Siberian prison, "the solemn prayers, the genuflections" which, he adds, "stirred up in my heart the memories of long, long ago, reminded me of the impressions of my childhood days and—I remembered how as a child I used to stand in church and look at the common people crowding at the entrance; they made way obsequiously for some army officer with thick epaulets or some gentleman or devout lady dressed showily, who walked to the front pews and were ready to pick a quarrel for them. I could not help feeling at the time that there they prayed differently from us, more fervently and with a full realization of their humble state."

Dostoevsky's parents were very fond of the writers of the sentimental, romantic and highly patriotic school who flourished at the time. Of these only two can be said to have had a permanent influence on Dostoevsky, the first, Nikolai Karamzin, historian, poet and novelist of the sentimental school, and the second, Alexander Zhukovsky, romantic poet and translator. Karamzin's *Letters of a Russian Traveler*, a diary of his journey in Western Europe, and his *History of the Russian Empire* were the books Dostoevsky's father was fond of reading to his children; they became young Dostoevsky's favorite books and were destined to play a determining part in shaping his political ideas. Karamzin had left on his European journey "a cosmopolitan," but returned "a Russian patriot." "My country," he wrote in his *Letters*, "I bless thee. I am in Russia at last and in a few more days, my friends, I shall be with you again." He was so glad to be back, he wrote, that he stopped passers-by in the street just to hear them speak Russian. In his famous *History*, Karamzin's ideas of Russia as "a bulwark against the contagion of Western Europe" and the comparison he drew between the state of Western Europe and the decline and fall of the Roman Empire—"the dying Rome"—made a deep and lasting impression on Dostoevsky, and though for the first ten years of his life in Petersburg he fell under the spell of the French Utopian socialists, he returned to them all the more fervently during the last years of his life.

Karamzin's novels, particularly his popular novel *Poor Lisa*, a great favorite of Dostoevsky's father, who used to interrupt his reading to expatiate on the moral aspects of the story, left a mark on Dostoevsky's early works. Aly, the hero of his novel *The Insulted and Injured*, bears a striking resemblance to Erastus, the hero of *Poor Lisa*. Erastus seduces Lisa, whom he first meets in the streets of Moscow "selling lilies of the valley," and then marries a rich, middle-aged widow, for after her seduction poor Lisa was no longer "the angel of chastity" who had "fired his imagination" and "enthralled his soul." Karamzin, like Dostoevsky, does not blame his hero, for, according to the tenets of the sentimental school, no one can be blamed for the many sad and unjust things in the world, since it has all been ordered by "a kind Providence" which man must trust blindly.

Karamzin's poetry, too, left its mark on Dostoevsky's writings, particularly a predilection for twilight, which Karamzin found "so much sweeter than bright days," and a liking "not for the enchanting gaiety of noisy Spring," or for "the gorgeous brilliance and ripeness of luxuriant Summer," but for "the pale Autumn when worn out / And with a languorous hand her wreath plucking / She for her end is waiting." Indeed, the only descriptive passage of any length to be found in Dostoevsky's writings unmistakably shows signs of Karamzin's influence. It is the description of autumn in the country in Dostoevsky's first novel, *Poor People,* one of the longest reminiscences of his childhood days on his parents' estate of Darovoye.

"How I loved the autumn in the country!" this remarkable autobiographical passage begins. "I was still a child, but even then I felt a great deal. And so it is autumn already! I loved an autumn evening more than an autumn morning. I remember there was a lake at the foot of a hill, a short distance from our house. This lake—I seem to see it even now—is wide and bright and as pure as crystal. When the evening is quiet—the lake is calm; there is not a rustle of the trees along its banks, the water is still as glass. Fresh! Cold! The dew falls on the grass, lights shimmer in the peasants' cottages on the bank, the herd is driven back—and just then I used to slip quietly out of the house to gaze at my lake, and I used to gaze at it for hours sometimes. The fishermen at the edge of the water had lit a campfire and its light could be seen far away reflected in the water. The sky is so cold, so blue and its edges are covered with fiery red shafts and these shafts of light grow fainter and fainter; the moon rises; the air is so resonant—you can hear everything so clearly: the quick flutter of a frightened little bird, the sharp ring of a pebble displaced by the light breeze, the splash of a fish in the water. A white mist rises over the blue water, thin and transparent. The distant objects grow dark; everything seems swallowed up in the mist, but close by everything stands out in sharp relief just as though it were carved by a chisel—the boat, the banks, the islands; a barrel, thrown away and forgotten at the edge of the water, rocking hardly perceptibly, a willow branch with yellow leaves entangled in the rushes, a belated gull, rising in the air and diving into the cold water, then again rising and disappearing in the mist. I kept gazing and listening—it was all so strange and wonderful. And yet I was still a child, a baby.

"Oh, I loved the autumn, the late autumn, when the corn had been harvested and the work in the fields brought to an end, when of an evening the village girls were gathering to play and sing in some cottage, when everyone was waiting for the arrival of winter. Then everything would grow much darker, the sky was overcast, yellow leaves were strewn like paths at the edges of the bared woods, and the pine forest grew blue and then black, especially in the evening, when a damp mist descended and the trees could be glimpsed through the mist looking like giants, like hideous and terrible apparitions. Every time I happened to lag behind during a walk, every time I dropped behind the rest and found myself walking alone, I felt scared and began to quicken my steps. I used to tremble like a leaf for fear that some terrible creature might suddenly thrust his face from inside the hollow of a tree; meanwhile, a wind would suddenly rise and rush through the woods, blowing, roaring, and howling so piteously, tearing hundreds of leaves from the lifeless branches and whirling them about in the air. Behind them a big flock of birds would sweep across the sky with a wild, piercing cry, covering it completely as though with a black pall. I used to get terrified, and just at that very moment I would hear someone—some voice—whispering: 'Run, run, child! Don't be late! Things will be awful here in a moment, run, child, run!' My heart would be gripped with fear, and I'd run and run till I was breathless and panting. I would come running home out of breath, and at home everything was gay and noisy. We, the children, would be given some work to do: shelling peas or poppies. The green logs crackled in the stove; our mother looked on happily at our work, our old nanny Ulyana [Alyona] told us stories about the old days or hair-raising fairy tales about sorcerers and dead men. We, the children, huddled closer to each other, though there was a smile on our lips. Then suddenly we would all fall silent: Hark, a noise! Someone's knocking! Not at all! That was Frolovna's spinning-wheel droning. Oh, the laughter that this would cause! And then at night we were too frightened to sleep; we would have such terrible dreams. I used to wake up and I did not dare to move, and lay shuddering under the blanket till the morning. But in the morning I would get up as fresh as a daisy. I'd look out of the window: the entire field was covered with hoarfrost; the thin, autumn hoarfrost hung on the bare branches; the lake was covered with ice as thin as a sheet of paper; a white mist was rising over the lake: the gay birds were twittering noisily. The sun shone from a cloudless sky and the bright sunbeams were breaking up the thin ice like glass. It was light, bright, gay! The fire crackled in the stove once more; we all sat down at the samovar, and our black dog Polkan, chilled to the marrow during the night, looked through the window, wagging his tail in friendly fashion. A peasant rode past the windows on a lively horse on his way to the woods for firewood. Everyone was so happy, so cheerful! Oh, what a golden time my childhood was!"

Apart from Karamzin's prose and poetry and Zhukovsky's romantic poems, most of them translations from German, a great favorite of Dostoevsky's parents was Anne Radcliffe's *The Mysteries of Udolpho*. In his *Winter Notes on Summer Impressions*, a series of articles about his impressions of his first journey abroad, Dostoevsky recalls how he longed to go abroad "almost from the days of my childhood, ever since the time when during the long winter evenings, still unable to read and write, I listened open-mouthed and faint with excitement and horror to my parents who before our bedtime used to read the novels of Mrs. Radcliffe, which afterwards gave me nightmares. . . ." In a letter to the poet Yakov Polonsky,[6] Dostoevsky also referred to Mrs. Radcliffe's "Gothic" novels. "How many times since the days of my early childhood," he wrote, "had I dreamed of being in Italy. Ever since the novels of Radcliffe,

[6] July 31, 1861.

all sorts of Alphonsos, Katarinas and Lucias stuck in my mind. And I am still raving about Don Pedros and Donna Claras. Then came Shakespeare —Verona, Romeo and Juliet—oh, the fascination of it all! To Italy, to Italy! But instead of Italy, I found myself in Semipalatinsk and before that in the House of the Dead. Won't I ever succeed in traveling all over Europe, now when there is still strength, passion and poetry left in me?" And in his novel *The Insulted and Injured* he refers to another book he read as a child, *Children's Reading for the Mind and the Heart*, published by Karamzin for "Young readers of noble descent," and particularly to *Alphonse and Dalinda or The Miracle of the Heart.* "Even today," he makes his hero declare, "I cannot recall this story without a sort of flutter of the heart and when a year ago I reminded Natasha of the first two lines, 'Alphonse, the hero of my story, was born in Portugal, Don Ramir, his father,' etc., I almost burst into tears."

Before he had learned to read, Dostoevsky observes in his *Writer's Diary*,[7] his mother read to him the stories from *The Lives of the Saints*, stories that imprinted themselves on his mind and were of great significance to his later development. There were, besides, the fairy stories he heard as a child from the wet nurses who used to visit their house twice a year, stories that stimulated his imagination to such an extent that they, too, like Mrs. Radcliffe's novels, gave him nightmares.

"The arrival of one of our wet nurses," Andrey records, "was a real holiday for us. In the evening when mother was busy in the sitting room and father was entering his prescriptions into the case notes of the hospital patients, we would wait in the dark drawing room for the arrival of the wet nurse. When she came in, we would all sit down in the dark room, and the telling of fairy stories began. This went on for about three or even four hours. The stories were told almost in a whisper so as not to disturb our parents. It was so still that we could hear the scraping of father's pen next door. And the stories we were told! There was one of the Fire Bird, another about the wily priest's son, Alyosha Popovich, a third about Bluebeard, and many others. All I can remember is that some of the stories were very terrifying. . . ."

Dostoevsky was rather backward in learning to read. In a letter to his wife from Ems (where he was undergoing a cure at the time)[8] Dostoevsky expressed the fear that his eight-year-old son Fyodor would be laughed at because he could not read. "I, too," he wrote, "was laughed at in my childhood because I lagged behind my brother in reading." Dostoevsky was taught to read by his mother, and his first reading book was a collection of Bible stories translated from the German, under the title: *One Hundred and Four Stories Chosen from the Old and New Testaments by Johann Huebner, with the Addition of Pious Reflections.* It had several crude lithographic illustrations, showing the Creation of the

[7] July-August 1877.

[8] *Letters*, September 1, 1879.

World, Adam and Eve in Paradise, the Flood, etc. Whether it was the Bible stories or the fact that his mother taught him to read from them or both, the book left a deep impression on him. "I vividly remember," Andrey records, "how not so long ago, towards the end of the seventies, in fact, I mentioned this book to my brother Fyodor while talking to him about our children and his excitement as he told me that he had succeeded in finding a copy of the same book and that he treasured it as something sacred."

Of Dostoevsky's first two teachers, one was a deacon who, according to Andrey, had a marvelous gift for telling Bible stories, and the other Nicholas Souchard, a French émigré, who became so ardent a Russian patriot that he changed his name to Drashusov. He taught the two elder boys French and composed their birthday greetings to the doctor, which they copied out on a clean sheet of paper and handed to their father neatly rolled up, and then recited by heart to his great parental delectation. It seems that on one such occasion, M. Souchard's inspiration gave out and he simply copied out some lines from Voltaire's *Henriade.*

Winter was the hardest time for Dostoevsky and his elder brother. Their father's strict regime kept them within doors most of the day. The doctor constantly reminded them that he was a poor man and that they would have to make their own way in the world. In summer this regime was relaxed and the children were allowed to take walks (under the supervision of Alyona Frolovna) in the hospital grounds or to sit down and make sand pies or play horses. Ball games were strictly forbidden as "improper." They were also forbidden to talk to the patients who were allowed out on a fine day. In the evening the whole family would go for a walk to a nearby wood, known as Mary's Copse. These walks, Andrey records, were also conducted in a very "proper" fashion. The children were not allowed to run about, and the doctor talked to them "about subjects conducive to their mental development," such as "acute, obtuse and right angles and curved and broken lines, which are met with at almost every step in Moscow." Still, even these rules were occasionally broken. "One day," Andrey records, "we were lucky to see during our walk a professional sprinter who was displaying his art for money and who, when running, held one end of his handkerchief, soaked in spirits, in his mouth. Imitating him, we all began running along the avenues of the hospital grounds holding the ends of our handkerchiefs in our mouths. We indulged in this game for quite a long time." Another summer diversion before the purchase of Darovoye was the annual pilgrimage to the famous Troitsky (Trinity) Monastery, which took five or six days. They attended all the church services and returned home with all sorts of toys bought in the shops and stalls in the monastery grounds. The doctor was too busy to go with them, and they traveled with their mother and one of their acquaintances.

Occasionally, though not too often, the doctor took his family to a show. "I can only remember one or two occasions," Andrey records, "when at Shrovetide or at Christmas, a box was taken at a theater for a matinee performance and we, the four elder children and our parents, went to see a play, which was chosen after careful consideration. Once, I remember, we saw *Jacqueau or the Brazilian Monkey*. I can't remember exactly what the play was about, except that the actor who played the monkey was a marvelous equilibrist. My brother Fyodor raved about him for a long time and tried to imitate him." Their mother's uncle, Vassily Kotelnitsky, a professor of medicine at Moscow University, also used to take them to shows at Easter, though of quite a different character. "Every Easter holiday," Andrey records, "we, the three elder brothers, had to go to dinner with our great-uncle on a day previously appointed by him. After an early dinner, about two o'clock in the afternoon, the professor and ourselves went to the fair, which at that time was right opposite the windows of our great-uncle's house. After walking past all the side shows and seeing all sorts of clowns, strong men, Punch and Judy shows and all sorts of street actors, our great-uncle would take us back to his house, where the carriage sent for us by our parents was already waiting, and we would return home full of the most varied impressions, and for a long time we would copy the street actors and re-enact the comedies we had seen." Dostoevsky himself, in a letter to a correspondent only a few months before his death, refers to another play he had seen as a child. "When I was ten years old," he wrote, "I saw a performance in Moscow of Schiller's *Robbers* with Peter Mochalov [one of Russia's great tragic actors] and, I assure you, the very strong impression I carried away from that performance has had a very good effect on my spiritual development."

VII

Dostoevsky was a boy of eleven when he found himself for the first time in the country among peasants. In the early spring of 1832, soon after the death of his grandfather, Fyodor Nechaev, he and his two brothers, Mikhail and Andrey, journeyed the 100 or so miles to their little estate of Darovoye in a large covered wagon, drawn by a team of three horses and driven by Semyon the Broad, the most competent driver in the village, who had come down specially to Moscow to fetch them. It had been agreed between the doctor and his wife that she should spend six months every year in the country, managing the estate. After a priest had held a service for the travelers (nothing in the pious doctor's house was undertaken without a special service), the huge conveyance started for the country, accompanied by the doctor in his carriage. The doctor saw them off to the tollgate, bade them a last goodby, his wife bursting into tears, as usual. The journey took two whole days. During that time, Andrey records, "Fyodor was in a kind of fever. He always chose the seat beside the driver on the box and there was not a single stop at which he would not jump down from the box, run round to have a good look at the place, and help Semyon the Broad with the horses."

The countryside round Darovoye and Chermoshnya, the two villages of the Dostoevsky estate separated from each other by about one mile, was, Andrey records, "pleasant and picturesque." The "country house" of the estate, however, was just a thatched, one-story cottage, the walls of which were made of wattles smeared with clay. It had three small rooms and stood in a rather large and shady linden copse. Across a small field was a dark birchwood thicket full of ravines and known as Brykovo, a name Dostoevsky preserved in *The Devils*, giving it to the place where Stavrogin and Gaganov fought their duel. On the other side of the field was a large orchard of about fifteen acres, which could also be entered from the linden copse and which was surrounded by a deep ravine with gooseberry bushes growing on the top of it. "These three places," Andrey records, "namely the linden copse, the orchard and the birchwood thicket, were nearest to our cottage and for that reason were in constant use by us as our playground. Near our house were two mounds with four old lime trees growing on each of them, and under these trees we had our breakfast, our dinner and our evening tea. My brother Fyodor took a liking for Brykovo from the very start and we later named it 'Fedya's copse.' Mother, however, was very loath to let us walk in that wood, because it was said that snakes hid in the ravines and that even wolves were to be found there."

It was, in fact, in the summer of 1832 that the incident with the imaginary wolf occurred which Dostoevsky described in 1876 in the February number of his *Writer's Diary* under the title of *The Peasant Marey*. Dostoevsky was eleven and not, as he claims, nine years old at the time. It happened in August. It was, Dostoevsky writes, "a dry bright day, though rather cold and windy. . . . I walked past the threshing floor and, going down a ravine, climbed up into the dense thicket of bushes which stretched from the other side of the ravine to the wood. I got among the bushes and I could see a peasant plowing by himself not very far away. . . . I knew almost all our peasants, but I did not know which of them was plowing now, nor did it really matter to me because I was occupied with my own affairs–breaking off switches from a hazel tree to thwack frogs with. . . . I was also interested in beetles and other insects and was collecting them; some of them were very beautiful and I liked the small, quick, red-and-yellow lizards, but I was afraid of snakes. However, there were fewer snakes than lizards. There were not many mushrooms there; to get mushrooms one had to go to the birch wood, and I was about to go there. For there was nothing in the world I loved so much as the wood with its mushrooms and wild berries, its beetles and its birds, its hedgehogs and squirrels, and its damp smell of well-rotted leaves. Even as I write this I can smell the fragrance of our birch wood:

these impressions stay with you all your life. Suddenly amid the dead silence I heard clearly and distinctly the shout, 'Wolf! Wolf!' I uttered a shriek and, panic-stricken, screamed at the top of my voice and rushed out to the clearing, making straight for the plowing peasant."

In the autobiographical passage from *Poor People* quoted earlier, Dostoevsky described the sudden panic that took hold of him even when lagging behind his mother and brothers during a walk in the country, but here he was by himself and he could never forget the peasant Marey, who had comforted him and dispelled his fears. "If I had been his own son," Dostoevsky writes, "he could not have looked at me with eyes shining with brighter love." Was it not because his own father never looked at him like that that the memory of his encounter with Marey stuck in his mind all his life? Marey, according to Andrey, was not a fictitious character. His real name was Mark. "He was a handsome peasant," Andrey recalls, "of over middle age, with a large black beard streaked with gray. He was known in the village as a cattle expert and whenever we had to buy cows at a fair, he was always the one whose opinion was consulted."

In recounting the story of the imaginary wolf so many years later, Dostoevsky was anxious to prove that "the savagely ignorant serf" really possessed "a high degree of culture." Yet as a child Dostoevsky does not seem to have worried about his father's brutal treatment of the serfs. An observant child like him must have been aware of the fact that the peasants, including "Marey," were regularly flogged at the stables at the behest of his father and in spite of his mother's intercession. There is a hint of it, however, in what he has to say about Marey. "Who compelled him to look like that? He was one of our serfs, a peasant who was our property, and after all I was the son of his master." But that was a reflection that came to him much later. At the time he soon forgot all about Marey. "Whenever I happened to come across him," he writes, "I never spoke to him either about the wolf or about anything else."

There was another person in the village who may not have interested him at the time, but whom he used as a prototype for one of the most harrowing incidents in *The Brothers Karamazov.* "In concluding my reminiscences of our estate," Andrey writes, "I cannot help mentioning the half-wit Agrafena. We had an idiot girl in our village who did not belong to any family. She spent all her time wandering about the fields and it was only at the time of hard frosts that she was made to shelter in some peasant cottage. She was by then a woman of 20 or 25. She spoke very little, unwillingly, unintelligibly and incoherently. All one could make out of her talk was that she was constantly recollecting a child of hers who was buried in the cemetery. I believe she was born an idiot but, in spite of it, had been raped and became the mother of a child that died soon after. Reading the story of Stinking Lisaveta in my brother's novel *The Brothers Karamazov*, I could not help remembering our idiot girl Agrafena."

There were many other things in the country to occupy Dostoevsky's mind. There was the fishing in the huge pond his mother had had made out of the dried-up river bed behind Brykovo and which she had put out of bounds for the peasants by having the local clergy go round it with icons and holy banners, thus "imposing a curse" on any poacher who dared to fish in it. "We went fishing very early in the morning, not later than 5 o'clock," Andrey records, "and every one of us had an 'aide-de-camp,' that is to say, a serf boy, who had to dig up worms and thread them on the hook. . . . In a word, there was the most loathsome lordliness!"

There were other games in which Dostoevsky always took the leading part. Andrey describes three such games and one "inexcusable prank." There was the "game of savages," invented by Dostoevsky, who had been reading many descriptions of life among savages. They built a hut in some inaccessible spot of the linden grove, which was to be the headquarters of the "savage tribes," then they stripped and dyed their bodies to resemble the tattooing of savages, made themselves hats and belts out of leaves and dyed goose feathers and, armed with handmade bows and arrows, raided the enemy tribes in Brykovo, that is to say, the peasant boys and girls, whom their little masters had placed in previously chosen spots. These were taken prisoner and kept in the hut till the appropriate ransom was received. "It was, of course, my brother Fyodor," Andrey writes, "who was the chief of the tribesmen. My brother Mikhail did not often take part in this game; it was not in his character, but, as he was beginning to paint at that time, he acted as our dresser and painted us." Even at so early an age, Mikhail, who, incidentally, was very shortsighted, played second fiddle to his younger brother.

Another game invented by Dostoevsky was based on his reading of *Robinson Crusoe*. Dostoevsky was Robinson and Andrey, "the little tail," as his elder brothers nicknamed him, was Man Friday. "We did our best," Andrey records, "to reproduce in our linden grove all the privations Robinson had experienced on his desert island."

The third game was perhaps not so innocent as the other two. "We contrived," Andrey observes, "to make it more interesting. Every one of us had a team of three horses, made up of a peasant boy and, as shaft horses, two peasant girls. We drove these 'troikas' not in the linden grove, but on the road from our village to Chermoshnya, and very often we had races with a prize for the winning team. While playing this game," Andrey rather guilelessly concludes, "we, who had watched the sale of horses at the fair in Zaraisk [the nearest country town], which we often visited, organized the same kind of exchange and sales of our horses with all the methods employed by the horse dealers, that is, looked at the horses' teeth, lifted their legs, examined their hoofs, etc." Andrey was four years younger than Dostoevsky, who must have been thirteen or even fourteen at the time, an age a little too advanced for playing at horses, unless, of course, there were little fillies to be "sold."

The "inexcusable prank" concerned a religious "procession" in which the boys, led by their sprightly maid Vera, took part after a visit to a dilapidated chapel near the cemetery. "Without giving it another thought," Andrey records, "we took down the icons from the shelves and, singing hymns, began walking round the field. This we repeated a few times, till someone told our mother about it and we were told off good and proper."

There was one more game Dostoevsky took part in, though only as a witness, a "game" that may have left a deeper impression on his mind than he himself suspected, a game in which he perhaps for the first time experienced the keen delight that is hidden in torture and cruelty. "As a child in the country," he wrote in his *Writer's Diary*,[9] "I used to know a little boy, the son of one of our serfs, who was terribly fond of torturing animals. He particularly enjoyed killing hens when they had to be prepared for dinner for his masters. I remember how he used to climb up to the thatched roof of the threshing barn to look for sparrows' nests: every time he found a nest, he would at once begin pulling the heads off the sparrows."

Many years later Dostoevsky was to accuse Turgenev of cowardice, or, as he expressed it, "coyness," for turning away at the last stages of the public execution of the murderer Tropmann in Paris. "No man," he wrote to his future biographer Nikolai Strakhov,[10] "has a right to turn away and ignore what is taking place on earth." And, indeed, *he* would have watched, open-eyed and pale-faced, the chopping off of a criminal's head as he did the tearing off of heads of sparrows as a boy—"so as to experience," as he put it in an expunged passage of *Netochka Nezvanova*, "during the very process of torture a sort of inexplicable yet deep sense of pleasure consisting of a feeling of repentance, pity and the consciousness of one's own inhumanity," the sort of "cruel sensuality" to which, as he declared in the *Dream of a Ridiculous Man*, "almost everyone on earth" was prone and which was "the only source of almost all the sins of mankind."

So far nothing is known of Dostoevsky's first knowledge of sex. "My father," Andrey writes, "was very careful in supervising his children's morals, and this was particularly true of my two elder brothers when they had grown older. I cannot recall a single instance when my brothers went out anywhere by themselves; my father regarded it as quite improper, and yet by the time they left home my elder brother was 17 and my brother Fyodor was almost 16. To their boarding school they were al-

[9] February 1876.
[10] *Letters*, June 23, 1870.

ways driven in my father's carriage and they also came back in it [at the weekends]."

The first young men to visit their house were the sons of their priest, Sergey and Yakov Barshev, who had paid a visit to the doctor's house on returning from their studies abroad and who afterwards became professors of jurisprudence at the universities of Moscow and Petersburg. Their visit was something of an event in the Dostoevsky household. Andrey recalls how his father used to repeat afterwards: "If I were to live not to see, but just to be sure, that my sons would be as successful as the Barshev boys, I'd die a happy man." Even when they were at the boarding school, no one of their classmates ever visited their house. "Only once." Andrey records, "a certain Kudryavtsev, one of my elder brother's classmates, paid him a visit. My brother was allowed to return the visit, but that, it seems, was the end of their acquaintanceship."

There was, however, a young boy who, with his mother, was a frequent visitor to their house. He was called Ivan or Vanichka Umnov, and was a pupil of the State Secondary School, where the doctor refused to send his sons, first, because corporal punishment was still practiced there, and, secondly, because he feared that his sons' morals might be corrupted by the day boys. Umnov was a little older than Mikhail and, according to Andrey, used to supply his elder brothers with the latest literary gossip and books that were not available at their house. It was Umnov who introduced Dostoevsky to Gogol, who was considered too frivolous and even too "obscene" a writer by the doctor. Umnov also had learned by heart *The Lunatic Asylum*, a satire on the writers of the day by Alexander Voeykov, a popular poet and critic. "My brothers," Andrey records, "learned a few stanzas of that satire by heart and recited them in my father's presence. My father was displeased and expressed the opinion that it was probably the work of some schoolboys. But when he was told that it was a poem by Voeykov, he still insisted that it was highly improper because it contained all sorts of insolent references to men of high standing and famous authors, particularly Zhukovsky."

Was it Umnov who first revealed to Dostoevsky the mysteries of sex as seen through the eyes of a rather depraved schoolboy? In his notebooks Dostoevsky often refers to some of his future characters by the names of people he had known well in his early childhood. These became the prototypes of many of his characters. Dostoevsky mentions Umnov twice in his notes in connection with his work on *The Devils*. Thus in February or March 1870, he noted: "He [Stavrogin] meets Umnov and proves to him that he knows a lot more than he. On his return home he tells the cripple that Umnov is a fool and knows nothing, and beats the cripple and then runs after Umnov again." This may well have been a reminiscence of Umnov at the time when he was chief purveyor of the facts of life to the two Dostoevsky brothers. The other reference to Umnov is even more explicit and could hardly have been made if Umnov had not discussed sexual matters with his two younger friends: "Dreams of will power. Umnov peeps through the keyholes at naked girls, tries to rape the cripple."

VIII

The names of Souchard and Chermak occur again and again in Dostoevsky's notebooks between 1869 and 1871, when he used to jot down random ideas for his unwritten novel *The Life of a Great Sinner* and *The Devils*. How clearly imprinted was Chermak's boarding school, where he spent three years from 1834 to 1837, on his mind, can be judged from a letter he wrote barely three months before his death[11] to Vladimir Kochenovsky, the son of a well-known historian and one of his former classmates. "Yes," he wrote, "there are only a few left of our Chermak schoolfellows, but I remember them all. In life I only met Lamovsky and Tolstoy afterwards. I never saw the Schumachers again, nor the Mulhausens. Anna Chermak (Lamovsky) I was very glad indeed to meet. Whenever I am in Moscow it always gives me a thrill to drive past the house in Basmannaya [where Chermak had his boarding school]. I remember you very well. You were a rather little boy with large, beautiful dark eyes. A pity we did not meet in the summer."

He himself, however, was apparently never happy either at Souchard's prep school or at Chermak's boarding school. This is what he had to say about his impressions as a boy at school in his *Writer's Diary*:[12]

"Before that the little boy lived only at home and he knew nothing but his home, and suddenly he is surrounded by a hundred boys like him, unfamiliar faces, a noise, an uproar, everything is different from what he knew at home—dear Lord, the horror of it! At home he may have been hungry and cold, but he was loved there, and even if he was not loved, he was *at home* there, he was among his own folk, but here—not one kind word from the school authorities, the teachers are so strict and severe, the subjects he has to learn are so difficult, the corridors are so long, and among his schoolmates there are such scamps, such bullies, such scoffers, and so pitiless: 'Just as if they had no heart, just as if they never had a father and mother!' He had been told that it was wicked and shameful to lie and hurt everyone's feelings, but here everyone lied, deceived, hurt his feelings and laughed at his terror as well. One day they disliked a boy because he cries about being away from home and is 'dishonoring' his class. Another day they start beating him mercilessly, all of them, all the time, without anger, just for amusement. Let me observe that as a child I met many such unhappy children in different schools—and what crimes are committed sometimes in our educational establishments of every type and name—yes, crimes! If a boy attempts foolishly to complain,

[11] *Letters*, October 16, 1880.

[12] February 1877.

he's beaten almost to death (he might, in fact, be killed too), schoolboys beat a boy for being a 'telltale' without pity and without thinking. They will point a finger at him for years, they will send him to Coventry, they will make a pariah out of him—and what heartlessness, what pitiless indifference on the part of the school authorities! I can't remember a single decent teacher in my childhood and I don't think there are many such teachers even today: they are all just civil servants in receipt of salaries. And yet it is just the children who, on their admission to school, pine for their families and their homes, who afterwards more often than not grow into remarkable men, persons endowed with great talents and abilities, while those who accommodate themselves quickly to their new environment and get used to anything at once, those who never pine for anything and, indeed, immediately assume a leading position among their schoolfellows more often than not grow into men without any spark of talent or simply into bad men, climbers, tricksters and intriguers already from the age of eight. . . ."

Dostoevsky and his elder brother spent only the mornings at Souchard's prep school, returning each day in their father's carriage for dinner. The subjects they were taught there included French and math, the teaching of Latin being left to the doctor. At Chermak's boarding school they spent the whole week, returning home only at weekends. The lessons at the boarding school began at 8 o'clock with breaks at 10 and 12 o'clock. After lunch there were lessons again from 2 to 6 o'clock with a break at 4 o'clock. From 6 to 9 o'clock the pupils were supposed to do their homework and at 9 o'clock they had supper, after which they went to bed. Dostoevsky made no friends at school. He was, as he himself admitted to Nikolai Strakhov, too quick to take offense and he resented the often coarse jokes and jeers of his classmates. Some of his teachers in the higher forms of the boarding school were university lecturers, but none of them was sufficiently outstanding to leave any impression on him. There was, however, one teacher, the teacher of German, who must have influenced him considerably in his blind adoration of Pushkin. In the Dostoevsky household, Pushkin, a contemporary poet, was not held in great regard, and it is, surely, ironical that Dostoevsky should have been made aware of Pushkin's greatness by a German, who used to recite his poems with immense enthusiasm, though with an atrocious German accent. The teacher, whose name was Goering, was fond of telling his class of a meeting he had had with the great poet, who had given him permission to translate his works into German. Pushkin became one of Dostoevsky's favorite poets from that time, and when the two elder brothers decided to regale their parents with a recital of two long poems, Dostoevsky chose Pushkin's poem *On the Death of Prince Oleg*, while his elder brother, a great admirer of Schiller, chose Zhukovsky's translation of Schiller's ballad *The Count of Hapsburg*.

Dostoevsky's choice of Pushkin's poem is interesting also because it throws a light on his character—the hidden sides of it in particular. The first stanza of the poem tells how "prophetic" Oleg lays waste the villages and fields of the "unreasonable" Khozars (a fate to which Dostoevsky many years later cheerfully consigned all the "unreasonable enemies" of Russia) and how an "inspired" soothsayer, whose "prophetic tongue is truthful and free," foretells that his shield will be "on the walls of Constantinople" (another fond dream of Dostoevsky's), but that his horse will be the cause of his death. The fortuneteller's prediction comes true, and although the Prince's horse is dead, the Prince himself is stung by a poisonous snake as he puts his foot on his horse's bones. Dostoevsky, too, had great faith in fortunetelling of any kind and resorted to it at every crisis throughout his life.

The arrival of the two brothers at home on a Saturday was a great occasion. Dinner was postponed till 2 o'clock, and the two boys were expected to tell their parents about their progress at school during the past week, about their teachers and schoolmates. After dinner the two brothers sat down to read the books they had brought with them. Dostoevsky, according to his first biographer, loved to read travel books, "and under the influence of this reading was filled with a passionate desire to visit Venice, Constantinople and the Near East in general." Andrey records that his brother was often seen reading Walter Scott, particularly *Waverley* and *Quentin Durward*, Pushkin's works and Karamzin's *History*, which he always read when there was nothing new to read. There were also the monthly supplements to the popular monthly *The Library for Reading* with the latest works of fiction by Russian and foreign writers.

The boys only spent the months of July and August in the country, and some of their dutiful letters written to their mother in Darovoye before their arrival there have been preserved. One of them, written in the spring of 1834, when Dostoevsky was still at Souchard's preparatory school, expresses his deep affection for his mother. "Darling Mama," he wrote, "when you left us for the country I felt so unhappy and every time I think of you now, darling Mama, such sadness comes over me that I cannot shake it off. Oh, if only you knew how badly I want to see you and how I cannot wait for that happy moment. Every time I think of you, I pray to God to preserve your health."

His mother's health was indeed in a perilous state. Andrey records that "beginning with the autumn of 1836, our mother got very ill. She was losing strength very rapidly and quite soon she could no longer comb her very long and thick hair and at last decided to have it cut off. From the beginning of 1837 our mother's condition worsened, and from the beginning of February she became bedridden." She died at 7 o'clock in the morning of February 27, 1837. "Before her death," Andrey writes, "she recovered consciousness, asked for the icon of the Redeemer, and first gave her blessing to us children, and then expressed the wish to give her blessing to father. It was a deeply moving scene and we all wept aloud." Her funeral was on Monday, March 1. Pushkin had died on January 29, but the news of his death reached Dostoevsky only after his mother's funeral. "I remember," Andrey writes, "that my brothers almost went out of their minds when they heard of Pushkin's death and all its circumstances. In his conversations with his elder brother, my brother Fyodor kept repeating that if we had not been in mourning for our mother, he would have asked our father's permission to wear mourning for Pushkin." Andrey goes on to quote a doggerel poem on the death of Pushkin that his two elder brothers kept reciting. The deaths of the only woman and the only poet he remembered with deep veneration all his life brought to an end the first period of Dostoevsky's life. He was not yet sixteen when he left for Petersburg, and eleven years later he was to leave it for a prison in Siberia—they were to be the most crucial and most dramatic years of his life.

[2]

THE YOUNG DREAMER AWAKENS TO FAME

In May 1837 the doctor took his two elder sons, Mikhail and Fyodor, to Petersburg, intending to place them in the Army Engineering College. The career their father had chosen for them appalled them, but so strictly were they brought up, so successfully had they been screened from outside influences, and so completely dependent were they on their father, that it would never have occurred to them to do what their father had done—challenge his decision and make their own way in life. They had never had any money to spend as they liked. "I don't remember a single occasion," Andrey records, "when my brothers were given pocket money and I suppose they first became familiar with money only after father had left them in Petersburg." And yet while the conflict between them and their father never came out into the open, it was there all the time. "My brother and I," Dostoevsky writes, recalling his journey to Petersburg with his father in *A Writer's Diary*,[1] "were dreaming of a new life, our heads were full of visions of 'the sublime and the beautiful,' when those words were still fresh and pronounced without irony. We believed passionately in something, and though we knew perfectly well what we should be required to know for the math examination, we only dreamed of poetry and poets. My brother was writing poems, three poems a day even during the journey, and I was composing a novel dealing with life in Venice."

A better idea of how completely divorced from reality the two brothers were at the time can be obtained from this letter Mikhail wrote to his father a year and a half later, on November 28, 1838: "Let everything be taken from me, let them leave me naked but give me Schiller, and I shall forget the whole world! What do I care for all these external things, when my spirit is hungry? He who believes in the beautiful is already happy! Well, papa, rejoice with me, I think I am not without poetic gifts. I have written many poems . . . and I am myself beginning

[1] January 1876.

to believe that there is poetry in them. Now I've begun to write a drama, and I think the first act is good. If you promise not to be angry, I'll send you some of my writings. My whole life is in my poetry, all my feelings, my joys and my sorrows are contained in it! . . ."

The poor doctor, befuddled with spirits most of the time, found a sober moment in which to express his contempt for his eldest son's poetic ambitions in a letter to Dostoevsky on May 27, 1839, the last letter he wrote before his violent death. "I am angry with him myself," he declared, "for wasting his time on his stupid verses." The doctor was, of course, right in a way, for Mikhail was neither poet nor dramatist, and when he realized it at last, his disappointment was such that he took to drink. But at the time Dostoevsky had his head in the clouds no less than his brother, and it was his father's complete lack of sympathy with the aspirations of his two elder sons that not only deepened the rift between them, but made any understanding between them impossible. "The greatest tragedy," Dostoevsky wrote,[2] "is that good, kind and generous people do not understand or, as a result of their environment and former life, cease to understand certain ideas and get into open conflict even with those they love and wish to make happy. This happens most often between fathers and sons."

Nothing perhaps illustrates better the difference between the highly romantic adolescent Dostoevsky and the mature genius of the great novelist he was to become than the change in his attitude to the inscription on the tombstone on his mother's grave. The doctor decided to put up a tombstone on the grave of his long-suffering wife after he had made up his mind to send his two elder sons to the Engineering College in Petersburg and to resign his post at the hospital and to go and live on his estate. "My father," Andrey records, "left the choice of the inscription to my brothers. Both of them decided that the tombstone should have only the name, surname, date of birth and death. On the back of the tombstone they chose the epitaph from Karamzin: 'Rest in peace, beloved dust, till the joyful morn.' And this beautiful inscription was engraved on the tombstone." Beautiful? Dostoevsky mentions the same inscription twice in his writings, and each time he cannot help jeering at what must have afterwards seemed to him to be a horrible cliché. It occurs for the first time in the fourth chapter of the fourth part of *The Idiot* (written at the beginning of 1869) in General Ivolgin's version of Lebedev's ridiculous story of how he lost one of his legs in the campaign of 1812, had it buried and erected on its grave a monument, which bore the inscription, "Rest in peace, beloved dust, till the joyful morn." He used it again four years later in *Bobok*, his first "fantastic" story, published in *The Citizen* in February, 1873. The story has been treated by some of Dostoevsky's biographers as proof of his "sexual obsessions," or what Strakhov in his

[2] *Letters,* April 17, 1877.

famous letter to Tolstoy of November 28, 1883, called his "animal voluptuousness." It is, in fact, a most grisly indictment of human carnality, comparable only to King Lear's outburst in Act IV: "Let copulation thrive." And in this hideous scene in which even the dead are anxious "to go to't with a riotous appetite," the most lecherous of them all, General Pervoyedov, has Karamzin's epitaph inscribed on his grave: "Rest in peace, beloved dust, till the joyful morn."

A mysterious illness nearly delayed Dostoevsky's departure for Petersburg. He had been taken with his elder brother by his aunt Alexandra Kumanin on her usual annual pilgrimage to the Troitsky Monastery, "to offer up prayers before the journey," as Andrey explains. On the journey to the monastery and back Dostoevsky and his brother, it seems, "regaled" their aunt with recitals of poems, but on his return to Moscow Dostoevsky fell ill with an infection of the throat, which defied all medical treatment, and he lost his voice. In desperation his father tried homeopathic treatment, making him dine at a separate table "so as not to inhale the smell of the food eaten by the rest of the family," as Andrey records. In the end the doctor decided not to wait for Dostoevsky's complete recovery in the hope that the journey in the month of May would be of benefit to him. But Dostoevsky never really completely recovered from the effects of this illness: his voice remained husky for the rest of his life.

Before they left for Petersburg, Father Barshev, who officiated at all their family occasions, held a special service at which he offered up prayers for the safety of travelers, but during the journey an incident occurred that brought Dostoevsky face to face with the terrible realities of Russian life and eventually landed him in a Siberian convict prison. Twenty-four years later, in the notebook he kept while writing *Crime and Punishment*, Dostoevsky commented on this incident: "My first personal insult. A horse. A Government Courier."

He described this "first personal insult" of his in his *Writer's Diary*:[3] "This incident," he wrote, "happened a very long time ago, in my prehistoric days, as it were, namely in 1837, when I was only fifteen years old [he was, in fact, sixteen at the time], on the way from Moscow to Petersburg. My elder brother and I were traveling with my late father to Petersburg to be enlisted among the officer-students of the Engineering College. It was in May; it was hot. We traveled very slowly so as not to change horses at the posting stations and stopped there for two or three hours at a time. I remember how sick and tired we got in the end of this journey which lasted almost a whole week. . . . One afternoon we stopped at one of the stations, at an inn, at some village in the province of Tver. It was a large and well-to-do village. We were due to leave in half an hour and meanwhile I looked through the window and I saw the following scene.

[3] January 1876.

"Directly opposite the inn, across the street, was the posting station. Suddenly a government courier's carriage, drawn by three horses, drove up to the front steps, and out jumped the courier, wearing the full-dress uniform with narrow coattails and a large tricorn with white, yellow and, I believe, green plumes (I forget this detail and could check it up, but I seem to remember catching a glimpse of green feathers too). The courier was a strong, tall, sturdily built fellow with a flushed purple face. He ran into the station and quite certainly 'knocked back' a glass of vodka. I remember our coachman telling me at the time that such couriers always drank a glass of vodka at every station as otherwise they would not be able to endure 'such torture.' Meanwhile a new fast troika drove up at the station and its coachman, a young lad of twenty in a red shirt and holding a peasant's cloth coat in his hand, jumped onto the box. The courier ran out of the station at the same moment and took his seat in the open carriage. The coachman drove off, but even before he had time to drive off, the courier half rose in his seat and silently, without uttering a single word, raised his huge right fist and, lowering it from above, crashed it down heavily on the back of the coachman's neck. The coachman lurched forward from the blow, raised his whip and lashed out at the shaft horse with all his might. The horses darted away, but that did not in the least satisfy the courier. It was method, not madness, it was something that had become almost a tradition, something that had been the result of hundreds of years of experience, and the courier's terrible fist rose again and another blow fell on the back of the coachman's neck. Then again and again and so it went on till the troika disappeared from sight. It goes without saying that the coachman, who could scarcely hold on to his seat because of the blows, would keep whipping up the horses until they tore along in a frenzy. Our coachman explained to me that nearly all the couriers drove like that, but that this particular courier made a feature of it and that everyone knew him already; that after drinking a glass of vodka he would jump into the carriage and start showering blows on the coachman and went on doing it without any excuse, in a most regular manner, raising and lowering his fist, and kept it up for a mile, after which he would leave the coachman in peace. Should he feel bored, he might start again at any moment during the journey, though sometimes the coachman might be lucky. But as soon as they got near the next station, he would start all over again, his fist beginning to go up and down about a mile from the station to make quite sure that everyone in the village was duly impressed by the dashing way in which he drove up to the front steps. 'From these blows,' our coachman declared, 'my neck hurt for a whole month afterwards.' When the lad comes home and everyone laughs at him—'Got a proper cudgeling from the courier, haven't you?'—he will probably give his young wife a beating that very day—'Let me work it off on you at least,' but perhaps also because 'she looked and saw' . . .

"This disgusting scene stuck in my mind all through my life," Dostoevsky concludes. "I could never forget the courier and many more of the cruel and shameful things about the Russian people which for a long time afterwards I could not help explaining a little too one-sidedly . . . At the end of the eighteen-forties, at the time when I indulged in most ecstatic and high-minded dreams, it occurred to me one day that if I were ever to found a philanthropic society, I would most certainly engrave this courier's troika on the society's seal as an emblem and a warning."

The most significant phrase in this account concerns Dostoevsky's oblique admission that "for a long time" he gave a "one-sided" explanation of this incident, or, in other words, that he blamed the Tsarist government for it. The society Dostoevsky was dreaming of founding at the end of the 1840's was a political one, in fact, a revolutionary one, and had nothing to do with philanthropy. Indeed, the word "philanthropic" was a euphemistic expression widely used at that time and even used by Gogol in that sense in the second part of *Dead Souls*. In 1880[4] Dostoevsky again recalled this incident, but by that time he had thought of a "satisfactory" explanation of it, namely, that the courier, though outwardly undoubtedly a Russian, was in reality a "European," as indeed was shown by his uniform! It took Dostoevsky forty-three years to reach such an amazing conclusion. At the age of sixteen he may have been a romantic dreamer who knew little of life, but the incident of the courier opened his eyes and provided the first impetus towards an understanding of the nature of man and the world he lived in.

Another encounter that had a lasting influence on Dostoevsky's works took place immediately on his arrival in Petersburg, at an inn where he stopped with his father and elder brother. There he met Ivan Shidlovsky, a twenty-three-year-old romantic poet who was continually torn between the promptings of the flesh and the spirit. Shidlovsky, Dostoevsky was to declare many years later to Vladimir Solovyov, the philosopher and mystic, had "a tremendous influence" on him. Writing to Solovyov's brother Vsevolod, the novelist and critic, Dostoevsky implored him to mention Shidlovsky in an article he was writing at the time. "It doesn't matter," he explained, "that no one knows anything about him or that he left no literary reputation. Please, mention him, for he was a man of the utmost importance to me and does not deserve that his name should be forgotten."

Shidlovsky attracted the young Dostoevsky not only because they shared the same romantic ideas about life and literature, but also because there seems to have been a kind of spiritual affinity between them, the same affinity of soul that existed between Dostoevsky and Vladimir Solovyov many years later. Indeed, Dostoevsky admitted as much at

4 *A Writer's Diary*, August.

his very first meeting with the young idealist philosopher in 1873. "You remind me strongly of one man," his wife records him as saying to Vladimir Solovyov, "a certain Shidlovsky, who had an enormous influence on me when I was young. You are so like him in face and character that at times I cannot help feeling that his soul has transmigrated into yours." In both of them Dostoevsky had divined a fundamental honesty of mind and heart that few people, and least of all he himself, possessed. "I used to spend whole evenings with him," Dostoevsky wrote to his brother,[5] "talking about all sorts of things. Oh, what a pure, open soul!"

Dostoevsky knew Shidlovsky for only a little over two years, for the poet soon left Petersburg for the provinces, then entered a monastery as a novice and went on a pilgrimage to Kiev, where, like Alyosha in *The Brothers Karamazov*, he was advised by an elder "to live in the world," which he did, veering between bouts of unbelief and piety, getting drunk and wandering about dressed as a novice and preaching the gospel outside country pothouses. He died in 1872, but it seems that Dostoevsky lost touch with him after he left Petersburg at the end of 1839.

The ten letters the two boys sent to their father between July 1837 and May 1839 throw an interesting light on their curious relationship, characterized, on the doctor's part, by a rueful realization that his sons were anything but frank and honest with him, and, on the part of Mikhail and Fyodor, by an insincerity that verged on hypocrisy. The first five letters seem to have been written entirely by Mikhail and only signed by Fyodor. They all begin with the stereotyped invocation to their "dearest papa" and end with the no less meaningless expression of their "deepest respect and devotion," occasionally fortified by an appeal to the Almighty "to preserve your health which is so precious to us." The Almighty's succor was most appealed to after a request for money. There is an interval of over six weeks between their first and second letters. In the first the doctor is given a brief account of their studies at the cramming school of Koronad Kostomarov, a rather formidable retired army engineer, and in the second he is informed that the entrance examinations for the Army Engineering College would be held on September 15th and that all Kostomarov's students, including Mikhail and Fyodor, had been presented to General Scharnhorst, the principal of the College. The boys also asked for fourteen rubles to defray the cost of new caps they were "compelled" to buy before the examinations. They had been to the Kazan Cathedral with Shidlovsky, a visit they had meant to pay "a long time ago, especially before the examinations."

Eleven days later the news the doctor received from his sons was less heartening. Fyodor, it is true, had passed his exams "with flying colors," having got full marks for geometry, history, French and Scriptures, but in spite of that he was only twelfth in order of admission, because, Mikhail

[5] *Letters*, January 1, 1840.

explained, those who got ahead of him had given money, that it to say, a bribe to the colonel. "Fyodor," Mikhail adds, "feels bad about this injustice. We have nothing to give, and even if we had, we should most probably not have given anything, because it is shameful and a disgrace to buy priority with money and not with deeds." But that was not all. Fyodor had also been refused a state scholarship, and where were they to get 950 rubles? "Dear Lord," Mikhail concludes, "what's going to happen to us? But He will not forsake us. Our only hope is in Him." But, as a matter of fact, their only hope was in the Kumanins, who, they knew, would not refuse to send them the money, but who, they also knew, were on very bad terms with their father, who might resent his sons asking them for money. In their next letter, of October 8th, the news of their approach to the Kumanins is carefully conveyed and the pious sentiment expressed that everything came about by the will of the Almighty. "He does everything for the best," Mikhail wrote, "and He is sure to settle our business too. Only, dear papa, do not take it to heart, and believe that God has settled it all for our good." A month later the news is gently broken of the receipt of the 950 rubles from the Kumanins, of the money having been paid in and a receipt given for it. As for Fyodor, army drill was not at all to his liking, and the Grand Duke, too, was very strict. "Shidlovsky," Mikhail added in a postscript, "sends you his best regards. He visits us or send for us on Sundays and we spend a whole evening with him."

II

On January 16, 1838, Dostoevsky entered the Army Engineering College, which was housed in the Mikhailovsky Palace, built by the mad Tsar Paul. The students of the Engineering College knew, of course, many of the stories handed down by word of mouth relating to the history of the palace and the august lunatic who was murdered in it. They knew, for instance, which room had been the Emperor's throne room and which his bedroom, dining room and kitchen. It was not so long since the door to the staircase leading from the first floor to the ground floor had been walled up and the corridor, at the end of which was the door opening onto the canal where a boat had been moored, had been demolished (this was, no doubt, the way by which the assassins gained access to the Emperor's bedroom). In one of the oval rooms there was still the hook on which had been hung the dove belonging to the sect of flagellants who performed their religious "rituals" under it.

During the sixteen months between his admission to the College and his father's violent death, Dostoevsky wrote five letters to the doctor, each of them full of demands for money and insincere protestations of a desire to share his thoughts and experiences with him. "Heavens," Dostoevsky begins his second letter to his father on June 5, 1838, after an interval of five months, "how long it is since I wrote to you, how long since I tasted those moments of truly heartfelt bliss, truly pure and exalted bliss, which only those of us feel who have someone with whom to share their troubles and their hours of ecstasy, who have someone to whom they can confide everything that is taking place in their souls. . . . Oh, how avidly am I now revelling in this bliss."

In one of the articles he contributed to *The Citizen* in 1873, Dostoevsky tried to explain "why," as he put it, "everyone without exception in Russia is a liar," a fact, he declared, "of which I am absolutely convinced." One of the reasons was, he thought, "the desire to give pleasure by producing an aesthetic impression on the listener." But it was hardly for that reason that, in his letter of May 5, 1839, Dostoevsky wrote to his father: "Having passed to a higher class, I find it *absolutely necessary* to take out a subscription to the French library. How many great works by men of genius—works on mathematics and military sciences—there are in the French language! I find it necessary to read them; for I am passionately fond of military science, though I can't stand mathematics. . . . I'd also like to tell you that I am sorry to have to give up Latin. What a wonderful language! I am now reading Julius Caesar and after having had nothing to do with it for two years I still understand absolutely everything." It was not Caesar or books on military science that Dostoevsky was reading at the time—the reason for these two thumping lies was something that was to plague him all his life and for which he never hesitated to tell a lie or make a rash promise—his perpetual need of money. In an earlier letter he had tried a more direct approach to his father. "If you send me 100 rubles," he wrote, "I shall do my best to pass my exams; if not, I shall stay in the same class for another year. It's for you to decide, dear papa; it makes no difference to me." That, too, was a lie. It did make a great difference to him, for he hated the Engineering College, and, as he confessed to his father in an unguarded moment, all he wanted was to get out of it.

Twenty years later, shortly after his release from prison, Dostoevsky referred in a letter to a friend to "the painful memories" of the time he had spent at the Engineering College. "What terrible examples have I not seen there?" he wrote. "I saw young boys who had already worked out what their whole life was going to be like: at what particular time they would obtain a certain rank, what would be more profitable to their career, what was the best way of making money, and how one could best attain to a position in the army in which one could count on being both independent and secure. This I saw and heard from more than one person." Six years later, in 1864, Dostoevsky enlarged these few "painful memories" into a long description of his experiences at the Engineering College in a famous passage in his *Notes from a Dark Cellar*. "My schoolmates," he wrote, "overwhelmed me with spiteful and pitiless derision because I was not like any of them. And derision was the one thing I could not stand. . . . I at once conceived a bitter hatred for them and withdrew into my own shell of wounded, timid and excessive pride. Their coarseness appalled me. They laughed cynically at me, at my ungainly figure. . . . Even at that time I was amazed at the pettiness of their thoughts, the silliness of their occupations, their games, their conversations. . . . They were not interested in anything that was out of the ordinary, in anything that was conducive to thought, so that I could not help looking on them as my inferiors. . . . They understood nothing. They had not the faintest idea of what life was really like. . . . On the contrary, they had a most fantastic and absurd notion of the most simple, most ordinary facts, and already at that age they were in the habit of admiring success alone. Everything that was just but looked down upon and oppressed, they laughed at shamelessly and heartlessly. Rank they mistook for brains. . . . Even at sixteen all they were discussing was soft jobs. . . . And they were abominably vicious. . . . I hated them. . . . They repaid me in the same coin and did not conceal their loathing for me. But I was no longer anxious for them to like me; on the contrary, I longed continually to humiliate them. To escape their ridicule, I began to apply myself more diligently to my studies and was soon among the top boys in my class. This did make an impression on them. However, they all began to realize that I was already reading books they could not read and that I understood things of which they had not even heard. They looked sullenly and sardonically upon all this, but they had to acknowledge my moral superiority. . . . Their jeering stopped, but their hostility remained, and henceforth our relations became strained and frigid. . . . The first thing I did on leaving school was to give up the career for which I had been trained so as to break all ties that bound me to my past, which I loathed and abominated."

The truthfulness of this account of his school days is vouched for by a great deal of contemporary evidence as well as by remarks in his own letters at the time, such as the following curt sentence in his first letter to his father after he had joined the Engineering College: "Thank God I am getting used to my life here; about my fellow students I can say nothing good."

Dmitry Grigorovich,[6] a contemporary of Dostoevsky's at the Engineering College who was to become famous as the first Russian novelist to give a realistic, albeit sentimentalized, description of the life of the Russian peasant, states in his reminiscences that "it is difficult to imagine that in

[6] Grigorovich was brought up by his mother, a Frenchwoman, the widow of a rich Russian landowner, and he knew very little Russian when he first entered the Engineering College. "I knew a Russian writer," Dostoevsky writes about him in the July-August (1876) number of his *Writer's Diary*, "who had made a name for himself" and who "had not only learned the Russian language, but had even learned to know the Russian peasant—and afterwards wrote novels dealing with the everyday life of the Russian peasant."

an army college customs could exist that were only possible in a most savage society." One of these customs was the whipping of new boys, or "hazel hens," as they were called. "The new boys," Grigorovich records, "had to crawl on all fours under a table, and on emerging on the other side, they were whipped with ropes without any regard for where the blows fell." Dostoevsky, unlike his classmates, who were mostly boys of fourteen, was an idealistic and rather priggish young man of seventeen at the time, and one can easily imagine his reaction to such treatment and to the singing of bawdy songs by the students of the lower and higher "officer" classes.

He did not apply himself with any particular enthusiasm to the subjects he was supposed to study. The curriculum of the "conductor" or lowest class included twelve subjects, of which only one—Russian literature—might have interested him had it not been for the fact that it was taught by a pedant to whom Pushkin was a mere rhymester and Gogol an indecent writer. For the more important subjects—architecture, topography, analytic and practical geometry, physics, artillery and fortifications—Dostoevsky had neither the inclination nor the ability. Writing to his father on June 5, 1838, about his lack of success in the third-term examinations, he confessed ruefully that he was no good at all at drawing and that this had had a bad effect on the final results. "As you know," he wrote, "I am very bad at drawing . . . and drawing is considered here more important than mathematics." Another of his weak points was army drill in the square before the Mikhailovsky Palace. He had to stand rigidly in line and at the drill sergeant's word of command "One!" stretch out his right leg with the foot pointing downwards and wait for the command "Two!" when he had to raise his leg very slowly and, as Grigorovich put it, "remain in that crane-like position" till the command "Three!" They were also put through the routine of marching in preparation for the reviews by the Grand Duke and the Emperor. "Just imagine," Dostoevsky wrote to his father in the same letter, "five reviews by the Grand Duke and the Emperor have completely exhausted us. We took part in the trooping of the color, marched on parade with the Guards and before every review our company was tortured by constant exercises in marching and drill. All the reviews were in preparation of the magnificent and brilliant May Parade, at which the entire royal family was present and in which 140,000 troops took part. This day exhausted us completely. During the next few months we shall be in camp. Owing to my height, I have been put into the company of skirmishers, so that I have to do double drill now—the battalion and the skirmishers." In 1848 Dostoevsky was five feet six inches tall (according to the official report of the prison authorities) and he most probably was not any shorter in 1838.

There are two descriptions of what he looked like at the time, one by a friend of his elder brother, Dr. Alexander Riesenkampf, who met him for the first time in November 1838, and another by the painter Konstantin Trutovsky, who joined the Army Engineering College in 1839 and who later shared rooms with Dostoevsky. Riesenkampf[7] describes him as "rather rotund, stoutish, fair, with a round face and a slightly tipped-up nose. His light chestnut hair was closely cropped, and under his high forehead and thin eyebrows was concealed a pair of small and rather deep-seated gray eyes; his cheeks were pale and freckled; his complexion was sallow, his lips rather thick. . . ." Trutovsky, who helped Dostoevsky with his drawing and who later became a talented artist, described him as "well-built, thickset, with a rather jerky way of walking, a kind of gray complexion, a thoughtful look and a somewhat concentrated expression. The military uniform," he concluded, "did not suit him at all."

Nor did the military discipline suit him at all. What annoyed him particularly was the way he had to salute a superior officer in the street. The army regulations laid it down that an officer-cadet or indeed any low-ranking officer should first stand at attention, throw off the cloak from his left shoulder, to expose his epaulet, and then touch his tricorn hat with his right hand—a complicated procedure that had to be repeated a dozen times during a walk on Nevsky Avenue. "Tell him," his father, who had learned of Dostoevsky's annoyance, wrote to Mikhail on November 11, 1838, "to put himself in his superior officer's place. I suppose he would be pleased to be saluted by officers of lower rank, and, above all, let him remember that he who does not know how to obey will never learn how to command." But, of course, it was not only saluting that Dostoevsky disliked. It was, in fact, his bad marks in the purely military subjects that failed him in his final examinations at the end of his first year and kept him in the third (that is, lowest) form for another year. Characteristically, Dostoevsky put the blame for his failure to pass to a higher class on someone else. "Some of my teachers," he wrote to his father on October 30, 1838, "did not like me . . . with two of them I had personal disagreements. One word from them and I was left behind." In his letter to Mikhail, however, he put the blame only on one master.

"The horrible exam!" he wrote.[8] "It kept me from writing to you and to father and from seeing Shidlovsky. And what was the result? I haven't been transferred. Oh horror! Another year, one whole year more! I would not have been so mad, if I did not know that villainy, black villainy alone defeated me. I should not have minded if the tears of our poor father did not scald my soul. Till now I did not know the meaning of injured pride. I would have blushed if I had succumbed to the feeling . . . but do you know, I wish I could crush the whole world with one blow. . . . I lost, wasted so many days before the examination, I fell ill, I lost weight, I passed the examination in every subject and—failed. . . . That was

[7] Mikhail had met Dr. Riesenkampf in Reval, where he had been admitted to a military engineering school in June 1838.

[8] *Letters*, October 31, 1838.

what one of our masters (the algebra master) wanted because I was rude to him during the year, a fact he had the meanness to point out to me in explaining the reason why I had not passed. . . . Out of 10 marks I got an average of 9½ [his marks were two out of twelve, not ten, as he claims, in the important military subjects] and I did not pass. . . . But to hell with it all. I shall just have to grin and bear it."

His injured pride blinded him also to the fact that most of his time was devoted to literary occupations and not to algebra. In recounting "the unforgettable hours" he had spent with Dostoevsky during their first meeting at the Mikhailovsky Palace, Dr. Riesenkampf writes: "He [Dostoevsky] recited to me with his usual enthusiasm passages out of Pushkin's *Egyptian Nights* and Zhukovsky's translation of Walter Scott's *St. John's Eve*, told me of his own literary efforts and was only sorry that the strict rules of the college prevented him from meeting me somewhere else. . . . He loved poetry passionately, but wrote only prose because he had not enough patience for the writing of verse. Thoughts sprang up in his head like the spray in a cascade of water. His natural, beautiful recital overstepped the bounds of artistic self-control."

It was no wonder Dostoevsky was thought to be "an eccentric" by his fellow students. They had nicknamed him "Photius" after an eccentric cleric, Peter Spassky (1792–1838), who had assumed the name of Photius on becoming a monk and regarded himself as "the militant instrument of Providence" and "the Savior of the Church and the fatherland." Dostoevsky was indeed an outsider among the 125 students of the Engineering College. Even his social status as "nobleman" seems to have been questioned by the College authorities, who sent in a request to the Herald's Office on May 19, 1838, to find out "the origin of the minor Fyodor Dostoevsky," and it was only a year and a half later, on November 29, 1839, that the Herald's Office found it possible to confirm that "one may consider the minor Fyodor Dostoevsky as belonging to the class of nobility."

There seems to have been only one student at the College whom Dostoevsky made friends with. His name was Ivan Berezhetsky, and he was a class higher than Dostoevsky. "I never saw Dostoevsky or his friend Berezhetsky taking part in the escapades of their fellow students or in their favorite games," one of the tutors, Alexander Savelyev, records. "They never went to the dancing class on Tuesday, which was very popular with the students. Often, on the excuse of not feeling well, they stayed in their dormitory reading together or walked through the rooms of the College. It is difficult to define the true significance of this friendship," Savelyev continues. "Berezhetsky was considered a rich man and he liked to show off his wealth (he wore diamond rings and a gold watch), his fine clothes and his fine manners. Dostoevsky, on the other hand, was the son of a poor doctor . . . and kept aloof from the school authorities and his fellow students, for he was one of those rare characters who find it difficult to accept the ideas and actions of society, if they are contrary to their own convictions." Curiously enough, no reference to Berezhetsky can be found in either Dostoevsky's letters or his notebooks, except perhaps the following obscure reference in a letter to Mikhail on January 1, 1840 (after Berezhetsky had been promoted to the rank of officer and had left the College): "I had one friend, a man I was very fond of."

What brought about the end of their friendship? Was it Dostoevsky's sensitivity, the "bitterness" in his attitude toward people that Savelyev had noticed already in his first year at college? Berezhetsky was always exquisitely dressed, while Dostoevsky had to depend entirely on the army issue of clothing. Did Dostoevsky borrow money from his friend, which later he was unable to pay, a circumstance which brought about the severing of relations with some of his closest friends throughout his life? A loan to Dostoevsky was the surest way of earning his enmity, for he could never repay it when promised, and this worried him so much that he began to hate the man who had lent him the money.

The morbid way in which Dostoevsky was conscious of the inadequacy of his clothes as compared with those worn by his fellow students becomes clear from his frantic letters to his father for money to buy himself "at least a new pair of boots." For a decent pair of boots, as Dostoevsky explains through the mouth of his hero in *Poor People*, "is necessary in support of one's honor and one's good name." In *The Double*, too, Dostoevsky speaks of new boots as the criterion of material well-being. When dressing, Golyadkin, the hero of the story, "looked lovingly at his boots several times, raising one foot one moment and the other foot the next, admiring their style and whispering something under his breath, and from time to time winking and grimacing significantly as though in reply to his thoughts."

On May 10, 1839, Dostoevsky wrote to his father: "I must willy-nilly conform to the rules of the society I live with. Why make an exception of oneself? Such exceptions are sometimes exposed to a great deal of unpleasantness. You understand it yourself, dear papa. You have lived among people. Now, every student of an army college has to spend at least 40 rubles when in camp. (I am writing to you about all this because I am talking to my father.) In this sum I am not including such necessities as, for instance, sugar, tea, etc. One has to have those anyway, and not only out of decency alone, but because one simply cannot do without them. When you are soaked to the skin in rainy weather in a canvas tent, when you come back from maneuvers in such weather, feeling tired and chilled to the marrow, you can fall ill if you have no tea, which is what happened to me last year on maneuvers. Still," Dostoevsky goes on, as if tea were some outlandish commodity that the army did not supply gratis to private and officer alike, "taking into account your present difficulties, I shall refrain from drinking tea. All I demand is 16 rubles for two pairs of ordinary boots, which I must have. At present my things—books, boots, pens, paper, etc.,—have to be put somewhere. For this purpose I must also have a trunk, for there are no buildings in a camp except tents. Our beds are just bundles of hay covered with sheets. The question therefore is where am I to put all my things if I have no trunk? You ought to know that the government does not care whether you have a trunk or not, since once the examinations are over, books are no longer needed. That is why I will not be given a place where I can put a trunk, which I must have. If I put it in my tent, it is sure to interfere with my comrade with whom I share the tent. I shall simply not be allowed to keep a trunk in a tent, for it just isn't done. I must therefore find a place for it somewhere else. This I can do by making an arrangement with one of our orderlies (as everyone does). But I shall have to pay him for this. So that I must have sixteen rubles for the boots, one ruble (at least) for the trunk, five rubles for transporting it to the camp and back, two rubles for a place for it, and five rubles for cleaning my boots. That is the usual charge. In town it's a different matter, but in camp one has to pay an orderly for everything he does."

Would Dostoevsky have made "an exception of himself" if his father had not sent him the money for his trunk and his boots? The testimony of one of his contemporaries at the Engineering College shows that there was no basis whatever for his exaggerated fears that his "honor and good name" might have suffered if he did not try to emulate the extravagant habits of his friend. "I lived in the same camp as he, in the same canvas tent," Semyonov Tyan-Shansky writes in his memoirs, "and managed without my own tea (we were given army tea in the mornings and evenings), without my own boots and without a trunk for books, though I used to read them no less than Fyodor Dostoevsky. So that it was not a real necessity, but was done rather in order not to lag behind those of his fellow students who had their own tea, their own boots and their own trunks."

Apart from Berezhetsky, Dostoevsky made no really intimate friend at the Engineering College. Grigorovich records that "already at the college he showed his well-known traits of unsociability, shunned everybody, took no part in games, sat absorbed in a book and looked for a place where he would be left in peace; soon he found such a place, and it became his favorite place for a long time: a deep recess in the fourth dormitory with a window looking onto the Fontanka; during breaks he could always be found there and always with a book." Trutovsky, too, remembered him as keeping aloof from everybody and always walking up and down with a thoughtful expression and discussing something for hours with Berezhetsky and another student. "He always looked serious," Trutovsky adds, "and I cannot imagine him laughing or looking cheerful." According to Savelyev, it often happened that Dostoevsky did not notice anything that was going on around him. "He put away his books and exercise books," Savelyev writes, "only when the drummer walked through the dormitories beating 'lights-out.' But I saw him many times in the middle of the night sitting at his table and reading some book. He would throw a blanket over his night clothes; he did not seem to be aware of the strong draft blowing in through the window. He used to say that the stillness of the night and the half-darkness of the dormitory lit by a tallow candle were conducive to quiet work, and this habit of working at night, remained with him to his last days."

While working hard at the Engineering College in the second or lower and third or higher officers' classes, where he studied differential and integral calculus, statics, descriptive geometry, physics, tactics, architecture, fortifications, theoretical and applied mechanics, chemistry, geometry and the art of military construction, Dostoevsky never for a moment gave up the idea of eventually resigning from the army and devoting himself to "solving the mystery of man." Already on August 16, 1839, that is, only a few months after the death of his father, he wrote to Mikhail: "Now I look much more often at my surroundings with complete indifference, but my awakening is all the stronger for that. My only aim is to obtain my freedom. I am ready to sacrifice everything for it. I must confess, though, that one has to possess great faith in one's future and a strong sense of one's own powers to continue living on one's hopes. But what does it matter? Whether they come true or not, I shall accomplish what I have set out to do. To learn the meaning of man and life is something I am making progress in. I have confidence in myself. Man is a mystery which must be solved, and even if you were to spend your whole life in solving it, you could not say that you had wasted your time. The solution of this mystery is my business, for I want to be a man."

Two years later, on February 27, 1841, he again confides to Mikhail his desire to achieve freedom. "Oh, my brother, my dear brother," he wrote, "how I wish to reach the haven of freedom as soon as possible. A man's freedom and his vocation are a great thing! I am dreaming of it again as never before. And one's soul expands in an effort to understand the greatness of life. . . ."

But freedom was still far off, and in the meantime his father's death had made it necessary to make sure that his allowance was not jeopardized. The first thing to do was to get in touch again with the rich Kumanins in Moscow. His uncle and aunt had undertaken to provide for his two younger brothers and three sisters, but to him, who was at the time immersed in contemplating "the sublime and the beautiful" as it appeared in the works of Schiller, they were nothing but "paltry souls," as he contemptuously described them in a letter to Mikhail.[9] He therefore hastened to resume the interrupted correspondence with the Kumanins in the florid style he had used in his letters to his father, though this time without invoking the deity as witness to his repentance. On December 25, 1839,

[9] *Letters,* August 16, 1839.

he admitted to them that his long silence "might" strike them as "black ingratitude," but that now "the thought that I have failed to carry out my obligations, that I did not perform my duty . . . this thought has completely destroyed me. . . . These pure effusions of a contrite heart," the eighteen-year-old hypocrite went on, "the grievous death of my father and the benefactions you have bestowed upon our family have aroused in me a feeling of shame and the pangs of repentance. . . ." He therefore hoped "to deserve your attention by a continual preservation of that sacred feeling of love, respect and devotion with which I have the honor of remaining your humble and obedient nephew, Fyodor Dostoevsky." A month later, on receiving a reply from his aunt, with the news of the engagement of his seventeen-year-old sister Varvara, upon whom the Kumanins had bestowed a dowry of 25,000 rubles, he dispatched an even more abject letter, in which he declared himself to be in debt to them, "a debt," he wrote, "which exceeds all I shall ever be able to do to repay it, and if my guilt has any redress, if my repentance and my devotion to you have any value in your eyes, I shall deem myself happy, for it will greatly relieve my conscience. . . ." His aunt had informed him of the death of his uncle, Michael Nechaev, who had been slapped by his father for trying to seduce their parlormaid, and that made him "shed a few sincere tears in his memory." He concluded by excusing himself for not replying earlier because of his examinations. "Now," he declared, "that they are over I am not wasting a minute. But," he added rather lamely, no doubt wondering whether even his aunt would swallow the lie of examinations at the *beginning* of a new term, "I feel that I am wearying you with my letter. And so permit your sincerely loving and devoted nephew to remain your ever humble and obedient Fyodor Dostoevsky."

In a letter written on the same day he assured his sister Varvara that he had never forgotten his brothers and sisters and impressed upon her in particular that their eldest brother, Mikhail, loved her sincerely though he had never written to her. "Don't forget," he added a little cryptically, "what he had to put up with in placating our father." He added truthfully enough that "the closest friendship binds me to him." He also expressed the hope that Varvara would remind their brother Andrey "to be grateful to our benefactors," that is, the Kumanins, who had agreed to pay for Andrey's tuition to enable him to pass his entrance examinations to the Army Engineering College. It had occurred to Dostoevsky that it would be a good idea if he could appropriate this money by undertaking to help Andrey with his studies. He concluded his letter to Varvara rather stiffly, considering the occasion: "Good-by, dear sister, your friend and brother, Fyodor Dostoevsky."

It is quite inconceivable that Dostoevsky should not have known that his seventeen-year-old sister was being married off to a man who was old enough to be her father and whom she had never seen in her life, a man who was marrying her for her dowry. The man was Peter Karepin, a forty-six-year-old widower with a four-year-old daughter. He occupied the important post of director of the Moscow Governor-General's office and was also honorary secretary to several charitable societies, but his largest income came from his post of chief manager of the estates of Count Golitsyn. Andrey, who was present at the first meeting of Karepin with his sister at the Kumanins', could not help observing how embarrassed and unhappy his sister felt, especially when, to break the ice, she was forced to play preference, a card game she knew nothing of, with her future husband and her uncle. "My sister Varenka," he records, "was made to sit down on the right of her fiancé. After the second deal Karepin fanned his cards out and showed them to my sister. But she, poor thing, could at that moment hardly distinguish a king from a knave. And, indeed, to see a man for the first time in her life and to be conscious of the fact that this man was her fiancé, her future husband!"

The truth is that Dostoevsky was so pleased at the time that at least one of his sisters had been comfortably "settled" and need concern him no longer that he never asked himself what his young sister must have felt to be married to a man almost three times her age, a man she had never seen before. It was only after he had quarreled with Karepin, who became his guardian, that the problem of such a marriage, common enough in those days, as the marriage of his own mother showed, presented itself to him in all its dramatic possibilities. It required an injection of hatred to rouse his sympathy for a young bride in such a situation, and in *The Christmas Tree and a Wedding*, written four years after his violent quarrel with Karepin, he gave an artistic treatment of the problem, together with a venomous and, according to all contemporary accounts, most unfair portrait of Karepin in the person of Julian Mastakovich.

III

After passing his examinations at the Army Engineering College on August 5, 1841, Dostoevsky was promoted to the rank of engineer-ensign and was allowed to live in his own quarters. Having obtained some of his longed-for freedom at last, he was not slow to enjoy to the full the many pleasures a city like Petersburg provided. His complete absorption in his literary work—he was writing feverishly by this time, although none of his early work has been preserved—and his absolute determination to become a writer made him entirely unscrupulous. As it happened, Mikhail, too, was just then greatly in need of money. He had fallen in love in Reval with a German girl, Emilia Ditmar, and was eager to marry her as soon as possible. The two brothers, therefore, decided that Mikhail, nominally one of the guardians of their father's estate, should go to Moscow to raise money for himself and his brother and bring back as many things as he could conveniently lay his hands on from Darovoye. This he did. "From Darovoye," Andrey states, "Mikhail took away everything that was of any value and sent it off to his bride in Reval. Some of the things, such as my father's fur coats, he sold in Moscow for next to nothing. All the china and silver was shared out by my two elder brothers and I saw it afterwards at their houses."

Mikhail brought his brother Andrey to Petersburg in the autumn of 1841 and installed him in Dostoevsky's lodings. "I cannot help feeling," Andrey writes, "that I was taken away from Chermak's boarding school simply for financial reasons, because, as I found out later, my uncle gave my brother Fyodor a considerable sum of money for my board and lodgings and for my coaching." It did not take Dostoevsky long to spend the "considerable sum of money," and he never really made any serious attempt to coach his brother for the entrance examinations to the Army Engineering College. In fact, he soon got bored with Andrey. "His lessons and his life at my place," he wrote to Mikhail on December 22, 1841, "have become intolerable to me, free, lonely and independent as I am. I can't work and I can't amuse myself—you understand what I mean. Besides, he has such a strange and shallow character that it would turn anyone away from him. I am really sorry I ever thought of that stupid plan of mine to let him live with me."

The first flat Dostoevsky rented on leaving the Engineering College consisted, according to Andrey, of two small, dark rooms with an entrance hall to which a kitchen was attached. He shared it with a fellow officer, Adolf Totleben, who soon after Andrey's arrival moved to other quarters but whose brief sojourn at Dostoevsky's flat proved to be of great importance to Dostoevsky after his return from Siberia eighteen years later. Adolf was often visited by his brother, Eduard Totleben, who had left the Engineering College a few years before Dostoevsky and who was to distinguish himself in the Crimean War as the defender of Sebastopol. It was on that short acquaintanceship that Dostoevsky relied when he enlisted Eduard Totleben's help in 1859 in obtaining permission to live in Petersburg and to resume his literary work there.

In December 1841, Andrey fell ill with typhoid fever, and Fyodor nursed him "very carefully." As soon as Andrey began to recover, Dostoevsky himself fell ill. According to Dr. Riesenkampf, Dostoevsky had been suffering from a hacking cough which became particularly bad in the morning, when his voice became so hoarse as to be inaudible. It was caused by his excessive smoking. "Even his doctor," Riesenkampf states, "had difficulty in persuading him not to smoke so much of the strong Zhukov pipe tobacco."

Riesenkampf's reminiscences were written long after Dostoevsky's death and, with the exception of a few verifiable facts, are quite unreliable. This is particularly true of his description of Dostoevsky's next flat as very large but without furniture except for a sofa, a writing table and a couple of chairs. Andrey describes the same flat as consisting of three small rooms with an entrance hall and a kitchen. It was in this flat that Dostoevsky was frequently visited by Trutovsky and Grigorovich. Trutovsky used to amuse him by his clever caricatures, and Grigorovich by his stage gossip and his gift for imitating the voices of famous actors. It was at this flat, too, that Dostoevsky gave frequent card parties. "My brother," Andrey writes, "was very keen on playing cards, preference or whist being followed by faro and other games of chance. At such parties, I remember, I used to look after my brother's guests, pouring out tea for them which was taken to my brother's room by his batman and myself. After tea, punch was usually served, a glass or two for each guest." This is the first mention of Dostoevsky's passion for gambling, which was to keep him in penury for many years.

On August 21, 1842, ten days after passing his examinations to the higher officers' class, Dostoevsky suddenly appeared at Riesenkampf's flat, looking cheerful and fit, and announced his promotion to second lieutenant, the receipt of a large sum of money from his guardian, which made it possible for him to pay off his debts, and, last but not least, his success in obtaining a twenty-eight-day leave to visit his elder brother, who had in the meantime married his Emilia, in Reval. To celebrate the occasion, he dragged Riesenkampf out of bed, took him to an expensive restaurant and treated him to an excellent dinner. Next morning he left by boat for Reval, where Riesenkampf met him again three weeks later, enjoying his visit but rather depressed by "the rigid caste spirit of the Baltic Germans and the lack of healthy symptoms of culture among them." This, Riesenkampf thought with some justification, was the reason why Dostoevsky was prejudiced against Germans all his life.

On his return to Petersburg, Dostoevsky had to face the disagreeable problem of his younger brother's future. Andrey had been completely unprepared for the entrance examinations to the Army Engineering College. He even failed to pass the preliminary examination in mathematics. However, through the influence of an army general, a relative of their guardian Karepin, he was admitted as a resident student to the Petersburg School of Architecture. Glad to get rid of Andrey at last, Dostoevsky celebrated the event by taking his brother out to dinner, at which, Andrey records, "we drank a bottle of wine in honor of the occasion." A few days after the dinner, having learned that Andrey had been sent a hundred rubles by the Kumanins through Karepin's relative, Dostoevsky began bombarding his brother with requests for a loan. At the end of 1842 Dostoevsky wrote: "Dear Andrey, if you have received the money, then for God's sake send me five rubles or even one ruble. I have had no fuel in my stove for three days and I haven't a penny. Next week I shall get 200 rubles (I am borrowing it) and I'll pay you back." A few weeks later, at the beginning of January 1843, having failed to obtain the loan, he wrote again: "If you have got the money, send me some at once. I have nothing. And let me know when you are coming to see me, for if you can't send me anything now, you could perhaps bring me some. Please!" This was followed by a third desperate note a few weeks later. "You wrote to me that you can't get the money before Shrovetide. So this is what I have thought of: with this letter I am sending you a note in which I ask you for a loan of fifty rubles. Show it at once to the general and ask him to let you have the money immediately. Tell him you've promised me the money on your word of honor. I promise faithfully to pay you back as soon as I get the money from Mikhail. You won't be without money. Take as much as you need from the fifty rubles. You don't want money now and I am in a terrible fix. Please help me. Your Dostoevsky. P.S. If I don't have any money by Strovetide, I'll get an advance from my salary and pay you back." Andrey must have lent him the money eventually, for a year later Dostoevsky was at last able to repay some of it. "I'm sorry it's so little," he wrote to Andrey, "but I'm afraid I can't afford more as I have not had a penny for a long time myself."

Dr. Riesenkampf, who returned to Petersburg in September 1843, after Dostoevsky had entered the government service as a draftsman in the Petersburg Engineering Corps, found him living on bread and milk, which he got on credit from a nearby shop. At the request of Mikhail, Riesenkampf agreed to share a flat with Dostoevsky "so as to influence him by his example of German neatness and orderliness." But Riesenkampf's example had little influence on Dostoevsky, who was just then studying the life of the Petersburg poor in search of material for his first novel and was consequently taking a particular interest in the doctor's poor patients. But, Riesenkampf writes, the huge monthly bill of the baker alone could not be explained by Dostoevsky's hospitality to the poor patients. In fact, Dostoevsky's batman, who had been keeping company with his laundrywoman, had been providing not only for her family, but also for her numerous friends, all at the expense of his master, and the same was true of Dostoevsky's tailor, bootmaker, barber, and so on, for it was not easy to convince him that a great many people to whom he was dispensing hospitality did not deserve his sympathy.

In November 1843, Riesenkampf records, Dostoevsky received his annual allowance of 1,000 rubles and began pacing up and down the drawing room, "not in the way he usually did, but noisily, self-confidently, almost proudly." Next morning he came into Riesenkampf's bedroom once more with his quiet, diffident gait and asked him to lend him five rubles. It seemed that the greater part of the 1,000 rubles had gone to pay his debts and the rest he had lost at a game of billiards, his last fifty rubles having been stolen by one of his partners whom he had left alone for a few minutes. In December 1843, Dostoevsky's financial position became desperate again. "Although," he wrote to Mikhail on December 31, "Karepin has sent me 300 rubles, I was forced to follow my former system and, owing money for household expenses, I am again in debt to the amount of 200 rubles." To pay his debts Dostoevsky was this time forced to borrow 300 rubles from a moneylender, a retired noncommissioned officer, receiving only 200 rubles, the remaining hundred rubles being retained by the moneylender as his interest for four months. In addition, he had to pledge a quarter of his annual salary and get the treasurer of his department to guarantee it.

The unreliability of Riesenkampf's account of Dostoevsky's financial position at that particular time is perhaps best illustrated by his claim that Dostoevsky had an annual income of 5,000 rubles. Actually, Dostoevsky received an annual allowance of only 1,000 rubles from Karepin, and his officer's salary did not amount to as much as that. In fact, Dostoevsky's income must have been much less than 2,000 rubles a year, which, taking into account his extravagant habits, explains why he was always in debt.

Dostoevsky continued to borrow from moneylenders at extortionate rates of interest while making fantastic plans for getting rich quickly by crashing into the translation market. "I must tell you," he wrote to Mikhail at the beginning of 1844, "that during the Christmas holidays I translated *Eugénie Grandet* by Balzac. (A miracle! A miracle!) The translation is first class. I shall receive at least three hundred and fifty rubles for it. I had a great desire to offer it for sale, but your future millionaire had no money to pay for copying out his manuscript. In the name of the heavenly angels send me thirty-five rubles (the price of copying), and by the Jew Yankel (a play I have just completed) and—by what else?—by my mustache which, I hope, will grow one day, I swear that half of what I get for *Eugénie* will be yours. *Dixi.*"

His translation of Balzac's novel was published in 1844 in the June and July issues of the monthly periodical *Repertoire and Pantheon* in a greatly abbreviated form, which, however, was sufficient to show that Dostoevsky had very little regard for Balzac's text.

The "future millionaire" had first broached his plan for getting rich quickly by translations of French novels in a letter to Mikhail on December 31, 1843. His plan was to publish 2,500 copies of a translation of Eugène Sue's *Mathilde*, which, he calculated, would net a profit of 7,000 rubles in six months. In his next letter he urged his brother to do the translation, while he would do the editing, but a fortnight later, in reply to Mikhail's request for more details, he had to inform him "with deep regret" that the whole thing had fallen through. He next urged his brother to start translating Schiller, beginning with *Don Carlos*, but he was no longer counting their profits in thousands; 350 rubles was all he could promise. He himself had been translating George Sand's *La dernière Albini*, but, he wrote to Mikhail in the summer of 1844, "imagine my horror—the novel has already been translated in 1837. How the hell was I to know that?" Meanwhile he made up his mind to resign his commission and devote himself entirely to literary work. "The point is," he wrote to Mikhail after he had sent in his resignation in September 1844, "that I never really intended to stay too long in the army, so why should I waste the best years of my life? Besides, they intend to send me to the provinces and, well, what on earth can I possibly do without Petersburg? . . . Don't worry about me," he went on, "I shall soon be able to earn enough to keep me going. I shall work devilishly hard. But what am I going to do now? That's the question. I owe 800 rubles—525 to my landlord. I wrote home [that is, to Karepin in Moscow] that I owed 1,500 rubles, knowing their habit of sending only one third of what you ask. . . . If the Moscow swine keep on delaying, I shall be lost. I shall most certainly be dragged off to jail by my creditors. A most comic business!"

Dostoevsky did not tell Mikhail about the 1,000 rubles he had received from "the Moscow swine" and lost on the same day. Having sent in his resignation, he could not very well ask Karepin to send him another 1,000 rubles. He therefore decided to give up his claim on his father's estate for a lump sum of 1,000 rubles in silver, half of which was to be paid at once and the rest at ten rubles a month. He made this proposal to Karepin at the end of August 1844, in a characteristic letter. He began by informing Karepin that he had been forced to resign his commission because of the "extremely unsatisfactory" state of his affairs. He had not written to him about it at once because he had not the money to post the letter. There followed a rather confused account of his critical position. "Everyone for himself and God for all," he went on, unable to restrain himself from making fun of Karepin's fondness for quoting proverbs. "Here you have a wonderful proverb invented by people who have been lucky enough to have had a good life. For my part, I am ready to admit that this wise rule is the height of perfection. But the trouble is that this proverb was changed at the very beginning of its existence. Everyone for himself, everyone against you, and God for all. After that it is natural that there is not much hope left for a man like me." After making the extraordinary claim that if he had not resigned he would have had to raise 1,200 rubles to cover the expense of his journey to Orenburg or Sebastopol (he did not seem to know himself where he was being sent or, indeed, if he was being sent anywhere), as though he would not have gone there at the government's expense, he went on:

"I wish to inform you, sir, that I have the greatest need for clothing. The winters in Petersburg are known to be very cold and the autumns to be very damp and harmful to one's health. From which, I suppose, it follows that it is impossible to walk about without clothes—you might find yourself being carried out of your house feet foremost. Of course, there is a noble proverb even to describe such a contingency: *it serves him right!* But this proverb is used only in extreme cases and I have not yet reached such an extremity. As I will have no lodgings, for I shall have to leave my present flat because I am unable to pay the rent, I shall have to live in the street or sleep under the colonnade of the Kazan Cathedral. But as this is unhealthy, I must have a flat. There exists a sort of proverb that in such a case one could find *Government* lodgings, but that is true only in extreme cases, and I have not yet been reduced to such an extremity. And, finally, one has to *eat*. For *not to eat* is unhealthy, but as there are no proverbs so far as eating is concerned, all one can do is to die of hunger; but that again is only possible in extreme cases, to which I, thank God, have not yet been reduced."

He went on to explain that he would be willing to renounce his claim on the share of his inheritance for only one payment of 1,000 rubles (in silver), provided that half of it was paid at once and the rest over a period of time. He threatened to sell his part of the estate to a stranger if his request was not granted, even if he were offered less than a thousand for it. "I simply must have the money," he wrote. "I shall not allow myself to be ruined completely. I must get settled. Now I am free nothing is going to stop me. . . . I want you to know," he concluded this extraordinary letter, "that in May I obtained an advance of the whole of my salary (I had to eat), hence I haven't a penny, neither have I any clothes, and, finally, I must pay my debts. I wish for nothing more than to wind up my affairs. They interfere with my life."

On September 7, 1844, he wrote another long letter to Karepin, repeating his demand for a lump sum in exchange for his share of the inheritance. "I shall be put on the retired list," he wrote, "my creditors will show me no mercy, particularly as I shan't even have any clothes, and I shall be exposed to great unpleasantness. . . . You must surely realize that I shall not go to jail humming songs out of stupid bravado. It's quite ridiculous. That is why for the last time I am writing to you, for the last time telling you of the extremity of my position, for the last time begging you to help me, and for the last time telling you I should rather rot in jail than re-enter the service without my affairs being settled."

Karepin is generally blamed for refusing Dostoevsky's request, but his reply to Dostoevsky's two letters hardly justifies such a reproach. "I am sending you fifty rubles without comment," Karepin wrote, "and instead of arrogance and rudeness, with which your letters are filled, I am enclosing two accounts for the last and the current years . . . which show that the income from your parents' estate amounts to about 4,000 rubles in notes [*i.e.*, 1,000 rubles in silver] and that it depends on the harvest and the prices of agricultural produce. Of this sum a certain amount has to be paid to the Trustees' Council Bank in repayment of a private loan of 1,000 rubles, so that each of your brothers can only receive from 700 to 800 rubles a year and only in a very good year about 1,000 rubles." He went on to explain that it was impossible to sell a part of the estate, because it was mortgaged, the private debt had not been repaid, and there were three heirs who were still minors. But even if it were possible to sell his share, there was not enough money to pay him the lump sum he demanded. This should have been sufficient to explain why Dostoevsky's plan was not practical. Unfortunately, Karepin went on to read Dostoevsky a lecture on his cold egoism and indifference" towards his parents' memory as well as towards his brothers and sisters. "You had hardly had time to feel the weight of your epaulettes on your shoulders," he declared, "before two words began to recur in your letters: your inheritance and your debts. I said nothing, attributing it to your youthful fantasy and knowing very well that experience would teach you to know better. But now I should like to point out that your inheritance is very minute: to be angry with it or to complain about it is a waste of time, for it does not depend on you and there are thousands of people in the world who have not got even that. Besides, considering the extent of your expenditure, it will not last for one year, and what of the future? . . . I do not doubt that you will agree with me that to exceed the degree of the possibility of repayment is an encroachment on another man's property. It is not your fault that you were not born a millionaire, but it is your fault if you are not satisfied with the means which God, your social position and the benefactions of the authorities have bestowed on you. Are you," he went on grandiloquently, "to abide by Portico sophisms and the abstract indolence and voluptuousness of Shakespearean dreams? What are they good for? Of what practical use are they? What are they but inflated, inflamed, puffed-out, exaggerated, bubble-like images? On the other hand, so far as material advantages are concerned, you have been shown and you have open before you the road to honor, of work for the benefit of your country, not in slavish imitation of someone else's visions, but in the works of your own intellect and the knowledge with which your work has for so many years adorned it."

"Portico sophisms," "Shakespearean dreams" and "inflated bubble-like images" were, of course, just what Dostoevsky wanted in order to get his own back on Karepin. "These Muscovites," he wrote to Mikhail,[10] "are inexpressibly vain, stupid, and love to preach. In his last letter K. without rhyme or reason advised me not to be carried away by Shakespeare. He says that Shakespeare and a soap bubble are one and the same thing. I do want you to understand this comic trait—this bitterness against Shakespeare. I mean, what has Shakespeare to do with it? You should have seen the letter I wrote to him! A model of polemics! I told him off properly. A *chef d'oeuvre* of letter writing!"

His letter, written on September 19, 1844, is also a model of rudeness and of complete inability to see anyone's point of view but his own. He would have been grateful for Karepin's sympathy and advice, Dostoevsky began, if it had not been for the tone of his letter, which might have deceived an ignoramus, but not him; he understood it very well and, because of it, he no longer felt the need to be grateful. He went on to deny that he was robbing his younger brothers, and accused Karepin of inciting his whole family against him. He further claimed that there was nothing wrong about his wishing to sell his share of his parents' estate and that the legal difficulties of such a sale had been invented by Karepin just to

10 *Letters*, September 30, 1844.

"stun" him. He even declared that he might withdraw his resignation from the army if his debts were paid, which of course he never intended doing.

"You are shocked by my egoism," Dostoevsky went on, "and would rather explain my demands by my youthful thoughtlessness. But it's none of your business. And," he added, ignoring the fact that Karepin was the legal guardian of his parents' estate, "I find it strange that you should take this work upon yourself without being asked or given the right to do so. You may be sure," he jeered, "that I revere the memory of my parents no less than you do yours." He then went on to accuse Karepin of "lack of civility," in ignoring his letters. "If, on the other hand," he went on, "you thought it beneath your dignity to discuss anything with me, no doubt, believing me to be an arrogant youngster who had only recently put on epaulettes, then you should not have expressed your superiority so naïvely and humiliated me so insolently by your admonitions and words of advice, which are becoming only to a father. As for your Shakespearean soap bubbles, I wonder why you should think it so necessary to give such a drubbing to Shakespeare. Poor Shakespeare!"

Having delivered what he thought to be a shrewd blow in defense of Shakespeare, Dostoevsky turned to the more pertinent matter of his debts and put the blame for them squarely on the shoulders of Jeremy Bentham. Referring to Karepin's statement that "to exceed the degree of the possibility of repayment is an encroachment on another man's property," he declared (quite wrongly, as is clear from his letter to Mikhail) that his debts only amounted to 1,500 rubles and that, anyway, he was not responsible for them. "I did not incur them and it is not my fault that in Petersburg more than anywhere else flourishes the commerce patronized by Bentham [a reference to the extortionate rates of interest charged by the Petersburg moneylenders]. At any rate, this naïve statement of yours (out of respect for your years I would not like to interpret it as an intentional rudeness and a desire to hurt my feelings) I must and indeed shall treat as belonging to the same category as your Shakespearean soap bubbles." The real sting Dostoevsky left to the tail of his letter. "The study of the life of man," he wrote, "being my primary aim and hobby, I have now become convinced of the existence, for instance, of Famusov, Chichikov and Falstaff. At any rate," he concludes, "the thing's done. I have sent in my resignation, I have not a farthing to repay my debts or," he added, as though still holding out the prospect that he might withdraw his resignation, "to get the necessary equipment. If you do not send me the money immediately, you will entirely justify my last letter."

Karepin, of course, ignored his letters. On September 30, 1844, Dostoevsky tried to get his own back on Karepin by being really rude to him in his letter to Mikhail. After calling Karepin "a swine" and "a damn fool," he even tried an uninhibited doggerel epigram: "Karepin's a drunkard, he f——s and sh——s, believes in God, has a high rank and d.t. fits." At the same time he was anxious that Mikhail should write to Karepin and vouch for him. "They do not *trust* me," he wrote in the same letter. "They think that I will deceive them. Please, vouch for me. Tell them *you are ready to offer everything you have as a guarantee that I will not make any more claims.* If they have not got so much money, 800 or 700 will be a great help to me in my present position, and, please, vouch for this too, namely that it will be taken into account as part payment for the lump sum of 500 rubles in silver and 500 rubles in silver to be paid in installments."

Even if Mikhail did write to Karepin, which is doubtful, since his own financial position was even more desperate than Dostoevsky's, his guarantee would not have impressed their guardian. In the end, of course, Dostoevsky had to eat humble pie and grovel before the man he so despised. On October 20, 1844, the day after he had been officially informed that his resignation had been accepted and that his rank on his retirement had been raised to that of first lieutenant, he appealed again to Karepin to reconsider his refusal to accept his proposal for the sale of his share of the estate. "You must know," he wrote, "that at the very moment that you are reading my letter my resignation has been gazetted (check it in the papers). I have no clothes, no money, and I will have no lodgings, either." To meet Karepin's objections to his plan, he now proposed to give an IOU as a guarantee for the sum advanced until the final division of the estate among its heirs. "This seems to me to be a simple and possible solution," Dostoevsky declared meekly, "and I can't express in words what a beneficent thing it will be for my whole future. I shall have no more financial worries," he went on astonishingly, "escape from the vile situation in which I have been for the past two years and," he added quite shamelessly, "I may be in a position to carry on in the service. . . . You are a *businessman*, you are dealing with us as a *businessman* and as a *businessman* I don't suppose you will have time to consider my affairs, though they are of no great consequence or just because they are of no great consequence. But if the entire salvation, the entire well-being, the entire hopes of a person depend on these unimportant affairs, then one must forgive this person's insistence and importunity. That is why I humbly request you to help me in the way I wrote to you earlier. . . . Since I can see from your account that there is no money, then, please, borrow some. . . . If you leave me without an answer and without help I am done for. And that is why I am forced to ask for an official confirmation that you are our guardian and what the income from my estate amounts to. I am asking you this because I may have to prove to my creditors that I possess the means of paying them. . . . Please, forgive me, first, for interrupting your work by my requests and, secondly, for insisting that I must have the money immediately, for if things come to a head I may have to borrow more money and let my creditors have everything at a rate of interest ten times higher than I had paid on my loans before. . . . You can imagine what the results will be—everyone will suffer. I therefore beg you once more in God's name to answer me as quickly as possible. Apart from everything else, I have not enough money to buy food. God forbid that you should ever experience what I am experiencing now. . . ."

Karepin accepted Dostoevsky's apology and sent him the 500 rubles in silver, that is, the first half of his share of the estate. This money, of course, did not last, but by this time Dostoevsky had finished his first novel that was to make him famous, and the question of money did not matter to him for a time at least.

IV

In 1847, ten years after his arrival in Petersburg, Dostoevsky, having tasted the intoxication of fame and the bitterness of failure, cast his mind back to those early, ecstatic days of his friendship with the poet Shidlovsky. He had spent the whole winter of 1839, he wrote to Mikhail on January 1, 1840, "in a wildly rapturous state," reading and discussing Homer, Shakespeare, Schiller, Hoffmann, with Shidlovsky, and it was then that "so many strange and wonderful things" had happened to him.

"Oh," he wrote in the same letter, "if only you had seen him last year. He lived a whole year in Petersburg without work and without a civil service post. Goodness only knows why he lived here. He was not so rich as to live in Petersburg for his pleasure. But it was clear that the reason he came to Petersburg was that he wanted to run away somewhere. To look at him—a martyr! Haggard, with hollow cheeks and eyes that were dry and fiery. The spiritual beauty of his face increased with his physical prostration. He suffered, he suffered grievously. Good Lord, how he loved some girl (Maria, her name was, I believe)! She married someone else. Without this love he would not have been the pure, exalted, selfless priest of poetry. . . . Making my way to his poor lodgings, sometimes on a winter evening (for instance, exactly a year ago), I could not help recalling Onegin's sad winter in Petersburg (8th chapter). Only before me was not a cold person, a person who is an ardent dreamer in spite of himself, but a beautiful, exalted person, the sketch of a man Shakespeare and Schiller have given us; but already at that time he was about to fall into the somber mania of Byronic characters. We often spent whole evenings together discussing goodness only knows what. Oh, what a frank, pure soul! My eyes fill with tears when I recall those evenings. He did not conceal anything from me, and what was I to him? He had to open up his heart to someone. . . . Oh, what a poor, pathetic creature he was! A pure, angelic soul! In that distressing winter he did not forget his love. It blazed more and more fiercely. Spring came, it revived him. His imagination began creating dramas, and what dramas, Mikhail! You would have changed your opinion of them, if you had read his revised *Maria Simonova*. He revised it all winter; he himself called its old form ugly. And his lyrical poems! Oh, if only you knew the poems he wrote last spring. For instance, the poem where he talks of fame. If only you had read it, Mikhail! . . ." Dostoevsky was seventeen at the time and Shidlovsky twenty-three. Unlike Onegin, they were both genuine "dreamers." But looking back upon those days ten years later, Dostoevsky, who, as he wrote to Mikhail in March 1845, was no longer "the same man in relation to literature," for "then it was just childishness, nonsense," gave an annihilating analysis in the fourth article he wrote for *The St. Petersburg Journal* in 1847 of the type of Russian "dreamer" Shidlovsky and, to a large extent, he himself had been.

"Do you know," he wrote, "what a dreamer is, gentlemen? It is a Petersburg nightmare, a personified sin, a mute, mysterious, sullen, wild tragedy, with all the frantic horrors, with all the catastrophes, peripeteias, dramatic beginnings and endings, and we say it not at all jokingly. You sometimes meet a man who gazes about him absent-mindedly, with a vaguely dull look, often with a pale, crumpled face, always apparently preoccupied with some weighty, brain-racking problem, sometimes looking utterly exhausted, as though he had been doing some terribly hard work, but actually producing absolutely nothing: such is the dreamer from the outside. A dreamer is always difficult because he is erratic to a degree: one moment he is cheerful, another over-morose, one moment rude, another—attentive and tender, one moment an egoist, another—capable of the noblest feelings. . . . They live mostly in complete seclusion, in inaccessible places, as though hiding from people and from the light, and, as a rule, you catch a glimpse of something melodramatic at the first sight of them. They are morose and taciturn with the people in the house, self-absorbed, and they show a great liking for anything that is indolent, light, contemplative, everything that touches their feelings or excites them. They love to read, and they read any kind of book, even serious, specialist works, but they usually do not read more than two or three pages, for they are completely satisfied. Their imagination, mercurial, volatile, ethereal, is already aroused, their feelings attuned, and a whole dream world with all its joys and griefs, its hell and paradise, its ravishing women, its heroic deeds and noble activities, always with some kind of gigantic struggle, crimes and all sorts of horrors, suddenly takes hold of the dreamer's entire being. The room vanishes, space is nonexistent, time stands still or flies so quickly that an hour passes in a minute. Sometimes entire nights pass imperceptibly in indescribable pleasures; often in a few hours they live through a paradise of love or a whole huge, gigantic unheard-of life, wonderful as a dream, grand, beautiful. And for some unknown reason the pulse quickens, tears gush out, pale, moist cheeks burn with a feverish fire, and when the rosy light of sunrise comes through the dreamer's window, he looks pale, sick, anguished and—happy. Almost unconscious, he flings himself on his bed and, as he falls asleep, he is aware for a long time of a painfully pleasant physical sensation in his heart. . . . The moments of sobering up are terrible; the unhappy wretch cannot endure them and at once takes his poison in new and larger doses. Again some book, a musical motif, an old memory from real life, in short, one out of a thousand of things and a most trivial one, too, and the poison is ready, and once more imagination plays freely, richly, on the magnificently ornamented and capricious canvas of the quiet and mysterious dream world. In the street he walks with downcast eyes, paying little attention to his surroundings, sometimes forgetting reality even there. If he does notice something, it is the most trivial detail. The most ordinary, insignificant fact immediately assumes a fantastic coloring. He just cannot help seeing something fantastic in everything. Closed shutters in daytime, a misshapen old woman, a man walking towards him in the street and waving his arms about and talking aloud to himself, a great many of whom, incidentally, one meets in the street, a family scene in the window of some poor wooden house, all these things are almost adventures. His imagination is aroused and immediately a whole story, a novel is born. . . . Quite often reality produces a painful, inimical impression in the dreamer's heart and he hastens to hide himself away in his sacred, golden little corner, which is actually very often dusty, untidy, disorderly, dirty. Little by little our mischievous fellow begins to shun the crowd, to shun the things everyone is interested in, and gradually, imperceptibly, his talent for life is blunted. He begins quite naturally to believe that the pleasures his willful imagination conjures up for him are fuller, more splendid, and more lovely than real life. In his delusion he at last completely loses the moral sense which enables man to evaluate the whole beauty of his immediate surroundings, and he becomes confused and lost, he lets slip the moments of real happiness, and, in his apathy, folds his arms and refuses to acknowledge that human life is a ceaseless self-contemplation of nature and the daily facts of existence. There are dreamers who celebrate the anniversary of their fantastic sensations. They often notice the dates when they were particularly happy and when their imagination had been active in a most delightful way, and if at the time they happened to walk in a certain street, or read a certain book, or see a certain woman, they do their utmost to try to repeat the same experience, and they copy and recall the minutest circumstances of their hollow, impotent happiness on the anniversary of their impressions. Isn't such a life a tragedy? Isn't it a sin? Isn't it horrible? Isn't it a caricature? And aren't all of us more or less dreamers?"

Dostoevsky was more, rather than less, of a dreamer during the early years of his life in Petersburg. This highly romantic phase of his life did not last long, but while it lasted it exercised a most potent influence on him. It was his passionate enthusiasm for Schiller, whom he revered as a great lover of humanity and as the source of everything that is great and noble in man, that best illustrates this particular period of his life. In reply to Mikhail, who reproached him for his ignorance of Schiller's works, Dostoevsky wrote on January 1, 1840: "You wrote to me that I did not read enough Schiller. You are mistaken. I learned Schiller by heart, I talked constantly of him, I raved about him, and I think that the best thing fate did for me was to let me learn to know the great poet at that time of my life. Never could I have learned to know him as I did then. Reading Schiller with *him*," he went on, referring not to Shidlovsky, but apparently to Berezhetsky, "I verified by *him* the noble and fiery Don Carlos, Marquis Posa and Mortimer. That friendship brought me a great deal of grief and pleasure. Now I shall never mention it; but Schiller's name became near and dear to me, a sort of magic sound that called forth so many dreams; they are bitter, Mikhail, that is why I never spoke to you about Schiller and the impressions he made on me: it gives me pain when I hear the name of Schiller."

In a country whose entire political and economic life was based on slavery and where every expression of liberal ideas was ruthlessly suppressed, the cult of Schiller among the more enlightened section of the nation and, particularly, among the young people in the higher schools and universities was widespread. "The French Convent of 1793," Dostoevsky wrote in 1876,[11] "in conferring honorary French citizenship *au poète allemand* Schiller, *l'ami de l'humanité*, may have performed a beautiful, great and prophetic action, but it did not suspect that in barbarous Russia this Schiller was much more national and much dearer to the Russian barbarians than in France of that time. Even later, during the whole of our present century, Schiller, the citizen of France and *l'ami de l'humanité*, was known in France only to professors of literature, and not to all of them, either, but only to a few." In an earlier essay, which he published in 1861 in his monthly periodical *Time*, Dostoevsky was even more definite about Schiller's influence on the younger generation of Russia. "Yes," he wrote, "Schiller really was absorbed into the blood of Russian society, especially in the last generation and the one before that. We were educated on him, he was one of our own and we owe everything in our development to him." It was, of course, in imitation of Schiller that Dostoevsky wrote his first original work, the play *Mary Stuart*. This, together with extracts from another play of his, *Boris Godunov*, written in imitation of Pushkin, he read to Mikhail and some of his friends during his brother's visit to Petersburg on February 16, 1841. (Neither of these early literary efforts of Dostoevsky's is extant.)

At the time, the romanticism of both Shidlovsky and Dostoevsky was of a deeply religious character and was in direct opposition to the rebellious ideas in the poetry of Byron. "Byron," Dostoevsky wrote to Mikhail,[12] "was an egoist. His idea of fame was contemptible and futile."

[11] *A Writer's Diary*, June.

[12] *Letters*, October 31, 1838.

Three months earlier,[13] he wrote to Mikhail: "If you have read the whole of Hoffmann, you will probably remember the character of Alban. How do you like it? It is terrible to see a man, who is in the control of inscrutable and incomprehensible powers, a man who does not know what to do, who plays about with a toy which is—God!" But in expressing his horror of Alban, a typically Byronic hero, who repudiates the accepted codes of behavior, the seventeen-year-old Dostoevsky, though fighting against them, admits the intoxicating powers of these revolutionary ideas as against the naïve beliefs of his childhood.

"I don't know," he writes to his brother in the same letter, "whether my sorrowful thoughts will ever cease. One condition only is given to man as his portion: the atmosphere of his soul is composed of a union of heaven and earth. What an unlawful child is man; the law of spiritual nature is broken. . . . It seems to me that our world is a purgatory of heavenly spirits, clouded over by sinful thought. It seems to me that the world has adopted a negative meaning and the sublime and refined spirituality turned into a satire. If a person who does not accept this idea or its effect in relation to the whole should happen to stray into this picture, what would happen? The picture will be spoiled and cannot exist. . . . But to see only the hard casing under which the universe languishes, to know that one explosion of will is enough to smash it and unite with eternity—this is terrible! How cowardly is man! Hamlet! Hamlet! When I recall those stormy, wild speeches, in which one hears the moans of the tortured world, then neither sorrowful complaint nor reproach constrict my chest. . . . My soul is so crushed with grief that it is afraid to comprehend it for fear of rending itself. . . ."

It was not Dostoevsky alone, but all the forward-looking people in the Russia of that time who felt that Hamlet's cry: "The time is out of joint: O cursed spite, That ever I was born to set it right," was a faithful description of their own dilemma, their own vacillations and uncertainties, their own tragic incapacity for doing something that would solve the social and political problems of their day in accordance with the ideas they believed in so passionately. It was their despair and disappointment that led to the spread of "Byronic" influence in Russian life and letters.

"Byronism," Dostoevsky wrote in 1877,[14] "though only of brief duration, was a great, sacred and necessary phenomenon in the life of European mankind and perhaps even in the life of mankind as a whole. Byronism appeared at the moment of man's terrible anguish, disappointment and almost despair. After the frenzied transports of the new faith in new ideals, proclaimed at the end of the last century in France, some-

[13] *Letters,* August 9, 1838.
[14] *A Writer's Diary,* December.

thing happened in the foremost European nation of the period, something so utterly different from what had been expected, something that so deceived men's expectations, that perhaps no sad moment comparable to this has ever happened in the history of Western Europe. And it was not only because of external (political) reasons that the newly created idols crashed, but also because of their inner bankruptcy, a fact which was clearly seen by those of perspicacious hearts and progressive intelligences. A new *way* had not yet come into view, a new valve had not yet been opened and everything was on the point of suffocation beneath the former horizon that contracted and descended terribly low over mankind. The old idols lay smashed to smithereens. It was just at that very moment, that there appeared a great and mighty genius, a passionate poet. Mankind's anguish and somber disappointment in its own destiny and the ideals that deceived it could be heard in his verses. That was a new and never-before-heard-of Muse of sorrow and revenge, malediction and despair. The spirit of Lord Byron's poetry seems to have suddenly spread over all mankind and all mankind responded to it. That was, as it were, the opened valve; amid the general hollow moans, most of which were quite unconscious, this was the mighty cry in which all the cries and moans of humanity merged as though by unanimous consent. . . . No powerful mind and no generous heart in our country could disregard the influence of Lord Byron's poetry. And this was not only because of sympathy for Europe and for Europeans from afar, but because in our country, in Russia, too, a great number of new, unsolved and acutely painful problems had arisen, and too many old disappointments. . . ."

In Dostoevsky this "Byronic" mood persisted for some considerable time, and it was accompanied by a feeling of the futility of hopes about the great vocation of a creative writer.

"It is sad to live without hope, Mikhail," he wrote to his brother:[15] "I look ahead and my future terrifies me. I seem to float in a kind of cold Polar atmosphere, where no ray of sunshine has ever penetrated. I have not experienced any burst of inspiration for a long time, while I am often in the same state of mind as that experienced by the Prisoner of Chillon after the death of his brothers in the dungeon. The heavenly kind of poetry will not fly to me, nor will it warm my heart that has grown cold. . . . You say I am secretive, but the truth is that my former dreams have left me and my wonderful arabesques, which I created formerly, have lost their gilding. The thoughts, whose rays set fire to my heart and soul, have now lost their fire and warmth, or else my heart has hardened, or—but I am afraid to go on. I am terrified to have to say that all my past has been just a golden dream, glittering daydreams. . . ."

[15] *Letters*, October 31, 1838.

V

It was at this early period that Dostoevsky fell under the spell of Lermontov, a poet who, Dostoevsky wrote in his *Writer's Diary*,[16] "was a follower of Byron, but because of his great and original poetic gifts a special sort of follower of Byron–kind of sarcastic, capricious and morose, always skeptical of his own inspiration, of his own Byronic moods." It was Lermontov and then Gogol, the two "demons," as Dostoevsky described them, who had, more than anyone else, brought about the great breach in the religious and romantic ideas of the young man who was to become an even greater "demon" than either.

"We, too, had demons, real demons," Dostoevsky wrote in one of the essays on Russian literature that he contributed to *Time* in 1861. "There were two of them, and how we loved them, how we still love and treasure them! One of them kept on laughing; he laughed all his life at himself and at us, and we all laughed with him and laughed so long that finally we began to cry with laughter. He grasped the true significance of Lieutenant Pirogov [a character in Gogol's *The Portrait*]; he made the loss of an overcoat by a civil servant into a most terrible tragedy. He told us in three lines all there was to know about the Ryazan lieutenant–everything to the last detail. He put before us a whole gallery of money-grubbers, land-sharpers, plunderers and all sorts of 'assessors.' All he had to do was to point a finger at them and at once a mark was branded on their forehead which stayed there forever, so that we never forgot who they really were and, above all, what their names were. Oh, he was a colossal demon such as you never had in Europe and whom you would perhaps have never allowed to be in your country. The other demon–but the other one we loved perhaps even more. He wrote so many excellent poems for us. . . . He cursed and suffered, suffered in earnest. He revenged himself and he forgave, he wrote and roared with laughter–he was generous and he was ridiculous. He liked to whisper strange fairy stories to a sleeping young girl, setting her virginal blood on fire and making her see visions which she really ought not to be seeing, particularly in view of the highly moral education she had received. He told us the story of his life and his love adventures: he seemed, on the whole, to try to mystify us–we never could tell whether he was speaking seriously or laughing at us. Our civil servants knew him by heart and as soon as they left their offices they all suddenly began posing as Mephistopheleses. Sometimes we did not agree with him; he made us feel depressed, vexed, sad and sorry for someone, and we were filled with bitterness and spite. In the end he got tired of us; he never felt happy for long with anyone or anywhere; he cursed us and laughed at us 'with the derisive laugh of a deceived son at

[16] December 1877.

the father who had squandered his fortune at cards,' and flew away from us—

> "And over the mountains of Caucasus
> The exile from paradise flew. . . .

"We followed his fortunes for a long time, but at last he perished somewhere—aimlessly, stupidly and even ridiculously. But we did not laugh. We were not in a laughing mood just then. . . ."

Dostoevsky was certainly not in a laughing mood when Lermontov's novel *A Hero of Our Times* was first published in 1840, for in Pechorin, the hero of Lermontov's novel, he found many features that corresponded strikingly not only to what he was feeling just then, but also to what was buried deep inside him—the dark traits of his character of which even he was only dimly aware. Pechorin deplored the squandering of his "unbounded powers" on trivialities and wondered whether he, too, belonged to the category of people who, "at the beginning of their lives, conscious of their unbounded powers, intend to end like Alexander the Great or Lord Byron, and yet remain low-grade civil servants forever." Dostoevsky, in his letter to Mikhail on July 19, 1840, two months after the publication of *A Hero of Our Times* practically paraphrases Pechorin's thoughts and sentiments. "And, indeed," he writes, "how sad is life and how wearisome the moments that are still left of it when man, aware of his errors and conscious of his unbounded powers realizes that they have been squandered on activities that were false, unnatural, and unworthy of his nature; when you feel that the fire of your soul is put out, extinguished by goodness only knows what; your heart is torn to pieces—why? Because of a life that is worthy of a pigmy and not a giant, of a child and not a man."

Pechorin deplored the fact that, as a young man, he was "a dreamer who loved to caress in turn gloomy and rainbow-colored images." Dostoevsky in the same letter deplored his "useless and aimless activity" and described himself as one "who is involuntarily seeking food for his mind, but is wasting himself on an unnatural yearning for an ignoble dream life." He, too, like Pechorin, felt that "there are two men in me: one lives in the full meaning of the word, and the other thinks and passes judgment on him." Again, he, too, like Pechorin, had "one passion" which he did not conceal—a passion for gambling. "At the card table," Lermontov wrote, and it really seems as though he were talking of Dostoevsky at the roulette table, "he forgot everything and usually lost; but his constant bad luck only intensified his stubbornness." And then there was that terrible confession of Pechorin's at the thought that the girl he had seduced would spend the night weeping: "This thought," Lermontov's hero declared, "gives me unbounded pleasure—there are moments when I understand the vampire. . . ." And so did Dostoevsky. Indeed, the sensual delight hidden in cruelty that Dostoevsky had first experienced in watching the serf boy pulling off the heads of sparrows was to figure a great deal in his novels, particularly in *Notes from a Dark Cellar*, when the young prostitute's tears gave the autobiographical, anonymous hero an even keener delight than that experienced by Pechorin.[17] It is, no doubt, this inner affinity with Lermontov's hero that made it easier for Dostoevsky to accept the interpretation of Pechorin by the great and influential Russian critic Visarion Belinsky as merely "a link in the process of the emergence of the type of revolutionary fighting for new ideals. Pechorin's passions," Belinsky wrote, "are the charms which purify the sphere of the spirit; his errors, however terrible, are merely acute illnesses in a wholesome body which fortify it for a long and wholesome life. Let him slander the eternal laws of reason, deeming pride to be the greatest good, let him slander human nature, seeing in it egoism alone; let him slander himself, mistaking certain momentary expressions of his spirit for its fullest development—the solemn moment will come and the contradiction will be resolved, the struggle will be at an end, and the discordant sounds of his soul will merge together into one harmonious chord." This language may seem a little obscure, "Aesopian," as the method practiced by the writers of that day for circumventing the censors was called, but to the young Dostoevsky, as to anyone of the radical movement of the time, it was clear enough. Indeed, many years later Dostoevsky was to regard Lermontov as the true representative of what he called "the movement of negation" in Russia. "The reason why we respected and thought highly of Pechorin," he wrote in 1876, "was because he seemed to us to be a man of *tenacious* hatred," and the chief object of this hatred was, of course, the brutal social and political conditions under which they all had to live during the reign of Nicholas I.

The other "demon," Gogol, helped to complete Dostoevsky's break with his romantic past. *Dead Souls* and *The Overcoat*, two of Gogol's finest works, which had exerted an enormous influence on Russian literature, were published in 1842. *The Overcoat* can be said to have created what was to be known as the "natural" school of writers, among whom Dostoevsky took the foremost place, creating the literary fashion of depicting the life of the lower classes of Russia, "the humiliated" and the downtrodden. "Dostoevsky," Dr. Yanovsky records, "never

[17] An interesting illustration of how Dostoevsky quite deliberately cultivated the sensual side of his feelings is provided by his confession to Mikhail of the strange method he had invented to increase the enjoyment of his letters. "You can't imagine," he wrote Mikhail on January 1, 1840, "the sensuous fluttering of my heart every time I receive a letter from you. Indeed, I have invented a new kind of pleasure—a most strange one—the pleasure of tantalizing myself. I take your letter, turn it over several times in my hands, feel it to make sure it is the right weight, and, having examined and admired it to my heart's content, put it in my pocket. You can't imagine what a sensuous condition of heart, soul and feelings it is! And having thus waited sometimes as long as a quarter of an hour, I throw myself avidly at last on the letter, tear off the seal and devour your lines, your dear lines!"

tired of reading Gogol. He often read him aloud. When he read *Dead Souls* he invariably exclaimed as he closed the book: 'What a great teacher for all of us Russians, but particularly for our Russian writers.'" As late as 1876, Dostoevsky stressed the revolutionary significance of *Dead Souls*, which he declared to be one of the most profound creations of Russian literary genius, because Gogol's characters "give rise in the Russian mind to the most turbulent ideas which one cannot help feeling it is impossible to solve now, if indeed ever." During his first Petersburg period, he deplored Gogol's defection to the reactionary camp. In a letter to Mikhail, he wrote:[18] "I am saying nothing to you about Gogol, but here is a fact. In the next issue of the *Contemporary*, an article by Gogol will be published containing his will and testament in which he disavows all his works and declares them to be useless, if not worse. He says that he will not take up his pen again because his business is to pray. Agrees with all the opinions of his opponents. Orders to print his portrait in an enormous number of copies, the profits from their sale to be used for giving financial aid to pilgrims to Jerusalem and so on. So now judge for yourself."

Of the non-Russian writers, apart from Schiller, those who had the greatest and most lasting influence on Dostoevsky during his first Petersburg period were George Sand and Balzac. Dostoevsky, of course, was a voracious reader from an early age. In a letter on August 18, 1880, he declared that "at the age of twelve, in the country during the holidays, I read the whole of Walter Scott." At the age of seventeen, he wrote to Mikhail[19] that he spent his free time in camp reading through "the whole of Hoffmann . . . almost the whole of Balzac (Balzac is great! His characters are the creations of a universal mind! Not the spirit of an age but whole millenniums have by their struggles prepared such a denouement in the soul of man). Goethe's *Faust* and his short poems . . . also Victor Hugo except for his *Cromwell* and *Hernani*."

Seven years later, on March 24, 1845, he wrote to Mikhail again: "You want to know what I do when not writing—I am reading. I read a terrific lot and the reading has a strange effect on me. Something I have read before, I read again, and I seem to be filled with new strength, I think everything over carefully, I understand it clearly, and extract the ability to create from it." Some of his early literary judgments were rather brash, and he subsequently altered them, while to others he never referred again. Thus of Homer he wrote to Mikhail on January 1, 1840: "Homer (a man perhaps as fabulous as Christ, incarnated by God and sent to us) can be considered as a parallel to Christ, but not to Goethe. Try to understand him well, Mikhail, try to understand the *Iliad*, read it well (you have not read it, have you?). You see, in his *Iliad* Homer gave to the whole ancient world absolutely the same

[18] *Letters*, September 5, 1846.
[19] *Letters*, August 9, 1838.

kind of organization of spiritual and earthly life as Christ did to the modern world. Do you understand me now? Victor Hugo, as a lyric poet, has a purely angelic character and a childlike Christian poetic tendency, and no one can compare with him in that, neither Schiller (inasmuch as Schiller is not a Christian poet), nor Shakespeare considered as a lyric poet, nor Byron, nor Pushkin. I read his sonnets in French. Only Homer, who has the same unshakable confidence in his vocation and childlike belief in the God of poetry whom he serves, is like Victor Hugo in the direction taken by the source of his poetry, but only in that, and not in the ideas which were given to him by nature and which he expresses, but I was not speaking about that. Derzhavin," he concludes, perhaps not so astonishingly when one considers that he knew no Greek and had only a very elementary knowledge of French, "I think, is higher than either of them as a lyric poet."

How continually Dostoevsky changed his opinion about Victor Hugo can be gathered from a letter he wrote in April 1877: "So far as Victor Hugo is concerned," he declared, "I can see that you are still too young if you talk of him in the same breath as Goethe and Shakespeare." And in a reference to *Les Misérables*, which he liked, he observed in the same letter: "How ridiculous are his [*i.e.*, Victor Hugo's] lovers, what typical French bourgeois in the worst meaning of the word."

Not too much should be made of Dostoevsky's views of Corneille and Racine at that highly romantic period of his life, for, curiously enough, except in the letter to Mikhail in January 1840, their names never occur in his correspondence again. Objecting to Mikhail's view that the Russians could never admire Corneille or Racine because their "form" was bad, Dostoevsky takes up the cudgels on behalf of the two French dramatists. "You poor fellow," he writes, "to say so cleverly to me: Do you really think they have any poetry in them? You can ask that? Why, have you read *Andromaque?* Have you? Have you read *Iphigénie?* Are you really going to tell me that this is not exquisite? Is not Racine's Achilles a Homer-like character? Racine may have stolen from Homer, but think how he has done it! Think of his women! Try to understand him. Racine no genius? He could not create drama? He could only imitate Corneille? And what about *Phèdre?* Is it not the highest and purest expression of nature and poetry? Why, it is a Shakespearean sketch, though only of plaster of Paris and not a marble statue. Now what about Corneille? . . . Don't you realize that his gigantic characters and his romantic spirit make him almost the equal of Shakespeare? . . . Have you read his *Cinna?* Before the divine sketch of Octavius such characters as Karl Moor, Fiesco, Tell and Don Carlos fade into insignificance. . . . Have you read *Le Cid?* Read it, you wretch, read it and grovel in the dust before Corneille. . . . What else could the romantic movement demand if its highest ideas are not developed in *Le Cid?* Think of his young son and his mistress! And what an ending!"

Chateaubriand, Pascal and the social satirist Barbier are other French writers the young Dostoevsky mentions in his letters to Mikhail that he has read; Grigorovich adds to this list Frédéric Soulié's *Memoirs of the Devil*, Fenimore Cooper's *Lake Ontario* and De Quincey's *Confessions of an English Opium Eater*, which Dostoevsky must have found particularly interesting, because it describes De Quincey's nocturnal wandering in the less savory streets of London and his involvement with prostitutes, similar probably to his own experiences in the Petersburg slums.

The foreign writer who left the most lasting impression not only on Dostoevsky's writings but also on his personal life was George Sand, whose early novels he tried to translate and to whom he was to pay a glowing tribute in his *Writer's Diary*.[20] Her novels acted as an antidote against the despair and mental suffering that Byron and Lermontov inflicted upon the idealistic younger generation of Russians in the first half of the nineteenth century. The death of George Sand on June 8, 1876, took Dostoevsky back to those early days and, he wrote, it made him realize what her name had meant in his life, how much "adoration and enthusiasm" she had exacted from him and how much "happiness and joy" she had given him.

"I put down each of these words without fear of contradiction because it is literally true. She was one of our, and I mean *our*, contemporaries in every sense of the word—an idealist of the thirties and forties. Her name is one of the names of our mighty, self-confident and at the same time sick century, full of the most obscure ideals and of the most insoluble desires—names which, having arisen then, in 'the country of holy miracles,' won from us too many thoughts, loves, sacred and noble impulses, vital and precious convictions. . . . Don't be surprised at these words of mine," explains Dostoevsky, who, at the time of writing George Sand's obituary, had gone over to the reactionary camp in Russia, "for while there can still be arguments about George Sand, who is already half or even nine-tenths forgotten, she has done her work in our country and who, if not we her contemporaries, ought to pay tribute to her on her grave? . . . The appearance of George Sand in literature," Dostoevsky recalled, "coincided with the years of my youth. . . . Her novels first appeared in Russian translations about the middle thirties. I believe I was only 16 when I read for the first time her novel *l'Uscoque*, one of the most charming of her earlier works. I remember I was in a fever all night afterwards. . . . What I, a young boy, as well as everyone else, was so impressed by at the time, was the chastity, the purity of her characters and ideals, and the modest charm and severe and restrained tone of her stories, and I think I am right in saying that, at least as far as I can remember, she occupied immediately almost the foremost place in the galaxy of new writers who had become famous throughout Europe. Even Dickens, who appeared in Russia almost at the

[20] June 1876.

same time as she, took second place to her in the attention of the public, not to mention Balzac, who had preceded her and who had given us in the thirties such works as *Eugénie Grandet* and *Le Père Goriot*. . . ."

Politically, Dostoevsky explains, George Sand's works were important because Russian readers could extract from them the ideas the Russian authorities tried so hard to "shield" them from. What were these ideas? In explaining them Dostoevsky incidentally reveals what made him join the revolutionary camp in Russia in the 1840's.

"After the end of the bloody French (or more correctly, the European) revolution," he writes, "attempts were made to express new desires and new ideals. Progressive minds [including his own] understood very well that all that had happened was a rebirth of despotism, or in other words: *Otes-toi de là que je m'y mette*, that the new conquerors of the world (the bourgeois) showed themselves to be perhaps worse than the former despots (the nobility) and that 'liberty, equality and fraternity' were merely high-sounding words and nothing more. Moreover, doctrines appeared according to which they were no longer high-sounding but forbidden words. The conquerors pronounced or rather recalled those three sacramental words with derision; even science (the economists) came along to the help of those who derided and condemned the utopian meaning of those three words, for which so much blood had been shed. Thus, next to the triumphant conquerors there began to appear those with dejected and sad faces, who frightened the victorious ones. It was just at this time that there suddenly arose a really new word and new hopes: people appeared who proclaimed that there was no reason in the world why the business [*i.e.*, the revolution] should have come to an end, that the political change had achieved nothing, that the business must be carried on, and that the renewal of mankind must be social and must be continued on radical lines. . . . The history of this movement," Dostoevsky concludes his cautious defense of his participation in the revolutionary movement of the 1840's, "is well known and it is still going on and it does not seem to me that it has any intention of stopping. I do not wish to say anything for or against it here, all I wanted to say . . . was that George Sand's place in this movement must be sought at its very beginning."

There was another aspect of George Sand's novels which had an even greater influence on Dostoevsky, both as a writer and as a man. It was George Sand's demand for the recognition of the equality of women as expressed in the heroines of her novels. "From the very beginning," Dostoevsky writes, "even as a sixteen-year-old boy, I was amazed at the strange contradiction of what people wrote and spoke about her and of what I actually saw for myself. Actually, many, or at any rate some of her heroines represented a type of so high a standard of moral purity as it is impossible to imagine without an even greater moral standard in the soul of the writer herself, without an understanding and recognition of the highest form of beauty in mercy, patience and justice. It is true that amid the mercy, patience and the recognition of the obligations of duty there was also a quite extraordinary pride in the way those demands and protests were made, but that pride was so precious just because it proceeded from the highest truth without which mankind would never have been able to maintain its high moral ideals. . . . Her heroines craved for sacrifices and acts of heroism. What I liked particularly at that time was . . . the pure ideal of an innocent girl—pure and so powerful just because of her innocence. . . . We meet a frank, honest, but inexperienced character, a young girl possessing that proud sense of chastity which does not fear and could not be besmirched by contact with vice, even if she suddenly found herself accidentally in the very den of vice. The longing for a generous sacrifice (as though such a sacrifice were expected from her) strikes at the heart of such a young girl and, without another thought and without sparing herself, she suddenly takes a fatal and dangerous step, selflessly, self-denyingly and fearlessly. She is not troubled or frightened by what she sees and comes across; on the contrary, it merely raises the courage in her young heart, which only now becomes aware for the first time of its real strength, the strength that comes from innocence, honesty and purity, redoubles her energy and points out new ways and new horizons to one who did not know them till that moment, but who has not yet become polluted by compromises with life."

This analysis of some of George Sand's heroines fits perfectly several of Dostoevsky's own, particularly Sonia in *Crime and Punishment*. Indeed, since it is hardly conceivable that Dostoevsky was not aware of it, the above passage can be taken as an acknowledgment of his indebtedness to George Sand. There was, however, this cardinal difference between Dostoevsky and George Sand. "It is true," he writes, concluding his tribute to her, "that she did not like to depict in her novels humble characters, good but yielding, weak-minded and oppressed, as in almost every novel of the great Christian Dickens; on the contrary, she set up her heroines proudly, just as if they were empresses. She liked that, and this peculiarity of hers must be noted; it is rather characteristic."

Although Dostoevsky makes a point of insisting in his article that "George Sand belonged to the whole movement and did not preach about the rights of women only," it was undoubtedly her fight for women's emancipation that made the greatest impact on Russian progressive opinion of the time and led to the emergence of the "emancipated" woman who appears in Dostoevsky's later novels in a somewhat dubious light. But that cannot be said of his earlier personal attitude towards what was known at the time as "free love." Indeed, even as late as the sixties, Strakhov records, no importance was attached among Dostoevsky's circle of friends to "physical excesses and deviations from the normal. People who were extremely sensitive so far as morals were concerned and cultivated an extremely lofty trend of thought, and even those who, as a rule, eschewed every kind of physical depravity, regarded misdemeanors of that kind with the utmost composure, spoke of them as amusing trifles in which it was quite permissible to indulge in a moment of leisure. Spiritual improbity was severely condemned; carnal improbity was dismissed as of no importance. This strange *emancipation of the flesh* had a seductive effect and in some cases led to consequences that are painful and terrible to relate."

If George Sand was responsible for some of the main traits in Dostoevsky's female characters, Balzac was responsible for some of the main ideas of his male characters, including Raskolnikov's idea of the superman to whom "everything was permitted," and who had the right to step over the threshold, to shed innocent blood, and to bring as a sacrifice on the altar of his egoism everyone he thought fit for the job of furthering his own advancement. According to Grigorovich, Dostoevsky considered Balzac to be "immeasurably higher than any other French writer." In fact, Schiller and George Sand were from the very start contrasted in Dostoevsky's mind with Balzac as well as with Hoffmann (and to a certain extent Dickens, too), who shook his belief in the perfectibility of man and occasionally made him wonder if there was not after all some truth in the Christian doctrine of original sin. Balzac, in particular, made so great an impression on the young Dostoevsky just because in his *Comédie Humaine* he provided so terrible a refutation of the idealistic beliefs of the utopian socialists of his time. It aroused an inner conflict within him which he was never able to resolve and which, perhaps, he never wanted to resolve. Balzac as "the devil's advocate," whose "basic idea," as an anonymous article in Dostoevsky's monthly, *Time,* declared, "was the worship of material powers, contempt for every ideal, the restoration of evil, the anatomic analysis of vice, and, finally, the absence of every moral ardor," exercised a violent attraction on the young Dostoevsky. "To study life," he had written in his letter to Karepin quoted earlier, "is my primary aim and hobby, so that I have now become fully convinced of the existence of Famusov, Chichikov and Falstaff." Hoffmann's novels, too, seemed to confirm him in the belief that evil is an ineradicable element in human nature.

On the whole, both Russian and Western European literature sustained in the young Dostoevsky his optimistic beliefs in the betterment of mankind and, particularly, the rehabilitation of the oppressed and downtrodden, "the social pariahs rejected by everybody," as he was to describe them ten years later. At that time, though, he was very far from associating this rehabilitation with the Christian faith. He was, in fact, moving inexorably towards his brief phase of active participation in a revolutionary conspiracy. That phase, however, was to be preceded by an even shorter period of literary fame following the completion of his first novel.

VI

Dostoevsky first mentioned *Poor People* almost as an afterthought at the end of his long letter to Mikhail on September 30, 1844, most of which was given up to his fantastic scheme of making a fortune out of his brother's translations of Schiller's plays and complaints against "the Moscow swine," that is, his guardian, Karepin. "I am finishing a novel of the length of *Eugénie Grandet*," he wrote. "The novel is rather original. I am already copying it out in its finished form. By the 14th I shall quite certainly know whether it is accepted or not. I am sending it to *Home Annals*. (I am very satisfied with my work.) I shall get perhaps 400 rubles for it," he went on, as usual counting his chickens, "that's all I can hope for."

In the meantime, he met Grigorovich, who just then had also finished his first short study of low life, *St. Petersburg Organ-Grinders*, and they decided to share Dostoevsky's flat. Neither had any money, and most of the time they lived on rolls and tea. Dostoevsky, who had finished *Poor People* in November, was still revising it in March. "I vowed," he wrote to his brother, never suspecting how often he would be compelled to break his vow[21] "to do my utmost not to write to order. . . . I want every work of mine to be perfect. Look at Pushkin and Gogol. They have not written a great deal, but both are waiting for memorials to be erected to them. Why, today Gogol gets one thousand rubles in silver for a printed page, and Pushkin, as you know, used to sell one line for a gold sovereign. But their fame, especially Gogol's, was bought by years of poverty and starvation. The old school is disappearing, the new writers daub and don't paint. The whole of a writer's talent," he went on, describing what Turgenev called the "pseudo-sublime" and ultrapatriotic best sellers of the day, "is wasted on one mighty swing, in which can be seen a monstrous, unfinished idea, the bare force of muscles, but only a particle of the thing that really matters. Béranger said about our present *feuilleton* writers that they are a bottle of Chambertin in a bucket of water. Here, too, they are imitating them: Raphael painted a picture for years, went on polishing it, and the result was a miracle! Gods were created by his hand. Vernet paints a picture a month, for which special exhibition halls are hired, the perspective is rich, the whole thing is bold and sweeping, but it isn't worth a farthing. They are all just decorators!

"In an article in the *Invalid*," he wrote in the same letter, "I have just read about some German poets who had died of hunger and cold and in lunatic asylums. There were twenty of them and what names! I still feel somehow terrified. One has to be a charlatan . . . !" Grigorovich records that intensive work and "stubborn refusal to go out" aggravated Dostoevsky's illness, which had already manifested itself several times

[21] *Letters*, March 24, 1845.

at school. "During our rare walks," Grigorovich continues, "he would sometimes have fits. Once we came across a funeral procession: Dostoevsky turned away quickly, wanted to go back home, but before we had time to walk a few yards, he had a fit so violent that, with the help of a few passers-by, I had to take him to the nearest shop and it took me some time before I could bring him round. Such fits were usually followed by depression lasting two or three days."

There can, in fact, be no doubt whatever that Dostoevsky's epileptic fits, though perhaps milder and less frequent than during the last twenty years of his life, began during the early forties. It is also not within significance that his severest fit should have happened at his encounter with a funeral procession, for overwork and depression had brought back his superstitious belief in bad omens and his disposition to hypochondria, from which he was to suffer more and more as his money troubles increased.

On May 4, 1845, after telling Mikhail that he had again been revising *Poor People*, he wrote: "I don't know what is going to happen to me. You are unfair to say that I am not worried about my situation. I am sick with worrying about it and very often I don't sleep at night because of my tormenting thoughts." He did not know what to do about his novel, whether to publish it in a periodical or to get a bookseller to publish it independently. Mikhail had invited him to visit Reval again, but he had first to dispose of the novel. He had plenty of new ideas and, if he succeeded in publishing his novel, his literary career was assured. As for money, "Alas," he wrote, "I'm hanged if I know where it has all gone. But I haven't too many debts. As for my lodgings, I still owe something to my landlord . . . and moving to new lodgings will cost me more than staying at the old ones. Lodgings, my novel, Reval—three *idées fixes—ma femme et mon parapluie!* . . . And if I don't place my novel," he concluded, "I will most probably drown myself in the Neva. What else is there left for me to do? I've thought of everything. I shall not survive the death of my *idée fixe!*"

But Dostoevsky need not have worried. Fate came to his rescue in the most unexpected way. Grigorovich found him one day brooding over the manuscript of his novel and asked his permission to show it to a friend, the young poet Nekrasov, who was planning to publish a symposium by different authors. Dostoevsky agreed. There are several versions of what happened afterwards, including one by Dostoevsky himself and one by Grigorovich. There are a few minor discrepancies between the two accounts. Dostoevsky for some reason concealed the fact that Grigorovich had been living with him at the time and claimed that he himself and not Grigorovich had taken the manuscript of *Poor People* to Nekrasov. But there is no discrepancy in their descriptions of the effect the novel had on Nekrasov. "I read it," Grigorovich records, "and on the last page where the old man Devushkin takes leave of

Varenka, I could no longer control myself and began to snivel; I stole a glance at Nekrasov: tears were rolling down his cheeks too. I told him excitedly that we should not waste time, but that we ought to go and see Dostoevsky at once (it was about four o'clock in the morning), tell him of the success of his novel and try to reach an agreement with him at once about its publication. Nekrasov, who was also very excited, agreed, dressed quickly and off we went. Dostoevsky answered the door and, seeing a stranger beside me, grew pale, looked confused, and for a long time could not reply to what Nekrasov was telling him. . . . After Nekrasov's departure, he shut himself up in his room and I could hear him pacing up and down for hours. . . ."

Dostoevsky's account is much fuller, but rather glosses over his own reaction at the meeting with Nekrasov. After declaring that he was "terrified" of "the party of *Home Annals*," to which Nekrasov belonged, Dostoevsky went on:[22] "I had been reading Belinsky with enthusiasm for several years, but he seemed terrifying and menacing to me and sometimes I could not help thinking that he would 'scoff' at my *Poor People*. But that was only sometimes: I wrote it with passion, almost with tears, and—was it possible that all those moments I had lived through with the pen in my hand while working at that novel—that all this was nothing but a lie, a mirage, a false feeling? But, of course, I thought that only for very short periods of time, though my anxiety kept recurring. The very evening I gave away my manuscript I went to see one of my former friends—who lived in some remote part of Petersburg—and we spent the whole night together discussing *Dead Souls* and reading it again for the hundredth time probably. This was the sort of thing that usually happened in those days: two or three young people met—'Come, let's read Gogol!' and down they sat and read Gogol all through the night sometimes. . . .[23] I came back home at about four o'clock. It was a 'white' Petersburg night, as light as day. It was a fine, warm night and, on entering my lodgings, I did not feel like going to bed, so I opened the window and sat down at it. Suddenly, much to my surprise, there was a ring at the front door, and a minute later Grigorovich and Nekrasov began embracing me rapturously and almost crying with excitement.

[22] *A Writer's Diary*, January 1877.

[23] The Russian mathematician Sofia Kovalevsky, sister of Anna Korvin-Krukovsky, whose stories Dostoevsky published in his magazine and to whom he had made a proposal of marriage in 1865, gives quite a different and, one must admit, much more convincing version of how Dostoevsky spent that historic May night. "The whole of that night," she reports Dostoevsky as saying, "I indulged in cheap and sordid debauch, without pleasure, simply out of anxiety. It was the month of May and one of the Petersburg 'white' nights. I never could endure those nights, for they always upset my nerves and brought on a kind of 'foul' fit of depression. But this was particularly true of that night. I came back home, but did not feel like going to bed. I sat down at the open window, feeling awful, and suddenly there was a ring at the front door. . ."

They had . . . taken my manuscript, begun reading it just to see what it was like, thinking that ten pages would be enough to reach a decision. But having read ten pages, they decided to read ten more, and then had sat through the whole night reading it aloud in turn. 'He was reading about the death of the student,' Grigorovich told me afterwards when left alone with me, 'and suddenly at the point where the student's father runs after his son's coffin, Nekrasov's voice cracked once or twice, and a moment later he just could not hold out any longer, and banged his fist on the manuscript: "Oh, damn him!" He meant you, and so we went on all through the night.' When they finished (seven quires!) they decided unanimously to come and see me at once. 'What does it matter if he is asleep? We'll waken him. *This* is higher than sleep!' Afterwards, having become more familiar with Nekrasov's character, I was often surprised at the way he behaved that time: he was reticent, almost mistrustful, careful and not very communicative. That, at least, is how he always seemed to me, so that our first meeting was in truth a revelation of his most profound feelings. They spent half an hour with me at the time and," Dostoevsky goes on, contradicting Grigorovich's testimony, "goodness only knows what we did not discuss during that half hour, catching each other's meaning at once, with exclamations, rapidly: we spoke of poetry, of truth, of 'the condition of the times,' of course, and of Gogol, quoting passages from *The Government Inspector* and *Dead Souls,* but most of all, of Belinsky. 'I'm going to take your novel to him today and you will see. Why, what a man he is, what a man!' Nekrasov said to me excitedly, shaking my shoulders with both hands. "You'll get to know each other, you'll see what a wonderful man he is! Now you'd better go to bed. Go to bed—we're going, but tomorrow you must come and see us!' As though I could sleep after their visit! What enthusiasm, what success! But most of all it was their feeling that was so precious at that moment. I remember that clearly. Someone else is successful, I thought to myself, well, he is praised, people are eager to meet him, he is congratulated, but those two came running to me with tears in their eyes, at four o'clock in the morning, to wake me, because this is *higher* than sleep. Oh, that is wonderful. That is what I thought. Go to bed, indeed!"

They were all in their early twenties at the time: Dostoevsky and Nekrasov were twenty-three and Grigorovich twenty-four. Belinsky, who was approaching the end of his career—he died three years later—was only thirty-four.

Nekrasov took Dostoevsky's manuscript to Belinsky on the same day. His first words, according to Dostoevsky, were: "A new Gogol has appeared!" "With you, Gogols grow like mushrooms!" Belinsky, still according to Dostoevsky, observed severely, but he accepted the manuscript. "When Nekrasov came to see him in the evening," Dostoevsky concludes, "Belinsky met him, looking terribly excited. 'Bring him, bring him quickly!' he said."

Dostoevsky, always prone to dramatize situations, may have telescoped a few days in his account, but he did not exaggerate the impression his first novel made on the critic. Pavel Annenkov, one of the most prominent literary historians of the day, who did not belong to Dostoevsky's circle of friends, left this description of Belinsky's excitement on reading *Poor People.*

"During one of my visits to Belinsky before dinner when he rested from his literary labors, I caught sight of him from the courtyard sitting at the window of his drawing room with a large manuscript in his hands and marks of agitation on his face. He, too, noticed me, and shouted: 'Come quick, I have something to tell you! From this manuscript,' he went on after shaking hands with me, 'I cannot tear myself away for the second day. It is a beginner's novel, but that of a highly gifted person. I don't know what the man looks like and what is the extent of his ideas, but his novel opens up such mysteries of life and such characters in Russia as no one before him has ever dreamed of. Just think, it is the first attempt at a Russian social novel, and so contrived as only an artist could. It is a simple matter: there are good-natured fellows who think that to love the whole world is something very nice and pleasant and, indeed, the duty of every man. But they are unable to understand anything when the wheel of life, with all its customs and usages, having knocked them down, crushes their limbs and bones in silence. That is all —but what a drama, what types! Oh, I forgot to tell you the artist's name: it is Dostoevsky, and as for the specimens of his motifs, here are a few of them.' And Belinsky began to read with feeling the passages from the novel which had struck him most, imparting an even more expressive shade of meaning by his intonation and nervous rendering. This was how he welcomed the first work of our novelist."

And here is Dostoevsky's own famous description of his first meeting with the "furious Visarion," as Belinsky was known to his friends and enemies: "And so (on the third day) they brought me to him. I remember that at the first sight I was struck very forcibly by his appearance, his nose, his forehead. For some unknown reason I had had quite a different idea of that 'redoubtable awe-inspiring critic.' He greeted me gravely and with restraint. 'Well,' I thought to myself, 'that's how it ought to be,' but in less than a moment everything had changed: the air of gravity did not belong to the person of a great critic meeting a twenty-two-year-old writer on the threshold of his career, but, so to speak, was assumed out of respect for the feelings he was anxious to communicate to me as soon as possible. . . . He began warmly, with burning eyes: 'Why, do you realize yourself,' he kept repeating to me several times in a high-pitched voice, 'what exactly you have written?' He always spoke in a high-pitched voice when deeply moved. 'You could have written it only by some intuitive sense as an artist, but do you comprehend yourself the terrible truth you have shown us? It is impossible that in your early twenties you should have understood it. Why, this unhappy wretch of a civil servant of yours has been in the service so long and has brought himself to such a point of humility that he dare not even consider himself unhappy and regards the slightest complaint almost as freethinking. He does not even dare to admit that he has a right to be unhappy and when, poor fellow, the general gives him a hundred rubles, he is crushed and annihilated with astonishment that a man like him could be pitied. . . . And that torn-off button, and that minute of kissing the general's hand—why, this is no longer compassion for the unhappy man, but horror! horror! There is horror in that nobleness of his. It's a tragedy! You have got to the very heart of the matter, you have pointed out the most important thing about it. We, publicists and critics, merely discuss things, we are merely trying to explain it all with words, while you, the artist, reveal the whole essence of the matter with one stroke, with one revealing trait of character so that you could touch it with your hand, so that even the most unthinking of your readers could understand it all immediately. This is the secret of creative art, this is the truth in art! This is an artist's service to truth! Truth has been revealed and announced to you as an artist, it was granted to you as a gift. Well, then, value your gift and remain true to it and you will be a great writer!'

"All this he said to me," Dostoevsky continues. "All this he said about me afterwards to many people who are still alive and who can bear witness to it. I left him in a state of ecstatic joy. I stopped at the corner of his house, looked at the sky, the bright day, the passers-by and I felt with all my being that a solemn moment had come to pass in my life, a radical change that had brought about a final break with my past, that something quite new had begun, something I had never anticipated even in my wildest dreams. (And I was a terrible dreamer in those days.) 'And am I really so great?' I thought shamefacedly to myself with a kind of shy rapture. Oh, don't laugh at me! Never afterwards did I think that I was great, but then—how could I resist it! 'Oh,' I said to myself, 'I shall be worthy of that praise, and what men, what men! That's where real men are! I shall be worthy of them, I shall try to be as fine as they are, I shall be *true!* Oh, how frivolous I am, and if only Belinsky knew the worthless, shameful things there are in me! And everyone says that these literary fellows are proud and vain. However, it's only in Russia you will find men like that.' All this, I thought, I remember very clearly," Dostoevsky concludes, "and I could never forget it. It was the most entrancing moment of my life. Recalling it in the Siberian prison, I grew stronger in spirit. Even now I recall it every time with delight. . . ."

"Am I really so great?"—the twenty-three-year-old Dostoevsky never doubted it for a moment.

VII

"In Russian literature there has not been any other example of fame so quickly won as the fame of Mr. Dostoevsky," Belinsky wrote in his *Review of Russian Literature for 1846*. Three years later Dostoevsky himself wrote to his brother: "This fame they have thrust upon me is of doubtful value, and I don't know how long this hell will go on—poverty, work that has to be finished by a certain date—oh, if only I could get some rest!" What had happened? "The success of *Poor People* and Belinsky's immoderately enthusiastic praises had a definitely harmful effect on Dostoevsky," is the cautious way in which Grigorovich tried to explain the final rift between Dostoevsky and Belinsky, Annenkov is much more specific about it. "Belinsky," he wrote in his *Marvellous Decade*, "constantly drew Dostoevsky's attention to the need for acquiring literary skill, because he could not apparently get used to Dostoevsky's diffuse style and ascribed it to the inexperience of the young writer. But Belinsky was mistaken," Annenkov shrewdly observes. "He was not dealing with a literary tyro but with a fully fledged writer whose working methods had become set. Dostoevsky listened to the critic's admonitions with an air of benevolent indifference. The sudden success of his novel did more than free him from the doubts and hesitations which usually beset the first steps of a writer: he accepted it as a prophetic dream holding out the promise of laurel wreaths."

This promise was not to be fulfilled for a long time. All too soon, Belinsky's friendly "admonitions" turned into hostile criticism, which Dostoevsky would not and could not stomach. At first, however, their friendship was very close. Both belonged to the same social class, both were sons of poor army doctors, a fact of which they must have been acutely conscious at a time when all cultural activities in Russia, including literature, were concentrated in the hands of aristocrats such as Prince Vladimir Odoevsky, the popular author of fantastic moral tales, and Count Vladimir Sollogub, the author of the popular tale *Tarantas*. "Dostoevsky," Belinsky wrote in a hasty note in June 1845, "my soul (the immortal one) yearns to see you. Please come at once. The man who will bring you this note will show you the way. You will meet *ours*, and please don't be shy of your host. He will be glad to see you at his house." This must have been the first invitation to visit his house for the purpose of meeting *ours*, that is to say, his closest literary friends, that Dostoevsky received from Belinsky.

After spending the summer of 1845 with his brother in Reval, where he began writing his second story, *The Double*, Dostoevsky was already able to write to Mikhail[24] that he was a frequent visitor at Belinsky's, who was "terribly well disposed" towards him and saw in him the justification of his views. "In general," he went on, as though in antici-

[24] *Letters*, October 8, 1845.

pation of what was to come, which, if anything, proves that success had not completely gone to his head, "my future (and not the very distant future, either) may be good or may be very bad indeed. Belinsky keeps nagging me to finish *The Double*. He has already told everyone in the literary world about it and almost sold it to Kraevsky [the editor of *Home Annals*]. As for *Poor People*, half of Petersburg is talking about it. Think what Grigorovich alone is worth! He told me himself: '*Je suis votre claqueur-chauffeur*.'" He next informed Mikhail that he was going to be one of the chief contributors to *The Scoffer*, a humorous monthly Nekrasov had planned to publish, the aim of which was "to laugh at everything and everybody." One of the proposed "news items" in the first issue would be a report of an imaginary meeting of the Slavophiles in Moscow at which "the important problem" of the origin of Adam would be finally solved. Adam would be "proved" to have been a Slav, "a discovery that was bound to be of great benefits to the whole Russian nation." Thirty years later, in his *Writer's Diary* and Pushkin speech, Dostoevsky outdid the Slavophiles by claiming almost the same thing not for Adam but for Christ!

In his next letter[25] Dostoevsky had even more exciting news to tell his brother. "Well, Mikhail," he wrote, "I don't think my fame will ever reach the same height of glory as it has now. Everywhere incredible respect and tremendous curiosity about me. I've become acquainted with scores and scores of really decent people. Prince Odoevsky is begging me to honor him by a visit, and Count S[ollogub] is tearing his hair in despair. Panaev has told him that there is a man of genius who will trample them all underfoot. S. has rushed all over the town and at last, on going to see Kraevsky, suddenly asked him: Who is this Dostoevsky? Where can I *get hold of* Dostoevsky? Kraevsky, who does not give a damn for anybody and tells everybody what he thinks, said to him that Dostoevsky would not condescend to honor him with a visit. And so it is: some silly little aristocrat clambers onto a pair of stilts and thinks he will annihilate me by the greatness of his favors. Everyone receives me as a miracle. I can't open my mouth without people in every corner repeating that Dostoev. said this or Dostoev. wants to do that. Belinsky likes me more than ever. The other day the poet Turgenev returned to Russia (you must have heard about it) and immediately became so deeply attached to me that Belinsky can explain it only by claiming that Turgenev had fallen in love with me. But, Mikhail, what an excellent fellow he is! I, too, have almost fallen in love with him. A poet, a man of talent, an aristocrat—handsome, rich, intelligent, well-educated, twenty-five years old—is there anything nature has denied him? Finally, an absolutely straightforward, fine character trained in the best school!"

In short, the intellectual elite of Petersburg were at his feet. His fame,

[25] *Letters*, November 16, 1845.

it is true, did not make him rich, for, in fact, he was penniless, but he hoped that his contributions to *The Scoffer* would bring him a lot of money. He had written an announcement for it in the press, which had "created a sensation" and for which Nekrasov had paid him twenty rubles in silver. While talking to Nekrasov he had an excellent idea, that of writing a story in nine letters, which he did that very night. He took it to Nekrasov next morning and got 125 rubles for it. "In the evening," Dostoevsky went on with his tale of glory, "I read my story at Turgenev's to our circle, that is, to about 20 people, and it created a sensation. It will be published in the first number of *The Scoffer* [which, incidentally, never appeared because the magazine was scotched at birth by the censors]. Belinsky said that he had complete faith in me now because I seem to be able to deal with any subject. The other day Kraevsky, hearing that I was penniless, succeeded in persuading me to accept 500 rubles from him as a loan. . . . Well, Mikhail, if I were to enumerate all my successes to you, I should run out of paper. Golyadkin [that is, *The Double*] is working out excellently; it will be my *chef d'œuvre*. Yesterday," he added, as though as an afterthought, "I went to see Panaev for the first time and, I believe, fell in love with his wife. She's clever and pretty as well as awfully kind and frank. . . ." He was sorry to be writing so much about himself, but, he explained "frankly," "I am absolutely in raptures about my own fame." On rereading his letter, however, he confessed that "first I am illiterate, and, secondly, a shameless braggart." His overexcitement, for which there was, no doubt, plenty of justification, brought about an overindulgence in sex. "The sweet Minnas, Claras, Mariannas, etc.," he writes, referring to the Petersburg prostitutes, most of whom were recruited from among the German girls in the Baltic provinces, "are prettier than ever, but they are damnably expensive. The other day Turgenev and Belinsky hauled me over the coals for my dissolute life. These fellows simply don't know how to show their love for me. They are all in love with me. My debts," he added gloomily, "are as big as ever."

Avdotya Panaev was a writer of some talent and the leading light among the "emancipated" women of the time. She had married Ivan Panaev, a rich landowner, in 1837, at the age of eighteen. By the time Dostoevsky met her on November 15, 1845, she had already become the mistress of Nekrasov, who, together with her husband, acquired *The Contemporary Review*, which they transformed into the most radical periodical in Russia. Dostoevsky's infatuation for her did not last. In his next letter to Mikhail[26] he declared that his love for P. was no joke, but that he thought it was already passing. It was, in fact, Dostoevsky's first experience of unhappy love. In her reminiscences Avdotya Panaev described Dostoevsky as "a terribly nervous and impressionable young man. He was thin, small, fair and with a sickly complexion," she wrote.

[26] *Letters*, February 1, 1846.

"His small gray eyes seemed to wander uneasily from one object to another and his pale lips twitched nervously. He knew almost all the people who were present at his first visit, but he looked terribly embarrassed and did not take part in the general conversation. We all did our best to help him overcome his shyness and to show him that he was a member of our circle."

Dostoevsky became a frequent visitor at the Panaev's literary *salon*, and quite soon, Mrs. Panaev records, "his shyness was gone and he even became rather aggressive, began to have violent arguments with everyone and to contradict everyone out of sheer stubbornness. Being young and nervous, he could not control himself and too openly displayed his author's vanity and the high opinion he had of his talents. Stunned by his unexpectedly brilliant success at the very outset of his career and showered with praises by competent men of letters, he could not conceal his pride before other young writers who had made a more modest start in their careers. With their appearance in our circle it was asking for trouble to get into their bad books, but, as though on purpose, Dostoevsky laid himself wide open to their jeers by his irritability, his supercilious tone and his assumption that he was infinitely more talented than any of them. So they started spreading all sorts of stories about him and exasperating him by their derisive remarks. Turgenev, in particular, was excellent at it—he purposely drew Dostoevsky into conversation and drove him mad with exasperation. Dostoevsky would lose his temper and would sometimes passionately defend some absurd idea he had expressed without thinking, while Turgenev egged him on and enjoyed himself hugely. One evening," Mrs. Panaev concludes, "Turgenev described in Dostoevsky's presence a meeting he had had in the provinces with a man who had imagined himself to be a genius. Dostoevsky went as white as a sheet, trembled all over and ran off without staying to hear the end of Turgenev's story. I asked them why they tortured Dostoevsky like that. But Turgenev was in a merry mood and infected the others with it, so that no one paid any attention to Dostoevsky's departure."

That, according to Mrs. Panaev, was the last time Dostoevsky came to see them, and, she adds, he even avoided meeting any of his former associates in the street.

Poor People was published in Nekrasov's *Petersburg Symposium* on January 15, 1846, and was greeted, Dostoevsky wrote to his brother,[27] "with violent abuse." But the abuse of the Petersburg papers was compensated for a hundredfold by the high praise of Belinsky, who, Dostoevsky was only too eager to tell Mikhail, found "that I have excelled Gogol." Belinsky and the others, he went on, "have discovered a new original literary trend in me, namely, that in my work I prefer

[27] *Letters,* February 1, 1846.

analysis to synthesis, that is, I penetrate deep into the heart of things and, analyzing each atom, try to get to the whole, while Gogol goes straight to the whole and is, therefore, not as deep as I. My future, Mikhail," he wrote in summing up this rather exaggerated account of his triumph, "is a most brilliant one." After enumerating the many reviews of *Poor People* that were being written just then ("Odoevsky is writing a special article about *Poor People*, Sollogub, my friend, also"), he adds this information: "I have crashed into high society, Mikhail, and after three months I shall tell you personally of my adventures." Alas, his adventures came to an ignominious end much sooner than he expected. According to Panaev, a young society girl expressed the wish to see Dostoevsky. But when they presented their "idol" to her and the girl was about to open her pretty mouth to pay him an exquisite compliment, he all of a sudden turned pale and began to sway. "We carried him to a back room and sprinkled eau-de-cologne on his face," Panaev concludes. "He recovered consciousness but refused to enter the drawing room again."

The publication of his second story, *The Double*, however, opened Dostoevsky's eyes to the pitfalls of literary fame. The main idea of *The Double* Dostoevsky summed up in a letter to Mikhail at the end of 1846, in the following words: "The *outward* must be balanced by the *inward*. Otherwise, with the absence of outward events, the inward will take too dangerous a sweep upwards. Nerves and fantasy will take up too much room. From want of habit every outward event will appear to be of colossal and, somehow, of frightening importance. One begins to be afraid of life." Golyadkin, the hero of *The Double*, the suspicious and apprehensive low-grade civil servant, bore, in fact, a strange resemblance to Dostoevsky himself. Indeed, some of the scenes he made in Belinsky's circle made Belinsky exclaim on one occasion: "Don't you think this is absolutely like a scene from *The Double?*" Recalling the circumstances surrounding the writing and publication of *The Double* in Kraevsky's *Home Annals* in February 1846, Dostoevsky wrote in 1877, in the November issue of his *Writer's Diary*: "I'm afraid I was most definitely unsuccessful with this story, but its idea was rather good and I don't think I have ever dealt with anything more serious than this idea in all my writings. But I was not successful in the form of the story. . . . All the same, Belinsky who . . . from the very beginning of the autumn of 1845 was highly interested in this new work of mine . . . insisted at the beginning of December 1845, that I should give a reading of at least two or three chapters of this story at his place. He even gave a party (which he hardly ever did) for this occasion and invited a number of close friends. Ivan Turgenev, I remember, was also at this party, but after listening to only half of what I read, he congratulated me and went away. . . . Belinsky liked the three or four chapters I read that evening very much (though they did not deserve it). But Belinsky did not know the end of the story and was under the influence of the fascination *Poor People* had exerted on him."

At the time, however, Dostoevsky was highly appreciative of Belinsky's enthusiasm. "*The Double*," he wrote to Mikhail on the day of the publication of the story, "is ten times better than *Poor People*. *Ours* say that after *Dead Souls* there is nothing like it in Russia, that it is the work of a genius and what do they *not* say about it! What great hopes they place in me!" It is clear that so carried away was Dostoevsky by his sudden fame that he was not able to see that *ours* were beginning to pull his leg. "I have received 600 rubles in silver for *The Double*," he told Mikhail in the same letter. "In addition, I got a lot more money; in fact I have spent three thousand rubles since returning from my visit to you. I'm leading a disorderly life—that's the trouble. . . . I am in a terrible state of health. My nerves have gone to pieces and I am afraid of a fever or a nervous breakdown. I can't live decently—I am so dissolute."

It was just then that he and Grigorovich parted company. "I don't know what it was about," Grigorovich writes in his reminiscences, "but one day we had a violent quarrel and we decided to live apart." Dostoevsky told Mikhail that he had left his old lodgings without any explanation of why he did so and that he was now living "in two excellently furnished rooms."

Two months later the sad awakening came: *The Double* was a failure! Though still insisting in his letter to Mikhail[28] that his fame had reached "the height of glory," he could not help revealing that "the horrible and agonizing fact is that *ours*, Belinsky and all, are dissatisfied with me for my Golyadkin . . . and the public as a whole, everybody, everybody, in fact, found Golyadkin so flabby and boring, so diffuse, that it is impossible to read it. . . . As for me, I have lost heart for a time. I suffer from a terrible vice: unbounded vanity and ambition. The thought that I have not come up to expectations and ruined the thing that might have been something really great, is killing me. I am sick of Golyadkin. . . . All this has given me hell for a time and I became ill with grief. . . ."

But he was not downhearted by any means: he was too conscious of his genius to be beaten by failure. Belinsky had left *Home Annals*, to which he had contributed regularly for a long time, and was planning to publish "a gigantic almanac," and Dostoevsky was writing two stories for it: *The Shaven Side Whiskers*, obviously intended as an attack on Nicholas I, who regarded whiskers and beards as a sign of French "freethinking," and *A Story of Destroyed Government Offices*, both, he explained to Mikhail, "of shattering dramatic interest. . . . The public," he added, "are waiting for something from me with impatience." There was another reason why he had to publish something new. "A

[28] *Letters*, April 1, 1846.

whole legion of new writers has appeared," he told Mikhail in the same letter. "The most remarkable of them are Herzen and Goncharov. . . . They are both highly praised. But priority still remains with me so far and I hope always."

A few weeks later he fell seriously ill. "I nearly died," he wrote to Mikhail.[29] "I fell ill with an acute irritation of the whole nervous system. The illness attacked my heart and caused it to be congested and inflamed, but I recovered after two bloodlettings and an application of leeches. I practically ruined myself on all sorts of decoctions, drops, powders, mixtures and similar nasty stuff. Now I am no longer on the danger list."

It was during the spring of 1846 that Dostoevsky met Dr. Yanovsky, who treated him for another purely "local" complaint. During his treatment, however, Yanovsky records, Dostoevsky often complained of very strong attacks of sick headaches which he feared were the first symptoms of heart failure. It was his constant fear of "sudden death," Yanovsky explains, that made him abstrain from all stimulants, including tea. The first examination showed that "there was nothing wrong with his lungs, but that his heartbeats were irregular and his pulse uneven and remarkably shallow, as with women and persons of a nervous temperament." Dostoevsky told him that he was very poor and had to live on the money he earned, and yet, Yanovsky remarks, he wore a beautifully cut black frock coat of excellent cloth and an expensive black cashmere waistcoat. His linen was fine and immaculate, and he carried a "Zimmermann" top hat (Raskolnikov also wore a "Zimmermann" top hat, only it was a battered one). His shoes, however, were not so fine, and, Yanovsky adds, he carried himself rather awkwardly.

Yanovsky was only twenty-eight at the time, and he and Dostoevsky soon became friends. Dostoevsky, like most hypochondriacs, showed a morbid interest in all sorts of diseases, and he used to borrow Dr. Yanovsky's medical textbooks, especially those dealing with the diseases of the brain and the nervous system. He was also interested "in the development of the skull according to the system of Gall," that is, in the then fashionable "science" of phrenology, and after an examination of his own skull he proclaimed proudly that it bore a close resemblance to the skull of Socrates.

On May 16, 1846, Dostoevsky again complained to Mikhail of having no money. He asked him to be nice to Belinsky's wife and sister who were on a short visit to Reval, because he "loved and respected" them. He was himself planning to spend the second part of the summer with his brother in Reval, but for the time being he was suffering from "boredom, attacks of sadness and apathy and a feverishly spasmodic expectation of something better. And on top of it there is my illness." His "ill-

[29] *Letters*, April 26, 1846.

ness" was, no doubt, due to the increasing rift between him and Belinsky's closest associates. Indeed, Dostoevsky began to look upon Belinsky himself with somewhat jaundiced eyes. Belinsky was very fond of a game of cards—it was, in fact, his only weakness, and yet Dostoevsky began to express aloud his contempt for an "idiotic occupation like that." "Really," Mrs. Panaev records him as saying, "it's quite impossible to distinguish between the society of civil servants and the society of writers: the same kind of stupid pastimes!" Belinsky was no doubt informed of Dostoevsky's remark, but all he would say was that it was a pity Dostoevsky, instead of working at his talent, was already imagining himself a genius. "He simply must get medical treatment," Mrs. Panaev records the critic as saying. "It's all the result of a terrible attack of nerves. Poor boy, life must have knocked him about badly. One must have the nerves of a bull to put up with the conditions of our life today. If there is no change for the better, we shall all in the end become mentally deranged." This remark was also no doubt immediately conveyed to Dostoevsky, who could hardly have relished the idea of being considered a "mental case."

What must have precipitated his nervous complaint was the constant waiting for something to happen that would restore his reputation. It is this waiting, coupled with the fear of another failure, that, twenty years later, he described in *The Insulted and Injured* as "mystic terror." In an autobiographical passage in this novel, Dostoevsky refers to it as "the most excruciatingly painful fear of something impossible to define, something incomprehensible and nonexistent in the natural order of things that will most assuredly come to pass, perhaps this very minute, as though against all rational arguments to the contrary, and confront me as an irrefutable fact—horrible, hideous and implacable. This sensation of fear usually grows more and more intense, despite all rational argument, so that in the end my mind, though it might at those moments acquire even greater lucidity, is deprived of every possibility of offering resistance to those sensations. It is not obeyed, it becomes useless, and this dichotomy is intensified even more by the fearful anguish of expectation."

In Reval his nervous complaint did not improve, although he had started on his third story, *Mr. Prokharchin*, published in *Home Annals* in October 1846, a desperate attempt to regain the applause his first novel had won by a harking back to the same environment and almost the same characters. Did he anticipate Belinsky's annihilating verdict, accusing him of insincerity and a desire to show how clever he was and finishing with the openly contemptuous sentence: "Of course, we have no right to demand from Mr. Dostoevsky's works the perfection of Gogol's works, but all the same we think that even a highly talented man may find it quite useful to follow the example of a man of greater talent." In any event, he had been beastly to everyone in Reval. "I remember," he wrote to Mikhail at the end of 1846, "how unkind and disobliging I was at your place in Reval. I was ill, Mikhail, I remember your telling me once that the way I treated you shows that I considered you as my inferior. My dear, that was absolutely unfair. But I have such a bad, repulsive character. I always regarded you as higher and better than I. I am ready to give my life for you and yours, but sometimes," he went on, revealing one of the most fundamental traits of his character, "when my heart overflows with love, you won't be able to get a kind word out of me. My nerves do not obey me at such a time. I am absurd and disgusting and for that reason am doomed always to suffer from being misunderstood. People say I am unfeeling and heartless. How many times was I rude to your wife, a most honorable woman and a thousand times better than I. I remember how sometimes I was deliberately beastly to your boy Fedya, whom at the same time I loved even more than you. The only time I can show that I am a man who possesses a kind and loving heart is when some chance circumstance snatches me out of the everyday banal routine of life. Till then I am disgusting. . . ."

On his return to Petersburg, Dostoevsky lived for a short time with his former fellow student Konstantin Trutovsky. "Every time Dostoevsky went to bed," Trutovsky records, "he asked me that if he should die, he should not be buried too quickly, for he was terribly afraid of lethargy, and he would describe to me the whole horror of awakening in the grave." He had been to see Nekrasov about the publication of his Almanac, for which he had contributed an introduction and collaborated with Nekrasov and Gigorovich in the writing of the humorous story *The Danger of Abandoning Oneself to Ambitious Dreams.* On October 5, 1846, he made the acquaintance of Alexander Herzen, who wrote to his wife on the same day: "I saw Dostoevsky today and I cannot say that the impression he made on me was particularly pleasant."

His financial situation was as bad as ever. "Kraevsky," he wrote to Mikhail,[30] "gave me 50 rubles in silver [an advance on *Mr. Prokharchin,* no doubt] and to judge from the way he looked, I don't expect he will give me more." But at least he was not starving, for in November he joined a small "association" of students and writers who had rented a large flat on Vassilevsky Island and who shared expenses for food and lodgings, so that Dostoevsky had to pay only fifteen kopecks for a good dinner. But his health was deteriorating ("Petersburg," he wrote to Mikhail on October 7th, "is hell for me"); and he was planning to go abroad, hoping that in Italy he might, like Gogol, write the long novel he had in mind and be able to get his own terms for it. "For," he told Mikhail in the same letter, "the system of constant indebtedness favored by Kraevsky is a system of literary slavery and dependence." But before

[30] *Letters,* September 11, 1846.

going to Italy he had to pay off his debts, which amounted to 1,600 rubles. He hoped to raise the money, but he was "in a panic" about his health. "I have terrible palpitations," he wrote, "as bad as during the first period of my illness."

Nothing came of his plan to go abroad, for he could not raise the money. His literary plans, too, came to nothing. Nekrasov did not get permission to publish *The Scoffer*, and Dostoevsky gave up writing *The Shaven Side Whiskers*. He was now writing *The Landlady* and planning to publish *Poor People* and *The Double* in book form, but in November he had to postpone their publication for lack of funds. In that month, too, he finally quarreled with Nekrasov and broke off his association with the *Contemporary*. Nekrasov, he wrote to Mikhail,[31] "is vexed with me for giving two of my stories to Kraevsky, to whom I am in debt, and for refusing to publish a statement that I have nothing to do with *Home Annals*. Having to give up the idea of getting a story from me in the near future, he abused me and incautiously asked me to return the advance he had given me. I took him at his word and promised to let him have a written acknowledgment of my debt with a promise to return the money by December 15. . . . When I told Nekrasov exactly what I thought of him, he just stammered and behaved like a Jew who is robbed of his money. In a word, a sordid business. Now they are spreading the story that I am infected with vanity, have exaggerated ideas about myself and have sold myself to Kraevsky because [Valerian] Maykov [who had succeeded Belinsky as literary critic of *Home Annals*: he was drowned in 1847 at the age of twenty-four] praises me. Nekrasov, on the other hand, is going to abuse me. As for Belinsky, he is such a weak character that even in literary matters he changes his mind continually. It is only with him that I keep up my former good relationship."

Mrs. Panaev gives quite a different version of Dostoevsky's break with Nekrasov and *The Contemporary Review*. "One day," she records, "Dostoevsky appeared at Nekrasov's office and demanded to have a talk with Nekrasov. He was in a highly excited state. I left Nekrasov's office and I could hear from the dining room that they were having a very heated argument. When Dostoevsky rushed out of the office into the entrance hall he was as white as a sheet and could not get his hand through the sleeve of his overcoat which the footman was holding out for him. Dostoevsky snatched the coat out of his hands and rushed out of the front door. When I entered Nekrasov's office I found him in the same state of intense excitement. 'Dostoevsky has simply gone off his head,' said Nekrasov in a voice shaking with agitation. 'He came to me with threats demanding that I should not print my criticism of his works in the next number. And who told him the lie that I am reading my skit in verse on him everywhere! He was mad with fury!' "

[31] *Letters*, November 26, 1846.

The skit in verse on Dostoevsky, the joint work of Nekrasov and Turgenev, was written with a venom that would have infuriated a man much less excitable than Dostoevsky. It described Dostoevsky as "a knight of mournful countenance blossoming on the nose of literature like a ripe pimple" and, referring to Dostoevsky's unhappy experience in high society, described him as "having dipped his nose before a Russian beauty and nearly perished in the prime of life." Dostoevsky, who never forgot an insult, repaid Turgenev in kind by his skit in *The Devils*. At the moment he damned them all.

Meanwhile he had made new friends and acquaintances, including the poet Apollon Maykov, brother of Valerian, who was to remain one of his closest friends throughout most of his life, and two others, who were to play a great part in the tragedy that was to overtake him so soon: Mikhail Butashevich-Petrashevsky, a twenty-five-year-old official of the Russian Foreign Office, and the twenty-one-year-old poet Sergey Pleshcheyev, both sons of well-to-do landowners. Dostoevsky met Petrashevsky in the spring of 1846. "Our first meeting was accidental," Dostoevsky stated after his arrest in his official deposition to the court. "I was, if I am not mistaken, with Pleshcheyev in a pastry cook's near the Police Bridge and was reading newspapers. I saw Pleshcheyev stopping to have a talk with Petrashevsky, but I was not able to examine Petrashevsky's face closely. Five minutes later I left the pastry cook's. Before I reached Bolshaya Nevskaya Street, Petrashevsky caught up with me and suddenly asked me: 'May I ask what's the idea underlying your next story?' As I had not observed Petrashevsky very closely in the shop, I thought at first that he was a stranger, who happened to come across me in the street, and not a friend of Pleshcheyev's. But at that moment Pleshcheyev came up and cleared up my misunderstanding. We exchanged a few words and, reaching Malaya Morskaya Street, took leave of one another. This was how Petrashevsky aroused my interest at our very first meeting."

In December of 1846 Dostoevsky was working hard on his story *The Landlady* and on *Netochka Nezvanova*, the novel he had just begun and was not destined to complete. "This letter," he wrote to Mikhail on December 17th, "I wrote at odd moments, for I am busy writing day and night, except that occasionally I go to the Italian opera. . . . I am feeling well . . . and am writing with zest. I can't help feeling that I have brought an action against the whole of our literature, the periodicals and the critics . . . and am firmly establishing my pre-eminence just to spite my ill-wishers. . . ." He was still seeing Belinsky while writing *The Landlady*, which, in his total inability to cast a critical eye over what he was doing just then, he thought was better than *Poor People*. "My pen," he told Mikhail, "is guided by a spring of inspiration that gushes out straight from my soul." But it was *The Landlady* that brought about his final break with Belinsky, who had been smarting for some time from Dostoevsky's critical (to put it mildly) attitude towards him. The break took place in the spring of 1847, a year before Belinsky's death. In a letter to Annenkov, Belinsky declared that *The Landlady* was "terrible rubbish" and that "every new work of Dostoevsky's is a new downfall. In the provinces," he went on, "they can't endure him and in Petersburg they speak badly even of *Poor People*. I tremble at the thought of rereading it. . . . We were bamboozled, my friend, about Dostoevsky–the genius! As for me, the old devil, I deserve to be beaten. I, the foremost critic, acted like a real donkey. . . ."

In his statement to the court Dostoevsky, who, it is true, was eager to emphasize his disagreement with Belinsky, gave the following account of the reasons that led to the break between them: "In the literary world quite a few people know of my quarrel and final break with Belinsky in the last year of his life. The reason for our disagreement is also well known: it arose from a difference in our views about literature and literary tendencies. My view was fundamentally opposed to Belinsky's. I reproached him with trying to impose a personal and unworthy purpose on literature, reducing it solely to a description, if one may express it so, of newspaper facts or scandalous incidents. I protested that you could not attract anyone by bitterness, but that you would only make everybody sick and tired of you if you seized every Tom, Dick and Harry in the street, stopped every passer-by by buttonholing him, and started forcibly to preach to him and teach him sense. Belinsky got angry with me and in the end we passed from coolness to a formal break, so that we did not even meet during the last year of his life."

Going over his association with Belinsky twenty-six years later, Dostoevsky wrote in his *Writer's Diary* in 1873: "During the last year of his life I no longer visited him. He no longer liked me; but I accepted passionately his teachings at that time."

[3]

THE REBEL: FORTRESS AND SCAFFOLD

The question how much Dostoevsky was influenced by Belinsky's radical ideas and, especially, by his atheism has never really been satisfactorily elucidated. There was a period in his life—the period during which he was writing *The Devils*—when no abuse was strong enough with which to bespatter Belinsky's reputation. He described the critic to Strakhov[1] as "the most stupid, shameful and evil-smelling phenomenon in Russian life." "This man," he wrote, "used most obscene words in swearing at Christ in front of me and yet he was never able to put himself or any of the leading men in the world on the same level as Christ. He was not able to realize how much petty pride, malice, impatience, irritability, meanness and, most of all, vanity there was in him and in them. He never asked himself: what shall we put in His place? Not us, surely not us who are so vile. No, he never gave a thought to the fact that he himself was vile; he was satisfied with himself to the utmost and that in itself was a personal, evil-smelling, shameful stupidity." He even refused to acknowledge that Belinsky had any talent. He forgot entirely that it was Belinsky to whom he owed his fame and that, though the critic made some reservations about some of his stories and roundly condemned his *Landlady* as something "monstrous, stilted and false," he never went back on his admiration for *Poor People*. One cannot help wondering whether he was so abusive about Belinsky in 1871 because he was about to return to Russia and knew that the Russian secret police were keeping an eye on him and opened all his letters. Two years later, having become the editor of the reactionary monthly *The Citizen*, he no longer felt constrained to enunciate his views with such vehemence, and in the very first number of his *Writer's Diary* he gave a much calmer account of his relationship with Belinsky. "My first novel *Poor People*," he wrote, "delighted him; (then, a year later, we parted company—for all sorts of reasons, which were, however, quite unimportant

[1] *Letters*, May 30, 1871.

in every respect); but at the time, having become attached to me with all his heart, he at once attempted with the most naïve haste to convert me to his faith. I am not in the least exaggerating his warm attachment to me, at least during the first months of our acquaintance." At the time Belinsky, according to Dostoevsky, was "a passionate Socialist" and he began Dostoevsky's conversion "straight away with atheism." He felt that, as a socialist, he had first of all to "depose Christianity," which created "the moral foundations" of the society he hated. He realized, no doubt, that by denying the moral responsibility of the individual, he also denied his liberty, but, Dostoevsky claims, "he believed with all his might that far from destroying personal liberty, socialism re-establishes it in unprecedented grandeur, but on new, and this time on adamant foundations." Belinsky, in fact, was an idealist, "an utterly ecstatic personality," but so set was he on destroying Christ's teaching that he even denied "the moral unapproachability and the marvelous and miraculous beauty" of Christ himself, "unlike Renan, who in his completely atheistic book *Vie de Jésus* proclaimed that Christ was still the ideal of human beauty."

" 'Do you realize,' " Dostoevsky records Belinsky as saying to him "in a squeaky voice" one evening, " 'do you realize that one ought not to pile up sins on a man and burden him with guilt and make him offer the other cheek when society is so basely organized that a man cannot help committing crimes, since he is led to crime by economic forces, and that it is absurd and cruel to demand of a man to do something that he could not possibly do, according to the laws of nature, even if he wanted to?' "

"We were not alone that evening, there was one of Belinsky's friends there whom he greatly respected . . . as well as a young writer who afterwards became famous.

" 'I can't help feeling deeply touched when I look at him,' Belinsky suddenly interrupted his vehement tirade and, addressing himself to his friend, pointed to me: 'for every time I mention Christ, a change comes over him and he looks as though he were going to burst into tears. Why,' he pounced on me again, 'don't you see, you naïve fellow, that if your Christ had been born today, he'd be the most inconspicuous and ordinary man. He'd be completely effaced when confronted with modern science and the modern intellectual leaders of mankind.'

" 'Well, no-o-o!' Belinsky's friend cut in. (I remember we were all sitting, while he kept pacing the room.) 'No. If Christ appeared today, he'd join the movement and be at the head of it.'

" 'Yes, of course, of course,' Belinsky agreed with astonishing rapidity. 'Yes, he would indeed have joined the socialists and gone along with them.' "

"These intellectual leaders of mankind whom Christ is supposed to have joined," Dostoevsky continued, "were all Frenchmen at the time:

first and foremost George Sand, the now completely forgotten Cabet, Pierre Leroux and Proudhon, who had only just then begun to be known. Those four, as far as I can remember, Belinsky respected most of all. Fourier was not respected in any comparable way. . . . This all-ecstatic man," Dostoevsky could not help adding, with a touch of malice, "who possessed such a wonderfully calm conscience, sometimes fell a victim to melancholy, but it was melancholy of a special kind—it did not arise from doubts, nor from disappointments—oh, no!—but from the thought—why not today, why not tomorrow? He was a man in a hurry, the most impatient man in all Russia. Once I met him at four o'clock in the afternoon at the Znamensky Church. He told me he had gone out for a walk.

" 'I come here often to see how they are getting on with the construction (of the Nikolayevsk Railway, which was just then being built). I may as well get some satisfaction out of standing here and watching how the work is progressing: at last we shall have at least one railway. You don't know how much this thought lightens my heart sometimes.'

"This," Dostoevsky concludes, "was warmly and well said. Belinsky never gave himself airs. We walked on together. On the way home, I remember, he said to me: 'When they bury me' (he knew he had T.B.) 'they will realize at last whom they have lost.' "

It was characteristic of the later Dostoevsky in his calmer moods to end the painful reminiscences of his association with Belinsky on this minor and far from rancorous note. He enlarged on the theme of his acceptance of Belinsky's ideas in a later issue of his *Writer's Diary* of the same year. "At the time," he wrote, "the whole affair was looked upon in a most rosy and paradisiacally moral light. It is absolutely true that the idea of socialism, which was in its first infancy just then, was being compared, even by some of its leaders, to Christianity and was understood to be merely a correction and improvement on the latter in accordance with the spirit of the age and the demands of civilization. All these ideas appealed to us in Petersburg tremendously and seemed to be in the highest degree sacred and moral and, above all, applicable to humanity as a whole as the future law of all mankind without exception. Long before the Paris revolution of 1848 we had all fallen under the spell of those ideas. In 1846 I had already been initiated by Belinsky into the whole *truth* of that coming 'renewed world' and the *sanctity* of the future communist society. All the convictions about the immorality of the (Christian) foundations of contemporary society and of the immorality of religion and the family; of the immorality of the rights of private property; all the ideas about the abolition of nationalities in the name of the universal brotherhood of man, about contempt for the love of one's country, which was regarded as a brake on the general development, etc., etc., all these were influences that we could not resist and that, on the contrary, took complete possession of our minds and hearts. . . . At any rate it seemed a grand idea to us, an idea that was higher than any other dominating idea of the time—and it was this that was so terribly fascinating."

Whether the complete acceptance of Belinsky's ideas led Dostoevsky to jettison his deeply rooted religious beliefs still remains uncertain. They certainly pushed them into the background for a time. In one of his last notebooks, in a reference to some of the radical critics of *The Brothers Karamazov*, Dostoevsky remarked: "They have no idea of the force of negation which *I experienced*. Even in Europe there has never been such a forceful expression of atheistic ideas." Indeed, it is very probable that the conflict between belief and disbelief, which, as Dostoevsky wrote to Apollon Maykov from Dresden on April 6, 1870, "tormented me, consciously and unconsciously, all my life," was one of the legacies left over from the period of his enthusiastic acceptance of Belinsky's ideas.

His estrangement from Belinsky had no effect on his newly won convictions. On the contrary, by joining the Petrashevsky group, he found himself amidst people some of whom did not shrink even before the idea of a revolutionary uprising in order "to restore" the dignity of man. "Man waits for his crown," a leading member of the Petrashevsky group declared in summing up its aims. "He has earned it and will soon take it and cover his tortured head with it and reveal himself as the king of the earth. . . . We are surrounded by hundreds of millions of people, who are all victims of crazy dreams and who do not realize that a new life awaits them and that they ought to be preparing to accept it. Our business is to reveal the falsehood and the pity of this situation to them and bring them the glad tidings of a new life. Yes, we must all do that and we must remember what a great thing we are undertaking. The laws of nature, trampled underfoot by ignorance, must be reinstated; the divine image of man must be restored in all its beauty and majesty; the great harmonious passions, crushed and suppressed, must be set free and organized; cities and towns must be razed to the ground and their materials used for the erection of new buildings, this whole life of torments, calamities, poverty, shame and disgrace must be transformed into a splendid and harmonious life of joy, riches and happiness, and the whole of the impoverished earth must be covered with palaces and fruits and adorned with flowers—this is our aim, our great aim, and there is no greater aim than this in the whole world."

Dostoevsky began visiting Petrashevsky's Friday at homes in March 1847, and he at once discovered, as he was to testify after his arrest, that, apart from their vague, if grandiose, aims, there was no unity among the members of the group. "One can state positively," he declared in his statement to the court, "that it was impossible to find three men among them who agreed on any one point. That is why there were constant arguments at their meetings and everlasting contradictions in their opinions. In some of these debates I, too, took part."

Petrashevsky, as a faithful follower of Charles Fourier, claimed that "man, like any other living creature, has a right and a duty to life, which for him, as for everything else in nature, means a free and many-sided development in accordance with the demands and the laws of his nature; the very fact of his birth imposes upon man the direct obligation of a harmonious, spiritual and material development; man's life must be absolutely sacred under all circumstances and at all times; every well-organized society must aim at the elimination of contradictions and differences of opinion between its members . . . so that the common and unanimous desire of all shall be the fostering of the well-being and prosperity of all. This should become universal law, and society itself should become a practical realization of the precept of brotherly love given to us by our Redeemer. In short, everyone should consciously love his neighbor as himself. Thus, the truths of positivist philosophy are identical with the true teaching of religion."

Dostoevsky, who had heard all this put with even greater passion by Belinsky, was never particularly impressed by Petrashevsky or his attempts to introduce phalansteries in accordance with Fourier's teachings, even though he occasionally resorted to quotations from the Bible. He knew perfectly well that this was only a manner of speaking and that Petrashevsky, like Belinsky, was an unbeliever. What he objected to most of all was Petrashevsky's shilly-shallying attitude towards more positive steps for bringing about the triumph of the ideals they were all preaching. "Fourierism," Dostoevsky wrote in his statement to the court, "is a pacific system: it casts a spell on the soul by its refinement and charms the heart by the love of mankind. This inspired Fourier when he composed his system, and astonished the mind by its harmony. It attracts men not by bitter attacks but by love of humanity. There is no hatred in this system. Fourierism does not propagate political reforms; the only reforms it preaches are economic. It aims at undermining neither the government nor private property, and indeed at one of the last sittings of the French Chamber, Victor Considérant, the representative of the Fourierists, solemnly denied that Fourierism intended to undermine the rights of the family. . . . Furthermore, it is a well-known fact that Fourier's system does not condemn an autocratic form of government."

This, indeed, was precisely the reason that made Dostoevsky join a more active revolutionary group, which met regularly at the flat of the minor poet Sergey Durov. But this was not to happen until a year after he became a frequenter of Petrashevsky's at homes and, more especially, a borrower of proscribed books from his library. Long before that time, in April and June 1842, he described, in one of the four articles he contributed to *The St. Petersburg Journal*, the different groups of "circles" that were so fashionable in Petersburg in those years. "The whole of Petersburg," he wrote, "is really nothing but a collection of an enormous number of circles, each of which has its own statutes, its own ideas of decorum, its own laws, its own logic and its own oracles. . . . In some circles, though," he went on, having, no doubt, circles similar to Petrashevsky's in mind, "more important matters are discussed: a few well-educated and well-meaning people come together with enthusiasm, banish vigorously all innocent pastimes, such as gossiping and card games (this is not true of literary circles, of course) and with inexplicable passion, debate all sorts of important matters. Having discussed and talked about them, and having solved a number of questions to the satisfaction of everyone and got each other to agree about everything, the whole circle relapses into a kind of irritable mood, into an unpleasant kind of depression. Finally, they start quarreling, they exchange a few harsh truths, a few harsh and strong personalities come to the fore, and then they all go their separate ways. . . ."

It was a most depressing time for Dostoevsky, too. Again and again in his articles there are references to his cheerless and comfortless existence. "I was walking along the Haymarket and thinking what to write about. I felt sick at heart. . . ." Or again: "I felt somehow dreary and vexed. . . ." Or: "Depression and doubt rend and gnaw at my heart. . . ." He was worried about his health. "I caught a cold yesterday," he wrote to Mikhail in April 1847, "after going out at night in an overcoat and without a jacket. The Neva was covered with moving ice floes. It's cold here, as cold as in November. And this is the sixth time I have caught a cold."

II

Towards the end of 1847 Dostoevsky was urging Mikhail to come and live in Petersburg with his family. "It is unthinkable," he wrote to him,[2] "that we should not elbow our way into the world—nonsense! Remember what the people who shake their heads deprecatingly are really like. The same salary you are getting now, you would always be able to earn here, and without having to work so hard, either. I shall stay at my present lodgings and wait for you. . . ." In an earlier letter he referred in even more scathing terms to the people who "shake their heads deprecatingly," a hint, no doubt, at Karepin and "the Muscovites," "I am thinking a lot about you," he wrote to Mikhail. "You have a great deal of sound common sense and sparkles of brilliant humor and gaiety. But, good Lord, how many disgusting, vilely limited gray-bearded sages there are, experts, Pharisees of life, who are *proud* of their experience, that is, of their lack of personality (for they are all cut to one and the same pattern), worthless people who are everlastingly preaching that one

[2] *Letters,* September 9, 1847.

should be content with one's fate, that one should set a limit to one's ambition in life and be content with one's place in it, without really attempting to grasp the meaning of those words—contentment that is like monastic self-restraint and self-mortification, people who condemn with inexhaustible and petty malevolence the strong, ardent heart that cannot endure their vulgar daily routine and calendar of life. They are infamous villains, the lot of them, with their farcical earthly happiness! Infamous villains!"

That was all very well, but Mikhail had a wife and three children to support, and his "sound common sense" must have told him to beware of his brother's optimism. He had already had a foretaste of Dostoevsky's absurd plans to get rich quickly. He resigned his commission just the same and arrived in Petersburg alone in the autumn of 1847 and brought his family over at the beginning of 1848. "Mikhail," Andrey records in his memoirs, "got a decent flat on Nevsky Avenue and Fyodor and I used to dine with him every Sunday and on every holiday, a custom which we kept up religiously till the end of 1849 when it was broken for reasons beyond our control."

The failure of his fantastic story *The Landlady* made Dostoevsky revert to his earlier, more naturalistic manner in his next three stories—*Polzunkov* (the Crawler), an anticipation of the type of hanger-on of his later novels, *A Faint Heart*, and *The Honest Thief*, published between February and April 1848. On May 26, 1848, Dostoevsky, Yanovsky records, burst into his room with the news that Belinsky had died that morning. "My dear fellow," Dostoevsky said, "a great misfortune has befallen us—Belinsky is dead."

There was a cholera epidemic in Petersburg in the summer of 1848, and Dostoevsky and Mikhail and his family fled to the holiday resort of Pargolovo, where they were joined later by Andrey and their youngest brother, Nikolai, who had arrived in Petersburg in May to study architecture. It was from Pargolovo that Yanovsky received the note from Dostoevsky in which he wrote that he was no longer worried about dying of a heart attack because he was very busy collecting money for a drunkard who was going from house to house offering himself to be flogged for money, a man, no doubt, after his own heart. Mrs. Panaev, who also spent that summer in Pargolovo, states that Dostoevsky never visited them and even stopped greeting Nekrasov and Panaev when he met them in the street, but looked sarcastically at them. "Dostoevsky," she goes on, "was often seen in the company of Petrashevsky, who always looked very somber. He was of less than medium height, with a large black beard, long hair, and always walked about in a cloak and a wide-brimmed soft hat and carried a thick stick." It was at Pargolovo, too, that Dostoevsky got on more intimate terms with Nikolai Speshnyov, a rich landowner and one of the more radical members of the Petrashevsky "circle," who advocated a violent seizure of power and believed in the proximity of a peasant revolution in Russia.

It was in October of that year that Dostoevsky and Pleshcheyev proposed to Speshnyov that they form their own revolutionary group apart from Petrashevsky. In December 1848, Dostoevsky was present at one of Petrashevsky's "Fridays" when another member of the circle, Konstantin Timkovsky, read a paper on Fourierism and communism in which he proposed, as an experiment, to "divide the world into two parts, one part of which was to be given to the Fourierists and the other to the communists," a proposal that shows perhaps better than anything how far from reality the "revolutionaries" of the Petrashevsky "circle" were and explains why Dostoevsky was so eager to form his own group of more active revolutionaries.

It was at one of these meetings of the new activist group of young revolutionaries at Pleshcheyev's that Dostoevsky made friends with Alexander Milyukov, a writer and teacher of literature and a friend of the poet Sergey Durov, at whose house the group usually held their meetings in 1849. According to Milyukov, Durov hired a piano and invited a few friends to his ostensibly musical parties on Saturdays. At these meetings, Milyukov records, the members of the group made violent speeches against the censorship and for the liberation of the serfs. "When someone expressed doubts as to whether it was possible to liberate the serfs in a legal way," Milyukov states, "Dostoevsky replied sharply that he did not believe in any other way." On the other hand, Alexander Palm, another member of the group and the author of a novel about the Petrashevsky group in which the hero, Alexey Slobodin, is a barely disguised portrait of the young Dostoevsky, records that when they were discussing at one of the meetings what should be done if it proved impossible to liberate the peasants without a revolution, Dostoevsky cried, "All right, then *with* a revolution!"

It would seem, in fact, that at the beginning of 1849 Dostoevsky was leaning more and more towards the outspokenly revolutionary views of Speshnyov. In January he went to see his friend Apollon Maykov and informed him that the members of the Durov "circle" intended to obtain an illegal printing press. "One day," Maykov wrote in a letter to a friend many years later, "in January, 1849, Fyodor Dostoevsky came to see me and stayed the night at my flat—I happened to be living alone just then. My bed was against one wall and Dostoevsky's bed was made up on a sofa along the opposite wall. And so he started telling me that he had been asked to approach me with a proposal. Petrashevsky, he said, was a fool, a cheap mummer and a chatterbox. He couldn't be relied on to do anything sensible and that was why a number of the more capable members of his circle had decided to form their own circle about which he would know nothing and into which he would not be admitted. They were Speshnyov, Pavel Philippov [a twenty-four-year-old student in the faculty of mathematics of Petersburg University], and five or six more, whose names I don't remember, including Dostoevsky. They decided to co-opt another seventh or eighth member, that is, myself. They had further decided to obtain a secret printing press for printing illegal literature. I tried to point out to him the improvidence and the danger of such an undertaking and I told him that they were running the risk of forfeiting their lives. I can still remember Dostoevsky sitting there—like the dying Socrates in front of his friends—in his nightshirt with an unbuttoned collar, exercising his eloquence to prove the sacredness of their undertaking and our duty to save our country, etc., so that in the end I began to laugh and joke. 'So it's no, is it?' he concluded. 'No, no, and no!' Next morning, after breakfast, he said to me as he was going out: 'Say nothing about it—not a word.' 'Of course not.' Afterwards I found out that the printing press had been ordered in different parts of the town, according to a drawing by Philippov, and assembled at a flat belonging to one of the members of the Durov circle a day or two before the arrest [of the Petrashevsky group]." In fact, the printing press was at Philippov's study when the police arrived to arrest him, on April 23, 1849, but, standing among the different scientific instruments in the room, it escaped notice and was later clandestinely removed by the members of his family.

A more outspoken version of his talk with Dostoevsky on that January night was preserved by another friend of Apollon Maykov, the poet Golenishchev-Kutuzov. In this account, which was published only in 1956, Maykov records that when he asked Dostoevsky what was the aim of the secret society of seven members he wanted him to join, Dostoevsky replied: "Why, our aim is to organize a revolution in Russia. We've already got a printing press. . . . Everything is ready."

In his letter to General Totleben from Siberia,[3] Dostoevsky acknowledged that he had been guilty of a conspiracy against the state. "I was convicted of an intention (but not more) to act against the government," he wrote. "I was found guilty legally and justly." And according to his first biographer, Orest Miller, Dostoevsky admitted to him the existence of "a conspiracy" the intention of which was "to spread general dissatisfaction with the existing order, beginning with the educational establishments, and make contact with every group that had the seeds of dissatisfaction in it—such as the religious dissenters and the serfs."

From the beginning of March to the middle of April 1849, Dostoevsky took a very active part in the Saturday meetings of the Durov group. On April 1 he spoke at a meeting of the Petrashevsky group and expressed himself in favor of the abolition of censorship, the liberation of the serfs and the reform of the law courts. At the meeting a fortnight later he read Belinsky's letter to Gogol attacking the reactionary views

[3] *Letters,* March 24, 1856.

Gogol had expressed in his *Selected Passages from the Correspondence with My Friends,* which the government had banned because it was considered to be "full of arrogant expressions against the church and the government." Dostoevsky had received a copy of the letter from Pleshcheyev and had read it once before, at a meeting of the Durov group. During the same month Dostoevsky was present at a dinner at Speshnyov's at which Nikolai Grigoryev, a lieutenant in a guards regiment and an enthusiastic member of the Petrashevsky "circle," read his *Soldier's Talk,* a pamphlet in which, according to the report of the public prosecutor, "he most arrogantly attacked army service, the orders of commanding officers and, especially, of your Imperial Majesty," and which, "to judge by its style and purport, was meant to lead to the undermining of the loyalty of the lower ranks of the army and their refusal to obey their superior officers."

All this time the meetings at Petrashevsky's were watched by a secret-police agent, a young student by the name of Antonelli, who sent in full reports of them to the Third Department, that is, the political secret police. His report of a dinner given by Petrashevsky in honor of Fourier on April 7, 1849, at which Dostoevsky was not present, clinched the case of the police against the members of the group and led to their arrest. At this dinner Petrashevsky concluded his speech with the words: "We have condemned to death the present social order; all that remains to be done is to carry out the sentence." Another speaker, the police spy reported, talked of "the necessity of abolishing the family, private property, the state, the laws, the army and the churches," while a third declared that "the transformation of the social and political order is at hand" and called those present at the dinner "to action."

Altogether, twenty-three men were arrested on the night of April 23, 1849, all but five of them young men in their twenties. Dostoevsky was considered to be "one of the most important" among them, chiefly, it would seem, because, as Speshnyov put it, he, more than anyone else, "gave the impression of being a real conspirator: he was taciturn, he liked to talk confidentially to people, he was secretive rather than outspoken, and, besides, he looked much older than his age."

The following order for the arrest of Dostoevsky was issued by the head of the political police, Count Alexey Orlov:

Third Department	Secret
of His Imperial Majesty's Office	To Major Chudinov,
St. Petersburg	C.O. of St. Petersburg
22nd April 1849	Gendarmerie Division
No. 675	

At the order of His Imperial Majesty I instruct you to arrest at 4 o'clock in the morning the retired engineer-lieutenant and writer Fyodor Mikhailovich Dostoevsky, who lives at the corner of Malaya

Morskaya Street and Voznesensky Avenue in the house of Shil, on the third floor, in the apartment of Bremer, to seal all his papers and books and to deliver them together with Dostoevsky to the Third Department of His Imperial Majesty's Office. In carrying out the arrest, you must take particular care that none of Dostoevsky's papers remains unaccounted for.

It may happen that you will find a large number of books and papers in Dostoevsky's rooms which may make it impossible for you to transfer them at once to the Third Department. If this should be the case, you should put them all together in one room, or, if necessary, two rooms, and after sealing the rooms, take Dostoevsky himself at once to the Third Department.

If while his papers and books are being sealed, Dostoevsky should point out that some of them do not belong to him, you should take no notice of it and seal those too.

In carrying out this order, you are to observe the utmost care and vigilance and you will be held personally responsible for its successful execution.

Lieutenant-General Dubelt, chief of staff of the Gendarmerie Corps, will see that you are accompanied by an officer of the St. Petersburg police and the required number of gendarmes.

Adjutant-General,
Count Orlov.

III

On April 23, 1849, Dostoevsky arrived home, as usual, in the small hours of the morning. In *Netochka Nezvanova,* the novel he was writing at the time, he expressed his feeling of black despondency that never left him as he struggled hopelessly against the general indifference and open hostility with which his writings were met after his first brilliant success. "No one," he wrote, "has any need of you now, no one wants to know you even—that is how the world goes. And things are sure to be much worse when they realize that you really have talent. Envy, petty baseness and, worst of all, stupidity will drive you to distraction even more than poverty will. A man of talent requires sympathy, he requires understanding, but even if you are a little successful in attaining your object, the evil faces will surround you still. They will consider your success of no importance and they will regard with contempt whatever you may have achieved by hard work, privations, hunger and sleepless nights. They will neither encourage nor comfort you; they will not point out to you the things that are good and true in you, but will seize on every mistake you make with gleeful malevolence. They will deliberately point to what is bad in your work, to what you are mistaken in, and, under the outward guise of indifference to you and contempt for you, will celebrate every mistake you make as though it were a festive occasion (as if no one had ever made mistakes in his life!). You, on the other hand, are arrogant, you are often proud when you shouldn't be, you can easily offend some ambitious nonentity, and then you are in real trouble—you are alone and they are many; they will torment you to death with their pinpricks. . . ."

How far the scorn of his former friends drove Dostoevsky to distraction can be seen from a letter he wrote to Eugénie Maykov, the mother of Apollon,[4] in which he apologized abjectly for a violent quarrel he had had at her house with some of Belinsky's friends and for rushing out of the house without saying good-by to her. "I ran away instinctively," he wrote, "knowing very well the weakness of my character which in extreme cases makes me lose complete control of myself and leads me to quite *hyperbolic* extremes." These "hyperbolic extremes" no doubt became more and more frequent after his new stories were ignored. The need to finish a story by a certain date, he wrote to Kraevsky,[5] made him write "such a bad thing as *The Landlady*," and every failure of his made him ill. He had published six stories between February and December 1848, without the least improvement in his reputation. His political activities, too, he confesses through the mouth of the hero of one of his most lyrical stories—*White Nights*, published in the December number of *Home Annals*—often plunged him into "black gloom." He was overwhelmed by the feeling that he would never be able "to start living in earnest," that he had lost all touch with life and all understanding of what was real and actual, and even when he did experience moments of returning sanity, they filled him with horror and dismay. Neither did his constant state of penury improve matters. Whenever he got an advance from Kraevsky, he spent it with an improvidence that was the despair of all his friends. He liked giving dinners at expensive restaurants. He would invite a large company and spend a ruble a person on them for food and much more on drinks—vodka before dinner and two glasses of champagne during dinner. "Dostoevsky," Dr. Yanovsky recalls, "did not drink vodka, but he had a quarter of a glass of champagne, which he would sip after the speeches he liked so much to make. The rest of the night he would spend drinking tea. 'It makes me feel happy,' he used to say, 'to see a poor proletarian sitting in a nice room, eating a good dinner, and washing it down with a glass of bubbly, and first-class bubbly, too!' After dinner, Dostoevsky used to walk up to each one of his guests looking very pleased, press his hand warmly, saying, 'The dinner wasn't too bad, was it? The fish and the sauce were very, very tasty, weren't they?' And he would even exchange kisses with some of them. . . ."

Next morning he was broke again, and again he had to run for an

[4] *Letters,* May 14, 1848.

[5] *Letters,* February 1, 1849.

advance to Kraevsky, in spite of the fact that Kraevsky, whose hack he had become, had agreed to pay him a regular advance of fifty rubles a month. Thus, a short while before his arrest, he sent a desperate note to Kraevsky, begging him to let him have only fifteen rubles as an advance for the fifth part of *Netochka Nezvanova.* "I am struggling with my small creditors." he wrote, "like Laocoön with the snakes. Fifteen rubles doesn't mean anything to you, but it's a lot to me. Please, have pity on me. I have not had a farthing for the past week. If only you knew how desperate I am!"

He was not only broke, he was also ill. On the day before his arrest, at 6 o'clock in the afternoon, his brother Andrey met him in the street. They stopped and chatted for five minutes. In reply to Andrey's inquiry about his health, Dostoevsky said:

" 'It's bad, Andrey, very bad. I feel that my illness is sapping my strength. I really ought to go somewhere for a rest this summer, get proper medical treatment, but I've no money. Why don't you come to see me?'

" 'But the day after tomorrow is Sunday and I'll see you at Mikhail's.'

" 'Will you be there?'

" 'Certainly.'

" 'Well, then, good-by.'

"But, as it turned out," Andrey concluded, "neither of us was to be at Mikhail's on Sunday."

Both of them, in fact, were arrested early in the morning of April 23, 1849. Dostoevsky wrote an account of his arrest in the album of Milyukov's daughter on May 24, 1860:

"On the twenty-second or rather the twenty-third of April (1849) I returned home at about four o'clock in the morning after a visit to Grigoryev, went to bed and fell asleep at once. In less than an hour I felt in my sleep that some strange and suspicious people had entered my room. I heard the clanking of a saber brushing against something by mistake. What was up? I opened my eyes with an effort and heard a soft and sympathetic voice saying, 'Get up, sir.'

"I looked up and saw the district superintendent of police, a man with handsome side whiskers. But it was not he who had spoken. The man who had spoken was dressed in a light-blue uniform and wore the epaulets of a lieutenant-colonel.

" 'What's the matter?' I asked, sitting up in my bed.

" 'At the order of . . .'

"I looked [at the official paper] and indeed it was 'at the order of . . .' At the door stood a soldier, also in a blue uniform. It was his saber that had clanked. . . .

" 'Oh, so that's it!' I thought. 'Won't you let me . . .' I began.

" 'Yes, yes, dress. We'll wait, sir,' added the colonel in a voice that sounded even more sympathetic.

"While I was dressing, they demanded to see all my books and began to rummage among them. They did not find much, but they made a thorough search of everything. They tied the books and letters very carefully with string.[6] The police superintendent showed a great deal of forethought during the search. He went straight for the stove and rummaged about in the ashes with my pipe. At his invitation the gendarme sergeant stood on a chair and tried to climb on top of the stove, but he lost his footing on the cornice and fell with a crash back to the chair and from the chair to the floor. It was then that the perspicacious gentlemen were satisfied that there was nothing on top of the stove.

"An old and bent fifteen-kopeck coin lay on the table. The police superintendent inspected it carefully and, at last, nodded to the colonel.

" 'You don't think it's counterfeit, do you?' I asked.

" 'Well, we'll have to look into that,' muttered the superintendent and added the coin to the other evidence.

"We went out. We were seen to the door by my frightened landlady and her servant Ivan, who, though frightened too, gazed at us with a kind of stupid solemnity proper to the occasion. . . . At the entrance of the house a carriage was waiting. A gendarme, the superintendent, the colonel and myself got into it. We drove in the direction of the Fontanka, towards the Chain Bridge by the Summer Gardens [*i.e.*, the building of the Third Department]. . . . There was a great deal of coming and going there, and lots of people. I met many acquaintances. They were all sleepy and silent. A certain gentleman, a civil servant of high rank, received [the arrested], and light-blue gentlemen [*i.e.*, members of the political police, who wore a light-blue uniform] kept coming in with new victims. 'Some St. George's Day!' someone whispered in my ear.[7] And April 23 was of course St. George's Day. We gradually surrounded the civil servant with the list in his hands. In the list we noticed before Antonelli's name a penciled note: 'agent of the discovered affair.' 'So it's Antonelli, we said to each other. We were then placed in different rooms in expectation of the final decision about where we were to be sent. There were about 17 of us in the so-called White Drawing Room. Then Lieutenant-General Dubelt came in. But here I interrupt my story. It's too long to tell. But I assure you that Dubelt was a most delightful man."

Andrey, who was arrested by mistake (the police were after Mikhail), gives a fuller description of the scene in the "White Drawing Room" of the Third Department in his memoirs. "To my great surprise," he

[6] Among the books confiscated by the police were two proscribed volumes from Petrashevsky's library: *Le Berger de Kravan* by Eugène Sue and *De la célébration du dimanche* by Proudhon, both of which attacked the monarchy and private property and extolled the ideas of socialism.

[7] Before the reign of Boris Godunov the serfs had the right to change their landowners on St. George's Day, a right Boris Godunov abolished. Hence "Some St. George's Day!" became a saying signifying some sudden calamity.

wrote, "I found about twenty men in the drawing room. They had apparently just been brought there and were talking noisily. . . . The number of arrivals increased every minute and they were all well acquainted with one another. I alone stood, looking dejected, knowing no one and unrecognized by anyone. The noise and conversation in the room grew louder, some people demanding tea, others coffee, and so on. Suddenly I saw my brother Fyodor.

" 'What are you doing here?' he asked, running up to me.

"But that was all he had time to say. Two gendarmes came up to us and took me and my brother to different rooms. . . . The whole of that day of April 23 we spent at the Third Department. We were placed in different rooms, 8 to 10 men in each room, and cautioned not to talk to one another. . . .

"About twelve o'clock Count Orlov arrived and addressed the prisoners in each room, telling them that since they did not know how to make use of the rights every Russian citizen enjoyed, they forced the government to deprive them of their freedom, and that after a detailed examination of their crimes, sentence would be passed on them. Their ultimate fate depended on the mercy of the monarch.

"We were given tea, coffee, lunch and dinner, all of it very beautifully served," Andrey continues. "In short, we were excellently fed as the guests of the Third Department. . . ."

At 11 o'clock a roll call took place and, after a brief interrogation by Dubelt, each of the prisoners was conveyed under guard to the Peter and Paul Fortress and placed in solitary confinement in a cell of the Alexis Ravelin. The door of the cell was opened five times a day: at 7 o'clock in the morning, when the prisoners had their wash and their cells were tidied; at ten, when the cells were inspected by the commander of the fortress; at twelve when the prisoners had lunch; at seven, when they had dinner; and at nightfall, when a lighted lampion was brought in. For lunch they were given cabbage soup with boiled beef and porridge with plenty of bread, and for supper one hot dish. To drink they had a pewter cup of water or kvass, which was constantly refilled, and they were also allowed to order their own drinks from outside.

Dostoevsky's arrest and incarceration may have been a great shock to him, but it must also have been accompanied by a great sense of relief: no more literary "slavery," no more writing desperate begging letters to Kraevsky, no more struggling with creditors, no more threats of imprisonment for debt. As a result, his health improved. "I am, thank God, in good health," he wrote to Andrey,[8] who had been released as soon as his mistaken identity had been discovered and Mikhail imprisoned in his stead, "and though unhappy, I am far from losing heart. Every condition has its consolations."

[8] *Letters,* June 20, 1849.

It was not for nothing that the government considered Dostoevsky "one of the most important" of the accused, for he carried himself with great dignity and conducted his defense with quite astonishing candor and courage, although he knew perfectly well that he could expect no mercy and that he would be sentenced, if not to hard labor in a Siberian prison, then at least to exile to a remote part of the Russian Empire. It was, in fact, his finest hour, and he knew it and was justly proud of it all his life.

IV

On May 6, 1849, the special investigating commission of five members, headed by General Nabokov, commandant of the Peter and Paul Fortress, submitted to Dostoevsky three "preliminary" questions: (1) What was Petrashevsky's character as a man and, in particular, as a politician? (2) What took place at the Petrashevsky at homes? (3) Did the Petrashevsky circle have any secret aims?

Instead of replying to these questions, Dostoevsky wrote a long "explanation" or statement in which he pleaded the cause of freedom of conscience in such outspoken terms that he condemned himself out of his own mouth. With regard to Petrashevsky, he merely stated the truth when he declared that he had never been on good terms with him, though he did frequent some of his Friday at homes. Since September he had been at Petrashevsky's only eight times and was never alone with him for over half an hour. He had gone there to meet people whom he liked and whom he did not see often. On the other hand, he frankly admitted that he had always respected Petrashevsky as an honest and honorable man. At the Petrashevsky at homes all sorts of contradictory opinions were expressed, and he, Dostoevsky, took part in many of the debates. What exactly was he accused of? That he took part in the discussions at Petrashevsky's house, that he had expressed freethinking views, that he read aloud Belinsky's letter to Gogol?

"Let me say quite frankly," he wrote, "that till now I have always found it the most difficult thing in the world to define the words 'freethinker' and 'liberal.' Does it mean a man who expresses unlawful opinions? But I have known people who are quite ready to give voice at every street corner to whatever idiotic things enter their heads. Who has looked into my soul? Who can define the degree of disloyalty, harm and insurrection of which I am accused? [So far nobody had accused him of anything, and the fact that he mentioned insurrection and disloyalty could not but have a very adverse effect on the court, for, of course, this was tantamount to an admission that he was guilty of both, and even the slightest suspicion of insurrection and disloyalty would be enough to condemn him.] Perhaps I am judged by a few words I uttered at

Petrashevsky's. I spoke there three times: twice about literature and once about a completely nonpolitical subject: about personality and about men's egoism. If the accusation against me is based on a few words torn out of their context and written down on a scrap of paper, I am not afraid even of such an accusation, though it is a most dangerous one, for there is nothing more dangerous, more fatal and more unfair than a few words snatched out of goodness only knows where, overheard in a hurry, understood in a hurry, and more often entirely misunderstood, and written down in a hurry. Indeed, if to wish for something better is liberalism and freethinking, then I am perhaps a freethinker in that sense. I am a freethinker in the same sense as any man can be called a freethinker who deep down in his heart feels that he has a right to be a citizen, that he has a right to wish his country's good, for in his heart he finds both love for his country and the consciousness that he will never do anything to harm it. But was this desire for something better a desire for something that was possible or impossible? Let them prove that I am guilty of desiring changes and upheavals by force, by a revolution, arousing malice and hatred. I am not afraid of such evidence, for no denunciation in the world can take anything away from me or add anything to me; no denunciation can make me out to be what I am not. Or has my freethinking manifested itself in my speaking aloud about subjects which others think it best to pass over in silence not because they are afraid to say something against the government (there can be no question of that!), but because the subject, according to them, is of a kind that it is considered not the done thing to speak of it aloud? Is that it? But this dread of uttering certain words always offended me, for it is more liable to be an affront than a compliment to the government. And, indeed, what reason can an innocent man have to be afraid for himself and for the words he utters? That can only mean," he declared, surely with his tongue in his cheek, "that the law does not sufficiently protect the individual and that it is possible to seal one's doom by some idly uttered word or some careless phrase. But why have we ourselves brought about a situation in which a frank word loudly uttered that bears some resemblance to the expression of an opinion, a word uttered honestly and without any afterthought, is already regarded as something eccentric? In my opinion, it would be much better for all of us if everybody were frank with the government.

"I have always felt sad to see that we are all instinctively afraid of something; that when, for instance, we meet together in a crowd in some public place, we look mistrustfully at each other, scowling and casting sidelong glances, suspecting everyone. If anyone starts talking politics, he will invariably lower his voice in a most mysterious way, though a republic were as far from his thoughts as France. Indeed, too great a suppression of opinions, too great a fear throws a kind of somber light on our everyday life, making it appear joyless and unfriendly, and the pity of it is that it is not true. . . . We ourselves are merely irritating the government without any reason by our mysteriousness and mistrustfulness. It has always been my belief that a conscious conviction is better and stronger than an unconscious, unstable and vacillating one which is likely to collapse at a puff of wind. It is we ourselves who shun all contact with one another, form separate circles or become callous in solitude. . . ."

Dostoevsky next went on to give this characteristic picture of himself: "I do not like to talk aloud, particularly in society where I have the reputation of being a reserved, taciturn and unsociable man. I have very few acquaintances. Half of my time is devoted to work, which is my only means of livelihood, and the other half is occupied by my chronic illness, attacks of hypochondria from which I have been suffering for the past three years. . . . This leaves me with little time for reading, or for friends and acquaintances. . . ."

But it was time, Dostoevsky felt, to take the bull by the horns and get down to the problem of the international situation and its influence on the policies of the Russian autocratic regime. "What exactly am I accused of?" he repeated. "That I talked about politics, the West, the censorship, etc.? But who did not talk or did not think of these questions in our time? Why," he went on, asking his seemingly innocuous but actually rather compromising questions, "why, then, did I study, why, then, did my studies arouse the desire for inquiry in me, if I have no right to express my personal opinion or refuse to agree with an opinion which by itself may be authoritative? In the West terrible events are taking place, an unprecedented drama is being played out there. The century-old order of things is cracking and collapsing. The most basic principles of society threatened to crash down and carry a whole nation with them in their fall. Thirty-six million people are endangering their whole future, their fortunes, their very existence and that of their children! And is this not a picture to stir your soul and arouse your attention, interest and curiosity? It is the self-same country that gave us our science, our education, European civilization—why, such a spectacle is a lesson to us all! It is, after all, history, and history is the science of the future. In view of all this, are we who have been given a certain amount of education and in whom the thirst for knowledge has been aroused, are we to be accused of having possessed so much curiosity as to talk sometimes of the West and of political events, to read contemporary books, to look closely at the movement in Western Europe and even to study it as much as possible? Am I really to be accused of taking a somewhat serious view of the crisis which afflicts and breaks poor France in two, of perhaps considering this crisis as historically necessary in the life of the French people as a transitory phase (who can now say it isn't?) that will bring better times at last? My freethinking about the West and the revolution did not go further than that opinion and these ideas. But does the fact that I talked about the French revolution and permitted myself to pass judgment upon contemporary events mean that I am a freethinker, that I am a republican, that I am against autocracy, that I am undermining it? So far as I am concerned, there is nothing more absurd than the idea of a republican regime in Russia. . . . If," he went on, letting the cat out of the bag, for the question of "reforms," that is, the liberation of the serfs, was considered "revolutionary" in the reign of Nicholas I, "reforms are to be introduced, they will have to come from an authoritative source which will even for a time have to be strengthened, for otherwise"—he added a concealed threat—"the thing will have to be put through in a revolutionary way. Indeed, everything that is good in Russia, beginning with Peter the Great, has always come from above, from the throne, and till now nothing has come forward from below except ignorance and stubbornness. This opinion of mine is known to many people. . . ."

He next turned to the question of censorship, trying again to anticipate the points of his indictment. Failing to realize how scared the Russian government was of any possible repercussions in Russia of the revolutionary events in Europe, in which so well-known a Russian nobleman as Bakunin was taking a leading part, he merely succeeded in making things worse for himself.

"I have spoken of censorship," he admitted, "about its excessive strictness in our time and I have deplored it, for I felt that a kind of misunderstanding had arisen which is responsible for the present strained and difficult position of literature. I could not help feeling sad at the thought that in our time the vocation of the writer should be degraded by dark suspicions and that the censors should look upon a writer even before he has written anything as a sort of natural enemy of the government, and that even before reading the manuscript, they should already be prejudiced against it. I cannot help feeling sad when I hear that a certain work is banned not because it has been found to contain anything liberal or freethinking or anything that offends morality, but, for instance, because the story or novel happens to have an unhappy ending, or that the picture it paints is too gloomy, although that picture throws no suspicion on anyone in society and although the tragic ending itself is due to some quite accidental and external cause. Let them analyze everything I have written and let them find in any of my writings one word that is adverse to morality and the established order. And yet it is I who have been the victim of such a ban because I painted a picture in too-somber colors. But if only they knew in what a somber situation the author had been placed by the prohibition of his work! . . . And what was it I was complaining about? About a misunderstanding! Is it at all possible to paint in bright colors only? How could the bright side of the picture be seen without the dark one? We get an idea of light because of the existence of shadows. We are told: describe bravery, virtue. But we should not recognize virtue without vice; the very conception of good and evil arose because good and evil have always lived together side by side. . . . I am not for the depiction of vice and the dark sides of life. Neither the one nor the other is particularly dear to me. I am saying this solely in the interests of literature. Literature cannot exist in so tense a situation. Whole genres of literature will have to disappear: satire and tragedy could no longer exist. . . . Satire derides vice but, most of all, vice masquerading as virtue. How can any deriding exist today? The censor suspects a hint in everything, suspects the presence of malice or personal attack—does not the writer hint at some person or some established custom or law? . . . I complained about all this and I prayed for this sad misunderstanding to be resolved quickly. I did so because I love literature and cannot help being interested in it, because I know that literature is an expression of the genius of a people, that it is the mirror of society. Without literature society cannot exist and I saw that it was dying. That was why I was worried by the misunderstandings that have arisen between literature and the censorship."

As for Belinsky's letter to Gogol, he freely admitted that he had read it, but claimed, rather unconvincingly, that no one could have guessed whose side in the controversy he had taken—Belinsky's or Gogol's. He admitted, too, that for a short time he had known Belinsky intimately. Belinsky, he declared, was an excellent man, but his illness "destroyed even the man in him—it embittered him, it hardened his soul and poured gall into his heart. . . ." In fact, he concluded even more lamely, he had read the letter merely "as a literary testament," and only now had he realized his mistake.

Turning, finally, once more to the two addresses he had delivered at the Petrashevsky at homes, he claimed that in his speech about literature his main contention had been that art had no need of any political tendency, that it was an aim in itself, and that all an author had to think about was the artistic value of his work, for its "idea" would come by itself, for it was "the necessary condition of a work of art."

V

Mikhail's arrest was another blow that Dostoevsky felt very deeply. Mikhail was eventually released after spending two months in the fortress. In his evidence before the investigating commission, Dostoevsky did his best to exonerate him of all blame. "My brother," he stated, "got to know Petrashevsky through me, so that I alone am to be blamed for this as well as for the misfortune that has befallen my brother and his family. For while I and the other accused have suffered from depression and anguish during these two months of imprisonment, he has suffered ten times more in comparison. For he is of a naturally weak constitution and has a disposition towards consumption. In addition, he is greatly upset about the desperate position of his family, which is in danger of literally perishing of starvation in his absence."

In 1876, in the April number of his *Writer's Diary*, Dostoevsky was much more outspoken about Mikhail's involvement in the Petrashevsky affair. "My brother," he wrote, "did not take part in the organization of the secret societies at Petrashevsky's or Durov's. He nevertheless visited Petrashevsky's at homes, and made use of the secret, illegal library at Petrashevsky's house. He was a Fourierist and studied Fourier passionately. . . . After his arrest he left behind a frightened wife and three children, the eldest of whom was only seven years old, and they were all left without any money. My brother loved his children tenderly and passionately and I can imagine what he must have suffered during those two months. And yet he gave *no incriminating evidence* which might have compromised others. . . . He could certainly have done so if he had wished, for though he had taken no part in anything, *he knew quite a lot.*"

Dostoevsky himself did much more than that. Not only did he refuse to implicate any of the accused, but he did his best to make things easier for them. "When I went to Siberia," he wrote to General Totleben on March 24, 1856, "I had at least the consolation of knowing that I had behaved honestly in court, that I did not put the blame on others, and indeed sacrificed my own interests when I saw the possibility of getting others out of trouble by my confession."

Many years later Dostoevsky recalled that General Rostovtsev, one of the five members of the investigating commission, had asked him to tell them everything. "I cannot believe," Rostovtsev said, "that the author of *Poor People* could have conspired with those depraved men. It's impossible. You can't be greatly implicated in this business and I am authorized by the Emperor to inform you that if you make a clean breast of the whole affair you will receive a complete pardon." Dostoevsky said nothing. Then Lieutenant-General Dubelt observed with a smile, "I told you so, didn't I?" Whereupon Rostovtsev cried, "I can't bear to look at Dostoevsky any more," rushed into the adjoining room, locked himself in and kept shouting: "Has Dostoevsky gone? Tell me when he's gone–I can't bear to see him!"–a theatrical outburst that Dostoevsky regarded as insincere and put on specially for the occasion. Apart from that scene, the interrogation proceeded normally.

Dostoevsky stoutly refused to admit any revolutionary intentions either by the members of the Petrashevsky "circle" or by those of the Durov "circle." He had never heard of any plans for an insurrection at Petrashevsky's, he stated in his testimony before the commission. In fact, he was firmly convinced that if Petrashevsky had permitted such a plan to be discussed, there would have been no visitors at his next at home. As for Petrashevsky himself, he was "ridiculous" rather than "harmful." He had always been convinced, Dostoevsky declared, that

"Petrashevsky was suffering from a certain kind of vanity. It was out of vanity that he invited people to his Friday at homes and it was because of his vanity that he did not get tired of them. It was also out of vanity that he had many books and, I think, he was pleased that people knew that he had rare books." Petrashevsky's socialist and revolutionary convictions, he further pleaded, were mere "theoretical abstractions." When reminded that one member of the Petrashevsky group had actually raised the question of a peasant revolt, Dostoevsky explained that he had spoken of it "not as a fact or as something he desired, for, granted the possibility of the liberation of the serfs, he was against the idea of insurrection or revolutionary action." When the question of the proposed illegal printing press was raised, Dostoevsky stated that Philippov had made his proposal merely out of bravado. "Almost everyone," he declared, "was appalled by his proposal. We all felt that things had gone too far and were waiting to hear what the others had to say. I don't know, I may be mistaken, but it seemed to me that half of those present did not express their opposition to Philippov's proposal because they were afraid that the other half would suspect them of cowardice, and wished to reject it not in a direct but in some oblique fashion. As a result," he concluded, not very truthfully, "Philippov's proposal was rejected."

Durov's "circle," Dostoevsky declared at his trial, was a purely artistic and literary one. Durov and some of his friends decided to publish a literary magazine and they began meeting regularly to discuss it. These meetings were soon transformed into "literary and musical evenings." It was true that at one of those meetings an "unfortunate" proposal was made "to lithograph" articles and stories without submitting them first to censorship, but that proposal was turned down.

"All that my own liberalism amounted to," he told the court, "was the desire that my country should prosper. . . . I always believed in autocracy as the only form of government for our country. . . . Perhaps I did occasionally express my views about it with a touch of bitterness, but that was only at rare moments. . . . I desired many improvements and changes, I deplored many abuses, but at the very basis of my political thinking lay the idea that those changes could be made only by an autocracy. All I wanted was that no voice should be stifled and that every crying need should be heard. . . . My desire for something better never went beyond what was possible. . . . I have never been a socialist, though I liked to read and study social problems. . . . I am passionately fond of history and that was why I followed the revolutionary movements in Western Europe with great interest. . . . I did sometimes talk about political questions, but seldom, hardly ever, made speeches about them. I admitted the historical necessity of the present revolution in the West, but only in expectation of better things. . . . Socialism offers a thousand measures for the organization of society and as all those books are written cleverly, ardently and not infrequently with a true love for mankind, I read them with great interest. But just because I do not adhere to any social system but studied socialism in all its systems, I can see the mistakes made by every socialist system (though, I admit, my knowledge of them is far from thorough)—that is the conclusion I have reached. Socialism is a science in a state of fermentation, it is chaos, it is alchemy before the advent of chemistry, astrology before the advent of astronomy though I cannot help feeling that out of the present chaos something harmonious, sensible and beneficial will eventually emerge for the good of mankind, just as out of alchemy emerged chemistry and out of astrology, astronomy."

The last avowal was in itself an admission that was enough to nullify Dostoevsky's profession of loyalty to the Tsarist autocratic regime.

To the last written question of the court, whether he had anything to add in exoneration of his guilt, Dostoevsky, realizing that it was a mere formality, replied that he had nothing to add except that he had never done anything with evil and premeditated intent against the government. "What I did," he declared, "was done thoughtlessly and much of it almost by accident, as, for instance, the reading of Belinsky's letter. If however," he concluded, "I did speak my mind freely, it was only in the circle of intimate friends, who could understand me and who knew in what sense I was speaking. But I always avoided the propagation of my doubts." He had written "thoughts" at first, but crossed it out and substituted "doubts" in its place. This last statement could only be viewed by his judges and Nicholas I himself as an admission of guilt.

VI

Dostoevsky spent eight months in the Alexis Ravelin of the Peter and Paul Fortress. During the first two months he was not allowed to do anything, but after that he was given permission to read books and to write. He was also allowed a quarter of an hour's exercise in the small courtyard under the supervision of an armed guard. His only communication with the other accused was by tapping on the wall to Philippov, his next-door neighbor. Dostoevsky, Orest Miller records, used to say that at the time he realized perfectly well that "if *their* side won, there was nothing left for him to do but bear his punishment. Moreover, he was quite ready to admit that from *their* point of view the government was right." To Mikhail he wrote:[9] "I am not losing heart. Of course, it's boring and sickening, but what's to be done? However, it isn't always boring. Time sometimes passes very quickly, but at other times it seems to drag on forever. Sometimes you even feel that you are growing accustomed to this kind of life and that it doesn't matter. I am doing my best, of course, to banish all temptations from my mind, but

[9] *Letters*, July 18, 1849.

you can't always get the better of them and my old life keeps breaking in with all its old associations and I relive my past again. . . . The days are bright and sunny now, at least most of the time, and I feel a little more cheerful. But the rainy days are unbearable, the casemate looks very grim indeed."

He had devised the plots of three stories and two novels and was writing one story (*A Little Hero*). "This work," he wrote in the same letter, "especially if one does it with enthusiasm (and I have never worked so much *con amore* as now), used always to exhaust me and I had to interrupt my work by all sorts of diversions, but here the agitation produced by the work has to pass by itself. I am quite well, except for my hemorrhoids and the state of my nerves which is growing steadily worse. At times I suffer spasms of the throat, as I used to before. My appetite is bad and I sleep very little, and when I do I have morbid dreams. I only sleep five hours out of the twenty-four and wake up four times in the night. This I find particularly painful. I find the time when it is getting dark most depressing. At nine o'clock it is quite dark here. I sometimes don't fall asleep till one or two o'clock in the morning and I find five hours of darkness almost insupportable. This more than anything else is affecting my health."

It was three months after his arrest and he still did not know how long his imprisonment in the Alexis Ravelin would last. He had been reading the seventeenth-century Metropolitan Dmitry Rostovtsev's religious and dramatic works and two travel books describing the holy places, but that was only a drop in the ocean. He would like some modern book, for, he wrote, "this would even improve my health, since I may be able to compare my ideas with someone else's or remold my ideas in accordance with someone else's turn of mind." He wondered whether the "Muscovites" knew about his arrest and imprisonment. He could only surmise that they would prefer not to know anything about it. All he desired was to be well. Boredom was a transitory thing and, after all, a cheerful disposition was something that depended on him alone. "There is an enormous amount of adaptability and vitality in man," he concluded. "I wouldn't have believed it, had I not learned it by experience now."

A month later, on August 27, 1849, he wrote to Mikhail again, still unable to say when the uncertainty of his position would be cleared up. "My *private* life," he wrote, "is as monotonous as before, but I was again allowed to take a walk in the garden in which there are about seventeen trees. This is real felicity to me. Besides, I am now allowed to have a candle at night—and this is another piece of good luck." He had nothing good to tell his brother about his health. "For a whole month now," he wrote, "I have had nothing but castor oil, which alone keeps me going. My hemorrhoids are driving me to desperation and I have a pain in my chest, which I have never had before. And, besides, my supersensitiveness becomes morbidly alert, especially towards evening; at night I have long, hideous dreams. Moreover, for some time now I cannot get rid of the impression that the floor is rocking under me and, sitting in my cell, I feel as though I were in a cabin on board ship. All this leads me to the conclusion that my nerves are getting more and more frayed. Whenever my nerves went to pieces before, I made use of it to carry on with my writing, for in such a state I could write much more and much better, but now I have to restrain myself for fear of a breakdown. For the past three weeks I have written nothing; now I have started again. But all this is nothing, one can still live," he concluded, as if in dread anticipation of much worse things to come.

In his last letter to Mikhail from the fortress, on September 14, 1849, two weeks before the beginning of his trial, he thanked his brother for sending him Shakespeare, the Bible and the latest number of *Home Annals*. "I have been rereading the books you sent me. I thank you particularly for Shakespeare. How did you guess?" He also found *Jane Eyre*, a translation of which was published in *Home Annals*, "extremely good." For five months he had been living "on his own resources," and so far "the machine has not fallen to pieces and is still in working order. However," he continued, "everlasting thinking and nothing but thinking, without any outside impressions to renew and sustain thought, is a hard thing. I feel as though I were under a bell glass from which the air was being pumped out. Everything in me has gone into my head and from my head into thought—everything, absolutely everything, and, in spite of it, this seems to be increasing every day."

A month later his trial came to an end. According to some reports, the court before which the accused were tried decided to acquit them for lack of evidence. The government then handed over the case to a court-martial, which found all but two of them guilty and sentenced them to be executed by a firing squad.

The sentence on Dostoevsky, passed on November 16, 1849, read: "The court-martial finds the accused Dostoevsky guilty of having received from Moscow in March of the current year a copy of the criminal letter of the writer Belinsky from the nobleman Pleshcheyev (one of the accused) and of having read this letter at public meetings, first at the house of the accused Durov, then at the house of the accused Petrashevsky, and finally, of giving it for reproduction in many copies to the accused Mombelli. Dostoevsky was present at the house of the accused Speshnyov during the reading of Lieutenant Grigoryev's outrageous work under the title of *A Soldier's Talk*. The court-martial, therefore, sentences retired Engineer-Lieutenant Dostoevsky for failing to inform the authorities about the circulation of the letter of the writer Belinsky, in which both religion and the government were attacked in a criminal manner, and about the pernicious work of Lieutenant Grigoryev, to be deprived of his rank, of all rights of property, and to be executed by shooting."

The death sentences were never meant to be carried out: it was a way of striking terror into the hearts not only of the condemned men, but also into those of their numerous known and unknown sympathizers. Like every other act of gross inhumanity, it failed singularly in its purpose and merely increased the hatred and contempt in which the regime of Nicholas I was held.

On November 19, 1849, the prosecuting counsel at the court-martial submitted a long statement to the Emperor suggesting that all the accused should be reprieved and their death sentences commuted to various terms of imprisonment. The ostensible reason for the reprieve was the existence of various entenuating circumstances, such as "the repentance of many of the accused, their voluntary admission of acts which, without their frank confessions, would have remained unknown, the youthful age of some of the accused and, finally, the fact that their crimes had no harmful consequences, having been forestalled at the right moment by the measures of the government." So far as Dostoevsky was concerned, the prosecuting counsel suggested that "he should be sentenced to hard labor in Siberia for eight years." Nicholas I reduced the sentence to "four years, then into the army as private."

None of the accused was informed of either their death sentences or their reprieves. Nicholas I decided to carry on with the mock execution of the condemned men "and to announce their reprieve only at the moment when everything is ready for carrying out the death sentences." On December 21st, therefore, the Minister of War and the Petersburg Governor General issued an order in which every detail of the mock execution was set down with fiendish exactitude, proving quite clearly that it had not only been "approved" but carefully drawn up by Nicholas I himself. According to this order, three posts were to be put up on the Semyonovsky Parade Ground "at a height of one *arshin*" (two feet and four inches), but no pits were to be dug. One battalion each of the Life Guards, Chasseurs and the Moscow regiments, and two squadrons of the Horse Guards were to be drawn up beside the posts. On December 22nd, at 9 o'clock in the morning, "the criminals" were to be brought there in carriages under the escort "in front and behind" of two squadrons of mounted gendarmes, one mounted gendarme in addition to ride at either side of every carriage, the whole procession to be headed by the Adjutant-Commander of the Peter and Paul Fortress. "The criminals," the order stated, "are to be driven up to the troops. On their descent from the carriages, they are to be met by a priest in funeral attire, carrying a cross and the Holy Testament, and then, surrounded by their guards, marched all along the lines and, finally, to the center of the drawn-up troops," where, incidentally, a kind of scaffold had been erected. After the presenting of arms and the beating of drums, the death sentences were to be read out. After that, the order to shoulder arms was to be given and "the ceremony of the deprivation of civic rights" performed, that is, the uniforms of the noblemen taken off and sabers broken in two over the heads of those who had been sentenced to hard labor. "Then," the order goes on, "long, white shirts are to be put on all the criminals. After giving his blessing, the priest is to retire. The criminals Petrashevsky, Mombelli and Grigoryev are to be blindfolded and taken to the posts. While these criminals are being tied to the posts, 15 soldiers, with loaded rifles, accompanied by noncommissioned officers, are to station themselves before each post at a distance of 15 paces. The remainder of the criminals are to stay with their guard. After which," the order concludes, "His Majesty's decision is to be carried out. . . . Petrashevsky is to be put in irons and sent from the place where his sentence has been read straight to his destination, accompanied by a gendarme and a government courier. [Petrashevsky was sentenced to life imprisonment in a Siberian prison.] The other prisoners are to return to the fortress and to be sent off in accordance with special instructions. . . ."

VII

At 6 o'clock in the morning of December 22nd the prisoners in the Peter and Paul Fortress noticed an unusual noise and tramping of feet along the corridors and they realized that something special was going to happen that day. At 7 o'clock they were put in carriages and driven out of prison, having first been told to change into their own clothes. It was a cold, frosty day. Snow fell at brief intervals from a lowering sky. The windows of the carriages were covered with hoarfrost, and the prisoners did not know where they were being driven. Speshnyov tried to rub the hoarfrost off to see where they were, but the soldier who sat beside him said: "Don't do it, sir, or I shall be flogged." No one, of course, dreamed that they had been sentenced to death or that Nicholas I had prepared a mock execution for them in order to frighten them into a more loyal frame of mind. At last they arrived at the Semyonovsky Parade Ground, and "the ceremony" proceeded according to the order issued the day before. Dostoevsky told Orest Miller that nine men were placed on one side of the scaffold and eleven on the other side. They were forbidden to talk, but they managed to whisper to one another, and, according to Mombelli, Dostoevsky, who was standing beside him, gave him a brief account of the story he had written in the fortress. Dostoevsky himself did not seem to remember this but, as Orest Miller remarks, he might have done it in his excitement and eagerness to say something. The death sentences were then read out by the prosecutor at their trial. Dostoevsky whispered to Durov, who stood beside him: "It's impossible that they should execute us," but Durov pointed to a cart where he supposed their coffins had been placed under a covering of straw (actually, their convict clothes had been placed there). After that, no doubt was left in Dostoevsky's mind.

The thing that stuck in his mind, Orest Miller records, was the way the prosecutor folded the paper and, placing it in his side pocket, got off the scaffold. The prosecutor's place was then taken by the priest, who was holding a cross in his hands. The priest invited the condemned men to come up to him and make their confession, but only one of them accepted the invitation: the rest merely kissed the cross when he held it out to them. The presence of the priest finally convinced Dostoevsky that the death sentences would be carried out, for, he thought, they could not possibly turn the priest, too, into "a decorative article."

After three of the accused had been tied to the posts, Dostoevsky, Orest Miller records, was overcome by "a mystical fear," feeling that in about five minutes he would pass into "another unknown world," but, "however much shaken he might have been, he did not go to pieces. Even when mounting the scaffold, he was not pale, but gave the impression of being in a hurry rather than of being crushed."

Dostoevsky gave his own immediate impressions of the mock execution "ceremony" in his letter to Mikhail on his return to his cell. "Dear, dear brother," he wrote, "everything has been decided. I am sentenced to four years' hard labor in a fortress (in Orenburg, I believe) and then to service in the army as a private. Today, on December 22, we were driven to the Semyonovsky Parade Ground. There they read out the death sentences to us, made us kiss the cross, broke sabers over our heads and put death garments (white shirts) on us. Then three of us were tied to posts to be executed. They had called out three men. I was therefore next to be called and I had no more than a minute to live. I remembered you, Mikhail, and all yours; at the last moment you, you alone, were in my mind and it was only then that I realized how much I loved you, dear, dear brother. I also had time to embrace Pleshcheyev and Durov, who were next to me, and take leave of them. At last the retreat was sounded, the men tied to the posts were brought back, and they read out to us that his Imperial Majesty had granted us our lives. Then our real sentences were read out. . . ."

Dostoevsky never forgot the scene on the Semyonovsky Parade Ground or what he had been through during the short time he had stood there "in terror of death." He gave a full description both of the scene and of what he had felt at the time in *The Idiot*. "I had better tell you of another meeting I had with a man last year," Dostoevsky makes Prince Myshkin say. "There was a strange incident in his life, strange because it so rarely happens. This man had once been taken, together with others, to a place of execution where a sentence of death was read out to him. He was to be shot for a political crime. Twenty minutes later his reprieve was read out to him, another penalty for his crime being substituted. Yet the interval between the two sentences—twenty minutes or, at least, a quarter of an hour—he passed in the absolute certainty that in a few minutes he would be dead. I very much liked to listen to him when he used to recall his impressions of those moments, and I questioned him several times about it. He remembered everything with most extraordinary distinctness, and he used to say that he would never forget anything he had been through during those minutes. Three posts were dug into the ground about twenty paces from the scaffold, which was surrounded by a crowd of people and soldiers, for there were several criminals. The first three were led to the posts and tied to them; the death vestments (long, white smocks) were put on them, and white caps were drawn over their eyes so that they should not see the rifles; next a company of soldiers was drawn up against each post. My friend was the eighth on the list and his would therefore be the third turn to be marched to the posts. The priest went to each of them with the cross. It seemed to him then that he had only five more minutes to live. He told me that those five minutes were like an eternity to him, riches beyond the dreams of avarice; he felt that during those five minutes he would live through so many lives that it was quite unnecessary for him to think of the last moment, so that he had plenty of time to make all sorts of arrangements: he calculated the exact time he needed to take leave of his comrades, and decided that he could do that in two minutes, then he would spend another two minutes in thinking of himself for the last time, and, finally, one minute for a last look around. He remembered very well that he had decided to do all this and that he had divided up the time in exactly that way. He was dying at twenty-seven, a strong and healthy man; taking leave of his comrades, he remembered asking one of them quite an irrelevant question and being very interested indeed in his answer. Then, after he had bidden farewell to his comrades, came the two minutes he had set aside for thinking of himself; he knew beforehand what he would think about: he just wanted to imagine, as vividly and as quickly as possible, how it could be that now, at this moment, he was there and alive and in three minutes he would merely be *something*—someone or something—but what? And where? All that he thought he would be able to decide in those two minutes! There was a church not far off, its gilt roof shining in the bright sunshine. He remembered staring with awful intensity at that roof and the sunbeams flashing from it; he could not tear his eyes off those rays of light: those rays seemed to him to be his new nature, and he felt that in three minutes he would somehow merge with them. . . . The uncertainty and the feeling of disgust with that new thing which was bound to come any minute were dreadful; but he said that the thing that was most unbearable to him at the time was the constant thought, 'What if I had not had to die! What if I could return to life—oh, what an eternity! And all that would be mine! I should turn every minute into an age, I should lose nothing, I should count every minute separately and waste none!' He said that this reflection finally filled him with such bitterness that he prayed to be shot as quickly as possible."

"Why," he makes Prince Myshkin ask a little earlier in the novel, "this cruel, hideous, unnecessary and useless mockery? Possibly, there are men who have had sentences of death read out to them and have been given time to go through this torture and then been told: You can go now, you have been reprieved. Such men could perhaps tell us. It was of agony like this and of such horror that Christ spoke. No, you can't treat a man like that!"

Seven years later, at a time when he had finally gone over to the reactionary camp in Russia, Dostoevsky still remembered the scene on Semyonovsky Parade Ground with an undisguised sense of pride: "We, the members of the Petrashevsky group," he wrote in his *Writer's Diary* of 1873, "stood on the scaffold and listened to our death sentences without the slightest feeling of repentance. No doubt, I cannot vouch for everybody, but I don't think I shall be mistaken in saying that at that moment, if not everyone, then at any rate the great majority of us, would have deemed it dishonorable to renounce our convictions. This happened long ago and therefore it is quite legitimate to ask whether that obstinacy and refusal to repent was due to our wickedness, to the fact that we were still intellectually backward young ruffians. No, we were not and perhaps not even wicked young men. The death sentences by a firing squad, read out to us at first, had not been read out as a joke; almost all the sentenced men were convinced that they would be carried out and went through at least ten terrible and infinitely horrifying minutes in expectation of death. During those last minutes some of us (I know that for certain), delving deep down into our minds instinctively and examining in a flash our lives, which were still so young, may have repented of some of our serious misdeeds (those which every man has lying in secret on his conscience all his life), but the cause for which we had been sentenced, the ideas and conceptions which held sway over our minds, we considered not only as requiring no repentance, but as something purifying, as a martyrdom for which a lot will be forgiven us. And so it went on for a long time. . . ."

The letter Dostoevsky wrote to Mikhail on his return to his cell is remarkable for the tremendous upsurge of his vitality and optimism. His first sensation on recovering from his ordeal was one of joy. He paced his cell excitedly, laughing and singing aloud. "Mikhail," he wrote, "I do not feel dispirited or discouraged. Life is life everywhere, life is in us ourselves and not outside us. There will be men beside me and to be a *man* among men and to remain a man forever, not to lose heart and give way in any circumstances, however painful or unhappy—that is the aim of life, that is its purpose. I have realized it. This idea has entered into my flesh and blood. Yes, it is true! The head that has been creating and living the higher life of art, that comprehended and got used to the higher needs of the spirit—that head has already been cut off. What remains is the memory and the images, created but as yet not embodied by me. It is true, they will plague me and prey on my mind, but I have still got my heart left and the same flesh and blood which can love and suffer and pity and remember—and that is also life. *On voit le soleil!*"

His manuscripts, including his story *A Children's Fairy Tale* (published under the title of *A Little Hero* in 1857) and drafts of a novel and a play, were taken away from him, but what worried him most was that he had to have some money to spend on the long trek to his Siberian prison. He asked Mikhail to send him some and he begged him also to tell anyone he had quarreled with or anyone on whom he might have left "an unpleasant impression" not to think badly of him. "There is no gall or malice in my heart," he declared, "and at this moment I wish I could love and embrace everyone I have ever known. This consolation I experienced today, taking a last farewell before death of those I loved. Oh, how cold it was today," he recalled with a shiver. His heart bled at the thought of how much time he had wasted, and how little he had prized it, how much he had sinned "against his heart and spirit." He now realized that "life is a gift, life is happiness" and that every minute of it could be "an eternity of happiness—*si la jeunesse savait!*" He assured Mikhail again that he had not lost hope and that he would keep his spirit and heart pure. Never before had he felt such a superabundance of healthy reserves of spiritual life. He could not tell whether his body would be able to stand the trials that were in store for him, but he had been through so much in life that nothing frightened him any more. The only thing that worried him was that during the next four years he would have to give up writing. "Dear Lord," he exclaimed, "how many images created anew by me will have to perish, to die in my head or dissolve like poison in my blood. Yes, I shall perish if I am not able to write. I'd rather go to prison for fifteen years if only they'd let me have a pen in my hands! . . . Life in the fortress," he concluded, "has already killed many of my carnal desires that were far from pure. I have taken little care of myself before. Now no privations can frighten me and that is why you should not be afraid that any material burden will kill me. This will never happen! Oh, if only I could have my health—if only I could preserve my health, everything would be all right. . . ."

Mikhail was allowed to take leave of Dostoevsky on December 24, 1849. He was accompanied by Alexander Milyukov, who left an account of that farewell meeting. "We were taken to a large room on the ground floor of the commandant's house," Milyukov records. "It was late and the room was lit by one lamp. We had to wait a long time, the fortress clock chiming two quarters before the door opened and Dostoevsky and Durov entered accompanied by an army officer. In spite of the eight months of prison they had hardly changed. Both were already wearing their traveling convict clothes as well as sheepskins and felt boots. Dostoevsky expressed his pleasure at his brother's acquittal, and at the leave-taking of the two brothers anyone could have noticed that the elder one suffered most. There were tears in his eyes and his lips trembled, while Dostoevsky was calm and kept consoling him. 'Even in a Siberian prison,' Dostoevsky said, 'I'll start writing again. . . . I have been through a great deal during the past eight months and I expect I shall experience many more things—I'll have plenty of material to write about. . . .' The meeting lasted a little over half an hour, but it seemed very brief to them. When they were told to say good-by, they embraced and shook hands for the last time. Hearing that they would be taken away in an hour, we waited for them to appear at the gate of the fortress. The night was bright and not too cold. The fortress clock struck nine when two sledges drove out of the gates, each one with a prisoner and a gendarme beside him. 'Good-by!' we shouted. 'Au revoir,' they shouted back."

In fact, the prisoners left much later than 9 o'clock, and there were not two, but four, sledges which left the fortress that night. In the first one sat the government courier, in the second and third Dostoevsky and Durov, who was also sentenced to four years' imprisonment, which he served with Dostoevsky in the Omsk fortress, and in the fourth Ivan Yastrezhembsky, a thirty-three-year-old teacher of political economy in the Institute of Technology, who had been sentenced to six years' hard labor.

Dostoevsky never forgot that night of Christmas Eve. In his first letter to Mikhail after leaving prison,[10] he gave an account of his departure for Siberia.

"As soon as you left me, we were led away—Durov, Yastrezhembsky and I—to be put in irons. Exactly at twelve o'clock, that is, exactly on Christmas Day, I put on fetters for the first time. They weighed ten pounds and they made walking extremely uncomfortable. Then they put us in open sledges, each one of us separately, with a gendarme, and, preceded by a sledge in which a government courier was traveling, we left Petersburg. I felt sick at heart, and confused in mind from the many different sensations of that day. My heart seemed to be 'fidgety' and for that reason it moped and ached dully. But the fresh air revived me, and as one usually feels a kind of animation and excitement before every new step in life, I was actually quite self-composed and looked intently at Petersburg as I was driven past the festively lit up houses and said good-by to every house individually. We were driven past the house where you lived, and I could see that Kraevsky's flat was lit up. You had told me that he was giving a Christmas party and that Emilia

[10] *Letters*, February 22, 1854.

and the children had been invited to it, and it was at that house that I felt unbearably sad. I seemed to be taking leave of your little children. . . ."

It was not only Mikhail's children, it was also his literary past he was leaving behind him that Christmas Eve. The fact that he could never resume his interrupted work on *Netochka Nezvanova* is perhaps the best proof of that. He had been trying in vain to find himself in the stories he wrote after his first novel, but they were all to a greater or lesser degree derivative, Gogol exerting the greatest influence on him, followed by Schiller, Hoffmann and Balzac, and, in his unfinished novel, George Sand. What they lacked most was depth and an authentic background. In *Netochka Nezvanova,* in particular, the plot as well as the melodramatic situations in which it abounds would lose very little if one substituted English, French or German names for the Russian names of its characters. Dostoevsky himself was dimly aware of these fundamental shortcomings of his novel. "I knew perfectly well," he wrote, shortly before his arrest, to Kraevsky, whose complete lack of literary flair he was to lampoon later in the epilogue of *The Insulted and Injured,* "that the first part of *Netochka Nezvanova* is a good literary work, so good that *Home Annals* can, of course, *give it space without being ashamed of it.* I know it is a serious work. For, after all, it is not I alone who am saying this, but *everyone* is saying it." Who was everyone? By that time Dostoevsky had lost the literary friends on whose judgment he could rely. He was, in fact, trying to persuade not only Kraevsky, but also himself that the novel on which he had spent over two years was something more than an echo of the works of the great novelists he admired. Why else should he try to persuade Kraevsky to print it *without being ashamed of it*—his own italics, by the way. Such a phrase he would never have dreamed of using in the first flush of his fame.

It was only during his solitary confinement in the Alexis Ravelin, when he was shut out by force from all outside literary influences, that he had found himself sufficiently to write a story with a convincing background. His imprisonment in Siberia was to strengthen this process of liberation of his innate creative powers.

[4]

A NIGHTMARE WORLD

Writing twenty-six years after his arrival in Siberia, Dostoevsky, in his sketch *The Peasant Marey*,[1] tells how after a particularly horrible scene in prison the memory of the humane treatment he had received as a boy of nine from a peasant on his father's estate banished "as if by some miracle all hatred and anger from his heart" and he could look "at those unhappy creatures," that is, the peasants who were his fellow convicts, "with different eyes."

The horrifying scene, which, as Dostoevsky described it, can certainly be taken as genuine, happened one Easter Monday. It was a particularly fine spring day, but Dostoevsky himself "was plunged in gloom." "I wandered aimlessly," he recalls, "behind the barracks in the prison yard, looked at the palings of the strong prison fence, counting them mechanically, though I did not particularly want to count them, but doing it more out of habit than anything else. It was the second day of 'holidays' in prison. The convicts were not taken out to work, lots of them were drunk, cursing and quarreling broke out every minute in different corners of the prison. Disgusting, coarse songs; groups of convicts playing cards under the bunks; several convicts who had run amok and had been dealt with summarily by their own comrades, were lying half dead on the bunks, covered with sheepskins, until they should recover consciousness; the knives that had already been drawn several times—all this had so harrowing an effect on me during the two-day holidays that it made me ill. I could never bear without disgust the wild orgies of the common people, and here in this place this was especially true. On such days even the prison warders never looked into the prison, carried out no searches, did not look for drinks, realizing that once a year even these outcasts had to be given a chance of enjoying themselves and that otherwise things would be much worse. At last blind fury blazed up in my heart. I met the Pole, M——ski [Mirecki], one of the political

[1] *A Writer's Diary*, February 1876.

prisoners. He gave me a black look, with flashing eyes and trembling lips. '*Je hais ces brigands!*' he hissed at me in an undertone and walked past me. I went back to the barracks, although I had rushed out of them like a madman only a quarter of an hour before, when six strong peasants had hurled themselves on the drunken Tartar Gazin in an attempt to quiet him and had begun beating him. They beat him senselessly—a camel might have been killed by such blows. But they knew that it was not easy to kill this Hercules, and they beat him therefore without any qualms. Now, on my return, I noticed Gazin lying unconscious and without any sign of life on a bunk in a corner at the other end of the barracks; he lay covered with a sheepskin, and they all passed by him in silence, knowing very well that if the man was unlucky he might die from a beating like that. I made my way to my place opposite the window with the iron bars and lay on my back with my eyes closed and my hands behind my head. I liked to lie like that: no one would bother a sleeping man, and meanwhile one could dream and think. But I found it difficult to dream: my heart was beating uneasily and M——ski's words were still echoing in my ears: '*Je hais ces brigands!*' . . .

"By and by I forgot my surroundings and became lost in memories. During the four years of my imprisonment I was continually recalling my past and seemed in my memories to live my former life all over again. These memories cropped up by themselves; I seldom evoked them consciously. It would begin from some point, some imperceptible feature, which then grew little by little into a complete picture, into some clear-cut and vivid impression. I used to analyze those impressions, adding new touches to an event that had happened long ago, and, above all, correcting it, correcting it incessantly, and that constituted my chief amusement. This time for some reason I suddenly remembered one fleeting instant in my early childhood when I was only nine years old."

After relating the incident with the peasant Marey, which performed the miracle of his "conversion," Dostoevsky concludes: "That evening I again met M——ski. Poor man! He could have no memories about Marey or peasants like him and he could have no other opinion of these people except, '*Je hais ces brigands!*' "

In his first letter to Mikhail, written only *one* week after his release from prison, Dostoevsky never mentions this miraculous conversion of his, which, he claimed in 1873 in his *Writer's Diary*, was owing to "the direct contact with the peasants [in prison], the fraternal union with them in our common misfortune, the realization that you have become the same as they, that you are like them—indeed, that you are like one of the lowest of them." In fact, it becomes quite clear from that letter that on leaving prison he shared the Polish political prisoner's sentiment: *Je hais ces brigands.* These *direct* impressions of his life in prison are absolutely genuine and can be taken as a true expression of his views at the time. "How can I convey to you," he begins, "any conception of what I have been through and the conclusions I have come to during all this time?"

To give Mikhail an idea of what his views on leaving prison were, and what he had experienced there, Dostoevsky starts his narrative from the day of his departure for Siberia.

"Our route lay via Yaroslav," he writes, "and, therefore, after three or four posting stations we stopped at daybreak at an inn in Schlüsselburg. We fell upon our breakfast as though we had not eaten for a whole week. After being imprisoned for eight months, we had got so hungry during the fifty miles of travel that even today I remember it with real pleasure. I felt gay, Durov kept talking without stopping, and Yastrezhembsky was full of all sorts of terrible and extraordinary premonitions. . . . We watched our courier very closely. We found that he was a fine old man, good-natured and extremely kind to us. He had had great experience of men and had traveled all over Europe with government dispatches. His name was Kuzma Prokofyev. The first thing he did for us was to provide us with covered sledges, which we appreciated greatly for the frosts were terrible. Next day being a holiday, the drivers had put on long peasant coats of gray German cloth and scarlet belts. There was not a soul in the villages we passed through. It was a glorious winter day. We were being driven over the empty highway through Novgorod, Yaroslav, etc. We drove through little towns at great distances from one another, towns of no particular importance. But as we were traveling during the Christmas holidays, there was always something to eat and drink everywhere. We were frozen stiff. We were dressed warmly, but after traveling for ten hours without leaving the covered sledge and stopping five or six times on the way, the cold became almost unbearable. I was frozen to the core and could scarcely get warm in hot rooms. But the marvelous thing was that the journey completely restored my health. One night in the province of Perm we withstood a frost of forty degrees below zero. That is the sort of thing I should not dream of recommending to you. It is rather unpleasant.

"Our passage across the Urals," Dostoevsky continues, "was very sad. The horses and the sledges sank in the snowdrifts. A blizzard was raging. It was at night and we had to leave our sledges and wait until they were dragged out of the snow. All around us the snow was falling and the wind was howling. It was the border between Europe and Asia, in front of us was Siberia and our mysterious future and behind my past life—it was very sad and tears started to my eyes. All along the roads entire villages rushed out to look at us, but, in spite of our fetters, they overcharged us shamelessly at all the posting stations. Prokofyev himself paid for almost half of our expenses from his own pocket, practically forcing us to agree to it, and so we spent only fifteen silver rubles each on the journey. On January 11 we arrived in Tobolsk and after being presented to the local authorities and searched, Durov, Yastrezhembsky and I were locked up in a cell by ourselves.[2] During the search all our money was taken away from us. Speshnyov and the others who had arrived before us were put in another cell and we hardly ever saw each other all that time. We spent six days in Tobolsk and there we were rewarded by the great sympathy shown to us by the exiles of the old days (that is to say, not by them, but by their wives) who took care of us, as though we were their own kith and kin. What wonderful people, people hardened by twenty-five years of sorrow and self-sacrifice. We saw them only for a moment because we were guarded very closely. But they sent us food, and warm clothing, and comforted and encouraged us. I had gone on the journey without taking anything with me, not even proper clothes, and now I realized what a mistake I had made. They even sent me clothes and at last we left Tobolsk and after three days arrived in Omsk.[3]

"In Tobolsk," Dostoevsky continues, "I had already learned about the people under whose orders we were to live. The commandant of the fortress was a very decent fellow, but the governor of the prison, Major Krivtsov, was a beast such as you rarely came across, a dis-

[2] According to Yastrezhembsky, they were taken on their arrival in Tobolsk "to a huge room in which parties of convicts were got ready for departure. About three hundred men, women and children of different ages and different nationalities were gathered there. Some of them were being put in chains, others had iron rods attached to them, and others still had their heads shaved. This scene," Yastrezhembsky declares, "produced a shattering and depressing effect on us." At the prison office, where they were taken next, they noticed that the copying clerks wore convict clothes and that some of them had the letters K.A.T. (*katorga*, *i.e.*, hard labor) and others had their nostrils torn out and the letters V.O.R. (*i.e.*, thief) branded on their faces and foreheads. During the search, Yastrezhembsky records, the prison governor "confiscated" his bottle of rum. The three of them were then taken to a narrow, dark and dirty cell with bunks on which, instead of mattresses, were three dirty sacks filled with straw and the same kind of pillows. "It was pitch dark," Yastrezhembsky continues, "and behind the door we could hear the sentry marching up and down in a forty-degree frost. We sat down and tried to get warm, Durov on the bunk, and I beside Dostoevsky on the floor. Behind the thin partition, as we learned later, prisoners awaiting trial were kept and we could hear them shouting, playing cards, clinking glasses, and swearing. . . . Durov had his fingers and toes frostbitten and his legs were badly chafed by the fetters. As for Dostoevsky, he already suffered from scrofulous ulcers on his face and in his mouth. The tip of my nose was frostbitten.

"Quite by accident we obtained a tallow candle, matches and hot tea which we found tastier than nectar. Dostoevsky had some excellent cigars, which the worthy prison governor had overlooked. We spent the whole night in amicable talk. Dostoevsky's sympathetic, charming voice, his tenderness and gentleness and even some of his capricious outbursts, which were absolutely like those of a woman, had a calming effect on me. I parted from Dostoevsky and Durov in the Tobolsk prison," he concludes. "We embraced and wept and never saw each other again."

[3] "When in Tobolsk," he wrote in his *Writer's Diary* in 1873, where he has something more to say about the reception he had received from the wives of the men convicted for their part in the military insurrection on December 14, 1825, "we were waiting to find out what was going to happen to us and had to spend some days in

gusting barbarian, a bully and a drunkard. He was everything loathsome, in fact, that one could possibly imagine. He began by calling Durov and myself damned fools for being involved in our affair and threatened to flog us at the slightest misdemeanor. He had been governor of the prison for the last two years and was responsible for the most horrible acts of injustice. Two years later he was himself put on trial. The good Lord saved me from him. He was always drunk when he came into the prison (I never once saw him sober) and he would immediately find fault with a convict who was quite sober and get him flogged under the pretext that he, the convict, was drunk. Once during one of his visits at night he ordered people to be flogged for not sleeping on the right side, for muttering in their sleep, for anything in fact that happened to enter his drunken head. And it was such a man who wrote reports and certificates of conduct about us every month and sent them to the authorities in Petersburg. I had met convicts already in Tobolsk, but here in Omsk I had to live with them for four years. They are a coarse, exacerbated, malevolent people. Their hatred of the nobility exceeds all limits and that is why they welcomed us, noblemen, with hostility, without concealing their malicious glee at our misfortune. They would have devoured us alive if we had let them. Not that we could really have organized any defense against them, for we had to live, eat, drink and sleep with people like that for several years and we did not even have anyone to complain to about the innumerable insults of all sorts they hurled against us. 'You noblemen have pecked us to death with your iron beaks. Before, when you were our masters you tortured us, and now when you have become even worse than the worst of us you want to be our brothers.' That was the sort of thing we heard almost every day for four years. We had one hundred and fifty enemies who were never tired of persecuting us. They loved it. It provided them with an occupation, a diversion, and the only way we could save ourselves from serious trouble was by showing our indifference and our moral superiority, which they could not but understand and respect, and by refusing steadfastly to give in to their will. They were always conscious of the fact that we were their superiors. They had no idea of the nature of our crime. We never spoke about it ourselves and that was why we never understood one another. We had therefore to

prison at the convicts' transportation point. The wives of the Decembrists appealed to the governor of the prison and succeeded in obtaining permission to meet us at his quarters. We saw those great sufferers who had voluntarily followed their husbands to Siberia. Though themselves guiltless of any crime, they suffered for twenty-five years the same privations as their convicted husbands. Our meeting lasted an hour. They gave us their blessings on our new journey, they made the sign of the cross over us and handed a New Testament to each of us—the only book a convict was allowed to have in prison. It lay for four years under my pillow. I read it sometimes myself and read some of it to others. I used it to teach one convict to read."

put up with their persecution and the feeling of revenge, with which they live and breathe, against the class of the nobility."

There were a few exceptions, though. "In prison too among brigands I found decent people during the four years I spent there," Dostoevsky explained. "Believe me, there are deep strong and beautiful characters among them and I was glad to be able to look for gold under a coarse exterior. . . . I taught a young Circassian (sentenced for an act of brigandage) Russian and he was deeply grateful to me. Another convict wept when he said good-by to me. I used to give him a little money and his gratitude was quite overwhelming. My character, though, I am sorry to say, has grown worse: I was capricious and impatient with them. They respected my moods and bore it all without a murmur."

He had brought enough material from prison to fill whole volumes. If he had not got to know Russia, he thought, he had got to know the Russian people, though, he admitted, it was probably his vanity speaking. As for his life in prison, it was very hard.

"Penal servitude," he wrote, "is much harder under military law than under civil law. All the four years I lived behind the four prison walls and only went out to work. The work we had to do was not always hard, but often I had to work till I was absolutely exhausted, and in foul weather, too, when the ground was muddy and in winter when it was unbearably cold. Once I had to spend four hours on some special job in forty degrees below zero when the mercury in the thermometer froze. One of my feet was frostbitten. We lived in a crowd, all of us together, in one room. Imagine an old, dilapidated wooden building, which should have been demolished long ago and which could no longer serve its purpose. In summer we were nearly stifled from the lack of air and in winter we suffered from unendurable cold. The floor boards were rotten and covered with filth an inch thick, so that one kept perpetually slipping and falling. There was an inch of ice on the tiny window panes so that one could scarcely read anything all day. From the ceiling water kept dripping incessantly, and there were drafts everywhere. We were packed like salt herrings in a cask. Even when they heated the stove with bits of wood, we scarcely felt the warmth (the ice in the room would hardly melt), and the room was full of poisonous charcoal fumes. That was how we lived all winter. The convicts did their washing in the same room and on that day the whole of the small barracks would be awash. There was no room to turn around. From nightfall to daybreak it was impossible to go out to relieve oneself, for the barracks were locked up. A small tub was put for that purpose in the corridor and the air became absolutely unbearable. All the convicts stink like pigs. They say that they have to behave like swine because, after all, they are 'alive.' We slept on bare bunks and were allowed only one pillow. We covered ourselves with our short sheepskins which left my legs bare. All night I shivered with cold. There were millions of fleas, lice and cockroaches. In winter we wore sheepskins, which often were of the worst quality and gave practically no warmth. On the feet we wore boots with low tops—you can imagine how comfortable they were when walking in frost. For food we were given bread and cabbage soup, which was supposed to have a quarter of a pound of minced beef in it, but I certainly never saw any in my soup. On holidays we were given porridge, but with hardly any fat. During Lent we had cabbage and water and very little else. I suffered terribly from indigestion and was ill several times. In circumstances like these it was impossible to live without money. In fact, without money I should most certainly have died, for no one, no convict, can possibly endure such a life. However, I drank tea and sometimes I had my own piece of boiled beef. That saved me. I could not possibly abstain from smoking, for one would have been suffocated in that stench. All this had to be done by stealth. I often had to go to the hospital because of illness. My nervous attacks sometimes resulted in epileptic fits, but that did not happen often. I am still suffering from rheumatism in my leg, but on the whole I am quite well. When you add to all these pleasures, the practical impossibility of getting a book and that whatever book you do get, you have to read it by stealth, as well as the everlasting enmity and quarreling around you, oaths, shouts, uproar, never alone, always under guard, and consider that it went on like this without any change for four years—I know you will forgive me if I say that it was bad. And, besides, the fear that you might be called to account for anything you did, the fetters and the vile air, and there you have a good picture of my life in prison. What happened to my mind, my beliefs and my heart during those four years I won't tell you. It's a long story. But this everlasting absorption in oneself, which I sought like a refuge from bitter reality, has brought its own fruits. I have now many desires and hopes such as I never thought of before. One thing I ask you: do not forget me and please help me. I must have books and money. Send me the Koran, Kant's *Critique de la raison pure* and Hegel, especially Hegel's *History of Philosophy*. My whole future depends on them.

"Before leaving for Sebastopol," he concluded, "Philippov made me a present of twenty-five rubles. He realized that I wouldn't have any money, good fellow. All our exiles are carrying on as well as they can. . . . Speshnyov lives in the province of Irkutsk where he has become very popular. . . . What a wonderful man he is.[4] Wherever he happens to be even the wost reserved people at once surround him with respect

[4] A great deal has been made by some of Dostoevsky's biographers of the fact that, as Yanovsky records, Dostoevsky, who had once borrowed 500 rubles from Speshnyov, referred to him as his "Mephistopheles." Dostoevsky was liable to call the people he borrowed money from all sorts of names, but, as the above passage shows, he admired and respected Speshnyov greatly.

and veneration. Poor Grigoryev [one of the three tied to the posts on the Semyonovsky Parade Ground] has lost his reason completely and is now in the hospital."

II

Dostoevsky arrived at the Omsk prison on April 23, 1850. In June he was formally entered in the list of prisoners of Omsk fortress as one of the "political criminals" sentenced to "second-degree hard labor." His occupation was given as "laborer" with the additional information that he could read and write. He wore the convict half-gray, half-black tunic with a large yellow diamond-shaped piece of material sewn on the back, and a soft yellow round cap in summer, with a sheepskin, ear muffs and mittens in winter. His head was shaved on one side. He looked like a strong, stocky laborer. Four iron rods fastened by a belt around his waist made his movements slow and clumsy. According to the evidence gathered from the inmates and prison officials, his pale, haggard face, covered with red spots, was never relieved by a smile and he opened his mouth only to give short and abrupt replies. He wore his cap pulled over his forehead and seemed always "self-absorbed, morose and unpleasant." He walked with his head "thrust forward" and his eyes "cast down."[5] The convicts did not like him; they looked at him darkly, but "without hatred" and made way for him in silence. Dostoevsky, the report continues, looked "like a wolf caught in a trap." He shunned his fellow prisoners, preferring to keep to himself and exchanging a few words with them only if it were absolutely necessary. When some of the younger prison officials tried to show him some kindness (contrary to prison regulations they obtained for him permission to work as a clerk at the prison office for three months) by inviting him to sit down and rest, he refused to do so, replied unwillingly to their questions, accepted every expression of sympathy mistrustfully, refused the books they offered him and only showed an interest twice, when they gave

[5] A remarkable confirmation of this can be found in the autobiographical passage at the end of *Crime and Punishment*, in which Dostoevsky describes Raskolnikov's first days in prison, where, he writes, "there was a great deal he did not notice and did not want to notice. He lived, as it were, with downcast eyes. He found it unbearable and loathsome to look. But in the end he could not help being surprised at many things, and he began, as though reluctantly, to notice things the existence of which he did not even suspect. But what generally surprised him most was the terrible, unbridgeable gulf that lay between him and all those other people. It seemed to him that they belonged to quite a different species of pople. He looked on them and they on him with distrust and hostility. He knew and understood the general reasons for this separation, but he would never before have admitted that those reasons were so deep-rooted or so strong. . . .

"He was disliked and shunned by everyone; in the end they even began to hate him. Why? He did not know. They despised him and they laughed at him."

him translations of *The Pickwick Papers* and *David Copperfield*, which he took to the hospital to read. The most extraordinary thing was his quarrel with Durov, who, unlike himself, was popular with the convicts for his sociable character and his readiness to crack jokes with them. He does not mention this, or what happened to Durov, at the end of his letter to Mikhail, but he does refer to him without mentioning his name in *The House of the Dead*. "I looked with horror," he writes, "at one of my comrades (of the nobility) whose life flickered out in prison like a guttering candle. He entered the prison together with me, looking young, handsome and cheerful, and he left it gray-haired, unable to drag his feet, short-winded, with his health ruined."

In his letter to Mikhail, Dostoevsky gave a true description of his impressions of prison life and the attitude towards him of the convicts, whom, as he expressed it, he imagined "out of vanity" to have at last understood. Before leaving Omsk he wrote a letter to Natalya Fonvisin, the widow of the Decembrist exile, who had given him a copy of the New Testament in Tobolsk, in which he again spoke of his loathing for his fellow prisoners. "It is almost five years now," he wrote,[6] "that I have not been alone for a single hour. To be alone is a normal need just like eating and drinking. Otherwise you become a hater of men in this forced communism. Indeed, the society of men has become a poison and an infection to me and it was from this unbearable torture that I suffered most of all during these four years. There were moments when I hated everyone I happened to come across whether he was right or wrong and looked on them all as thieves who were stealing my life with impunity. The most unbearable misfortune is when you yourself become unjust, vicious and disgusting. You realize all this, you even reproach yourself, but you are unable to master yourself. I have experienced it. . . ."

In *The House of the Dead*, which he published in full in 1861 and 1862 in his periodical, *Time*, but had already begun writing in Siberia, Dostoevsky repeats verbatim the sentence in which he described to Mikhail the hatred of the convicts for the "noblemen."

The extent to which the convicts refused to have anything to do with Dostoevsky is illustrated by the story he tells in *The House of the Dead* about a complaint the convicts had agreed to lodge about the poor quality of their food. Dostoevsky wanted to join them, but the convicts refused to have anything to do with him. "Iron Beak" and other uncomplimentary names were hurled at him. "Never in my life have I been so insulted," Dostoevsky wrote. He felt sick at heart at the time, but was even more depressed after talking the incident over with one of the convicts.

[6] *Letters*, February 20, 1854.

"Why do you want to complain?" the convict asked him, as though trying to understand him. "You always eat your own food."

"But, good Lord," objected Dostoevsky, "there are also many of your people who eat their own food and yet they did join the protest, so I suppose we too have to do so out of a—a feeling of comradeship."

"*But what sort of comrade are you to us?*" the convict asked Dostoevsky with a look of surprise.

"I glanced at him quickly," Dostoevsky writes. "He really did not understand me. He simply did not understand what I was talking about, but I understood him perfectly at that moment. For the first time an idea, which had been stirring dimly in my mind and would not leave me, became clear to me, and I suddenly understood something which I had hitherto only vaguely apprehended. I understood that they would never accept me as one of themselves, even if I were a hundred times worse than they, even if I spent my whole life in prison. What stuck in my mind particularly at that moment was the look the convict gave me. In his question: 'What sort of comrade are you to us?' I could detect such a genuine naïvety, such a good-natured feeling of bewilderment, that I thought at first: Isn't there in his words a kind of irony, or malice, or mockery? But not a bit of it: I was simply no comrade of theirs and that was all there was to it. 'You go your way and we shall go our way. Why don't you mind your own business?' "

Even when at work the convicts refused to have anything to do with him. "With regard to myself," he writes in *The House of the Dead*, "I noticed one peculiarity. Whenever I tried to assist them in their work, I seemed not to be wanted, I was always in their way, everywhere they drove me off with curses." Still, he did not shirk work, whether it was the burning and pounding of alabaster, the shoveling of snow (which he enjoyed very much), the unloading of bricks from barges on the Irtysh or the turning of a grindstone wheel. "I felt," he writes, "that work could save me, improve my health and strengthen my body. Constant mental anxiety, nervous irritation and the close air of the barracks could have destroyed me utterly. 'Try to be in the open air as much as possible,' I told myself. 'Get tired every day, get used to carrying heavy loads—at least that will save me, strengthen me, and when I leave prison I shall be strong, healthy and not aged.' I was not mistaken: work and activity were very useful to me."

At the beginning of 1852, the commandant of the Omsk fortress asked the Ministry of War to transfer Dostoevsky and Durov from the category of hard-labor convicts to the easier category of short-term prisoners. This would have meant that, among other privileges, they would have been released from wearing iron rods. On April 3rd the Ministry replied that the appeal had been presented to the Emperor, who "did not deem it necessary to give his consent to it."

III

Dostoevsky was kept in prison from January 23, 1850, to February 15, 1854. He had entered prison in winter and in winter he left it. "With what impatience," he writes in *The House of the Dead*, "have I waited for winter, with what delight have I watched my last summer in prison drawing to an end, the leaves on the trees turning yellow and the grass in the steppe withering. At last the longed-for winter came. But, strange to tell, the nearer the day of my release, the more and more patient I grew. . . . Let me observe in passing," he adds, "that as a result of constantly dreaming of freedom and missing it for so long a time, freedom seemed to me in prison much freer than real freedom, that is to say, freedom as it is in reality. . . . On my very last day in prison," he continues, "I went around the whole stockade of our prison *for the last time*. Here, behind the barracks, I used to wander during my first year, broken-hearted, all alone, without a soul to talk to. I remembered how I counted the many days still left for me there. Early next morning, before the convicts were led out to work, I walked through the barracks to say good-by to the prisoners. Many strong, callused hands were stretched out amicably to me. A very few shook mine in a comradely fashion, others realized very well that I should become quite a different man soon and though they, too, took leave of me amicably and in a kindly way, it was not as of a comrade, but, as it were, of a gentleman. Some turned away from me sternly and did not reply to my words of farewell. Some, indeed, gazed at me with hatred. . . ."

Dostoevsky was later on to base his entire philosophy of life on the idea that, as he put it in his *Writer's Diary* in 1873, "the need for suffering in its most extreme form" was "the fundamental need of the Russian people," which, he maintained, "has been infected with the desire for suffering since time immemorial." This curious idea of his stems, no doubt, from his experiences of prison life, though at the time he certainly had little use for a belief in suffering as something "from which the Russian people derive acute enjoyment." On the contrary, his observations of corporal punishment in prison and later in the army, as becomes all too clear from *The House of the Dead*, showed that it was the people who inflicted the suffering who derived the keenest enjoyment from it. "I tried to imagine the psychological state of the prisoners who were about to undergo corporal punishment," he writes. "Before their punishment it is seldom that any of them is calm, and this is true even of those who had been beaten many times before. The condemned man, I observed, was generally overcome by a kind of acute, though purely physical terror, a terror that is involuntary and uncontrollable and that crushes the whole moral being of a man."

This is the sort of thing that happened at one of the usual punishments of the time—running the gantlet, at which the condemned man was bared to the waist, had his hands tied in front of him on the butts of two rifles, and was then dragged by two noncommissioned officers through "the green street," that is, two lines of soldiers armed with sticks with which he was mercilessly belabored. Dostoevsky knew the consequences of that sort of punishment (which, by the way, earned the Emperor the nickname of Nicholas the Stick), for he had not only watched the lifeless body of the prisoner who had been thus punished slowly recovering from his terrible wounds in the prison hospital, but had to administer such punishment himself while serving as a private in the army in Semipalatinsk. "At the moment when he is bared to the waist and his hands are tied to the butts of the rifles," he writes in *The House of the Dead*, "the prisoner as a rule begins to implore the officer-in-charge not to punish him too severely. 'Sir,' the poor wretch cries, 'please, have mercy on me, be like a father to me, sir! I shall pray to God for you all my life! Don't destroy me, sir! Be merciful, sir!'

" 'My dear fellow,' the officer replies, 'what am I to do with you? It is not I who am punishing you, is it? It is the law!'

" 'But, sir, it all depends on you. Please, don't be too hard on me!'

" 'Do you think I am not sorry for you? Do you think it gives me pleasure to see you being beaten? I am a human being, too, am I not? Am I a human being or not? Answer me!'

" 'Why, of course, you are, sir. You're our father and we are your children. Be a father to me, sir!'

" 'But, my dear fellow, just think. You've got brains, haven't you? Well, don't you think that I know perfectly well that as a human being I must look leniently and mercifully upon you, miserable sinner that you are. . . .'

" 'Perfectly true, sir. It's the truth you've spoken, sir!'

" 'Yes, certainly, I must look mercifully upon you however greatly you've sinned. But it's not me, you see, it's the law! Think! I serve God and my country and I shall take a grevious sin upon my soul if I weaken the law—think of that!'

" 'Sir!'

" 'Oh, well, all right. I'll do it for you. I know I shouldn't do it, but so be it. I'll be lenient with you this time. I won't punish you severely. But what if you should take it into your head that I'd deal as leniently with you again and then commit another crime? Why, I shall be responsible for it, shan't I?'

" 'Sir, I swear as before the throne of God Himself . . .'

" 'Oh, well, all right. But are you willing to swear to me that you will behave yourself in future?'

" 'May God strike me dead on the spot, may . . .'

" 'Don't swear, it's a sin to swear. I'm ready to take your word for it. Do you give me your word?'

" 'Sir!'

" 'Very well, listen. I'm taking pity on you just because of your orphan tears. You are an orphan, aren't you?'

" 'Yes, sir, I am an orphan. I have neither father nor mother, sir. I'm alone in the world, sir. . . .'

" 'Very well, just because of your orphan tears, then. But, remember, this is the last time. Take him,' he adds in so tender a voice that the prisoner does not know what kind of prayers will do for such a kind-hearted man.

"He is led away, the drum begins to beat a loud tattoo, the first sticks start coming down. 'Hit him!' the officer roars. 'Beat him! Sting him! Harder! Harder! Hit him harder, the orphan, the scoundrel, harder! Thrash him! Baste him! Pitch into him!' And the soldiers rain blows on him with all their might, and the poor wretch starts screaming, while the officer runs after him, laughing at the top of his voice, holding his sides and unable to straighten himself, so that in the end one feels sorry for the poor man. He is enjoying himself, he is hugely amused and only from time to time does he burst into roars of laughter and once more his shouts can be heard: 'Thrash him! Sting him, the scoundrel! Sting him, the poor orphan!' "

There could, indeed, be no doubt as to who derived the greater pleasure from suffering: the soldier who was being mercilessly beaten or his officer who was administering the beating.

"I don't know how it is today," wrote Dostoevsky, summing up his views on corporal punishment in *The House of the Dead*, "but in the not so distant past there were certainly gentlemen who derived the sort of pleasure out of flogging their victims that was reminiscent of the Marquis de Sade and the Marquise de Brenneville.[7] I think there is something in that sensation that gives these gentlemen a thrill that is both delightful and painful. There are people who, like tigers, yearn for a taste of blood. He who has once experienced this power, this immense power over the body and soul of a fellow man like himself . . . and the possibility of humiliating another human being created in God's image, involuntarily becomes completely incapable of controlling his own sensations. Tyranny is a habit; once rooted, it grows like a disease. I am firmly of the opinion that the best man in the world can grow coarse and insensitive from habit to a point where he becomes indistinguishable from a wild beast. Blood and power intoxicate: they lead to callousness and depravity; the most abnormal phenomena become accessible and, finally, enjoyable mentally and emotionally. Man and citizen become totally lost in the tyrant, and a return to human dignity, repentance and regeneration becomes almost impossible for him. Besides, the example and the possibility of such a willful exercise of power acts as an infection on society as a whole. A society that regards such a

[7] The Marquise Maria Madeleine Brenneville was executed in 1676 for poisoning her father, two brothers and a few more of her relatives, in order to inherit their fortunes.

phenomenon with indifference is already infected to the core itself. In short, the right of corporal punishment granted to one man over another is in itself one of society's festering sores and one of the most certain ways of corrupting the sense of civic duty until it finally decays."

Such a view of the mental and physical effects of corporal punishment is certainly incompatible with the idea of suffering as a general panacea for the regeneration of man. Nor is it compatible with "the need for suffering" which the Russian people, according to Dostoevsky, seemed to feel. Tolstoy once remarked that being a sick man himself, Dostoevsky thought that the whole world was sick, an aphorism that perhaps goes too far, but that has more than a grain of truth in it. Dostoevsky certainly derived a morbid enjoyment from both suffering and the infliction of suffering and he came gradually to invest the whole Russian people with this unhealthy trait. But it was not, as he later claimed, a lesson he learned from close contact with his fellow convicts. The only fact he had brought out of prison was the hatred of the Russian peasant for his masters, the nobility. In prison he realized for the first time how terrible and how deeply rooted this hatred was, and this realization was the first step towards his subsequent contention that, instead of trying "to enlighten" the common people and lift them out of their ignorance and filth, it was the duty of the Russian educated classes, as he wrote in 1876 in his *Writer's Diary*, "to fall down before the common people and wait for everything from them—ideas and images, to fall down before the sense of truth and justice of the common people and recognize them as true and just."

If, therefore, the hatred of the "people" towards the nobility and the overwhelming feeling of guilt arising from it led Dostoevsky eventually to idealize the mass of the illiterate Russian peasantry as the sole repository of truth and righteousness, his atheistic convictions, derived from Belinsky and his Petrashevsky associates, superimposed on the religious background of his childhood, led to the religious doubts which tormented him all his life. The period of his "doubts" began in prison and was accompanied by an idealization of the person of Christ as the man-God and the identification of the Russian people as a God-bearing people.

This he makes abundantly clear in his remarkable letter from Omsk to Natalya Fonvisin. "I have heard from many people," he wrote, "that you are very religious. It is not, however, because you are religious, but because I have myself experienced and been through the same thing, that at such moments (when you live through once more all your past misfortunes in your mind) you thirst 'like parched grass' for faith and you find it because truth becomes clear to you when you are unhappy. But let me tell you this about myself: I am a child of this age, a child of unbelief and doubts to this very day, and shall be (I know it) to the very day when I am laid in my grave. This longing to believe has cost and still does cost me terrible torments; it is a longing that is all the stronger in my heart the more arguments I have against it. And yet God sometimes vouchsafes me moments during which I am completely calm; at such moments I love and I find that I am loved by others; at such moments I have laid up in myself a symbol of faith in which everything is clear and sacred to me. This symbol is very simple. It is: to believe that there is nothing more beautiful, more profound, more sympathetic, more reasonable, more courageous and more perfect than Christ, and not only is there not, but, I tell myself with jealous love, there cannot be. Moreover, if anyone were to prove to me that Christ was outside truth and that truth really was outside Christ, I would still rather remain with Christ than with truth." And he meant it, too: he was nothing if not extreme.

He was sent to Semipalatinsk, a fortress town near the border of China, on the high bank of the Irtysh and built on the ruins of "seven palaces" of the Mongols, where he had to serve as private in the Seventh Siberian line regiment. He realized very well, as he wrote to Mikhail, that "in a soldier's coat I am the same sort of prisoner as before," but he knew, too, that, as he wrote to Andrey,[8] there was a great difference and that "the indescribable, never-ending suffering" he had experienced in Omsk had come to an end. He was, he told Natalya Fonvisin in his letter from Omsk, "in a state of expectation. . . . I cannot help feeling, that very, very soon something is going to happen which will be of decisive importance to my future, that I am approaching a turning point in my life, that I have apparently grown ripe for something, that what is going to happen will be something gentle and bright, perhaps something ominous, but in any case inevitable. Otherwise my life will be a failure. But perhaps all this is nothing but morbid dreams. . . ."

His presentiment this time turned out to be quite true. Two things happened to Dostoevsky in Semipalatinsk that were to be of decisive importance to his future: his meeting with Baron Alexander Wrangel, the twenty-two-year-old public prosecutor of the district, and his first great love affair, with Maria Dmitriyevna Isaev, the wife of a poor local official.

[8] *Letters*, November 6, 1854.

[5]

THE MEEK LOVER: FIRST MARRIAGE

Semipalatinsk, as described by Baron Wrangel, had a population of about 6,000, composed of Russians, Tartars and seminomadic Kirghizes. It had one Russian Orthodox church, seven mosques, army barracks, a hospital, government offices and a large market place surrounded by a palisade where caravans of camels and horses used to unload their merchandise. Tradesmen sold their wares in tents or open stalls. The houses were of one story and timbered. Wooden fences stretched for miles along deserted streets. At night the town was plunged in darkness and, but for the desperate barking of the watchdogs, it would have appeared dead. The streets were unpaved and covered with dry sand. Dostoevsky was to spend over four years there, from March 1854 to July 1858.

At first Dostoevsky lived in the army barracks. There he was befriended by a seventeen-year-old soldier called Nikolai Katz, a converted Jew, who did some tailoring on the side and possessed a samovar. Katz treated the silent and morose thirty-three-year-old ex-convict to tea and could not help admiring the uncomplaining way in which he bore the rigors of army life. "Poor Dostoevsky," Wrangel writes, "had to stand for two or three hours during the army exercises; the slow march in particular exhausted him." Dostoevsky himself wrote to Mikhail on July 30, 1854: "I suppose you know what I am doing now. Drill, inspections by the brigade and division commanders and preparations for them. I arrived here in March. I knew practically nothing about army service and yet in July I was on parade with the others and I knew the business no worse than they. What it cost me and how it tired me out is a different matter, but they are satisfied with me, thank God. . . . However strange this may all seem to you, I think you will realize that serving as a private in the army is no joke, that a soldier's life, with all the duties of a soldier, is not very easy for a man like myself whose health is far from good and who has long got out of the habit of such service. It cost me a great deal of labor to acquire this habit. I am not complaining, it is my cross, and I deserved it. . . . To tell the truth, I have no other occupations except those connected with the army. As for what has been going on in my heart and soul and mind—what has grown up there, what has ripened and what has withered away and been thrown out together with the weeds—it is something you cannot convey on a scrap of paper. I live a very solitary life here and as usual am shuning people. Besides, you must remember that for five years I have been constantly under guard, and that is why it is a real joy to me to be alone sometimes."

By that time, however, his life was not as solitary as he pretended. His commanding officer, Lieutenant-Colonel Belikov, learning of the presence in his company of "a literate private," invited him to his house to read the newspapers to him. That was the beginning of Dostoevsky's introduction into Semipalatinsk "society." His entry into this exclusive circle of high officials and their wives was certainly facilitated by the fact that, as Wrangel noted, he "never showed the slightest sign of wishing to ingratiate himself with people, or flattering people, or desiring to crash into society. At the same time, he was very reticent and modest, as though not realizing his outstanding qualities, and it was thanks to his tact that he gained general respect." From the very beginning of his army career, in fact, Dostoevsky had made up his mind that the only way he could hope to get back to Russia was, as he advised the Moscow students twenty-four years later, "by bending down to the ground like a blade of grass." It was his first lesson in the efficacy of submissiveness to the will of authority, which he was to propagate with such militant fervor towards the end of his life. "Oh, what a meek man he was," the chief regimental bugler recalled naïvely many years later. "He always tried to put himself beneath everyone else. Whenever he met me in the street, for instance, he would draw himself up and salute. He always showed you the respect due to your higher rank, and when you addressed him, he always replied civilly and respectfully."

Having gained the favor of his superiors, Dostoevsky was given permission to live in his own lodgings. He rented a room in a cottage in the most desolate part of the town and paid five rubles a month for it. "The cottage," Wrangel records, "was just a timber cabin, lopsided, without foundations and without a single window facing the street, so built as a safeguard against robbers and thieves. The two windows of Dostoevsky's room looked out onto the courtyard, which was rather large, with a well and a sweep and a small kitchen garden with a few raspberry and black-currant bushes. It was surrounded by a high fence with tall gates and a low wicket gate and was guarded by a very ferocious watchdog. Dostoevsky's room was fairly large, but with a very low ceiling. It was always in semidarkness. The walls were smeared with clay and had once been whitewashed. Along two walls was a large bench. On the walls were cheap popular prints, soiled by flies. Behind a large Russian stove to the left of the door was a bed, which was divided off by a cotton curtain. There was also an ordinary deal box, which served as a chest of drawers, a table, and a tiny looking glass in a frame. On the window sill were flowerpots with geraniums. The faded curtains on the windows had originally been red. The whole room was indescribably dirty. Cockroaches were running about in hordes on the table, the walls and the bed. In summer there were besides hundreds of fleas and cockroaches."

Dostoevsky's room, his washing, darning, and so on, was done by the elder daughter of his landlady, a pretty twenty-year-old girl. Her sixteen-year-old sister, too, was beautiful, and Dostoevsky was on very good terms with her. Indeed, their relations must have been much closer than that, for, as Wrangel puts it, "the mother quite openly exploited the youth and beauty of her daughters, and when Dostoevsky reproved her, she told him: 'Why, sir, they would have become the mistresses of some battalion clerk or noncommissioned officer for two cakes or a pound of nuts. It's an honor to serve a gentleman. After all, not every girl has the good luck to go to bed with a civil servant.' "

It was in the spring of 1854, however, that Dostoevsky met the woman with whom he was to fall desperately in love and whom, to his great misfortune, he was to marry. Her name was Maria Dmitriyevna Isaev. She was twenty-nine when he met her. "A fairly beautiful woman of medium height," Wrangel describes her. "She had fair hair and was very thin, but had a passionate, *exaltée* nature. Even at that time an ominous hectic flush covered her pale face. . . . She was well-read, fairly well-educated, had an inquiring mind, was kindhearted and quite unusually vivacious and impressionable." She was the wife of Alexander Isaev and had a son, "a bright boy of nine," Wrangel records. "Isaev," he goes on, "was a sick man; he had T.B. and he was a hard drinker. He was a gentle and quiet man." He was a former teacher of the secondary school in Astrakhan, the principal of which was Maria's father. He took a job in the civil service and was transferred to Semipalatinsk, where he spent most of his time drinking in low pubs. He soon lost his job. There was something inherently good and helpless about him, and this appealed strongly to Dostoevsky, whom he might have reminded of his unlucky uncle in Moscow, who had also been an inveterate drunkard and who had been so atrociously treated by his father. "Perhaps I am the only one here who knew how to value him," Dostoevsky wrote to Wrangel.[1] "If he had any faults, it was his unhappy life that was to a large extent to be blamed for it. I should like to see anyone who could have borne up to such persistent bad luck, but then —such goodness, such true nobility. . . ." "I shake your husband's hand warmly and I embrace him with all my heart, like a friend, a brother, but I wish he kept better company," he wrote to Maria after Isaev had obtained a civil-service job in Kuznetsk, where he died a short while

[1] *Letters*, August 15, 1855.

after. "Will he really be as indiscriminating in Kuznetsk as he was in Semipalatinsk? And are these people really worth bothering about? Ought he to eat and drink with them and put up with their abominations? After some such company one feels unclean oneself." And to Mikhail he wrote two years later: "He [Isaev] lived a disorderly sort of life and his nature too was rather disorderly, passionate, stubborn and a little coarse. His reputation suffered a considerable decline here, and he was involved in a great many unpleasant incidents, but many of the attacks against him were unwarranted. He was as irresponsible as a gypsy, vain, proud, unable to control himself, and, as I have already said, went to seed terribly, but he was a highly intelligent man and very goodhearted. He was well-educated and understood everything you talked to him about. In spite of his sordid surroundings, he was an extremely honorable man."

This type of "honorable" drunkard, who, when in his cups, liked to discourse on all sorts of lofty themes, was later to appear in Dostoevsky's great novels under different names—Marmeladov in *Crime and Punishment*, General Ivolgin in *The Idiot* and Captain Snegiryov in *The Brothers Karamazov*.

As for Maria herself, she took a warm interest in Dostoevsky and was extremely kind to him, but, Wrangel writes, "I don't think she had really any idea of his great talents: rather she took pity on an unhappy man whom fate had treated so scurvily. It is possible that she got attached to him, but she was never in love with him. She looked upon him, as she used to say, as 'a man without a future.' Dostoevsky, on the other hand, mistook her feeling of pity and compassion for love and fell in love with her with all the ardor of a young man."

Dostoevsky spent his evenings with the Isaevs, and he agreed to give lessons to their young son, Pasha, who was subsequently to become the bane of his life.

The other great event in Dostoevsky's life in Semipalatinsk took place on November 20, 1854. It was the arrival of the twenty-two-year-old public prosecutor Alexander Wrangel, who had been present as an onlooker at the mock execution of the Petrashevsky "rebels" on the Semyonovsky Parade Ground and who, before his departure for Siberia, had been to see Mikhail and had got letters and money for Dostoevsky from him. "Baron Wrangel," Dostoevsky wrote to Apollon Maykov,[2] "is a very young man with excellent qualities of heart and soul, who arrived in Siberia straight from the Lycée with a *generous* dream of learning to know the region, of being useful, etc. We became close friends and I grew very fond of him. . . . He is extremely good-natured and has a tender heart, though at first glance his exterior gives the impression of a certain unapproachability. He belongs to a semiaristocratic circle, which is not entirely to my liking, but he does not like it either, for he has excellent

2 *Letters*, January 18, 1856.

qualities, though a great deal of his social background still shows. . . . Finally, he is a little oversensitive, very impressionable, and sometimes rather secretive and somewhat moody."

To Mikhail he recommended Baron Wrangel a few days earlier as "a very young man, with a strongly developed *point d'honneur*, quite incredibly kindhearted, a little proud (that's from the outside, I like that), with a few youthful faults, well-educated, but not brilliant or profound, fond of study, a weak character and as impressionable as a woman, a little hypochondriac and rather oversensitive; the things that make a man mad and angry merely grieve him—a sign of an excellent heart. *Très comme il faut.*"

That was not Dostoevsky's first impression of the young public prosecutor with the carefully tended ginger sidewhiskers. "I found out where Dostoevsky lived," Wrangel records, "and sent someone to ask him to come to see me in the evening and have tea with me. Dostoevsky did not know who I was or why he was being asked to see me, and when he came into the room he was extremely reticent. He wore a gray soldier's greatcoat, with a red stand-up collar and red shoulder straps. He was above medium height and looked morose. His complexion was pallid, his face freckled, and his fair hair cropped short. Examining me keenly with his intelligent, gray-blue eyes, he seemed to be trying to penetrate into my very soul in an attempt to find out what kind of a man I was. He admitted to me afterwards that he was very worried when my messenger told him that the public prosecutor wished to see him. But when I apologized for not coming to see him myself first and gave him the letters and parcels from Moscow and the regards from his relatives and spoke affably to him, he at once became cheerful and began to trust me. He realized instinctively that he would find a real friend in me."

It was Wrangel who introduced Dostoevsky to the military governor of the province, and from that moment he was received in all the best houses of Semipalatinsk. But most of his time was spent at the Isaevs'.

"For five years I had lived without people all by myself, literally without having anyone I could pour out my heart to," he wrote to Maria,[3] but you received me as if I were one of the family. I felt at home at your place. Your husband treated me better than if I had been his brother. Think what a nuisance I was to you with my impossible character, but you and your husband were fond of me. I understand it very well and I feel it, for I am not without a heart, am I? . . . The very fact that a woman stretched out her hand to me was a landmark in my life. . . . A woman's heart, a woman's compassion, a woman's sympathy and infinite goodness about which we have no idea and which, fools that we are, we often do not notice, are quite indispensable. I found it all in you. A sister would not have been more kind to me and to my faults than you

[3] *Letters*, June 4, 1855.

were. . . . If you had not been there, I should have grown apathetic, but now I am a man again. . . ."

Every time Dostoevsky returned from the Isaevs', Wrangel records, he was in a kind of ecstatic state. "She came to me," he was to write to Wrangel himself two years later, "in the saddest period of my existence and brought me back to life. She revived in me the will to live." Not that their relations were unclouded. Because she was not in love with him, her responses to his ardors could not by the very nature of things be particularly satisfying, and even this unsatisfactory state of affairs was made worse by the fact that since she was the wife of one of his best friends, his love for her had to be kept secret and seemed quite hopeless. As a result there were often "outbursts of anger," as Dostoevsky put it, between them. "Alas," he wrote to Wrangel,[4] "I never told you that, but while you were still here, I drove her to despair *par ma jalousie incomparable*."

In April 1855 Wrangel took a country house for the summer in the vicinity of Semipalatinsk known as Kazakov Garden. It was not far from where Dostoevsky's battalion was stationed in its summer quarters, and Dostoevsky often stayed there. They would busy themselves with the flower beds, Dostoevsky, with beads of perspiration streaming down his face, helping Wrangel to water the young plants. He would take off his gray soldier's coat and remain in his faded pink waistcoat with a long watch chain of smoke-blue beads and an enormous, onion-shaped watch attached to it. They would bathe in the river and have tea or dinner on the terrace, where they read the week-old newspapers, smoked long pipes, talked of their Petersburg friends and, adds Wrangel, "curse Europe." They also went for long walks in the dense forest and occasionally went for rides on horseback. Once Dostoevsky even took part in a hunt, but refused to follow the hounds to the kill.

"One day in May," Wrangel records, "Dostoevsky came looking gloomy and upset and told me with despair that Isaev was being transferred to Kuznetsk about four hundred miles from Semipalatinsk. 'You see,' he kept saying to me bitterly, 'she has agreed to go there! She isn't against it. That's what's so galling!' " For a brief moment he must have realized that she did not really care for him, and that was why, as Wrangel records, his despair was boundless and he walked about like a madman, for it seemed to him that there was nothing left for him to live for. "I shall never forget the scene of their parting," Wrangel continues. "Dostoevsky sobbed like a child. (Many years later he reminded me of this scene in his letter of March 31, 1865. 'You, the witness of my infinite happiness and of my terrible grief,' he wrote, 'do you remember that night in the forest a few miles from Semipalatinsk when we saw them off?') We left late at night. It was a wonderful May night. I took Dostoevsky in my trap. The Isaevs got into an open cart. They had not

4 *Letters,* March 3, 1856.

enough money to buy a covered one. Before their departure they stopped at my house and had some champagne. Wishing to give Dostoevsky the chance of exchanging a few sweet nothings with his Maria before their parting, I treated her husband to several glasses. I gave him some more for the road and, since he was entirely in my power, I then transferred him to my carriage, where he soon fell asleep. Dostoevsky changed seats with the husband. The road was smooth and even. All around us was thick pine forest, soft moonlight and the air was sweet and balmy. We drove on and on, but at last the time for parting came. The two lovers embraced, both of them wiped away their tears, while I dragged the sleeping and drunken Isaev to his cart. He at once began to snore. Pasha too was asleep. Their cart drove away and was soon lost to sight. The harness bells died away in the distance. Dostoevsky was standing on the same spot as if rooted to the ground, speechless, his head bowed, tears rolling down his cheeks. I went up to him, took his hand, and he seemed to awake as though from a deep slumber and, without uttering a word, sat down beside me in my carriage. We arrived home at daybreak. Dostoevsky refused to go to bed and kept muttering something under his breath. After returning from camp, he went to bed and stayed there for the rest of the day, refusing to eat or drink and merely smoking one pipe after another nervously."

II

Maria's departure for Kuznetsk made Dostoevsky feel, he wrote to her on June 4, 1855, as lonely as when he was arrested in 1849 and buried in prison, "torn away from everything I loved." He did not know what to do with himself. "I remembered everything," he wrote, "and felt sad when I thought of my future. . . . Shall we really never see one another again?" And, indeed, it seemed that Dostoevsky's first genuine love affair was destined to come to an end for the very unromantic reason that the husband of the woman he loved had got a job 400 miles away, that he was prevented by his army service from seeking a meeting with her and that she did not seem particularly keen to arrange one with him. Then the unexpected happened: poor drunken Isaev died in Kuznetsk on August 4, only three months after his departure from Semipalatinsk. "A man who is in love," Vsevolod Solovyov records Dostoevsky as saying to him a long time later, "does not reason. Do you know," Dostoevsky went on in a passionate whisper, his voice trembling, "how one loves? If your love is pure and you love purity in your woman and you suddenly realize that she is a loose and immoral woman, you will love her immorality, you will love the nastiness in her which you loathe so much—this is what love is like." He spoke from his experience of the two love affairs he had had in his life—both of them unhappy. At the time of his first love affair he certainly did not stop to reason: he was incapable of reasoning. On August 14, 1855, Dostoevsky rushed off a letter to Wrangel, who happened to be away at the time, asking him to send Maria some money. "She is penniless," he wrote. "She asked me what she should do," he wrote again on August 23. "At the moment she thinks of selling some of her things to raise a little money."

The correspondence with Kuznetsk continued, but, as Wrangel records, it did not give Dostoevsky joy. He felt that something was wrong. He was losing weight, looked thinner, was gloomy and irritable and walked about like a shadow. On a warm evening he would lie on the grass in Kazakov Garden and gaze for hours at the stars—that seemed to calm him. Wrangel tried to distract him by dragging him off to see people, and one day he took him to some mines in the country and introduced him to the mining engineers. But nothing was of any avail. Dostoevsky, Wrangel writes, suddenly became very superstitious and began telling him stories about clairvoyants and went to consult fortune-tellers. The trouble was that he had nothing to offer his Maria. She was impressed by his friendship with Wrangel and by the way he was received by all the important personages in the region, but he was still only a common soldier, with no prospects whatsoever, "a man without a future," as she herself had described him. In the circumstances he dared not even talk to her of marriage.

He had indeed taken steps to convince the Petersburg authorities of his loyalty to the throne: in May 1854 he persuaded Lieutenant-Colonel Belikov to forward to the chief of staff of the region a most loyal poem, *On the European Events of 1854*, that is to say, the outbreak of the Crimean War, and on August 13, a week after Isaev's death, General Hasford, Commanding Officer of the Siberian Corps, forwarded another loyal poem, *On July 1, 1855*, to the authorities in Petersburg, and in September a third, on the Empress's birthday, and added a recommendation for his promotion to the rank of noncommissioned officer. On November 20, the Ministry of War informed Hasford that his recommendation had been accepted. To Dostoevsky this promotion seemed the first gleam of hope towards the full restoration of his civic rights, and he felt justified in making a proposal of marriage and in informing his relatives and, above all, Mikhail about it.

He first broached the news of his intention to marry Maria as soon as his circumstances changed "even a little" for the better in a letter to Mikhail on January 13, 1856. But it is clear from this letter that although he was determined to carry out his intention "even if the earth should open up under his feet," as he quaintly put it, he was not confident that Maria would accept him. "It may and it may not happen. I am an honest man," he went on, "and I shall not make use of my influence to force this noble creature to sacrifice herself for me. But when it becomes possible, even in five years' time, I shall carry out my intention." In the meantime he implored Mikhail not to breathe a word about it to their sisters, for he was afraid that they might at once get anxious about him and start giving him "sensible advice." "Sensible advice" was the thing he dreaded most just then, for at the back of his mind he realized very well what a desperate gamble the marriage might turn out to be.

In the meantime Wrangel returned to Petersburg, and Dostoevsky gave him a letter to General Eduard Totleben, his former fellow student at the Engineering College, who had distinguished himself in the defense of Sebastopol and had become a very popular and influential figure. Dostoevsky rightly felt that Totleben might be very useful to him in pleading his cause before the Petersburg authorities and, indeed, before the new Tsar, Alexander II, who had just ascended the throne and was known to be in favor of progressive reforms, including the liberation of the serfs.

Dostoevsky began his letter to Totleben by reminding him of their old acquaintanceship and by admitting that he had been guilty "of the intention (no more) of acting against the government. . . . Long experience," he went on, "hard and agonizing, has sobered me and changed my views on many things. But *then*—then I was blind and believed in theories and utopias." He further pointed out that the army had never been his vocation and that what he wanted most was to obtain permission to publish his works. "The vocation of a writer," he concluded, "has always seemed to me a most honorable and most useful one. I am convinced that it is only as a writer that I could be truly useful, and could once more acquire a good name for myself."

Wrangel carried out his mission and reported back to Dostoevsky that both General Totleben and his brother, Adolf, were taking the warmest interest in his affairs. The news from Kuznetsk, however, was not so good. There was, as Dostoevsky told Wrangel in a long letter on March 23, 1856, "an ominous piece of news." Maria, it seems, had at last made up her mind to be "frank," but instead of telling him the truth, she posed a hypothetical question: What if a middle-aged man of excellent character, a civil servant with a good job, made her an offer of marriage—what should she tell him? She was alone with a child far away from anybody, and her father, who supported her, was old and likely to die.

She had, in fact, fallen in love with a young, impecunious teacher, and her hypothetical question was merely her way of making a final break possible without hurting Dostoevsky too much. But the mere possibility of such a marriage of convenience for a woman he loved and for whom he was ready to sacrifice his life threw him into greater despair than ever. "I was struck insensible," he wrote to Wrangel. "I swayed, fainted and wept all night long. Great are the joys of love, but its sufferings are so terrible that it would have been better not to have loved at all." He felt even more deeply the situation in which his poor Maria supposedly found herself, for it reminded him of the terrible position in which he had placed his own heroine in *Poor People*. "She is," he told Wrangel, "in the position of my own heroine in *Poor People*, who marries Bykov." And he added characteristically: "I brought it upon myself!"

It never occurred to him that Maria had invented the story of her middle-aged suitor because she had read *Poor People* and thought that, faced with a situation that was so familiar to him, he would be more liable to acquiesce in it. But if she did think that, his letter must have disabused her. "I wrote her that very evening," Dostoevsky told Wrangel, "a terrible letter full of despair. My dear angel! She is so sick and I tore her to pieces. I said that I should die if I lost her. There were threats, endearments, humble supplications. . . ." But the fact remained that she could not possibly marry a common soldier. What, then, were his prospects? Believing that she loved him ("*Mais elle m'aime! Elle m'aime!* I know that!" he keeps repeating in his letter to Wrangel in a kind of desperation, which perhaps reveals more than anything else the nagging doubt at the back of his mind), he naturally concluded that if his affairs took a turn for the better, she would prefer him to anyone else.

"Let me tell you," he writes in the same letter, "what we in our language (she and I) regard as my future career: transfer from the army to the civil service, a civil-service job with some sort of a salary, a rank in the service (even the lowest, the fourteenth) in the near future or some kind of possibility of obtaining money that would last us at least till my affairs are finally settled. These are my hopes: what I need most *urgently* to keep her suitors away and still appear as an honorable man to her is: (1) to obtain some kind of favor at the conclusion of peace or at the coronation, (2) a transfer from the army to the civil service, if nothing else comes as a result of the manifesto, (3) an officer's rank or a rank in the civil service. I don't believe that my career is at an end. I believe that in two years' time, even if nothing happens now, I shall be able to go back to Russia. The most important thing is money. I have two things ready for publication, an article and a novel. I want to apply for permission to publish. If I get it, then I am provided for for the rest of my life. Now it's different from what it used to be. I have many things carefully thought out and carefully written and such a strong will for writing. I hope to write a novel by the beginning of September which will be much better than *Poor People*. You see, if I am allowed to publish (and I do not believe, do you hear, I do not believe that it will be impossible to obtain such permission) it will create a sensation, the book will be sold out, it will bring me in money and earn me a reputation and the government's attention and then my return to Russia, too, will be accelerated. After all, what I want is two or three thousand rubles a year. This ought to be sufficient to keep us going here. In two years' time, we shall return to Russia, she will live well and, who knows, perhaps we shall make a fortune. Do you really think that, having shown so much courage and energy during the last six years in fighting against unheard-of sufferings, I will not be capable of earning enough money to keep myself and my wife? Nonsense!" And as though feeling that he was once more indulging in fantastic dreams which would convince neither Wrangel nor Maria, he added quite soberly: "You see, the main point is that no one has any idea of my powers or of the degree of my talent, and that is the main thing I pin my hopes on." However, if the worst came to the worst, there was still Kumanin, his rich uncle in Moscow, who would lend him a thousand rubles to restart his career with, and they could live on that for a year, "after which," he added inconsequentially, "my affairs will be settled." For the time being, though, "*la dame* (*la mienne*)," he wrote to Wrangel, "is depressed, in despair, ill, has no faith in my prospects, in our future. . . ." He had asked her, "since she could not possibly marry anyone before the end of the period of mourning, before September, to wait and give no definite answer to anyone." In the meantime he implored Wrangel to write to her to confirm that the golden prospects Dostoevsky had written to her about were no idle invention of a lovesick man. "Save me from despair," he concluded his letter to Wrangel. "You more than anyone else can understand me."

From Mikhail, who had raised objections to his marriage, he was not going to stand any nonsense. "This attachment, this feeling for her, is everything in the world to me now!" he wrote on March 24, 1856. "I live, breathe only with her and for her." And to make quite sure that his brother made no further objections to his proposed marriage, he went so far as to tell him that he and Maria "exchanged vows and promises" and that "she gave me her word that she would be my wife. I shall die of despair if I lose her," he went on, without explaining why, if she had really given him her word to be his wife, he should lose her. "I want to devote all my life to making her happy. This woman is worth it." And he concludes by inadvertently revealing what was certainly the trump card which eventually made Maria agree to marry him: "When she promised to be my wife, I promised her that I would ask my relations to see that her son is placed in a good school."

A month later the situation was still as desperate as ever. It is true that Maria did not any longer pretend that she was contemplating marriage to a middle-aged civil servant (she had concocted the story, Dostoevsky informed Wrangel rather guilelessly, because he had told her that he had danced at a Shrovetide party and she was beginning to imagine he was running after other women). But, realizing "how deeply" he was in love with her, she now refused to meet him altogether. "The trouble is," he wrote to Wrangel,[5] "that in all her last letters, in which there are still expressions of tenderness, attachments and even something more, she

[5] *Letters*, April 13, 1856.

hints that she will never make me happy and, since both of us are so unhappy, it would be best for us to part." He had, therefore, made up his mind to go and see her himself "and decide everything once and for all." He went to Kuznetsk at the beginning of June, and it was only there that he learned the dreadful truth.

What happened is best described in Dostoevsky's own words. "I was there, I saw her," he wrote to Wrangel.[6] "How it all happened I do not understand even now. I had a permit to go to Barnaul, but I took the risk and went to Kuznetsk. . . . I saw her! What a noble, what an angelic soul! She wept, she kissed my hand, but she loves another! I spent two days there. In those two days she remembered our past and her heart again turned to me. Whether I am right or wrong in saying this I don't know. But she said to me: 'Don't weep, don't be sad. Everything is not decided yet. You and I and no one else.' Those were her very words. I spent two days with her and it was both bliss and unbearable torment. At the end of the second day I left full of hope, but it is quite likely that it is the absent ones who are to blame. So it happened. One letter after another and I can see again that she is miserable. She weeps, but again she loves him more than me. I am done for, and she too. You can't imagine what she's doing and what she has made up her mind to carry out—she, with her quite extraordinary and remarkable common sense. She's twenty-nine; she's educated, clever, she has seen the world, she knows people, she has suffered, her last years in Siberia have made her ill, she is seeking happiness, she has a mind of her own, she has a strong will and—she is determined to marry *now* a youth of twenty-four, a native of Siberia, a man who has had no experience of life, who knows nothing, who has had no proper education, who is only just on the threshold of life, while she is perhaps about to take her last step in life. A man of no importance and without anything in the world, a teacher in a district school who hopes (very soon) to get a salary of 900 rubles a year. What is going to happen to her, living in poverty with a lot of children and condemned to stay in Kuznetsk all her life? Who knows how far their quarrels, which I foresee are inevitable in future, will lead them? For however idealistic a youth may be, he is far from being a man on whose steadfastness one could rely. And, as a matter of fact, far from being idealistic he . . . Anything may happen afterwards. What if he should insult her with some mean reproach when . . . What if it was only his youth that attracted her, that what she wanted was merely sexual satisfaction . . . I should not be surprised if she—pure, beautiful angel that she is—would have to listen to all this from him! . . . I care more for her happiness than mine. I discussed it all with her, that is, not all, for I could not say it all, but some of it. She listened and was impressed. But with women feeling takes precedence

[6] *Letters,* July 14, 1856.

even over the obvious dictates of common sense. All my arguments failed because she thought that I was attacking him, that I was trying to blacken his character (I didn't really mind her thinking that), but when I tried to defend him and said that I did not think he could be as bad as that, I did not convince her and left her still doubting my motives: she wept and was unhappy. . . . She is a knight in woman's clothes, she has a knightly heart: she will ruin herself. She does not know herself, but I do know her. She defied me to write to *him* about everything, about what I thought of it all, and I have decided to do so; for at our parting she again turned to me with all her heart. I made friends with him: he wept at my place, but all he knows is how to weep. I realized my false position; for were I to begin to dissuade them, to show them what their future will be like, they would tell me that I was only exerting myself on my own behalf and that I was deliberately inventing all sorts of future horrors. Besides, he is with her and I am far away. And so it was. I wrote a joint letter to both of them. I let them see what might be the consequences of a marriage of two ill-matched people, but I am afraid that what happened to me was what happened to Gil Blas and the Archbishop of Granada when Gil Blas told him the truth. She replied by defending him warmly, just as though I had been attacking him. And he, truly like a native of Kuznetsk and *stupidly*, took it all as a personal attack and an insult—I mean, my friendly appeal to him that he should think what he was trying to do, whether he was not going to ruin a woman for his own happiness; for he is 24 and she 29, he has no money or any prospects for the future, and they would have to live in a hole like Kuznetsk all their lives. Just imagine, he actually took offense at that! Moreover, he got her up in arms against me by turning an idea of mine inside out and persuading her that it was insulting to her. He abused me in his answer to my letter. He has a wicked heart, I can't help thinking. But after her first outbursts, she is quite ready to make it up, she writes to me herself, she is tender again, she is affectionate again. . . . What will be the end of it I don't know, but she will ruin herself and my heart sinks at the thought of it. Her happiness is dearer to me than my own. I am walking about like a madman in the fullest meaning of the word. We have had a military parade and I am bodily and mentally exhausted and walking about like a shadow. . . . My heart will never recover from this blow. . . . I don't know what will be the end of it. . . . I feel like tearing my heart out and burying it and with it everything else. Please write to her. She must not suffer. If she does marry him, she must at least be provided for, and for that he has to get some post. He must be transferred to some other place. Now he's getting only 400 rubles and intends to sit for an examination in order to get a higher post as teacher in Kuznetsk. Then he will have 900 rubles. I don't know yet what can be done for him, but I'll write to you about it. Try to have a talk with General Hasford about him (as a young man of excellent abilities). Praise him up to the skies. Tell the General that you knew him personally and that it would not be a bad idea to give him a higher post. His name is Nikolai Vergunov. He is a native of Tomsk. I am doing it all for her, for her alone. At least she should not live in poverty—that's all I am concerned about."

A week later he wrote to Wrangel again to remind him to speak to General Hasford about Vergunov. It was clear that he had given up all hope of marriage and was genuinely concerned about Maria's future. He was still hopelessly in love with her. "If only," he exclaims in the same letter, "I could see her again, even for only one hour. And though nothing would have come of it, I should at least have seen her!"

In the meantime he had written two more loyal poems: *On the Conclusion of Peace* and *The Dread War Is Over*. The first was sent to General Hasford by the military governor of the Semipalatinsk region on May 19, 1856, and Hasford himself tried to obtain permission for the second to be published in the Petersburg press. At last Dostoevsky's patriotic verses and Wrangel's yeoman service on his behalf in Petersburg official circles bore fruit: on October 1, 1856, he was promoted to second lieutenant in his old battalion, a promotion that meant that his civic rights had been restored and that he was again a nobleman.

Wrangel was anxious to learn whether his promotion had made any change in his relations with Maria, but Dostoevsky wrote to him[7] that their relationship was still the same. "Every week I receive letters from her, letters full of the most sincere protestations of her attachment. But in her letters she often calls me her brother." However, it seemed that her marriage "to the other one" was out of the question, for poor Vergunov's salary was not 400, but only 300, rubles a year, and she herself had to live on the money her father sent her. As for himself, she was still everything in his life. "My promotion to the rank of officer has pleased me just because it may make it possible for me to see her as soon as possible. I have no money and I haven't been to see her yet. My brother has promised to send me some and I am expecting to get it next week, and then I'll go at once. My commanding officer has promised to let me go. Worrying about her would have literally killed me or driven me to suicide. Don't shake your head, don't condemn me. I know that what I am doing is not sensible, since I have practically no hope. But whether I have any hope or not makes no difference to me. I am not thinking of anything any more. All I want is to see her, to hear her talk. I am an unhappy madman. Such love is a disease. I am aware of it. . . ."

He assured Mikhail in a letter he wrote to him on the same day that he was not supporting Maria. "She's not that sort of woman," he wrote. "She would rather live on a few pennies than accept any money from me. She's an angel whom I met on my way and to whom I am bound

[7] *Letters*, November 9, 1856.

by suffering. Without her I would have lost courage long ago. What will be will be. You are very upset about the likelihood of my marriage to her. My dear fellow, I don't think it is very likely to happen, though she does love me. But what will be will be."

Within seven weeks, however, the situation changed completely. What happened during this short period is difficult to say. In his letter to Wrangel at the end of December, Dostoevsky merely says that his Maria became "quickly" disappointed in her "new attachment." By that time the "attachment" was not particularly "new," nor was Maria's disappointment particularly "quick." However, when Dostoevsky again appeared in Kuznetsk, on Christmas Day, exactly seven years after his departure in chains and under a convoy to Siberia, "she herself," he wrote to Wrangel, "said 'yes' to me." They were going to be married before Shrovetide, "if a certain circumstance does not prevent it. But this," he added mysteriously, "has nothing to do with my marriage and," he underlined, "*I do not think it will happen*, and if it does not happen, then by the time you get my next letter, it will be all finished." At the moment, he had not a penny and he had to raise at least 600 rubles to defray the cost of the wedding (which he raised eventually by borrowing the money from a Semipalatinsk acquaintance). What the "certain circumstance" was, none of Dostoevsky's biographers has succeeded in uncovering. It may have had something to do with Maria's discarded lover (according to Dostoevsky's daughter, Maria never really discarded him, but that is mere malice). In the letter to Wrangel announcing his engagement he begs the baron "on my bended knees" to do something for Vergunov. "He is dearer to me than a brother now," he writes. "It will take too long to tell you about my relations with him. His only hope to improve his position is for him to sit for an examination in Tomsk to obtain a civil-service rank and a post for one thousand rubles a year, which he will get if he passes his exam." He therefore implored Wrangel to ask any of his relations at the Ministry of Education "to influence" the decision of the principal of the Tomsk secondary school in Vergunov's favor. "For Vergunov," Dostoevsky assures Wrangel, "it is not sinful to ask. He deserves it." Why? Because Vergunov agreed to give up Maria if he got a good job? Was that the "certain circumstance"?

There was one circumstance, however, that Dostoevsky unfortunately did not take into account before rushing into marriage: his epilepsy. According to Wrangel, his epileptic seizures began three months after his arrival in Semipalatinsk. "I was never present when Dostoevsky had his epileptic fits," Wrangel records. "But he had them very often and usually his landlady let me know. After a fit he would feel jaded, dispirited, unable to collect his thoughts. He always felt the approach of an attack and he used to say to me that before its onset his whole body was seized with an inexpressible feeling of voluptuousness, but after it he looked helpless and pitiful."

As late as November 9, 1856, he wrote to Wrangel that one of the reasons why he was anxious to return to Russia was "to consult specialists about the nature of my illness (epilepsy) and of the attacks which are still recurring and after which my memory and all my faculties seem to go numb. These attacks make me fear that I may go insane." To Mikhail he wrote on the same day: "I was rather ill in the autumn. My attacks do not cease. They recur again and again and every time after an attack I lose courage and feel that my memory and my faculties have gone. Depression and a kind of morally humiliating condition—that is the result of my attacks."

Maria no doubt knew something of his "nervous attacks," but she certainly did not associate them with epilepsy; nor did Dostoevsky disabuse her on that score. Was it because he feared the disclosure of his illness that he wrote to Mikhail,[8] after announcing that his decision to marry Isaev's widow was "irrevocable": "All possible arguments, even the most reasonable ones," he declared, "will be like the famous cry: *mais qu'allait-il faire dans cette galère?* I quite agree that it was stupid of the son of Orontes to find himself on a galley as a prisoner of the Turks. I am ready to agree with every argument, but say what you like, be sorry for me as much as you like, I shall still be *dans cette galère*. I got there, and whatever you may say, it is an undeniable fact." A galley is certainly a strange place for the consummation of one's happiness.

To his sister Varvara, the widow of his former "enemy" Karepin, who had died in 1850, he gave another rather curious reason for his marriage. "Please tell Uncle," he wrote,[9] "that my marriage is not an absurdity. I am still under police supervision and I shall always be under police supervision, for the government will never trust me. Now, a married man who has changed his ideas and settled down will be believed more than a man who is free. The government is sure to take into account the fact that a married man will not wish to sacrifice the future of his family and will not be carried away by pernicious ideas."

There Dostoevsky, who by now should have known everything about the police, was wrong: even when his loyalty to the government was no longer in question, even when he became the bosom friend of the most reactionary men in Russia and had been considered "safe" to act as a sort of semitutor to two royal princes, the police continued to keep private correspondence.

III

On January 25, 1857, Dostoevsky got his loan of 600 rubles, and two days later he left for Kuznetsk. Curiously enough, he was still uncertain whether Maria would marry him after all. He had to act "decisively,"

8 *Letters*, December 22, 1856.
9 *Letters*, December 22, 1856.

he wrote to Wrangel on January 25, for he could not put off the wedding till after Easter "because of certain circumstances" (Vergunov landing his job after all and Maria going back on *her* word to marry Dostoevsky?). "Somehow," he continued cautiously, "I hope it will come off. In all the decisive moments of my life I have been lucky. . . . You say that I am too lazy to carry on with my writing; no, my friend, I am not, but my relationship with Maria Dmitriyevna has taken up all my time during the last two years. At least I have *lived.* I may have suffered, but I have lived."

He need not have worried: in Kuznetsk no more objections were raised, and everything there was ready for a quiet wedding, which took place on February 6, 1857. It was on his return to Barnaul, where he and his bride stopped for the night—their wedding night—on the way back to Semipalatinsk, that the blow fell that disrupted their married life even before it had begun. "In Barnaul," he wrote to Wrangel on March 9, 1857, two and a half weeks after his return to Semipalatinsk, "I had an epileptic fit and I had to stay there another four days. (My fit crushed me both bodily and mentally: the doctor told me that I am suffering from real epilepsy and warned me that if I did not take immediate steps, that is to say the prescribed treatment, which I can only get when I am completely free, my fits may take a turn for the worse, and in one of them I may suffocate from a spasm of the throat, which almost always happens with me during an attack.)"

His epileptic seizure, he wrote to Mikhail on the same day, "frightened my wife to death." To realize how great a shock his unsuspecting bride had got, one has only to recall Dostoevsky's own description of such an attack and, what is perhaps even more to the point, his second wife's account of first witnessing one. Dostoevsky described his epileptic fits in *The Idiot.* "It is a well-known fact," he wrote, "that epileptic fits, the *epilepsy* itself, comes on instantaneously. At that instant the face suddenly becomes horribly distorted, especially the eyes. Spasms and convulsions seize the whole body. A quite incredible, bloodcurdling scream breaks from the chest; in that scream everything human seems to be suddenly obliterated, and it is quite impossible, at least very difficult, for an observer to imagine and to admit that it is the man himself who is screaming. One gets the impression that it is someone inside the man who is screaming. This, at any rate, is how many people describe their impression; the sight of a man in an epileptic fit fills many others with absolute and unbearable horror, which has something mystical about it."

Anna, Dostoevsky's second wife, who when she married him was twelve years younger than Maria, who did not go through any emotional crisis before marrying him and who knew that he was an epileptic, left a very careful description in her reminiscences of the first of his epileptic fits that she witnessed. It happened shortly after their marriage, at a dinner party given by her sister. "Dostoevsky," she writes, "was very animated and was telling something very interesting to my sister. Suddenly he interrupted his speech in the middle of the sentence, went pale, raised himself from the sofa and began leaning towards me. I looked with astonishment at his changed face. But suddenly there came from him a terrible, inhuman scream, or rather, a wail, and he began falling forward. At the same time came a loud scream from my sister, who was sitting beside my husband. She sprang from her chair and rushed out of the room, sobbing hysterically. My brother-in-law ran out after her. Many times later I heard this 'inhuman' scream which seems to be common with epileptics at the beginning of a seizure, and this scream always terrified and shocked me. But at that time, to my surprise, I was not frightened, though it was the first time in my life that I had seen an epileptic attack. I seized my husband by his shoulders and forced him to sit down on the sofa; but picture my horror when I saw the unconscious body of my husband slipping down the sofa and felt that I was not strong enough to stop it! Pushing away the table with a lighted lamp, I let my husband sink to the floor. I myself, too, sank down and kept his head on my knees all through his convulsions. There was no one to help me: my sister was in hysterics, and my brother-in-law and the maid were bustling around her. Gradually the convulsions ceased and my husband began to regain consciousness. But at first he did not seem to realize where he was and he even lost the power of speech: he wanted to say something, but instead of one word he uttered another and it was impossible to understand him. It was perhaps after half an hour that we were able to raise my husband from the floor and put him on the sofa. We decided to give him time to calm down before taking him home, but to my extreme grief the fit recurred an hour after the first and this time with such force that, after regaining consciousness, my husband screamed with pain for over two hours—that was something terrible."

What Maria's feelings were at the sight of the writhing, unconscious body of her newly wed husband can be easily imagined. She must have been more than terrified; she must have been appalled at what she had let herself in for. Anna had married Dostoevsky at a time when he was a famous writer; indeed, she married him *because* he was a famous writer. When Maria married Dostoevsky he was practically unknown and she had never had any great opinion of him as a writer; she had married him chiefly for the sake of her son, whom he had promised her to care for, and she sacrificed her own love as a result (whether Vergunov would have been a satisfactory husband for her is beside the point, since, as it turned out, Dostoevsky was most certainly not). She was, Dostoevsky wrote in his letter to Mikhail on March 9, 1857, "a little quick-tempered, greatly impressionable, and her past life had left scars on her soul." He had added another "scar on her soul" on their wedding night, a scar that must have made any intimacy between them a terrifying experience to her.

Indeed, their marriage was doomed from the very start, a fact that Dostoevsky had soon to admit to himself. She was not only "a little" quick-tempered, but also sharp-tongued, and, like Mrs. Marmeladov in *Crime and Punishment*, given to expressing her disappointments in loud lamentations. It was not long before she began calling him "jailbird." Contemplating his shattered married life as early as the end of 1857, Dostoevsky wrote to Maria's sister: "You know I have a premonition that I shall soon die. Such premonitions, nearly always, are the result of anxiety over one's health, but I assure you that it is not so in this particular instance. And my certainty of imminent death is completely calm. I can't help feeling that I have already experienced everything in life and that there is nothing more to live for." A year later, on December 13, 1858, he confessed to Mikhail: "My life is hard and bitter. I am not writing a single word about it to you now."

And a year after his first wife's death, he summed up his married life with her in one sentence (in a letter to Wrangel on March 31, 1865): "I was positively unhappy with her."

IV

The first thing Dostoevsky had done on leaving prison was to fill the gaps in his reading. "I began to read all the literature that had been written while I was in prison for five years," he recalled in 1877 (in the November issue of his *Writer's Diary*). "*A Sportsman's Sketches*, which had just begun to appear before my arrest, and Turgenev's first short stories I remember reading at one go, at a gulp. I was in raptures over it all. It is true, the steppe sun was shining over me just then, it was early spring and with it a new life dawned for me, prison was behind me, freedom!"

But even in Semipalatinsk, as he wrote to Apollon Maykov on January 18, 1856, there were not enough books for him. The books he had asked his brother to send never reached him because the acquaintance to whom Mikhail had addressed them was afraid to acknowledge that he knew a political ex-convict and refused to accept them. "During the current year," he told Maykov, "I have read practically nothing. But let me tell you my impressions. I like Turgenev most of all—the pity is that, possessing so enormous a talent, there is not enough firmness in him. L.T. [Leo Tolstoy] I like very much, but in my opinion he won't write a great deal (however, I may be mistaken). About Ostrovsky I don't know at all. He may know a certain class of the Russian population very well, but I can't help feeling that he is *a poet without an ideal.* Disabuse me, please, and send me some of his best work, so that I may know him not only by the reviews. Pisemsky I like very much. He is clever, good-natured and even naïve. But one thing about him I cannot help deploring: he is too much in a hurry. He writes too quickly and too much. One must have more self-esteem, more respect for one's own talent and for art, more love of art. When you are young, ideas swarm in your head, but it isn't every one of them that you should seize in a hurry, or be in a hurry to express your view about. It is much better to wait for a greater synthesis; to think more, to wait till a great deal that is petty and expresses only one idea is gathered into one large, solid, distinct image, and then give expression to it. The colossal characters created by colossal writers were often created and developed over a long period and with great persistence. After all, a writer need not give expression to all his intermediate experiments and sketches. As for our lady novelists, they write like lady novelists, that is to say, cleverly, charmingly, but they are in too much of a hurry to tell you what they think. Why is it that a lady novelist is hardly ever a true artist? Even such an incontestable and great artist as George Sand has many a time done great harm to herself by her feminine qualities. . . . I am sorry for the incoherence of my letter. That's why I can't stand Madame de Sévigné. Her letters are a little too well written."

He enlarged on his reluctance to write for money and in a hurry (a thing he hated but was never able to avoid) in his first letter to the editor of *The Russian Herald*, Mikhail Katkov, on January 11, 1858, "Working for money and working for art are for me incompatible," he declared. "During the three years of my literary work in Petersburg, I suffered a great deal because of it. I was loath to prostitute my best ideas and the best plots of my stories and novels by working in a hurry and by having to finish it by a certain date. I loved my characters too much and was anxious to create them without haste, to create them with love. I'd rather have died than dishonor them. But, being constantly in debt to Kraevsky (who, though, never forced me to deliver my work by a specified time) I was tied hand and foot myself. For instance, knowing that he had nothing for the next number of his periodical, I sometimes forced myself to think out the plot of some story on the 26th of the month, that is, four days before publication, and very often wrote it in four days. The result was sometimes very bad, sometimes not so bad, judging at least by the reviews which appeared in other journals. Of course, I often had several months to prepare something better, but the trouble was that I never knew myself how many months I could count on to finish a certain work. As a consequence, I always set myself a time limit of no more than one month, for I knew that I would have to come to Kraevsky's rescue in time for his next month's issue. But one month passed, five months passed, and I merely tormented myself by trying to think of a better plot for a story, for I did not want to publish anything that was bad, apart from the fact that it would have been dishonest of me to do so. At the time I was a victim of hypochondria, from which I at times suffered badly. It was only the fact that I was young that saved me from wearing myself out completely and losing my enthusiasm and love for literature."

He was writing his first novel after his release from prison at the time, a novel which, he told Mikhail (as he had so often claimed about any work he happened to have written), was *the best thing* he had ever written, and he was anxious not to repeat the mistakes he had made before when working for Kraevsky; for this novel had to re-establish his literary name and consolidate his reputation as one of Russia's foremost writers. That was the main reason why he was so anxious to make his theories about the process of fiction writing clear not only to his correspondents, but perhaps even more to himself. He challenged Mikhail's idea that a work of art ought to be created all at once. "Where did you get such a notion?" he wrote to him on May 31, 1858. "Believe me, everywhere hard work is necessary. I assure you that a light and elegant poem of a few lines by Pushkin appears to have been written at one go simply because Pushkin worked over it for so long. He most probably had to rewrite it several times. These are facts. It took Gogol eight years to write *Dead Souls*. Everything written at one go is immature. Shakespeare, they say, never blotted his manuscripts. That is why there are so many monstrosities and so much bad taste in his plays, whereas had he worked longer at them they would have been much better. You seem to be unable to distinguish between inspiration, that is to say, the first and instantaneous creation of an image, and the process that goes on in one's mind while working on it (as always happens). For instance, I write down a scene at once just as it occurs to me for the first time and I am glad to do so, but afterwards I keep working at it for months and get inspired by it not once but several times (because I love the scene), adding several times to it or taking something away from it. This used often to happen to me and believe me, the result was much better. Of course, one has to have inspiration. Without inspiration there can be nothing."

These theories were all very well, but the problem that faced Dostoevsky immediately on his return to Semipalatinsk after his wedding was how to carry them out, or, in other words, how to stage his literary comeback with a successful novel when he had not enough means to keep himself, his wife and his stepson while writing his masterpiece. "My situation is critical," he told Mikhail on March 1, 1858. He wrote to Katkov, giving him a general idea of the novel he had in mind and asking him for an advance of 500 rubles. To his surprise, Katkov sent him the money. But it was barely enough to pay his debts. A month or two later (on July 19, 1858) he again wrote to Mikhail: "I have no money. All that I have left is literally a few rubles. I have no one to borrow from because the people I used to borrow from are no longer here. . . ." On May 9, 1859, he ruefully confessed that he had not enough money to live on for the eighteen months he needed to write "a long novel" for another publisher. There was, furthermore, the question of the amount of money a publisher of a periodical could be expected to pay him for a printed folio page. "You keep writing to me," he declared in the same letter to Mikhail "that Goncharov, for instance, got seven thousand rubles for his novel and that Katkov paid Turgenev four hundred rubles for a folio page[10] of his *Nobleman's Nest* (I have read it at last; it is very good). And I am only asking a hundred rubles for a page. My friend, I know very well that I write worse than Turgenev, but not so much worse, and after all, I hope to write something which will not be at all worse. Why then do I, who am in such straitened circumstances, receive only a hundred rubles, while Turgenev, who owns two thousand serfs, gets four hundred? It is my poverty that forces me to be in a hurry and write for money, which means spoiling my work for certain."

The reason Turgenev got four times as much for a folio page (Dostoevsky realized it very well) was not because he wrote so much better than Dostoevsky, but because he was the most talked-of writer of the day, while after his ten years of absence from the literary scene hardly anyone remembered Dostoevsky's name. Writing to Annenkov as early as January 10, 1853, Turgenev refers to Dostoevsky as "the semideceased." During his imprisonment the censorship saw to it that Dostoevsky's name did not appear anywhere in print. The first difficulty Dostoevsky had therefore to surmount was the right for his name to appear. His patriotic poems were written in the sycophantic style he considered most likely to make the biggest impression on the persons nearest the throne, since it was with the monarch that the final decision lay. But apart from the adulatory, ingratiating tone, which seems to be the customary mode of address in the rarefied atmosphere of royal courts, the sentiments expressed in the poems were not very different from those he quite genuinely held. In prison, he wrote to Maykov on January 18, 1856, he could not help rethinking a great many things, "perhaps," he added cautiously, "too many things," and he hoped Maykov would do him the justice of admitting that he never acted against his conscience and that whatever beliefs he held, he always gave himself up to them entirely. "Do not think," he went on, "that I am hinting at the events that have brought me here. I am speaking about the things that came after them. . . . Ideas change, but the heart remains the same. . . . I am referring to patriotism, the Russian idea, the feeling of national duty and honor, everything you yourself write about with such enthusiasm. I always shared the same feelings and convictions as you. Russia, duty, honor?—yes! I have always been truly Russian. . . . I fully share your patriotic feelings about the *moral* liberation of the Slavs. This is the role of Russia, noble and great Russia, our sacred mother. . . . Yes, I quite agree with you that Russia is destined to put the finishing touch to Europe and her destiny. This has been clear to me for a long time. . . . You must agree

10 Sixteen printed pages or approximately 8,000 words.

that all right-thinking people, that is to say, all those who set the fashion in these things, have always regarded French ideas with scientific detachment, while they themselves always remained Russians. . . . I assure you that I, for instance, am so closely related to everything Russian that even the convicts did not frighten me—they too were Russians, my brothers in misfortune, and I have had the good luck to find a streak of generosity even in the heart of a brigand, because, being myself a Russian, I could understand him. My misfortune has taught me a great many practical things, but most of all I learned that I have always been a Russian at heart. . . ."

Dostoevsky would go a great deal further than that in his political evolution, but for the time being he merely reverted to some of the ideas he had imbided from Karamzin as a child. The Crimean defeat added a more emphatic note to his patriotic sentiments, and the *moral* liberation of the Slavs (whatever that might mean) was still a long way off from their actual "liberation" under the aegis of Russia, which he was to demand so vociferously during the last years of his life.

He had, indeed, written an article on Russia embodying these ideas, but, he wrote to Wrangel, it turned out to be a purely political pamphlet, and he did not think the authorities would allow him to resume his writing with the publication of a political pamphlet, however patriotic. He therefore decided to write an article on art instead and dedicate it to the dowager Empress, who was the president of the Russian Academy of Art and Sciences. "My article," he wrote in his letter to Wrangel, "is the fruit of ten years of thought. I thought it out very carefully while I was still in Omsk. There's going to be a great deal of original and exciting stuff in it. I vouch for its exposition. Perhaps many people will disagree with me about many things, but I believe in my ideas and that's enough for me. Some chapters dealing with the role of Christianity in art will contain whole pages from my pamphlet."[11]

The only trouble was that he was not sure whether any of the existing periodicals would accept an article by him. The left-wing *Contemporary* had been, he thought, hostile to him ever since his quarrel with the Belinsky circle, and although (he wrote to Mikhail on September 13, 1858) he felt no ill-will towards them, he could not forget that they had treated him spitefully and dishonorably; *Moskvityanin*, the organ of the conservative Moscow Slavophiles, would have nothing to do with him at that particular period, when he was still supposed to be tarred with the revolutionary brush; the conservative *Russian Herald* had published articles which contained ideas diametrically opposed to his; and *Home Annals* he did not care to approach because he still owed Kraevsky money advanced for *Netochka Nezvanova*, which he certainly did not intend to finish. It was different, of course, with a novel, but then what

[11] *Letters*, April 13, 1856.

he was after was permission to publish his works, and he could not help feeling that, unlike a "serious" article, a novel was still regarded with contempt by the people on whom the decision to allow him to publish his works depended.

As it turned out, it was his comic novel, *My Uncle's Dream*, that marked his return to literature. He began to write it as a comedy, he told Maykov in his letter of January 18, 1856, and many of the descriptive passages in the novel still retain their original form of stage directions. Wrangel records that at the time Dostoevsky was working at his comic novel he was "in an infectiously merry mood" and that he would roar with laughter as he recounted the adventures of the uncle to him. He sent the novel to *The Russian Word*, a new monthly periodical, at the beginning of 1859, and, as he wrote to Mikhail, was very eager to learn of the impression it would produce. "This," he wrote, "is very important to me. . . . I should also like to know whether or not the censorship has blue-penciled anything."

The novel, with its amusing descriptions of the goings-on in the "high" social circles in remote provincial towns such as Semipalatinsk, is certainly one of Dostoevsky's most high-spirited creations, but it was completely ignored by the literary critics, chiefly because it appeared at a time when everyone in Russia was too preoccupied with the impending great reforms introduced by Alexander II at the beginning of his reign. Dostoevsky himself became too preoccupied with the burning issues of the day to care much for it. In September 1873, when he was just beginning to fancy himself as a prophet, he refused to have anything to do with a proposal to adapt it for the stage. "Let me tell you this," he wrote to the dramatist who asked his permission to turn the novel into a play: "I dare not and I *cannot* set about revising the novel. I have not read it for the last fifteen years and, having reread it now, I found it rather bad. I wrote it in Siberia, soon after leaving prison, and my only reason for writing it was to re-enter literature. Besides, I was terribly afraid of the attitude of the censorship towards me, a former political exile."[12]

He was perfectly well aware that it was only as a novelist that, as he told Wrangel, he could "make a name" for himself and "make people take notice of him." While writing *My Uncle's Dream*, he was, therefore, working at *The Village of Stepanchikovo*, another novel for Katkov's *Russian Herald*, which he was convinced had great merits.

He had got the idea of the novel, he told Katkov,[13] during his "stay" in Omsk, and it was very dear to his heart, though, he was quick to add, he realized that that was no guarantee of its merit, "for it often happens that a writer's favorite work turns out to be one of his worst." Still, he assured Mikhail on April 11, 1859, he considered it much better than

[12] *Letters*, September 14, 1873.
[13] *Letters*, January 11, 1858.

My Uncle's Dream, because it had two "serious" characters in it which had never appeared in any novel before. "There is," he went on, "very little romantic stuff in the novel (that is, the passionate element, as in *A Nobleman's Nest,* for instance), but it has two enormous and typical characters which I have been creating and writing down for five years, and which, in my opinion, are perfectly realized, characters which are completely Russian and have so far been scarcely dealt with in Russian literature. I don't know whether Katkov will realize its value, but should the reading public receive my novel coldly, I may give way to despair. My best hopes and, above all, the consolidation of my literary name are all based on it. . . ."

If, therefore, *My Uncle's Dream* was merely a lighthearted literary romp in which his own opinions, such as his anti-Slavophile sentiments of that particular period, rarely come to the fore, *The Village of Stepanchikovo and Its Inhabitants* was a novel into which, as he told Mikhail in the same letter, he had put his "whole soul," his "flesh and blood," though he had not, of course, said everything he had to say in it. In view, however, of his anxiety to avoid anything that might awaken the suspicions of the authorities or in any way offend the vigilant eye of the censorship, he tried to conceal his "flesh and blood" under the cloak of a comic narrative.

The ideas which were so dear to him at the time and which he hoped would "consolidate" his literary reputation were, on the whole, the same as those which had so dramatically interrupted his literary career ten years earlier. Indicted for reading Belinsky's letter to Gogol, he now returned to the attack on Gogol's *Selected Passages* by making one of his characters, the sanctimonious hypocrite Foma Opiskin, repeat the most absurd views Gogol had expressed in them, which Belinsky had so vigorously attacked. Moreover, he made Opiskin adopt the same mixture of grandiloquent and coarse language used by Gogol in his ill-fated book, and reminded even Kraevsky, as Mikhail wrote to Dostoevsky, "of Gogol during the sad period of his life." Dostoevsky even got his own back on the Tsar himself, whose distaste for whiskers, as an expression of French "liberalism," he had tried to lampoon in *The Shaven Side Whiskers,* the tale he had intended to write for Belinsky's Almanach. "I know for a fact," the narrator of the novel declares, "that at the behest of Foma, my uncle had to shave off his lovely brown whiskers, for Foma thought that in his whiskers my uncle looked like a Frenchman and therefore had little love for his country. My uncle obeyed because he too believed that there was 'little patriotism' in whiskers."

The uncle, Colonel Rostanev, is Dostoevsky's first sketch of "the perfect man," who was ten years later to be given a much more satisfactory embodiment in Prince Myshkin, the hero of *The Idiot.* The colonel thinks that his aim in life should be to make all people "happy and contented," a formula beloved of the utopian socialists of Dostoevsky's revolutionary period. In his mouth Dostoevsky puts his own most cherished notion of how one should treat people to whom one does a favor. "One has to be doubly careful," the colonel says, "with a man who has had a run of bad luck. One has to be doubly considerate to a person one has done a favor to." Dostoevsky expressed the same thought in a letter to Wrangel. "A person one had done a favor to," he wrote, "must be treated with great care; he is suspicious, he can't help feeling that by treating him familiarly and in an offhand fashion, one wants to make him repay the favor done him. You know it as well as I do. If God has given us good sense and a sense of honor we cannot do otherwise." Incidentally, the contemptuous way in which Dostoevsky in this novel dismisses the famous holy lunatic Ivan Koreysha, religiously consulted by "grand ladies" at his Moscow lunatic asylum, and the reverence with which he treats him in the second chapter of the fifth book of *The Devils*, illustrates perhaps better than anything else to what strange conclusions his faith (so far only in its embryonic state) in the innate wisdom of the Russian common people would eventually lead him.

The novel fell between two stools: Katkov, for whom it was originally intended, refused to publish it because of its attacks on the conservative camp, to which he belonged, while Nekrasov, to whom Dostoevsky offered it next, would not have it because these attacks were no longer valid. Gogol's *Selected Passages* had been forgotten after Gogol's death in 1852, and even the materialist "utilitarian" Nikolai Chernyshevsky, who had taken Belinsky's place on *The Contemporary Review*, had in his articles *On the Gogol Period in Russian Literature*, published in 1856, treated it merely as an unimportant aberration of a man of genius. On the other hand, Dostoevsky's attempt to placate the censorship by providing an idyllic ending to the novel could not but arouse the antagonism of the revolutionary and liberal parties in Russia, especially on the eve of the liberation of the serfs. The novel, like *My Uncle's Dream*, was so completely ignored by the critics when it was eventually published, at the end of 1859 in Kraevsky's *Home Annals*, that Nekrasov, who in August 1858 had let Dostoevsky know that he was ready to publish anything by him, is said to have exclaimed: "Dostoevsky is finished!"

But Dostoevsky had not yet even begun.

V

On April 17, 1857, shortly after his return to Semipalatinsk, Dostoevsky had been officially notified of the restoration of his status as nobleman. He had still two more years to serve in Siberia, a service that was beginning to be more and more onerous to him with the regular recurrence of his epileptic attacks. His financial position was as bad as ever. His wife seemed to have as little practical sense as he, and the fact that nothing had come of the wonderful prospects he had held out to her must have given her plenty of material for her incessant nagging. One of Dostoevsky's pupils in Semipalatinsk (he was forced to give private lessons to supplement their meager income) records that during her lessons in winter her teacher used to cough badly and cover up his threadbare clothes with his greatcoat. Luckily, he succeeded in obtaining a free place for his ten-year-old stepson, Pasha, in the Siberian Cadet Corps in Omsk. "Although I find it hard," he wrote on July 29, 1857, to the second master of the Cadet Corps, Ivan Zhdan-Pushkin, at whose house he and Durov had stayed for a short time after their release from prison, "to send away a little boy of his age whom I have vowed to take care of out of respect for the memory of his father, I cannot possibly refuse to take advantage of such an opportunity, particularly as the corps commander has made an exception for him by admitting him while still underage." Dostoevsky was quite sincere about Pasha. He got attached to the boy, who was certainly bright enough to grasp his stepfather's weak points as well as his mother's contempt for him.

In August 1857 *A Little Hero,* which Dostoevsky had written while in solitary confinement in the Peter and Paul Fortress, was published anonymously in *Home Annals.* It was the first thing of his to appear in print for eight years. In September 1857, he wrote to his sister Varvara Karepin: "I am not through with my illness yet. On the contrary, my fits occur much more frequently now. In April I had three seizures while on duty and three or four more while asleep. After them I always feel weak and depressed." In December 1857 he obtained a certificate from his battalion doctor to the effect that, owing to chronic epilepsy, he was unable to carry out his regimental duties. "Mr. Dostoevsky," the certificate states, "is thirty-five years old, of indifferent physique, had his first attack of epilepsy in 1850, which manifested itself in a scream, loss of consciousness, convulsions of limbs and face, foaming at the mouth, stertorous breathing and a racing and weak pulse. The fit lasted fifteen minutes. It was followed by general weakness and a return of consciousness. In 1854 the attacks recurred and since then one occurs at the end of every month. At present Mr. Dostoevsky suffers from general weakness, emaciation, and very often from facial neuralgia as a result of an organic ailment of the brain. Although Mr. Dostoevsky has received regular treatment for epilepsy during the last four years, there is no improvement in his condition and for that reason he cannot continue in his Majesty's service."

A month later, on January 16, 1858, Dostoevsky sent in his resignation from the army. His epileptic fits were also interfering seriously with his work. In July he wrote to Mikhail that he was not having any treatment for his illness, for he was afraid that the local doctors might "bungle things." He wanted to consult the best Moscow doctors and only then make up his mind what to do. In September 1858 he wrote to Mikhail: "My illness is not getting better, but is growing worse. Last month I had four seizures, which has never happened before—and I did practically no work. . . . But I have to pay my debts. I'm afraid," he concluded only too prophetically, "I shall have to write for money all my life." A month later he wrote to a friend: "I am sick and tired of my life in Semipalatinsk—even my literary work has become a torment to me."

In December 1858 he at last received permission to return to Russia, but was not allowed to live either in Moscow or in Petersburg. He chose to live in Tver (present-day Kalinin) because it was near Moscow, where he still hoped to be able to consult specialists. On March 18, 1859, he was officially notified that his resignation from the army had been accepted. Six days later the Ministry of War sent secret instructions to the Ministry of the Interior to place Dostoevsky under constant police surveillance. In April Dostoevsky received the order releasing him from army service and a month later he applied to the principal of the Omsk Cadet Corps for permission to take away his stepson, who had not been much of a success at the school. In June Dostoevsky wrote to Mikhail from Semipalatinsk: "I am leaving here with a heavy heart and with practically no money. The expenses of the journey have crushed me. The thousand rubles I received from the editor of *Russian Word* have melted away like wax. Please, send me 200 rubles in Kazan. . . ."

Dostoevsky and his wife left Semipalatinsk on July 2, 1859, in a tarantas he had bought specially for the journey. "I shall never forget our last day in Semipalatinsk," Dostoevsky wrote to his former company commander from Tver on October 23, 1859, "when, incidentally, I clinked glasses with everyone. . . . At last we arrived in Omsk, the weather was glorious and the road excellent. In Omsk we stayed three or four days. We took Pasha from the cadet corps and I paid a visit to some of my old friends and superiors. . . . Omsk, I am sorry to say, I did not like at all. It brought back many sad memories to me. When we left Omsk I really took leave of Siberia. The road was very bad, but Tyumen is an excellent town. We spent two days there. During the first half of the journey I had two epileptic fits, but since then I have had no more. Our coachman Nikolayev, an excellent fellow, though a bit of a boaster, cried like a child when he took leave of us. . . . The weather was very pleasant and our open carriage did not break down once. There was no delay in getting fresh horses, but the prices at the posting stations were terribly high. The wonderful forests in the Perm and Vyatka provinces were the height of perfection. We spent a whole day in Yekaterinburg and I'm afraid we were tempted there: we spent forty rubles and bought all sorts of articles, including thirty-eight different minerals, cuff links, buttons and so on. We bought them for presents and, truth to tell, they were very cheap. . . . One beautiful afternoon at about five o'clock, wandering through the foothills of the Ural mountains in the middle of a forest, we at last came across the border between Europe and Asia. There was an excellent column with an inscription to mark the spot. An old retired soldier was guarding it. We got out of the carriage and, making the sign of the cross, I thanked God for making it possible for me to see the promised land at last. Then we took out our rush-covered flasks filled with bitter orange liqueur and drank a farewell toast to Asia. Nikolayev, too, had a drink with the old soldier and our new coachman. We had a chat and then went for a walk in the forest to gather wild strawberries. We gathered quite a lot of them. . . . In Kazan we stayed for some time. All we had left was 120 rubles in silver which was obviously not enough to take us as far as Tver. We decided to wait for the two hundred rubles from my brother. We waited ten days and spent fifty rubles. . . . We arrived in Nizhny-Novgorod at the height of the fair. We arrived at night and wandered about the town for two hours trying to find a hotel room, but all the hotels were full. At last we found a kind of dog kennel and were jolly glad of it. I went at once to have a look at the fair. Well, it certainly was worth seeing. I walked round it for two or three hours but only saw a small part of it. Still, the effect was considerable. If anything, it was too effective. It seems that its fame is fully justified. We left the town the same day and arrived in Vladimir where I met the commanding officer of our brigade who told us all about his adventures abroad. We had quite a few drinks that evening. I talked a lot to him and we discussed all sorts of interesting things. At last we left Vladimir and, bypassing Moscow [where he did not relish the idea of meeting his sisters], arrived at the Serpukhov Monastery. On the way there the coachman made me pay three times as much as I would have paid had I traveled on government service. But the monastery rewarded us completely. I hadn't been there for twenty-three years. What architecture, what memorials, Byzantine halls, churches! The sacristy filled us with wonder. There are amazing pearls there of enormous size, emeralds more than half an inch in size, and diamonds worth half a million each. The vestments are all the work of Russian empresses and royal princesses who made Ivan the Terrible's clothes. There are also collections of old coins there, old books and all sorts of rarities—I could not tear myself away. At last we arrived in Tver and found a flat of three small furnished rooms for eleven silver rubles a month. . . ."

[6]

BACK TO LIFE: A NEW MESSAGE

Dostoevsky spent four feverish months in Tver. He arrived there on August 19, 1859, and immediately began making plans for obtaining permission to live in Petersburg. His meeting with Mikhail took place almost on his arrival. Mikhail had been making valiant efforts to provide for his large family, as well as for his mistress and his illegitimate son, by turning himself into the owner of a cigarette factory and offering "free gifts" to the purchasers of his wares. (Dostoevsky had learned about it in Siberia from Mikhail's advertisements in the papers.) But his business did not thrive, and his drinking habits grew worse, so that by the time Dostoevsky arrived from Siberia he had just recovered from a serious attack of cirrhosis. "My brother has been dangerously ill," Dostoevsky wrote to his former company commander in Siberia. "He came to see me here—you can imagine my joy! The railway station is about two miles from the town and I went there at night to meet the train. We talked over lots of things—why, you cannot describe moments like these! . . ."

The meeting between Mikhail and Maria, however, was far from cordial. Hard drinking had accentuated Mikhail's nervous twitches, from which he had suffered as a child, and now his head kept jerking violently and uncontrollably, a fact that must have intensified Maria's apprehensions about the family she had married into. For his own part, Mikhail could not but regard with distaste and ill-concealed horror the consumptive woman his unfortunate brother had married, for she could disguise the nature of her illness as little as she could her contempt and hatred of her husband. Nor was it particularly hard for Mikhail to guess that his brother, too, was no longer in love with his wife. In fact, Dostoevsky no longer cared to conceal the fact that his marriage was a failure. "If you want to know how I am," he wrote to Wrangel,[1] "all I can say is that I have saddled myself with all sorts of family cares and am dragging them along on my back. But," he added, "I firmly believe that my life is not finished yet and I do not want to die."

[1] *Letters*, September 22, 1859.

In his first letter to Mikhail after their meeting, Dostoevsky, though he had only twenty rubles left, implored his brother to go to one of Petersburg's fashionable milliners and buy his wife a hat. On the following day, he wrote to Mikhail again, enclosing a sample of the ribbons for the hat. "The color of the hat," he was careful to point out, "is to be the same as the gray stripe on the ribbon." Maria's chief complaint against her husband after their arrival in Tver was that she had no decent clothes to walk out in. (Dostoevsky's contemptuous description of women's dresses as "rags" in his great novels is, no doubt, due to Maria's constant demands for female fineries.) She refused to accompany him on his visits to some of the prominent people in the town, to whom he was introduced by an old friend (a former member of the Petrashevsky circle), whom he met by chance in Tver. His new acquaintances included Count Baranov, the governor of the province, and his wife. It was the countess, Dostoevsky wrote to Mikhail,[2] who asked him "several times *most earnestly* to visit them without ceremony in the evening. I am afraid," he added, "I shall have to visit them. She seems to be an old acquaintance of mine. Sollogub (she is his cousin) introduced me to her twelve years ago. . . ."

Count Baranov proved of great assistance to Dostoevsky in removing the ban against his residence in Petersburg. But Dostoevsky did not rely on him alone. He got Wrangel to help him too. "Tver," he wrote to Wrangel,[3] "is much worse than Semipalatinsk. Gloomy, cold, stone houses, no movement, no interests—there is not even a decent library—a real prison!" He wrote to Eduard Totleben again and, as before, got Wrangel to deliver his letter to the general. And, finally, on October 18, 1859, he wrote to Alexander II and got Count Baranov to forward the letter to the palace. "I, a former state criminal," it began, "take the liberty to drop my humble petition before your great throne." He went on to inform the Emperor that his literary work was his only means of livelihood, but that his serious illness interfered with his work and he had to settle in Petersburg, where he could obtain the necessary medical treatment. "Bring me back to life," he pleaded, "and grant me the possibility of being useful to my family and perhaps also to my country. . . . You, Sire, are like the sun, which shines upon the righteous and unrighteous alike; gladden the hearts of a poor orphan and his mother and an unhappy, sick man, and lift the ban from one who is ready this very minute to give his life for the Tsar."

The "poor orphan," that is, his stepson, Pasha, was beginning to be a real nuisance to him. Maria, Dostoevsky wrote to Wrangel,[4] "is worried to death about her son's future. She keeps on saying that if I were to die, she would be left in the same hopeless position with a growing son

[2] *Letters,* October 1, 1859.

[3] *Letters,* September 22, 1859.

[4] *Letters,* November 2, 1859.

as after the death of her first husband. She is terrified of it and, though she does not tell me everything, I realize how greatly worried she must be." He therefore included in his letter to the Emperor a "humble request" that his stepson should be given a secondary-school education at the government's expense, a request that was eventually granted.

On November 1, 1859, Dostoevsky received a letter from General Totleben, who wrote that he had had a talk with the Minister of the Interior and the chief of the gendarmerie, and that they did not raise any objection to his residence in Petersburg. On November 25, Count Baranov notified Dostoevsky officially that his request had been granted. On December 2, the Petersburg military governor-general ordered the Petersburg commissioner of police to institute a secret surveillance over Dostoevsky. About a fortnight later Dostoevsky at last returned alone to Petersburg to rent a flat and get everything ready for the arrival of his wife and stepson.

II

In Tver, Dostoevsky had found a letter from Pleshcheyev waiting for him. "Nekrasov and Panaev," his old fellow revolutionary wrote to him, "have been asking me about you with great interest and they told me that if you want money they will send it to you at once and that they will not worry you until you have something for them. I undertook to give you their message. Goncharov, too, inquired after you." The *Contemporary* was not only the most progressive, but also the most widely read periodical at the time, and Dostoevsky felt that to be published in a journal, which had "hounded" him before, was, as he wrote to Mikhail,[5] "very important to my reputation." The news that Nekrasov had rejected *The Village of Stepanchikovo* "surprised" him. Had he not read it at all, he wondered. "I hear," he wrote to Mikhail,[6] "that Nekrasov is gambling heavily at cards and that Panaev is too worried to care about his journal, and," he added, "that but for Chernyshevsky and Dobrolyubov they would have gone to wrack and ruin long ago." Chernyshevsky and Dobrolyubov were both seminarists turned atheists, the two of them "utilitarians" and leaders of the renascent revolutionary movement, but there certainly seems to be no indication that for the time being Dostoevsky regarded them with the vicious dislike that he showed for the "seminarists" later on, particularly in *The Brothers Karamazov*. He was writing *The House of the Dead*, which, he told Mikhail,[7] would have "something serious and somber and something humorous as well as a great deal of colloquial speech including prison slang (I read to you some of the slang expressions I had written down on the spot), and

[5] *Letters,* October 11, 1859.
[6] *Letters,* October 4, 1859.
[7] *Letters,* October 9, 1859.

characters never before heard of in literature, and something touching and, above all, my name." He was planning a long novel with a strong "passionate" element. Both *The House of the Dead* and his new novel he would like to give to the *Contemporary*, but even these inducements did not make Nekrasov change his mind about the novel Katkov had rejected.

In the same letter Dostoevsky wrote to Mikhail that what he wanted most was "to work, to fight, and to create a literary name" for himself. "I challenge them all to a fight," he wrote four days earlier to Mikhail. It seemed, indeed, that he would have to fight hard to carve out a name for himself in the literary world. He put all his hopes on the novel with "the passionate element," which he hoped to start writing in December. "It will be, first, effective and passionate," he wrote to Mikhail,[8] "and, secondly, my entire heart's blood will be put into it. I planned it while lying on my bunk in prison at a most distressing moment of sadness and self-analysis." But to write this novel "with an idea," which would give him "a new start," he told Mikhail, he had to be free of money worries for at least one year. He therefore proposed to issue his published works in three volumes, the first to include *Poor People*, *Netochka Nezvanova*, *White Nights*, *A Little Hero*, *The Christmas Tree and a Wedding*, a revised *Honest Thief* and *The Jealous Husband*, the second, a completely revised version of *The Double* and *My Uncle's Dream*, and the third, *The Village of Stepanchikovo*. The first volume, he thought, was sure to sell, since it contained his best work. As for the initial expense, he asked Mikhail to get a loan of 300 rubles on a promissory note, which, "I swear," he wrote, "I shall repay if I have to get the money from under the ground."

This fantastic plan of raising money, like his other fantastic plans, came to nothing, since Mikhail's financial position was such that he could not raise the required sum. It is interesting, though, because of Dostoevsky's intention to revise *The Double*. "The revised story," he wrote to Mikhail,[9] "together with an introduction will be worth as much as a new novel. They'll see at last what *The Double* is! I hope to arouse tremendous interest. In short, I challenge them all to a fight," he went on with tremendous faith in his own powers even at the lowest ebb in his career, "and, after all, if I do not revise *The Double* now, when shall I do it? Why should I give up an excellent idea, the greatest type according to his social importance, whom I was the first to discover and whose existence I was the first to proclaim?"

He never revised the story, although between 1861 and 1864 he jotted down his plan for a radical revision in his notebooks. He wanted to make Golyadkin a follower of Fourier, introduce him into the Petra-

[8] *Letters,* October 1, 1859.
[9] *Letters,* October 4, 1859.

shevsky circle, make him dream of taking a leading part in a Russian revolution while his double was planning to betray him. This would have meant rewriting and not just revising the story, but by that time Dostoevsky was fully occupied with writing *Crime and Punishment* and *The Gambler*, and when he came to include the story in the third volume of the edition of his works, he merely abbreviated its text. This "revision" did not satisfy even Dostoevsky, who wrote:[10] "This story is one of my positive failures, but its idea was excellent and I have never dealt with a more serious idea in my literary work. It is the form of this story that I completely failed to master. I revised it thoroughly about fifteen years later for the full edition of my books issued at the time, but even then I convinced myself once more that it had completely miscarried and that if I were to take up the idea of the story again now and attempt to write it anew, I should have chosen quite a different form; but in 1846 I did not discover that form and did not get the most out of the story."

In 1859 most of his literary plans, with the exception of *The House of the Dead*, were rather hazy, chiefly because he had been away too long from the center of things. This is also true of the "long novel with the passionate element" and the provisional title of *Confession*, which he planned to write and offer to Nekrasov. But now that Nekrasov had finally rejected *The Village of Stepanchikovo*, he was no longer willing to have anything to do with the man whom he now dismissed (in a letter to Mikhail[11]) as "a literary peasant." It became clear to him now that when he finally settled in Petersburg he would have to fight the established literary world by launching a monthly periodical of his own in which he could publish his own works. He was now going to challenge them all "to a fight" in good earnest. He jotted down the following list of subjects he hoped to deal with in the course of 1860: (1) *Mignonne*, (2) *Spring Love*, (3) *The Double* (revise), (4) *The Diary of a Convict* (fragments), and (5) *Apathy* and *Confession*.

With the exception of *The Diary of a Convict*, whose title he soon changed to *The House of the Dead*, and which he began writing in the autumn of 1859, he made no attempt to carry out the rest of his program. "There was no end to Dostoevsky's plans and projects," Strakhov remarks in his biography of Dostoevsky. "He always carried several subjects in his head which he hoped to make use of as finished works of art, but only later, when he had more leisure, when times were quieter." But he never found time for them, for there were always new things happening around him, things that demanded immediate treatment.

He arrived in Petersburg for the second time as a complete stranger. "When I returned to Petersburg after so many years," he told Vsevolod Solovyov eighteen years later, "many of my former friends did not even

[10] *A Writer's Diary*, November 1877.
[11] *Letters*, October 18, 1859.

want to know me." Many of his old "friends" were, no doubt, afraid to have anything to do with a man who was still a political suspect, but many more, as Dostoevsky told Vsevolod Solovyov, were merely fair-weather friends. "Friends," he declared, "appeared only when I had had some success. When my success was gone, my friends, too, were gone. It's absurd, of course, and it's nothing new, and yet every time it happened, it hurt me terribly. I could always tell how successful a work of mine was by the number of friends who came to see me, by the extent of their attention and the frequency of their visits. And I was always right. Oh, people can sense it, they have a good nose for it! I remember how everyone rushed to know me after the success of *Crime and Punishment*. People I had not seen for years suddenly appeared and were so kind to me, and then they were suddenly gone again. Only two or three remained. . . . Success, you know, is a queer thing. A man suddenly becomes blind and weak, anyone can cheat him in the grossest possible way—he'd believe anything, take everything at its face value."

But Dostoevsky himself had alienated many of his former friends and well-wishers by his eagerness "to fight them all." He was never a clean fighter: he got as much pleasure out of hurting an opponent as out of defeating him in an argument. Besides, while some of his former friends were not particularly anxious to know him, others were only too willing to do so. One of the latter was Dr. Stepan Yanovsky, who came to Tver to meet him. But this old friendship did not last either, though this time the cause was not ideological, but personal: Dostoevsky, on his return to Petersburg, became, in his own words, "too greatly attached" to Yanovsky's wife, the actress Alexandra Schubert, an attachment that lasted for about a year.

Alexandra Schubert was thirty-three at the time. She had married Yanovsky in 1855 after the death of her first husband, and three years later went on the stage against Yanovsky's wishes. She left Yanovsky shortly after Dostoevsky's arrival in Petersburg and went to Moscow, where she continued her theatrical career. Dostoevsky's first letter to her is dated March 14, 1860. He envied her her new life. "Do you remember," he wrote, "how at dinner at my brother's you told me that I had such a dull 'Lenten' face and how you poked fun at it. If I had the slightest talent for writing a comedy," he went on, "I'd have written one for you." She knew about his unhappy family life, and all he could tell her was that, but for the "hopeless nastiness" of his life, he would have been able to get on with his writing. Alexandra Schubert seemed to him the first woman who might, if she wished, help him to a "new life" by making him forget the ghastly mistake of his marriage. He rushed off to Moscow after her, but the lady, it seems, was not willing.

On his return to Petersburg, he described to her his trip to Moscow as just "a dream." He had seen her husband, who promised to send her money (again, as in the case of Isaev, he had found himself in an ambivalent position towards a friend). He himself was in "a feverish position" because of the novel he was writing (probably *The Insulted and Injured*, whose hero was in a similar ambivalent situation). "I want to write it well," he went on, "because my whole literary career depends on its success. I shall have to work at it day and night for three months, but think of the reward when I have finished it. Perhaps, as a reward to myself, I shall go abroad for two months, but before that I shall certainly pay another visit to Moscow. What will our meeting be like then? . . . I should very much like to be worthy of your friendship. . . . You are kind, intelligent. . . . You have such a charming character. . . . You laugh so much at everything prosaic, ridiculous, supercilious and stupid, that it is a pleasure to listen to you." And after telling her that he and his brother were planning to start a monthly magazine, he repeated that what he liked about her so much was her faith in life and in her vocation, the fact that she had devoted herself so wholeheartedly to art and had not become disappointed with it. "Don't be angry with me for foisting my friendship upon you," he begged her. "Still," he concluded, as if looking for a reason why his advances had been rejected, "I have a most vile character—not always, though, but spasmodically."

Dostoevsky's last letter to Alexandra Schubert, written on June 12, 1860, is even more characteristic, not only of this brief encounter, but also of Dostoevsky's attitude towards the problems of love and jealousy. The relations between Alexandra Schubert and Dr. Yanovsky had by then reached a critical stage, Yanovsky threatening to take legal steps, as her husband, to force her to leave the stage, and Alexandra replying that if he did so, she would open a tavern in a Petersburg slum under her married name of Yanovsky. Dostoevsky offered to act as an intermediary between them and found himself faced by a jealous husband who suspected him of being his wife's lover (a situation which he was to use nine years later in a more dramatic form in his short novel *The Eternal Husband*). He met Yanovsky in Pavlovsk. "Do you really intend," he asked him, "to force your wife to leave the stage? Why, this means depriving her of light, air, and sun! . . . This is tyranny! What do your rules and convictions amount to after that?" Yanovsky, Dostoevsky wrote to Alexandra, got very excited and said it would not come to that. "He is jealous," Dostoevsky went on. "He seems to be convinced that we are writing to each other daily and that you do what I tell you. . . . He believes that I have betrayed our friendship. You seem to have confirmed his suspicions when you said to him in Moscow: 'You don't know Dostoevsky, he isn't your friend at all,' " a significant remark, revealing perhaps more than anything else Dostoevsky's attempts to seduce her and her own complete indifference to his advances. Dostoevsky, too, made things worse by revealing to Yanovsky "as a secret" something of his own domestic circumstances. "This was an important thing to me," he wrote to Alexandra, "it broke out of my heart, but he, I'm afraid, thought that I was in love with you. Noticing your portrait on his table, I glanced at it, and when I went up to the table a second time, looking for a match, he turned your portrait face down while speaking to me, which seemed silly. . . . There are two kinds of jealousies," Dostoevsky continued, "a jealousy of love and a jealousy of hurt pride—he has both. How I wish that you would separate, for instead of your love (which no longer exists), he would have got a warm feeling of gratitude, friendship and respect, which surely is worth everything else."

By this time Dostoevsky felt that he had to get himself out of a situation that seemed to lead nowhere. "Let me tell you frankly," he wrote to Alexandra in conclusion: "I love you very much, so much so that I can tell you now that I am not in love with you, for I prize your correct attitude toward me and I was greatly upset when I thought that you had deprived me of your confidence. I blamed myself. It was torture. I am so glad that I am quite sure now that I am not in love with you. This makes it possible for me to be even more devoted to you without being afraid for my heart." Having got this off his chest, he bade her a lasting farewell. "Good-by, my darling. I kiss your pretty mischievous little hand with veneration and trust and press it with all my heart. All yours, Dostoevsky."

A year later he was to meet the woman who was destined to leave a much deeper and more permanent impression on his heart and writings. Meanwhile he was too busy with his new adventure in the world of journalism—the world of the so-called "fat" journals—to worry too much about a love affair that was too like his first love for Mrs. Panaev in that it was quite hopeless from the very start.

III

Dostoevsky arrived in Petersburg in the second half of December 1859, almost exactly ten years after he had left the city in chains and under guard. He was met at the station by the two men who had come to say good-by to him at the Peter and Paul Fortress on the very day of his departure for Siberia—his brother Mikhail and Alexander Milyukov. "We spent the evening together," Milyukov records. "Dostoevsky did not seem to have changed physically: indeed, he seemed to look more cheerful than before and had not lost a whit of his usual energy. . . . That evening we only exchanged news and impressions and recalled the old times and our former friends. After that we saw each other every week." They met every Tuesday evening at Milyukov's house, and it was there that Dostoevsky met Nikolai Strakhov, who was to become for many years one of his closest collaborators and his biographer.

Strakhov left this description of Dostoevsky on his return to Petersburg: "He wore only a mustache in those days and, in spite of his immense forehead and beautiful eyes, he looked like a common soldier, that is to say, his features were those of a Russian peasant." Dostoevsky's wife, Maria, of whom Strakhov had only caught a passing glimpse, made "a very pleasant impression" on him "by her pallor and the delicate features of her face," in spite of the fact that they were "irregular and small." One could see at once, he adds, her predisposition to the illness that soon "brought her to her grave."

Strakhov was most struck by "the superabundance" of Dostoevsky's ideas, the warmth with which he expounded them, and the "special manner" of his conversation. He often talked to the person he was addressing in an undertone, almost in a whisper, until something happened to excite him, then he grew animated and raised his voice sharply. "At that period, though," Strakhov remarks, "he was usually extremely cheerful and there was a great deal of gentleness in him, in contrast to what he was like during the last years of his life after all the hard work and agitation he had gone through."

The subjects discussed by the intimate circle of friends who met at Milyukov's house were mostly concerned with social and political problems, but Strakhov, brought up on Hegelian philosophy, could not help noticing with dismay that what they were all interested in, and particularly Dostoevsky, was not the "eternal," but "the temporary and particular," aspects of those problems. To study those aspects, "it was the usual practice of writers," Strakhov records, "to visit the filthiest slums, enter into friendly conversation with people with whom neither merchants nor civil servants would dream of associating, and regard the most savage occurrences with compassion." These "*physiological* considerations" seemed to have been the main subject of debate among Dostoevsky's friends. "At first," Strakhov writes, "I could not help being surprised to hear opinions about men's qualities and actions enunciated not from the height of moral standards, not by applying the criteria of reason, humor and beauty, but from the point of view of the inescapable pressure of various influences and the inescapable frailty of human nature." Strakhov admits that even at that early date, Dostoevsky refused to accept the full implications of such a "physiological" theory of literature (he later completely repudiated it), but he insists that what he calls "the French influence" of the 1840's was still felt very strongly among the Petersburg *literati,* although the political situation had undergone a complete change since those days: for in the early 1860's, while Europe was in the grip of reaction, Russia was, or seemed to be, on the brink of great liberal reforms, chief among which was, of course, the liberation of the serfs. Strakhov asserts that he was appalled by "the narrowness of the prevalent theory" that the writer should serve "the latest fad." Brought up "on German theories of the freedom of the artist," he was astonished "to hear talks about the modern meaning of different literary schools and the efforts to catch the latest and newest expressions of social life." He was appalled even more, of course, by the loose morals of the writers among whom he found himself, "the emancipation of the flesh" to which Dostoevsky had succumbed and what, in his letter to Tolstoy of November 28, 1883, Strakhov was to call his "animal sensuality."

That Strakhov, never particularly happy in his relations with women, should in his letter to Tolstoy have used somewhat exaggerated language in describing Dostoevsky's "immoral" life is not surprising. But excerpts from his tiresome letter to Tolstoy, published for the first time in 1913 in the October issue of *Sovremyonny Mir* (*Contemporary World*), have been so often quoted and misquoted by Dostoevsky's biographers, both reputable and disreputable, that it is only fair to quote it in full:

"I shall write you, dear Leo Nikolayevich, a short letter, though the subject it deals with is very rich. But I am not feeling well and it would take me too long to develop it. I expect you must have received now my Biography of Dostoevsky—I beg your attention and indulgence—please, tell me what you think of it. And I'd like to take this opportunity of making a confession to you. All the time I was writing it I wrestled with myself, I wrestled against the feeling of disgust that arose within me and I tried to smother this evil feeling. Help me to find a way out of it. I cannot consider D. either a good or a happy man (which, as a matter of fact, is the same thing). He was spiteful, envious, immoral and spent all his life in such a state of agitation that it made him look pitiful and would have made him look ridiculous if at the same time he had not been so spiteful and so clever. Like Rousseau, however, he regarded himself as one of the best and happiest of men. While writing his Biography I could not but vividly call to mind those traits of his character. In Switzerland he treated a waiter so disgracefully in my presence that the man's feelings were hurt and he said to him: 'Don't you think I am a human being too?' I remember that what surprised me at the time was that this was said to a preacher of humanity and that here we had an example of the conceptions of the *rights of man* in a free country like Switzerland.

"Such scenes constantly occurred with him because he could not control his spiteful nature. Many times I ignored these ill-mannered outbursts of his, during which he behaved like a woman, unexpectedly and indirectly; I, too, could not help once or twice making some rather offensive remarks to him. But then, so far as insults were concerned he had a great advantage over ordinary mortals and the awful thing about it was that he enjoyed it, that he never completely repented of any of the dirty tricks he played on people. He could not help being attracted by them, and he boasted about them. Viskovatov started telling me how he boasted about having had intercourse in a bathhouse with a little girl who was brought to him by her governess. Observe in this connection that with all his animal sensuality he had neither good taste nor any appreciation of a woman's beauty and charm. This can be seen in his novels. The characters who are most like him are the hero of *Notes from a Dark Cellar*, Svidrigaylov in *Crime and Punishment* and Stavrogin in *The Devils.* One scene dealing with Stavrogin (rape, etc.) Katkov refused to publish, but Dostoevsky read it to many people.

"With a nature like that he had a great penchant for cloying sentimentality and lofty and humane dreams, and these dreams constitute his whole philosophy of life. They were his literary Muse and his literary path. In essence, however, all his novels are merely essays in self-justification and prove that noble sentiments can live side by side with all sorts of abominations in man.

"I feel so awful not to be able to get rid of these thoughts and not to be able to find some point of reconciliation. Am I angry? Do I envy him? Do I wish him ill? Not at all. I am merely ready to weep that this memory of him which *could have been* bright merely oppresses me.

"I remember your saying that people who know us too well quite naturally do not like us. But sometimes it is different. It is possible in the case of a close (long) acquaintanceship to discover some trait in a man's character for which you will forgive him everything afterwards. *A feeling of genuine goodness, a spark of genuine warmth of heart*, even one moment of sincere repentance—can make amends for everything; and if I had remembered anything like that about D. I would have forgiven him and rejoiced over him. But just putting oneself on a pedestal as a model of a good man, mere cerebral and literary humaneness—Lord, how disgusting it is!

"He was a truly bad and unhappy man, who imagined himself to be a happy man, a hero, and he loved tenderly only himself. Being conscious of the fact that I myself am capable of arousing disgust and having learned to understand and forgive this feeling in others, I thought that I might find a way of understanding and forgiving D. too. But I do not find it. I do not find it.

"This is a brief comment on my Biography. I could have written and told about this side of D. too, for there are many incidents I remember much more vividly than those I have described, and my story would have sounded much truer, too; but let that truth be lost; let us show off only the façade of life as we do everywhere and in everything."

It is not true that in his biography Strakhov did not betray any ill-feeling towards Dostoevsky. There is a phrase in it that practically repeats the insinuation in his letter to Tolstoy that Dostoevsky was like his most discreditable characters (whom, incidentally, Dostoevsky did not attempt to justify in any way). "Nearly always," Strakhov wrote, "the characters Dostoevsky created were in his own image." He resented the way Dostoevsky presumed to edit his (Strakhov's) articles because they "destroyed their tone" and were not to his taste. They seem to have had many "warm" disputes about it. Even at the time of their closest friendship, their relations, Strakhov remarks, "did not overstep a certain line. Each of us," he explains, "draws a line beyond which he does not admit anyone, or rather cannot admit anyone." One cannot help wondering if with Strakhov this forbidden territory did not include his attitude towards women, which Dostoevsky, no doubt, tried to discuss frankly with him, as he did with everyone else. Strakhov further accuses Dostoevsky in his biography of "moments of suspiciousness" during which he used to say: "Strakhov has no one to talk to and that is why he holds on to me." Indeed, Strakhov himself admits that the success of *Time* made him give up his teaching, which he detested, and gave him his chance of devoting himself to writing. He resented the "impatient way" in which Dostoevsky asked him to read his articles to him. "At the time," he tries to justify himself, "I did not realize how flattering this impatience really was for me!" He also resented the fact that Dostoevsky never praised him and never expressed his approbation of him—and there was no doubt a good reason for that, too. He did not appreciate Dostoevsky's jokes. "His humor," he writes, "did not appeal to me particularly," which indicates that Dostoevsky must have enjoyed pulling the leg of his "philosophic" friend. But he, too, as he frankly admits to Tolstoy, could not help making "some rather offensive remarks" to Dostoevsky from time to time.

In his biography Strakhov admits going out of his way to make Dostoevsky realize how little he knew of philosophy. When they were discussing "abstract" questions, he would point out that what Dostoevsky thought to be his own original ideas had long been discussed by philosophers "known to us from the history of philosophy." Dostoevsky, Strakhov remarks, was "amused" and jokingly consoled himself with the thought that his ideas were "identical with those of one or another great thinker." Considering how hypersensitive Dostoevsky was, one can only wonder whether his amusement was not put on to disguise his vexation at Strakhov's assumed air of self-complacent superiority.

That Strakhov was only too eager to show off his philosophic training becomes apparent from his quite unnecessary disclosure that Dostoevsky had made him a present of his copy of Hegel's *History of Philosophy* because, not knowing German, he could make nothing of it. Strakhov's ill-will towards Dostoevsky is best illustrated by his behavior in the spring of 1878. Both Dostoevsky and Tolstoy were present on March 10th at a lecture given in Petersburg by Vladimir Solovyov on some aspects of religion from his *Readings of Godmanhood* (described by Tolstoy afterwards as "the ravings of a lunatic"). Dostoevsky had gone to the lecture hoping that Strakhov would introduce him to Tolstoy, but Strakhov ignored him on the ground that Tolstoy had begged him not to introduce him to anybody. Dostoevsky, Anna states in her reminiscences, was greatly distressed not to have been able "even to have a look at Tolstoy."

But then the whole spirit of Strakhov's letter to Tolstoy bewailing his inability "to forgive" Dostoevsky is tinged with hypocrisy. Dostoevsky himself, of course, many times bewailed his "vile" character, which was most probably due to his chronic illness more than to anything else and as such was completely beyond his control. As for Dostoevsky's loose morals, Tolstoy, who had gone through a period of much looser morals, was hardly the man to whom to complain about it. It is, besides, rather curious that having tried to blacken Dostoevsky's character by a story that Viskovatov, an obscure professor of Russian literature, whom Dostoevsky had only met a few times, "started to tell him," he should not have mentioned the nature of the other disgraceful incidents he only hints at. Strakhov knew, of course, that his letter to Tolstoy would eventually be published and his insinuations made a great deal of by future biographers of Dostoevsky. All Tolstoy said in reply was that Dostoevsky suffered from "a constitutional nervous defect." As for Dostoevsky's portraying himself in some of his characters, Tolstoy merely replied that "the deeper a writer penetrates into the human heart, the more universal he becomes and the more familiar and kindred he is to us all. The result is that even in those exceptional characters not only we, but also foreigners, recognize ourselves and our own inner being."

But it is, of course, the story Viskovatov "started to tell" Strakhov about Dostoevsky "boasting" of having had intercourse with "a little girl" a governess had "brought" to him that crops up again and again in biographies of Dostoevsky. What substance is there in such a story? Is there any evidence for it? And is it likely that Dostoevsky would have "boasted" about it? What was the age of the "little girl?" Ten, thirteen, fifteen? To support this vague story, Strakhov, as Dostoevsky's second wife justly remarks, quotes the scene from *The Devils* which Katkov refused to publish and which, it is only fair to observe, Dostoevsky himself did not include (something he could have done if he wished) when the novel was published in book form.

Anna, who deals with Strakhov's letter to Tolstoy in an appendix to her reminiscences, records that after Katkov's refusal to publish the scene of the rape, Dostoevsky wrote several other scenes for, as she put it, "the artistic characterization of Stavrogin," and among them was a scene in a public bathhouse, "a true occurrence," she writes, "about which someone had told my husband," in which a "governess played a criminal part." When Dostoevsky read this revised scene to several of his friends, "including," Anna points out, "Strakhov," they objected to it on the ground that the introduction of "a governess" in so unsavory an incident might involve Dostoevsky in a public controversy as "an opponent of the woman's question" in the same way as formerly Dostoevsky had been accused of an attack against the younger generation because he made Raskolnikov an ex-student of Petersburg University. "And it is this version of the scene," Anna writes, "this odious part played by Stavrogin, that Strakhov, in his malice, did not hesitate to ascribe to Dostoevsky, forgetting that the carrying into effect of such an act of depravity demands a great deal of money and can be afforded only by very rich people, while my husband was all his life in financial straits. Strakhov's reference to Viskovatov is all the more astonishing to me because the professor never came to our house, and Dostoevsky did not think much of him, anyhow. . . ."

Anna's statement about the expense of such "an act of depravity" is hardly convincing, but her disclosure about one of the new versions of Stavrogin's adventures certainly shows how Viskovatov, who bore a grudge against Dostoevsky, whom he accused of disliking him, might have deliberately misinterpreted the story and "started" telling it in his own version to Strakhov, who was only too eager to believe it.

What makes Strakhov's story completely incredible is the fact that the one thing Dostoevsky was consistent about all through his life was his condemnation of cruelty to children. The rape of a little girl was regarded by him as an act of brutality for which there could be no excuse or forgiveness. The rape of a little deaf and dumb girl who later drowned herself Dostoevsky regarded as Svidrigaylov's most heinous crime. In one of his recently published notebooks dealing with *Crime and Punishment*, he gives this characterization of Svidrigaylov: "The main thing–Svidrigaylov knows that he is obsessed by all sorts of mysterious horrors. He tells no one about them, but he discloses them unintentionally by his deeds: it is a spasmodic and bestial need to torture and kill–he is coldly passionate. A wild beast. A tiger." Even Strakhov, had he known of this entry, would hardly have identified Svidrigaylov with Dostoevsky, as he does in his letter to Tolstoy. In fact, long before Dostoevsky had even contemplated writing *The Devils* or written *Crime and Punishment* he had been planning to make the rape of a girl of ten the culminating point of a novel.

Sofia Kovalevsky records in her reminiscences that Dostoevsky often discussed the plots of his novels with her and her sister. "Occasionally," she writes, "Dostoevsky was very outspoken in his conversation, completely oblivious of the fact that he was talking to young girls. My mother was sometimes horrified by his stories. For instance, one day he began telling us of a scene from a novel he had conceived when he was still a young man. Its hero was a middle-aged landowner of excellent education, who had traveled abroad, read intelligent books and was a collector of pictures and engravings. As a young man he had led a rather dissolute life, but afterwards he got married, settled down with his wife and children in the country, and became a highly respected person.

" 'One day,' Dostoevsky said, 'he woke early in the morning, the sun was shining through the windows of his bedroom, everything around him was tidy, nice and cozy. And he, too, felt such a tidy and respectable person. A sensation of peace and contentment spread all over his body. As a true sybarite, he was not in a hurry to get up, for he was anxious to prolong this pleasant state of vegetative well-being.

"'His mind fixed upon some point midway between sleep and wakefulness, he went over various happy moments of his last journey abroad. He saw once more the marvelous shaft of light falling upon the naked shoulders of St. Cecilia in the Munich gallery. Very brilliant passages from a book *On World Beauty and Harmony* also passed through his head.

"'Suddenly, at the very height of those pleasant dreams and experiences, he began to feel uneasy—it was a strange feeling of physical pain and anxiety. It was the sort of thing felt by people who had old bullet wounds from which the bullets had not been extracted: a minute before he felt no pain and suddenly the old wound began to ache and went on aching.

"'The landowner started thinking and wondering. What could it mean? There was nothing wrong with him physically and he had no troubles or worries of any kind. And yet he felt sick at heart and it was getting worse and worse.

"'He began to feel that he ought to remember something, and he did his best to remember and began searching his memory. . . . Suddenly he did remember, vividly and realistically, and the feeling of disgust that took hold of him was so strong that the whole thing might have happened yesterday and not twenty years ago. And yet during all those twenty years this thing had never worried him in the least.

"'He remembered,' Dostoevsky said, ending his story, 'how egged on by his friends once after a night of dissipation he had raped a ten-year-old girl. . . .'

"My mother," Sofia Kovalesky continued, "threw up her hands in horror when Dostoevsky said it.

"'For goodness' sake,' she implored him in a voice of despair, 'there are children here!'

"At the time," Sofia Kovalevsky, who was then only fifteen, added, "I did not understand what Dostoevsky was talking about, and it was only from my mother's tone of indignation that I realized that it must have been something dreadful."

Dostoevsky always held that children should be told everything, and he may not have anticipated the effect his story would have on the mother of two young daughters. Be that as it may, there can be no doubt that even during his first period as a writer he had been contemplating writing a novel in which the rape of "a little girl" was to be the pivot round which the action of the narrative turned. The appalling rape of the half-wit Agrafena in Darovoye must have burned itself into Dostoevsky's conscience very early in his life, and the rape of a helpless creature, and especially of a child, became fixed in his mind as one of the most heinous crimes a man could commit. Would he have boasted about it even if he had committed it?

Today we know much more than Strakhov knew about Dostoevsky's involvement with women, and considering how abominably he was treated by the women he loved, one is bound to feel sympathy for him rather than the hypocritical indignation Strakhov pretended to feel. As for Strakhov's failure to understand (as he asserts in one of his letters to Tolstoy) how Dostoevsky, who had been married twice and had run after so many women, could not delineate a single trait of a man's passion for a woman in spite of his description of "the improbable complications of such passions," one can only observe that a man like Strakhov, who was never married, who never ran after women, and whose romantic notions of women were as false as they were ridiculous, could hardly set himself up as a judge of a man's passion for a woman as Dostoevsky delineated it. To his rhetorical questions: "Did I envy him? Did I wish him evil?"—the only answer is: "Yes, of course, you did!" It is with this in one's mind that one must turn to Strakhov's biography, which contains so much invaluable information about Dostoevsky's first attempts to rehabilitate himself after his return from Siberia.

IV

Dostoevsky had not been entirely forgotten. In referring to his "interesting" name in his letter to Mikhail on October 1, 1859, Dostoevsky had in mind the fact that as a former political convict his name would arouse a great deal of interest, if not enthusiasm, among the numerous adherents of the radical movement in Petersburg. This was exactly what happened. He was in great demand at public readings, which were so popular at the time. Orest Miller records that the first time he saw Dostoevsky, he was reading the extract from his *House of the Dead* describing the death of a convict in the prison hospital. "He realized very well," Orest Miller writes, "that he was being invited to read extracts from *The House of the Dead* for one reason only, namely, for the sake of a political demonstration."

Dostoevsky's first appearance in public took place in April 1860, at a reading of *The Government Inspector* in aid of the Russian Literary Fund, founded a year earlier. Wrangel, who was present, writes that the hall was packed and the appearance of Dostoevsky was greeted with thunderous applause. Dostoevsky had to read the rather important part of Shpekin, the postmaster, but, Wrangel observes, he was not at his best. He looked embarrassed and his voice was low and dull. Strakhov also records that although Dostoevsky read very well, his somewhat dull, low voice betrayed his inexperience. Turgenev, who was at the height of his fame and popularity just then as the author of *A Nobleman's Nest* and *On the Eve*, took the part of one of the merchants. The two old enemies could not have avoided meeting each other, and one can only imagine the bitter memories this meeting must have brought back to Dostoevsky. But whatever his feelings, he suppressed them, since he realized only too well how important Turgenev's name would be among the contributors to *Time*, the new monthly he and Mikhail were planning to publish.

Turgenev had just broken with the *Contemporary*, which was conducting a bitter campaign against him, and Dostoevsky was quick enough to take Turgenev's part by writing two articles in his defense; this was greatly appreciated by Turgenev, who, when approached by Dostoevsky to contribute to *Time*, promised not to publish his next story in any other periodical. Three months later, the Petersburg Censorship Committee informed Mikhail, the official editor (Dostoevsky, as an ex-convict, could not fill that post), that he had been granted permission to publish the periodical. In September 1860, Dostoevsky sent out to the press an announcement of the forthcoming publication of *Time* in January 1861. The announcement was accompanied by a long statement, or "manifesto," as Dostoevsky called it, outlining the aims of the new journal. For the time being, he tried to avoid the appearance of having joined either of the two extremist camps into which the educated and politically conscious section of the Russian population was divided—the Westerners and the Slavophiles—and, by his apparent moderation, to acquire a sufficiently large reading public to put his journal firmly on its feet during the first year of its existence. In this he succeeded beyond expectation.

In his "manifesto" Dostoevsky was careful to dissociate himself from the extremist views of the Slavophiles, who repudiated Peter the Great's reforms as having inflicted untold harm on the Russian people by severing them from their own national past. He did agree that they had cost Russia too much by creating a gulf between the educated classes and the vast majority of the Russian population—the 43,000,000 illiterate and ignorant peasants—but he maintained that this cleavage was coming to an end. "All those who have followed Peter the Great," he wrote, "have got to know Europe and have adopted a European mode of life, but they have not become Europeans. Once upon a time we reproached ourselves for our incapacity to transform ourselves into Europeans. Now we think differently. Now we know that we cannot be Europeans, that we cannot squeeze ourselves into any of the Western European forms of life, which Europe has developed out of its own national sources which are alien to us—in the same way as we cannot wear clothes not cut to our size. We have become convinced at last that we, too, are a separate nationality, independent of all outside influences, and that our task is to create a new form for ourselves, our own native form, drawn from our own soil, our national spirit and our national resources. But," Dostoevsky was quick to point out, fearful lest he should be taken for a Slavophile, "we did not return vanquished to our native soil. We do not reject our past: we recognize that Peter the Great's reforms widened our horizon, that through them we reached an understanding of our future significance in the great family of nations. We know," he went on, "that we cannot now put up a Chinese Wall against mankind. *We foresee, and foresee with a sense of reverence, that the character of our future activity must be international to the highest degree, that the Russian idea is, perhaps, to become the synthesis of all those ideas which Europe is developing with such pertinacity and such courage within its separate nationalities, that, perhaps, everything that is hostile will find its reconciliation and further development in the Russian national spirit.*"

Dostoevsky was to expatiate on *his* idea of "the Russian idea" in a more and more uncompromising and chauvinistic form as time went on, expressing, finally, not merely his belief, but his conviction, that the Russian people had been endowed with spiritual powers to bring about *a world synthesis*, to reconcile the European contradictions and bring about a union of all nations under the aegis of Russia. For the moment, however, he was very careful twice to insert a "perhaps," proving that he himself was not yet ready to out-Slavophile the most diehard of the Slavophiles. Indeed, in one of his essays published in *Time* in 1861, he admitted that his belief "that the Russian nation is an unusual phenomenon in the history of mankind" could not be proved, but he thought that there could be no doubt that the Russian people possessed "an instinct for grasping the general nature of mankind," a "highly-synthesizing" capacity, the capacity of "general reconciliation and universality."

Dostoevsky had not so far been abroad, nor, as far as is known, had he had any personal contacts with foreigners; he knew foreigners merely from the study of literature, and the fact that he himself was able to extract the universal significance of some character in a Balzac or a Dickens novel and to find "a point of union and reconciliation in completely contrary rival ideas of two different European nations" led him to the curious belief that this personal quality of his, stemming from his peculiar genius, was peculiar to all Russians. He himself could never master a foreign language, and yet so convinced was he of "the universality of the Russian national spirit" that in the same essay he stated as a matter of sober fact that "every Russian can speak all foreign languages and learn the spirit of any foreign language just as though it were his own Russian language—which," he added, "you do not find among any other European nation *in the sense of a general national aptitude*."

At the time nobody in Russia took his idea of the universality of the Russian spirit seriously. Ideas, Strakhov pointed out in his biography, were apprehended by Dostoevsky only in their most generalized aspect. "The most abstract and general ideas," he wrote, "had a tremendous effect on him and he got very excited about them. He, as it were, *felt* ideas extremely vividly. . . . He was always carried away by the impetuosity of his ideas and was ready to think that what he saw so clearly in his own mind was inevitable and was bound to come to pass soon."

There was another reason why Dostoevsky had decided to found "a new, independent literary organ." This was, as he pointed out in his "manifesto," the general lack of a critical attitude towards literary authorities. "There are still in our literature," Dostoevsky declared, "a number of established ideas and opinions which have not the slightest trace of originality, but which exist in the form of incontrovertible truths solely because at one time or another some literary pundit has determined it like that. . . . Mediocrity sometimes quite selflessly regards with awe the opinions established by some literary luminaries, especially if those opinions are expressed boldly, arrogantly and brazenly. Sometimes it is just this brazenness and arrogance that give authority to a writer who, not being a fool, knows how to make the best use of the circumstances that provide him with quite an extraordinary, though temporary, influence upon the masses. Mediocrity, for its part, is almost always extremely timid and . . . timidity begets literary slavery, and there must be no slavery in literature. . . . We have therefore decided," Dostoevsky concluded, "to found a journal which would be completely independent of literary authorities–in spite of our respect for them–and challenge all literary eccentricities of our times. . . . We shall not evade polemics. We shall not be afraid occasionally of 'teasing' the literary geese; for the gaggle of geese is sometimes useful: it forecasts the weather, if it does not always save the Capitol."

The "program" of the new periodical did not differ essentially from the "programs" of similar periodicals, including the indispensable "literary" section, the critical and bibliographical section, the section dealing with economic, financial and philosophic problems, the latest government edicts and internal news, letters from foreign correspondents, "political rumors" and miscellaneous items, such as short stories, etc. Making a virtue of necessity, Dostoevsky refused to follow the accepted usage of publishing the names of his contributors. "For all our respect for famous literary names," he explained, "we realize that it is not they who constitute the strength of a journal."

Dostoevsky himself claimed to have contributed about one hundred folio pages to *Time* during the first two years of its existence, but, apart from that, nothing of any particular importance was published in *Time* or its successor, *Epoch*. The first number of *Time* contained the first installment of *The Insulted and Injured*, translations of three Edgar Allan Poe stories and an episode from Casanova's memoirs, a story by a Russian woman writer and an article by Strakhov.

What Dostoevsky found so attractive about Poe was what he called his "indirect fantastic genre." If one tried to imagine something that was not quite ordinary, he wrote in his footnote on Poe, something that, though possible, one did not come across in real life, the image one conjured up in one's mind was either a rather blurred outline of the whole or only some particular aspect of it. "But in Poe's stories," Dostoevsky pointed out, "you see all the details of the image or the event presented to you so clearly that in the end you are apparently convinced of its possibility, though that event is either completely impossible or has never yet happened anywhere in the world. . . . If there is any fantastic element in Poe, it is a kind of material one, if one may express it so."

V

Strangely enough, and contrary to what Strakhov described at "the regime of literary terror" carried on by the *Contemporary*, Chernyshevsky, who was at the time the actual editor of the monthly, at first expressed himself in very friendly terms about the new periodical. "We wish it success," he wrote, "because we have always welcomed the appearance of a new journal which promises to be the representative of an honest and independent opinion however much it differs from our own way of thinking." Dostoevsky never forgot this generous gesture on the part of one of his most dangerous rivals, and he always had a soft spot for the man whose "utilitarian" views he ruthlessly attacked in his novels. It is, thus, not without significance that in 1873, during one of the most reactionary periods of his career, when he edited *The Citizen*, Dostoevsky should have published in his *Writer's Diary* a warm tribute to Chernyshevsky in connection with an incident that occurred in May 1862. The disappointed expectations of the great "reforms" initiated by Alexander II caused a wave of revolutionary propaganda to sweep over Russia. One morning Dostoevsky found a revolutionary leaflet at the door of his flat. The leaflet, issued by a terrorist organization calling itself "Young Russia," denied the efficacy of "peaceful reforms" and called for a revolutionary uprising even if it meant the shedding of blood. "It is the destiny of Russia," it declared, "to be the first to realize the great cause of socialism."

Dostoevsky had met Chernyshevsky, whom he knew to be one of the leaders of the revolutionary movement and who was generally believed to be chiefly responsible for the revolutionary leaflets, soon after his return to Petersburg. "We met again," he wrote in his *Writer's Diary*, "though not often. But we always shook hands. Herzen told me that Chernyshevsky had made a bad impression on him, that is, by his appearance and his manner, but I liked Chernyshevsky's appearance and manner.

"One morning," Dostoevsky continued, "I found at the door of my flat, attached to the door handle, one of the most extraordinary leaflets ever to appear in those days, and quite a number of them did appear at that time. It was addressed 'To the younger generation.' One could not imagine anything more absurd or more stupid. . . . I felt terribly vexed and sad all that day. It was all still very new at the time and so close at hand that it was difficult to obtain a good idea of those people, difficult because one could hardly believe that beneath all that turmoil there was nothing of any importance. I am not talking about the revolutionary movement of that time as a whole, but of the men at the head of it. So far as the movement is concerned, it was something painful and unhealthy, though crucial in its historic context, and it will certainly have a serious page in the Petersburg period of our history. Besides, this page, I cannot help thinking, is very far from having been written yet.

"And so I, who have long been in profound disagreement with those people and the aims of their movements, suddenly felt vexed and almost ashamed of their clumsiness: Why, I thought, must they be so stupid and clumsy? Not that it was any business of mine. It was not their lack of success I felt sorry for. Actually, I have never known any of those who were responsible for scattering the leaflets, but the reason why I felt so sad just then was that I realized that it was not a question of a stupid escapade of some foolish people who did not matter. It was the total lack of understanding of reality of people with a high level of education and mental development that was so depressing. Though I had lived in Petersburg for about three years and studied certain facts carefully, this revolutionary leaflet shook me that morning. It came to me like quite a new and unexpected revelation: never till that day had I dreamed of such utter ineptitude. Before the evening I suddenly thought of going to see Chernyshevsky. I had never before been to his place and neither had he been to mine.

"I think it was about five o'clock in the afternoon. I found him alone at his home, his servants having gone out, and he answered the door himself. He welcomed me very cordially and showed me into his study.

" 'Nikolai Gavrilovich,' I said, 'what's the meaning of this?' and I took out the leaflet.

"He took it as something he had never seen before and read it through. It only had about ten lines.

" 'Well,' he said with a faint smile, 'what about it?'

" 'Are they really so foolish and ridiculous? Is it impossible to stop them and put an end to this loathsome business?'

"He replied very impressively and weightily:

" 'Do you suppose that I am in sympathy with them and do you think that I could have had any part in the writing of this leaflet?'

" 'Of course not,' I replied, 'and I don't even think it necessary to assure you of it. But it is necessary to stop them at all costs. Your word carries some weight with them and it goes without saying that they are afraid of your opinion.'

" 'I don't know any of them.'

" 'I'm sure of it. But it isn't at all necessary to know them or talk to them personally. You have only to declare your condemnation aloud somewhere and it will reach them.'

" 'It may not have any effect. Besides, such things are unavoidable.'

" 'And yet they do a lot of harm to everyone and everything.'

"Just then another visitor rang the doorbell, I don't remember who. I went away. I consider it my duty to state that I spoke frankly to Chernyshevsky and I believed and still believe that he was not 'in sympathy' with those distributors of revolutionary leaflets. I could not help feeling that my visit was not unwelcome to Chernyshevsky; a few days later he confirmed it by calling on me. He spent an hour with me and, I confess, I rarely met a more gentle or more affable man, so that even then I could not help being surprised at some stories about his character which was said to be harsh and unsociable. I realized that he wished to get acquainted with me and, I remember, I appreciated it. Then I called on him again and he on me too. Soon, because of certain circumstances, I went to live in Moscow and spent nine months there. Our acquaintanceship ceased. After that Chernyshevsky was arrested and exiled. I never could discover the reason for his arrest and exile; I don't know it even now."

The political disorders first began in 1861 at Petersburg University. Many students were arrested; some of them were even imprisoned in the Peter and Paul Fortress (*Time* sent them a huge joint of roast beef and bottles of red wine to show its sympathy with the "liberal" ideas of their movement), and exiled to Siberia. Finally, the university was closed down, though the authorities permitted extramural lectures by its professors at the Council Chamber of the Petersburg Municipality. But these too ceased after a disorderly meeting, "the famous literary and musical evening," as Strakhov calls it, which took place on March 2, 1862, in celebration of the 1,000th anniversary of the foundation of the Russian state. Dostoevsky, who gave one of his public readings at the meeting, gave a more or less exact description of it in *The Devils.* The chief speaker was a professor of Petersburg University, who in his lecture (which had been approved by the censorship) referred to the bitter cup the Russian people had had to drain during the thousand years of Russia's history. "On the ascension to the throne of our present safely reigning monarch," he went on, "the cup was full to the brim. . . ." He was not allowed to finish the sentence in which he declared that the Emperor had removed some of its bitter contents by the liberation of the peasants. His words were interpreted to mean something quite different, and the rest of his sentence was drowned in thunderous applause and cries of "Bravo!" The curious thing was that those who shouted most vociferously were not, as Orest Miller points out, "nihilists," but the adherents of the right-wing Slavophile camp, and when the lecturer reached the phrase: "Our administrators are standing on the edge of a precipice," the enthusiasm of the extreme Slavophiles merged with the enthusiasm of the revolutionary "nihilists," although each extremist party understood "administrators" to mean something different.

It was to drive home the fact that the group of writers gathered round *Time*, including the former Slavophile critic Apollon Grigoryev, had nothing to do with either camp that Dostoevsky thought it necessary to publish on the back cover of the first number of his periodical a further "announcement," attacking the Westerners for their idea of Russia as "a piece of ballet scenery, beautiful but abstract and unjust" and the Slavophiles for donning ancient Russian costumes and imagining that by doing so they achieved a union with the common people of Russia. But even in the attempt to dissociate themselves from both the Westerners and the Slavophiles there was no complete agreement between the *Time* contributors, Apollon Grigoryev feeling much closer to his old friends of the Slavophile camp. Indeed, Mikhail's question "What kind of profound philosophers are Kireyevsky and Khomyakov?" (the two intellectual leaders of the Slavophiles) so offended the critic that he left for Orenburg and for a time refused to have anything to do with the Dostoevskys. Later he accused Mikhail of "working Dostoevsky's great gifts like a stagecoach horse" by demanding that Dostoevsky should finish *The Insulted and Injured* by July 1861, that is, six months after the publication of its first installment. Dostoevsky, who was well aware of the shortcomings of his semiautobiographical novel with its chain of improbable and mysterious events, wrote in a note published in 1864 in the November issue of *Epoch*: "If I have written a magazine novel (which I confess I have) it was my own fault and no one else's. I have written like that all my life, all I have ever published was written by me like that, except *Poor People* and a few chapters of *The House of the Dead*. It often happeneed in my literary life that the beginning of a chapter of a novel or short story was already set up in type at the printer's while the ending was still in my head but *had* to be written without fail by next day. Having got accustomed to working like that, I did the same with *The Insulted and Injured*, forced by no one but of my own free will. A new journal, whose success was more important to me than anything else, had to have a novel and I had offered to write one in four parts. I assured my brother that I had worked out the plot long ago (which was not true), that I should find it easy to write and that the first part had already been written. This time I did not do it for the sake of money. I am quite ready to admit that many of the characters of my novel are puppets and not living people, stock characters (as Grigoryev put it) and not characters who had assumed an artistic form (which really required more time to mature in heart and soul). I naturally realized it, though perhaps only vaguely. But what I did know for certain when I began writing it was (1) that though my novel might not turn out as well as I liked, it would have poetry, (2) that it would have two or three strong and passionate passages, and (3) that two of its more serious characters would be delineated perfectly and *even* artistically. That certainty was enough for me. What resulted was a rather crude novel, but it has about fifty pages of which I am proud."

The novel was received coldly by the critics, except by Chernyshevsky, who declared it to be "the most important thing" in the new periodical, and by Nikolai Dobrolyubov, the brilliant young literary critic of the *Contemporary*, who liked the "social discords" in the novel and hailed Dostoevsky as a remarkable novelist of "the humanist movement."

Quite different was the effect produced by the publication of *The House of the Dead*, the first installment of which had appeared in *The Russian World* on September 1, 1860, but which was published in full in *Time*, from April 1861 to December 1862. It a letter to Dostoevsky on January 7, 1862, Turgenev expressed his admiration for the book. "I am very grateful to you," he wrote, "for sending me the two numbers of *Time* which I am reading with great delight. Your *House of the Dead*, in particular. The picture of the *bathhouse* is simply Dantesque and in your characterization of the different persons (for instance, Petrov) there is a great deal of subtle and true psychology. I am sincerely glad of the success of your journal and, I repeat, I am ready to help you in any way I can."

In *The House of the Dead* Dostoevsky challenged Chernyshevsky's theory of "enlightened egoism" for the first time without referring, however, to any of the "utilitarians" by name. "Some people say," he wrote, "that the highest love of your neighbor is also the highest egoism. What egoism has to do with it I shall never understand." In this book he goes even further than in *The Insulted and Injured* in his admiration of religious meekness and "active" love, to two qualities that were to become the most distinguishing characteristics of two of his favorite heroes—Prince Myshkin in *The Idiot* and Alyosha in *The Brothers Karamazov*. In *The House of the Dead* it is the twenty-two-year-old Aley, a Muslim from the Caucasus, whom he admires most for those two "Christian" virtues. "He was as chaste as an innocent little girl," he writes about Aley in the fourth chapter, "and every time he saw a vile, sordid, violent, cynical or unjust action in prison his beautiful eyes used to blaze up with indignation and grow more beautiful because of that. He avoided quarrels and never used bad language, though he was not one of those who allowed themselves to be insulted with impunity, for he knew how to stand up for himself. But then, no one picked a quarrel with him: everyone loved him and was nice to him. . . . There are people who possess such beautiful natures and who have been so richly endowed by God that the very thought that they could at some time or another change for the worse never occurs to you. You feel that you never need worry about them. I, too, feel now that I need not worry about Aley. . . ."

It was these idealized qualities of religious meekness and Christian love that Tolstoy found so appealing about the book. "The other day," Tolstoy wrote to Strakhov on September 26, 1880, "I did not feel well and I reread *The House of the Dead.* I had forgotten a lot of it and I can honestly say that I don't know of a better book in the whole of our modern literature, including Pushkin. It is not its tone, but its point of view that is so marvelous: it is sincere, natural and Christian. It is a good, edifying book. If you see Dostoevsky, tell him I love him."

In Dostoevsky's public readings, too, it was the extracts from *The House of the Dead* that evoked the greatest applause from his enthusiastic young audience. Orest Miller remarks that Dostoevsky used these readings for propagating his views on "a return to the soil" as the only way to bridge the existing gulf between the mass of illiterate peasants and the educated section of the Russian population. "I vividly remember the first time I saw and heard Dostoevsky at a literary evening," he writes. "He read about the death of a convict in the prison hospital from *The House of the Dead.* I do not know whether Dostoevsky had chosen that scene intentionally, for it clearly expressed the difference between his attitude towards the peasants from that of those who had invited him to give his reading—the difference which made him declare in *The House of the Dead*: 'Our wise men cannot teach our people a great deal . . . it is they themselves who need to learn from them.' It was only after Dostoevsky's death," Orest Miller concludes, "that I learned that he greatly disliked reading in public because he was usually asked to read from his *House of the Dead.* 'It looks,' he once said to Strakhov after such a reading, 'as though I am always complaining to the public—that is no good.' It is clear that he realized very well that he was asked to read just that simply as a demonstration." But Orest Miller is exaggerating "the torture," as he put it, Dostoevsky must have felt on realizing that particular aspect of his public reading. He was not at all appalled by what he called "the interest" his name aroused. Nor was he averse to the applause of the multitude. On the contrary, he reveled in it.

VI

The success of *Time,* which doubled the number of its subscribers in one year, was due chiefly, as Strakhov rightly points out, to Dostoevsky's "interesting" name. "My name," he told Strakhov when traveling with him in Switzerland in 1862, "is worth a million." But it was also due to the hard work Dostoevsky put in for *Time* during the first months of its existence. He wrote, in addition to his novel, many of the articles published in its first three issues—hard work that resulted in a violent attack of epilepsy, which laid him low for three whole days. His epileptic seizures, Strakhov records, usually took place once every month, though occasionally he had two attacks in one week. Strakhov only witnessed one such attack. It was on Easter Eve of 1863: "Dostoevsky came to see me at eleven o'clock," Strakhov writes, "and we began an animated conversation. I can't remember what exactly it was we were discussing, but I know that it was an important abstract subject. Dostoevsky grew very excited and began pacing the room, while I remained sitting at the table. He was saying something grand and gay and when I made a remark in support of what he was saying, he turned to me with an inspired face, showing that his animation had reached a climax. He stopped for a moment as though searching for words to express his thought and had already opened his mouth. I looked at him with keen anticipation, feeling that he was about to say something unusual, that I was about to hear some revelation. Suddenly a strange, drawn-out, senseless sound issued from his opened mouth and he sank unconscious to the floor in the middle of the room. This time it was not a violent attack. His body merely kept twitching and at the corners of his mouth were flecks of foam. Half an hour later, he came to and I saw him off to his home which was not far off."

Dostoevsky, Strakhov records, did most of his writing at night, from midnight only, when the whole house had gone to bed and he remained alone with the samovar. Sipping his not too strong and almost cold tea, he wrote till 5 or 6 o'clock in the morning. He got up at 2 or even 3 o'clock in the afternoon and spent the day receiving visitors, going for walks, or visiting friends. His usual reading, according to Strakhov, consisted of Russian journals and newpapers. His attention was always directed towards his fellow writers and the criticisms of them and himself. He set great store on any kind of success and any kind of praise, and was greatly upset when he was attacked or abused.

The editorial offices of *Time* were in Mikhail's flat, and Dostoevsky's flat was only a few blocks away. Strakhov describes the district as dirty and thickly populated by the poor of the metropolis. "In many of his novels, especially in *Crime and Punishment*, Dostoevsky gives a marvelous picture of those streets and their inhabitants. In those depressing streets that filled us with disgust we all spent several happy years." Strakhov and Dostoevsky usually met at the editorial offices of *Time* at 3 o'clock in the afternoon, read the newspapers and journals, went for walks, then met again at 7 o'clock at Strakhov's. Their friendship at that time was very close. "It was a feeling," Strakhov writes, "that passed into tenderness. After an epileptic attack, Dostoevsky would at first lapse into a state of black depression. Everything irritated and frightened him and the presence of those nearest to him was a burden to him. It was then that his brother or wife sent for me—he felt at ease with me and he gradually recovered."

It was Dostoevsky himself who broke the uneasy truce between *Time* and the *Contemporary* in his article *[Dobrolyu]bov and the Problem of Art*, published in 1861 in the February issue of *Time*. In it he attacked the "utilitarians" for demanding of art "direct, instantaneous, immediate usefulness, strictly in accordance with the prevailing circumstances and in obedience to them, so much so that if at a certain time society is preoccupied with the solution of a certain problem, then art must not have any other aim than the solution of that problem." While such an aim may be desirable, an artist must not be forced to pursue it, because "the first law of art is the freedom of inspiration and creation. . . . Art," Dostoevsky wrote in concluding his article, "will be true to man only if its freedom of development is not hampered. That is why art must never be constrained by all sorts of aims, no laws must be prescribed for it, nothing must be done to disconcert it, for it has, as it is, to deal with many underwater rocks, many temptations and deviations which are inseparable from the historic life of man. The freer its development, the more normal is it bound to be and the sooner will it find its true and *useful* path. And since its interest and aims are identical with the aims of man whom it serves and with whom it is indivisibly united, the freer its development is, the more benefits will it bring to mankind."

This challenge to the "utilitarians" could, of course, not be permitted to go unanswered, and the full fury of the *Contemporary*, which had just then launched its attack on Turgenev's *Fathers and Sons*, was turned on *Time*. Dostoevsky responded by publishing an article by Strakhov in which Turgenev was extolled as "a truly objective artist" and Bazarov, the hero of *Fathers and Sons*, declared to be "a truly observed character." The praise of Turgenev's novel was taken up by Dostoevsky himself in the February 1863 issue of *Time* in his *Winter Notes on Summer Impressions*, in which he attacked the *Contemporary* writers for their supercilious claim to have solved all problems. "With what an air of calm self-complacency," Dostoevsky wrote, "we have given Turgenev a thrashing for having refused to remain quiescent and dissatisfied with our majestic personalities or to accept them as an ideal, and for looking for something better than us. Better than us? Good Lord! Can there be anything better or fairer than us under the sun? So they attacked him for his Bazarov, the restless and yearning Bazarov (a sign of a great heart), in spite of all his nihilism. Why, we have given him a thrashing even for his Kukshina, the progressive louse Turgenev has combed out of Russian life, and we did not hesitate to add that he was against the emancipation of women. . . ."

There was no love lost between Dostoevsky and Turgenev, but during that short period when both of them found themselves adrift in Russia, they did their best to forget the past and be friends. When Turgenev arrived in Petersburg in the spring of 1862, he paid a visit to the editorial offices of *Time* and invited Dostoevsky, Mikhail and Strakhov to dinner at his hotel. "The storm raised against him," Strakhov observes, "quite obviously disturbed him." At dinner he talked "with great animation and charm" and, learning of Dostoevsky's proposed trip abroad, warned him against "the clever and mean tricks" employed by foreigners to inveigle the innocent Russians to part with their money, a warning singularly inappropriate in the case of Dostoevsky, not only because he had not enough money to interest the lurking foreigner, but also because he was only too ready to part with his money at the first roulette table that came his way. All the same, considering Dostoevsky's professed belief, as expressed in one of his first articles in *Time*, "that the Russian nation is an extraordinary phenomenon in the history of entire mankind" and that "the character of the Russian people is so unlike the character of all modern European peoples that the Europeans are unable to understand it," such a warning could have scarcely passed unheeded by him.

[7]

FIRST JOURNEY ABROAD: BAAL AND THE BOURGEOIS

Dostoevsky left for his first journey abroad on the morning of June 7, 1862. He spent two and a half months abroad, visiting Berlin, Dresden, Wiesbaden, Baden-Baden, Paris, London, Lucerne, Geneva, Genoa, Florence, Milan, Venice and Vienna. In his letter to Andrey on June 6th he gave as the reason for his journey his desire to consult specialists about his epilepsy. The same reason he had no doubt also given to his wife, Maria, who, always afraid that he might die and leave her penniless, had insisted on his making over to her the 2,500 rubles a Petersburg publisher owed him for the book edition of his *House of the Dead*. He told Andrey that he had to leave his wife in Petersburg because he had no money for her to travel with him and because she could not leave her son, who was just then working for his exams—none of which was true. "I have longed to go abroad many times," he wrote a few months after his return to Petersburg in his *Winter Notes on Summer Impressions*, "almost since my childhood. . . . The whole land of 'holy miracles,' " he continued, quoting a line from an early poem by Khomyakov, "seemed to me like the promised land. . . . In short, I was seized by an unquenchable thirst for something new, for a change of place, for general, synthetic, panoramic, perspective impressions. . . ." There was another reason he does not mention: the lure of roulette. It was true that, as he wrote to Andrey, the affairs of *Time* were going "incredibly well" and that they had 4,200 subscribers that year, but they had incurred many debts the year before, and they could expect to achieve financial stability only in two or three years. It was a long time to wait, and, as he confessed in *The Gambler*, the novel in which he described his first impressions of roulette, "however ridiculous it may seem that I should be expecting so much for myself from roulette, the opinion held by everyone that it is absurd and stupid to expect something from gambling is even more ridiculous. Why should gambling be worse than any other method of acquiring money—trade, for instance? It is true that only one out of a hundred wins, but what has that got to do with me? . . . I really don't see anything sordid in the desire to win as quickly as possible and as much as possible. I always thought it was very stupid of a certain well-fed and well-to-do moralist who said to a man who had tried to justify his gambling by pleading that he gambled only for small stakes: 'More's the pity, it's a sign of petty greed!'—as though petty greed is not the same as great greed. It's all relative. What is a trifle for Rothschild is a lot for me, and as for making money or winning it, people do it everywhere, and not only at the roulette table. All they do, in fact, is take away or win something from one another. Whether winning money or making a profit is good or bad is another question."

He knew, of course, from his own experience that he had not the necessary firmness of character for gambling, but he could not resist the thrill of staking everything on a certain number. "With what avidity," he wrote in *The Gambler*, "do I look at the gaming table with the scattered louis d'ors, friedrichsdors and thalers, at the little piles of gold coins forming small heaps of glowing metal when raked in by the croupier or the tall columns of silver coins grouped around the wheel. As soon as I catch the sound of jingling money, even if I am two rooms away from the roulette chamber, I am almost seized with convulsions." What was even worse, he felt overcome with a strange sensation during the game: "I remember distinctly," he wrote, "that I was suddenly seized by a terrible craving to take a risk. Perhaps after experiencing so many strange sensations, one's soul is not satiated and demands more and more powerful sensations until at last it is too tired to wish for anything. . . ." And even when he happened to win there arose in him "a strange sensation to challenge fate, a kind of desire to give it a punch on the nose, to stick out my tongue at it," with the inevitable result that he lost everything he had and left the gaming table "stunned." That was exactly what happened on his first visit to the casino in Wiesbaden on his way to Paris.

He was so eager to try his luck there that he spent only one day in Berlin. (The weather was very bad, he explained in his *Winter Notes*, and one look at Berlin showed him that it was quite incredibly like Petersburg.) We learn of his bad luck at Wiesbaden from Mikhail's letter to him on June 26, 1862. "For God's sake," Mikhail implored him, "don't gamble any more. Why challenge fate with our kind of luck? What you won't earn with your head, you won't get by luck." And a month later: "After your debacle in Wiesbaden your letters have assumed a sort of subdued tone."

Smarting under the stings of misfortune, Dostoevsky did not even stop to admire Cologne Cathedral, which, he recalled in his *Winter Notes*, he had drawn with such veneration during his lectures on architecture at the Army Engineering College. He got angry at being asked to pay for walking across the new Cologne toll bridge. "Hang it all," he thought, "what are they so proud of their bridge for? Haven't we Russians invented the samovar?" And off he went to Paris. Of "the wonders of nature" he had so far only seen the banks of the Rhine, which, he wrote to Strakhov from Paris,[1] really were "a wonderful sight." Paris itself, he told Strakhov in the same letter, "is a most boring city." If there had not been so many really remarkable things there he would have died of boredom. The French, he went on, just made him sick. The Frenchman was quiet, honest, polite, but false at heart, and money was everything to him. He had no ideals whatever. The level of general education was low to a degree. "You will perhaps laugh," he added, realizing that he was talking a little wildly, "that I am passing judgment on the French after spending only ten days in Paris. I admit it, but (1) what I have seen during the ten days so far confirms my idea and (2) there are certain facts that one can observe and understand within half an hour, but which, by the very fact that such things exist and are possible, clearly reveal whole aspects of the social conditions of a people." Fifteen years earlier, as he confesses in his *Winter Notes*, he had worshiped Western Europe and, especially, France with a veneration that was "almost eccentric." But now he was no less certain that there existed "a chemical fusion of the human spirit with the native soil" and that it was quite impossible "to tear oneself away from it."

The truth is that, whereas in 1847 he would have gone abroad to admire and worship, he went abroad in 1862 for the sole purpose of finding fault and critizing. Though many years were still to pass before, like Ivan in *The Brothers Karamazov,* he was to look upon Western Europe as "a graveyard," he was now moving very close to the Slavophiles, though still condemning them for thinking that they could achieve a spiritual union with the Russian peasant by purely external means. Herzen, whom Dostoevsky went to see in London, was struck by the rather confused nature of his political ideas. "Yesterday," he wrote to the radical poet Nikolai Ogaryov on July 17, 1862, "Dostoevsky came to see me. He is naïve, a little confused, but a very nice man. Believes with enthusiasm in the Russian people."

The fact that he still associated with Herzen, that he went to see Bakunin, who had just arrived in London after escaping from Siberia, and had a soft spot for Chernyshevsky, whose utilitarian ideas he abominated, shows that he was still sitting on the fence, a political attitude quite incomprehensible to any Russian politician and incredible in a man like Dostoevsky, who could not help going to extremes.

II

Dostoevsky arrived in London on July 9, 1862 and stayed eight days. "I was in London," he wrote in his *Winter Notes*, "and did not see St.

[1] *Letters,* July 8, 1862.

Paul's. It's true. I did not see St. Paul's. . . . There you have the first adventure of mine that does not redound to my honor (that is, I did see it from a distance, but was in a hurry to get to Pentonville, so I just gave up the idea of seeing it and drove past it)." What Dostoevsky wanted to go to Pentonville for, he does not say. Herzen lived in a different part of the town, in Orsett House, Westbourne Terrace, and he had no other acquaintances in London. Was he anxious to have a look at Pentonville Jail and compare it with the prison he had been at in Siberia? Dostoevsky, as Strakhov, who spent some time with him in Italy, remarks, "was not particularly interested in nature, or in historical monuments, or in works of art, with the exception perhaps of the greatest, all his attention being directed to people, *their* nature, and perhaps also the general impression of the life of the streets." It was the latter, in fact, that he found so enthralling in London.

"Everything in London," he writes in his *Winter Notes*, "is so vast and so jarring in its originality. Every jarring note, every contradiction seems to live peacefully side by side with its antithesis, and they go forward hand in hand, contradicting each other, but without apparently excluding each other. . . . And yet here too one becomes aware of the same hard, stubborn, inveterate fight, a fight to the death between the general Western European individualistic principle and the necessity of somehow or other living together, of somehow or other establishing a community and settling down in one anthill; to turn themselves into an anthill so long as they could live together without devouring each other, for the only other alternative is to turn themselves into cannibals. Here one becomes aware of the same thing as in Paris: there is the same desperate tendency to preserve the *status quo* out of sheer despair, to tear out with one's flesh all desires and hopes, to execrate one's future, in which even the leaders themselves perhaps have not sufficient faith, and prostrate themselves before Baal." Realizing, however, that in his analysis of the industrial revolution, as it unfolded itself before his eyes in the London of the World Exhibition, he may have gone a little too far, Dostoevsky hastens to point out the difference between Paris, where the "bourgeois" is quite unconsciously pleased with himself, and London, where the general atmosphere is so "crushing." He then goes on to give a truly Dantesque picture of London in the toils of Baal that was to affect all his thinking to the end of his life.

"This city bustling day and night, unbounded like the sea, the whine and growl of the machines, the trains running over the houses (and soon under the houses too), this boldness of enterprise, this seeming disorder, which, in fact, is capitalist order of the highest degree, this polluted Thames, this air impregnated with coal fumes, these magnificent squares and parks, these terrible slums, like Whitechapel with its half-naked, savage and hungry population, the City with its millions and world trade, the Crystal Palace, the world exhibition. . . . Yes, the exhibition is amazing. You feel the terrible force which here unites all those numberless people from all over the world into one fold; you are conscious of some gigantic idea; you feel that here something has already been achieved, that here is victory, triumph. You even begin to fear something. However independent you may be, you can't for some reason help feeling terrified. 'Is this really the attained ideal?' you ask yourself. 'Is this the end? Is this really "the one fold"? Will one really have to accept this as the final truth and fall down before it, mute and silent for ever?' All this is so triumphant, so victorious, so proud that you are rendered breathless. You gaze at these hundreds of thousands, at these millions of people, who so meekly gather here from every corner of the globe—people who came with one single thought, quietly, doggedly and silently thronging this enormous Crystal Palace, and you feel that here something has come to pass for good and all, it has come to pass and come to an end. It's a kind of Biblical picture, something like Babylon, a kind of prophecy from the Apocalypse which is being fulfilled before our very eyes. You feel that one must possess an immense amount of spiritual resistance and a great force of denial not to give in to this impression, not to accept the fact and deify Baal, that is to say, not to accept the existing state of things as your ideal. . . ."

Was all this "nonsense, morbid nonsense, exaggeration"? A picture conjured up out of the Apocalypse by "a well-fed dilettante" as a sop to his strained nerves? Dostoevsky admits that he might have been carried away by "the scenery," but, he goes on, "if you saw how mighty is the spirit that created this colossal scenery and how proudly this spirit is convinced of his victory and his triumph, you would have stood aghast at his pride, his obstinacy and his blindness, and felt alarmed for those over whom this proud spirit soars and reigns. At such hugeness and such enormous pride of the ruling spirit, at such a triumphant finishing touch of the creation of this spirit, a hungry soul too is quite often abashed, humbled, looks for salvation in gin and dissipation and begins to believe that all this is as it should be. . . ." He then proceeds to give this Hogarthian scene of dissipation of the London working classes.

"In London you can see crowds so vast, and in such a setting as you will not see anywhere else in the world. For instance, I was told that every Saturday night half a million workers, men and women, with their children, pour into the streets like a flood, mostly flocking to certain quarters of the town, and all through the night, till five o'clock in the morning, they are taking part in a bacchanalian revel, eating and drinking like beasts, to last a whole week. All this, of course, means going short for the rest of the week, saving up their meager earnings gained with toil, sweat, and curses. In the butchers' and grocers' shops flaring gas jets light up the streets brightly. It is as though a ball had been prepared for these white Negroes. The people swarm round the open taverns and in the streets where they eat and drink. The public houses are as gay as palaces. All are drunk, but not cheerfully; everything is somber, dull and somehow ominously quiet. Only from time to time is this brooding silence, which weighs so heavily upon you, broken by loud curses and bloodthirsty fights. All seem to be set on getting dead drunk as quickly as possible. Wives are no better than their men and get drunk with them; the children run about and crawl between them.

"On such a night, at two o'clock in the morning," Dostoevsky relates, "I lost my way and wandered about for hours in the streets among the countless multitudes of this gloomy people, driven to ask the way almost by signs as I don't know a word of English. I found my way at last, but the impression of what I had seen haunted me for the next three days. The common people are the same everywhere, but here everything is so overwhelming, so startling, that what existed before only in your imagination, now confronts you as palpable reality. Here you are no longer aware even of people, but of an insensible human mass, a general loss of consciousness, systematic, resigned, encouraged. When you look at these outcasts of society, you feel that for a long time to come the prophecy will not be fulfilled for them; that for a long time there will be no palm branches for them, nor white robes; that for a long time they will call in vain to the throne of the Almighty, 'How long, O Lord?'

"But they know this themselves, and till now they have been protesting against the wrongs society has inflicted on them by forming all kinds of dark religious sects. We are surprised at the folly of people embracing such superstitions, but we fail to realize that what we see here is a rejection of our social formula, an obstinate, unconscious, instinctive separation, a separation at all costs, for the sake of salvation, a separation accompanied by a feeling of disgust with us, and fear, too. These millions, abandoned and driven away from the world's feast, jostling and crushing each other in the outer darkness into which they have been flung by their more fortunate brothers, are groping blindly to knock at the gates—any gates, looking desperately for a way of escape from the suffocating dark cellar. Here we are witnessing a last desperate attempt to huddle together into one mass, prepared to abandon even the semblance of human beings, so long as they can have a life of their own, so long as they can keep away from us.

"Anyone who has ever visited London has probably been to the Haymarket, if only once. This is the quarter which at night is crowded with women of the street. The streets are lighted by clusters of gas jets of which we have no idea in our country. Magnificent coffeehouses, ornamented with mirrors and gold, at every step. There are crowds of people here. One cannot help feeling terrified making one's way through them. And how odd they are. Old women and beautiful young girls before whom you stop dead in sheer astonishment. In the whole world you won't find such beautiful women as in England. . . .

"There is no room for the crowds on the pavements and they spill over into the roadway. All of them are intent on some booty and rush with shameless cynicism upon the first man who crosses their path. There the ragged and the resplendent, the extremes of youth and age—all jostle together. In this terrible crowd you will find a drunken tramp and a rich man of title. You hear curses, quarrels, touting, and the gentle, inviting whisper of a still timid pretty girl. And what beauties you sometimes come across! Faces as though out of keepsakes. I remember one day I went into a 'casino.' A band was playing, people were dancing, the whole place was packed. Everything there was magnificent. But their somber character did not leave the English even amid their merrymaking: they looked serious even while dancing, even gloomy, and they went through their steps as though it were a sort of duty. Upstairs in the gallery I caught sight of a girl and I stopped dead in astonishment. Never before have I come across such ideal beauty! She was sitting at a table with a young man who seemed to be a rich gentleman, but who did not appear to be a habitué of the casino. . . . He spoke little to her . . . their conversation was often interrupted by long pauses. She too looked very sad. Her features were tender, delicate, and there was something suppressed and melancholy in her beautiful and rather proud eyes, some hidden thought, a yearning for something. She looked consumptive. She was, she could not but be intellectually superior to all that crowd of unfortunate women: otherwise what is there in a human face? And yet she drank gin, for which the young man paid. At last he got up, pressed her hand, and they parted. He left the casino, while she, her pale cheeks covered by hectic spots from the liquor she had drunk, went out and was lost in the crowd of prostitutes.

"In the Haymarket I saw mothers who had brought their young daughters, girls still in their teens, to be sold to men. Little girls of about twelve seize you by the hand and ask you to go with them. One night I remember seeing among the crowd of people in the street a little girl who could not have been more than six years old. Her clothes were in tatters. She was dirty, barefoot, emaciated and beaten black and blue. Her body, which could be seen through the holes in her clothes, was all bruised. She was walking along aimlessly, hardly knowing where she was, and without apparently being in any hurry to get anywhere. Goodness knows why she was roaming about in the crowd; perhaps she was hungry. No one paid any attention to her. But what struck me most about her was that she looked so wretched and unhappy. Such hopeless despair was written all over her face that to see that little creature already experiencing so much damnation and despair was somehow unnatural and terribly painful. She kept shaking her disheveled head from side to side, as though debating some highly important question with herself, waving her little hands about and gesticulating wildly, and then, suddenly, clapping them together and pressing them to her bare chest. I went back and gave her sixpence. She seized the small silver coin, gave me a wild look of startled surprise, and suddenly began running in the opposite direction as fast as her little legs would carry her, as though terrified that I should take the money away from her. Altogether titillating subjects. . . ."

Dostoevsky never forgot the little girl in the Haymarket. Fourteen years later he was to use her as a symbol of the pitiful and as an object of mercy in one of the most imaginative of his "philosophic tales," *The Dream of a Ridiculous Man.*

"But when night has passed and the day dawns," Dostoevsky concluded his impressions of London, "the same proud and somber spirit once more majestically sweeps over the gigantic city. He is not disturbed by what has taken place at night, neither is he disturbed by what he sees around him by day. Baal reigns and does not even demand submission, because he is sure of it. His faith in himself is boundless; he hands out organized charity disdainfully and calmly in order to be left in peace, and that is why it is impossible to shake his self-confidence. Baal does not hide from himself, as they do in Paris, for instance, certain savage, suspicious and disturbing facts. The poverty, the suffering, the murmur and the torpor of the masses do not disturb him in the least. He contemptuously permits all these suspicious and ominous facts to live next to his own life, beside him. He does not try, like the Parisian, pusillanimously and strenuously to shut his eyes to facts, to encourage himself and pretend that everything is peaceful and as it should be. He does not hide away the poor as they do in Paris, so that they should not disturb and frighten him while he is asleep. The Parisian likes to bury his head in the sand like the ostrich so that he should not see the hunters who are catching up with him. In Paris. . . ."

But the French bourgeois was easy game to Dostoevsky, and his strictures against him are neither very profound nor very original. The remarkable fact about his first journey to Western Europe is that he saw what he had intended to see all along. He was convinced long before he had started on his journey that Western Europe had nothing more to offer to Russia, but that, on the contrary, it was Russia which had the right solution for the ills that afflicted Western Europe. "The Western European," he writes in his *Winter Notes*, "talks of brotherhood as of the great moving force of mankind, but he does not suspect that one cannot get brotherhood if it does not exist. What, then, is to be done? One has to achieve brotherhood at all costs. But it appears that it is impossible to achieve brotherhood, that it achieves itself, it is given, it is found in man's nature. But in the nature of Western European man it is not found to be present; instead there is a personal element in it, the element of private ownership, of intense self-preservation, of considering one's own self as of equal value to everything that exists beside it. From such a conception no brotherhood can emerge. Why not? Because in brotherhood, in real brotherhood, it is not the individual who has to worry about his right to be deemed of equal value and of equal weight with all the rest, but all the rest who must come to this individual demanding his rights, and, without being asked, recognize him to be of equal value and weight to the rest in the world. Moreover, this rebellious individual ought first to sacrifice all of himself to society, he must not only abstain from demanding his rights, but, on the contrary, give himself to society without any demands. But the Western European is not used to such a procedure: he demands his rights, he wishes to *have a share*—and the result is that there is no brotherhood. But could he not become regenerated? Well, regeneration is a matter of thousands of years, for such ideas must first pass into the flesh and blood before they can become real. . . . One can do nothing about it, it must come to pass by itself, it must be part of man's nature, it must be contained unconsciously in the nature of the whole tribe, in short, for a brotherly, loving element to exist, one must love."

The only way of achieving such a brotherhood of man Dostoevsky held to be the Russian way, in which he believed "man himself is instinctively drawn to brotherhood, to a life in a commune, to a life of mutual concord. In spite of the barbarous coarseness and ignorance which have taken root in his nation, in spite of the age-long slavery, the invasion of alien hordes. In short, in his case the need for a brotherly commune is inbred in his nature, for he had this habit from time immemorial."

The Slavophiles, too, were all for reviving the ancient Russian peasant "commune," but they never went so far as to claim it as the only way of bringing about the universal brotherhood of man. No wonder Herzen thought Dostoevsky naïve. What Herzen did not suspect was the fierceness with which Dostoevsky was going to defend this idea of the Russian common people as the sole depository of the mystery of the brotherhood of man. Indeed, Dostoevsky was to go even further than that: he was to persuade himself that this innate capacity for brotherhood was the result of the Russian people's centuries-long suffering and submission, and that, therefore, suffering and submission were the only means of achieving happiness. True brotherhood, he writes in his *Winter Notes*, "must say to the man who offers to sacrifice himself for the good of the brotherhood: 'You are offering too much to us. We have no right to accept it, for you say yourself: that is what all your happiness consists of. But what can we do if our hearts ache incessantly also for your happiness? Therefore, take everything from us too. We shall try with all our might that you should have more personal liberty and more self-expression. Do no longer be afraid of any enemies, neither of man nor of nature. We are all for you, we all guarantee your safety, we shall all be exerting ourselves on your behalf, for we are all your brothers and there are many of us and we are strong; so keep absolutely calm and cheerful, fear naught and put your trust in us.' After which," Dostoevsky concludes, "there can be no question of sharing anything, for everything will be shared out automatically. . . . What a utopia, gentlemen! Everything based on feeling and nature and not on reason. Why, it seems even to be a degradation of reason. What do you think? Is it a utopia or not?" Dostoevsky did not think it was utopian, because of his belief in the innate feeling for brotherhood in the Russian peasant. He was no less strongly convinced that this "element of brotherhood" was absent from the nature of the "West European man" and that, therefore, the attempt of the Western socialists "to persuade man to accept the idea of brotherhood" was doomed to failure. As for the "lure" of living on a purely rational basis, man being promised a job and guaranteed a proper wage in exchange for "a tiny drop of his personal freedom for the good of all," it is, in Dostoevsky's opinion, all an illusion, for no man would agree to live on such terms, because "even a tiny drop will seem heavy to him. Fool that he is," Dostoevsky writes, "man can't help feeling that his freedom is best of all. The socialist, of course, just throws up his hands in despair and tells him that he is a fool, that he has still to grow up, that he is not mature and does not understand where his own advantage lies; that an ant, a mute and insignificant ant, is cleverer than he, because in an anthill everything is so good, everything is so well ordered, all are well fed and happy, everyone knows his job, in short—man is still a long way off from the anthill."

III

During the next eighteen years Dostoevsky did nothing more than develop this argument. For the time being he kept the Orthodox faith out of it, for so far religion did not play any part either in his writings or in his private life. Indeed, Strakhov stated quite definitely that he did not remember Dostoevsky referring to religion in any of his private conversations with him at that period. And there were many occasions during which Dostoevsky could have discussed religion with him if he had felt as strongly about it as he did during the last ten years of his life. In July 1862 they traveled together in Switzerland and Italy. In a letter from Paris,[2] in which Dostoevsky had invited Strakhov to travel with him, he complained of terrible loneliness, aggravated by bad weather. "Oh," he wrote, "if only we could travel together! We shall see Naples, go for walks in Rome, and who knows?—perhaps make love to a young Venetian girl in a gondola. (Eh? Nikolai Nikolayevich?) But, 'nothing, nothing, silence,' as Poprishchin [the hero of Gogol's story *The Diary of a Madman*] says in a similar contingency."

The bantering tone, on which some of Dostoevsky's biographers have pounced so avidly as further evidence of his uncontrollable sexual im-

[2] *Letters*, July 8, 1862.

pulses, shows how gently he treated Strakhov's incompetence where women were concerned and contrasts with Strakhov's assumption of a high moral tone towards his less inhibited colleague. They met in Geneva, where occurred the scene with the hotel waiter described by Strakhov in his letter to Tolstoy. Anna, in her defense of her husband, declares in her reminiscences that because of his illness Dostoevsky was sometimes very quick-tempered and that it was quite possible that he shouted at the waiter who had been too slow to serve him, but that this was not "ill nature," only "impatience." Unfortunately, she goes on: "And how improbable the waiter's reply: 'I too am a man!' In Switzerland the common people are so rude that a servant, in reply to an insult, would not have confined himself to a few plaintive words, but would have known how to reply with redoubled arrogance, counting entirely on his impunity"—a perfect giveaway, throwing light on her own as well as on Dostoevsky's real attitude towards "the common people," as against his idealization of the Russian peasant, whom he did not really know and who never appears in his novels, and perhaps justifying Strakhov's strictures on the contrast between Dostoevsky's humanitarian sentiments and his temperamental outbursts.

Dostoevsky, Strakhov records, found Geneva too "gloomy and boring" a city, and they traveled to Lucerne, where they had a trip on a steamer on "the lake of four cantons." The weather was beautiful and they enjoyed the incomparable scenery enormously. From there they traveled to Turin and Genoa, where they took ship to Leghorn and then went by train to Florence. In Florence they spent a week in "a modest pension in Via Tornabuoni." There too, Strakhov reports, they did nothing that ordinary tourists did, but besides their walks they read a great deal. Victor Hugo's *Les Misérables* had just been published, and Dostoevsky bought it volume after volume and read three or four volumes during that week. Once Strakhov succeeded in inveigling him into the Uffizi, far as the Medici Venus. However, they enjoyed their walks in Florence, though Dostoevsky thought that the Arno was very like the Petersburg Fontanka. It was at dinner at their pension that the conversation about Garibaldi which is recorded in the *Winter Notes* took place. It was shortly before the battle of Aspromonte, on August 28, 1862, and the general view at the table was that Garibaldi was taking a great risk (he was, in fact, wounded and taken prisoner by the French). What enraged Dostoevsky and made him rush out of the room was the astonishment expressed by a Frenchman that while enjoying unlimited powers in Naples Garibaldi should not have appropriated any of the 20,000,000 lire of the city's funds. His keen dislike of the French, a consequence of his enthusiasm for the French utopian socialists in the 1840's, made him describe the scene, and particularly the French speaker, in much more violent terms than were warranted—such at least is Strakhov's view.

Mikhail Andreyevich Dostoevsky, Dostoevsky's father, and Maria Fyodorovna Dostoevsky, his mother

The Alexis Ravelin in the Peter and Paul Fortress, where Dostoevsky was incarcerated during his trial in 1849

F. M. Dostoevsky, 1847

Anna Grigoryevna Dostoevsky, nee Snitkin, Dostoevsky's second wife

Но вы какъ бы уже ...
рые прочтутъ здѣсь описанное и зовете ихъ въ бой? Не стыдясь признаться въ преступленіи, зачѣмъ стыдитесь вы покаянія? Пусть глядятъ на меня, говорите вы; ну, а вы сами какъ будете глядѣть на нихъ? Иныя мѣста въ вашемъ изложеніи усилены слогомъ; вы какъ бы любуетесь психологіей вашею и хватаетесь за каждую мелочь только бы удивить читателя безчувственностью которой въ васъ нѣтъ. Что же это какъ не горделивый вызовъ отъ виноватаго къ судьѣ?

— Гдѣ же вызовъ? Я устранилъ всякія разсужденія отъ моего лица.

Тихонъ смолчалъ. Даже краска покрыла его блѣдныя щеки.

— Оставимъ это, рѣзко прекратилъ Ставрогинъ.—Позвольте сдѣлать вамъ вопросъ уже съ моей стороны: вотъ уже пять минутъ какъ мы говоримъ послѣ этого (онъ кивнулъ на листки) и я не вижу въ васъ никакого выраженія гадливости или стыда... вы кажется не брезгливы!...

Онъ не докончилъ и усмѣхнулся.

— То-есть, вамъ хотѣлось бы чтобъ я высказалъ вамъ поскорѣе мое презрѣніе, твердо договорилъ Тихонъ. Я предъ вами ничего не утаю: меня ужаснула великая праздная сила ушедшая нарочито въ мерзость. Что же до самаго преступленія, то и многіе грѣшатъ тѣмъ же, но живутъ со своею совѣстью въ мирѣ и въ спокойствіи, даже считая неизбѣжными проступками юности. Есть и старцы, которые грѣшатъ тѣмъ же и даже съ утѣшеніемъ и съ игривостью. Всѣми этими ужасами наполненъ весь міръ. Вы же почувствовали всю глубину, что очень рѣдко случается въ такой степени.

— Ужь не уважать ли вы меня стали послѣ листковъ? криво усмѣхнулся Ставрогинъ.

Facsimile of galley proof with corrections in Dostoevsky's handwriting of ninth chapter of *The Devils* (the unpublished chapter "At Tikhon's," describing Stavrogin's rape of a young girl)

Facsimile of Dostoevsky's first draft of *The Brothers Karamazov*

Dostoevsky's writing desk

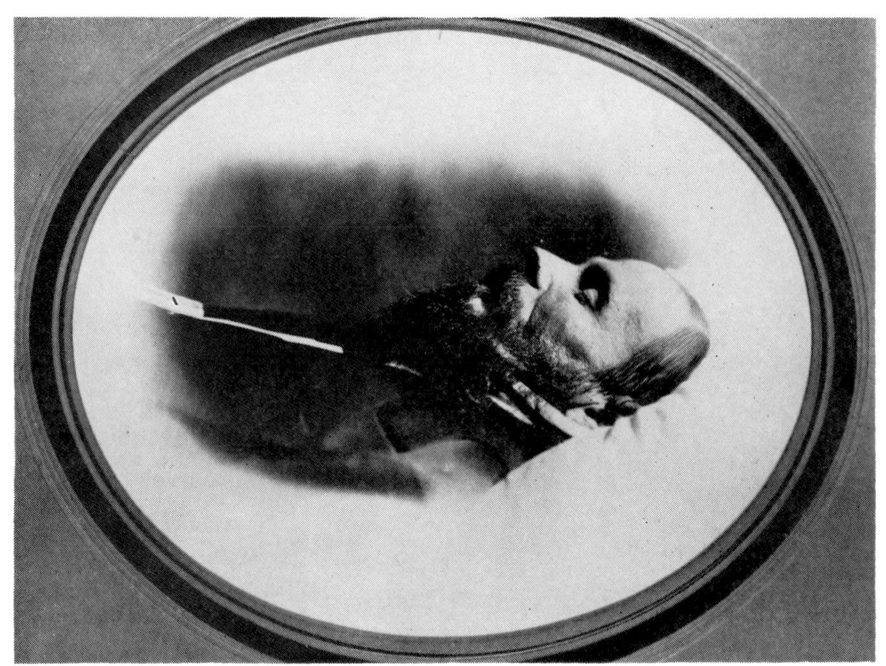

Dostoevsky on his death-bed, January 29, 1881

Dostoevsky's personal belongings

The sofa on which Dostoevsky died, with photograph of the Sistine Madonna over it

Dostoevsky's funeral in Petersburg, January 31, 1881

On his return to Petersburg in September 1862 Dostoevsky first of all wrote his third "manifesto," in which he again outlined the policy of his journal to its subscribers. For the first time he went over to the attack of the "utilitarians," who, after Turgnev's novel *Fathers and Sons,* were now generally known as "nihilists," though in his manifesto Dostoevsky preferred to dub them (after Apollon Grigoryev) "theoreticians." The "theoreticians," he maintained, never really knew "the people," that is, the peasants, and, indeed, always despised them. "We are absolutely certain," he wrote, "that the more intelligent of them think that the people will understand everything, while the people will most probably refuse to listen to them." As for the orthodox liberals, whom Dostoevsky, again after Grigoryev, called "doctrinaires," they want to teach the people, write popular books for them, but they do not realize that "the people will start reading their books only when they themselves become indistinguishable from the people, that is to say, when their interests become the people's interests and vice versa." But all they wanted, Dostoevsky claimed, was "to raise" the people to their own level. His own remedy, Dostoevsky repeated, was "to unite with the people as closely as possible; to merge with them completely and to become morally fused with them as one unit." There were incomparably more vital and sound guarantees for progress and regeneration "in some *natural* principles of the character and customs of Russia" than "in the dreams of the most ardent restorers of the West who have already condemned their own civilization and are looking for a way of escape from it." He merely pleaded that this "union with the people" should be brought about "without leaps and bounds and without a dangerous *salto mortale*"; he only hoped that the general enthusiasm for such a union, which he claimed to exist, would be allowed to grow unhampered by legal means, although he himself was sure that freedom granted "in natural development" to such a solution as he advocated, even, he added cautiously, in the form of the freedom of the press (an old demand of his for the abolition of censorship), would by itself be enough to bring it about. Little did he dream that within eight months his mild appeal would be answered by the closing down of his journal!

He concluded his "manifesto" by an open declaration of war against the *Contemporary* as well as the more moderate "liberals"—his first defection from his attitude of neutrality in the political strife between the two camps of extreme radicals and diehard conservatives. "We hate," he declared, "the inane, brainless people who shout at the top of their voices and who discredit everything they touch, soil any pure and honest idea by the very fact that they are in its favor; the whistlers who whistle for their bread or merely for the sake of whistling; the people who ride astride a stolen phrase as though it were a stick, whipping themselves up with a little switch of hidebound liberalism."

The "whistlers" were the contributors to *The Whistle,* the satirical supplement to the *Contemporary*, edited by the young critic Dobrolyubov. Dostoevsky followed up his attack on the *Contemporary* in the September number of *Time* by publishing in November his short story *An Unpleasant Incident*. In this he lampooned the "liberals" in the person of the high official who, in an excess of "liberal" sentiments, condescends to go uninvited to the wedding of one of his lowly subordinates, satirized the left-wing "exposers" of *The Whistle* and, finally, extolled the innate virtues of the common people in the person of the mother of the unlucky official, whose "heavenly pleasures" on his wedding night were spoiled by his superior, who had got drunk and had been put to sleep in the bridal bed.

Dostoevsky's third "manifesto" and his short story brought to an end the uneasy truce between him and Nekrasov. The *Contemporary* had been suspended for eight months on June 15, 1862, and Chernyshevsky arrested three weeks later. Dostoevsky invited Nekrasov to become a regular contributor to *Time*. Nekrasov declined on the ground that it would brand him as a reactionary. Dostoevsky did not seem to realize how much his virulent attack on the "theoreticians" and the "doctrinaires" had compromised him in the eyes of both the liberals and the revolutionaires. Curiously enough, he still regarded himself as a "progressive" who had not broken with his own revolutionary past. Indeed, in his reply to the letter he received in January 1863 from Belinsky's widow, he recalled his early days in Petersburg with pleasure. "I loved and respected your unforgettable husband so much," he wrote, "that I thank you for having reminded me of those best years of my life." But if Dostoevsky still had any illusions about his standing with the left-wing parties, they were dispelled with the reappearance of the *Contemporary* in March 1863. For from its very first issue Nekrasov's journal embarked on a bitter campaign against *Time*, and the satirist Saltykov-Shchedrin, its new editor, launched a personal attack on Dostoevsky in the following (April) number of *The Whistle* under the all too transparent title of *Presumptuous Fedya*, which Dostoevsky parodied four years later in the eighth chapter of the second part of *The Idiot* as "an epigram invented by one of our most famous humorists."

Within the next sixteen months Dostoevsky was to suffer three of the cruelest blows of his life: the closing down of *Time*, the death of Mikhail and a disastrous love affair.

[8]

LOVE AND ROULETTE

Dostoevsky's brief and abortive love affair with Apollinaria, or Pauline, Suslov is usually treated by his biographers in a way that would be more appropriate to some of the more violent characters of his novels, Rogozhin, for example, than to a man who, though a writer of genius, was by no means a monster of cruelty in ordinary life. Writing after the end of their love affair to Pauline's sister Nadezhda, who was studying medicine in Zurich at the time, Dostoevsky denied that he enjoyed "the sufferings, tears, etc., of other people. You have seen me," he wrote,[1] "in my most sincere moments and you can therefore judge for yourself whether I thrive on other people's sufferings, whether I am coarse (inwardly), whether I am cruel?" All this was, of course, what Pauline wanted her sister to believe about Dostoevsky, for it was Pauline who made Dostoevsky suffer and not the other way around. "Do you know," Dostoevsky makes his anonymous hero of *Notes from a Dark Cellar* say, "that one can deliberately torture a person because of love? It is mostly women who do that." And he wrote the *Notes* shortly after the final break between himself and Pauline.

Pauline was twenty-two when she first met Dostoevsky in 1861. She was the daughter of a former serf who had become the manager of his master's estates and subsequently a well-to-do factory owner. His two daughters received a first-class education, first in Moscow and then in Petersburg, where Pauline became an external student of Petersburg University and her sister a student at the Medico-Surgical Academy. Both of them were followers of the extreme radical movement—the nihilists—and Dostoevsky was often to be seen in their company and in the company of their friends engaged in heated arguments with them, some of which he later recorded in his novels. The exact date of Pauline's meeting with Dostoevsky is not known. Dostoevsky's daughter, Lyubov,

[1] *Letters*, April 19, 1865.

claimed that Pauline had written her father "a simple, naïve and poetic letter in which she told him that she was in love with him. Her letter showed her to be a young and naïve girl dazzled by the genius of a great writer. This letter excited my father, for it came just at the moment when he felt a great need for such a declaration of love." Like everything else in Lyubov's reminiscences, this story is apocryphal. For one thing, Dostoevsky, though acclaimed by the radical youth of the time at his public readings as a victim of the autocracy, was not then considered to be "a writer of genius" and Pauline was certainly not "dazzled" by Dostoevsky's genius. "What scandalous story are you writing now?" she asked him flippantly in a letter written in June 1864, apropos of his *Notes from a Dark Cellar*. "We shall all read it . . . but I don't like it when you write cynical things. It does not suit you at all; it doesn't suit you as I imagined you to be before."

Dostoevsky was known to her primarily as the author of experimental tales of Petersburg slums, and it was in that genre that she, too, had written her first story, *For the Time Being*, the hero of which "mentally lifts the miserable rags of the city, peers into all its corners, and there arise in his mind's eye many tragic and heart-rending scenes and his ears are filled with curses and suppressed moans." When Mikhail protested against the publication of such stories, Dostoevsky hastened to explain that he realized very well that they were not literature and that it would be silly to regard them as such, but that stories like that contained "*facts*" which were useful. Dostoevsky published Pauline's story in 1861 in the September number of *Time*, and presumably made the acquaintance of Pauline and her sister during the autumn of the same year. In her diary Pauline records Dostoevsky as saying to her: "You fell in love with me by mistake, because you have such a great heart. You waited till you were twenty-three. . . ." This seems to indicate that Dostoevsky had been her first lover and that they only became lovers in the winter of 1862 when Pauline was twenty-three. If Dostoevsky's description of her in his semi-autobiographical novel, *The Gambler*, is anything to go by, she was at the time tall and slender with reddish hair and "real cat's eyes."

Dostoevsky was forty-one at the time, and his attraction to her was intellectual rather than physical. "You are angry with me," she wrote to him when their affair was over, "and you ask me not to write to you that my love for you makes me blind. But I can assure you that I have never written or even thought of writing that, for I never blushed on account of my love: it was fine and beautiful. I could have written to you that I blushed for our former relationship. But there should be nothing new for you in that. I have never concealed it and many times wished to put an end to it before my departure abroad. . . . But you never could understand what I quite understand now: you regarded it as essentially right and proper. You behaved like a serious man who was too busy to think of what I was feeling and understood his obligations in his own way, not forgetting to get as much pleasure out of life as possible on the ground that, as some doctor or philosopher maintains, it is necessary for one's health to get drunk once a month."

Nothing, indeed, could have been clearer: Pauline had never really been in love with Dostoevsky, and the longer their intimate relationship continued, the more anxious she became to put an end to it. Dostoevsky, on the other hand, though at first treating his affair with her rather lightheartedly, grew more and more deeply involved in it the cooler she grew towards him.

In the spring of 1863 *Time* was banned by the authorities because of an article by Strakhov on the Polish insurrection, which had broken out at the beginning of the year and which the Russian government was ruthlessly suppressing. This was the first tangible defeat suffered by Dostoevsky, in his "return to the soil" agitation. The idea of the article, published under the title *The Fatal Question*, Dostoevsky wrote to Turgenev on June 17, 1863, was that the Poles despised the Russians as barbarians and were so proud of their own European civilization that for a long time there could be no question of any "moral reconciliation" between them and Russia. Since the Russian government was all in favor of European civilization, it "misinterpreted" Strakhov's article as pro-Polish. The situation being too explosive for half-measures, it closed down Dostoevsky's journal.

The closing down of *Time* meant financial ruin not only for Dostoevsky, but also for Mikhail, who had been so sure of the success of the journal that he had sold his cigarette factory. A further complication was the growing deterioration of Maria's health. Dostoevsky had to take her to live in Vladimir, where the climate was considered to be less harmful for consumptives, and this, of course, involved him in further expenses.

Pauline went abroad (a trip she and Dostoevsky had planned earlier) in the hope, no doubt, that a long separation would make the break she wished for much easier for both of them. She was mistaken about this, for separation only made him realize how much he missed her. There was, in addition, his desire to retrieve his financial position by trying his luck at the roulette table. "Yes," he admitted to Mikhail in a letter from Turin,[2] "I went abroad with the idea of saving you all as well as myself," for he had by now invented an "infallible" system for breaking the bank. This system, he explained to his sister-in-law, Varvara Konstant, in a letter from Paris,[3] was really very simple. All one had to do was not to get excited and keep oneself under control whatever turn the game might take—two conditions that, owing to his mental make-up, Dostoevsky found quite impossible to fulfill. Indeed, it was probably just

[2] *Letters*, September 30, 1863.
[3] *Letters*, September 1, 1863.

because he found it so impossible to control himself and not to get excited that he never lost faith in the infallibility of his "system." But before going abroad in pursuit of love and riches, Dostoevsky had to raise the money for the journey. On February 2, 1863, he had been elected to the Committee of the Russian Literary Fund and made its secretary. On July 23 he tendered his resignation from both posts and applied for a loan of 1,500 rubles to enable him to go abroad for three months for the improvement of his health and to consult European specialists. He promised to repay the loan by February 1864, by which time he hoped to finish a novel, and, in case of his death, ceded all the rights in his works to the Literary Fund. He only got 1,000 rubles and, leaving some of it for his wife, went abroad at the beginning of August. Before going, however, he engaged a tutor, a former seminarist and contributor to *Time*, to look after his stepson, Pasha, and prepare him for his examinations.

Pauline was in Paris, but Dostoevsky was in no hurry to join her. He first stopped at Wiesbaden to try his luck at roulette. "On the way to Paris," he wrote to his sister-in-law, who of course knew of his affair with Pauline, "I spent four days in Wiesbaden and, well, had a shot at the roulette—won a little bit—yes, won—don't tell anyone about it, above all, not Pasha, he'll get it into his head that one can make a career of gambling. After all, he got it into his head that he need not waste his time on his studies because he intended to get a job as a shop assistant—he told me so himself. . . . I won 5,000 francs, that is, at first I won 10,400 francs, brought them back home and put them away in my traveling case, intending to leave Wiesbaden the very next day. But I could not restrain myself and lost half of my winnings." He sent 300 rubles for his wife, 60 rubles for his stepson, and the rest to Mikhail to be kept for him till his return.

It was characteristic of his attitude towards his wife that while hurrying to meet his mistress he quite sincerely expressed his anxiety about her health. "I'm not feeling too bad," he concluded his letter to his sister-in-law. "I may go to Italy. Everything depends on circumstances." Did he suspect anything? A repetition of his experience in June 1856, when he was suddenly faced with the fact that the woman he was so desperately in love with had herself fallen in love with a younger man? Maria was only a few years younger than he, whereas Pauline was almost twenty years younger. Why, though they had planned to go abroad together, had she been so anxious to go there first? Was she so glad to get away from him? Why, again, did she insist that when he arrived in Paris he should not go to see her at her rooms without letting her know beforehand of his arrival? He did send off a note to her as soon as he got to his hotel, but he could not wait for an answer and rushed off to see her. It was a mistake. For Pauline had written to him several days before his arrival in Paris, and if he had waited for her letter, he would have been spared an extremely painful scene. She sent off her letter as soon as she received his note, but he was already on the way to her rooms.

"You have arrived a little too late," Pauline had written. "A short while ago I still dreamed of going with you to Italy and have even begun learning Italian, but everything has changed in a few days. You said to me once that I could not give my heart away quickly. I have given it away in a week at the first call, without a struggle, without any assurance, almost without hope that I am loved. I was right when I used to be angry with you whenever you began expressing your admiration of me. Don't think I am blaming myself. I merely want to say that you don't know me, and, indeed, that I don't know myself.

"I would like to see you, but what's the use? I would very much like to talk to you about Russia."

Pauline felt very sorry for Dostoevsky (she states in her diary), for she realized how distressed her letter would make him, and she was only afraid that he might come to see her before her letter reached him, which he did.

"I caught sight of him through the window," Pauline writes in her diary, "but waited until they came to tell me of his arrival. For a long time I could not make up my mind to go down to see him. 'Hullo,' I said to him in a trembling voice. He asked me what was the matter with me, but that only intensified my agitation and, at the same time, increased his uneasiness. 'I thought you would not come,' I said, 'and that's why I wrote you that letter.'

" 'Which letter?'

" 'To ask you not to come.'

" 'Why not?'

" 'Because it's too late.'

"He lowered his head.

" 'I must know everything,' he said. 'Let's go somewhere and tell me or I shall die.'

"I proposed that we should go to his hotel. All the way there we did not utter a word. *I did not look at him.* He merely shouted at the driver from time to time in a desperate and impatient voice, '*Vite, Vite,*' making the latter turn around and look at him in bewilderment. I did my best not to look at him and he did not look at me either, but all the way he kept my hand in his, pressing it occasionally and making convulsive movements.

" 'Please, don't,' I said to him. 'I am with you, am I not?'

"When we went into his room, he fell at my feet and embracing my knees tightly, burst into loud sobs.

" 'I have lost you! I knew it!' he said.

"Having calmed down, he began to ask me what sort of man it was.

'Perhaps,' he said, 'he's handsome, young, a good talker. But you will never find a man who loved you as much as I.'

"I did not want to say anything to him for a long time.

" 'Have you given yourself to him entirely?'

" 'Don't ask,' I said. 'It's unfair.'

" 'Polya,' he said, 'I don't know what's fair or what's unfair. Who is he? A Russian, a Frenchman? Not my doctor?'

" 'No, no.'

"I told him that I was very much in love with the man.

" 'Are you happy?'

" 'No.'

" 'How's that? You're in love and not happy? Is it possible?'

" 'He does not love me.'

" 'He doesn't!' he cried, clasping his head in despair. 'But you don't love him like a slave, do you? I must know that! You won't follow him to the ends of the earth, will you?'

" 'No,' I replied, crying bitterly, 'I—I'll go back to—to my village . . .'

" 'Oh, Polya,' he cried, 'why are you so unhappy? It had to happen that you would fall in love with another man. I knew it. You see, you fell in love with me by mistake because you have such a great heart. You'd waited till you were twenty-three, you're the only woman I know who does not make any demands. But think what it costs: a man and a woman are not the same. He takes, she gives.'

"When I told him the sort of man he was [*i.e.*, Salvador, the young Spanish medical student she had fallen in love with], he said that it gave him a bad feeling: he was glad he was not a serious man, a Lermontov. We talked about all sorts of things. He said that, anyway, he was happy to have known such a person as I. He asked me to remain his friend and to write to him when I felt particularly happy or unhappy. Then he proposed that we should go to Italy together, promising to behave as though he were my brother. When I told him that I expected he would be writing his novel, he said: 'Who do you take me for? Do you think all this will pass without leaving any trace?' I promised to go and see him next day. I felt better after having talked to him. He understands me."

How much can one rely on Pauline to have given a truthful account of what passed between her and Dostoevsky during their first meeting in Paris? There is certainly nothing in this or her subsequent accounts of her journey with Dostoevsky to Italy and across Germany to indicate that "tone of undisguised malice" with which Dostoevsky insists that the hero of his autobiographical novel, *The Gambler*, had been treated by the semifictitious Pauline. "She knows, for instance," he writes, "that I am madly in love with her and she even lets me speak of my passion, but, of course, she could not have expressed her contempt for me more than by this permission to talk freely and quite frankly to her about my love."

Both of them found themselves in the position of betrayed lovers, but it was she who humiliated him and made him suffer for her own hurt pride. "Apollinaria is a great egoist," Dostoevsky wrote to her sister in Zurich.[4] "Her egoism and vanity are colossal. She demands *everything* from people, all perfections, and does not forgive a single imperfection out of consideration for a person's other good traits of character, while she herself thinks that she has no responsibilities towards anyone. She still reproaches me for not having been worthy of her love and never ceases to complain about me. Yet she herself greeted me in 1863 with the words: 'You've arrived a little too late,' that is to say, she had fallen in love with someone else, while only two weeks before she was still writing that she loved me very much. It is not for having fallen in love with another man that I reproach her, but for the few words she sent me to my hotel in Paris with the harsh phrase: 'You've arrived a little too late.' I still love her. I love her very much, but I wish I did not love her. She is *not worthy* of such love. I am sorry for her, because I can foresee that she will always be unhappy. She will never find a friend or happiness. A person who demands everything from someone else while considering herself free of any obligations will never be happy. She thinks it was rude of me to contradict her, to dare to tell her how badly she had treated me. She always treated me with disdain. Now she is offended because at last I felt like answering back, complaining, contradicting her. She does not admit equality in our relationship. There is no trace of human feeling in her relations with me. She knows I still love her, then why does she torture me? Don't love me, but don't torture me. . . ." In *The Gambler*, too, Dostoevsky harps on Pauline's delight in torturing the man who loves her. "Pleasure is always desirable," the hero of the novel says to Pauline, "and savage, boundless power—even over a fly—is also pleasure of a kind."

In her diary Pauline does not, of course, admit to having derived any pleasure from torturing Dostoevsky. On the contrary, she seems bent on creating the impression that he enjoyed being tortured, but one remark of hers fully confirms Dostoevsky's analysis of her character. In his anxiety to get rid of her, her Spanish lover asked a friend of his to tell her that he had contracted typhus. But on the following day she met him in the street. His deception so infuriated her that she decided to kill him. She made all the necessary preparations and even burned his letters, which, as she puts it, might have "compromised" her. Having taken this decision, she felt "wonderful." She did not sleep all night and early next morning went to see Dostoevsky. "He was asleep," she writes in her diary. "When I came in, he woke up, unlocked his door, and went back to bed. He looked at me with surprise and fear. I was quite calm. I told him to come to my place at once. I wanted to tell him everything and

[4] *Letters*, April 19, 1865.

ask him to be my judge. . . ." When Dostoevsky arrived at her rooms, she told him what had happened and he warned her against doing anything stupid. "I don't think," she replied, "that I'd really like to kill him, but I should very much like to torture him a long time."

The "peninsula" (as Dostoevsky darkly referred to the Spaniard in his conversation with Pauline) being unamenable to such treatment, she meted it out in full to Dostoevsky, who had the first foretaste of it on their arrival in Baden-Baden on their way to Rome.

II

Before leaving Paris, Dostoevsky went to the Papal Embassy to obtain a visa for his entry to the Pope's Roman dominions. It was there that his first and only direct clash with the authorities of the Catholic Church occurred.

Already, during his first journey abroad, Dostoevsky had come in contact with Catholic propaganda. In London, he relates in his *Winter Notes on Summer Impressions*, walking one night "in the crowd of lost women and rakes," he was stopped by a woman dressed in black, who thrust into his hand a leaflet, issued by the Catholics and written in French specially for foreign visitors in London. This incident made Dostoevsky reflect on the fact that, unlike the Anglican priests, who "eschew the poor," the Catholics seemed to make a special effort to convert them. At the Papal Embassy in Paris he got into even closer contact with the Catholic Church. He was met, he relates in *The Gambler*, by "a little abbot of about fifty, thin and with frost in his face," who asked him courteously to wait. But he noticed that several people, who came after him, were immediately shown upstairs. This infuriated him. "I got up," he writes, "went up to the abbot and told him firmly that as the Monsignor was receiving visitors, he could also deal with me. Suddenly the abbot recoiled from me with an expression of the utmost surprise. He seemed quite unable to understand how an insignificant Russian could put himself on the same footing as the Monsignor's visitors. He looked me up and down in a most insolent manner, as though glad of the opportunity of insulting me, and cried: 'Do you really think that Monsignor would give up his coffee for you?' Then I shouted in an even louder voice than he, 'I don't care a damn for your Monsignor's coffee! If you don't visa my passport at once, I'll go and see him myself.' 'While the cardinal is with him?' the little abbot cried, pushing me aside with horror and rushing to the door, where he stood with arms crossed as though indicating that I'd only pass over his dead body. Then I told him that I was a heretic and a barbarian, *que je suis hérétique et barbare*, and that I don't care a rap for any of their cardinals, archbishops, monsignors, etc., etc. In short, I made it quite clear that I would not budge. The abbot gave me a look full of hatred, then snatched the passport out of my hand and took it upstairs. A minute later it was returned to me visaed."

Pauline found her journey with Dostoevsky (they left Paris on September 3, 1863) "very amusing. While obtaining visas for our passports," she records in her diary from Baden-Baden on September 6, 1863, "he had a row in the Papal Embassy and all the way here he spoke in verse. At last we found two rooms with two beds, he registered as *officier* which made us laugh a lot. . . . On the way, he told me that he still had hopes, though before he had said that he had none. I said nothing to him, though I knew that it would never be. He liked the fact that I left Paris without any fuss. He did not expect it. But you can't build on that–quite the contrary. Last night these hopes of his were made particularly obvious. At ten o'clock we had tea. After tea, being particularly tired that day, I lay down on the bed and asked Dostoevsky to sit down closer to me. I felt good. I took his hand and held it in mine a long time. He said he felt happy to sit like that. I told him I had been unjust and rude to him in Paris because I seemed to be thinking only of myself, but I had been thinking also of him. I had not told him that because I had not wanted to offend him. Suddenly he got up, was about to go out of the room, but tripped over my slippers, which were lying beside the bed, and came back as suddenly and sat down.

" 'Where were you going?' I asked.

" 'I wanted to close the window.'

" 'Close it, if you like.'

" 'No, I don't think I will. You don't know what happened to me just now,' he said with a strange expression.

" 'What?'

"I looked at his face: it was agitated.

" 'I just wanted to kiss your foot.'

" 'Whatever for?' I said in great embarrassment, tucking in my feet almost in terror.

" 'I just felt like it and I decided to kiss it.'

"Then he asked me if I wanted to go to sleep, but I said, no, I wanted to sit a little longer with him. Thinking of going to bed and undressing, I asked him if he thought the maid would come to take away the tea things. He said she would not. Then he gave me such a look that I felt uncomfortable and I told him so.

" 'I, too, feel uncomfortable,' he said with a strange smile.

"I hid my face in the pillow. Then I asked him again if he thought the maid would come and he again said that she would not.

" 'Well, you'd better go to your room,' I said. 'I want to go to bed.'

" 'Presently,' he said, but stayed for some time. Then he kissed me passionately and, at last, began lighting his candle. My candle was going out.

" 'You won't have a light,' he said.

" 'I will,' I replied, 'I have a candle.'

" 'But that's mine.'

" 'I have another.'

" 'You always find answers,' he said with a smile and went out.

"He did not close the door and soon came in again under the pretext of closing my window. He walked up to me and advised me to undress.

" 'I'll undress,' I said, pretending only to wait till he was gone.

"He went out again and once more came back upon some pretext, after which he went away for good and closed his door. Today he reminded me of last night and said that he was drunk. Then he said that he supposed I disliked his tormenting me like that. I said I didn't mind and did not mention the subject again so that he should remain in a state of suspense. He said I had a very cunning smile, that he supposed I thought he was a fool, that he realized his folly, but that he could not help it."

She found this cat-and-mouse game amusing because it compensated for her hurt pride: she never for a moment forgot the Spaniard or her plans to revenge herself on him. For the time being she revenged herself on Dostoevsky.

III

In Baden-Baden Dostoevsky went to see Turgenev. "I saw him twice," he wrote to Mikhail from Turin.[5] "But Turgenev did not meet Apollinaria. I concealed the fact that I was traveling with her. Turgenev is depressed, though he has recovered from his illness. He lives with his daughter. He told me all about his moral torments and doubts, philosophic doubts which have become of vital importance. Partly a fop. I did not conceal from him that I am gambling. Gave me his *Phantoms* to read, but I'm afraid I was too busy at the tables and I returned it unread. He says he wrote it for our journal and that if I wrote to him from Rome, he'd send it to Rome. But what do I know about our journal?"

Mikhail was moving heaven and earth to obtain permission to publish *Time* under another name, suggesting *Pravda* (Truth) at first, and when it was turned down as being too provocative, if not presumptuous, settling on *Epoch*, the first number of which appeared on March 21, 1864. In the meantime their rich Uncle Kumanin died in Moscow, an "important" piece of news about which Mikhail immediately informed Dostoevsky, for they each expected to be left something in his will.

In Baden-Baden, Dostoevsky told Varvara Konstant, he had lost "everything" at roulette. "Of the three thousand francs," he wrote,[6] "I

[5] *Letters*, September 20, 1863.
[6] *Letters*, September 8, 1863.

have only 250 francs left in my pocket." He therefore asked her to send him back one hundred rubles of the three hundred he had sent to his wife, and he only prayed that his wife should not find out. "There are all sorts of adventures," he concluded, "and but for them life would be boring."

Pauline took Dostoevsky's losses very calmly: "Dostoevsky," she noted in her diary on September 6, "has lost a lot of money and is upset to have so little left for our journey. I am sorry for him partly because I cannot repay him for these worries of his but what's to be done?—I can't. Do I really have any responsibility towards him?—no, that's nonsense."

Mikhail, on the other hand, was appalled at the news. "I can't understand," he wrote to Dostoevsky from Petersburg, "how you can gamble while traveling with a woman with whom you are in love." Dostoevsky did not think it necessary to let his brother into the secret of his curious relationship with Pauline. All he told him in his letter from Turin,[7] in which he asked him to send back the money he had won in Wiesbaden, was that there were all sorts of "adventures," but that he was terribly bored "in spite of" Pauline. "Here," he went on, "one accepts even happiness grudgingly, because one finds oneself separated from everybody one has loved and whom one has missed so much. To look for happiness, having abandoned everything, even when one might have been useful, is egoism, and this thought poisons my happiness, if, that is, there can be any question of happiness." As for his brother's objections to his gambling, he reminded him that he had an "infallible" system and that he had actually won 600 francs in a quarter of an hour. "This excited me and all of a sudden I began losing and could no longer stop myself and lost every penny I had. Then, having sent off my letter to you, I took the *last* few coins I had and went back to the casino; I staked 4 gold pieces and won 25 in half an hour. My unusual run of luck intoxicated me and I risked all the 35 gold pieces I had on me and lost them all. After paying our landlady, we only had 6 gold pieces left for our journey. In Geneva I pawned my watch. . . . *She* pawned her ring. . . ."

Pauline had only two entries in her diary from Turin. On September 14th she noted that some young Frenchmen looked "very impudently" at her while she was having dinner with Dostoevsky, which made him furious and "put him in a difficult position because he might find it very difficult to defend me in case of need." They therefore decided to dine at a different hotel. On September 17th, she noted that after having "reproached" Dostoevsky for something, she realized that she was being unfair to him and, wishing to make amends, she "became tender" with him. "He responded so joyfully," she continues, "that I became doubly tender with him. When I sat beside him and looked at him with affection,

[7] *Letters,* September 8, 1863.

he said: 'Now this is a familiar look. I haven't seen it for a long time.' I put my hand on his chest and burst out crying."

There seems to have been no further development of this sentimental interlude. All Pauline records of their further stay in Turin is a remark made by Dostoevsky at dinner on observing an old man giving a lesson to a little girl: "Just imagine such a little girl with an old man, and suddenly some Napoleon says: 'Destroy the whole town,' it was always like that in the world," and the fact that she was reading some philosophic treatise about Kant and Hegel and "contrary to all expectation" understood something.

From Turin they traveled to Genoa and from there by sea to Leghorn and Rome, where, Pauline noted on September 29th, Dostoevsky again "pestered" her. He wished, she explained, to know the reason of her "stubbornness," thinking that it was her "wish to torment him." He told her that a man must not be "tormented" too long, for in the end he would give up trying to get what he wanted so much.

"I could not help smiling," Pauline writes, "and almost asked him why he was telling me this.

" 'There is one main reason for all this,' Dostoevsky began firmly (later I found out that he was not so sure about it), 'a reason that fills me with disgust—namely, the peninsula.'

"This unexpected reminder agitated me very much.

" 'You're still hoping,' he said.

"I made no answer.

" 'You're not denying it,' he said. 'You're not saying it isn't that.'

"I made no answer.

" 'I have nothing against that man because he's just a shallow person.'

" 'I'm not hoping at all, I've nothing to hope for,' I said after thinking it over.

" 'That's nothing. You cannot suppress your hopes by your reason. Reason has nothing to do with it.'

"He waited for a denial, but there was none, for I felt the justice of his words.

"He suddenly got up and went out to lie down. I began pacing the room. . . . I really began quite shamelessly to hope again.

"On awakening Dostoevsky became unusually jaunty, gay and importunate. Just as though he wished to overcome his painful inward sadness by teasing me.

"I looked in bewilderment at his strange behavior. He seemed to wish to treat everything as a laughing matter so as to hurt me, but I just looked at him in surprise.

" 'You're not nice today,' I said at last simply.

" 'Why? What did I do?'

" 'You were better in Paris and Turin. Why are you so gay?'

" 'I'm gay because I feel vexed,' he said and went out, but he soon came back again.

" 'I'm unhappy,' he said seriously and sadly. 'I'm observing everything as though it were a duty, as though I were learning a lesson. Anyway, I thought I'd amuse you.'

"I flung my arms round his neck and said that he had done a lot for me and that I appreciated it very much.

" 'No,' he said, 'you're going to Spain.'

"I felt somehow terrified and—thrilled by his hints of Salvador. . . . Dostoevsky again turned everything into a joke and, as he walked out, said that he felt it was humiliating to leave me like that (it was about one o'clock in the morning and I was lying undressed in bed). 'For,' he declared, 'Russians never retreat.' "

In *The Gambler* Dostoevsky expressed his feelings rather more frankly. "Do you know," the autobiographical hero of the novel addresses Pauline in a similar situation, "do you know that one day I shall kill you. Kill you not because I shall fall out of love with you or out of jealousy, but because I sometimes feel like devouring you. . . . I have many times," he asserts, "been overcome by an uncontrollable desire to strike you, to maim you, to strangle you. . . . You're driving me mad. . . ."

It was, in fact, in Rome that the idea of *The Gambler* occurred to him. He asked Strakhov[8] to raise some money from the publisher of the *Library for Reading* as an advance on a projected novel. "The novel," he wrote, "will deal with a certain type of Russian living abroad. . . . I shall take . . . a man who has lost faith in everything and who *dares not to believe,* a man who defies authority but is afraid of it. He reassures himself by the thought that there is nothing for him to do in Russia and hence his harsh criticism of the people who are calling our Russians abroad to return to their country. But it's impossible to describe everything. He is a living person (he seems to be standing before me right at this moment). . . . But the chief thing is that all his vitality, all his strength, his violent temper, his boldness—are spent on roulette. He is a gambler, and not an ordinary gambler, either, just as Pushkin's miserly knight is not just a miser. (I do not mean to compare myself to Pushkin. I'm just saying this for the sake of clarity.) He is a poet of sorts, but the point is that he is ashamed of his poetry, for deep down he feels how contemptible it is, though the fact that there is a risk ennobles him in his own eyes. The whole story is the story of how he has been playing roulette for three years in gambling houses. . . ."

Unfortunately, when he came to write *The Gambler* three years later, he introduced his own unhappy love affair with Pauline into it, and this autobiographical theme, and the necessity of disguising it, distorted his original plan. It is interesting, though, that even at that early

[8] *Letters,* September 30, 1863.

date, when religion did not seem to loom very much in his thoughts, he was already contemplating writing a novel whose hero had lost faith and *dared not* believe, a rebel against authority—a theme that plays an important part in all his great novels. It is true that he had to write *The Gambler* in a hurry to get out of the clutches of an unscrupulous publisher who would have obtained the copyright of all his works if he had failed to deliver it by a certain date. But even that hardly explains why the gambler theme itself, which, he told Strakhov, he intended to represent as "a sort of hell, a sort of 'bathhouse' of a Siberian prison," remains artistically unconvincing. By introducing the autobiographical love element he may have tried to shake off the woman who, by refusing to resume an old relationship, possessed the terrible gift "of attraction, enslavement and domination" over him, but even in that he was not successful.

In Rome Dostoevsky visited St. Peter's, which, he wrote to Strakhov, made "a strong impression" on him, and "with a shiver down the spine," inspected the Forum and the Colosseum. "Well," he concluded a little lamely, "what can I say?"

From Rome he also wrote to his stepson, Pasha, expressing his concern at having had no news from his wife, who no doubt knew very well whom he was traveling with and did not write to him. He deplored the fact that Pasha did not pass his exams. "My friend," he wrote to the sixteen-year-old boy a little incautiously, as it turned out, "while I am alive and well you can depend on me to support you—but afterwards? To be deliberately an ignoramus, to lag behind one's own generation, to be worse and lower than others and, lacking education, fail to understand what is going on around you and be always aware of it—this you will find awful. . . ."

From Rome Dostoevsky and Pauline went by sea to Naples. On board ship they met Herzen with his family. Again, there seemed to be no violent political disagreements between them. Dostoevsky still refused to follow Strakhov into the camp of the reactionary Slavophiles, who, he wrote to Strakhov in his letter from Rome, had "a kind of remarkable *aristocratic repletion* in the solution of several problems." Dostoevsky could not very well hide Pauline from Herzen, but, Pauline records, he introduced her "as a relation, in a very vague sort of way." Resenting this, she flirted with Herzen's young son, which infuriated Dostoevsky. They had had a quarrel over the emancipation of women before leaving Naples, but by the time they parted, Pauline going back to Paris and Dostoevsky to Petersburg, their relationship, in Pauline's phrase, was *almost* as before, and she was sorry to say good-by to him.

On his way home, Dostoevsky stopped at Homburg and tried his luck at roulette again and lost most of the advance on *The Gambler* he had received in Turin. Pauline records in her diary on October 27th: "Yesterday I received a letter from Dostoevsky. He has lost again and asked me to send him some money. I decided to pawn my watch and chain." She got 300 francs for them and sent them off to Dostoevsky. It was all over between them, though two years later Dostoevsky was again to appeal to her for money in a similar situation, and they were to meet again in Petersburg at the end of 1865.

[9]

PROPOSALS OF MARRIAGE: TWO YOUNG GIRLS

On his return to Russia towards the end of October 1863, Dostoevsky had to hurry off to Vladimir, for his wife's condition had become critical. He decided to take her to Moscow where she could be looked after by his second sister's husband, Alexander Ivanov, who was a doctor and whom he greatly respected. He was, in fact, greatly attached to his second sister, Vera, and her large family of ten children, the oldest of whom, Sofia, was his favorite. His financial position had improved slightly, his late uncle Kumanin having left him 3,000 rubles in his will. "We are renting a flat here," he wrote to Mikhail from Moscow. "I have had two epileptic attacks here, the second a violent one."

Pasha came over to see his mother in January 1864, but his visit seems to have been a mistake. "He did not produce the effect here which he had evidently expected," Dostoevsky wrote to his sister-in-law, Varvara Konstant. "He was rather obnoxious to his mother, who, I am afraid, is becoming very irritable, because of her illness. I am terribly sorry for her. She thinks continually about dying and falls into despair. Her chest is bad and she's grown as thin as a rake. It's terrible. It's painful and dreadful to look at her." In February he wrote to his stepson that his mother was getting very weak, and a month later[1] he wrote to Mikhail that he did not think she'd live till Easter. Her mental faculties, too, were deteriorating rapidly. She was imagining that her bedroom was full of devils, and Ivanov had to open the window and pretend to drive them out. Six days later he wrote to Mikhail that Ivanov expected her to die any day. She refused to see her son until she felt that she was about to die, "but," Dostoevsky went on, "she might die tonight and yet this morning she was planning to take a house in the country for the summer and go to Taganrog or Astrakhan after another three years.

[1] *Letters*, March 20, 1864.

If I were to remind her of Pasha, she'd get frightened, for she would think that there was no hope for her and that she was about to die at any moment. Why torture her during what may be the last hours of her life?" He asked Mikhail to prepare Pasha for his mother's death, but, he added, "don't frighten him too much (though I don't think he is likely to be frightened at all)."

On April 15, 1864, he wrote to Mikhail: "Last night Maria had a hemorrhage: blood gushed from her throat and she began to choke. We were all expecting the end. We were all beside her. She took leave of us all, made peace with all, and expressed her last wishes. She sends her regards to all your family and wishes you all a long life. Especially Emilia. She expressed her wish to make peace with you. (You know, my friend, all her life she was convinced that you were her secret enemy.) She spent a bad night. This morning Ivanov told me *definitely* that she would die today. There can be no doubt about it." She died at 7 o'clock in the evening, Dostoevsky added in a postscript. She asked him to take care of Pasha and give her blessing to him. "She died fully conscious," Dostoevsky wrote to Wrangel a year later,[2] "and taking leave of us all, remembered you too. . . . Oh, my friend," he went on, overcome with contrition, and forgetting how badly he had treated her after practically forcing her to marry him, "she loved me boundlessly and I, too, loved her dearly, but I did not live happily with her. I shall tell you all when I see you, but in spite of the fact that I was positively unhappy with her (because of her odd, oversensitive and morbidly fantastic character), we never ceased loving each other. However strange it may sound, it was so. She was the most honest, the most honorable and the most magnanimous of all the women I have known in my life. When she died, though I suffered (all the years) watching her die, though I appreciated and felt painfully what I was losing with her, I never imagined how empty my life would become after they had buried her. And now a year has passed, and I still feel the same. . . ."

Wrangel knew nothing of Dostoevsky's promiscuous life in Petersburg, or of his affair with Pauline Suslov, but even then he could hardly have taken Dostoevsky's protestations of undying love seriously. Would he have felt his life to be so empty if his affair with Pauline had not ended so unhappily? But there is more in his tribute to his wife than a mere desire to justify to himself his treatment of her. The great void he felt in his life when he wrote his letter to Wrangel was not due to Maria's death alone; his brother, too, had died three months later, and with Mikhail's death on July 10, 1864, the fate of the new journal was sealed: it ceased publication in June 1865. Dostoevsky tried to save it by getting his rich Moscow aunt to advance him 10,000 rubles, which was the money she left him in her will. "But," he wrote to Wrangel, "it was

[2] *Letters,* March 31, 1865.

too late. . . . I began printing *Epoch* in three printing houses, I spared neither money, nor my health, nor strength. I was the only editor, I read the proofs, dealt with the contributors, corrected the articles, raised money, worked till six o'clock in the morning and only slept five hours a day. . . . But I myself did not publish a single line in my own journal. The reading public did not come across my name even in Petersburg, let alone in the provinces. . . ."

His brother had left debts amounting to 15,000 rubles, of which Dostoevsky guaranteed to repay 10,000. He had counted on getting 2,500 subscribers, but got only 1,300. "At the beginning of the subscription," he wrote to Wrangel, "the debts, mostly incurred by my late brother, had to be paid. We paid them out of the subscriptions, thinking that, having paid them, there would be enough left over to carry on with the publication of our journal. But the subscriptions came to an end and we were left with nothing. . . . Now . . . we cannot carry on with the publication of the journal and we have had to declare ourselves temporarily bankrupt and, in addition, I was left owing 10,000 rubles on bills of exchange and 5,000 rubles on my word of honor."

Dostoevsky's second wife Anna records how easy it was for people to make him sign a promissory note by claiming that he had promised them on his word of honor to refund a certain sum of money he had never borrowed from them; but it is Strakhov who provides a convincing analysis of this "unpractical" side of Dostoevsky's character. "This," he writes in his biography, "is chiefly due to the fact that such people *live for the moment*, that their past as well as their future can suddenly disappear from their minds. Such people can never introduce regular order into their lives. They make their decisions or their promises with the utmost sincerity, but can rarely carry them out. In case of nonfulfillment of the obligations undertaken on their own behalf or on behalf of others, they either suddenly discover thousands of the most obvious excuses or torment and reproach themselves bitterly; but once the crisis is over, they will again just as sincerely make more promises and as sincerely refuse to keep them. They very often make most wonderful plans and get very excited about them, but they soon forget to do what is necessary for their execution. They are genuinely sorry for their mistakes and failures and at the first temptation commit them again. They are perpetually either cast down or elated; when good fortune smiles on them, their past is erased from their minds and the future hardly exists for them at all. . . . In spite of his quick intelligence, in spite of the lofty aims he always kept before him in his activities and behavior, or rather because of them, he suffered from being unpractical; when he was engaged on some business, he did it well; but he did it in brief spurts, got easily satisfied and every moment the chaos round him increased."

Dostoevsky could be "practical" when it came to getting his rich, senile aunt to give Mikhail (and himself, too, later on), ostensibly as a loan, the money she was leaving him in her will. His letter to Mikhail,[3] outlining the procedure of blackmailing their aunt into letting him have the 10,000 rubles on pain of Christ's displeasure, is very characteristic. "You must put it to her," he wrote, "that she will not be ruined, but that she will ruin you and your family by her refusal. At first she will not be able to make up her mind, she'll start moaning and groaning. Let her. All you have to do is to take her by surprise, to press her hard morally, so that she should plainly realize the dilemma. 'To give is dangerous, for he won't repay; not to give—you may be responsible for a man's death and commit a grievous sin.' . . . All you have to say to her is: 'It's your money, you can give it to me if you want to, or refuse to give it if you don't want to. But if you don't, you will *ruin* me, and, after all, I am your nephew, your godson, who has never received anything from you and never asked you for anything. You are on the brink of the grave and you may be committing a sin: what will you say to Christ and your late sister? . . . You have 150,000 rubles and you are afraid to be ruined!' All this," Dostoevsky points out, "must be spoken harshly, particularly as it is *true* and *had* to be said. . . . I am quite willing to say it. One must not appear as a humble petitioner. Nor is it possible to get a great deal out of *them* by assuming a dry, businesslike tone. One has to work on them morally, not act pathetically, but severely. That is more likely than anything to lay them by the heels." And it worked, too.

It was of no avail. The death of Mikhail and the failure of *Epoch*—a failure that was not entirely due to lack of funds, but mainly to the lack of a policy more appealing than the rather vague call to the educated classes to "return to the soil"—made him declare to Wrangel "that only a miracle can save me now. Of all the reserve of my strength and energy there is left something confused and disturbing in my heart, something very near despair. Anxiety, bitterness, the most senseless rushing about, a most abnormal condition for me, and, in addition, loneliness—there's no one left of those who were beside me. . . . And yet I can't help feeling that I am still about to begin to live. Funny, isn't it? A cat's vitality."

II

Much of it was not funny at all. He *was* only beginning his career as a writer, though the direction which his genius was to take was already clearly indicated in his latest work—*Notes from a Dark Cellar*,[4]

[3] *Letters*, April 9, 1864.

[4] The Russian title of this short novel—*Zapiski iz Podpolya*—is variously translated as "Notes from the Underground" or "Notes from the Underworld," but the Russian word *podpoyle* simply means the dark cellar under a house used for the preservation of food in summer. It was used by the revolutionaries for hiding illegal printing

published in *Epoch* in 1864. Dostoevsky wrote the first part in January and February while looking after his dying wife in Moscow. Work on the second part was interrupted by his wife's death on April 15 and was most probably finished in Petersburg. Its first part is a closely reasoned attack on the scientific determination of the utilitarian thinkers and more particularly on the vision of a socialist society described by Chernyshevsky in his Utopian novel, *What Is to Be Done?*

Chernyshevsky wrote his novel while imprisoned in the Peter and Paul Fortress. It was finished in April 1863 and published in the *Contemporary* in the spring and summer of the same year. Chernyshevsky was defending the doctrine of "enlightened self-interest" and argued that a "correctly conceived" egoistic desire for happiness was bound to lead to a state of universal happiness. He summed up his vision under the symbol of a Crystal Palace, "a huge edifice which does not so far exist, though there does exist a hint of what it will be like—the palace which stands on a hill in Sydenham: glass and iron, glass and iron—and that is all." Dostoevsky had been to the Crystal Palace during his visit to the World Exhibition in London. In his *Winter Notes* he had already formulated his objections to the lure of material prosperity leading to the exploitation of the weak by the strong; in his *Notes from a Dark Cellar* he went further; he denied the very premise upon which the philosophy of scientific determinism was based as entirely inimical to human nature. "Why are you so firmly convinced," his anonymous hero asks, "that only material well-being is of benefit to mankind? . . . Is it not possible that man loves something besides material well-being? Perhaps he is just as fond of suffering. Perhaps suffering is as beneficial to him as material well-being . . . for suffering is doubt, and what sort of Crystal Palace would it be if one were to have any doubts about it?" And turning more directly to Chernyshevsky's vision of mankind cooped up in some grandiose Crystal Palace of the future, Dostoevsky describes it as "an idle dream" which is "against all laws of nature." He refuses to accept "as the epitome of all desires a big house with model flats for the poor on a lease of ninety-nine hundred and ninety-nine years" even if free treatment by "the dental surgeon Wagenheim" were thrown in. "You believe in the Crystal Palace, forever indestructible," he tells the utilitarians, "that is to say, in one at which you won't be able to stick out your tongue even by stealth or cock a snook even in your pocket. Well, perhaps I am afraid of this palace just because it is made of crystal and is forever indestructible and just because I shall not be able to stick out my tongue at it even by stealth."

---

presses and literature (there is a good description of it in Gorky's *Mother*). Dostoevsky, however, does not use it in its political, but in its ordinary, sense of a dark cellar—a place of retreat for the intellectual who denounces the *avant-garde* ideas of his time, who scoffs at "the sublime and the beautiful" and whose attitude towards men is one of embittered contempt.

In *The Insulted and Injured* Dostoevsky expressed his conviction through the mouth of the villian of this novel, Prince Valkovsky (he often expressed his most secret thoughts through the mouths of his negative characters), that "if only it were possible that every one of us should reveal the most secret desires of his heart . . . such a stench would rise in the world that we should all be suffocated." In his *Notes from a Dark Cellar* he does make his "paradoxical" hero do just that in the second part of the novel, and he does it to prove the limitations of the scientific approach to the ethical problems of mankind which he had expounded in the first part. In rejecting the panaceas of the utilitarians, Dostoevsky did not give up the hope that man, though seemingly bent on "destruction and chaos," could in the end be redeemed. This redemption, he claimed, could only be brought about by religion. That part of his argument in the tenth chapter of the first part of the novel was excised by the censors. "It would have been much better," Dostoevsky wrote to Mikhail,[5] "not to have published the penultimate chapter (the most important, in which my chief idea is expressed) than to have published it just as it is, that is, with sentences dragged out of their contexts and contradicting themselves. But what can one do about it? The swine of censors left the passages in which I scoffed at everything and sometimes blasphemed for the sake of form and cut out those in which I argued the need for a belief in religion and Christ. What's the matter with the censors? They are not plotting against the government, are they?"

But even with the excised passages, it was clear to everyone, and most of all to Nekrasov and Saltykov, that Dostoevsky had gone over to the conservative Slavophile camp. The *Contemporary*, which had so far been sniping good-humoredly at Dostoevsky, now launched a bitter attack on him. The article, published in July 1864, and partly written by Saltykov, was entitled *To the Swifts: A Message to the Chief Swift, Mr. Dostoevsky*. In this article Dostoevsky was described as "the gloomy novelist" who had just written a new novel under the title of *Notes on the Immortality of the Soul.* "These notes," Saltykov wrote, "are supposed to be written by a sick and malicious Swift. At first he talks about all sorts of unimportant things, such as his being ill and bad-tempered, that everything in the world is in a state of chaos, that he has a pain in the small of his back, that no one can tell whether or not it is going to be a good summer for mushrooms, and that every man is a good-for-nothing knave and will never become a decent human being until he admits that he is a good-for-nothing knave, and in conclusion, naturally goes on to expatiate on the real objects of his cogitations. He gets his proofs chiefly from Thomas Aquinas, but as he does not mention it, the reader believes that these ideas are his own."

Coming at a time when the whole future of *Epoch* was in jeopardy,

[5] *Letters,* March 23, 1864.

this personal attack on Dostoevsky, whose morbid sensitiveness made him particularly vulnerable, must have hurt him very much. He must, besides, have realized the harm such an attack in an influential monthly must do to the circulation of his own journal. He did not reply to it till November, when he published his unsigned article, *To Put an End to It: A Final Reply to the Contemporary*, in the ninth issue of *Epoch*. It was not his final reply, though. Goaded by the continuous pinpricks in Nekrasov's journal, he published in 1865 in the February issue of *Epoch* his unfinished fantasy, *The Crocodile, an Extraordinary Event, or an Amusing Incident in the Amusement Arcade*, in which he attacked the liberal and left-wing press. The liberal daily *Golos* (*Voice*) immediately retorted by accusing him of lampooning Chernyshevsky, who had only recently been exiled in Siberia. "Mr. Dostoevsky," the paper wrote, "will not of course accept our advice, but we would all the same advise him to stop at the fourth chapter of this extremely tactless story, about which rumors highly damaging to the reputation of his journal *Epoch* and Mr. Dostoevsky himself as its author are already circulating. . . . You will be condemned by everyone, friend and foe," the paper concluded, "and will have rendered no service to anyone."

The reason why Dostoevsky made so light, at the time, of these rumors was that he was too busy scoring off his opponents to realize that his joke had gone a little too far. Besides, his financial troubles were occupying his thoughts more and more and clouding his judgment. He was forced to sell his books and pawn his clothes, he told one of his creditors in a letter on April 29, 1866. "My money," he wrote, "was taken from me by my creditors, for otherwise they would have hauled me off to jail, and I could not have finished my work there, not in a debtors' jail, at any rate, and then I should never have been able to pay a penny to anybody. What was there left for me to do? Besides, I had in addition to provide for my stepson and my late brother's widow. . . . Still, do not imagine that I am particularly upset about it all. No. I have many happy moments. Life and hope are still strong in me."

III

During the next two years, in fact, he not only wrote *Crime and Punishment* and *The Gambler*, but made an offer of marriage to another young contributor to *Epoch*, and in the end, having been rejected, married his eighteen-year-old stenographer, Anna Snitkin.

In August 1864, Dostoevsky received a story from a young girl, the daughter of a rich landowner, a retired general, an aristocrat who was sufficiently interested in the latest literary trends to subscribe to the most important literary monthlies of the time, including the *Contemporary*, *Epoch*, *The Athenaeum* and *Revue de deux Mondes*. The girl was only twenty, and her name was Anna Korvin-Krukovsky (the family claimed descent from an ancient Hungarian royal house). The story, entitled *The Dream*, was trite enough. It concerned a middle-class girl who falls in love with a young, impecunious student (a stock figure of Russian fiction in those days, culminating in the hero of Dostoevsky's future novel, Rodion Raskolnikov), but refuses to have anything to do with him until she has a dream in which the student tells her that he, too, is in love with her and reproaches her for not marrying him. In her dream she sees herself "united" to him and living "a decent, hard-working life with him." She then tries to find the student, but, not very surprisingly, discovers that he had died a short while earlier with her name on his lips.

Ever since his childhood, dreams had exercised a great influence on Dostoevsky. He believed in the "prophetic" nature of dreams, and, no doubt, the title of the story and the part the heroine's dream plays in its plot appealed to him as well as its "youthful charm" (as he wrote to Anna in accepting her story), in spite of its "naïvety" and even its "transgressions against Russian grammar."

What must have appealed to him even more was the possibility—remote as it seemed at the time—of repeating his experience with another young girl with literary ambitions and so breaking the spell which Pauline still exercised over him. He met her early in March 1865. By that time Anna had written another story for Dostoevsky. Its hero, Mikhail, was brought up in a monastery by his uncle who was a monk. Anna's sister, Sofia, who was fifteen at the time, declares in her reminiscences that Alyosha Karamazov bore a certain resemblance to Mikhail, a fact that Dostoevsky acknowledged when many years later she reminded him of it. Anna concealed her literary success from her father, but the receipt of her fee for the story revealed her secret and provoked an explosion from the General. The letter with the money had been addressed to the housekeeper and was discovered by the General, who made the poor woman open it. "The fact that my sister was clandestinely receiving money from a man who was a stranger to her," Sofia writes, "appeared so shameful to my father that he fainted. He had a weak heart and suffered from gallstones and the doctors had warned him that any excitement might be fatal to him. And now—such a blow!" He at once sacked the housekeeper and told Anna that "anything can be expected from a girl who is capable of receiving money from a man without the knowledge of her father and mother. Today," he thundered, "you are selling your stories and tomorrow for all I know you will be selling yourself!"

However, the storm died down in a few days and the General's first concession was to agree to hear his daughter's story. The whole family was present and Anna read her story "in a voice trembling with agitation." When Anna, hardly able to contain her tears, reached the end of *The Dream* and read out the passage where the dying heroine was bewailing her wasted youth, tears started to the General's eyes and he left the room without uttering a word. He never mentioned her story to Anna again, but, Sofia records, he treated her "extraordinarily tenderly and gently" and they all realized "*que sa cause était gagnée.*" The disgraced housekeeper was re-engaged and the General gave his permission for Anna to see Dostoevsky during their next visit to Petersburg.

"Remember, Lisa," he warned his wife, though, "that Dostoevsky does not belong to our social set. What do we know of him? Only that he is a journalist and an ex-convict—some recommendation! You'll have to be very, very careful with him."

Anna wrote to Dostoevsky immediately on her arrival in Petersburg to invite him to pay them a visit. The visit took place on the appointed day and was not a success. The General, who did not accompany his family to Petersburg, had made his wife promise to be always present at Anna's meetings with Dostoevsky. Sofia, too, had asked to be present, and every now and then the two elderly aunts (at whose house they were staying) would come into the room to have a peep at a writer and ended up by sitting down on the sofa and staying till his departure.

"Anna," Sofia writes, "was furious that her first meeting with Dostoevsky, of which she had been dreaming so much, was taking place under such absurd circumstances. She looked cross and was obstinately silent. Dostoevsky felt awkward and ill at ease in that strained atmosphere; he felt embarrassed in the company of these old ladies and became irritable. He looked old and ill that day, as always when he was in a bad mood. He kept fingering his fair, scanty beard and biting his mustache and, as he did so, his whole face twitched." Anna's mother did her best to put him at his ease, but her refined manners of the born society hostess made things worse, and after half an hour Dostoevsky picked up his hat and, taking leave awkwardly and hastily, but without shaking hands with anybody, left the house.

As soon as he was gone, Anna rushed into her room, threw herself on the bed and burst into tears. "They always, always make a mess of everything," she kept repeating, sobbing convulsively.

Five days later Dostoevsky turned up again. This time Anna's mother and aunts were not at home, and the wooing of the rich girl who, by becoming his wife, could easily have got him out of his financial troubles could proceed undisturbed, the only person present being Anna's fifteen-year-old sister, who sat without interfering in their conversation and eagerly absorbing every word he uttered. "He seemed to me quite a different person," Sofia writes. "He looked so young and so simple, charming and clever. Is he really forty-three? I thought. Is he really three times as old as I and more than twice as old as my sister? Besides, he is a great writer: one can treat him just as a friend! And I felt at once," she concludes, "that he became very dear and close to me."

Anna, too, was pleased that a great writer like Dostoevsky should treat her as an equal. She was at the time, her sister records, very pretty: tall and slender, with a lovely complexion and a mass of fair hair reaching to her waist in two thick plaits. They talked animatedly together, joking and laughing, Anna even showing Dostoevsky her little sister's poems and Dostoevsky smilingly reading two or three extracts from them. The visit, which lasted for three hours, was interrupted by the arrival of their mother, who looked dismayed at first but in the end invited Dostoevsky to dinner. "After that day," Sofia writes, "he came to see us three or four times a week. . . . We loved it most in the evening when there were no other visitors. Then he grew animated and became extremely charming and fascinating. Dostoevsky disliked general conversation; he spoke only in monologues and only if those present listened to him with rapt attention. . . . Sometimes he told us the plots of his future novels and sometimes scenes and experiences from his past life."

If Sofia's version of these episodes is to be credited, Dostoevsky did not hesitate to varnish a tale in order to produce the greatest possible effect on the two young girls, the youngest of whom quite obviously listened to him with unconcealed love and adoration. Thus the story of his first epileptic attack caused by the visit on Christmas Eve by an atheistic friend, with Dostoevsky interrupting their conversation by an ecstatic cry: "There is, there is a God!" just at the moment when the church bells of a neighboring church began to peal, is highly apocryphal. On the other hand, the following description he gave them of his feelings before the onset of an epileptic seizure has probably a great deal of truth in it.

"You, normal people," Sofia records Dostoevsky as saying, "have no idea what happiness means; I am referring to that feeling of happiness we epileptics experience a second before a fit. Mahomet assures us in his Koran that he had seen Paradise and been in it. All the clever fools are convinced that he is simply a cheat and a liar. Not at all. He is not lying. He was in Paradise during an epileptic fit, from which he suffered as I do. I don't know if that feeling of bliss lasts a few seconds or several hours or even months, but, believe me, I would not exchange it for all the joys that life could give me!"

The wooing of Anna assumed a different character after a party at which Dostoevsky appeared in an ill-fitting frock coat and, conscious of the poor figure he cut, conceived a sudden raging hatred for a handsome cuirassier officer who was paying court a little too assiduously to Anna. To his disgust, Anna had refused previously to stay with him in a corner of the room, but let her mother whisk her off to entertain the guests. Dostoevsky listened gloomily to a discussion of a recently published book by an English clergyman who drew a parallel between Protestantism and the Greek Orthodox Church. Anna's mother, who was

German, observed that one of the advantages Protestants had over the Russian Orthodox was that they read the New Testament more often.

"Why," Dostoevsky suddenly exploded, mixing up his texts and involuntarily betraying his own anxiety, "was the New Testament written for society women? There it is written: In the beginning God created man and woman, or again, man shall leave his father and his mother, and shall cleave unto his wife. This is how Christ understood marriage. And what will all society mothers, who are only thinking of how to get their daughters married off to their best advantage, say to that?" And, glaring viciously at the assembled guests, he retired to his corner and did not utter another word the whole evening.

This attack on her mother, who never thought of marrying her off to anyone and least of all to the handsome cuirassier, angered Anna, who was no longer impressed by him and began contradicting and teasing him every time he demanded to know whom she was spending her free time with. After such a scene, he would arrive next day looking angry. Anna pretended not to notice his bad humor and picked up her sewing. This made him angrier still and he sat down in a corner of the room, gloomily silent. Anna too was silent.

"Will you stop your sewing!" he would finally explode, snatching the sewing out of her hand.

Anna would fold her arms obediently, but still kept silent.

"Where were you yesterday?" Dostoevsky asked angrily.

"At a ball," Anna replied indifferently.

"Did you dance?"

"Yes."

"With the cuirassier?"

"With him and with others."

"And you find this sort of thing amusing?"

Anna shrugged.

"For lack of anything else, I suppose I do," she replied, picking up her sewing again.

Dostoevsky looked at her in silence for a few minutes.

"You're just an empty-headed, stupid girl!" he exploded again.

But the subject that really set them quarreling was nihilism. They would discuss it angrily till midnight. Anna, who, like Aglaya in *The Idiot*, eventually married a French revolutionary, defended it, and Dostoevsky screamed his objections.

"Our entire youth is stupid and undeveloped," he shouted. "They think black boots are more important than Pushkin."

"Pushkin is really old-fashioned today," Anna replied calmly, knowing very well that the thing that was quite certain to infuriate Dostoevsky was disrespect for Pushkin.

In reply, Sofia records, Dostoevsky would pick up his hat and, after announcing solemnly that he considered it a waste of time arguing with a girl nihilist, declare that he would never darken her door again. But next day he would appear as though nothing had happened and resume his war of words with the girl who, like Pauline, seemed to enjoy driving him mad. Once he told her that she had a cheap, worthless mind, while her sister, though still a child, understood him. Sofia, whose infatuation with Dostoevsky was growing more intense the more violent his quarrels with her sister became, blushed with pleasure and, she writes, would gladly have let herself be cut to pieces to prove that she understood him. "Lord," she prayed, "let the whole world admire Anna; only make Dostoevsky think that I am the prettiest girl in the world!" Once Dostoevsky praised her piano-playing and, as he had told her and her sister that his favorite piano piece was Beethoven's *Sonata Pathétique*, she spent days practicing it and was only waiting for the right moment to play it for him. It came a few days before their departure from Petersburg. One evening they were again left alone, her mother and aunts having gone to a reception at the Swedish Embassy, and when Dostoevsky came she offered to play his favorite sonata for him. Dostoevsky seemed to be very strange that evening, not irritable, as usual, but sweet and tender. Sofia began playing and became so absorbed that she did not notice that Dostoevsky and her sister had left the room long before she had finished. She went into the next room. There was no one there. "At last," she writes, "raising the curtain which covered the door of the dining room, I saw Dostoevsky and Anna sitting on the small sofa. The room was faintly lighted by a lamp with a large shade. My sister's face was in shadow and I could not see it clearly, but Dostoevsky's face I could see very clearly indeed: it was pale and excited. He held Anna's hand in his and, leaning over her, spoke to her in the passionate, excitable whisper I knew so well.

" 'Darling Anna, please understand that I fell in love with you the first moment I saw you. Even before—I felt it from your letters. And I don't love you as a friend, but passionately, with all my being. . . .'

"I felt dizzy," Sofia writes. "I was seized by a feeling of bitter loneliness and dull resentment, my blood seemed to rush to my heart and in a hot stream to my head. I let fall the curtain and rushed out of the room. . . . My soul was full of a feeling of bitterness, resentment and shame, but, above all—shame and resentment. Till that moment I did not realize that I was in love with Dostoevsky. And now, I kept repeating to myself, everything, everything is finished!"

Dostoevsky did not come to see them next day, and when Sofia asked her sister whether she really did not care for him, Anna replied that she did not love him sufficiently to marry him. "You see," she said, "I am sometimes surprised at myself for not being able to love him. He is so kind. At first I thought that I might fall in love with him. But he wants quite a different person for a wife. His wife must devote herself entirely to him, she must give up her whole life to him, she must think only of him. And I can't do it. I want to live myself. Besides, he's so nervous and demanding. He seems always to wish to get me entirely to himself, to swallow me up. I am never at ease in his presence."

Dostoevsky came again to take leave of them before they left for their country estate, but he stayed only a short time. According to his second wife, it was Dostoevsky who realized that Anna would never make a good wife for him because "she lacked the ability to give and take which is so necessary in every successful marriage, especially when married to such a sick and irritable man as Dostoevsky was so often. . . ." She quotes Dostoevsky as saying that while Anna was a very intelligent and highly educated girl, her opinions were diametrically opposed to his own and that she would never have agreed to give them up. "Our married life," he declared, "would hardly have been a happy one. I gave her back her promise and I wished with all my heart that she should meet a man who shared her views and be happy with him." But, of course, Anna had never promised to marry him and, in fact, he had never been in love with her. He had proposed to her because the match would have been financially profitable to him. He may also have been carried away a little by her youth and beauty, but her refusal did not affect him very much. His financial position was becoming desperate, and very soon *Epoch* ceased publication. It seems significant that during his wooing of Anna Korvin-Krukovsky he never mentioned the critical position of *Epoch*—the real reason for his constant visits would have become all too clear if he had.

IV

On June 5, 1865, Dostoevsky received from the police a notice of distraint for a debt of some 700 rubles, and the next day he applied to the Literary Fund for a loan of 600 rubles, for, he wrote, "it was only by promising to pay 600 rubles by July 9 that I could persuade my creditors not to sell my belongings or have me hauled off to jail." A month earlier he had sent in his resignation from the committee of the Literary Fund because, he wrote to the Fund's secretary: "I am worried by the thought that I am expecting to get a loan not because I have to go abroad for medical treatment but chiefly because I am a member of the committee." He had earlier tried to raise money by selling the copyright of a complete edition of his works to a publisher, a certain Stellovsky, who was well known for the harsh terms he offered to writers and musicians. Stellovsky offered him 3,000 rubles for his three-volume edition, but insisted on including a clause in the agreement for the delivery of a new novel within twelve months, that is, by November 1, 1866. By failing to deliver it by that date Dostoevsky would incur a heavy fine, and if he failed to deliver it by December 1, 1866, he would forfeit the copyright of all his published and unpublished works "forever." Stellovsky had made quite sure that Dostoevsky would agree to his iniquitous terms by buying up the bills of exchange he had so thoughtlessly given to his creditors and threatening through his agents, in whose names he had bought up the bills, to present them for immediate payment. Most of the money, therefore, returned to Stellovsky without in any way alleviating Dostoevsky's financial position. The failure of *Epoch* aggravated it, for his creditors became even more pressing. He tried to induce Kraevsky to give him an advance of 3,000 rubles for a novel, but Kraevsky, whom he had now twice lampooned in his writings, refused to have anything to do with him.

The proposed novel, *The Drunkards*, was never written, but its theme is generally taken to have been incorporated in *Crime and Punishment* in the incident of Marmeladov and his luckless family. Dostoevsky had, of course, a great deal of experience of confirmed drunkards—members of his own family, his first wife's husband, and various contributors to his journal, including the critic Grigoryev, who had died of alcoholism a short time earlier. The proposed novel, he wrote to Kraevsky,[6] "will deal with the present problem of drunkenness. Not only will this problem and all its ramifications be analyzed, but also the effect it has on family life, the education of children, etc. . . ." Kraevsky not being forthcoming, there seemed only one way open to him if he was to get money quickly: roulette. He had his infallible "system," and no disaster could shake his faith in it: if it failed him, that was not its fault, but the fault of his own "impossible" character. If only he could keep calm!

There was another powerful and no less preposterous reason that made him decide to go abroad for the third time: he actually hoped to make it up with Pauline, whom, as he had told her sister in April, he still loved very much, though he wished he did not. It would seem that his letter had impressed Pauline's sister, who did not relish Pauline's promiscuous life in Paris and no doubt did her best to persuade her to patch things up with Dostoevsky. Pauline was still swearing vengeance on her Spanish lover, but that did not prevent her from seeking distraction elsewhere. "People," she writes, thinking of her sister, "are talking to me about Dostoevsky. I simply hate him. He made me suffer so much at a time when there was no need for suffering." How had Dostoevsky made her suffer? Pauline is never specific on this point, but one can legitimately surmise that the source of her hatred of Dostoevsky was not so much physical disgust as intellectual defeat. "When I think what I was two years ago," she wrote in her diary on December 14, 1864, "I begin to hate Dostoevsky, for he was the first to kill faith in me." And when about two months later a young Russian revolutionary urged her to marry Dostoevsky and take his *Epoch* in hand, meaning that

[6] *Letters*, June 6, 1865.

she should make it into a left-wing journal, she replied: "I don't want to marry him."

"Take *Epoch* in my hands, indeed!" she added after recounting this conversation. "What kind of Iphigenia does he take me to be?"

She was quite sure, it seems, that Dostoevsky would still marry her, but also knew that no sacrifice on her part would have made Dostoevsky change his ideas or let her influence them.

At the end of June, at the time when Dostoevsky had finally decided to go abroad and patch up his affair with Pauline, she had arrived in Zurich to discuss the matter with her sister and must have been persuaded to agree to Dostoevsky's wish to meet her in Wiesbaden. Dostoevsky arrived in Wiesbaden on August 11, 1865. She arrived there some days later, but it was she who was now " a little too late," for by that time Dostoevsky had lost every penny he had and, as she had no money, either, both of them found themselves in an impossible situation. Strangely enough, Pauline does not mention her second meeting with Dostoevsky in Wiesbaden in her diary. The entry before the meeting is dated Zurich, June 30, and the next one is dated Spa, September 17. Not a word about what happened between those two dates. Of Dostoevsky's disaster at roulette we learn from his letter to Turgenev from Wiesbaden on August 15. "When I saw you in Petersburg about a month ago," Dostoevsky wrote, "I was in the process of selling my works for anything I was offered, for I was threatened with jail for the debts I incurred for my journal. . . . My works were bought by Stellovsky for 3,000 rubles, part of which was in bills of exchange. . . . All I had left for my journey abroad was 175 rubles in silver. Two years ago I won about 12,000 francs in one hour's play. Though I never intended to improve my present circumstances by gambling, I did want to win 1,000 francs. I have been five days in Wiesbaden and have lost everything, including my watch, and even owe money in my hotel. I am terribly ashamed to trouble you, but, apart from you, there is no one to whom I can appeal for help and, besides, you are so much more intelligent than anyone else and it is therefore morally easier for me to appeal to you." He asked Turgenev for a loan of one hundred thalers, promising to repay it within three weeks (it was not till 1876 that the debt was actually repaid). "I feel awful," he concluded his letter, "and, above all, I am ashamed to trouble you; but when one is drowning, what is one to do?" Turgenev sent him fifty thaler, and on August 20, Dostoevsky thanked him in a short note, adding that he had caught a cold while traveling from Berlin and still felt feverish every day.

Of his other "adventures," as he called them, in Wiesbaden during that short and disastrous trip abroad we learn from his letters to Pauline and Wrangel. His letters to Pauline are couched in very friendly but hardly ecstatic terms. They are certainly not the letters of an ardent lover. In the first, dated August 22, 1865, he describes his parlous position. He had written for money to Herzen, with whom, he declared, he was "on excellent terms"—an interesting admission, showing that even at that late date he had not yet gone over entirely to the conservative camp—but had so far had no reply. "Meanwhile," he continued, "my position has deteriorated to an unbelievable extent. Immediately after your departure, early next morning, they told me at the hotel that they had been ordered not to let me have any dinners, or any tea or coffee. I went to ask for an explanation and the fat German proprietor told me that I did not 'deserve' to have dinner and that he would let me have tea only. And so since yesterday I have had no dinner and keep going only on tea. And the tea, too, is horrible, served in a glass. They don't clean my clothes and boots, they don't answer my calls, and all the servants treat me with most inexpressible, typically German, contempt. . . . All this would have been amusing were it not so confoundedly inconvenient. So that if Herzen doesn't send me the money, they'll probably seize my things and kick me out or do something worse. Disgusting." He begged her to send him some money, if she did manage to get to Paris and was able to borrow some from her friends. "*Au revoir*, my dear," he concludes, "I can't believe that I won't see you before your departure from Paris. As for my position, I hate to think about it; I am just sitting in my room and reading so as not to waken my appetite by some movement. I embrace you warmly. For God's sake do not show my letter to anybody and don't tell anybody about my position. It's disgusting. All yours, F.D."

Two days later he wrote to her again. "My affairs," he declared, "are in so horrible a state that I don't think they could get much worse." He had had no reply from Herzen, and he was beginning to wonder whether anyone had been telling Herzen "nasty things" about him. "I am tormented," he went on, "by my inactivity, the uncertainty of my position, the loss of valuable time and this cursed Wiesbaden, of which I am so sick that I can't bear to look at it. Meanwhile you are in Paris and I shan't see you. I am also worried about Herzen, for if he did get my letter and *does not want* to answer—think of the humiliation! Have I deserved it? Because of my disorderly way of life? I admit it, but what a bourgeois morality!" He begged her again to send him some money, and he was beginning to wonder if she, too, did not want to reply to his letters. "I still have no dinners," he continued, "and keep going on my morning and evening tea for the third day and—strange to say—I don't seem to be so very hungry. What is bad is that they keep persecuting me and sometimes even refuse to let me have a candle at night, especially if a tiny candle end has been left over from the night before. However, I usually leave the hotel at three o'clock and come back at six so as not to let them know that I had no dinner. A real Khlestakov!" He still hoped to see Pauline in Paris, little realizing that on her return there she had resumed her promiscuous life. "Good-by, my dear," he wrote, concluding what he thought would be his last letter to her. "If I have no more very special adventures I shall write no more. *Au revoir.* All yours, Dos. PS.—I embrace you again very warmly. Has your sister arrived? Give her my regards." He added another postscript to tell her of the friendly reply he had received from Herzen, who did not enclose any money, though. He surmised that Herzen himself must be hard up. He begged her to send him 150 gulden, signed himself this time: F. Dostoevsky and added: "Now I simply don't know what's going to happen to me."

Receiving neither a reply nor any money from Pauline, he wrote at the beginning of September to Alexander Milyukov in Petersburg, imploring him to sell the serial rights of the novel he was planning to write (*Crime and Punishment*) for 300 rubles. "I am sitting at my hotel," he wrote.[7] "I am up to my neck in debt, everybody is threatening me, and I haven't a penny." But Milyukov was unlucky: no one wanted Dostoevsky's novel even at such a ridiculously low price. In desperation he wrote to his old friend Wrangel, who was at the time first secretary at the Russian Embassy in Copenhagen. He asked Wrangel for a loan of one hundred thaler. "I am applying to you for his loan," he wrote,[8] "because I still remember you as you were when I knew you and because there were so many moments which united us in our lives that, though we have been separated by life, we can never be strangers to one another." He wanted the money, he explained, for a trip to Paris which was very important to him. Five days later he wrote to Wrangel again, repeating his request for a loan, for his position had become twice as bad, as he was now being threatened with the police. He got the money from Wrangel a week later, but, he wrote to Wrangel, "informed about the money, the landlord took away almost *everything*, leaving me only 15 gulden." However, he was hoping to get some money from Katkov, to whom he had offered his new novel for publication in *The Russian Herald.* His past experience with Katkov, though, had not been a very happy one, for Katkov had refused to publish his *Village of Stepanchikovo* in spite of the fact that he had sent him an advance for it. That advance Dostoevsky had repaid, but after that *Time* and *The Russian Herald* had conducted a campaign against each other, and he was wondering whether Katkov bore him any ill will on that score. "And yet," he wrote to Wrangel, "the novel I am writing now will perhaps be the best I've ever written, if I am given time to finish it. Oh, my friend, you can't imagine the torment of writing to order! . . . But what can I do? I owe 15,000 rubles, while only a year ago I did not owe anyone a penny. I have not only sacrificed 10,000 rubles of my own for the benefit of my brother's family, but have also undertaken to repay my brother's debts, and now I am in danger of spending several years in a debtors' jail for somebody else's

[7] *Letters,* September 17, 1865.

[8] *Letters,* September 28, 1865.

debts. What's going to happen to my poor Pasha? And to my sick brother Nikolai?" He hoped to pay Wrangel a visit and then return to Petersburg by sea.

The 10,000 rubles he had "sacrificed" for the benefit of Mikhail's family were his part of the expected inheritance left him in her will by his rich aunt, Alexandra Kumanin. Like Mikhail, he had got the money in advance from his aunt to save his journal, and, like Mikhail, did not succeed in saving it. The thought of it rankled, for he had learned that his aunt had added a codicil to her will to the effect that her nephews Mikhail and Fyodor, having received their share of the inheritance, "are not entitled to any further share of the money left in this will."

Dostoevsky left Wiesbaden at the end of September after Yanyshev, the local Russian priest, had lent him enough money for his personal expenses and guaranteed to pay his hotel bill. Yanyshev warned him (for which Dostoevsky never forgave him) that he would be placed in a very difficult position if Dostoevsky "deceived" him. He did not go to Paris, for Pauline had left Paris on September 16, having decided to put an end to her "sad and coarse" life there. Instead he went to Copenhagen, where he arrived at Wrangel's house on October 1, 1865. He spent ten days there. Wrangel found that he had aged a great deal. "My wife," he records, "liked him very much and he spent a long time playing with my two children."

Dostoevsky never mentioned his affair with Pauline to Wrangel, which shows how estranged they had become since their Siberian days. But he summed up his relationship with her without mentioning her name in these words: "Let us always be grateful for the days of happiness we have received from the woman we love. We must not demand of her to be always thinking of us. This is unworthy egoism, which we must do our best to overcome."

He had intended it, no doubt, as an epitaph on his relationship with Pauline, but, as it turned out, he met her again in Petersburg in November. They argued and contradicted each other interminably, Pauline noted in one of the last entries in her diary. "Dostoevsky," she wrote, "has been offering me his hand and his heart for a long time, but he merely makes me angry. Talking of my character, he said: 'If you ever marry, you will hate and run away from your husband on the third day after your wedding.' Then he added: 'One day I'll tell you something.' I kept pestering him to tell me. 'You can't forgive me,' he said, 'for having once given yourself to me and you keep revenging yourself on me for that: it is the sort of thing a woman does.' "

Vindictiveness was indeed one of the most prominent traits of Pauline's character. She proved it after her marriage in 1880 at the age of forty to the twenty-eight-year-old critic Vassily Rozanov, when she ran away from him six years (not three days!) after their wedding and refused to give him a divorce for the next seventeen years, although by that time he was living with another woman and had two children by her. Dostoevsky realized, too, that, as he wrote to her from Dresden,[9] she would always find it difficult to be happy. "Oh, my dear," he wrote, "it is not cheap and *necessary* happiness that I mean. I respect you (I always did respect you) for demanding such a great deal from people, but, you see, I know that while in your heart you cannot help demanding much from life, you yourself think that people are either knights in shining armor or complete scoundrels and vulgarians." In fact it was Pauline's capacity to be so exacting and uncompromising that Dostoevsky admired in her most, and it is this trait that is most prominent in the characters of some of his heroines, such as Sonia in *Crime and Punishment,* Nastasya Filippovna in *The Idiot* and Grushenka in *The Brothers Karamazov.*

V

"Life and hope have not yet come to an end for me," Dostoevsky wrote to Yanyshev on April 20, 1866, in returning him the money he had borrowed eight months earlier. "I'll prove to you," he wrote to the priest in November, "that I am an honest man," and in the same letter he added that he had been punished already, for "the thought of what you must be thinking of me drives me mad." The year 1866 indeed provided ample proof that "life and hope" had not "come to an end" for Dostoevsky. In that year he finished *Crime and Punishment,* which revived his fame throughout Russia, and at last married a woman who gave him "the great and only human happiness" (as he wrote to Wrangel) he had so far lacked—a family of his own.

Not the 1866 opened propitiously for him. He had outlined his first draft of *Crime and Punishment* in his much quoted letter to Katkov, which he sent off while still immured in his room in the Wiesbaden hotel in September 1865. He was so anxious to raise money that he agreed to accept as little as 125 rubles for a folio page. Katkov, to his great relief, accepted his offer. "Later I found out," Dostoevsky wrote to Wrangel,[10] "that he was only too glad to accept my offer because he had nothing else for that year: Turgenev has not written anything and he has quarreled with Leo Tolstoy."

Dostoevsky began making notes for the novel even while on board the *Viceroy,* on which he sailed from Copenhagen to Petersburg, where he arrived on October 15. In Petersburg his epileptic seizures started again. "When I arrived," he wrote to Wrangel,[11] "I had an attack on

[9] *Letters,* May 5, 1867.
[10] *Letters,* February 18, 1866.
[11] *Letters,* November 8, 1865.

the very first night—a very violent one too. Five days later, as soon as I recovered from it, I had another and even more violent attack. I had a third one three days ago not so violent, but it took me three days to recover from it. All the same," he went on, "I am not relaxing for a moment and working away at my novel. Katkov sent me my advance of 300 rubles to Wiesbaden. Yanyshev forwarded them to me here. But my late brother's family, who are in a state of complete disorder, were only waiting for me to come back: I gave them all the money I had and borrowed another 100 rubles for them the other day." Mikhail's widow, Emilia, held him responsible for "squandering" her husband's money (the 10,000 rubles he had received from his rich aunt in Moscow) and looked on him as in duty bound to support her and her children. "She alone," he wrote to Yanyshev,[12] "still talks to me. Her children don't even exchange greetings with me."

His stepson, Pasha, was no great comfort to him, either. The tutor with whom he had left him during his previous journey abroad and while staying in Moscow with his dying wife had conducted himself, as Dostoevsky wrote to him at the end of 1864, "immorally and dishonestly." He spent the money Dostoevsky sent him on himself, letting his charge roam about the streets, making him pawn his watch and sending him to his relations for his dinners. "You brought prostitutes to your rooms," Dostoevsky went on, "and, following your example, Pasha also got himself a prostitute. . . . You accuse me of flying into a temper. I know very well my bad, morbid, and to some extent even ridiculous traits of character, but I also know that I am incapable of offending anyone without good reason. . . . I have written you this letter," he concluded, "because I have been wishing for a long time to point out to you, a so-called progressive, that progress has nothing to do with a fine phrase, that a fashionable phrase is not sufficient to salve your conscience or to cover up scandalous behavior. . . ." Dostoevsky considered his stepson "a sacred trust," but, as his letter to Pasha's "tutor" shows, he was hardly the man to bring up a conceited and rather stupid boy, who was quick-witted enough to realize the weak sides of his stepfather's character and exploit them at every favorable opportunity.

By the end of November Dostoevsky decided that the form of a "confession," that is, the first person singular, in which he had been writing *Crime and Punishment*, was quite inappropriate for the mass of material that had gradually accumulated in his mind, and, he wrote to Wrangel,[13] he burned "everything" and started writing it from scratch. "I am working day and night," he told Wrangel in the same letter, "but it is still not enough. . . . A novel is something poetic, something that demands for its composition a calm spirit and imagination. And I am worried by my

[12] *Letters,* April 20, 1866.
[13] *Letters,* February 18, 1866.

creditors who threaten to haul me off to jail. . . . You can imagine my agitation and nervousness. It puts a strain on one's spirit and one's heart, puts one off work for several days, but you have to sit down and write. Sometimes it is impossible." Then there were his epileptic seizures and, more recently in February and March, an attack of hemorrhoids. "For fifteen days," Dostoevsky complains, "I had to lie on my sofa and could not hold a pen in my hand. To lie down because I could not stand or sit from the convulsions which began immediately I got up! . . . I have grown nervous and irritable and my character has become spoiled. I don't know what will be the end of it. The whole winter I did not visit anyone and saw nothing and no one. I've been only once to the theater, to the first performance of *Rogneda.* And so it will go on to the end of my novel—if I'm not dragged off to jail, that is."

The first twelve chapters of the first part of *Crime and Punishment* were published in the January number of *The Russian Herald.* In March he took part in a public meeting of the Literary Fund and read the scene in the tavern between Marmeladov and Raskolnikov. On April 4 an attempt was made on the life of Alexander II by Dmitry Karakozov, an event that greatly upset Dostoevsky, who burst agitatedly into Maykov's flat to tell him of the shot fired at the Tsar.

But, though upset, Dostoevsky did his best to prevent repressive measures against the so-called nihilists. On April 25, 1866, he wrote a long letter to Katkov, a man of immense political influence, who had direct access to the Tsar himself and whose daily *Moscow News* had been conducting a violent campaign against any manifestation of liberalism in high places. Dostoevsky began with the rather questionable assertion that he had always been a Slavophile. He went on to point out that "the teaching to shake everything up *par les quatre coins de la nappe* so that there should at last be a *tabula rasa* for action" had always been one of the dearly held beliefs of the nihilists, who, he declared, were all socialists. "Socialism," he went on, "(especially in its Russian version) means the severance of all connections. For they are absolutely convinced that they would at once build Jerusalem on a *tabula rasa.* Fourier was quite sure that all he had to do was to form one phalanstery for the whole world to be covered with phalansteries—these are his very words. And our Chernyshevsky used to say that he only had to talk to the common people for a quarter of an hour to convert them to socialism. But," Dostoevsky put in his plea at last, "we must not forget that our poor, defenseless boys and girls have their own basic article of faith, namely their enthusiasm for goodness and the purity of their hearts. It is on this that socialism in Russia will for a long time be based. There are, of course, plenty of scoundrels and mischief-makers among them. But all these schoolboys and young students, and I have seen a great many of them, have been converted to nihilism selflessly and innocently in the name of honor and truth and because of a desire to be genuinely useful.

We must remember that they are utterly defenseless against all those absurdities which they accept as the last word of perfection. . . . The poor fellows are convinced that nihilism provides them with the fullest possible scope for their social and civic activities and for liberty." He followed up this plea for understanding and leniency by a warning that any attempt by the authorities to impose "a constraint on thought and word" would merely hamper the fight against nihilism. "Even if the nihilists are given full freedom to express their views," he told Katkov, "it would turn out to the advantage of the authorities, for they would merely make a laughing stock of themselves throughout Russia by *positivist* explanations of their doctrines, whereas now they are invested with an air of mystery and looked upon as sphinxes and enigmas and the sole depositories of wisdom, which of course exercises a great influence on the inexperienced." Finally, he put in a plea for a public trial of those accused of complicity in the attempt on the Tsar's life. He doubted whether any of the officials engaged in the investigation of the present conspiracy were able even to talk to a nihilist. "People," he declared, "suspect that the government is still attached 'to the old forms' and quite naturally have no confidence in it and are beginning to fear the advent of reaction."

This letter is certainly remarkable for showing that, though Dostoevsky was now moving rapidly to the right, he did not forget his own past as a "nihilist," nor did he overlook the purity of the motives of the majority of the young Russian revolutionaries and the incapacity of the government to deal with them in a way that might avert a recurrence of terrorist acts.

At Easter Dostoevsky rushed off to Moscow to get another advance of 1,000 rubles from Katkov. He intended to go to Dresden and there finish his novel without any interruptions from his creditors or his late brother's family. However, his trip abroad did not come off, chiefly because of a fall in the Russian currency, and he returned to Petersburg to carry on with his work on the novel, which, he wrote to Wrangel,[14] was his only hope.

While in Moscow he resumed his correspondence with Anna Korvin-Krukovsky. "You spoke so little about yourself while in Petersburg," he wrote, "that I could not help concluding (and, I think, rightly) that there was something in myself that prevented you from being sincere with me. And yet, my dear, good, noble Anna, if only you knew how sincerely I wished to agree with you about many things. I wanted so badly that you should respect me more because I could not help feeling that you don't seem to respect me at all." Was he trying to resume his wooing of Anna? In his next letter, from Moscow,[15] where he had

[14] *Letters,* May 9, 1866.

[15] *Letters,* June 17, 1866.

run away from his creditors again to be able to concentrate on his novel, he implored her not to leave him. He was now beginning to be worried by the clause in his agreement with Stellovsky under which he had undertaken, upon pain of a heavy fine, to deliver a new novel by November. "I want to do something eccentric and unheard of," he wrote to Anna, "namely, to write thirty folio pages in four months of two different novels, one in the morning and the other in the evening. You know, such extraordinarily eccentric things still appeal to me greatly. I'm afraid I don't fit into the category of sedate and solid citizens. Sorry, I'm boasting. . . . But I am convinced that not a single one of our writers, past and present, has ever written under the same conditions as I am *always* writing. Turgenev would have died at the very thought of it. But if you only knew how terrible it is to spoil an idea which has been born in you, delighted you, which you know is good, and to be forced to spoil it consciously."

The idea to which Dostoevsky was referring was the close parallel he originally meant to draw between the raising of Lazarus by Christ and the "raising" of Raskolnikov by Sonia, whom he conceived as the embodiment of the Christian principle of atonement through suffering. In the original version of the novel this parallelism was hinted at in various ways. It was on the fourth day after Raskolnikov had killed the old woman moneylender that Sonia read to him the passage from the Gospels about Lazarus. Lazarus had been dead for four days before his raising from the tomb, and in her reading Sonia put great emphasis on the word *four* when she read: "for he hath been dead four days." During her first visit to Raskolnikov's room, his mother observes that it it "just like a coffin," to which Raskolnikov replies with "a queer smile": "Mother, if you only knew what a strange thing you said just now!" And a few pages later, Raskolnikov remarks to Sonia, who had been describing her father's plain deal coffin: "Why do you look at my room like that? My mother has just said that it is like a coffin." At the end of the novel Dostoevsky refers again to this parallel after pointing out that the New Testament Raskolnikov had picked up from under his pillow "was the same book from which Sonia had read of the raising of Lazarus to him." And in the original text as published in *The Russian Herald* Sonia, when persuading Raskolnikov to go to the crossroads, bow down to the people and proclaim in a loud voice to the whole world: "I am a murderer!"—added: "Then God will bring you back to life and raise you. He raised Lazarus from the dead by a miracle and he will raise you too. Will you go? Will you go?" Finally, in his first draft notes of the novel Raskolnikov's confession is preceded by "a vision of Christ" to be used possibly as another parallel to Christ's visit to Lazarus.

Dostoevsky was "forced to spoil" this whole idea of Raskolnikov's "resurrection" at the very outset by Katkov, who demanded a thorough revision of two chapters and who took particular exception to the *fourth* chapter of the *fourth* part containing the crucial passage in which Sonia reads the Gospel to Raskolnikov. Writing to Milyukov,[16] Dostoevsky declared that he had written the offending chapter "with intense inspiration, but perhaps it is not as good as I thought—they are afraid it offends against the accepted *moral standards* and, besides, they see in it traces of *nihilism.* This revision," Dostoevsky went on, "was much harder than writing three new chapters. I don't know what's going to happen in future, but I am beginning to be worried by this first sign of a clash between my views and theirs. . . ."

In his letter to Katkov,[17] however, Dostoevsky, while deploring some of the cuts, admitted that others were necessary. "I have a strange peculiarity, namely, having written something, I completely lose my critical sense, for some time at any rate." And in a postscript he repeated that some of the cuts had improved the chapter to which Katkov had taken objection. "For the last twenty years," he wrote, "I have felt agonizingly—and I see it more clearly than anyone, that my chief literary defect is—*verbosity*, and I simply cannot get rid of it."

Dostoevsky was, in fact, apt to get too excited at first about his ideas and drive them to a point where he was in danger of toppling over into the morass of mysticism (as some of his more enthusiastic interpreters have done time and again). "Every moment of the story," Dostoevsky wrote in his preliminary notes for the novel, "must be absolutely clear." And in the third notebook on the novel, he wrote: "Always facts, no arguments."

Another powerful reason why Dostoevsky was so careful to avoid any accusation of indulging in what he called "abstract intellectual arguments" is that in *Crime and Punishment* he continued his attack on the dialectical "utilitarians" which he began in his *Notes from a Dark Cellar.* As in his earlier work, he constantly contrasts "life" with "theory." On the last page of the novel he sums up his position against the materialists in the statement that so far as Raskolnikov was concerned "life had taken the place of dialectics." Earlier in the novel (in the fifth chapter of the third part) he puts his objections to the theories of the utilitarians into Razumikhin's mouth. "They reduce everything to one common cause—environment," Razumikhin-Dostoevsky declares. "Human nature is not taken into account at all. Human nature is banished. Human nature isn't supposed to exist. They deny that, following the lines of historical development, mankind will at last be transformed into a healthy society. On the contrary, they maintain that a social system, emerging out of someone's mathematical brain, will at once organize mankind and transform it in an instant into a righteous society. . . . That's why they dislike the living process of life so much. They don't want a *living soul.* A living soul makes demands, it

[16] *Letters,* July 10, 1866.
[17] *Letters,* July 19, 1866.

scoffs at mechanics, it is suspicious, it is retrograde. . . . They reduce everything to . . . the planning of rooms and corridors in a phalanstery. The phalanstery, of course, is all ready, but unfortunately human nature is not ready for the phalanstery. Human nature wants life. . . . You can't jump over human nature by logic alone. Logic can foresee only three possibilities, but there is a whole million of them! . . ."

There might be a million of them, but these certainly do not include so close a parallel with the Gospel story of the raising of Lazarus as his original idea demanded. Already in April 1866, the satirical left-wing magazine *Iskra* (*The Spark*) had published a parody on *Crime and Punishment* under the title *The Double* and dedicated it to Dostoevsky. He simply could not afford, even if his artistic flair had deserted him completely in this instance, to jeopardize his whole case against the left-wing utilitarians by indulging in fictitious miraclemongering.

He felt no such contraint in dealing with the "Napoleonic theme" in the novel. The theme had been touched on by Pushkin as well as by Balzac, but it became a topic of general discussion in the European press after the publication of Napoleon III's book, *The History of Julius Caesar*, in March 1865. The book, in which Napoleon III argued that "Providence sends such men as Julius Caesar, Charlemagne and Napoleon to pave the path which the people have to follow and thus complete the work of several centuries in a few years and then stamp their genius on a whole era," was generally interpreted by the Russian press as "a self-defense of its royal author"; but the *Contemporary*, in a long review of the book, drew a more general conclusion from Napoleon III's theory. "There are, therefore," the reviewer wrote, "two different human logics and moral laws. One logic and one set of laws according to which one should judge the actions of ordinary men and another logic and set of laws according to which one should judge world geniuses, heroes, demigods. But if the great geniuses of history are above the laws which apply to ordinary mortals, the laws of ordinary logic are inapplicable to them, the question arises how we are to recognize these persons. We may consider a certain person as an ordinary mortal, while he will turn out to be a genius; or we may think that a certain person is a genius, while he will turn out to be a common or garden person."

In the fifth chapter of the third part of *Crime and Punishment* Dostoevsky reproduces almost verbatim this passage from the *Contemporary* article, but he puts it into the mouth of Porfiry Petrovich, the investigating magistrate, while he lets Raskolnikov himself give a brilliant exposé of all the implications of the "Napoleonic" theory.

[10]

THE STENOGRAPHER: SECOND MARRIAGE

To be able to work on his novel without constant interruptions by creditors and the never-ending demands and recriminations from Mikhail's widow, Dostoevsky decided to spend the summer of 1866 in Moscow. But he stayed there only a week, driven out by the "unbearable and oppressive heat, the torrid winds and the clouds of dust," as he wrote to Milyukov on July 8 from Lyublino, a small town near Moscow where his favorite sister, Vera, and her family had a country house and where he, too, had taken a cottage. Apart from working at *Crime and Punishment*, he wrote to Milyukov, he had drafted a plan for the novel he had to deliver to Stellovsky before November. "A highly satisfactory little novel," he hoped it would turn out to be, "even with a faint semblance of living characters. Stellovsky is worrying me to death and he even pursues me in my dreams." In a postscript he added: "Haven't had any fits so far. Am drinking vodka. How's the cholera?"

The cholera epidemic in Petersburg made him rush off a letter to Pasha who, as usual, wrote to him only when he was in need of money. "There's cholera in Petersburg," he wrote. "I'm worried about you. Are you ill? Are you really such a monster as not to reply to my letters—if I don't get one from you soon I'll give up everything and go to Petersburg myself. What are you doing to me?" But Pasha ignored his stepfather's demands to join him at his country cottage, and Dostoevsky was soon having too good a time at his sister's in Lyublino to worry about him.

Vera Ivanov's house was full of young people, including her own numerous brood and the twenty-five-year-old Alexander Karepin, her eldest sister Varvara's only son, a professor of medicine and a medical prodigy of a sort, though otherwise, as Dostoevsky's daughter Lyubov put it, "so stupid as to verge on idiocy." He was the constant butt of

Dostoevsky's good-humored wit (his uncle did not visit on him the anger and contempt he had felt for his father). Dostoevsky wrote all sorts of humorous verses and even a whole "ode" on him, in which he described him as "tiny, rotund, a little like Humpty Dumpty." One day Dostoevsky improvised a play—*The Trial of Karepin and His Future Wife*—in which he took the part of the judge. He put on one of his niece's red coats and a pair of paper spectacles. On his head he wore a bucket. His favorite niece, Sofia (to whom he was to dedicate *The Idiot* two years later), sat beside him as the clerk of the court. He made a brilliant speech in defense of Karepin's supposed wife, who, he declared, wished to follow the example of the heroine of Chernyshevsky's novel, *What Is to Be Done?*, and run away to Petersburg to learn sewing on a sewing machine. Her husband, Karepin, is sentenced to exile at the North Pole. Karepin is furious and rushes on Dostoevsky. Curtain. The second act takes place at the North Pole. Karepin is discovered sitting on a snowdrift and bewailing his fate. Dostoevsky, in the shape of a polar bear, steals up behind him and eats him up. Dostoevsky seemed to enjoy this horseplay very much. "He amused himself with us like a child," von Vogt, a friend of the Ivanovs, records, "probably finding that they had a restful and calming effect on him after the intense mental work on his great novel." (Dostoevsky was working on the fifth part of *Crime and Punishment* at the time.)

"Dostoevsky," von Vogt continues, "was also very fond of music. He was constantly humming some tune, which was an unmistakable sign that he was in a good mood. In this respect his niece Maria, Vera's second daughter, who was a student of the Moscow Conservatoire, gave him many pleasurable hours by her excellent piano playing. On one subject, however, they did not agree. Maria was a great admirer of Chopin, while Dostoevsky did not altogether enjoy the music of the Polish composer which he described as 'consumptive.' He liked Mozart and Beethoven most of all and of the Russian composers he preferred Glinka and Serov, especially the latter's opera, *Rogneda*. . . . Once in Dostoevsky's presence I played a German song on the well-known verse by Heine:

"*Du hast Diamanten und Perlen. . . .*

"Dostoevsky liked the song very much and asked me where I had heard it. I replied that I had several times heard Moscow organ-grinders play it in the streets. Dostoevsky had heard it for the first time and kept humming it quite often. It is likely it occurred to him later to make the dying Katerina Marmeladov repeat the words of this song in the fifth chapter of the fifth part of his novel." This, indeed, is more than likely.

Dostoevsky left a description of the high jinks at his sister's country house in his short novel *The Eternal Husband*, written six years later.

II

On his return to Petersburg in the autumn, Dostoevsky suddenly realized that he had only about two months in which to write the novel for Stellovsky. His friends—Maykov, Milyukov and others—proposed to write the novel for him, each of them a part of it, but Dostoevsky, who had already worked out the plan of *The Gambler*, would not hear of it. They then advised him to employ a stenographer and dictate the novel to her. Milyukov, who knew a well-known teacher of shorthand, took it upon himself to ask him to send Dostoevsky one of his best pupils. Thus it was that on October 4, 1866, Anna Snitkin, a twenty-year-old girl, knocked at the door of his flat at 13 Stolyarny (Carpenter) Lane.

"Dostoevsky's flat," Anna writes in her reminiscences, "was on the second floor. The door was opened by an elderly maid, who wore a green check shawl round her shoulders. I had read *Crime and Punishment* so recently that I immediately wondered whether this shawl was the original of the green *drap-de-dame* shawl which figured so largely in the life of the Marmeladov family. . . . I had scarcely time to take off my detachable hood when the door leading into the hall was flung open and against the background of a room flooded with light appeared a young man with a head of tousled black hair, a bare chest, wearing slippers. Seeing a stranger, he uttered a cry and vanished in a flash through a side door."

The dining room, into which she was shown by the maid, was, Anna writes, "very modestly furnished. There were two large chests, covered with rugs, along the walls. At the window was a chest of drawers covered with white pieces of knitted lace. Against another wall stood a sofa and over it hung a clock. . . . Two minutes later Dostoevsky came in, asked me to wait in his study and went out, as it later appeared, to order tea for us. Dostoevsky's study was a large room with two windows, very light on that sunny day, but at any other time rather dismal: it was silent and dark and one could not help feeling depressed by that darkness and silence. At the opposite wall was a soft sofa, covered by some brown, rather threadbare material; in front of it was a round table covered by a red cotton napkin. On the table stood a lamp; there were also two or three albums on it; round it were upholstered chairs and armchairs. Over the sofa hung a portrait in a walnut frame of a very thin woman in a black dress and a black bonnet. 'Dostoevsky's wife, I suppose,' I thought to myself, not knowing that he was a widower. Between the windows hung a large mirror in a black frame. The distance between the walls being much larger than the mirror, it had been moved nearer to the right window, which was not particularly nice, I thought. The windows were adorned by two large Chinese vases of a very beautiful shape. Along the other wall was a large sofa upholstered in green velvet and beside it a little table with a decanter of water. Opposite it, across the room, was a writing desk, at which I used always afterwards to sit when Dostoevsky dictated to me."

Dostoevsky put a few questions to her, then dictated a few paragraphs from *The Russian Herald*, and was rather put out by the long time she took in writing out her notes. When he looked over what she had written, he pointed out somewhat sharply that she had omitted a full stop. "He was obviously irritable," Anna writes, "and could not collect his thoughts. He asked me my name and then forgot it, then he began pacing the room and seemed to forget all about me." At last he told her that he could not dictate anything at the moment and asked her to come again at 8 o'clock in the evening. On saying good-by to her, he remarked:

" 'I am glad you're a woman and not a man.'

" 'Why?'

" 'Because a man would be quite sure to get drunk, but you, I hope, won't.'

"I felt amused, but I suppressed a smile.

" 'You can be sure of that,' I replied, keeping a straight face."

How did Dostoevsky, who was forty-five at the time, strike her? "At the first glance," she writes, "he struck me as rather old. But the moment he began talking, he looked younger and I thought that he could not be more than thirty-seven. He was of medium height, but kept himself very erect. His light chestnut, even slightly ginger, hair was smothered with pomade and carefully plastered down. But what astonished me was his eyes: one was brown and the other had its pupil so enlarged that the iris could not be seen. (During an epileptic attack, Anna explains in a footnote, "Dostoevsky fell on some sharp object and injured his right eye badly. The oculist put some atropine into it which greatly enlarged the pupil.") This gave Dostoevsky's look an enigmatic expression. His face, pale and sickly, seemed very familiar to me, probably because I had seen his portraits before. He was wearing a blue cotton jacket, rather threadbare, but his linen (collars and cuffs) were spotlessly white. . . . I left Dostoevsky's flat feeling very sad. I did not like him and he left a painful impression on me. I did not think we'd be able to work together, and my dreams of independence were shattered. . . ."

The "painful impression" Dostoevsky left on the young girl is confirmed in a somewhat longer note she wrote on May 26, 1883: "I must make one observation," she wrote. "No other man in the world, either before or after, ever made such a painful and truly depressing impression on me as did Dostoevsky at our first meeting. I saw before me a terribly unhappy man, careworn and worried to death. He looked like a man who had lost someone he dearly loved; like a man who had been struck down by a terrible calamity. When I left him, my rosy, happy mood had disappeared like a puff of smoke. My optimistic hopes were shattered and I walked along the streets feeling sad and crushed. . . ."

But at 8 o'clock in the evening she returned, and Dostoevsky did his best to put her at ease. Her serious bearing and her businesslike tone made a good impression on him. "He was used to meeting nihilist girls," Anna explains, "and the way they behaved in mixed company aroused his indignation. He was therefore all the more pleased to meet a person like me who was so utterly different from the prevalent type of young girls."

Dostoevsky again offered her tea and a cigarette (which she naturally refused) and regaled her with pears. Then, instead of starting his dictation, he trotted out the story of his mock execution, a story that he knew, from his experience with Anna Korvin-Krukovsky, made a great impression on young girls. He told her how happy he had felt after the return to his cell and how he kept singing at the top of his voice. Anna was duly impressed, and what struck her most of all was that he should be so frank with a young girl, almost a child, whom he had met for the first time in his life. His frankness, she records, produced a marvelous impression on her. But Dostoevsky went on talking, asking her about her family (her father had died shortly before, and her mother was Swedish), what school she studied at (she had finished her secondary school with a silver medal), what made her take up shorthand, and so on. She was beginning to be worried by the lateness of the hour, but, fortunately, Dostoevsky remembered what she was there for and began his dictation. While dictating, Anna writes, "he kept pacing the room rapidly, diagonally from the door to the stove, and every time he reached the stove he knocked twice on it. He was smoking all the time, often stubbing out his unfinished cigarette in the ashtray on the very edge of his writing desk."

The dictation of *The Gambler* went on daily from October 5 to October 29. Anna came punctually at 12 o'clock and went home at four to transcribe her shorthand. The work proceeded slowly at first, but later Dostoevsky prepared the material for dictation at night and it proceeded much more quickly.

The first clash between Anna and Pasha occurred a few days after she had begun working for her future husband. He stopped her at the gates as she was coming out to go home. "I recognized the young man I had seen in the hall during my first visit to Dostoevsky," she writes. "At close quarters he looked even more unprepossessing than from a distance. He had a dark, almost yellow face, black eyes with yellowish whites and teeth gone yellow with smoking.

" 'Don't you know who I am?' the young man asked me impudently. 'I saw you at my father's. I don't want to disturb you during your work, but I'm very interested to find out what sort of thing shorthand is, particularly as I shall be starting to study it myself shortly. May I?' And, without asking permission, he snatched my portfolio out of my hand, opened it and began examining my shorthand notes. I was so taken aback by his impudence that I did not even protest. 'A curious business!' he drawled indifferently as he gave me back my portfolio. . . ."

The poor fellow did not dream how very soon his whole future would depend on that slip of a girl. At the time Anna did not know that Pasha was only Dostoevsky's stepson, but, as the dictation went on, Dostoevsky became more and more outspoken with her about his private life and, as she put it, "every day revealed some sad picture of his life to me." Soon he began addressing her as "darling" (his usual mode of address, she later found out) and "sweetheart," which she took merely as endearments one would expect a middle-aged man to address to a young girl who was "almost a child." She stopped being afraid of him, "the famous author," and began talking to him freely and frankly "as to an uncle or an old friend." Gradually, he acquainted her with the whole story of his life, showed her his late wife's portrait, and even told her of his unsuccessful wooing of Anna Korvin-Krukovsky (the significance of which she did not realize at the time), giving her his own version of it, according to which Anna had agreed to marry him, but he had given her back "her word" because he realized that "holding such contrary opinions, they would never be happy." He never mentioned his affair with Pauline Suslov: that she had to find out by herself after her marriage.

She became aware of Dostoevsky's precarious financial position when she noticed one day that one of the Chinese vases she had admired so much on her visit had disappeared. Dostoevsky had told her that the vases were a present from his friends in Siberia, and she asked him whether the one that was missing had been broken. "No, it has not been broken," Dostoevsky replied. "It's been pawned. I badly needed 25 rubles so I had to pawn it." A few days later, "the same fate befell the other vase." Another day Anna noticed, as she passed through the dining room, a wooden spoon on the table laid for dinner. "I can see," she remarked laughingly, "that you're going to have buckwheat porridge today, for I'm told buckwheat porridge tastes better when eaten with a wooden spoon." "You're wrong," Dostoevsky replied. "You see, I had to have some money, so I pawned my silver spoons." Dostoevsky, Anna remarks dryly, always treated his financial difficulties with high good humor.

As they were approaching the end of their work, Dostoevsky, who seemed to be "in a strangely agitated mood," told her that he was at the parting of the ways at the moment: he had to decide whether to go east, to Constantinople and Jerusalem, and stay there perhaps for good, to go abroad and give himself up entirely to gambling, or to get married a second time and try to find happiness in married life. The first two alternatives were clearly advanced as a smoke screen to cover up his desire to find out what she thought of his idea of a second marriage. "I admit," Anna writes, "that his . . . desire to go east or become a gambler seemed rather vague and fantastic to me, but knowing that there were happily married families among my relatives and acquaintances I advised him to marry a second time and try to find happiness in family life.

" 'So you think,' Dostoevsky said, 'that I could still get married? That someone might agree to marry me? What kind of wife should I choose: a clever one or a kind one?' "

"Of course, a clever one," Anna replied, little dreaming of what he was driving at.

"Oh, no," Dostoevsky declared, little suspecting in his excitement that he was giving himself away. "If I am to choose, I'd rather choose a kind one, so that she should love and pity me."

Dostoevsky then went on to ask her why she did not get married. Anna replied that two men had proposed to her, but that, though she respected them greatly, she did not love them and that she would like to marry for love.

"Yes, yes," Dostoevsky, a little dashed, no doubt, by her reply, agreed "warmly," "certainly for love! Respect alone is not enough for a happy marriage."

On October 30, Dostoevsky's forty-fifth birthday, Anna brought the last copied-out pages of the manuscript of *The Gambler*. In honor of his birthday she arrived in a long lilac silk dress (she had worn black before because she was in mourning for her father). Dostoevsky thanked her for her attention and told her she looked taller and more slender in her silk dress. "But," Anna writes, "my pleasure was spoiled by the arrival of the widow of Dostoevsky's brother, who came to wish him many happy returns of the day. . . . Emilia Fyodorovna treated me condescendingly and I felt surprised and hurt. . . ." From their very first meeting, therefore, a gulf opened between Dostoevsky's dependents and his future wife, a gulf that Anna did her best to widen.

The relations between Dostoevsky and his young stenographer became closer with his visits to her home. A week after the completion of *The Gambler* he proposed to her. "November the eighth, 1866," Anna writes, "was one of the most significant days of my life: on that day Dostoevsky told me that he loved me and asked me to be his wife." He had engaged her services again to help him finish *Crime and Punishment*, and when she arrived he looked very excited. He had, she records, "almost a rapturous expression on his face, which made him look very young." She asked him what was the matter and whether he had some good news.

"Yes," he replied. "Tonight I had a wonderful dream."

"Is that all?" she asked and burst out laughing.

"Don't laugh, please," he begged. "I attach great importance to dreams. My dreams are always prophetic."

"Tell me your dream."

"Do you see this large rosewood box? This is a present from my friend Chokan Velikhanov and I prize it highly. I keep my manuscripts in it as well as my letters and the things I value most because of the memories attached to them. Well, so I dreamed that I was sitting in front of this box and sorting out my papers. Suddenly something flashed between them, a sort of bright little star. I kept sorting my papers and the little star kept appearing and disappearing. This aroused my curiosity: I began sorting the papers more slowly and between them I found a tiny diamond—very bright and sparkling."

"What did you do with it?"

"That's the trouble, you see. I can't remember. Then I started dreaming of something else and I don't know what happened to it. But it was a lovely dream!"

"I believe," Anna remarked and was immediately sorry she had said it, "I believe that dreams ought to be interpreted the other way round."

Dostoevsky's expression changed. His face darkened.

"So you don't think that anything will happen to make me happy?" he cried sadly. "That I have nothing to hope for?"

Anna, who still did not guess what he was driving at, felt sorry for him and did her best to restore his high spirits. When he asked her to tell him her dreams, she told him that she usually dreamed of her old headmistress, "a majestic lady, with old-fashioned curls over her temples," who was always giving her a dressing down. She also dreamed of a marmalade cat which once jumped on top of her from a fence and frightened her to death.

"Oh, you child, you child!" Dostoevsky kept repeating, laughing and looking tenderly at her. "Your dreams, too, are childish ones."

He asked her how she had enjoyed her godmother's birthday party the night before, and, still completely unaware of the coming proposal, she innocently told him of two very gay and charming students she had met there.

Dostoevsky's face became overcast, and Anna was beginning to fear that he might have an epileptic fit. She hastened to ask him what he had been doing lately.

"I have been thinking of a plot for my new novel," he said, quickly taking advantage of the opening her question had presented him with.

"Oh? An interesting novel?"

"Yes, very interesting, only I have been having some trouble with the ending. You see, it's a question of the psychology of a young girl. Had I been in Moscow, I'd have asked my niece Sonia about it. But now I'm going to ask you to help me."

Anna was greatly flattered. "Who is the hero of your novel?" she asked.

"An artist. No longer young. A man of my age, in fact."

"Tell me, tell me, please," Anna exclaimed, greatly interested in his new novel.

In reply, Dostoevsky embarked on "a brilliant improvisation," and

Anna soon realized that he was telling her the story of his own life. His hero, Dostoevsky explained, trying his best to paint as somber a picture as possible so as to make reality appear all the brighter, was a prematurely aged man, suffering from an incurable disease (paralysis of the arm), gloomy and suspicious; a man with a tender heart, but unable to express his feelings; a talented artist, but an unsuccessful one, who was never able to embody his ideas in the forms he wished and who was perpetually tormented by his failure to do so.

"But why are you so hard on your hero?" Anna asked, suddenly realizing that Dostoevsky had been rather overdoing his self-portrait.

"I see you don't like him," said Dostoevsky.

"Not at all. I do like him. He has a very kind heart. Think of the calamities that befell him and how uncomplainingly he put up with them. Anyone else would have grown hardened after so many troubles, but your hero still loves people and tries to help them. I'm sorry, but you are quite unfair to him."

"Well, yes, I quite agree he has a kind, loving heart," Dostoevsky said. "And I'm glad you have understood him so well."

"And so," Dostoevsky went on with his story, "at this decisive moment of his life the artist meets a young girl of your age or a year or two older. Let's call her Anna. It's a nice name."

By this time Anna was convinced that Dostoevsky had in mind Anna Korvin-Krukovsky, from whom she knew he had recently had a letter from abroad. "At that moment," she writes in her reminiscences, "I had completely forgotten that my name was Anna too."

Anna, the heroine of the imaginary novel, was quite different from its hero. She was gentle, intelligent, kind, full of life, and showed great tact in her relations with people.

"But," Anna asked with bated breath, the truth beginning to dawn on her, "is she beautiful?"

"No, not beautiful," replied Dostoevsky, "but not very plain, either. I like her face."

"I can't help thinking," Anna said, still uncertain whether he meant her or the other Anna, "that you've idealized your Anna too much. Is she really like that?"

"Yes, she is," Dostoevsky replied firmly. "I've come to know her very well. The artist," he went on with his story, "used to meet Anna in artistic circles and the more he saw of her, the more he liked her and the more strongly did his conviction grow that he could be happy with her. And yet the idea seemed almost impossible to him. And, indeed, what could he, an old, sick man, burdened with debt, give to that young, healthy, high-spirited girl? Wouldn't love for the artist be a terrible sacrifice on the part of that young girl and wouldn't she be bitterly disappointed afterwards for having bound up her fate with his? And, anyway, is it at all possible that a young girl who was so different in age and character from my artist could fall in love with him? Won't such a situation be psychologically improbable? That's what I'd like to know your opinion about."

"Why isn't it possible?" Anna asked warmly. "If, as you say, your Anna is not an empty-headed flirt and has a kind and responsive heart, why shouldn't she fall in love with your artist? What does it matter if he is sick and poor? Does one have to love a man only if he is handsome and rich? And what sort of sacrifice is it on her part? If she loves him, she will be happy and still never have cause for regret."

"And you seriously believe," Dostoevsky asked, looking agitatedly at her, "that she could love him sincerely and all her life?" He paused, as if uncertain whether he should go on. "Put yourself for a moment in her place," he went on in a trembling voice. "Imagine that I am that artist, that I have told you I loved you and asked you to be my wife. Tell me, what would your answer have been?"

He looked very embarrassed and there was such an expression of pain on his face that Anna at last realized that it was not, as she puts it, "a literary discussion" and that it would be "a terrible blow to his self-esteem and his pride" if she gave "an evasive" answer. She glanced at his excited face and said:

"I'd have replied that I loved you and would love you all my life."

After the "unforgettable moments" that followed her acceptance of his proposal, he saw her to the door, promising to spend the next evening with her and her mother.

"Anna," he said to her, "I know now where the little diamond is."

"Why, have you remembered your dream?"

"No, I haven't. But I've found it at last and I shall keep it all my life."

"You're mistaken," she retorted with a laugh, "you haven't found a diamond, but an ordinary pebble."

"I'm sure I'm not mistaken this time," Dostoevsky said gravely.

And he was right, of course, though at the time he could hardly have realized how well his second marriage would turn out. Anna's age worried him, though. "I began assuring him," Anna writes, "that I should soon be getting old myself, and though," she adds, "this promise was meant as a joke, it soon became a fact—that is to say, I did not get old, but I did my best to convey that impression by the way I dressed and talked so that the difference between the ages of my husband and myself became almost imperceptible."

III

Although they decided to keep their engagement a secret, the news of it soon leaked out, and a week later Pasha appeared in Dostoevsky's study wearing his Sunday best and a pair of blue spectacles which he only put on on solemn occasions. He told Dostoevsky that he had learned of his impending marriage, that he was astonished, dumfounded and shocked, that he was particularly hurt that, in taking so serious a step, Dostoevsky had not asked the advice and consent of his "son." He then begged his "father" to remember that he was "an old man" and that it was too late for him to think of starting a new life with a young girl, that he had other obligations, etc.

It was early in the morning. Dostoevsky, as usual, had been working all night and had only just got up. It was the worst time Pasha could have chosen to admonish him, for at that early hour Dostoevsky, as Anna was all too soon to find out for herself, was "a fiend incarnate." He lost his temper, screamed at his stepson, and threw him out of his study. Two days later he had an epileptic seizure; when Anna came to find out how he was, Pasha did not come out to speak to her. But during her next visit a week later he did appear (at Dostoevsky's order), congratulated Anna "dryly and officially" and sat with them for ten minutes without uttering a word and looking hurt and aggrieved. However, noticing, on later occasions, that his attitude only angered Dostoevsky without having the slightest effect on him, he made a virtue of necessity and became polite and obliging to Anna, without, however, missing any chance of saying something nasty to her when they were alone.

On December 9, 1866, Dostoevsky sent Pasha—to teach him a lesson, no doubt—to Anna with a letter and a present of a gold bracelet. He had been working on the fifth chapter of the last part of *Crime and Punishment* till 2 o'clock in the morning, he wrote, and was not feeling very well. He signed his letter: "Your infinitely loving and infinitely trusting —you are my whole future—my hope and faith and happiness and bliss —everything." This superfluity of endearments was most probably evoked by a call he had paid to his doctor, who has taken a very pessimistic view of his marriage and strongly advised him not to go on with it as such a difference in age could not possibly be conducive to a happy married life. He raised the question again at one of his visits to Anna's house. "Just think," he told Anna, "I am almost an old man and you are almost a child. I suffer from an incurable illness, I'm morose and irritable, while you are healthy, full of life and high spirits. I am almost at the end of my life and there has been a great deal of grief in my life. You, on the other hand, have had a happy life and your life is still all before you. I am, finally, poor and burdened with debts. What can we possibly hope for in face of such a disparity? We shall either be unhappy and, after tormenting each other for a few years, part, or we shall find that we suit each other and be happy for the rest of our lives." Anna assured him that he was exaggerating. What worried her, she said, was that he was marrying a stupid young girl who could hardly be called educated when compared to him, though, she added, she did get "a large silver medal" on finishing her school. It would seem that they were equally unsuited to each other—a reflection that, strangely enough, made them regard their future life with more equanimity. "I can see now," Dostoevsky told her, "that the novel I had invented was the best I have ever written: for it was at once successful and produced the desired effect!"

Only once, according to Anna, was their engagement clouded by a serious quarrel over the demands made on him by his stepson and his sister-in-law. One evening at the end of November he arrived as usual at 7 o'clock, chilled to the marrow, and asked for a glass of brandy. Anna offered him some sherry instead; it was only after he had drunk three large glasses of sherry and two glasses of hot tea that he felt warm. Puzzled why he should have felt so cold, she found, on going out into the hall for something, that he had come in his autumn overcoat instead of his winter fur coat. Pressed to explain why he had not been wearing his fur coat, he at last confessed that he had had to pawn it. It seemed that his sister-in-law had come to see him in the morning and asked him for fifty rubles to pay some pressing debt. Pasha, too, demanded money, and he had to send more money to his younger brother Nikolai. He had no money, and Emilia and Pasha decided to pawn his fur coat, assuring him that it was warm and thawing outside and that he could safely go out in his autumn coat until he got the money for the last installment of his novel from Moscow.

"I was profoundly shocked by the heartlessness of his relations," Anna declares. "I told him, quietly at first, that while understanding his desire to help his relations, I didn't think he ought to sacrifice his health and perhaps also his life for them. With every word I uttered, my anger and distress grew. I lost all control over myself and went on talking, like one demented, without choosing my words, trying to prove to him that he had also obligations to me, his fiancée. I told him that I would not put up with it. I cried, screamed, sobbed hysterically. Dostoevsky looked very upset, he kissed my hands and begged me to calm down. My mother, hearing my sobs, brought me a glass of water. I felt ashamed and apologized to Dostoevsky, who explained that he had pawned his fur coat a dozen times before and that was why he did not think it important now." He promised never to pawn it again, but it took several such "scenes" to make him break completely with his stepson and his elder brother's family.

At the end of December 1866, Dostoevsky went to Moscow to try to get an advance of 3,000 rubles on his next novel from Katkov to defray the expenses of his wedding. He was seen off at the station by Anna, Pasha and two of his nephews, representing Mikhail's widow, Emilia. They all trooped into the compartment to help him find a comfortable place for a journey which in those days took about twelve hours. Wishing to show how anxious he was for his "father's" comfort, Pasha said in a loud voice: "Papa, don't for heaven's sake lie on the upper berth. Should you get an epileptic fit, you'd fall down on the floor and you'd never get up again!" This expression of solicitude produced a rather unfortunate effect: Dostoevsky, who hated people to know of his affliction, glared angrily at his stepson and a woman passenger immediately asked a porter to take her things to another compartment. When Anna later asked Pasha why he had angered his stepfather, Pasha, characteristically, replied: "What do I care whether he is angry or not? I am taking care of his health and he ought to be grateful to me for that." It is only fair to add that Anna had been very assiduous in collecting any evidence she could lay her hands on in justifying her plan of action against Pasha, to whom Dostoevsky was attached, not only because he considered him to be his "sacred trust," but because he became genuinely fond of him and, perhaps, also because he knew that he himself was largely responsible for not bringing him up properly.

Dostoevsky spent twelve days in Moscow. His mission was successful. In view of the great success of *Crime and Punishment*, which, according to Strakhov, was the only novel people read and discussed in 1866, Katkov could not very well refuse an advance on Dostoevsky's next novel, though he only agreed to give him 2,000 rubles. There was, however, another and perhaps even more pressing reason for his trip to Moscow. In his desperate search for a wife he had proposed marriage to his sister's sister-in-law, Yelena Ivanov, whom he had met during his stay in Lyublino the previous summer. At the time Yelena's husband was still alive, but was expected to die any day. To his question whether she would marry him if she were free, she did not give him a direct answer, but there certainly seems to have been a tacit understanding between them. On his arrival in Moscow, he told his niece Sonia of his engagement and asked her whether Yelena had mentioned him during his absence. Sonia replied: "Why, of course. She is always talking about you. But I don't think she is in love with you." Dostoevsky concluded that since Yelena's husband was still alive, he need not worry about it. All the same, as he wrote to Anna,[1] he often felt "very sad, just as though I had committed some crime against somebody. . . . I thought I might dream of you, but did not. I tried to find out about our future by opening a book at random and reading the first line on the right-hand page and it was very much to the point. . . . Good-by, my darling, I kiss your sweet little hands and lips (which I think of often) a thousand times. . . ." On January 2, 1867, he wrote to her about the way Yelena had taken the announcement of his engagement to her at a New Year's party at the Ivanovs'. "Yelena," he declared, "took the news really well. She just said to me: 'I am very glad I stood firm last summer and did not give you a definite answer. I should have been ruined

[1] *Letters*, December 29, 1866.

otherwise.' I, too," Dostoevsky concluded, "am glad, she takes it all like that and now I feel *absolutely* easy in my mind on that score."

IV

The wedding of Dostoevsky and Anna Snitkin took place in the Troitsky Cathedral on February 15, 1867, at 7 o'clock in the evening. The reception at their new flat (the old flat Dostoevsky put at the disposal of Emilia and her family) went on till midnight. "Dostoevsky," Anna remarks, "loved to entertain in grand style and there was therefore plenty of champagne, fruits and sweets."

The real tug of war between Anna and Dostoevsky's relations and, especially, Pasha, began immediately after the wedding. "My love of Dostoevsky was boundless," Anna confesses, "but it was not a physical love, which might have existed between people of the same age. My love had nothing to do with my emotional life. It was not so much love as adoration, admiration for a man who was so highly talented and possessed such high spiritual qualities. It was a sort of soul-stirring pity for a man who had suffered so much, who had never known happiness and who was so neglected by those nearest to him, who should have repaid all he had done for them throughout their lives with love and care. . . . But I could not help being indignant with him," she concludes, "that so great an expert of the human heart as he should not realize how hard my life was, should do nothing to make it easier for me, but should foist his dull relatives on me and defend his stepson whose attitude to me was so unfriendly."

Pasha, as Dostoevsky explained to Katkov in a letter from Geneva,[2] "is a good, honest boy, but unfortunately he has a most extraordinary character: since his childhood he seems to have taken a vow *never to do anything*, while having no fortune of his own and the most absurd notions of life. He was expelled from school for some childish prank. After that he had about five tutors, but he did not want to do *anything* in spite of my repeated entreaties and he still does not know his multiplication table. He is, however, quite convinced that he could find a job as manager of a large estate any time he liked. All the same, I repeat, he is a charming, kind, obliging boy, entirely honorable, a little arrogant and impatient, but absolutely honest." Pasha, in fact, seems to have taken after his father; nor can there be any doubt that Dostoevsky himself was to a large extent responsible for Pasha's more than lackadaisical attitude to life. But the trouble with Pasha, as Anna saw it, was not that he was particularly stupid or unkind, but that "he never realized his position." He was convinced, she felt, that his "father" must live exclusively for him. He never did anything himself to help Dostoevsky, but often angered him by his "thoughtless actions." He looked upon his

[2] *Letters,* March 3, 1868.

stepfather as "an old fogy," and he quite openly declared that it was absurd for a man of his age to expect "personal happiness." As for Anna, who was only a few months older than he, he regarded her as an interloper, as one who had forced her way into their family where he had hitherto been the boss, Dostoevsky being too busy with his writing to look after his household. Anna was quite convinced that Pasha had made up his mind to make her life unbearable and, by engineering constant quarrels between her and her husband, to force them to part. Each incident was, perhaps, too trifling to justify her complaining to Dostoevsky, but since she knew that behind it was the barely concealed intention to excite her anger and insult her, she could not help being angry and feeling insulted. Pasha would, for instance, deliberately send their only maid off on an errand so that she could not tidy Dostoevsky's study and so cause a scene; he would drink the cream before Dostoevsky was due to appear for lunch and so make his stepfather angry because he could not have his coffee; or he would make sure that there was not a single matchbox in the house and again make Dostoevsky, a heavy smoker, shout at their maid. While Dostoevsky was in the room with them, Pasha made a point of being attentive to Anna, so much so that Dostoevsky even remarked what a wonderful effect her presence had had on him and how well-mannered he had become; but as soon as Dostoevsky left the room, Pasha's attitude to her would change and he would become insolent, make rude remarks about the way she carried out her household duties, accuse her of persecuting him, "a poor orphan," and even of begrudging him every bit of food he ate; he kept complaining about the way she treated him to Dostoevsky, who kept telling her not to hurt Pasha's feelings, for he was really a good boy. When she asked how she was supposed to have hurt Pasha's feelings, he would cut her short by saying that the whole thing was not worth discussing, but he begged her all the same to be kind to Pasha. In addition, she had to cope with Emilia, who came to see them almost every day and, "thinking she is an excellent housewife herself," gave her advice about how to run a house, always choosing a moment when Dostoevsky was present. Worse still, she constantly held up Dostoevsky's first wife as an example to her, which, Anna remarks dryly, was rather "tactless" on her part.

It was obvious that such a state of affairs could not go on very much longer, particularly, Anna confesses in her journal, as Dostoevsky used to get so exasperated by his relatives and shouted at them so furiously that sometimes she was "simply afraid" for her future life with him. One day Dostoevsky's pencils mysteriously disappeared from his desk, he shouted at the maid, and looked particularly cheerless and dejected and scarcely exchanged a word with Anna. The same day they had been invited to Maykov's, but Anna said she had a headache and Dostoevsky had to go by himself. After he was gone, Pasha told her that he did not believe she had a headache, but merely wanted to anger his "father." He went on to say that Dostoevsky had made a frightful mistake in marrying her and that she was responsible for his fits, which he had noticed had increased since their marriage.

It was the last straw. On his return from Maykov, Dostoevsky found Anna lying in bed, crying and sobbing. This second "scene" was even more effective than the first. Dostoevsky denied all knowledge of the way she had been treated by Pasha and agreed that it was time to put an end to "the turmoil" in which they were living. He had been thinking of going to Moscow to ask Katkov for a further advance on his next novel (which, by the way, he had not even begun planning), and he proposed that she should go with him. If Katkov gave him the advance, they might even go abroad together. Next morning Pasha and Emilia were, as Anna puts it, "disagreeably surprised" on hearing of their decision to go to Moscow together, but knowing that there was hardly anything left of Dostoevsky's previous advance, they raised no objections. As a parting shot, however, Pasha told her that while she was away he would see to it that her "neglected housekeeping" was put right. This time she was not offended: she was too glad to be rid of them all even for a short time.

In Moscow disappointments awaited her. In spite of Dostoevsky's assurance that his Moscow relatives were dying to make her acquaintance, her reception by the Ivanovs was more than cool. They had all hoped that he would eventually marry Yelena and then come to live in Moscow. As Anna did not know the reason for their coolness at the time, she felt even more upset and, trying to show how little she cared what they thought of her, she laughed and chatted merrily with a young student at a party given by the Ivanovs, arousing Dostoevsky's jealousy. On their return home, seeing how upset Dostoevsky was (he was pacing the hotel room and refusing to talk to her), she went up to him and tried to embrace him. But he pushed away her hand and gave her such "a fierce and evil" look that her heart sank.

"Are you angry with me?" she asked. "What have I done?"

At that question Dostoevsky exploded angrily and, as she puts it, "poured out the vials of his wrath" on her. He told her she was a heartless flirt and had flirted all the evening with the young student just to torment him. Her attempt to justify herself merely "poured oil on the flames" and, forgetting that they were at a hotel, he started shouting at her at the top of his voice. She was beginning to fear that he might have an epileptic seizure or that he even might kill her. She burst out crying and her tears at once mollified her maddened husband, who, rushing from one extreme to another, began comforting her and accusing himself.

"He kissed my hands," Anna records, "wept and cursed himself for making such a scene. . . . The impression of the incident of that night has burned itself in my mind. It made me reflect deeply about our future relationship. I realized the deep suffering that jealousy inflicted on Dostoevsky and I vowed never to expose him to such a painful experience again." In that she did not succeed, for the difference in their ages alone was a constant irritant that aroused his jealous nature (his unhappy experience with his first wife and with Pauline Suslov still further strengthened this disposition to jealousy), but the terrible scene at the hotel made Dostoevsky do his utmost to be as kind to Anna as he could, and Katkov's generosity in letting him have another advance of a thousand rubles still further soothed his ruffled temper. He showed Anna the sights of his native city, took her to his mother's grave, where they ordered a service in her memory at the cemetery chapel, and went with her to visit his rich old aunt, Alexandra Kumanin, who, Anna records, received them very amiably. But her mind had deteriorated so greatly since Dostoevsky had last seen her two years before that she did not know who they were. (A year later Dostoevsky was to describe this visit in *The Idiot*, his aunt appearing under the guise of Rogozhin's mother.)

On their return to Petersburg, they were met by Dostoevsky's relatives, including his dipsomaniac brother, Nikolai, who were waiting to hear how much money he had been successful in getting from Maykov. At dinner Emilia remarked that she had heard of a splendid country house near Pavlovsk, with an excellent garden, large enough not only for Dostoevsky, his wife and stepson, but also for her entire family.

"Anna," she added, with an ingratiating smile, in her broken Russian, "will feel much happier in the company of young people and, as for me, I don't mind sacrificing myself to look after the house which our dear hostess finds so difficult."

Dostoevsky frowned, but whether at Emilia's transparent hint at his young wife's inadequacy or at the suggestion that she would be happier in the company of young people, Anna could not tell.

"There's no reason why we should be looking for a country house," he said. "Anna and I are going abroad."

A dead hush fell over the company, but their attempt to turn it into a joke did not succeed. When Dostoevsky explained to them the plan of his proposed journey, they fell silent again and, unable to bear their mute protest, he retired to his study, where he was at once followed by Emilia. Left alone with Anna in the dinning room, Pasha turned furiously on her.

"I can see through your dirty tricks!" he said angrily.

"What dirty tricks?"

"You don't understand, do you? Why, this absurd trip abroad. But you'll find you're mistaken in your calculations. If I permitted your journey to Moscow it was only because papa was going to get money there. But the trip abroad is a whim of yours, and I do not intend to permit it."

"Ah," Anna replied jokingly, "but perhaps you will take pity on us."

"Don't count on that," Pasha replied firmly. "A trip abroad costs money, and all our family needs money, not you alone: we all share the money, you know."

Half an hour later Emilia emerged from Dostoevsky's study. She looked angry and, telling her children to come home with her, bade Anna a curt good-by. After they had gone, Pasha rushed into Dostoevsky's study, but his stepfather for once refused to listen to his indignant protests and sent him packing. He told Anna that all his relations were against their journey, but if he insisted on going abroad with her, they demanded that he should leave them enough money to live on for several months. As it was, Dostoevsky intended to leave 200 rubles for Emilia, a hundred for Pasha and another hundred for his brother Nikolai. He hoped to have a clear 500 for their expenses abroad, after which he hoped to write an article on Belinsky, for which he had already obtained an advance of 200 rubles from a Petersburg publisher. But Emilia was demanding 500 rubles, and, no doubt at Pasha's instigation, a creditor to whom he owed 2,000 rubles and who had hitherto been very reasonable about his repayments, demanded the payment of 500 rubles on a bill of exchange that had fallen due, threatening to issue a summons if the money was not forthcoming immediately. Dostoevsky was forced to give up the idea of the trip, but Anna contrived a plan of her own. She decided to pawn the furniture, as well as her silver and gold things, her lottery tickets and her fur coats, which were all part of her dowry. At first Dostoevsky would not hear of it, but faced by another bout of weeping and the threat that she might have to leave him, he gave in. When next evening all the relatives again came to dinner, Dostoevsky told them that he and Anna were leaving in two days' time.

"But, papa," Pasha, taken completely aback, protested, "you don't know that . . ."

"I don't want to know anything," Dostoevsky said angrily. "You will all get as much as you have demanded and not a penny more."

"But I forgot to tell you," Pasha cried, "that my summer overcoat is no longer fashionable and that there are a few more things I want."

"You won't get more than agreed," Dostoevsky for once was firm. "I have no right to dispose of Anna's money."

That settled (Anna persuaded Dostoevsky to let Pasha have his new summer overcoat, which did not propitiate him, for he threatened "to measure swords with her" when she returned in the autumn), they left for Europe at 5 o'clock in the afternoon on April 14, 1867, exactly two months after their wedding. They planned to return to Russia after three months, but they stayed abroad for over four years, returning to Petersburg on July 8, 1871.

[11]

FOUR YEARS IN THE WILDERNESS

When they started on their trip to Europe, neither Dostoevsky nor Anna could have had any idea how important it was to prove to the success of their marriage. Anna herself, in trying to explain this success many years after Dostoevsky's death, concluded her reminiscences with the following striking analysis of their married life: "My husband and I represented people of quite different temperament, quite different turn of mind, but we always remained ourselves, without ever echoing one another or making up to one another or meddling with each other's inmost thoughts and feelings—I with his and he with mine. In this way my dear husband and myself—both of us—felt unhampered and free. Dostoevsky, who had thought so deeply about the profound questions of man's soul, probably prized this noninterference of mine in his emotional and mental life, and that was why he sometimes used to say to me: 'You are the only woman who understood me' (that is to say, understood what was more important than anything to him). His relationship to me always constituted a kind of rock against which (he felt) he could lean or rather rest on, and which would not collapse but comfort him. This, in my view, explains the remarkable confidence my husband reposed in all my actions, though nothing I did was in any way unusual. It is this relationship that made it possible for both of us to spend the fourteen years of our married life as happily as is possible for people."

The thing that helped Anna to preserve her independence and that prevented Dostoevsky from interfering with her personal life (something Pauline Suslov could never achieve) was, paradoxically enough, the very thing that had brought them together—her knowledge of shorthand. For from the very first day of their journey abroad Anna kept a journal in shorthand in which she put down everything that happened to her as well as her own observations and criticisms, which would have infuriated Dostoevsky had he been able to read it. This journal, in fact, created a permanent place of refuge, a haven into which she could retire in safety from the storms that at first blew up all too frequently between them. In her reminiscences Anna gives many reasons for writing her shorthand diary, such as that she had to practice shorthand, that her husband was such a mystery to her that she decided to put down his sayings and thoughts (which she did not do, as a matter of fact), and, finally and most convincingly, that her diary was her "friend" to which she confided her thoughts, hopes and apprehensions. Dostoevsky, she records, asked her many times what she was writing "with her squiggles," but she never told him.

Their first quarrel occurred on April 18 in Berlin. They were sightseeing and Dostoevsky made some uncomplimentary remarks about her fur hat and old gloves. She replied tartly that if he thought she was badly dressed, they had better not be seen together and walked away. It was raining and the people in the street looked with astonishment "at the young girl who was walking in the rain without an umbrella and not paying any attention to anything around her." When she returned to their hotel Dostoevsky was not there. She at once imagined that he must have discovered what a bad girl she was and had thrown himself into the river in despair, or that he had gone to the Russian Consulate to start divorce proceedings against her. She kept jumping up from her seat and looking out of the window till, at last, she caught sight of him walking in the street "with a most independent air, with his hands thrust in his pockets." When he came into the room, she threw herself "on his neck, crying and sobbing," and when she told him about her imagining that he had drowned himself, he laughed and said: "A man can have little self-respect to drown himself in such a paltry little stream as the Spree."

Their second serious quarrel also arose out of some insignificant incident about a week after their arrival in Dresden where they had rented a flat of three rooms. Dostoevsky, Anna records on May 16, woke up in a bad mood and gave her a sharp scolding. "This," she writes characteristically, "seemed very funny to me, but I pretended to be hurt and refused to talk to him." Dostoevsky looked vexed, but Anna decided to teach him a lesson, and went out, merely saying that she was going to see the local teacher of stenography for whom she had a letter from her Petersburg teacher. She returned home rather late and found Dostoevsky still not dressed and scowling. She still refused to talk to him. "But," she writes, "when he started dressing, I decided to put an end to our quarrel and asked him whether he was not going to speak to me all day. It appeared that it was all my fault, but I didn't mind. I was tired of quarreling." After lunch Dostoevsky picked another quarrel with her. They had asked a German the way to the nearest pastry cook's (they wanted to get some ice cream), and were misdirected. Dostoevsky, as usual, began abusing the Germans for their stupidity, and, Anna writes, "when we happened to meet a Saxon hussar, Fedya became so incensed that he began cursing the King of Saxony for maintaining forty thousand guardsmen. I remarked that if he had the money there was no reason why he should not maintain them. It made no difference whatever to me whether the King of Saxony maintained guards or not; I replied simply in order to say something. But Fedya got terribly angry, this time with me too, and told me that if I was so stupid I had better shut up." When they got their ice cream at last, it was so bad that Dostoevsky started cursing again—the avenues for being too straight, the pond for being in the wrong place, and so on, till she got tired of it and wished to go home. On the way they passed through the *Grand Jardin* and Dostoevsky stopped at a shooting gallery. Anna, forgetting his army service, remarked that he would never hit the target. But Dostoevsky hit it first time and kept on hitting it again and again. Then, turning to her "in triumph," said, "Well?" adding that this merely confirmed an old idea of his that a wife was the natural enemy of her husband. They stopped at their favorite restaurant overlooking the banks of the Elbe, where she had a cup of coffee and he an ice followed by coffee. The sun was setting and they went up to the balustrade and began looking at it. "There we quarreled again over the sunset," Anna writes. "Fedya told me I was a fool and we went home furious with one another." They made it up, though, Anna, as usual, bursting into tears and Dostoevsky blaming himself and saying that she must be sorry to have married him, "and all sorts of other stupid things. . . ."

Anna usually went to bed rather early while Dostoevsky sat up till 2 o'clock or later reading magazines and books banned in Russia—*The Pole Star* and *The Bell* published by Herzen in London as well as Herzen's *Reflections on My Past.* "Before turning in," Anna writes, "Fedya wakes me 'to say good night.' We start talking, exchanging tender words, laughter, kisses, and this half-hour or hour is the happiest time of our day. I tell him my dreams, he tells me his impressions of the day, and we are terribly happy."

II

They arrived in Dresden on May 1, and on the very first day paid a visit to the famous picture gallery, which they visited again and again during their stay. Dostoevsky's favorite picture was Raphael's *Sistine Madonna,* before which he used to stand for hours, Anna records, "deeply moved and in rapt admiration." One day he even insisted on standing on a chair to examine the Madonna more closely. A gallery attendant pointed out to him that this was not permitted. "As soon as the attendant left the room," Anna writes, "Fedya told me that he was going to stand on the chair even if they threw him out and that if I did not like it I could go to another room. I did that, not wishing to irritate him; a few minutes later he joined me and said that he had had a good look at the Madonna. Fedya went on to say that it did not matter even if they did throw him out, that a lackey had a lackey's soul, etc. But at heart I did not agree with him: a lackey is not to blame if he is told not to permit all sorts of irregularities, and, indeed, what would happen if everyone were permitted to look at pictures in a way he considered most convenient for himself."

The other pictures Dostoevsky greatly admired in the gallery included Titian's *Christ with the Coin*, Murillo's *Maria and Child*, Correggio's *Holy Night*, Carrache's *Christ*, Holbein's *Madonna*, Ruysdael's *The Chase*, Claude Lorrain's *Acis and Galatea*, Rembrandt's *Rembrandt and His Bride*, and Van Dyck's *Charles I of England*. It was Lorrain's picture that left its greatest mark on Dostoevsky's writings. It represents a landscape lit on the left, by the slanting rays of the setting sun, the trees and sea merging into the sky and, on the right, dark cliffs, lit from above. In the foreground is the tent of Acis and Galatea. The sun lights up only Galatea's white figure and the figure of the cupid on the right. Above, on the lower cliff, is the figure of Polyphemus, merging into the shadow of the overhanging cliff to the left of him. The slanting rays of the setting sun had a deep emotional appeal to Dostoevsky, going back to his early childhood. It was this that fascinated him as he stood before the picture in the Dresden gallery, and the last meeting of Acis and Galatea —the unsuspecting happiness of their love-making before Polyphemus descends upon them and kills Acis—became associated in his mind with the golden age of "the first and the last day of mankind," one of the most sinister of the prophetic visions to be found in his works. He used it originally in *The Devils*, then transferred it to *A Raw Youth*, and finally came back to it again in his philosophic tale, *The Dream of a Ridiculous Man*.

"In the Dresden Gallery," he makes Versilov say in *A Raw Youth*, "there is a picture by Claude Lorrain which in the catalogue is called *Acis and Galatea*, but which I always called *The Golden Age*. I don't know why. . . . It is this picture I dreamed of, not as a picture, but as a legend. I can't remember my dream exactly, but, as in the picture, there was a corner of the Greek archipelago, time having receded three thousand years; caressing blue waves, islands and cliffs, a rich foreshore, a magical panorama in the distance, the setting sun—it is impossible to put it into words. It was the cradle of the nations of Europe and the thought of it seemed to fill my soul with love for my native land. Here was mankind's paradise: the gods came down from heaven and became related to men. . . . Oh, beautiful were the people who lived there! Happy and innocent they rose and went to sleep; the woods and meadows resounded to their songs and happy cries; their superabundance of unused strength was spent on love and good-natured gaiety. The sun poured its light and warmth upon them, rejoicing in her beautiful children. . . . A wonderful dream, mankind's lofty delusion! The golden age—the most improbable dream of any dreams for which men have sacrificed their lives and their strength, for which they have died and for which their prophets have been killed, without which nations do not want to live and, indeed, cannot even die. And all this I seemed to live through in my dream; the cliffs and the sea and the slanting rays of the setting sun. I still seemed to see all this when I woke up and opened my eyes, literally drenched in tears. I remember I was happy. A sensation of happiness hitherto unknown to me went through my heart till it hurt—it was love for all mankind. . . . And, you see, my friend, this setting sun of the first day of European man, which I saw in my dream, was transformed at once—as soon as I awoke—into the setting sun of the last day of European man—I seemed just then to hear the tolling of the funeral bell over Europe. . . ."

Though *A Raw Youth* was published in 1875, Dostoevsky had put the same description into the mouth of Stavrogin in *The Devils* five years earlier and only three years after he had stood before Claude Lorrain's picture for the first time with Anna at the Dresden Gallery. Ten years later, in *The Dream of a Ridiculous Man*, the figure of one-eyed Polyphemus, hovering over the scene of the happy, love-making pair as a foreboding of doom, became associated with man, the golden age being conceived as possible only for some beings on a remote planet—godless and sinless—until man arrives from the earth and corrupts them.

But while their visits to the picture gallery, their long walks, their nightly interludes of happy chatter and love-making and, perhaps most of all, the fact that for the time being they had no money worries, made their first month in Dresden happy, it was not as "serenely happy" as Anna claims. One of the reasons Anna gives for their happiness is that "there were no people standing between me and my husband." This is quite true, so for as Pasha and Emilia and her children were concerned, but there was someone else who still seemed to be standing between them and who was certainly responsible for the undercurrent of mistrust in their relationship and who was the real cause of their quarrels —Pauline Suslov! Anna never mentions her in her reminiscences, but the few references to her in her diary make this abundantly clear. Who could have told Anna about Pauline? Certainly not Dostoevsky himself. He was the last person to follow Tolstoy's example and hand to his young bride a written confession of his past love affairs. But he did dictate *The Gambler* to her, and even if no one had told her whom the heroine of the novel stood for (and Pasha was always on the spot to enlighten her, which may account for her keen dislike of him), it would not have taken her long to find out with whom Dostoevsky had traveled abroad two years earlier and what his relations with her had been.

The first indirect reference to Pauline occurs in Anna's diary on May 5. "Today," she wrote, "the sky is overcast, but it is not raining and I don't suppose it is going to rain. Fedya is very cross today, I don't know with what and with whom. I, too, am feeling irritable. This morning my head ached so badly that I could not do anything. Fedya wrote a letter." The letter has been preserved: it was to Pauline Suslov. He had had a letter from her the day before, and Anna must have guessed whom it was from. That was why she had not felt well that morning. The reason why Dostoevsky was cross is also not difficult to guess: Pauline did not seem to have heard of his marriage, and the prospect of informing his "eternal friend" (as he signed himself) of it presented a rather ticklish problem—and the way he told Pauline about it would hardly have made pleasant reading to Anna.

"I got married in February," he wrote. "Milyukov advised me to employ a stenographer. Olkhin, the professor of stenography, lent me his best pupil—a young and fairly good-looking girl of twenty, of a good family, who had finished her secondary school excellently, of a kind and bright disposition. At the end of our work on the novel, I noticed that my stenographer loved me sincerely . . . and I, too, liked her more and more. My life growing terribly painful and depressing after my brother's death, I asked her to marry me. She agreed and so we got married. The difference in our ages is terribly great, but I am getting more and more convinced that she will be happy. She has an understanding and sympathetic heart and she knows how to love. Besides," he repeated, as though apologizing to Pauline for his marriage and blaming *her* first, "life became very depressing after my brother's death. I still hoped to find someone with an understanding and sympathetic heart who would have responded to me, but I did not find her. . . ." After telling her that *Crime and Punishment* had brought him 14,000 rubles, which helped to reduce his debt to 3,000 rubles, he assured her that he had always respected her, but that he feared that she would never be happy because she demanded so much of people. He asked her to reply "at once." Did he still hope to see her? He had concluded his letter: "*Au revoir*, eternal friend!"—which seemed to indicate a desire to meet her again, perhaps even sooner than he dared hope.

Anna certainly suspected it, as the entry in her diary on May 9 shows: "This morning we left the house together: Fedya went to the *Café Français* to read the papers and I went to get the address of the library in which one could borrow Russian books. I soon learned what I wanted and went back home to read the letter which I had found in Fedya's writing desk. (It is, of course, wrong to read one's husband's letters, but I'm afraid I could not help it!) The letter was from S. Having read it, I became so agitated that I did not know what to do. I felt shivery, I trembled all over and even cried. I was afraid that his old attachment would be renewed and that his love of me would disappear. Lord, don't send me such a calamity!"

Dostoevsky found her in tears, but she told him she had a stomachache. "He said," she writes, "that there are some things I ought not to eat. (He thinks he can cure mental tortures by prescribing a diet!)" However, she went out to have a meal with him, but she could not shake off her feeling of unhappiness. In the evening she went to bed early and Dostoevsky kept coming in and asking how she was "He is obviously alarmed at my condition," she wrote. "I think he suspects that I know about the letter because he asked me if I were not jealous. I replied jokingly that I was jealous of the Englishwoman we had seen in the restaurant. There was a terrible thunderstorm tonight—awful peals of thunder and the rain cascaded down in huge drops."

On May 16 Dostoevsky left for Homburg to try his luck at the roulette table again, and, after seeing him off at the station, Anna went to buy some rolls from a bakery, but found herself outside the post office. "I had a feeling," she writes, "that there would be a letter from *her* and I was very glad that Fedya was away and I could read it. I paid six silver thaler and six pfennig for the letter, which had not been stamped, at once recognized the handwriting and went home without any sign of agitation. But on the way I felt ill. I hurried home, unable to suppress my premonition, fetched a knife and carefully opened the letter. It was a very stupid and rude letter, which did not reveal any particular intelligence in that person. I am sure she is very vexed at Fedya's marriage and that she expressed her disappointment by the tone of the letter. . . ."

When she went up to the looking glass, she saw that her face was all blotchy, but, on second thoughts, realized that Pauline's vexation was a good sign. Dostoevsky returned from Homburg on May 27, and when he asked her if there were any letters she handed him the letter from Pauline. "He either did not really know who the letter was from or pretended not to know," Anna wrote in her diary on the same day, "but as soon as he opened the letter, he glanced at the signature and began to read. I watched his face all the time he was reading that famous letter. He kept reading the first page a long, long time, as though unable to make out the meaning of what was written there, then at last he threw the letter down and blushed crimson. I thought his hands were trembling. I pretended not to know who the letter was from and asked him if it was from his Moscow niece Sonia. He replied that it was not from Sonia and seemed to smile bitterly. I had never seen him smile like that before. It was either a smile of contempt or of pity. I really don't know which, but it was such a pitiful, forlorn smile. Then he became very absent-minded and hardly knew what I was talking about. . . ."

Next day Dostoevsky was still unable to recover from the blow Pauline's letter had inflicted on his pride. "Fedya," Anna writes, "keeps pacing the room all the time, looking lost. He kept searching for something among his letters. It was quite evident that the letter from S. greatly affected him and that he felt hurt. I should very, very much like to know what he thought about it." Next day, Dostoevsky was still in "an awfully bad mood," Anna noted. "He seemed to be grieving for something, he was terribly impatient . . . and during our walk we kept quarreling, but our quarrels generally end in my laughter." Anna was obviously enjoying his discomfiture and at night, after she had gone to bed, he kept coming in and asking her all sorts of questions. "So it went on several times," Anna writes, "and I always woke when he asked me something and then fell asleep again. At last, an hour later, Fedya got angry and called me; I went into his room, my eyes heavy with sleep, and began assuring him that I had not been asleep. He grew indignant and said that if I did not want to sit with him, I'd better go. He was furious, but I burst out laughing and told him that it was absurd and idiotic to scold and talk to someone who was so sleepy that she did not know what she was saying and who was so tired that she was unable to stand on her feet. Fedya realized that he was unjust and asked me only not to laugh at him. Then I forced myself to sit in his room for hours and he came to the conclusion that I was sitting there with him 'out of revenge.' "

Yes, he knew she had read Pauline's letter, but he was too hurt by its "tone" to assert himself. Anna's triumph did not last long, though. When, a month later, on June 26, he asked her where she was going she replied that she was going to the post office, but that he need not worry as she would not read his letters. "He came up to me quickly," Anna writes, "and, with a shaking chin, began to tell me that he now knew what I meant, that I was hinting at something, that he reserved the right to correspond with anyone he liked, that he had dealings with all sorts of people, and that I should not dare interfere with him." Anna, who had by then learned how to deal with his outbursts of rage, did not laugh this time. Instead, she looked him straight in the face and said quite calmly that she did not care who was having dealings with him, but that if they could have been more frank with one another she would, perhaps, have been able to put an end to "a very boring correspondence" she had been forced to start. Dostoevsky asked who had written to her and she replied: "A lady." However fantastic the notion that his discarded mistress should have started a correspondence with Anna, Dostoevsky seemed to believe it, for after all was it not the "fantastic" element in his novels that he always claimed was true to life? "He was awfully curious to know who the lady was," Anna went on with her tale in the entry in her diary of June 28. "He had probably already guessed who it could have been and therefore he looked very upset and began trying to find out from me who she was and whether it was because of our marriage that our correspondence began, and that he would like to know very much in what way I had been insulted. I gave him evasive answers, but he advised me quite seriously to tell him because he could help me by telling me what I had to do. I replied that this correspondence was of no particular importance and that therefore I could very well do without his advice." He went on pestering her to tell him without result. All night he wakened her "to say good night," and she could not sleep after that, which vexed her so much that she began crying. But at about a quarter to six she heard Dostoevsky give his terrible shriek that always preceded an epileptic seizure, and she jumped out of bed and rushed up to him. It seemed that the excitement of that day had proved too much for him. "He soon stopped screaming," Anna records, "but his convulsions were terrible, his hand was all twisted and also his feet. Then he began to gasp, which never happened to him before. Then he opened his eyes and stared at me for several minutes, just as he does at the beginning of a fit. I prayed to God that his fit should not be repeated, for I simply did not know what to do, whether I should call a doctor, what to tell him if I did, and whether there were such doctors here. In general, every time he has a fit I am terribly upset, I start crying, praying, give way to despair. Fortunately, the fit passed and Fedya turned on his side and fell asleep and did not waken till morning." That was the end of the Pauline episode. Dostoevsky never corresponded with her again, while Anna kept a close watch on her through her relatives in Russia where Pauline had returned for a time to run a school for peasant children.

III

Dostoevsky's "adventures" at the roulette tables in Homburg, Baden-Baden and Saxon-les-Bains between May and November 1867 were an expression of his nervous indecision about his literary plans rather than of his passion for gambling or even his desire to improve his financial position. He confided his state of mind to Maykov, the only man with whom he exchanged his inmost thoughts at the time. He had left Russia, he wrote to Maykov,[1] "with death in my soul. I did not believe in abroad," he went on, "that is to say, I believed that the moral influence of life abroad would be a very bad one: I was alone, *without material*, with a young creature, who was ready to share my wandering life with naïve joy, but I realized, of course, that there was a great deal of inexperience and feverish excitement in this naïve joy and it disturbed and worried me. I was afraid that Anna would be bored alone with me. . . . I had no confidence in myself: I have a morbid character and I foresaw that she'd be worn out living with me. . . . But she proved to be much stronger and better than I thought, though I am still not easy in my mind about her. I was also worried about our meager means and the THREE (!) thousand rubles I had taken as an advance from Katkov. It is true I had hoped to start work immediately I settled somewhere abroad, but what happened? I have done nothing or practically nothing so far . . . I have, no doubt, felt a lot and *run over many things in my mind*, but there is still precious little written down, there is very little

[1] *Letters*, August 28, 1867.

in *black and white*, and it is *black and white* that counts; it is this they pay you for. . . ."

Anna, of course, noticed that Dostoevsky was "bored," and she did not object to his going to Homburg for a few days. "If I am glad that he is going," she wrote in her diary on May 13, "it is not at all because I think he is going to win (for to tell the truth I don't believe he will), but I can see that he is beginning to feel miserable and is getting irritable. This," she declared bravely, little realizing what was really worrying her husband, "is understandable: he is always alone, he has not a single acquaintance, not a single man he can exchange a word with. It's a good thing we can get something to read, or he would have died of boredom. To go there is his wish, his idea, so why not satisfy him, otherwise it will go on running in his head and give him no peace. . . . He told me that if he wins, he will come for me and we will live there. That would be nice. I don't know, though, perhaps it is not true, perhaps it would be better not to go there at all." She was also worried by the thought that, as she wrote in her diary on May 19, "to win money at roulette is not an honest way of making a living," but she decided that it was "better not to go too deep into such feelings."

Dostoevsky left Dresden for Homburg in the afternoon of May 16. In his very first letter to Anna from Homburg he admitted that his journey was a piece of folly and a sign of weakness, but "even if there is the tiniest chance—but to hell with it, I won't say another word. . . ." He had left in his light summer overcoat and his summer trousers and was chilled to the bone in the train. His hotel room cost him five francs a day, and, he added, "I can see that they are all brigands here. . . ." He assured her that he loved her and expressed the rather extraordinary view that God had sent her to him "to expiate his sins" and concluded that he was sure the two of them were beginning "to grow together." His next letter announced his first winnings and his renewed faith in his "system": "If one remains sensible, that is, as though made of marble, one will *most certainly* win as much as one desires. But," he added, "one must spend a great deal of time and be satisfied with little if one has a run of bad luck. . . . In short, I'll try and make a superhuman effort to be sensible," a sentiment that filled Anna with dismay, for she knew very well that Dostoevsky could never contrive to be sensible under such circumstances, particularly as he himself confessed that he was tortured by the thought that he might return poorer than he had left. "Anna," he concluded, "promise me never to show these letters to anyone. I do not want this abominable position of mine to become the talk of the town. . . . The sun is shining, it's a wonderful day. . . ."

The next day, however, was not so wonderful. He had lost "considerably," he wrote to Anna on May 19, and he hinted that he might have to stay "a little longer" to test his system for the last time. "As soon as I begin winning," he declared, "I begin to take risks—can't control myself—what an absurd situation—oh, if only all this would come to an end soon. . . ." But he seemed to be in "an excellent state of mind," for his "nature" sometimes demanded "a state of anxiety and excitement." The Homburg pleasure gardens were magnificent and the music excellent. "I wish we could live here were it not for the damned roulette!" he concluded. His next letter, written at 10 o'clock in the morning of May 20, began—an ominous sign—with a whole string of endearments followed by the announcement of another "vile and rotten" day. He realized, he wrote, that the whole thing was "absurd, stupid and despicable," but he just could not get rid of his idea. He had lost everything, pawned his watch, for which the "mean Germans" only gave him sixty-five gulden, gone back and won because he absolutely did not let himself be carried away. He thanked her for not reproaching him by word or thought. "When we are together," he wrote, "I am unsociable, morose and completely lack the gift of expressing myself entirely, without keeping anything back. I lack the social graces. My late brother Mikhail often reproached me bitterly with this." (A few months later he was to put almost the same words into the mouth of Prince Myshkin.) "But," he concluded ominously, "our brief parting is very useful for our happiness."

Anna, who had been doing a lot of sight-seeing in the surrounding countryside, realized at once that he was going to stay in Homburg a little longer. "I have had a presentiment of bad news," she wrote in her diary on Thursday, May 23. "I walked slowly to the post office, got the letter, read it and realized that Fedya apparently wanted very much to stay and have another go at roulette. I wrote to him at once that he could stay if he wanted to and that I would not expect him till Monday or Tuesday. I suppose he will stay. I suppose it can't be helped. I'd rather he got the hopeless idea of winning money out of his head. . . ."

He did, of course, lose again. My "hands trembled, my thoughts wandered," he wrote to Anna,[2] "and even while losing I seemed to be glad and muttered, 'Let it, let it!' " He pawned his watch again, lost most of the money, and asked her to forward him enough money for his hotel bill and his fares. "Now," he wrote, "I won't gamble any more." He was going to write to Katkov for a further advance of 500 rubles and sit down to write his article on Belinsky. "Then we shall go to Switzerland—perhaps it's all for the best: I'll get rid of this damned idea of mine—this monomania—about gambling. . . ." The day after, though, he was beginning to wonder whether it was not Anna who was responsible for his losses. It was, he wrote to her, because he had missed her so much that he could not concentrate on the game. "I usually began with forty gulden," he wrote, "took them out of my pocket, sat down

[2] *Letters,* May 21, 1867.

and staked one or two gulden. A quarter of an hour later I had usually (*always*) won double that amount. It was at that point that I should have stopped and left to calm my agitated nerves (I can keep calm at the roulette table for *no longer than half an hour.*) But I left only to smoke a cigarette and at once ran back. Why did I do that knowing that I was quite certain to lose? Why? Because on getting up in the morning I vowed that it was going to be my last day in Homburg, that I would leave the very next day and that therefore I . . . had to win as much as possible, at one go, in one day, with the result that I lost my *sangfroid*, my nerves became strained, I took a chance, I got angry, staked without thinking and–lost. My whole mistake you see, is that I did not take you with me." He had only twenty gulden left the day before and won 300 gulden in an hour. This made him wish to finish everything that very day and win twice as much again, and he rushed madly back to the gaming table and lost "everything, everything to the last penny. . . . I've only 2 gulden left to buy tobacco with." And yet he knew that if he had another four days he would be sure to get it all back. But, of course, he was not going to gamble again. "Dear Anna," he concluded, "please understand I am not blaming you; on the contrary, I'm blaming myself for not taking you."

Next day he rushed off another letter to her, addressing her as a "saintly soul" and complaining of toothache. If he received the money from her that day he was afraid he would not be able to leave at once, for what was the use of returning home "with moans and groans." This letter amused Anna greatly. She, of course, saw through his subterfuge at once. "Thinking that Fedya would be coming back today," she wrote in her diary, "I got up earlier, but before going to the station I went round to the post office and received Fedya's letter. He writes that he got my letter, but had not yet received the money from the bankers' and therefore was not yet leaving Homburg. Is that an excuse for staying there longer? Fedya has written me an amusing letter in which he complains of terrible toothache and asks me to wait a little longer. Well, so I wrote back to him that he could stay longer if he wished. What else could I do?"

But worse news awaited her. He had received the money and lost it all. Could she forgive him? Could she respect him any more? And what was love without respect? He overwhelmed her with rhetorical questions in his next letter as well as promises never to gamble again. "Now after such a lesson," he wrote, "I am no longer worried about my future. Now it's going to be work and again work. I'll prove to you what I can still do." He had lost 350 rubles altogether and he was asking her to send him more money at once. It was true he still suffered from toothache, but he promised faithfully to leave the same day he got the money. "My angel," he wrote, "don't think for a moment that I shall lose it again, don't think so basely of me. I, too, am a man! Don't try *to come here yourself*—this lack of confidence in me will kill me. *I give you my word of honor* that I shall leave at once." She sent him the money. In his next letter, he repeated that his only hope was work and that his new novel would be "more excellent" than *Crime and Punishment.* "Then," he wrote, little suspecting how coldly *The Idiot* would be received, "the reading public of Russia and the booksellers will be mine." In the meantime he hoped that Anna's mother would send them some money. He could not pay his hotel bill, and he wondered if he would get enough to settle it. The weather was terrible, but he was going to put on two shirts, etc., and, as soon as he returned, he would write to Katkov and ask for another advance of 1,000 rubles. Then they would go at once to Switzerland. In his last letter of May 26 he acknowledged the receipt of the money and promised to leave for Dresden the same day.

Anna received his letter on May 27. "My heart sank when I got his letter," she wrote in her diary. "I don't suppose he will come today." But she was mistaken. He did come back at 6 o'clock in the afternoon, but, as already mentioned, his arrival was spoiled for both of them by Pauline's letter, and for the next few days they quarreled continuously. He wrote to Katkov and to Pasha. He asked Pasha not to tell anyone where he was because he feared his creditors might find him even in Germany. Mikhail's mistress had written to ask him to send her some money, but all he could do was to ask Pasha to give her his regards. He warned his stepson not to incur any debts, for he would not pay them. "It is a pity," he concluded "you don't seem to be anxious to do something for yourself but are merely letting your imagination run away with you." If one is to believe Anna, whose evidence so far as Pasha is concerned is highly suspect, Dostoevsky used harsher words, but crossed them out at her insistence.

IV

Dostoevsky and Anna left Dresden on July 3 for Baden-Baden, where they stayed till August 23. Their last weeks in Dresden—apart from their usual quarrels and reconciliations and three epileptic seizures—were notable for two events: the attempt on the life of Alexander II in Paris by a Polish patriot on June 6, 1867, to which, as usual, Dostoevsky reacted violently, and on June 16, a scene in the Russian consulate which seems to throw a rather strange light on Dostoevsky's patriotism: in answer to an official's request to produce his passport, Dostoevsky, offended by the official's overbearing, patronizing tone, flared up and remarked that he could expect no better manners from a Russian official and, on leaving the consulate, said "in a terribly angry voice" (as Anna records): "A Russian Government office!" The whole of that evening he kept flying into such a rage at the recollection of this incident that

Anna was frightened. "Then," Anna writes, "he told me that when we were sitting at the consulate, he suddenly saw his dead brother Mikhail —he could distinctly see his head and shoulders suddenly appearing from behind the door; he said that perhaps he was going mad." His nerves were indeed getting overstrained by his financial worries, aggravated by the news that Anna was pregnant, by his seeming inability to write his promised article on Belinsky or make up his mind whether or not to make the main theme of his novel for Katkov (who had just advanced him another 500 rubles) the portrayal of a perfect man.

"The idea of my novel," he wrote to his favorite niece, Sofia Ivanov, and he wrote almost in the same words to Maykov, "has been worrying me for a long time, but it is so difficult that I dared not take it up, though I was so enamored of it, and if I do take it up now, it is because I'm in a desperate position. The main idea of the novel is to depict a positively perfect man. There is nothing more difficult in the world than this, especially now. All writers, not only ours, but even European, always made a hash of it, because it is an eternal problem. Perfection is an ideal, and the ideal—neither ours nor of civilised Europe—is far from being realized."[3]

It is characteristic of Dostoevsky's attitude towards his niece and his wife that, though they were of the same age, he shared his thoughts about his literary work with Sofia and not with Anna. He did not hesitate to tell Anna to "throw away that rubbish" when he saw her reading a French novel he did not approve of, and it never occurred to her to protest or to express an opinion of her own of the novel she was reading.

In Baden-Baden Dostoevsky's repeated attempts "to try his luck" at the gaming tables ended as disastrously as in Homburg in spite of the fact that this time he had Anna with him. This time he blamed all sorts of things for his "bad luck": an Englishman who was standing beside him at the roulette table, his old purse, a rich Pole behind him who kept winning, or Anna herself, whom he took with him and who spoiled his "new system" of putting his stakes on zero by the unexpected discovery that she had an "unlucky hand." In the end they were driven to pawn their few valuables. Here is a typical passage in Anna's diary describing the ups and downs of Dostoevsky's gambling, ending almost invariably in loss. Dostoevsky had just borrowed twelve gulden from Goncharov, who had also been gambling rather heavily. "We got up this morning," Anna wrote in her diary on July 22, "with a dreadful premonition that this money too would be lost. Usually Fedya never succeeds in winning the first time he goes there. We have noticed it very well. Usually his luckiest time is between two and three and later in the evening, about 6 o'clock. Fedya went and I had already prepared myself for the news that this money would be lost. And, to be sure, when he came Fedya said that he had a terrible run of bad luck: zero came

[3] *Letters*, January 13, 1868.

up four times, so how was he to know which number to put his money on. He thought that zero could not possibly come up again, and yet it kept coming up. So, of course, he lost. I felt awful; I simply lost control of myself and said several times: 'Oh damn, damn—the infamy of it!' And, indeed, I felt very miserable and also, somehow, hurt that we should be so unlucky not to be able to win just enough money for our daily requirements. All I had left in my purse was a five-franc piece, a two-gulden piece and some small change. Fedya took the five-franc piece and went out, but soon came back because he had lost it at once. There was nothing to be done about it; we should, of course, have left the money to buy food with, but we did not do so. He asked me to give him my last coin. I gave it to him and he went. Then I began praying to the Holy Virgin to help me as She had always done before, which I do not deserve. I was, somehow, confident that this time Fedya would win. It seemed to me that if I had this confidence, he would most certainly win. I was so firmly convinced of it that when Fedya came in, I said to myself: 'He has won!' So it was. He told me that he had put on that precious coin and won, then again, and at last won 17 two-gulden pieces on it, but afterwards lost 5, and came home with 12. It was the same amount he had borrowed from Goncharov. I was indescribably glad of that money, for it would have kept us for some time. Having brought the 12 two-gulden coins, Fedya took two from me and at once went back to the roulette, though I had told him most firmly not to do so, because I had noticed that when he went to the roulette after a win, he never succeeded in winning a single gulden. But he told me that he had to win enough for a bottle of wine and if he did that he'd be completely satisfied. Fedya went, but soon came back looking vexed because he had lost. We spent one gulden on wine and all sorts of other things and he was left with 9 silver coins, with which he went back to play after dinner. . . . Fedya came home after a while, having lost everything, so that we had not a farthing left. Fedya was in despair. He said he had ruined me, that everything was lost. He was in such terrible despair, that I did not know how to console him. At last, he as well as I decided that it was a waste of time to go to the roulette any more and he would therefore never go again; for it was clear that fate did not want us to win; after all, we had been lucky—we had won 168 gold pieces, but that was not enough for us, so we must make up our minds that we shall never get any money that way; however many things we pawned, however much money we borrowed—it would all be lost. Today, for instance, we were quite happy. The Holy Virgin helped us, gave us 17 gulden and then 12, but we did not know how to appreciate it, we wanted to get more, so now we have been punished. . . ."

This simple faith was characteristic of Anna, and it also had its influence on Dostoevsky, whom it took back to the early days of his childhood, to the equally simple faith of his mother. Anna, in fact, played a great part in at least his outward return to a belief in God and his gradual acceptance of the idea that the Greek Orthodox faith was the only religion capable of bringing salvation not only to Russia, but also to the whole world. Anna's constant quarrels with Dostoevsky merely intensified her influence over him. "I have absolutely no feeling of spite in my heart against Fedya," Anna wrote in her diary on July 25, "not the slightest ill will or vexation, but when he starts arguing with me I immediately find ten words for every one of his and I talk so impudently to him that it simply horrifies me, and I could not stop even if I were beaten, but when I finish calling him all sorts of names, it is as though nothing had happened, as though I never said a cross word. Fedya says that this is quite true and that nothing I do angers him." Dostoevsky was used to being called all sorts of names by his first wife, but there was all the difference in the world between Maria and Anna; for Maria's heart was full of malice and ill will against him, and if *her* scoldings did not anger him, they aroused in him a feeling of guilt that was much worse than anger. What a relief it must have been to him to be called names by Anna, and how greatly he must have appreciated that after their violent quarrels "it was as though nothing had happened!"

V

Baden-Baden was the scene of the famous quarrel between Dostoevsky and Turgenev, a quarrel which was to a large extent responsible for the frenzied violence with which Dostoevsky was soon to repudiate his former liberal views. The meeting between the two novelists took place on July 10, 1867, six days after Dostoevsky's arrival in Baden-Baden. He would have gone earlier but for the gambling fever which infected him on the very first day of his arrival in Baden-Baden. Summing up the four months of their nightmarish sojourn in that city, Anna wrote in her diary on August 21, ten days before their departure for Switzerland: "I forgot to say that we had 400 gulden besides the 234 florins my mother sent us, a total of 1,300 francs. That was the time we should have left. But then we are dreamers—that is a fact; we can never stop, we must go to the bitter end, we could not possibly take advantage of the certainty which would have solved our present difficulties. God gave us the money—we ought therefore to have left at once, for we should have had nothing to worry about for at least three months, after which we would have found some way of getting more money. But, then, we are dreamers—how should we know when to stop? Are we capable of it? Why, of course, we at once remarked that we must win money and that we shall most certainly win 10,000 francs. So how could we possibly not go on gambling after that—we had to go on and, of course, lose everything. . . ." On July 7, Dostoevsky kept losing and rushing back to Anna for more money, promising to leave Baden-Baden if he lost again. On their way from the casino, they met Goncharov, to whom Dostoevsky introduced his young wife. "Goncharov told me," Anna wrote in her diary, "that Turgenev saw Fedya yesterday, but did not go up to him because he knew that people do not like to be interfered with while playing. As Fedya owes Turgenev 50 rubles he must go and see him, for otherwise Turgenev will think that Fedya does not want to pay him a visit because he is afraid to be asked to repay his debt. Therefore Fedya wants to go and see Turgenev tomorrow." It is not surprising that Turgenev did not go up to Dostoevsky, for, according to Anna, when playing, Dostoevsky "looked terrible, just as though he were drunk: his face was red and his eyes bloodshot."

Dostoevsky did go to see Turgenev on the next day after meeting Goncharov, but did not find him at home. The following day he got up too late. Their meeting therefore took place on the morning of July 10. Dostoevsky described this meeting at length in a letter to Maykov six weeks later.

In the six weeks he had worked himself up into such a fury against Turgenev that all his dormant hatred of the man was aroused. The reason for it is perhaps best explained in a sentence by Anna in her diary on the day of Dostoevsky's visit to Turgenev. Dostoevsky had won forty-six gulden that day, and Anna wrote: "I was very, very glad that his winnings will help us to hold out for a little while and Fedya will not have to go to Turgenev to ask him to lend us money until we get some from Katkov." So the real reason why he went to see Turgenev was to keep up his seemingly friendly relations with him so as to be able to fall back on him if he should again, as two years earlier, be in dire straits. Unfortunately, he had won a little money the day before, and every time he won, the prospect of breaking the bank seemed nearer and more alluring. When he got to Schillerstrasse, "the charming little street with lovely front gardens," as Anna described it, he must have felt quite elated that he had not to ask Turgenev for another loan, though the thought that Turgenev could afford to live in a handsome house in such a fine street while he had to make do with two little rooms over a smithy must have aroused all his dormant resentment against his luckier literary rival.

It was 12 o'clock, and Turgenev was having his lunch—"his morning cutlet and half a glass of red wine," as Dostoevsky later described it in *The Devils*, in which Turgenev appears under the guise of Karmazinov. Turgenev continued his meal without inviting Dostoevsky to join him. After the cutlet, a small cup of coffee was brought in. The footman, who served the food, wore a frock coat, soft, noiseless boots, and gloves. This aristocratic milieu still further enraged Dostoevsky. "I tell you frankly," he wrote to Maykov, "I did not like the man even before. What made things worse was that I still owed him from Wiesbaden 50 thaler (which I haven't paid him back yet!). I don't like his aristocratic-Pharisaic embrace with which he comes to kiss you, but merely offers you his cheek.[4] What horrible patrician impudence! But what exasperated me most of all was his novel *Smoke*. He himself told me that the chief idea, the fundamental point of his book is summed up in the sentence: 'If Russia were to sink to the bottom of the sea, there would be neither loss nor agitation among men.' He told me that this was his fundamental conviction about Russia. I found him terribly irritated by the failure of *Smoke*. But, as a matter of fact, I had no idea of all the details of this failure. I did not know that he had received a beating everywhere and that in Moscow, in the English Club, I believe, they were collecting signatures to protest against his *Smoke*. He told me so himself. I tell you I could not imagine anyone displaying all the wounds of his injured pride so naïvely and so maladroitly as Turgenev did. And these men are, incidentally, boasting that they are atheists." What atheism has to do with injured pride Dostoevsky does not explain; the question of atheism was now becoming one of the most predominant problems in his writings, a problem he himself never solved, and he merely uses Turgenev as a whipping boy for all his opponents of the right-wing and left-wing liberal camps.

"Turgenev," he went on, "told me that he was a most decided atheist. But, dear Lord, deism gave us Christ, that is to say, so lofty a conception of man that it is impossible to fathom it without a feeling of awe and it is impossible not to believe that it is an eternal idea of mankind. And what have they—the Turgenevs, Herzens, Chernyshevskys—given us? In place of the supreme beauty of God, on which they spit, they are all without exception nastily self-loving and so shamelessly irritable and frivolously proud that one simply wonders what they are hoping for or who will follow them. Turgenev abused Russia and the Russians most horribly and hideously. But that's what I noticed: all these rotten liberals and progressives, mostly still of the Belinsky school, find their greatest enjoyment and satisfaction in abusing Russia. The only difference is that the followers of Chernyshevsky simply abuse Russia and quite frankly wish it at the bottom of the sea (mostly that!), while these offsprings of Belinsky add that they *love* Russia. And yet they not only hate anything that is typically Russian and deny its existence and at once gleefully caricature it, but were they really at last presented with a fact which could not be repudiated or caricatured and which one simply had to acknowledge, they would be desperately unhappy. Secondly, I noticed that Turgenev (just like all the rest who left Russia a long

[4] In *The Devils* Dostoevsky described his feelings at being offered Turgenev's cheek as follows: "I wondered which of us was more contemptible at that moment: he who was embracing me with the idea of humiliating me or I who despised him and his cheek, but who was kissing it, though I might have turned away." But did Turgenev intend to humiliate him? Was it not just his conventional way of greeting anybody?

time ago) simply does not know the facts (though they read the papers) and is so grossly ignorant of Russia that he fails to understand even such facts as are understood by the Russian nihilist, albeit he may be caricaturing them in his own way. Turgenev, incidentally, told me that we ought to crawl before the Germans, that there is only one unavoidable road before everyone, namely, civilization, and that all attempts of the Russophiles at independence was swinishness and stupidity. He told me," Dostoevsky went on, "that he was writing a long article against all Russophiles and Slavophiles. I advised him for the sake of convenience to order a telescope from Paris. Whatever for? he asked. Russia is far from here, I replied. You would be able to train the telescope on Russia and observe us; otherwise it really is difficult to see what is happening there. He got terribly angry. Seeing him so annoyed, I said to him with what really sounded like genuine naïvety: 'You know, I really did not expect that all these criticisms against you and the failure of *Smoke* would have annoyed you so much. I assure you *it isn't worth it*. Don't pay any attention to it!' 'But,' he said, 'I'm not at all annoyed! Who gave you that idea?' and he blushed. I changed the subject, spoke of my personal affairs and then picked up my hat and, without any intention, just at a venture, told him what for the last three months had been accumulating in my heart against the Germans: 'You know, I suppose, the kind of scoundrels and cheats one meets here. Really, the common people here are much worse and more dishonest than ours, and there certainly can be no doubt that they are stupid. Now, you've been talking about civilization. Tell me, what has civilization done to them and what is it they can boast so much to us about?'

"He turned pale (literally, I am exaggerating nothing, nothing) and said to me: 'In saying this, you offend me personally. I want you to know that I've decided to settle here for good, that I consider myself to be a German and not a Russian and am proud of it!' I replied: 'Though I have read *Smoke* and have been talking to you for a whole hour, I still did not expect to hear you say that and I'm therefore sorry to have offended you.' Then we parted very courteously and I vowed never to visit Turgenev again. Next morning, exactly at ten o'clock, Turgenev paid me a visit and left his visiting card for us with the landlady. As I had told him myself that I could receive no visitors before 12 o'clock because we do not get up before eleven, I interpreted his arrival *at ten o'clock* as a clear hint that he did not want to meet me again. . . . During the seven weeks of our stay in Baden-Baden I met him only once at the casino. We looked at one another, but neither he nor I had any intention of exchanging greetings with one another. . . ."

Dostoevsky must have felt that he had let his personal feeling of hatred for Turgenev color the account he gave of their meeting, for he thought it necessary to add the following explanation: "Perhaps the spitefulness with which I have described Turgenev to you and the way we kept on insulting one another will seem disagreeable to you. But really I can't help it; he hurt me too much by his convictions. Personally, I don't care a damn, though he is not particularly attractive with those aristocratic airs of his; but one simply can't listen to such abuse of Russia from a Russian traitor, who could have been useful. His kowtowing to the Germans and hatred of the Russians I noticed a long time ago, four years ago, in fact. But his present exasperation and frenzied foaming at the mouth against Russia is solely a result of the failure of *Smoke* and the fact that Russia has dared not to recognize his genius. It's just a matter of injured pride and it's all the nastier for that. But to hell with all of them!"

With Dostoevsky, of course, it was all a matter of gleeful spite (it is not for nothing that Turgenev was to call him the most spiteful Christian he had ever met); but the truth is that both Dostoevsky and Turgenev had allowed their dislike of one another to get the better of their good sense. Dostoevsky carefully refrained from telling Maykov the way he himself had attacked Turgenev's novel, which, according to Turgenev, he said should have been burned by the public hangman. He was all too quick to assume that Turgenev was not only played out as a writer, but that he had cut himself off completely from Russia and was serious in stating (if, indeed, he did state it) that he had become a German. It is, however, in this interview that one must look for the clue to the extraordinary outpouring of the most vicious and often unprintable abuse against the Russian radicals that fill Dostoevsky's letters for the next three years. "I'm so disgusted with our clever fellows," he wrote to Maykov from Geneva,[5] meaning the Russian revolutionaries, including Herzen and Bakunin, "that I do my best not to *meet* them, even in *the street*. Oh, the poor fools, oh, the worthless fellows, oh, the rubbish swollen with self-love, oh, the sh——, oh, the disgusting crew! I met Herzen by chance in the street and we spent ten minutes talking together in a sort of hostile-courteous tone interspersed with sneers and then each went on his way." In the same letter he declared that the Russian autocratic regime was based on "the mutual love of the monarch for the people and the people for the monarch. Yes," he explained, "love and not coercion lies at the basis of our state (a discovery first made by the Slavophiles, I believe) and this we shall proclaim to Europe which has no idea of it. Our unhappy class of clever men, uprooted from the soil—alas! cannot be re-educated (think of Turgenev!). It is to the new generation we must turn. . . . Here abroad I have finally become a convinced monarchist. . . . Our common people have always given their love to the Tsar and have always put their trust in him alone. For the common people—this is a mystery, a sanctification, an anointing. . . ." And he followed up this apparently *newly* found faith in the sanctity of an autocratic monarchy by expressing the wish that the Russian

[5] *Letters*, April 2, 1868.

"political," that is, strategic, railways should be built "as soon as possible" and, he added, "modern rifles, too, as soon as possible!"

In an earlier letter to Maykov[6] he revealed quite clearly what the "modern rifles" were meant for. After declaring that in Russia "the spontaneous and noble faith in goodness" pursues quite a different purpose from the attempts to solve the problem of comfort in the bourgeois West, he went on: "The whole world is facing a renascence through the Russian idea (which is firmly fused with the Greek Orthodox faith —you are right) and this will come to pass in about a century—this is my passionate belief. But for this great thing to come to pass it is necessary that the *political right and supremacy* of the Great Russian people over the entire Slav world should be accomplished finally and indisputably." So that even as early as 1868, Dostoevsky propagated the absorption by Russia of all Slav states, a demand that was to become one of the principal points of the policy he was to advocate with such intransigent passion in his *Writer's Diary* ten years later.

The idea of publishing a journal of his own in the form of a diary in which he could combat the ever-growing revolutionary movement in Russia occurred to him, as becomes evident from his letter to Sofia Ivanov[7] after attending one of the meetings of the First Congress of the League of Peace and Freedom, which took place in Geneva from the 9th to the 12th September, 1867, with the participation of Garibaldi and Bakunin. Dostoevsky and Anna were present at the triumphal reception given to Garibaldi on his arrival in Geneva. "My husband and I," Anna records in her reminiscences, "also went to rue du Mont Blanc through which Garibaldi had to pass on his way from the station. The houses were magnificently decorated with flags and flowers and there were masses of people in the street. Garibaldi, in his original costume, stood in the carriage and waved his little hat in reply to the rapturous welcome from the crowd. We managed to see Garibaldi at close quarters and my husband found that the Italian hero had a very sympathetic face and nice smile. . . ."

Garibaldi, Dostoevsky was pleased to tell his niece, soon left the Congress, but "the nonsense these socialists and revolutionaries talked in front of 5,000 spectators is beyond belief. The bathos, feebleness, muddle, disagreements, contradictions are quite unimaginable. And this trash is agitating the unhappy working classes! That is sad. They began with the argument that for the achievement of peace on earth one must destroy the Christian faith. Large states are to be destroyed and made into small states; all capital to be abolished, everything to be held in common by order, etc. All this without the slightest proof, all this has already been learned by heart twenty years ago and it has remained unchanged. And, above all, fire and sword, and after everything has been

[6] *Letters*, March 1, 1868.

[7] *Letters*, October 11, 1862.

destroyed, then in their opinion there will be peace." To Maykov he described the Congress in his letter of September 15th as "four days of shouting and lying."

What must have infuriated Dostoevsky particularly during the two hours he had attended the Congress as a spectator was Bakunin's speech in which he demanded the breaking up of the Russian Empire into its constituent parts of separate national entities, and declared that the existence of the Russian Empire was the only hindrance to peace. "He who loves freedom," Bakunin declared, "ought to realize that it could only be achieved by a free federation of provinces and peoples, that is to say, the annihilation of the empire" whose "successes and glory have been and always will be incompatible with the happiness and freedom of Russian and non-Russian peoples, her present-day victims and slaves. . . ." Dostoevsky had met Bakunin in London, but there is no evidence that he resumed the acquaintanceship in Geneva.

Quite different was his relationship with Bakunin's closest revolutionary collaborator, the poet Ogaryov, who, Anna records, "often came to see us and sometimes even lent us a few francs, which we returned to him as soon as we could. My husband had a high opinion of the poems of this sincere poet and we were both very glad of his visits. Ogaryov, a very old man at the time [he was fifty-four, that is, only seven years older than Dostoevsky], was particularly nice to me and, to my surprise, treated me almost as a little girl, which, in fact, I was just then." That Ogaryov's loans were much more substantial than "a few francs" can be gathered from Dostoevsky's letter to Anna from Saxon-les-Bains,[8] after he had, as usual, lost all the money he had brought with him at roulette: "I'll ask Ogaryov to lend me 500 francs till December 15. To begin with, he is not Herzen and, secondly, I shall not bind myself morally. I shall make this quite clear to him when asking for the loan. . . . After all, he is a poet, he has a kind heart and, besides, he comes to me himself and seeks something from me, so that he must respect me. . . ."

There was another and much more potent reason for Dostoevsky's close association with Ogaryov at the time. For Ogaryov had been conducting a lively correspondence with Konstantin Golubyov, a Russian peasant and a former sectarian turned philosopher, who was editing the journal *Truth* in Johannesburg. Ogaryov tried to convert the ex-sectarian to his own materialistic views, but in his replies, published in his journal, Golubyov, who always referred to himself as a peasant, did his best to refute those views, advocating the necessity of an autocratic monarchy for Russia and a union of the Old Believers with the Orthodox Church.

What did Ogaryov seek from Dostoevsky? What could he seek from a man who had gone over to the reactionary camp of the Maykovs and Katkovs and was even more extreme than they in his political demands?

[8] *Letters*, November 17, 1867.

Is it possible that Ogaryov, a close associate of Herzen and Bakunin and as uncompromising a revolutionary as they, with his poetic intuition divined the dichotomy, the tragic cleavage, between Dostoevsky's present religious and political views and his profound and ruthlessly candid vision of man? Dostoevsky himself hints at it in one of the rare passages of complete frankness in his correspondence. Writing to his niece Sofia from Geneva,[9] he commends her restraint and feeling of personal dignity. "Oh," he goes on, "never be false to it, follow a straight road without compromises in life. For you have only to compromise once with your honor and conscience and there will remain for a long time a weak spot in your soul, so that the moment you are faced with the choice between something difficult and something profitable you will at once retreat before the difficulty and follow the profitable. I am not stating a platitude; what I am telling you is what hurts me now; and of the weak spot I spoke to you perhaps from personal experience. What I love about you most is perhaps what I myself lack—everything in my nasty character has to be explained by some petty reason, by some moment of irritation. . . ." Even Dostoevsky, then, was aware that his outbursts of spleen and spite were caused by some deep-seated irritant, the consciousness that, having compromised once by writing those fulsome "odes" to the Tsarist family, he had been driven from one extreme to another till he found himself propagating policies that seemed to run counter to the humanitarian ideas he had believed in and still believed in at heart.

It was, indeed, the extreme nature of his present views that, paradoxically, aroused the suspicions of the Russian secret police, who were, of course, informed of his association with Ogaryov (who had taken over the editorship of *The Bell* from Herzen) and of his presence at the Congress of the League of Peace and Freedom. Thus, on November 28, 1867, the chiefs of the frontier police received an order from the chief of the notorious Third Department of the Emperor's Private Office to carry out a thorough search of Dostoevsky, should he attempt to return to Russia, and, if necessary, to arrest him and bring him under armed convoy to Petersburg. In the summer of 1866, Dostoevsky received an anonymous letter informing him of this order. "I am under police supervision," Dostoevsky wrote to Maykov from Vevey.[10] "The Petersburg police open and read all my letters, and as the Russian priest in Geneva is an agent of the secret police, some of the letters I receive from Russia are detained by the post office in Geneva with which, I know for certain, he has a secret understanding. . . . But how can a man who is pure in heart and a patriot, a man who has so completely given up his former convictions as to justify an accusation of betrayal, one who adores the Emperor—how can a man like that endure the suspicion of having relations with some wretched Poles or with *The Bell*.

[9] *Letters*, January 13, 1868.
[10] *Letters*, August 2, 1868.

Oh, the fools, the stupid fools! How can one have the heart to serve them? How many really guilty persons have they let slip through their fingers in Russia, but they suspect Dostoevsky!" It was not for the first time that Dostoevsky had the very unpleasant experience of being hoist with his own petard.

VI

Dostoevsky and his wife arrived in Geneva on August 25, 1867. On the way there they stopped for a day in Basle, where they inspected the cathedral and the museum (Anna was a born tourist). There they saw Hans Holbein's picture of Christ taken from the Cross. The realism of the painting horrified Anna, and she went to another room, while Dostoevsky was so impressed by it (he described the picture in *The Idiot*) that on her return she found him still standing before it "as though rooted to the ground. On his agitated face," Anna writes, "I noticed the frightened look which I had seen many times on it during the first moments of his epileptic fits. I took his arm, went with him to another room and made him sit down on a bench, expecting him to have a fit any moment. Fortunately, it did not come: Fedya calmed down gradually but insisted on going to see the picture again, this time," Anna states in her diary, "he stood on a chair and I was terribly afraid he might have to pay a fine, for here we have to pay fines for everything."

In Geneva they spent their first day hunting for rooms and only in the evening found one on the corner of rue Guillaume Tell and rue Bertelier on the second floor, with a view of the bridge over the Rhone and the Isle Jean-Jacques Rousseau. After paying a month's rent in advance they were left with only eighteen francs. By this time Dostoevsky had received an advance of 4,000 rubles from Katkov and had not even started writing his novel. He rushed off a long letter to Maykov, giving an account of his life abroad, including his meeting with Turgenev, and asking for a loan of 150 rubles. Maykov sent him 125, which, Dostoevsky wrote to him,[11] "absolutely saved us."

Their life in Geneva soon slipped into its usual routine. Dostoevsky worked at night and got up at eleven. After breakfast Anna, who was expecting her baby in about five months, went for a walk, while Dostoevsky went back to his writing. At 3 o'clock they went to a restaurant to have their dinner, after which Anna went back to their room for a rest, while Dostoevsky went to a café in rue du Mont Blanc, and spent two hours reading Russian and foreign papers. About seven in the evening they went for a long walk, stopping at the shop windows, Dostoevsky pointing out the expensive presents he would have bought her if he had the money. "To do him justice," Anna remarks, "my husband

[11] *Letters*, September 15, 1867.

possessed artistic taste and the precious articles he pointed out were exquisite." The evenings were spent either in dictation of Dostoevsky's new work or in reading French novels, Dostoevsky doing his best to cultivate his young wife's literary taste by forcing her to read systematically through the work of one writer, such as Balzac or George Sand, while he himself kept rereading Victor Hugo's *Les Misérables.*

Before starting on his new novel, Dostoevsky finished his article on Belinsky. "I have finished the damned article *My Acquaintance with Belinsky*," he wrote to Maykov.[12] "I could not possibly put if off any longer. And yet I have been writing it since summer, but I found it so harassing and difficult to write that I had to keep pegging away at it till at last I finished it with gnashing of teeth. The trouble was that I agreed to write it in a moment of aberration. As soon as I started writing it, however, I realized that it was impossible to write it in such a way that it would be passed by the censorship (for I wanted to tell everything). It would have been easier to write ten printed folio pages of a novel than these two folio pages. I have, in fact, written this thrice-cursed article *five times* and then still kept crossing out whole passages and writing them again. At last I managed to finish it, but it is so rotten that it makes me sick. The number of most precious facts I had to throw out! And, as was to be expected, what was left is quite worthless and mediocre. Disgusting!"

But was it only the censorship Dostoevsky dreaded in writing his ill-fated article, which for some mysterious reason got "lost" in Moscow and was never found again? Could it not be that in his present frame of mind it was quite impossible for him to be fair to the memory and achievements of the great critic, and he was afraid of alienating even conservative opinion in Russia by the vehemence of his attacks on the man to whom he owed so much of his own fame?

Having disposed of his "thrice-cursed" article, Dostoevsky sat down to his novel, and it was here that the real trouble began. "I worked and tormented myself," he later wrote to Maykov, describing his first attempts to write *The Idiot.*[13] "Do you know what it means to *write a novel?* No, thank God, you don't! You have never, I believe, written to order and by the yard and so have never experienced this hellish *torment.* Having obtained so much money in advance from *The Russian Herald* (oh, horror! 4,500 rubles), I hoped at first that poetic inspiration would not leave me, that at the end of the year a poetic idea could flash into my mind and unfold itself and that I should be able to satisfy everybody. This seemed all the more probable as a great many rudimentary artistic ideas always keep flashing through my head and making themselves felt. But, then, they just appear for a moment, while what I was after was their fullest possible embodiment, which always happens accidentally and

[12] *Letters,* September 15, 1867.

[13] *Letters,* January 12, 1868.

suddenly, though it is never possible to anticipate when this embodiment will take place; and it is only after this, after having got the full image in my heart, that I can start realizing it. At this point I can count on it unmistakably. . . . All the summer and autumn I kept arranging all sorts of ideas (some of them most diverting ones), but a certain experience I had acquired in these matters made me feel in good time either the falseness or difficulty or immaturity of some idea. . . ."

The mental strain of the initial stages of the composition of his new novel was so great that he soon broke under it and sought relief in the excitement of roulette. In her reminiscences Anna claims that it was she who gave Dostoevsky the idea of trying his luck again at the nearest casino in Saxon-les-Bains. But from his letters to her it becomes clear that, far from acquiescing, she did all she could to prevent him from making a journey which she knew could only end in disaster. He had to shout at her (for which he asked her abjectly to forgive him) before she would agree to let him go. He only spent two days—October 5 and 6—during his first visit at Saxon-les-Bains, with the inevitable result. "I am worse than a beast," he wrote to Anna on October 6, 1867. "At half-past seven last night I had won 1,300 francs and today I haven't a penny. Lost everything! Everything! And all because the scoundrel of a waiter in Hotel des Bains did not wake me as I had ordered him, so that I could leave at 11 o'clock for Geneva. As my next train was at 5, I went to the casino at two and lost everything. I am pawning my ring. . . . Tomorrow morning I'll be back in Geneva. Anna, fate is persecuting me. . . ."

Back in Geneva, he was getting bored with Anna's company. "Always alone—we are always alone—enough to go off one's head with boredom. . . ." Worse still, his epileptic fits now recurred almost every week, and he was also beginning to suffer from palpitations. Geneva, too, was getting on his nerves. "It's a horror and not a city," he wrote to Maykov. "It's Gehenna. Wind and whirlwinds all day long, and even on ordinary days the most sudden changes in the weather three or four times a day. And this for a man who suffers from hemorrhoids and epilepsy. . . ."[14]

His disgust with Geneva naturally led to his even greater disgust with the natives. "And what self-satisfied little boasters the Swiss are!" he went on with his jeremiad in the same letter. "For to be always satisfied with everything is a sign of particular stupidity. Everything here is horrible, rotten, everything here is dear. Everything here is drunken! Even in London there are not so many rowdies and loud-voiced drunkards. And everything they have, every post in the street, is elegant and grand. You ask them the way to somewhere. *Voyez, monsieur, vous irez tout droit quand vous passerez près de cette majesteuse et élégante fontaine en bronze, vous prendrez*, etc. And this *élégante fontaine* is the most flimsy, insubstantial rococo rubbish that you can

[14] *Letters*, October 21, 1867.

imagine, and he can't help boasting about it, though all you want him to tell you is the way. They have planted a rotten little garden consisting of a few bushes (not a single tree), something like two front gardens in Moscow, if joined together, and they photograph it and sell it as The English Garden in Geneva. But to hell with the scoundrels!" His novel, he told Maykov, was his only salvation. "I am sitting down seriously to my novel," he wrote to his niece Sofia in Moscow two days later, "but what I fear most is mediocrity. I'd rather it turned out either very good or completely bad. Mediocrity in 30 folio pages is something quite unforgivable. . . ."[15]

But the novel refused to write itself. He had prepared several versions, but none satisfied him, and again he found himself in a hopeless state of dejection, for which he knew only one remedy—the excitement of the roulette table. He arrived at Saxon-les-Bains on November 17 and left on November 19. He had brought 125 francs with him, lost them, won them again plus another one hundred francs, wondered whether he should send the one hundred francs to Anna, instead promised her[16] "to play in a most sensible way," apologized for being angry and shouting at her, and, next day, lost everything again. "Now," he wrote to Anna,[17] "my novel, only my novel can save me. Never, never, shall I gamble again." He had got fifty francs by pawning his winter coat and ring and lost that money too. Anna sent him his fares back to Geneva, and on his return he at last succeeded in getting his novel moving.

"At last," he wrote to Maykov,[18] "I took up one idea, wrote a lot, but on December 4 scrapped it all. . . . I began worrying myself to death by trying to think of a new plot for my novel and on December 18 began to write, working at it day and night. I wrote the first part in 23 days and have just sent it off. The second part, which I am sitting down to write now, I hope to finish in a month. . . . The first part is really only introductory. I only hope it will arouse some interest in what is to follow. I am afraid I am quite unable to say whether it will or not. I have only one reader—Anna, who likes it very much, but, then, she is no judge of my business." He had arranged with Katkov to be sent one hundred rubles each month, and he was glad to tell Maykov that he was no longer in such great need. They had also changed their quarters: they lived in two rooms in a house in rue du Mont Blanc, near the English church; one room was large with four windows and for that reason very cold, but the other was small and warm, "so that it is still possible to live."

In his letter to his sister Vera,[19] he described how he and Anna had

[15] *Letters*, October 23, 1867.
[16] *Letters*, November 17, 1867.
[17] *Letters*, November 18, 1867.
[18] *Letters*, January 12, 1868.
[19] *Letters*, January 13, 1868.

celebrated the Russian New Year the evening before by opening half a bottle of champagne exactly at half past ten (midnight Moscow time), clinked glasses "and drunk to the health of all our dear ones." On the same day he also wrote a more detailed letter about his novel to his niece Sofia. He referred to the great theme of what was to become one of his greatest masterpieces—the delineation of a perfect man and the fact (as he claimed) that there was only one positively perfect man in the world—Christ, the very appearance of whom was in itself a miracle.

"In Christian literature," he wrote, "the most perfect character is Don Quixote, but he is perfect simply because he is at the same time also ridiculous. Dickens's Pickwick (an infinitely weaker conception than Don Quixote, but enormous all the same) is also ridiculous and that is the only reason why he appeals to everybody. One feels a sense of pity towards a man who is unaware of his own perfection and who is being constantly held up to ridicule, and hence the reader's sympathy is aroused. This arousal of compassion is the secret of humor. There is nothing comparable in my novel and that is why I am afraid that it will be a complete failure. The title of my novel is *The Idiot* and I am dedicating it to you. . . ." He concluded with a reference to the woman question which, he hoped (and in this he differed radically from his new political friends), would soon take "several great and wonderful steps forward" in Russia. "The other day," he wrote, "I read in the papers that a former friend of mine, Nadezhda Suslov (Pauline Suslov's sister), had passed her finals at the medical faculty of Zurich University and defended her doctorate thesis brilliantly. She is still a very young girl, she is only 23, a rare personality, noble, honest, high-minded!"

On March 1, 1868, Dostoevsky wrote to Maykov that he was immersed in writing the second part of *The Idiot*. "Though we live quite contentedly together," he went on, "and are both busy, I at least feel terribly bored. More recently Anna has been feeling wretched, afraid to die in labor . . . we have very little money left . . . with the coming of spring my epileptic fits occur more frequently. . . ." Three days later he had two epileptic seizures, the second one, on the night of March 3, being so violent that he could hardly stand on his feet next morning. He went to bed early that day, and during the night Anna's labor started. She woke him at 7 o'clock, and he rushed out at once to fetch the midwife. Their first daughter, whom they decided to name Sofia after Dostoevsky's favorite niece, was born at 5 o'clock in the morning on March 5. "The midwife told me," Anna records in her reminiscences, "that never in her long practice had she seen a father of a newly born baby in such a state of violent agitation as my husband and she kept repeating, *Oh, ces, russes, ces russes!*" It seems Dostoevsky spent the night either kneeling in prayer or sitting in an easy chair, sunk in thought, his face buried in his hands. At the age of forty-six he had at last become a father.

"For the past month," he wrote to Maykov,[20] "I have become aware of quite new sensations, from the very first moment I caught sight of my Sofia for the first time to the moment when, a while ago, we bathed her. Yes, indeed, an angelic soul has flown into our house. . . . We want you to be her godfather. . . . Your goddaughter is a very beautiful baby, in spite of the fact that she resembles me to a degree that seems incredible and almost ridiculous. She has even inherited my quirks, my expression, my wrinkles on the forehead–she is lying there just as though she were making up a novel! Not to mention her features–her forehead especially is a replica of mine. From this, of course, it ought to follow that she is not particularly beautiful (for I am *beautiful* only in the eyes of Anna). But you are an artist yourself and you know very well that one can resemble a face that is far from handsome and yet be very charming. . . ."

He had now been working for a whole month, and the second part of the novel was giving him great trouble. He was in despair and tearing up the pages as soon as he wrote them. On April 3 he was in Saxon-les-Bains again. An hour after his arrival he had gone to the casino and lost all his money. "Forgive me, Anna," he wrote to his wife on the same day, "I have poisoned your life for you! And now I have Sonia,[21] too." He begged her to send him more money. "Come to my rescue, my guardian angel," he pleaded. "I love you dearly, but fate has decreed that I must torment those I love. Send me as much money as you can manage. Not for gambling–I should have sworn to you that I would not gamble again, but I dare not, for I have already lied to you a thousand times. . . . My angel, send me 100 francs. That will leave you 20 francs or less, but you could pawn something. . . ."

He was, of course, lying to her again and both he and she were perfectly well aware of it. That he did intend to gamble again he made clear by his statement that he intended to stay for another two days. He had pawned his watch and immediately went to the casino and lost the money. He was left with fifty centimes. "My friend," he wrote to Anna on April 4, approximately at 9:30 P.M.," "let this be my last and final lesson–yes, a dreadful lesson! Still," he perked up again–his powers of resilience after a bout of self-deprecation were indeed prodigious, "but for this loss of 220 francs I should not have got this wonderful, excellent idea which is quite certain to result in our general salvation!" What was the idea? It was simply to write another letter to Katkov to ask him for another advance of 300 rubles! "Oh, away with grumbling now!" he continued in the dithyrambic vein which so vividly recalled his father's

[20] *Letters*, April 2, 1868.
[21] Sonia is the Russian pet name for Sofia.

letters to his mother. "The cursed mirage—nothing of the kind will ever happen again!" They would leave windy Geneva for Vevey, he would finish his novel, and they would return to Russia via Italy and Austria, because he was anxious to show her Florence, Naples, Venice and Vienna. "In Russia, of course, we shall arrive without money," he went on, no longer obsessed, it seems, by the idea of sudden riches, "but if my novel is a success I shall get offers and I shall be able to sell *The Idiot*. I shall tell my creditors straight: if you are going to send me to jail, that is, if you demand that I shall sell my novel now, I'll sell it for next to nothing. Wait no more than another four months and I shall pay all I owe you. So, you see, everything depends on my novel and our journey to Vevey. Perhaps our whole future. Three years hence we shall perhaps at last be able to stand on our feet. But you must agree, my darling, that but for this horrible loss I should not have dared to take this *step* which will save us from everything. . . . Why, perhaps we really ought to thank God for this occurrence which has finally decided me to put my trust in my work. . . . This wonderful idea came to me at nine o'clock or thereabouts, after I had lost everything and gone for a stroll down the avenue (just as in Wiesbaden after I had lost everything, I had thought of the idea of *Crime and Punishment*). It's either fate or God!" he concluded, with a meaningless phrase that he knew would impress his silly wife. But in matters of money, Anna was not at all as silly as that. She was one of those methodical women who put down the price of every article they buy and are ready to haggle for hours over a penny. So far she had been unable to wean her husband from the "mirage" of getting rich quickly. It required a violent shock to make him pull himself together for a time.

Six weeks after his return from Saxon-les-Bains, on May 24, 1868, his baby daughter died of pneumonia. "I cannot describe our despair at the sight of our dead daughter," Anna records. "Deeply shaken and grieved by her death, I was terribly afraid for my unhappy husband: his despair was stormy, he wept and sobbed like a woman as he stood before the cold body of his darling and covered her pale little face and little hands with ardent kisses. Such stormy despair I have never seen. We both felt that we would not be able to endure our grief. For two days, without parting for a moment, we visited all sorts of offices to obtain permission to bury our baby, together we made all the necessary arrangements for her funeral, together we put a white satin dress on her, together we put her into the white coffin, lined with satin, and wept, wept uncontrollably. It was terrible to look at Fedya, he had grown so thin and haggard during the week of Sonia's illness."

Three days after Sonia's funeral Dostoevsky wrote to Maykov:[22] "My Sonia has died . . . two hours before her death I did not know that she would die. Three hours before her death the doctor said that her

[22] *Letters*, May 30, 1868.

condition had improved and that she would live. She was only ill a week; she died of pneumonia. Oh, my dear friend, my love of my first child may have appeared ridiculous, I may have expressed myself ridiculously in reply to the many congratulations I received on her birth. I alone was ridiculous in their eyes, but to you, to you, I am not afraid to write. This three-month-old little creature, so pale and so tiny, was already a personality and a character to me. She was beginning to recognize me, to love me and to smile at me when I came near her. When I sang her songs in my ridiculous voice she loved to listen to them. She did not cry and she did not frown when I kissed her; she stopped crying when I went up to her. And now I am told as a consolation that I will have other children. And what about Sonia? Where is that little person for whom—and I mean it—I am ready to be crucified if only that would bring her back to life? But let's leave it. My wife is crying. Tomorrow we shall at last part from our grave and go away somewhere. Anna's mother is with us: she arrived only one week before Sonia's death."

Dostoevsky concluded his letter with "a big request" to Maykov not to divulge the news of his little daughter's death to any member of his family, and particularly to Pasha. "It seems to me," he wrote, "that none of them will have pity on my child, but perhaps be glad of her death, and the very thought of it makes me angry. What has this poor creature done to offend them? Let them hate me, let them laugh at me and at my love—I don't care. . . ."

The campaign which Anna had been conducting very subtly to undermine his family's, and particularly Pasha's influence over Dostoevsky was beginning to fear fruit. Anna dreaded to return to Petersburg before, as she expressed it in her diary on July 31, 1867, "our love has grown much stronger," for, she wrote, "Pasha and the whole family would of course have succeeded in separating us, and, unable to put up with their insults and not expecting any firm defense from my husband, I should most certainly have not been able to bear it and would have gone away to my mother with my child. I am saying this confidently, knowing my character at the time." She began by intercepting Pasha's letters, while her mother, who was only too eager to help her, spread the story that Pasha had gone to Moscow to demand money from Katkov. "I have been informed and informed positively." Dostoevsky wrote to Katkov from Geneva,[23] "that my stepson, Pavel Isaev, a young man of about twenty-one, left Petersburg for Moscow at the end of February with the idea of coming to you and demanding money—whether in my name or not, I don't know. . . . He had been employed in Petersburg for the last two months at the address bureau (a post, of course, in accordance with his abilities). Suddenly I am informed that he has quarreled with his superior and gone off to Moscow to obtain money from you on the grounds that I am bound to keep him." He asked Kat-

[23] *Letters*, March 18, 1868.

kov not on any account to advance any money to his stepson. "I shall never leave the silly boy," he concluded, "while I am able to help him, but, please, forgive him for troubling you. You have been so good to me that I was very sorry to hear of it."

Though furious with Pasha, Dostoevsky hastened to dispatch a letter to him in which, to prevent any further trips to Moscow, he assured him that "while I live, you will be my son and a son who is dear to me. I vowed to your mother before her death never to leave you. I called you my son while you were still a little boy. How can I, then, leave you or forget you? When I got married and when you hinted to me at the time that your role would be different in future, I said nothing to you, because I was *hurt* by your supposition. Now I can confess it to you. I want you to know that you will always remain my son, my *elder* son, and not from duty but from the heart. If I frequently shouted at you and was angry with you, that is because of my unfortunate character, for I am fond of you as I have rarely been fond of anyone. When I return to Petersburg, I shall do all I can to obtain a good post for you and I shall always assist you *while I live* and whenever I have any money. . . ."

Dostoevsky was to regret these assurances, which were made on the spur of the moment and, as usual, went much too far. He was not, of course, entirely unaware of Anna's endeavors to bring about a complete breach in his relations with Pasha (in which she eventually succeeded), and he was from the very beginning suspicious of the story of Pasha's trip to Moscow. On March 14 he asked Maykov to find out whether there was any truth in it, and on June 9, having at last received a letter from Pasha, he realized that he had been unfair in suspecting him and wrote him a very affectionate letter, in which he himself informed him of Sonia's death. "The Lord has smitten me," he echoed Job, "my Sonia has died and we have already buried her. Oh, Pasha, I feel so bitter and wretched that I wish I was dead."

Reconciled to Pasha, Dostoevsky agreed to his suggestion to raise a loan of 200 rubles for him from a Petersburg printer and indeed asked him to raise another 800 rubles for himself from the same man.

VII

Dostoevsky left Geneva for Vevey with his wife and mother-in-law at the end of May, having had to pawn his own and Anna's clothes, but Vevey did not come up to his expectations. "In all the fourteen years of our married life," Anna wrote in her reminiscences, "I cannot remember such a sad summer as the one we spent in Vevey in 1868." Dostoevsky was working hard at his novel, "literally, day and night," he wrote to Maykov,[24] "in spite of my epileptic fits." There were still twenty-seven folio pages left to the end, but he was "crawling like a crab." He

[24] *Letters*, June 22, 1868.

blamed the Vevey air, which the Geneva doctors had warned him had a bad effect on the nerves. "Oh," he went on, "if only you had any idea how I loathe living abroad, if only you had an idea of the dishonesty, baseness, incredible stupidity and intellectual backwardness of the Swiss! The Germans are worse, of course, but the Swiss, too, aren't much better. They look upon a foreigner here as a means of making a living; all they are out for is to deceive and rob you. But worst of all is their uncleanliness! A kirghiz in his black tent leads a more cleanly life. I am simply horrified; I'd have laughed outright if I had been told that before of Europeans. But in Geneva I had at least Russian papers, while here I have nothing."

He was particularly annoyed with the "Europeans" because Maykov had told him of a book entitled *Les Mystères du Palais de Czars sous l'Emperor Nicholas I* in which he was said to have joined a secret revolutionary society after his return from Siberia, been rearrested, sent to Siberia and died on the way, while his unhappy wife committed suicide. "What astonished me most," he wrote to an unknown correspondent in connection with this book, "is the utter ignorance of Europeans of almost anything that has to do with Russia. . . . The wildest and most extraordinary reports of contemporary life in Russia are faithfully believed by the public. People, who regard themselves as civilized, are ready to pass judgment on life in Russia with extraordinary thoughtlessness, having no idea of our geography, let alone our civilization. . . . The other day I came across a stupid book purporting to describe the history of my life . . . and everything there is so distorted that you can't believe that such shamelessness can exist. . . ."

He had just written Chapters nine and ten of the second part of *The Idiot*, describing, in his own words, "an episode concerning our contemporary positivists belonging to the extremist youth." He knew, he wrote to Maykov,[25] that it was true, for he had written it from his own observation and experience. He also expected to be abused by everybody for it. And yet the Pavlishchev affair he so brilliantly described and, particularly, the article written by one of these "positivists" are, surely, no less shameless and fantastic than the most shamelessly fantastic stories spread about Russia abroad. His own extreme xenophobia was hardly likely to foster international understanding.

At the beginning of September Dostoevsky had still the last part of *The Idiot* to write, but he had to postpone work on the novel again, having decided to go to Italy. They traveled via the Simplon Pass, partly on foot, "myself," Anna writes, "walking with my husband beside the enormous coach, going on ahead of it, climbing up the mountain paths and picking wild flowers." The first time she saw him smile after the death of their daughter was in a small Italian village, where a shopkeeper, thinking he was a rich tourist, asked him 3,000 francs for a

[25] *Letters*, June 22, 1868.

small gold chain which supposedly went back to the days of Vespasian.

They lived in Milan for about two months, "for," he wrote to his niece Sofia on November 7, "we had not enough money to go any further. Though it often rained, the climate in Milan was remarkably good for my health. Milan is famed for its frequent heart attacks, but perhaps I won't have one here. Life is rather expensive; the city is large and important, but not picturesque and scarcely looks Italian. . . . The only remarkable thing in the city is the famous Milan cathedral, a huge marble Gothic building, all carved *à jour* and as fantastic as a dream. Its interior is extraordinarily beautiful." One day, Anna records, they even climbed to its roof to have a look at the view and the statues.

While in Milan, Dostoevsky came across an account in *The Russian Herald* of the annual meeting of the British Association in Norwich at which its president, Joseph Dalton Hooker, spoke of the possibility of the peaceful coexistence of science and religion. "You simply must read this article," he wrote to his niece. It was, indeed, a subject that interested him very much, for it provided him with ammunition against the "nihilists" and atheists, whose beliefs he was now determined to attack in a novel he was contemplating writing under the title of *Atheism.*

Dostoevsky was further cheered by the news he received first from Maykov and then from Strakhov of the foundation of a new monthly journal, *Zarya* (*Dawn*), in which Strakhov was to play a leading part and which was to continue with the policies he had advocated in *Time* and *Epoch.* "It would be advisable," he wrote to Maykov[26] from Milan, "that the new journal should express *the Russian spirit* as you and I understand it, though not entirely Slavophile. In my view," he added significantly, "we must not run after the Slavs, not *too much.* It is necessary that they should come to us themselves. . . . For many Slavs, in Prague, for instance, judge us entirely from the Western European point of view and are even surprised that our Slavophiles do not greatly care for the generally accepted forms of Western European civilization."

At the end of November Dostoevsky, with his wife and mother-in-law, both of whom were now busily engaged in persuading him to break with his family, went to live in Florence and took rooms near the Pitti museum. "The change of place," Anna writes, "has again had a good effect on my husband and we began together to inspect churches, museums and palaces. I remember how Fedya was delighted with the *Cathedrale*, the church of Santa Maria del Fiore and the small Capella del Battistero, where babies are usually christened. The bronze doors of the Battistero (especially Detta del Paradiso) by the famous Ghiberti, entranced him, and every time he passed the Capella he stopped and examined them. My husband used to say that when he got rich he would most certainly buy a full-length photograph of them and hang it in his study. My husband and I often went to the Palazzo Pitti where he

[26] *Letters,* October 7, 1868.

greatly admired Raphael's *Madonna della Sedia.* Another Raphael picture in the Uffizi gallery, *S. Giovan Battisto del Deserto,* was also greatly admired by my husband and he used to stand for hours before it. After a visit to the gallery, he always went to see in the same building the statue *Venere de Medici,* the work of the famous Greek sculptor Cleomenes. This statue my husband considered a work of genius." In his letter to Maykov in December,[27] he wrote about Raphael's picture in the Pitti: "I saw the *Madonna della Sedia* in 1863, looked at it for a week, but it is only now that I *saw* it."

"In Florence," Anna further records, "we found to our great delight a large library and reading room with two Russian papers and my husband always went there to read after dinner. Among the books he took home with him for the whole winter were the works of Voltaire and Diderot in French, which he knew well."

The new year brought them "the happy news" that Anna was pregnant again. "Our joy was boundless," she writes, "and my dear husband's care of me was so great that, having read the volumes of *War and Peace,* sent to him by Strakhov, he hid from me the part of the novel in which the death in childbirth of Prince Andrey Bolkonsky's wife is so artistically described."

Their financial position was still bad. For *The Idiot,* Anna explains, Dostoevsky received 150 rubles per folio page, which amounted altogether to 7,000 rubles, of which 3,000 had been advanced before Dostoevsky's marriage, and the remaining 4,000 had not only to keep them, but also to support Mikhail's family and Pasha, not to mention the payment of the interest on their pawned furniture in Petersburg. "But," she declares, completely ignoring Dostoevsky's escapades at the roulette tables in Homburg, Baden-Baden and Saxon-les-Bains, "we put up with our comparative poverty not only without a murmur, but often with complete unconcern. Fedya called himself Mr. Micawber and me Mrs. Micawber. We lived in complete harmony and concord." The "harmony and concord" was the result of Dostoevsky's complete capitulation to Anna's demands for his abandonment of Pasha and Mikhail's family. "Oh, you don't know how much unpleasantness they have caused me," Dostoevsky wrote to his niece Sofia from Florence. "Spite, calumny, jeers—and all this against me. They blamed me for all their misfortunes—me alone. Emilia assures everybody that they had a factory and that, till my arrival, they were rich, and after I arrived and started our monthly journal, they all became poor. It's all a lie. They maintain sarcastically that the reason I founded the journal was to be able to publish in it my works which no one wished to accept. I suppose they are saying this about *The House of the Dead* and *Crime and Punishment.* Now they are screaming that I have abandoned them, I who have given them all I had! . . . How spitefully they regarded my marriage, how they jeered then, the disgraceful

[27] *Letters,* December 26, 1868.

things they told my wife in secret about me, how they tried to frighten her, how they tried to make her loathe me! (All this I have just found out; these are facts, I assure you.) I have spent 2,000 rubles on them, while they abuse and defame me (I know that for a certainty) because, they claim, I have abandoned them while my brother had kept me in Siberia. . . . My Petersburg relations are tormenting me a little too much. . . ." This, of course, sounds more like Anna than Dostoevsky—she had now got what she wanted, though, to make quite sure, she thought it necessary to keep him for at least another year in the wilderness. Mikhail's widow, he told Maykov earlier in his letter from Florence on December 23, how now become his "mortal enemy." He sent Emilia another fifty rubles, but after that "I shall go on strike." He wrote to Emilia, telling her that he was very sorry, but he could not let her live in his Petersburg flat any longer. About Pasha he was not so certain: after all, it was only a few months earlier he had promised never to abandon him. "I must help Pasha," he wrote to Maykov in the same letter, "just a little bit."[28]

Dostoevsky did not finish *The Idiot* till January 1869, and, as usual, felt a little deflated. "I am not satisfied with my novel," he wrote to his niece Sofia.[29] "It does not express a tenth part of what I wished to express, though I do not disown it and still like my idea. . . . The last chapters I wrote day and night in anguish and terrible anxiety. I myself fixed the deadline for the last part for January 15—and what do you think happened?—two epileptic attacks and I was 10 days late. The climate here in Florence is much worse for me than in Milan and Vevey; my fits are more frequent. My last two fits happened with only an interval of six days. . . . Besides, it rains a lot in Florence; but, on the other hand, when the sun shines it is almost paradise. You can't imagine anything lovelier than this sky, air, and light. For two weeks it was a little cold, but because of the disgustingly poor construction of the apartments here we froze like mice in a cellar."

VIII

Dostoevsky's dissatisfaction with *The Idiot* was perhaps due not so much to his fear that he had not fully explained his "idea" as that, with the exception of Myshkin's speech in the seventh chapter of the fourth part of the novel, he had put forward as its exponents such unconvincing characters as Lebedev, Mrs. Yepanchin and Radomsky. This was a trick he was to use again and again in his last novels: realizing that some of his views were so extreme and even perverse that he would risk making himself ridiculous if he advocated them seriously by making his heroes into their exponents, he put them into the mouths of his avowedly

[28] *Letters*, February 6, 1869.
[29] *Letters*, March 20, 1868.

ridiculous characters, such as Lebedev. It was only when he felt very strongly about a subject he knew would not arouse violent criticism in Russia that he did not hesitate to make his hero the exponent of his own ideas, as he did in *The Idiot*, in which Prince Myshkin, quite contrary to his character, appears as a violent detractor of the Catholic Church. In his correspondence Dostoevsky was not as reticent, especially when writing to such pillars of conservatism as Maykov and Strakhov. And yet even there he sometimes felt uneasily that he was overdoing things. Thus, in his letter to Maykov from Florence,[30] in discussing Maykov's poem on the capture of Constantinople by Mahomet II, he proceeded to give his own dramatic version of it. He himself, he pointed out, would not have hesitated to treat it as a part of *Russian* history. He would have related "the whole of that catastrophe in a naïve and compact story: the Turks besiege Constantinople; the last night before the storming of the city, which took place at dawn; the last Emperor walks through the palace ('The king walks with large steps')—he is going to pray before the icon of the Vlakhern Virgin; the prayer; the storming of the city, the fighting; the Sultan enters Constantinople with a bloodstained saber; at the behest of the Sultan they look for the Emperor's body in a pile of dead bodies, they recognize him by the eagles embroidered on his shoes; St. Sofia, the trembling patriarch, the last mass; the Sultan, without dismounting, gallops over the steps into the cathedral (*historique*), reaching the middle of the cathedral, he pulls up his horse in confusion, looks round in consternation and dismay and utters the words: 'This is a house of prayer for Allah!'; then the icons and the communion table are thrown out, the altar is smashed, the mosque is established, the emperor's body is buried, while in the Russian Empire the last Paleologue princess arrives with the two-headed eagle instead of a dowry; a Russian wedding; Prince Ivan III in his wooden cottage instead of a palace, and into this wooden cottage passes the great idea of the significance of Russia as the head of the Greek Orthodox Church and the first stone is laid of her future supremacy in the East, the circle of Russia's future is enlarged, the conception is born of Russia not only as a great state but of a whole new world, which is destined to revive Christianity by an all-Slav idea of the Orthodox faith and introduce a new conception to mankind, when the West will rot away, and it will rot away when the Pope finally perverts Christ and thereby gives birth to atheism in the polluted and defiled Western man. . . . I would have gone even further, till the time of the liberation of the peasants, till the time of our aristocrats scattered all over Europe with the last rubles obtained on credit, their wives fornicating with foreigners, the seminarists propagating atheism, the Russian counts turned into great humanitarians and world citizens and writing novels and criticisms, etc., etc. The Poles would occupy a great deal of space. Then I should have ended

[30] *Letters*, May 27, 1869.

with a fantastic picture: Russia in two hundred years' time and, next to it, Europe and her civilization fallen into darkness and decay and brutalized. I should not have stopped here before any fantasy. I expect," he concluded, "that at this moment you must of course think that I have gone mad. . . . I'm afraid I have got carried away in my excitement. . . ."

He may have got carried away, but those were the ideas he was going to enlarge on in his *Writer's Diary* and in his famous Pushkin speech a few months before his death. His chief idea he had already formulated in a letter to Strakhov on March 30, 1869: it was that the main point of Russia's mission consisted of "the revelation to the world of the Russian Christ, unknown to the world, whose origin is contained in our own native Orthodox faith. In my view, it is in this that the whole essence lies of our future great civilizing mission and even the resuscitation of Europe and the whole essence of our future mighty existence."

It was with these ideas in mind that Dostoevsky conceived an "enormous" novel under the title of *Atheism* for which, he wrote to Maykov,[31] he would first have to read a whole library of atheist, Catholic and Greek Orthodox writers. "It cannot be ready before two years," he continued, "even if my livelihood were completely guaranteed during my work. I have the chief character. A Russian who is a member of our social set, *elderly*, not very educated, but of quite a good social position, who *suddenly*, at his age, loses his belief in God. All his life he served in the Civil Service, never leaving the beaten track and without distinguishing himself before the age of forty-five. (A psychological explanation: profound feeling, a man, a Russian.) His loss of belief in God affects him enormously (actually, there is a great deal of action in the novel and the situations, too, are very varied). He moves about among the younger people trying to find out what they are thinking about as well as among the atheists, the Slavophiles and Europeans, the Russian fanatical sects, hermits and priests; falls rather badly under the influence of a Jesuit propagandist, a Pole; descends from him into the very depths by becoming a member of the flagellants, but in the end he finds Christ and the Russian soil, the Russian Christ and the Russian God. (For God's sake don't say anything about it to anyone; for me it means: to write this last novel even if it kills me—I'm going to say everything I have on my mind.) Oh, my friend," he concluded, "I have quite different ideas of realism from our realists and critics. My idealism is more real than theirs. . . . Their realism will never explain a hundredth part of the facts that have really happened. And with our idealism we have even predicted facts. My dear fellow, don't laugh at my vanity; I am like Paul: if I am not praised, I shall praise myself."

Substitute "idealism" for "creative imagination" and Dostoevsky is to a large extent right. The dichotomy in his nature, on which he was so

[31] *Letters*, December 23, 1868.

fond of expatiating towards the end of his life, can be best seen in the difference between his thinking as a creative artist and as an ordinary man. In the first capacity he was capable of a profundity of thought and foresight unequaled among his great contemporaries, while in his capacity as a political propagandist he allowed his prejudices and spite to blind him to the most obvious consequences of the evils perpetrated by the Tsarist regime. Even though he himself had been a victim of the Tsarist secret police, all he could say about them (in a letter to Maykov from Vevey)[32] was: "Oh, the scoundrels, don't they know that for the last three years the nihilists and the liberals have been bespattering me with mud and that I have broken with them, that I hate Poles and love my country? . . ." But the "scoundrels" were the agents of the Tsarist government!

Dostoevsky never wrote his "enormous" novel, though he did refer to it again to his niece Sofia on February 6, 1868, as one which, even if his *Idiot* was not a success (as, in effect, it was not), was bound to create a sensation because of its theme. Since he knew, however, that his niece did not share his extremist view he characteristically hastened to assure her that its title, *Atheism,* was not "an exposure of modern ideas, but something quite different. . . . Two or three characters have already taken shape in my head, including a Catholic priest, an enthusiast, something like St. Francis Xavier. . . ." Is this the first inkling of what was years later to become the Grand Inquisitor in *The Brothers Karamazov?* Be that as it may, his assertion that "it was something quite different" was probably just his way of adapting himself to the views of his correspondent.

A year later the "theme of atheism" was to assume the form of an even more "enormous" novel, which, too, was left unwritten, and perhaps for the same reason: the constant conflict in Dostoevsky's mind between the propagandist and creative artist. "A work of art," he wrote to Maykov,[33] "in my opinion, first makes its appearance in the mind of the writer like a diamond, completely ready-made in all its essential parts, and this is the first function of the writer as a creative artist, the first part of his work. If you wish, it is not even he who is the creator, but life, the mighty substance of life, the living essence of God who reveals His strength in the very diversity of creation, but mostly in the great heart of the poet, so that if the poet himself is not the creator, his soul is the mine in which the diamond originates and without which it cannot be found. It is after that that the second function of the poet follows, a function which is not so profound and mysterious, namely, having obtained the diamond, to set and mount it. Here the poet is only a jeweler." Unfortunately, neither *Atheism* nor its successor, *The Life of a Great Sinner*, sprang out of the mind of Dostoevsky the "poet"—and no amount

[32] *Letters,* August 19, 1868.
[33] *Letters,* May 27, 1869.

of "setting" or "mounting" would make them into works of art or "poems," as, following Gogol's nomenclature, he called his novels.

IX

Dostoevsky and his wife left Florence at the beginning of August 1869, but did not return to Russia till two years later, in July 1871. The reason Dostoevsky invariably gave for his reluctance to return to Russia, although he repeatedly claimed that he found it impossible to write abroad, was that he was afraid his creditors would put him in jail. But by the time he returned, his debts had increased from 3,000 to 4,000 rubles, his furniture and valuables had been sold at public auction, and his creditors were no less eager to get paid than when he had left Russia for his voluntary exile. The truth, of course, is that Anna, who had forced him to go abroad to get him away from his "family," refused to let him go back until she was quite sure of her power over him. It was not before the end of the fourth year of their wanderings in foreign lands that she began to suffer from homesickness. By that time she and Dostoevsky had "grown together" (as she expresses it in her reminiscences), that is to say, Dostoevsky, who in the past had only felt secure with his elder brother, now felt even more secure with his wife; besides, her unsophisticated faith, uninhibited by reason and untroubled by doubts, approached the ideal he now accepted as the highest expression of the spirit of the Russian common people—the illiterate peasants, embodied by him (not very flatteringly, if Anna could only have seen the connection) in the half-witted cripple Maria Lebyatkin, whom he even endowed with the supernatural gift of clairvoyance. Like Maria Lebyatkin, Anna had little control over her natural feelings and gave way to tears on the slightest provocation. In Venice, where they stopped for two days to admire the sights, she lost her fretted Swiss fan, and, Dostoevsky wrote to his niece Sofia from Dresden,[34] "Good Lord, how she cried!"

From Venice they went to Vienna, where they also stayed for two days, and from there to Prague, "where," Dostoevsky wrote to Maykov, "we nearly died of cold (compared to Florence) and where we could not find lodgings. Yes, that's true. We intended to spend the winter in Prague and not in Dresden, but we could not find furnished rooms there. *That's why we left.* They let only single rooms for bachelors. We should have had to buy furniture, hire servants, and sign a lease for 6 months." In Prague, according to Anna, Dostoevsky wished to get in touch with "the leaders of the Slav world," though, since he had so little regard for the Westernizing Czechs, it is difficult to see how he and the "Slav leaders" could possibly have got on together. However, he and Anna

[34] *Letters,* September 10, 1868.

moved on to Dresden, which they knew so well and where they arrived in August 1869. Anna's mother joined them there again, and they rented three rooms in the English quarter, 5 Victoria Street. It was there that Dostoevsky's second daughter, Lyubov (the future author of a completely unreliable and for the most part scandalous biography of her father, written, incidentally, in German), was born on September 14, 1869.

On December 21, 1869, he sent his niece Sofia this description of his daily routine in Dresden: "I get up at one o'clock in the afternoon because I do my work at night. I work from 3 to 5 P.M., then go for a half hour's walk to the post office and back through the Royal Gardens—always the same route. We dine at home and then I go out for another walk and back home through the Royal Gardens again. At home I have tea and at half past ten sit down to work and usually work till five o'clock in the morning. Then I go to bed and punctually on the stroke of six fall asleep. That is my life."

In his notebooks, Dostoevsky, contrary to his usual practice, put down a careful description of his epileptic seizures for the period 1869–1871. There was, he observed, an "unheard-of" increase in the number and the frequency of his fits, and he attributed it to the fact that his illness was entering into a new "malignant" phase. The aftereffects of the fits, such as "loss of memory, heaviness in the head and even headaches, unsettled nerves, nervous laughter and mystical sadness," also lasted much longer. It was in connection with such a fit occurring in the afternoon in a Homburg hotel in May 1870 that he incidentally mentions spending a whole week gambling at the casino there. Anna did not preserve any letters he wrote to her during that week. Indeed, she never mentions his visit there at all. She does mention his trip in April 1871 to Wiesbaden, from where, again losing heavily, he wrote to her a number of frantic, self-abasing letters. Anna states that it was at her own suggestion that he went there. She hoped that it would not only help "to dispel the gloomy thoughts that prevented him from concentrating on his work," but also that "the cruel torments" he would suffer on losing the money that would have provided for his wife and child would at last make him give up gambling. But, in fact, his trip to Homburg a year earlier, which Anna is so careful to conceal, should have proved to her that the thought of jeopardizing the existence of his wife and child would never have weaned him of his "mad passion." It was true he never gambled again, but that was due to quite a different reason: by the time he went abroad again, his affairs (thanks to Anna's resolute dealing with his creditors) had improved considerably, and, secondly, he went abroad (to Ems) for a cure. His bronchial condition, the first symptoms of which appeared as early as 1868, had by then deteriorated to such an extent that he had not the physical strength to indulge in what he described in his *Writer's Diary* as an exciting experience, "a kind of obsession" of "half hanging over an abyss so as to peer into its very depths and–in certain, though not frequent cases–flinging oneself headlong into it."

X

Dostoevsky spent the first three months of 1869 working on a story for the monthly *Zarya* (*Dawn*), "a story," he wrote in his notebook, "like one of Pushkin's (short, without explanations, psychologically outspoken and good-natured)." The story was never written, but its plan, as outlined on six pages of his notebook, contains the first draft of some of the chief characters and episodes of *The Devils*. It concerns an adopted daughter of a rich woman landowner, who promises to leave her 20,000 rubles in her will, but dies intestate. Her fortune passes to her next of kin, a former hussar officer, who had squandered his patrimony. When at last he arrives, he strikes everyone as very strange. He is suspicious and, like Dostoevsky's father, looks under the beds and behind cupboards at night, "mistrustful and sardonic." He dismisses the housekeeper, an old relative, and engages a pert and insolent woman in her place. She tells him that the adopted daughter is expecting "a reward," to which he replies enigmatically, "We'll see!" When he meets her, he is struck by her beauty, while she becomes aware of his injured vanity. There follows "a light, short, wittily sarcastic" conversation between them. "He is a *type*. His main characteristic: the need to confide in someone which peeps through his terrible misanthropy and his hostile, insulting distrustfulness. . . . But this need is compulsive and impatient, so that he suddenly throws himself at people and, of course, is treated with disdain; having been once treated like that, he never forgives, *never forgets anything*, suffers, turns it into a tragedy." A very revealing autobiographical portrait, in fact, confirmed, perhaps, by two references to Durov, the man who had stood beside him on the scaffold and whom he had heartily disliked for being so popular with the convicts in their Siberian prison. Thus, describing the adopted daughter's father, he writes: "Her father is an *elegant* man, a sponger when abroad, *Durov*."[35] At the house of the adopted daughter, the hero of the projected story meets "either the aesthetic Durov or a colonel of an artillery regiment. . . ." The hero of the story "gradually" falls in love with the young girl, promises to give her the 20,000 rubles, tells her the story of his life, "smiting his breast," puts her to the test, while she, having been taught by him not to trust anyone, "even eavesdrops." He is very jealous, "naïve in his suspicions and nobly proud; truthful, pure to a degree, but unable to open up his heart to be understood and loved, and suffers accordingly." (Another autobiographical characteristic.) He looks too

[35] Durov died in Poltava on December 6, 1869, in the house of Alexander Palm, another member of the "Durov" circle.

crudely upon the world, because he demands extreme purity from it and does not forgive anything, a Christian, but shows no Christian charity. "I forgive everything, but leave me alone, I want to retire to my own dark hole." At last she cannot stand his treatment of her any longer, and "there are tears between them, etc." The main thing, Dostoevsky emphasizes, is that "he is in love with her, but has never been able to trust her sufficiently to propose to her. Even her relatives tell him scandalous stories about her and he is so base as to listen to them, he goes to investigate all sorts of fantastic episodes, believes all sorts of dreadful and mean imputations against her and suffers acutely at his own meanness when he realizes that it is all nonsense. Confesses his sins. . . . Tells her. . . . Once she speaks to him about cowardice, about a slap in the face [the first reference to the scene between Shatov and Stavrogin in *The Devils*], he gets suspicious, falls silent and next suffering, darkness and coldness. Then they make it up. A great house in Moscow—the mistress of the house, a friend of the late woman landowner, the young girl's godmother, wants to see her. She goes to live with them. Varya and father." (Another autobiographical reference, the great house, no doubt the Kumanin house in Moscow, in which Varya, Dostoevsky's eldest sister, lived, after running away from her father.) In Moscow the young girl falls in love with a count "or seems to," she is disgracefully treated, the hero takes her part, gets slapped, fights a duel, but refuses to fire at his opponent (another episode worked out in great detail in *The Devils:* the duel between Stavrogin and Gaganov), but the girl refuses to marry him, "though she loves him to distraction (or he can't forgive her and she knows that). Generally, tragic but also continuously comic, gay, diversified and subtle. N.B. Also possibly thus: when she left him and went to live with the rich Moscow woman, he went to the young cripple [the twelve-year-old daughter of a commissionaire he had met earlier] intending to make love to her, a public scandal, he is again humiliated. [The first version of the cripple episode in *The Devils.*] Another possibility: the crippled girl, unable to bear the thought that he is still in love with the heroine and wants to go back to her, runs away from him, out of sheer hatred and jealousy (vain and egoistic). He chases after her in the streets at night. The crippled girl is dead, drove herself to death out of malice. Crippled from being unmercifully beaten. . . . During their happy moments he tells her marvelously gay and charming stories, in which he plays the hero, comicality and dichotomy. . . . N.B.—Either a charming type or a serious murderer out of a dark cellar. . . . N.B.—There is a princess (a high-society flirt) who had claims on him *before*. Now that he has got his inheritance, she goes to him. (That is what he is afraid of and is waiting for.) The princess arrives at the great house. *She* insults the young girl. *He* takes the young girl's part; his face is slapped. A duel. But the young girl is all the same unmasked with her lover. N.B.—Or so: *She* was attracted to him both by character and compassion. She refuses the young man's offer. The princess takes the young man under her protection. The young man spreads slanderous stories about her. Meanwhile the princess forces him to marry her *after all.* He gets to a point of offering the young girl money. She refuses to take it and runs back to her own house. The young man, who slandered her, drowns himself. The hero is in despair; but his brother persuades him to elope with her. They get married. He is happy that he need not now be afraid of the princess. . . . As soon as the woman landowner dies, the brother of her adopted daughter arrives unexpectedly—a drunken hussar. Counts the money, not enough. She brings him her last 100 rubles. He stares at her in surprise; true? true? you're giving me? Very well, I'll pay you back! And he pays her back (1) by being the hero's second and forcing him to fight and (2) when she confesses to him—I love him, first tells her then jeers at her: what a man to fall in love with, and then forces the hero to marry her by elopement. . . ."

This rough sketch is interesting as showing the biographical elements a Dostoevsky novel is usually composed of. Some of the chief characters of *The Devils* that it contains include Stavrogin, the cripple (Maria Lebyatkin) and the young girl whom Stavrogin, in the original version, rapes, both of whom for the time being lead a sort of Siamese-twins existence, and Dasha, the adopted daughter.

The sketch, containing so many variants of the plot of the story, must have raised all sorts of doubts in Dostoevsky's mind about his ability to get it ready in time for *Zarya*, from which he had already received a considerable advance. He, therefore, decided to write a different story for it, taking for its theme a situation he found in *Madame Bovary*, which Turgenev had recommended that he read at their meeting in Baden-Baden: a husband who after his wife's death discovers that she had been unfaithful to him and that his daughter was not his child at all. Unlike Charles Bovary, however, Dostoevsky's hero does not take to the bottle and die, but decides to revenge himself on his wife's lovers and, particularly, on Velchaninov, the father of Lisa, whom he had thought of as his daughter.

Unlike Dostoevsky's other novels of this period, this short novel, published under the title of *The Eternal Husband* in 1870 in the January and February issues of *Zarya*, has very little political significance, but it does contain a great deal of autobiographical material, such as a description of his stay in 1866 in Lyublino near his sister Vera's family, whom he depicted under the guise of the Zakhlebin family. He even introduced Pasha into it, as Alexander Lobov, the only extant portrait of his stepson: "A young man of nineteen or even a little less—so young did his handsome, self-confident, and impertinent face look. He was not badly dressed, at least everything on him fitted well; of over medium height; his thick, black, tousled hair and large, bold, dark eyes stood out particularly in his countenance. Only his snub nose was a little broad, but for that he would have been really handsome." Velchaninov himself suffered from Dostoevsky's bad memory for faces: "My husband," Anna writes in her reminiscences, "had such a bad memory for faces that he sometimes did not recognize my brother, of whom he was very fond. His bad memory made him many enemies, for people took his failure to recognize them as a personal affront. He even forgot most recent events, while he remembered all sorts of things that happened in the remote past, astonishing his relatives by the vividness of his reminiscences."

Dostoevsky began writing *The Eternal Husband* in August 1869. At the end of October "two thirds of it," he wrote to Maykov, "have already been written and finally copied." He spent three months writing it. "You cannot imagine," he wrote to his niece from Dresden,[36] "the hard work it involved, particularly as I hated this vile story from the very beginning." He hated the story for two reasons: first, Kashpiryov, the editor of *Zarya*, was so remiss in sending him the promised advances on it that once he had to pawn his trousers to raise two thaler for a telegram; secondly, he had meanwhile conceived the idea of a great novel in several independent parts, "to which," he wrote to his niece Sofia,[37] "I am entirely dedicated, although I cannot, indeed, I must not, begin writing it, because I am not ready for it; I have not thought it out properly and I lack material—I therefore have to force myself to invent new stories, which I find absolutely vile."

The idea was an elaboration of his proposed "huge" novel *Atheism*. The new title of the novel, he wrote to Maykov,[38] was going to be *The Life of a Great Sinner*, and the book would consist of five separate novels. The first, which he planned to write for *Zarya* (having, in fact, already obtained an advance of 900 rubles for it), would deal with events in the 1840's. "The chief question which will be discussed in all the sections," he wrote, "is the same as the one that has worried me, consciously and unconsciously, all my life—the existence of God. In the course of his life the hero is sometimes an atheist. The second novel will take place in a monastery. On this second novel I pin all my hopes. Perhaps they will realize at last that I have not been writing a lot of rubbish all my life. (I will confess to you alone: as my chief figure in this second novel I want to present Tikhon Zadonsky,[39] under a differ-

[36] *Letters*, December 26, 1869.

[37] *Letters*, September 10, 1869.

[38] *Letters*, April 6, 1870.

[39] Tikhon Zadonsky (1724–1783), son of a poor sexton, real name Timofey Kirilov, educated in Novgorod seminary, became rector of Tver seminary and in 1763 bishop of Voronezh, retired in 1767 for health reasons and after 1769 lived in Zadonsky monastery. Famed for his Christian meekness and forgiveness. Once engaged in an argument with an agnostic nobleman who slapped his face; Tikhon knelt before him

ent name, of course, but he, too, will be a bishop who spent his retirement in a monastery.) A thirteen-year-old boy, who had taken part in a criminal act, intelligent and corrupt (I know the type), the future hero of my novel, is put in a monastery by his parents (an educated set) to be educated. The wolf cub and nihilist of a boy makes friends with Tikhon (you know Tikhon's character and personality, don't you?). In the same monastery I shall put Chaadaev[40] (under a different name, of course). Why shouldn't Chaadaev be put in a monastery for several years? Suppose, that after his first article, for which doctors had to examine him every week, he could not restrain himself and, for instance, published a brochure in French abroad—he could then be put into a monastery for a year, couldn't he? Chaadaev may be visited by Belinsky for instance, as well as Granovsky,[41] and even Pushkin. (For it isn't really Chaadaev in my novel, but a type like him.) In the monastery is also Pavel the Prussian,[42] as well as Golyubov and the monk Parfeny.[43] (In this world I am an expert and have known the Russian monastery since childhood.) But the main thing is Tikhon and the boy. Please, don't tell anyone the contents of the second part. I never tell the themes of my novels to anyone, I feel ashamed somehow. . . . Perhaps I may be successful in creating a majestic, *positive*, holy figure. This is no Kostanjoglo [the idealized landowner in the second part of Gogol's *Dead Souls*] or the German (I forget his name) in *Oblomov*. . . . It is true, I shall not create anything but merely exhibit the real Tikhon, whom I have taken into my heart with enthusiasm long ago. If I am successful, I shall consider this alone an important achievement."

This novel, he wrote to Strakhov,[44] would be as long as Tolstoy's *War and Peace*, and "is the goal of my entire future literary career, for I cannot count on living and writing for more than another six or seven years." To his niece he wrote:[45] "Oh, Sonia, if you knew how difficult it is to be a writer, that is, keep at it for a long time. Believe me, I know for certain that if I had two or three years without financial worries, like

---

and asked his forgiveness. (In *The Brothers Karamazov* the elder Zossima kneels before Dmitry Karamazov.)

40 Chaadaev, Peter (1796–1856), philosopher and essayist, a Catholic convert, famous for his *Philosophic Letters* attacking the stagnation of Russian society, for which he was "officially" certified insane by Nicholas I and put under house arrest.

41 Granovsky, Timofey (1813–1855), a famous liberal professor of history at Moscow university, prototype of Stephan Verkhovensky in *The Devils*.

42 Pavel the Prussian (1821–1895), a former Old Believer, sent by his sect to Prussia to found a central office of the persecuted sectarians, founded a sectarian monastery near the Russian frontier, in 1868 went over to the Orthodox church and settled in Moscow.

43 Parfeny, died in 1868, a monk in Athos, author of pamphlets against sectarians and a book describing his voyages in Russia, Turkey and Palestine.

44 *Letters*, April 5, 1870.

45 *Letters*, July 14, 1870.

Turgenev, Goncharov and Tolstoy, I should have written something people would talk about 100 years hence! I am not boasting. . . . The idea of the novel is so good, so significant that I am full of admiration for it myself. But do you know what will happen? I know it beforehand: I shall write the novel in 8 or 9 months, make a hash of it and spoil it. Such a thing must be written in 2–3 years. The details may not be so bad, the characters will be sketched out—but roughly. There will be a lot of unevenness, unnecessary prolixity, thousands of beautiful things (I mean it literally) won't get into it at all, for inspiration depends a great deal on time. But I shall be sitting down to write it all the same. Isn't it torture deliberately to lift one's hands against oneself?"

XI

At the time Dostoevsky was engaged in writing quite a different novel for *The Russian Herald*, a novel which arose out of a political murder in Moscow and with which he hoped to settle his accounts with the left-wing revolutionists in Russia. "I am working on a fruitful idea," he wrote to Maykov,[46] "one of those ideas, which are quite sure to have an effect on the public. Something like *Crime and Punishment*, but much more urgent and much nearer to reality with a direct relation to an important problem of contemporary life. I shall finish it by the autumn; I am not in a particular hurry, though. I'll try to have it published in the autumn, too, but if not, it won't matter. I hope to get at least as much money for it as for *Crime and Punishment*. . . . I have never worked with such zest and with such ease," he concluded, a little prematurely, as he soon realized. A month later he wrote to Maykov:[47] "What I am writing now is a tendentious thing, I want to express myself more warmly. I can imagine the nihilists and Westerners screaming at me that I am a *reactionary!* But to hell with them, I am going to say exactly what I think. And to show you how perplexed I am, I need only say that I simply do not know whether it's going to be a success or not. One moment I imagine that it will work out very successfully and I shall get a lot of money for the second edition and another that it will be a failure. But I'd rather it was a complete failure than only a moderate success. You've dealt me a shrewd blow by your remark that you had noticed an 'overworked imagination' in *The Eternal Husband*. What anguish it cost me! However . . . without hoping for success it is impossible to work with ardor. And I am working with ardor. So I am hoping."

By August his hopes of success had gone and, as usual, he started the novel afresh. "I have now decided," he wrote to Kashpiryov,[48] "to destroy all that I have written, to alter the novel radically and, though

[46] *Letters*, February 24, 1870.
[47] *Letters*, April 6, 1870.
[48] *Letters*, August 15, 1870.

some of what I have written will be included in the new version, it will also be radically changed." Two months later he gave Strakhov a more detailed account of this radical change in his novel: "At first," he wrote,[49] "that is, at the end of last year I looked down upon this novel as something contrived and uninspired. Then true inspiration came—and suddenly I grew fond of the thing, took it up with enthusiasm and began crossing out what I'd already written. Then in the summer another change: a new character came forward with a claim to be the real *hero* of the novel, so that its former hero (an interesting character, but not really deserving of the name of hero) retired to the background. The new hero appealed to me so strongly that I started altering it again. And now, when I had already sent off the beginning to *The Russian Herald*, I've got cold feet: I am afraid that the theme is beyond my powers. I am seriously afraid of it. It worries me. And yet I haven't introduced the hero without rhyme or reason. I have just written down his entire part in my plan of the novel (my plan covers several printed folio pages) and it is written down in scenes, that is, action, and not in lengthy explanations. That is why I believe that it will be a living person, perhaps, even a *new* one; I hope, but I am afraid. It is high time I wrote something decent and serious. But, perhaps, I shall fail. Whatever happens, I must go on writing, for by these alterations I have lost a great deal of time and have written terribly little."

To Maykov he wrote two months later:[50] "Having thought of writing an enormous novel (with a political tendency—a preposterous thing for me) I imagined at first that I'd manage it easily. And what do you think happened? I wrote almost ten versions and realized that the theme *oblige* and therefore became overanxious about the novel. I've finished the first part with difficulty and have sent it off. I don't think one would guess from it what I am driving at or what direction the action will take. . . . The title of the novel is *The Devils* with an epigraph from the gospels. I want to express myself quite openly and without currying favor with the younger generation. . . ."

At first, therefore, Dostoevsky intended *The Devils* to be quite a separate work from *The Life of a Great Sinner*. Its genesis was political or "tendentious," as Dostoevsky called it. The idea of the novel owed its existence to the murder on November 21, 1869, of Ivanov, a student of the Moscow Agricultural College by Nechaev, the twenty-two-year-old leader of the revolutionary group to which he belonged. Nechaev, who had taken an active part in the student disturbances at Petersburg University in 1868 and 1869, had joined Bakunin in Geneva and helped him to publish a number of revolutionary pamphlets and two issues of *People's Retribution*. He told Bakunin that he was a member of a non-existent revolutionary Central Executive Committee. Supplied by Bakunin

[49] *Letters*, October 21, 1870.
[50] *Letters*, December 27, 1870.

with a membership card of the Russian Section of the World Revolutionary Union, Nechaev returned to Moscow where he organized a number of revolutionary groups consisting of only five members. Ivanov, who belonged to one of these groups, disobeyed Nechaev's orders, and Nechaev decided to make an example of him. He lured him to a secluded spot in the grounds of the college where, in the presence of the other members of the group, he strangled him, then shot him through the head and, with the help of the rest, threw his body into a pond. By the time Dostoevsky learned of the murder from the Russian papers, Nechaev had rejoined Bakunin in Geneva.

According to Anna, Dostoevsky obtained firsthand information about Ivanov and the locale of the murder from her brother, who was also a student at the Moscow Agricultural College and who had lived with them in Dresden for some time. But, as Dostoevsky explained to Katkov in his letter of October 20, 1870, he knew neither Nechaev nor Ivanov and had gathered the circumstances of the murder from the papers. "But even if I had known them," Dostoevsky wrote, "I should not have copied. All I am taking is the fact of the murder. My imagination may conjure up quite a different picture from what really happened and my Peter Verkhovensky may not be at all like Nechaev; but it seems to me that in my mind my imagination has created the person, or rather the type, who might have committed that murder. No doubt it's not inexpedient to depict such a man; but it was not him that I found interesting. In my view these miserable monstrosities are not worthy of being made into heroes of a work of literature. To my own astonishment, this character has turned out to be a semicomic character. And that's why though the whole of this incident occupies an important place in the novel, it is nonetheless only an accessory and the background for the creation of another character who can really be called the chief hero of the novel. This other character (Nikolai Stavrogin) is also a dark character, is also a villain. But it seems to me that this character is tragic, though I expect many people will say after reading the novel: 'What on earth is that?' I sat down to write a novel about this sort of person because I had wanted to portray him for a long time. In my view, this person is both Russian and typical. I shall be very sorry indeed if I am told that it is a stilted character. I took him from my heart. Of course, it is a character that appears seldom in all its typicalness, but it is a Russian character (of a well-known social set). . . ."

What Dostoevsky finally decided to do in altering his first scheme of the novel was to give up the idea of writing his series of novels dealing with the Life of a Great Sinner (an idea that would have taken him many more years that he first planned) and make the "great sinner," whose main characteristics he had already jotted down in his notebook, the chief character of *The Devils*. In this, too, he eventually failed, not only because Katkov refused to print the chapter describing the rape by

Stavrogin of an eleven-year-old girl, but because the whole scene of Stavrogin's visit to Tikhon fell short of his original plan and, indeed, is very weak dramatically compared with many another scene in the novel. Of the secondary characters (apart from those adumbrated in the extract of the story he had first intended for *Zarya*), the governor of the province, von Lembke, is particularly interesting as showing Dostoevsky's hostility to the German bureaucrats (all of them Lutherans) who played such an important part in the Tsarist administration—which perhaps explains the real reason for his hatred of Germans as a nation. In his notebook there is this revealing paragraph: "N.B.—Sh[atov] says: the German is the natural enemy of Russia; he who refuses to see that, sees nothing. What have they done for us that they are so proud of? They are lower than us in everything. Their coalition in Russia merely helps one of them to replace another. A conspiracy that goes back 150 years. Owing to certain circumstances [namely, that after Peter the Great the Tsarist family was itself of German origin] they were always on top. All of them third-raters occupying the highest offices of state and looking upon the Russians with asinine contempt. They have sucked out Russian strength. They are a real coalition, etc. . . ."

None of this was included in the novel, since it was much too dangerous a view to express. Indeed, he afterwards even eliminated from the serialized version of the novel such an innocuous-sounding phrase as "hundreds of Lembkes occupy important posts and everything seems to go well."

Dostoevsky was getting more and more deeply involved in the religious and political issues raised in the novel, and by the time he at last left for Russia in July 1871, the greater part of it was still unwritten.

XII

The most important international event during Dostoevsky's two last years in Dresden was the Franco-Prussian War. Of war he wrote to his niece from Dresden:[51] "I completely disagree with you. Without war man grows apathetic in comfort and riches, completely loses the faculty of generous thoughts and feelings and quite inevitably becomes brutalized and declines into barbarism. I am speaking of nations as a whole. Without suffering there can be no happiness. The ideal has to pass through the crucible of suffering as gold through fire. The kingdom of heaven is attained through hard work. This future new life and transformation are so important that suffering, however painful, is of no consequence. Don't you really see the hand of God in it? What does temporary suffering amount to? You write: 'First they wound and injure and afterwards they bandage and nurse.' Remember the greatest words in the world: I will have mercy and not sacrifice." The advocacy of war as "necessary,

[51] *Letters,* August 29, 1870.

for without it the world would collapse or at any rate be turned into slime, a sort of foul stink infected with festering wounds," was resumed by Dostoevsky at greater length five years later, in the second chapter of the April number of his *Writer's Diary*. But, as always when expressing some extremely reactionary view, he did not do so directly, but through the mouth of a fictitious friend of his, a "paradoxical fellow." It was not true, he claimed, that in war people went to kill each other; on the contrary, "they go to sacrifice their own lives. . . . A long peace produces cynicism, indifference and boredom . . . baseness of thought, depravity, and inertness of feelings. . . . Science and art, in particular, always develop during the first period of a war . . . which . . . invigorates and stimulates thought." As for the Christian view on war, it comes as no surprise to find that Dostoevsky, through his "paradoxical" friend, claims that "Christianity itself recognizes the fact of war and predicts that the sword 'shall abide' till the end of the world," which, he remarks, without, however, this time giving chapter and verse for it, "is extremely significant and striking. Oh, without a doubt, in the highest moral sense, it [*i.e.*, Christianity] repudiates war and demands brotherly love. I shall be the first to rejoice when the swords are beaten into plowshares, but the question is—when is it going to happen, and, is it worth while beating swords into plowshares? For the world as it exists today is . . . worse than war, so much so that it is immoral to support it, and it is no use preserving it and, indeed, shameful and vulgar to preserve it. . . . May I add that cowardice and dishonesty are most evident during a period of peace. Man is by nature terribly disposed to cowardice and shamelessness and he knows it himself only too well; that is why he so greatly thirsts for war and so greatly loves war: he feels a remedy in it. War," Dostoevsky's friend concludes paradoxically enough, "develops brotherly love and unites peoples, by making them respect one another. . . ."

A year later, in the April number of his *Writer's Diary*, on the eve of Russia's declaration of war on Turkey, when there was no longer any need for disguising his real views, he boldly declared that "we ourselves need war for our own salvation, for war will clear the air we breathe and in which we were in danger of suffocating."

As for Dostoevsky's attitude to the Franco-Prussian War, his dislike of Germans seemed for a moment to make him forget his own ideas about war. Thus he asked Maykov[52] to remember the text from the gospels " 'For all they that take the sword shall perish with the sword.' No," he went on, surprisingly, "whatever the sword conquers cannot endure. And after this they shout: 'Young Germany!' On the contrary, it is a people that has spent its strength, for after such a spirit, after such science, to put one's trust in the sword, bloodshed and violence, and not even to suspect that such a thing as spirit and triumph of spirit exists

[52] *Letters*, February 5, 1871.

and to laugh at it with the coarseness of a corporal! It is a dead people without a future. And if it is alive, then, believe me, after the first moments of intoxication, it will discover in itself a protest towards a better life and the sword will fall out of its hands by itself."

Five years later, recalling the events of 1870-1871 in his *Writer's Diary*, Dostoevsky contrasted what he had thought at the time to be the "civic" spirit of the German troops going to war and the "arrogance" of the same troops on their victorious return. In the first instance he could not help admiring them for their "remarkable military bearing" and their "firm resolution apparent in their every step and gesture. . . . I confess," he writes, "that at the time I was terrified for the French, although I was firmly convinced that they would thrash the Germans." But a year later he noticed that the boastfulness, so typical of the Germans, had assumed the no less national characteristic of arrogance. "Indeed the Germans had felt so triumphant that they began to insult the Russians. There were many Russians in Dresden at the time and many of them told me afterwards how even the German shopkeepers, when talking to a Russian customer, invariably put in the remark: 'Now that we've finished with the French, we're going to start on you!' "

As for the events in Paris, Dostoevsky had no doubt that the Commune was bound to fail. "Are you really one of those who maintain that the Paris Commune failed because it had not enough men, resources, etc.?" he wrote to Strakhov from Dresden.[53] "During the whole of the nineteenth century this movement was either dreaming of heaven on earth (beginning with the phalansteries) or, while almost about to put their ideas into practice (1848, 1849–till today), displayed a humiliating impotence to say anything positive. As a matter of fact, it is the same Rousseau all over again and the dream to recreate the world by reason and experiment (positivism). And yet one would think there are enough facts to show that their impotence to utter a new word is not an accident. They cut off heads–why? Only because it's the easiest thing to do. To say something is incomparably more difficult. They desire the happiness of mankind and remain with Rousseau's definitions of the word 'happiness,' that is, a fantasy unjustified even by experience. The fire of Paris is an enormity: 'We've failed, then let the world perish,' for the Commune is more important than the happiness of the world and of France. But to them (and to many others) this wild fury does not appear as an enormity, but as something *beautiful*. It is thus that the aesthetic idea about the future of mankind has grown turbid. The moral basis of society (taken from positivism) not only gives no results, but cannot even find a definition for itself and gets confused in its desires and ideals. Are there really not enough facts already in existence to show that this is not the way to organize society, that these are not the roads to happiness and that happiness does not come from such remedies, as it

[53] *Letters*, May 30, 1871.

was thought till now. From where does it come? Many books will be written about it, but the main thing will be overlooked." He concluded with the idea that had by now become an obsession with him: "In Western Europe they have lost Christ (this is the fault of the Catholic Church) and that is why the West is in decline—that is the only reason. The ideal has changed—this is so clear! And the fall of papal power next to the fall of the heads of the Romano-German world (France and others)—What a coincidence!" And after his furious attack on Belinsky, who, he surmised, would have regarded the Paris Commune as a mere deviation, he concluded his letter with an expression of satisfaction with Strakhov's last article on Turgenev—"the scoundrel who is artistically true to himself, for," he added, recalling the way Turgenev had treated him at the very beginning of his literary career, "I know him from the way he pitched into me." He was at that moment on the point of repaying his debt to Turgenev by introducing him into *The Devils* and even going so far as to suggest that Turgenev sympathized with the Russian terrorist movement. Turgenev's contribution to literature he dismissed as merely a "landowner's literature. It said," he wrote, "all it had to say (excellently so far as Tolstoy is concerned). But this typically landowners' word was the last. A *new* word to replace the landowners' does not exist as yet, and there was hardly time for it." There is, of course, a great deal of truth in that, and it is Dostoevsky who replaced "the landowners' word."

XIII

The two important events in Dostoevsky's private life before his return to Russia were the death of his aunt in Moscow on March 29, 1871, and his stepson's marriage. His aunt's death had been preceded by a false report received from Maykov, who added that, according to his informant, his aunt had left 40,000 rubles to a monastery. Dostoevsky's first reaction to the news was that his relatives in Petersburg must have been left some money in his aunt's will and that they did not want him to know about it. Anna, no doubt, was only too pleased to support that view, if, indeed, she was not the first to suggest it to him. "Emilia," he wrote to Maykov on August 26, 1869, "did not mention Anna in her last letter although I had written to her that Anna was again pregnant, which means that they are really angry with me." To his niece Sofia he wrote on September 10, 1869, that since he could testify that his aunt was not in her right mind at the time she made her will, he was ready to start an action in the courts for its annulment.

The truth only reached him in December in a letter from his brother Andrey, who told him that there was no truth in the story that their aunt had left 40,000 rubles to a monastery and that it was quite impossible to annul her will. His Moscow relatives, who stood to gain most from his aunt's will, accused him of being "a litigious moneygrubber." In reply, he pointed out, a little too emphatically as it proved, that he expected to receive nothing from his aunt's will since he had already received everything. He repeated it in a letter to Sofia.[54] "Everything I should have got under her will," he wrote, "I have, as you know, already received—the 10,000 rubles I spent on my brother's journal. I cannot, therefore, be called a robber of someone else's money eager to start an action to take it away from others. I repeat," he concluded, "I received *everything* in 1864 and have no claim whatever on her estate." This unfortunate admission was to be followed by a breach between him and Sofia, the only relative he corresponded with, when he did start an action for the annulment of his aunt's will in his favor.

The death of his aunt, incidentally, seems to have been preceded by another of his "prophetic" dreams, which only shows how eagerly he was waiting for the news of the old lady's death. "This is the dream I dreamed about three weeks before my aunt's death," he wrote to Sofia:[55] "I entered their Moscow drawing room; they were all sitting down and among them was also my mother. I was talking to my aunt when, suddenly, I noticed that the pendulum of the clock had stopped. I said it must have caught on something, it couldn't have stopped so suddenly like that. So I got up, walked up to the clock and gave it a push with a finger; it gave a couple of ticks and suddenly stopped again. Then I woke up and wrote down my dream. In the evening I told it to an acquaintance and she advised me to find out whether anything had really happened. And now it is true: my aunt is dead, the pendulum has stopped." And he added this postscript: "My aunt has been of enormous importance in our life, from our childhood to the age of 16 she did a great deal for our mental development, you knew her too late."

His reaction to Pasha's marriage was one of sadness rather than rejoicing. "Your Pasha is getting married," Maykov wrote to Dostoevsky. "He came to see me, beaming with happiness, well dressed, with a mustache just breaking through on his upper lip and an engagement ring on his finger. Getting married. He wants me to put in a word for him with you." To Pasha Dostoevsky wrote:[56] "The moral influence of a woman even on a man strong in spirit is not only beneficial and not only always necessary, but also natural. It is the second and final education of a man. . . . And one more thing, my friend: all the relationships must be based throughout life on an inward, mutual and reciprocal respect for one another. One thing I still feel for you," he concluded, "a sincere, warm and ever friendly sympathy and an inner

[54] *Letters,* September 10, 1870.
[55] *Letters,* April 10, 1871.
[56] *Letters,* January 18, 1871.

anxiety and love for you. . . . But all the same I am terrified for you. However, don't take me for a croaking raven. . . ."

His worst expectations were to be justified, but Pasha, too, knowing perfectly well how little "mutual respect" there had been between his mother and stepfather, could hardly have taken Dostoevsky's sermon seriously. But at the moment both of them were engaged in a correspondence about the publisher Stellovsky, who had published *Crime and Punishment* without the agreed payment of over 1,000 rubles to Dostoevsky. Pasha seems to have botched the business, and Dostoevsky was forced to engage a lawyer. Maykov, who was also roped in on the unequal fight with Stellovsky, advised Dostoevsky to return to Petersburg and approached the Literary Fund for a loan of one hundred rubles to cover their fares. But with the failure of *The Idiot* and the publication of *The Devils*, the liberal members of the Fund's committee were reluctant to advance even so small a sum to their former secretary. Dostoevsky was terribly upset when informed by Maykov of their refusal. "You see," he wrote to Maykov,[57] "how haughtily the Fund has treated your request for a loan for me, what guarantees they are demanding and in what an arrogant tone their reply is couched. If a nihilist had asked them, they would not have answered like that."

After the failure of his last attempt to win money at roulette a week later, he dispatched another begging letter to Katkov.

At the end of June, the advance of 1,000 rubles from Katkov arrived at last, and "without losing another day," Anna records, "we began winding up our affairs in Dresden (redeeming our pawned articles and payment of debts). Two days before our departure my husband called me in, gave me a few thick bundles of papers covered with writing and told me to burn them. Although we had discussed it earlier, I was so loath to destroy the manuscripts that I began begging my husband to take them with us. But he reminded me that at the Russian frontier he would most certainly be searched and that his papers would be taken away and that they would be lost as all his papers had been lost after his arrest in 1849. It was also possible that while our papers were being examined, we would be detained in Verzhbolovo, which might be dangerous in view of the approaching birth of our second baby. However sorry I was to part with the manuscripts, I had to give in to my husband's persistent arguments. We lit a fire in the grate and burned the papers. Thus were destroyed the manuscripts of *The Idiot* and *The Eternal Husband*. I was particularly sorry to lose that part of *The Devils* which was the original version of that tendentious novel. I could save only the notebooks of the above-mentioned novels and give them to my mother who was returning to Russia a few months later. She refused to

[57] *Letters*, April 18, 1871.

take a whole trunkful of manuscripts, for she was afraid that it might arouse suspicion and the papers be confiscated. . . . It happened exactly as we had expected: at the frontier all our trunks and bags were opened and their contents painstakingly examined and the papers and a bundle of books put aside. All the passengers had been allowed to leave the customs shed and only the three of us and a number of officials remained. The officials crowded round the table and were examining the books and the papers. We were beginning to be worried that we might miss the Petersburg train, when Lyuba came to our rescue. She got very hungry and began crying so loudly that the officials soon got tired of her cries and decided to let us go in peace and gave us back all our books and papers."

They returned to Petersburg on July 8, 1871, after an absence of exactly four years, three months and four days.

[12]

THE LAST YEARS: THE PROPHET

Unlike Prince Myshkin, Dostoevsky, who to a large extent shared his hero's simple-heartedness ("The only thing I can boast about," he wrote to his wife), arrived in Petersburg after a long absence abroad, not on a cold November morning, but on a hot and sunny day of July. For two days he stopped at a hotel with his wife and little daughter (they could not afford to stay there longer) and then moved to two furnished rooms on the third floor of 3 Yekaterinhof Avenue, which they chose because it was not far from Yusupov Park, where they could take Lyuba, or Lilla, as they called their little daughter, for a walk on a hot day. On July 18 Anna gave birth to her third child, a boy named Fyodor after his father. Their financial position was desperate. "On their return from abroad," Maria Stoyunin, a schoolfriend of Anna's, writes in her reminiscences, "the Dostoevskys were for a long time in dire straits. They were forced to pawn their things and at times they were positively destitute." To make things worse, Dostoevsky caught a cold and, he wrote to his Moscow niece on August 9, 1871, was rather seriously ill. Fortunately, the meeting between Anna and Dostoevsky's Petersburg "relatives," which she had dreaded so much, went off peacefully. Emilia's grown-up children were now able to support her, and, as Anna remarks, she got used to the idea that Dostoevsky had a family of his own and could help her only "in a case of emergency." Pasha was a more difficult problem: he still clung to the idea that his "father" was "obliged" to support him and his family, but Anna liked his wife and, feeling sorry for her, was not anxious to make trouble between Pasha and his stepfather. The situation became a little more strained when, after receiving another small advance from Katkov, they decided to move to an unfurnished flat (Anna, anticipating a practice so widespread today, having obtained the furniture for it on a hire-purchase agreement). Having got the furniture, she set about looking for a flat. Pasha volunteered to help her and, to her astonishment, told her the same evening that he had found an excellent flat of eight rooms for only a hundred rubles a month.

"What do we want such a large flat for?" she asked.

"Large? It isn't large at all," he replied. "There will be a drawing room, study, bedroom and children's room for you and a drawing room, bedroom and study for us, while we shall share the dining room."

"You're not counting on living with us?" Anna asked, "amazed," as she writes, "at his arrogance."

"Why, of course," Pasha replied. "You see, I told my wife that when father returned we should all live together."

Anna, for whom the four years of independent life had not passed in vain, had no hesitation in making it clear to him that under no circumstances would she agree to share a flat with him. Pasha, as usual, was rude to her (he had, as Dostoevsky wrote to him six years later, a nasty habit of "laughing insolently in a person's face"), but, when he complained to Dostoevsky, he was curtly told that Anna had the last word in their domestic affairs.

But this rebuff did not shake Pasha's firm conviction, for which Dostoevsky himself was to a large extent responsible, that he had a right to his stepfather's financial support.

"Well, how's father?" he would ask Anna whenever he came for more money. "I'd like to have a talk to him. I simply must have forty rubles."

"But you know Katkov hasn't sent us any money," Anna would object. "We have no money. I had to pawn my brooch today for twenty-five rubles. Look, here's the ticket."

"Well, pawn something else."

"But I've nothing more to pawn!"

"I'm afraid there's something I have to buy."

"Wait till we get some money."

"I'm sorry, I can't wait."

"But I have no money!"

"What do I care? Get it from somewhere."

His impudence paid off: he walked off with fifteen rubles, leaving Anna (so she claims) with only five rubles and wondering what else she could pawn. But for this, too, Dostoevsky was largely to blame. He was fond of his Khlestakov-stepson, as he called Pasha in a letter to his niece.[1] Six months later he wrote to Anna, who was living with their children in Staraya Russa at the time, from Petersburg, that he had been to see Pasha and found him "terribly funny in the bosom of his family." Pasha had a little daughter—"poor little thing, so thin and so pretty," Dostoevsky wrote in the same letter. "I was so sorry for her."

Two years later, however, he warned Pasha that he was sending him thirty rubles for the last time, as he could no longer support him.

[1] *Letters*, January 31, 1872.

"Did it never occur to you," he wrote, "that I might lost patience at last?" Pasha never could keep his jobs longer than a few months, and in January 1876, Dostoevsky, after sending him another thirty rubles, pointed out to him that he was taking that money away from his own "unhappy" children. "I know," he wrote, "that I shall soon be dead and that when they are left alone not a single hand will give them a farthing. When your mother was dying," he concluded, "she said to me: Don't desert Pasha. I did not desert you till now, but you are almost thirty and it is not I but you who are to blame for your circumstances. I am afraid I am no longer in a position to support you. . . . I want you to know that." A year later he wrote to Pasha: "I warn you that I shall never again ask anyone for a job for you. Your self-conceit is quite astonishing. You have a much higher opinion of yourself than is warranted by your previous occupations or by your education." A year and a half later the rift between them had widened so much that Dostoevsky addressed him (on August 22, 1878) formally as if he were a complete stranger: "Believe me, sir, that you will find it extremely disadvantageous for yourself if I choose a certain way of obtaining satisfaction. . . ."

But if Pasha, as well as Dostoevsky's youngest brother, Nikolai, a hopeless dipsomaniac who had also to be financially supported, were a constant source of annoyance to him, Anna herself, contrary to the impression she tries to convey in her reminiscences, was not an unmixed blessing, either. Her efforts to bring some order into her husband's chaotic finances—her negotiations with his creditors, her attempts to act as publisher of his novels beginning with the publication of *The Devils* in January 1873, or, towards the end of his life, to go into the bookselling business under the firm of Fyodor Dostoevsky—were never very successful, not at least to the extent of freeing Dostoevsky from relying on his advances to make ends meet. Indeed, when in 1877, that is, three years before Dostoevsky's death, they decided to buy the house in Staraya Russa, the health resort near Lake Ilmen, where they had been spending the summers since 1872, they could not raise the astonishingly low price of 1,000 rubles for which it was being sold, and had to borrow the money from Anna's brother, who was only repaid a year after Dostoevsky's death.

Nor was she particularly successful as a housewife. Her school friend, Maria Stoyunin, records that she did not even look after her children properly. "Their clothes," she writes, "were in holes and their heads unclean." In his letters Dostoevsky had constantly to beg her to take proper care of their children as well as to show some respect for their old nanny, who, he had to remind her, was "such a frail old woman." Writing to her from Ems,[2] where he was undergoing a cure for his lung

[2] *Letters*, June 16, 1874.

condition (emphysema), he cautiously drew her attention to her "little faults," such as her "absent-mindedness, negligence and—untidiness." Five years later, again in a letter from Ems,[3] he was more outspoken. "You have very many faults," he wrote, "mistrust of me, inability to appreciate me and my love of you and nerves—nerves, nerves, no better than mine." He also complained of her secretiveness. "Again secrets," he wrote to her,[4] only fifteen months before his death, "again your everlasting secrets." Anna refers to these complaints in her reminiscences and explains that she could not always be frank with Dostoevsky because "he had to be left in peace to enable him to carry on with his work," but it was not while he was working that he made those complaints.

The remarkable thing about Dostoevsky's letters to his wife is that he never discussed with her any of the ideas that occupied his mind at the time he was writing his great novels, ideas that he discussed freely not only with Strakhov, Maykov and Pobedonostsev, the powerful reactionary statesman and tutor to the future Alexander III who became one of his closest friends, but also with all sorts of correspondents who showed an interest in them. Anna herself relates how Dostoevsky once tried to explain to her the meaning of his Legend of the Grand Inquisitor and how he had to give it up in the end because of her utter inability to follow his argument. But her inability to take an intelligent interest in his work did not really matter in view of her primitive religiosity and superstitiousness, which was perhaps one of her strongest bonds with Dostoevsky; for his lapse into an extremely chauvinistic kind of religion was accompanied by a relapse into the superstitions of his childhood days. His letters to Anna are full of descriptions of dreams in whose vaticinal powers he firmly believed. For instance, in one letter[5] he told her how "among other nightmares" he dreamed that their two-year-old son Fedya "climbed onto the window sill and fell down from the fourth story into the street. As he fell, turning over and over, I closed my eyes and shouted in despair, Good-by, Fedya! and immediately woke up. Write to me at once about Fedya, whether anything happened to him on the night of Saturday to Sunday. For I believe in second sight, particularly as it is a fact, and I shan't rest till I receive your letter." Six years later, on receiving the news of his sister-in-law's death, he wrote to Anna: "The news of poor Emilia Fyodorovna's death has greatly saddened me. . . . With her death an end has come to everything that still remains of my brother's memory for me on earth. . . . Imagine, I had a dream on the 5th (I wrote down the date) in which I saw my brother lying on a bed, bleeding profusely from a cut vein in the neck. In dismay, I was about to run for a doctor but was stopped by the

[3] *Letters*, August 16, 1879.

[4] *Letters*, September 5, 1879.

[5] *Letters*, July 23, 1873.

thought that he would bleed to death before the doctor's arrival. A strange dream, and what is so strange is that it happened on August 5th, the day before her death."[6]

He was also a firm believer in fortunetelling. Vsevolod Solovyov reports him as saying after a visit to a popular fortuneteller in 1878: "You see, it is quite impossible not to believe in the predictions of fortunetellers. Not only has a great deal of it been preserved in history, but every man knows it for a fact from his own experience. Everyone believes in it and if people do not acknowledge it, it is only out of cowardice from which we all suffer so much. A man believes in it perhaps even more than he should, but at the same time he laughs at and derides the honest man who declares frankly that he believes in it."

Anna was also, needless to say, a great believer in dreams. As for second sight, she claimed to possess it herself. "I knew," she writes, "that I possessed the faculty of expressing some supposition, of making some remark (quite by accident, just as though it escaped from me involuntarily in conversation) which came to pass almost literally. Usually this faculty of mine became apparent when my nerves were highly strung. . . . I read somewhere that the faculty of 'clairvoyance' is habitual with northern women, that is, Norwegians and Swedes. Do I owe this faculty of mine, which has caused me not a few unpleasant moments, to the fact that my mother is by origin a Swede?"

But, though of Swedish origin, she also shared Dostoevsky's hatred of foreigners, especially Germans, as well as of her own Polish and Jewish compatriots. Strangely enough, the more secure Dostoevsky felt with her, the less secure she felt with him. By the time they had returned from abroad she was no longer afraid of his relatives, but the specter of his past continued to haunt her. Besides, the inequality in their mental outlook made her distrust him, while the inequality in their ages made him distrust her. It would seem that about three or four years after their return to Russia she confessed to him that she had fallen in love with some man. "I was jealous only once," he wrote to her from Ems,[7] "and that was of . . . [two and a half lines inked out by Anna] with whom you told me you had fallen in love two years ago." Her distrust of him came to the surface several times during their sojourn abroad, notably when she opened Pauline Suslov's letters to him. No doubt, the readiness with which she agreed to let him gamble, although she realized very well that he was bound to lose in the end, was also an expression of her desire to exert a hold over him, for of course she knew that he would come crawling back to her. It was quite in character that in Russia, too, she should contrive something to undermine his sense of security in order to reassert her hold over him. Thus on May 18, 1876,

[6] *Letters*, August 25, 1879.
[7] *Letters*, July 3, 1876.

she played a "joke" on him, as she relates in the chapter of her reminiscences entitled "My Joke." Disguising her handwriting, she copied out an anonymous letter from a novel serialized in *Home Annals* in which the hero is warned of his wife's infidelity and told to ask her to show him the locket she was wearing "over her heart." At the time when this "mischievous" thought occurred to her, she states as an excuse, she had been "in a most good-humored frame of mind," her children having just recovered from scarlet fever and Dostoevsky himself having had no epileptic fits for some time. But it does not seem to have been a mere coincidence that just at that time Dostoevsky had entered into a correspondence with two women, one of them a young girl, both of whom were great admirers of his and both of whom he had been seeing at his office (he had just begun publishing his *Writer's Diary*). Is it not possible that just as ten years earlier she had opened Pauline Suslov's letters because she had got into a panic, so now she had got into a panic and copied out the anonymous letter so as to shake Dostoevsky out of his sense of security and bring him crawling back to her? Be that as it may, she posted the letter in the morning, knowing that it would be delivered before he arrived home from his office. Dostoevsky arrived rather late that afternoon and went straight to his study. Anna waited till he had read the letter. Then she went into the study and sat down at her usual place at his writing desk and, she records, "purposely" asked him some questions which he would ordinarily have answered at once. But he kept pacing the room "with heavy steps" in gloomy silence. She asked him why he looked so gloomy.

"Are you wearing your locket?" he asked, in a strangled voice.

"Yes."

"Show it to me."

"Why?" she asked innocently. "Haven't you seen it many times before?"

"Give it me!" he roared and, without waiting for her to unbutton the collar of her blouse, rushed up to her and tore the thin chain he had bought her himself in Venice from her neck. The locket, after he had managed to open it with his trembling fingers, had two pictures in it: his own and their son's. He glared stupidly at them for some time without uttering a word.

"Well, what did you find there?" Anna asked, and she told him about copying out the anonymous letter.

"But why did you send it to me?" he asked, still bewildered.

"I did it just for a joke," she replied.

"A joke? But think what I've been through during the last half hour!"

Dostoevsky, Anna writes, was thoroughly ashamed of his fit of anger, while she herself was "infinitely happy" that her "stupid joke" had ended so "satisfactorily." She vowed never to play such a joke on him again, "having found out by experience that in moments of jealousy my dear husband can be driven into a state bordering almost on insanity." But only two months later she forgot all about her "vow" and played a similar joke on her "dear husband" again. It is true that at the time he was at a safe distance, undergoing his cure at Ems. He had been to see the doctor (he wrote to Anna on the second day of his arrival), who had found an improvement in the upper parts of his chest, "though, on the other hand, below the right nipple under the fifth rib, where I had a pain sometimes last winter and where Dr. Botkin had eleven years ago diagnosed the beginning of serious trouble —that spot has grown worse and maybe very much so. Then at my urgent request he said that death was still far off and that I shall live for a long time yet, but that, of course, in view of the Petersburg climate I should have to take precautions, etc., etc."

Having received this reassuring news, Anna felt confident enough to add the following postscript in her reply: "My dear, whom do you think I met yesterday? Him!!! Guess who and be jealous! Details in my next letter." Dostoevsky guessed that the man she had met was the very man she had told him she had fallen in love with a year or two earlier. In her next letter, though, Anna explained that it was the man who had asked her to marry him before she met Dostoevsky. But Dostoevsky did not believe her. He had noticed that her handwriting in the postscript was different and concluded that she must have gone out before adding it and, excited by the unexpected meeting, dashed off the postscript "in a trembling hand." It never occurred to him that Anna might have invented the whole thing and purposely faked her excitement so as to arouse his jealousy as she had done only two months earlier. "You know perfectly well," he wrote back, "that I was never jealous of N——v, but you have written—Guess who and be jealous. I simply explain it as follows: you met the man, the good dancer who, you said, resembled me, you were carried away, your heart gave a flutter (which is very charming because it is so innocent and gay), and just to tease papa you wrote: Guess who and be jealous. Having sent the letter off, you changed your mind, felt sorry for papa who, as you thought, might be jealous, and so you wrote about N——v. I expect you probably met him too in the Arcade and now he has come in useful as an excuse. . . . I cannot help drawing this conclusion," he went on, "but I cannot help feeling unhappy all the same that you should deprive me of your confidence, because it is a bad sign. . . ." And, as Anna had anticipated, the fear for his security made him crawl back to her in the humiliating fashion that was so characteristic of him and that gave her the glowing feeling of having him completely in her power. "Don't be too hard on me, Anna," he pleaded. "Please, don't forget me, Anna, you who are my ideal, my divinity. Don't forget me. I adore every atom of your body and your soul and I kiss all of you, *all*, because it is mine, *mine!* Do tell me all the details (though I know that you won't tell me all). . . . Anna, my divinity, don't do anything to hurt me. . . . I kiss you again, I kiss you every minute and even your letter, that same letter, I kissed fifty times. . . ."

She was deeply touched by his letter and, regretting the way she had made him suffer, wrote back: "I was so touched by your last letter that I nearly burst into tears. I am so happy and so grateful to you for your letter. My dear, I am terribly proud of your love, but I often think that I do not deserve such a love. I am such an ordinary woman, so mediocre, full of petty caprices and demands, who perhaps has only one merit of loving the four of you [her son Alexey had been born on August 10, 1875] sincerely and wholeheartedly. . . . I have always told you that you are my sun, that you are on a mountain and I am lying below and only worshiping. . . . If only you knew how sorry I was for some of the stupid things I said and how worried I am about it. . . . And I have also to get rid of my stupid jealousy which sometimes begins to torment me. . . . I am surprised at you, Fedya," she concluded, "how can you love an old and ugly woman like me. . . ."

But three years later, with the increasing inroads his illness was making on his health and his virility, he still felt—at the age of 58—that he could not trust her, who was only 32—"in the prime of a woman's life," as he wrote to her. He was shocked to discover that for a time he had been transformed into "a mummy," and the feeling of his own incapacity made him more outspoken than ever before in his passionate avowels of love, which forced Anna to ink out many lines in his letters that must have shocked even her. "I am drinking coffee and tea and thinking only of you," he wrote to her from Ems,[8] "not only in this but in every sense. Now, Anna, I am convinced I not only love you but am in love with you and you are my only mistress—and that after twelve years. I mean it in the most *earthy* sense in spite of the fact that you, too, have of course grown older since I first knew you as a girl of nineteen. But now I like you in that sense *incomparably* more than before. It may sound improbable, but it is so. [Five lines inked out.] . . . this alone irresistibly attracts a man like me. If only you were frank with me, it would be perfection. I kiss you every moment in my dreams, *every moment, all of you,* without tearing my lips away from your body. I especially love that about which it is written: And with this delightful thing he was enchanted and enraptured. This thing I kiss every moment and I intend to go on kissing it all my life. Anna, darling, in this sense I can never and under no circumstances lag behind you, for it is not only the love-making itself, but the readiness, the fascination, the intimacy with which you make love that I find so delightful. . . ." Three days later, he concluded his letter: "You write that you have still got the bruise from the last

[8] *Letters,* August 16, 1879.

time I pinched you, but I pinched you from love, and as my love has grown much stronger here I promise to pinch you in future too till I am no longer in love with you. . . . In my thoughts I kiss you every minute and I also kiss 'the thing with which I am enchanted and enraptured.' Oh, how I kiss it, how I kiss it! Anna, don't say I am being coarse. I can't help it. I am like that and it is no use blaming me. You are yourself . . . [a word inked out], my darling, and all I hope is that you will understand it to the utmost degree and refinement. Au revoir, my angel, I kiss your darling toes and then your darling lips. . . . To me you are beautiful, and indeed you are beautiful to everybody, to everybody you are beautiful. . . ."

A week before he left Ems for the last time he wrote:[9] "You write, 'Love me,' but don't I love you? Why, my constant delight in you (which is, moreover, growing stronger every year) could have proved many things to you, but either you don't want to understand it or you are quite unable to understand it because of your inexperience. Why, show me any other marriage where this sort of thing has been felt as strongly after twelve years as in our married life. And my delight and admiration are inexhaustible. You will say it is only one side and the coarsest one at that. No, it is not, for everything, in fact, depends on it. It is this you don't want to understand. To conclude this tirade, I bear witness that I long to kiss every little toe of your feet and I shall do it, too. You'll see. You write: And what if someone reads our letters? Of course, I realize that, but let him read. Let them all envy us."

Dostoevsky's second marriage, painted by his wife in such roseate hues as based on mutual trust and respect, was, it appears on closer examination, not as happy as she would have liked her readers to believe. A young girl of a typically middle-class family, with little knowledge and even less understanding of the terrible social and political events that were taking place around her, married to a middle-aged genius, an epileptic, burdened with debt and doomed to a life of perpetual penury, she faced life with him bravely enough. But as the years passed and he grew more and more to depend on her, the fundamental incompatibility of their characters and mental make-up made itself more and more felt. The mystery, which Anna found so difficult to explain, namely, that Dostoevsky should, as she puts it, "not only love and respect" her, but also "worship" her as though she were "a special kind of human being specially created for him," was no mystery at all. The very fact that he "worshiped" her in such a humiliating fashion shows that she was a perfect foil for his deep-seated masochism, but not that at heart he felt any particular respect for her. The sexual side of their marriage (as he explained to her in the above extract from his letters) formed the strongest bond between them. Everything, as he declared, depended on it.

[9] *Letters*, August 28, 1879.

"Love," he wrote in what is certainly one of the most revealing autobiographical passages in his *Notes from a Dark Cellar*, "is a mystery that God alone comprehends and should be hidden from all eyes whatever form it takes. It is much better and more holy because of it."

II

On July 1, 1871, a week before Dostoevsky's return from abroad, the Petersburg Criminal Court began hearing the case against the four men who, with Sergey Nechaev, had murdered the student Ivanov in Moscow and their alleged fellow conspirators. Dostoevsky followed the trial closely for the two months it lasted. He incorporated the salient facts (including the widely publicized *Catechism of a Revolutionary*, laying down a policy of ruthless political terror, generally believed to have been drawn up by Bakunin jointly with Nechaev) in the second and third parts of *The Devils*. Two years later, after the arrest of Nechaev in Zurich and his incarceration in the Peter and Paul Fortress, Dostoevsky was anxious to point out that the character of *his* Nechaev did not resemble the real Nachaev. "All I wished to do," he wrote in his *Writer's Diary*, "was to supply the answer to the question how in our present transitory society not a particular Nechaev, but people like him are possible, and how it happens that such people succeed in getting so many followers." Those followers, he claimed, were not good-for-nothing scoundrels. "I myself was an old Nechaev revolutionary," he wrote. "I, too, stood on the scaffold under sentence of death, and, let me assure you, I stood there in the company of educated men." He denied that so monstrous a murder as that of the student Ivanov could not have been committed by idealists. "Nechaev," he declared, "no doubt represented that murder as a political act which was useful for the triumph of their great cause at some future date. Otherwise it is impossible to understand how a few young men (whoever they were) would have agreed to commit so dark a deed. In my novel, *The Devils*, I attempted to bring to light the different motives which lead even the purest hearts to perpetrate so monstrous a crime. For the whole horror of the situation is that not only in our country but all over the world the most foul and most disgusting actions can be committed by people who are anything but scoundrels. Our trouble today is that a man may commit a most atrocious crime without considering himself to be and, indeed, without actually being a scoundrel."

At the end of 1871 the whole of part one of *The Devils* and seven chapters of part two had been published in *The Russian Herald*. However, Katkov having taken strong exception to the eighth chapter, entitled "At Tikhon's," which included Stavrogin's confession of the rape of a little girl, the publication of the remaining part of the novel (the end of part two and the whole of part three) was postponed for a whole year. This seriously affected Dostoevsky's always precarious financial position, particularly after a notice of his return to Russia in the Petersburg papers had set all his creditors on his trail. While he was rushing about from one creditor to another in an attempt to pacify them, he tried to think of a way of saving the substance of the banned chapter. "To correct the chapter," he wrote to his niece Sofia from Petersburg on February 4, 1872, after his return from Moscow, where he tried in vain to persuade Katkov to alter his decision, "is out of the question. But while driving to my creditors I thought of four different plans and worried myself to death for three weeks trying to make up my mind which of them to adopt. In the end I rejected them all and thought of a new change which may satisfy the chastity of the editorial offices of *The Russian Herald*. I am going to send them an ultimatum to that effect. If they will not agree, I don't know what I shall do." They did not agree, and in the end he had to give up the idea of the rape and the meeting between Stavrogin and the saintly Tikhon.

In the meantime the published chapters of *The Devils* attracted general attention. In liberal and left-wing circles Turgenev's view (expressed in a letter to the poet Yakov Polonsky in May 1871) that Dostoevsky was a madman was generally approved with all sorts of uncomplimentary variations on the same theme.[10] But he became the darling of the conservatives, including Prince Vladimir Meshchersky, the ultraconservative editor of the weekly *The Citizen*. It was at Prince Meshchersky's Wednesday at homes, in the winter of 1872, that Dostoevsky met Konstantin Pobedonostsev, at the time a member of the State Council. It was also at one of these at homes "over a cup of tea," Prince Meshchersky records, "that Dostoevsky turned to me with a kind of good-natured and at the same time inspired look on his face and said: 'Would you like me to be editor of *The Citizen?*' " Prince Meshchersky, naturally, jumped at the chance. A month later, in December 1872, the appointment was approved by the authorities. He was to receive an annual salary of 3,000 rubles and in addition was paid seven kopecks a line for every article he contributed to *The Citizen*. The real reason why Dostoevsky was so eager to undertake the editorship of the weekly was that it gave him the chance of starting his own *Writer's Diary*, which he was later to publish independently. He warned Meshchersky "not to indulge in daydreams," for his name would not increase the circulation of the journal. "The hatred of *The Citizen*," he said, "is stronger than my popularity. And, anyway, what sort of popularity do I enjoy? They have found me out, they have decided that I'm going against the stream. . . ."

[10] "Everyone in the literary world has turned away from me," Dostoevsky wrote to his wife as late as June 25, 1875, after the publication of the first chapters of his next novel, *A Raw Youth*, "but I shall not run after them. . . . I can see that my novel will be buried with all honors."

A description of Dostoevsky at the time he assumed the editorship of *The Citizen* was left by its secretary, V. T. Pochinkovskaya. "He was of medium height," she records, "and wore a fur coat and galoshes. He spoke in a low, muffled voice. A very tired or sick man, with a gloomy, haggard face, he seemed, as it were, all locked up inside—no movements, no gestures, only his thin, bloodless lips twitching nervously when he spoke. He walked unhurriedly, with short, measured steps, shifting heavily from one foot to another, as convicts do whose feet are fettered. . . . He was always smoking and I can still see his thin, pale hand with its stumpy fingers stubbing out a thick cigarette in a sardine tin, filled to the top with the ends of his 'cannons.' "

Vsevolod Solovyov, who, early in 1873, at the beginning of his own career as a historical novelist, wrote Dostoevsky a fan letter, described him as "a stooping figure of medium height, thin, but rather broad-shouldered, who looked much younger than his age (he was 52 at the time), with a sparse, fair beard, a high forehead, his soft hair grown thin, but showing no signs of having gone gray, with small, light-brown eyes and a face that was far from handsome and, at the first glance, peasant-like, with a thin skin and a pale, almost waxen, complexion."

Dostoevsky's study Solovyov described as "a rather poorly furnished corner room, with a small writing table at the window, on which were two candles, a few books and newspapers, a cheap, old inkstand and a tin box with tobacco and cigarette wrappers in it. Near the table stood a small cupboard and at the opposite wall a sofa, upholstered in cheap, reddish rep on which he slept. Another smaller table completed the entire furniture of the study. During the last eight years of his life, Dostoevsky moved to several flats, each one gloomier than the one before, and he always had an uncomfortable study in which there was hardly room to turn round. In the morning I usually found him sitting before his small writing table, having only just washed and combed his hair. He wore an old overcoat and was filling his thick cigarettes and smoking them one after another, sipping strong tea or, very often, strong coffee. Almost every time I came to see him I found him in a most gloomy frame of mind: his brows knit, his eyes shining, his lips tightly compressed. . . . Sometimes he would begin to dream aloud, passionately and rapturously, about the future of mankind and of Russia. Those dreams of his were quite often unrealizable and his conclusions paradoxical. But he spoke with such passion and conviction, with such inspiration and, at the same time, in so prophetic a voice, that I too sometimes became infected with his enthusiasm and eagerly followed his dreams and images. In the evening I usually found him after his late dinner and here, too, was repeated the morning scene of silence, both of us pretending to be unaware of each other's presence. But at that time he was usually much calmer and more cheerful. The same black coffee, the same brick-red tea, the same thick cigarettes which he kept lighting one after another. After a time he would walk up to the small cupboard, open it and take out all sorts of sweetmeats: a tin of royal plums, crystallized berries, raisins, grapes. He would put them all on the table and invite me very insistently to do justice to them. . . . At literary gatherings," Solovyov concludes, "he would appear looking hunched up, glaring gloomily at everybody and greeting them as though they had been his mortal enemies. But he would soon relax, start talking and almost always became the center of general attention."

Between the end of April and the middle of May 1872, Dostoevsky sat for his portrait to the painter Vassily Perov, a portrait that was commissioned by Peter Tretyakov for his great private collection (later to become Moscow's great picture gallery). It is by this rather idealized portrait that Dostoevsky is generally known.

Earlier he received the first request for the dramatization of one of his novels (*Crime and Punishment*), a request that he granted, with the following cautionary note equally applicable to all the subsequent dramatizations of his novels: "There is a kind of mystery, according to which an epic form of narrative can never find a correspondingly satisfactory dramatic form. I am even of the opinion that for each art form there exists a corresponding series of poetic ideas so that not one of these ideas can be expressed in a form that does not correspond to it."

From the very start of his editorship of *The Citizen*, Dostoevsky realized that the daily grind such work entailed was killing his own creative powers. Already in January 1873, he wrote to his niece Sofia that he cursed himself for his decision to undertake the editorship of a weekly journal. On July 12 he complained to Anna, who was again spending the summer with the children in Staraya Russa, that he seemed to be getting more and more "stupid" and that he was finding it very hard to do any writing. "Already a month ago," he wrote, "I began to notice the difference between the ease with which I did my writing in Dresden and the difficulty with which I do it here. I ascribe it to the continual petty worries and the rush and bother my editorial duties entail. They are so exhausting that I shall have to take a long rest after this damned year."

His relations with Prince Meshchersky were also getting strained. The prince was not much of a writer, and Dostoevsky had to edit and quite often rewrite his articles. On July 20 he told Anna that he had received a very "rude" telegram from Meshchersky and that he was going to give him so sharp an answer that "in future he will think twice before lecturing me." On August 13, he told her that his "penal servitude" was making him ill. The final rift between him and Meshchersky came at the beginning of November with his curt refusal to publish an article by the prince on the latest arrest of students following the discovery among them of revolutionary leaflets sent from Switzerland. "To destroy this evil," Meshchersky proposed that all students should be compelled to live in government-controlled hostels where they could be kept under constant police supervision. "I have my reputation as a writer to consider," Dostoevsky wrote to Meshchersky, "and, besides, I have children. I do not therefore intend to *ruin* myself. Your whole idea, anyway, is entirely repugnant to my convictions."

On top of it all, Dostoevsky had been fined twenty-five rubles and had had to serve a sentence of two days' imprisonment for an article by Meshchersky in which the prince, always eager for a scoop, quoted a remark made by the Emperor to the head of a Kirghiz delegation without having first obtained permission to publish it. His trial took place on June 11, 1873, but it was not till March 21, 1874, that the police came to fetch him to serve his sentence. He was taken to the guardhouse in the Haymarket, Anna records. "I found him in a good-humored mood," she writes. "He inquired after the children and asked me to get them some presents and tell them that he had gone to Moscow." Vsevolod Solovyov, who visited Dostoevsky on March 22, found him in a large and fairly clean room, at the other end of which was " a young man, badly dressed and with a colorless face. Dostoevsky sat at a small deal table, drinking tea, smoking his cigarettes and reading a book. He was glad to see me and embraced and kissed me." The book Dostoevsky was reading was Victor Hugo's *Les Misérables*. "What a good thing," he told Anna on his release, "they had locked me up, for otherwise I shouldn't have found the time to renew my old marvelous impressions of that great work."

Dostoevsky resigned his editorship of *The Citizen* at the beginning of 1874. The only permanent result of this ill-considered attempt to renew his journalistic activities was his close friendship with Pobedonostsev. By this time he fully shared Pobedonostsev's views that "absolute truth reposes only in religion" and that "it is only the common people [*i.e.*, the illiterate peasants] who intuitively understand that absolute truth cannot be perceived in any material way, or represented palpably, or defined by a number or measure, but that one must believe in it."

"We became close friends," Pobedonostsev wrote to the Slavophile poet Ivan Aksakov two days after Dostoevsky's death, "during his editorship of *The Citizen*, when, out of pity for his desperate position, I worked the whole summer together with him. I kept Saturday evenings specially free for him and he very often spent them with me. His Zossima, too, he conceived according to my suggestions and we had many heart-to-heart talks together."

Dostoevsky described one of his visits to Pobedonostsev on July 26, 1873, to Anna: "Yesterday Pobedonostsev arrived from abroad. He came to see me at the office, waited for me, but I was not there. I went to see him yesterday and stayed till midnight. He wrapped a rug round me and saw me off down three dark flights of stairs with a candle in his hand. On the Isle of Wight he had read my *Crime and Punishment* at the recommendation of an exalted personage [the future Alexander III, who was staying with Queen Victoria at the time] whom he had accompanied to England."

It was, no doubt, also at the instigation of Pobedonostsev that Dostoevsky sent a copy of *The Devils* to the heir to the throne in February 1873.

III

The issues of *A Writer's Diary* published in *The Citizen* reveal Dostoevsky's still-ambivalent attitude towards the Russian peasant. On the one hand, the peasant is depicted as an inhuman beast in the terrible description of the way a peasant had flogged and tortured his wife till she hanged herself, and, on the other, as a human being whose "only love is Christ whose image he loves to the point of suffering." But the really remarkable thing is his attempt to re-establish himself in the eyes of the liberal and left-wing writers whom he had alienated by *The Devils*. Belinsky, about whom only a short while ago he had not had a good word to say, now appeared as an exceedingly good-natured man who could enjoy a joke against himself and who "understood more profoundly than anyone that science and realism alone can create nothing except an anthill and certainly not a social 'harmony' in which man could live happily. He knew," Dostoevsky astonishingly admitted, "that moral principles must be the basis of everything." He complimented Herzen on being "a good husband and father." As for Chernyshevsky, who was still languishing in Siberia, he never met "a more gentle and kindhearted man."

He had still to placate Nekrasov, the left-wing poet and owner of the *Contemporary*, his archenemy, whom he had so delighted to attack in *Time* and *Epoch*, and to him he devoted a whole article in which he analyzed one of his poems and proclaimed it to be "marvelously good." Writing to Strakhov on April 5, 1870, from Dresden, while working on the first versions of *The Devils*, Dostoevsky had expressed his regret that Strakhov's articles attacking the "utilitarians" were "too mild." "For them," he declared, "one must write with a whip in one's hand." According to Pochinkovskaya, who was in close touch with some of the chief contributors of the *Contemporary*, it was Dostoevsky himself who hinted to her that he would not mind publishing his next book in that journal. Whether this is true or not, the fact remains that one April morning in 1874 Nekrasov appeared at Dostoevsky's flat and, to the great astonishment of Anna, asked to see her husband. Knowing that Dostoevsky had not met his "literary enemy" since his return from abroad, Anna was very curious to find out what Nekrasov had come about and began listening at the door of her husband's study. "To my great delight," Anna writes, "I heard Nekrasov inviting my husband to publish his next novel in his journal and offering to pay him 250 rubles for a folio page, for which my husband had received only 150 rubles so far."

Seeing their "modest interior," Anna added, Nekrasov probably thought that Dostoevsky would jump at the offer, but instead she heard him say: "I cannot give you a positive answer for two reasons: first, I have to get in touch with *The Russian Herald* to find out whether they are in need of a work of mine. . . . Katkov has always treated me fairly and it would be indelicate on my part if I were not to offer them the first refusal of my work. . . . I should also like to point out," Dostoevsky added, "that I always get an advance of two to three thousand rubles."

Nekrasov agreed to let him have such an advance.

"Secondly," Dostoevsky went on, "I must consult my wife about your offer. She's at home and I shall ask her at once."

Anna quickly left her listening post and rushed back to her room. When Dostoevsky came, she records, a "curious incident" occurred. Without waiting to hear what he had come for, she blurted out:

"Why ask me? Accept it, of course. Accept it at once!"

"Accept what?" Dostoevsky asked in surprise.

"Why," she replied, "Nekrasov's offer."

"How do you know about it?"

"I've been listening to your conversation. I was standing behind the door," she said, without for a moment realizing that she had been doing anything disgraceful.

"So you've been eavesdropping! Aren't you ashamed of yourself?" cried Dostoevsky sorrowfully.

"Ashamed? Why should I be ashamed? You have no secrets from me and you'd have told me all about it, anyhow. What does it matter if I did eavesdrop?"

Dostoevsky, Anna remarks, just threw up his hands in dismay and went back to his study. Anna immediately glued her ears to the door again.

"I have discussed it with my wife," she heard Dostoevsky say, "and she's very glad that my novel will be published in the *Contemporary*."

Nekrasov, obviously taken aback by Dostoevsky's insistence on consulting his wife, said: "I'd never have thought that you'd be under your wife's thumb!"

"What is so strange about that?" Dostoevsky retorted. "We live very amicably together and I let her deal with all my financial affairs, for I have faith in her business abilities. I had therefore to consult her on a matter of such importance to both of us."

"Yes, yes, of course," Nekrasov was quick to assent and changed the subject.

At the end of April Dostoevsky left for Moscow to see Katkov. But

Katkov, who had just bought the serial rights of Tolstoy's *Anna Karenina* for 20,000 rubles, could not afford to advance 2,000 rubles to Dostoevsky,[11] who consequently accepted Nekrasov's offer.

Dostoevsky spent the month of May with his family in Staraya Russa, and on June 4 he left for Petersburg to consult his doctors before his departure for Ems. His bronchial condition showed no improvement after treatment by compressed air, and they all advised him to try the Ems waters. His epileptic fits, too, were becoming more frequent. The notebook in which he put down his plans for his next novel, *A Raw Youth*, contains an account of his epileptic fits for 1873 and 1874, showing that while in 1873 he had six fits, he had nine fits in 1874.

On the way to Ems he stopped in Berlin. It was Sunday, and he went to the Royal Museum to see an exhibition of pictures by Wilhelm Kaulbach who had died that year. He found nothing but "cold allegory" in them. He thought Berlin, as during his former visits, a horribly boring city and the Germans "coarse and uncouth." On the way to Ems in the train, however, he was entranced by "the most fascinating view in the world of mountains, hills, castles, and cities like Marburg and Limburg." In Ems he found "a terrible crush of visitors from all over the world." He wanted to buy a hat, but found the goods in the shops "worse than in the Petersburg flea market." His nerves, he complained to his wife, were in a terrible state. He had been to see the doctor and was told that four weeks of the Ems waters would be sufficient. What worried him most was his novel. "If only I could begin writing my novel," he wrote to Anna, "or just get something started—to start is half the work. . . ." In his next letter he wrote that he did a lot of walking and in the evening went to concerts. "So far," he wrote, "I have been reading only Pushkin and every day I find something new in him. . . . Occasionally a sad thought comes into my head: what if I am no longer capable of writing? Still, we shall see."

He was meeting many Russians, including a forty-year-old headmistress and her beautiful fifteen-year-old daughter. "The mother," he wrote to Anna, "is the biggest fool on earth, a cosmopolitan and an atheist, a chatterbox and fond of arguing. I told her candidly that she was an intolerable person and did not understand a thing, laughingly, of course, and cautiously, but in all seriousness. We parted civilly but," he assured Anna, who might have wondered about the beautiful girl, "I shall never meet them again. At night, I even had a nightmare. . . ."

In a postscript he added, "Yesterday on the promenade I saw the

[11] "We are not thought of very highly, Anna," Dostoevsky wrote on December 20, 1874. "Yesterday I read in *The Citizen* that Leo Tolstoy had sold his novel to *The Russian Herald* for 500 rubles a printed folio page, that is, for 20,000 rubles. They could not make up their minds whether to offer me 250 rubles a page, but they paid Tolstoy 500 rubles without a moment's hesitation. They do not think much of me because I live by my work."

Emperor Wilhelm for the first time: a tall and imposing-looking old man. Here everyone (even the ladies) get up, take off their hats and bow. He bows to no one, just waves his hand. Our Tsar, on the other hand, bowed to everyone here and the Germans appreciated it very much. Wilhelm was talking to a girl—mother and father following two steps behind, while the people thronged behind them, some in dresses trimmed with lace as at a ball—I can imagine how they must have envied the girl!"

On July 5 he wrote to Anna: "Began to work (alas, only at the plan, and even that is hard going)." And in his next letter, on July 6, he explained the chief problem of all his plots: "A superabundance of plans is my chief defect. When I went over the plot of my novel, I realized that there was enough material in it for four novels. Strakhov always regarded this as my defect. . . . I am terribly worried how we shall be able to carry on next autumn. (It is quite im-pos-sible to ask Nekrasov for another advance. I don't think he will give it, anyway. He is not Katkov.)"

Before he left Ems he had prepared two different "plans" for his novel, and, he wrote to Anna on August 1, "I don't know which one to adopt. . . . I shall start writing at the end of August, and do you know I am wondering if I shall have enough health and strength for the sort of work I used to undertake in the past. What has been the result of it, anyway? I finished the work but, on the whole, ruined my health. . . . And what's going to happen to us now—again live from hand to mouth, and what's worse: we've still got debts. . . ."

The problem was solved at least temporarily by Anna's proposal to save 1,000 rubles in rent and fuel by staying the winter in Staraya Russa. "The winter of 1874–1875 which we spent in Staraya Russa," Anna records in her reminiscences, "has left me one of my most wonderful memories. The children were well and my husband, too, felt quite well. As a result of his Ems treatment his cough had improved and his shortness of breath, too, had abated considerably. His epileptic fits occurred less frequently and were less severe. As a result, he seldom lost his temper, and he spent a great deal of time running about and playing with the children, even dancing the quadrille, mazurka and waltz with them and with me. To do him justice he danced the mazurka very dashingly like a 'real Pole,' and he was very pleased when I told him so. . . . Working at night, my husband got up at 11 A.M. During coffee he chatted to the children, and after 12 o'clock he called me to his study to dictate to me what he had written the night before. After lunch, he read (that winter) *The Wanderings of the Monk Parfeny* or attended to his correspondence and at half past three went for a walk, whatever the weather. He almost always went into Plotnikovs' shop (described in *The Brothers Karamazov* as the shop in which Mitya made his purchases before leaving for Mokroye) and bought all sorts of snacks and sweetmeats, though in small quantities. At five o'clock we had dinner with the children and after dinner my husband stayed with the children for half an hour, telling them fairy stories or reading Krylov's fables. At seven my husband and I went for our evening walk and invariably looked in at the post office on our way back. At nine the children were put to bed and my husband always came to give them his blessing and say their prayers with them. At ten silence reigned in the house, everyone having gone to bed early. My husband went back to his study to read the papers, while I retired to my room to lay out patience. My husband used to join me there quite often to read something out of the papers or help me finish my game of patience. At eleven I usually went to bed, while my husband worked at his novel till three or four o'clock in the morning."

At the end of October, Dostoevsky wrote to Nekrasov[12] that he hoped to be able to let him have the first chapters of *A Raw Youth* in time for publication in the January issue of the *Contemporary*. It was not finished till November 1875. Its main theme Dostoevsky formulated in one of his early notes as "the disintegration of family life." In a later note he wrote: "Drunkards in the streets. No one wants to work. A schoolboy commits suicide because he finds schoolwork too hard. A feeble, mean generation. No duties or obligations." As usual, Dostoevsky made use of some of the more sensational court cases, including the trial in July 1874 of the members of a small revolutionary "secret society" accused of inciting the population to revolt against the established order. On the whole, Dostoevsky treated this incident with a great deal less rancor than the trial of Nechaev's followers in *The Devils*, chiefly perhaps because he was writing for the left-wing *Contemporary*, though he does make the adolescent hero of his novel tell the revolutionary group: "All you are going to get is a barracks, common apartments, atheism, and wives shared by everybody with no children—that is your final goal." In his notes, however, his argument against the utilitarians of the day is much more advanced. He makes Versilov say to his adolescent son: "I shall know all the discoveries of the exact sciences and through them I shall acquire all sorts of comforts. Today I am sitting on *drap* and tomorrow we shall all be sitting on velvet, so what? Still the question remains: what shall we do then? With that amount of comfort and living on velvet, what is there to live for? What aim? Mankind will still yearn for a great idea. I admit that to feed and to share out equally, so far as the feeding of mankind is concerned, is also at the moment a great idea. But it is all the same a minor and subsidiary idea, for after man has been fed he will most surely ask what he has to live for." The argument had not so far been formulated as profoundly as it was going to be four years later in *The Brothers Karamazov*, but it is already there.

Dostoevsky himself was aware that he was not yet ready for his great

[12] *Letters*, October 20, 1874.

argument and that is perhaps the real reason why *A Raw Youth* is a failure; it was written without the inspiration of a great moral argument which always aroused his creative powers. "When a year and a half ago Nekrasov asked me to write a novel for the *Contemporary*," Dostoevsky wrote in January 1876 in his *Writer's Diary*, " I almost began writing my 'Fathers and Sons,' but, thank God, I restrained myself; I was not ready for it. In the meantime I wrote *A Raw Youth*—the first tryout of my idea. But, then, the son had already emerged from childhood and appeared as an immature man, who timidly and insolently wished to take his first step in life as soon as possible. I took a soul that had not yet sinned but that was already soiled by the terrible possibility of corruption, by an early hatred of its own insignificance and 'incidental' nature as well as by that wholeheartedness with which a still-chaste soul consciously admits vice into its thoughts, already commits it in its heart, admires it in its still-shamefaced but already impudent and wild dreams—all this left solely to its own devices and its own comprehension and, besides, to God too. All these are the miscarriages of society, the 'incidental' members of 'incidental people.' "

The way Dostoevsky reacted to the unfavorable reviews of his latest novel is described by Vsevolod Solovyov, who wrote a review of it, but had to say something of its "shortcomings" too. "I came to see Dostoevsky a few days after the publication of my review," he writes. "He met me as a man who had greatly offended him, and we had a somewhat heated interchange of words which made me pick up my hat and make for the door. But he kept me back, locked the door and began to justify himself, trying to prove to me that I was mistaken. He spoke for two hours, perhaps even longer, and I was only sorry there was no stenographer in the room to take it all down."

IV

Dostoevsky left Staraya Russa for Petersburg at the beginning of February 1875 and stayed there for a fortnight. He was anxious to get a further advance from Nekrasov after the publication of two installments of his novel (Nekrasov advanced him another 2,000 rubles), but the chief reason for his trip was to take an intensified course of compressed-air treatment, as his lung condition was deteriorating rapidly. Vsevolod Solovyov, whom he visited a few times during the fortnight, found him looking "ill and exhausted and getting more and more tired physically." Dostoevsky was also anxious to find out how his old friends Maykov and Strakhov reacted to his reconciliation with Nekrasov. When he told them of the compliments Nekrasov had paid him on his novel, "Maykov," he wrote to Anna,[13] "looked sad, and Strakhov was very cold. No, Anna," Dostoevsky dismissed the philosopher, "he is just a

[13] *Letters*, February 11, 1875.

nasty seminarist; he has already deserted me once in my life, namely after the closing down of *Epoch,* and only came running back to me after the success of *Crime and Punishment.* Maykov is much better, he may feel annoyed for a time, but he will become friends again. He is a good man and not a seminarist. . . ."

By the end of May his bronchial condition had deteriorated so much that his doctors warned him that unless he went to Ems again he might not live to the end of the year. "Last year," he wrote to Yelena Ivanov from Ems,[14] "Ems was of great help to me and I realize now that if I had not gone to Ems last summer I would most certainly have died last winter. From this illness," he added, all too truly as it turned out, "one sometimes dies suddenly, from the slightest cold, even from a cold in the head, if the illness takes a real hold of one's organism. Here I am taking the waters and am so bored that I'm afraid I'll go mad." He was writing to her because he was anxious that she should put in a good word for him with his niece Sofia, who refused to have anything to do with him after he had started the action for the annulment of his aunt's will. He also asked her whether his stepson, Pasha, was in Moscow. "He is, of course, angry with me for refusing to lend him 150 rubles," he wrote, "but, first, I did not have the money and, secondly, I helped him quite a lot last winter and even quite recently, on passing through Petersburg, paid a debt of his of 25 rubles. However," he was quick to add, "please don't tell him that I inquired after him. I've grown very fearful of people. It is certainly our duty to disregard what people think and say about us and the slanderous stories they spread about us, but there is a point beyond which it does a great deal of harm. . . . However," he concluded, "I do not think Pasha has been saying anything bad about me (he'd be too ashamed to do so), but his wife is a different matter." He was not sure, though, that even Yelena, with whom he had always been on good terms in spite of not having married her, would reply to his letter. "But if you do not send me an answer to this letter," he wrote in a postscript, "I shall always think of you as before and I shall pray God for your happiness."

In his letters to Anna he kept complaining that the waters did not seem to be doing him much good: ". . . the wound in my chest," he wrote, "still makes itself felt." He was planning to resume the publication of his *Writer's Diary* next year, but was wondering whether he would have enough money to start it. "Here," he wrote,[15] "everything is dull and dead. At the Kurhaus and in the park there is an awful crush of people (someone has already poured a glass of the mineral waters on my overcoat). Horrible faces! . . . Last evening I went for a walk outside the town—the countryside is lovely but sad. . . ." Two days later he wrote: "I think I'll go off my head from boredom or commit some

[14] *Letters,* June 11, 1875.
[15] *Letters,* June 16, 1875.

act of violence. . . . I am reading the Book of Job which throws me into a state of morbid rapture: I put it away and pace the room for hours, almost in tears, and but for the most contemptible notes of the translator, I might have been happy. This book, Anna, strange to say, was one of the first that made a tremendous impression on me—I was only a child at the time. . . ." At the beginning of July he still failed to notice any improvement in his condition. *The Petersburg News* even published a story that he was seriously ill, which made Anna send him a telegram, the sight of which, he wrote to her on July 5, made him collapse in a chair. He had been to see the doctor, who assured him that his chest was "in an excellent condition." Who could have published the silly story, he wondered. "Oh," he sighed, "what a nuisance it is to be a 'great man!' "

He arrived back in Petersburg on July 19. Meeting Turgenev's close friend, the memoirist Pavel Annenkov, in the train, he at last "could hold out no longer," he wrote to Anna, and gave Annenkov for transmission to Turgenev the fifty thaler he had borrowed ten years before. He had intended to send Turgenev the money a year earlier, but at the last moment he changed his mind, for he was afraid that he might not have enough money for his Ems trip. At the time (on June 4, 1874) he had even drafted a letter to Turgenev, apologizing for the long delay and declaring that he could find no argument to justify it. It is interesting, in view of the demand they received a year later from Turgenev for an additional payment of fifty thaler, which so outraged Anna and disturbed Dostoevsky, that in his draft letter of June 4 Dostoevsky himself admitted that he was not sure whether Turgenev had lent him one hundred or fifty thaler.

After spending a few days in Petersburg in a vain attempt to find a flat, since he was determined not to spend another winter in the country, Dostoevsky left for Staraya Russa, where he continued to work on *A Raw Youth*. He stayed there till the middle of September. On August 10, 1875, Anna gave birth to their second son, Alexey, who inherited his father's epilepsy and died in May, 1878. On his return to Petersburg Dostoevsky completed his novel, the last installments of which were published in the *Contemporary* in November and December of 1875. The last months of the year Dostoevsky was busy collecting material for the first number of his *Writer's Diary*. On December 22, 1875, he sent in an application to the Press Department for permission to publish his monthly journal, "in which," he stated, "I wish to publish an account of all my real experiences as a Russian writer, an account of everything I see, hear and read." On January 11, 1876, he explained in a letter to Vsevolod Solovyov that the accounts of contemporary events he was going to publish in his *Writer's Diary* were to be more in the nature of personal views on current events. "It is going to be a diary in the full meaning of the word," he wrote. But three months later he admitted in a letter to a woman correspondent, a well-known educationist, that "I was too naïve when I thought that it would be a real diary. A real diary is almost impossible. . . ." As for her accusation that he was wasting his talents on trifles, his reply was that "a creative writer must know the reality he depicts in his works to the smallest detail. Among our writers," he went on, "only one man, in my opinion, is conspicuous for it—Count Leo Tolstoy. Victor Hugo, whom I esteem highly as a novelist (for which the late Fyodor Tyutchev even got angry with me once, declaring that *Crime and Punishment* was a greater novel than *Les Misérables*), may be occasionally very long-winded in his studies of details, yet but for him those wonderful studies might have remained unknown to the world. That is why," he wrote, at last admitting the *real* reason why he began publishing his *Writer's Diary*, "getting ready to write a long novel, I have decided to immerse myself in the study—not of reality itself, for I know it, as it is—but of the details of current life. One of the most important problems of current life, for instance, concerns the younger generation and the Russian family, which I cannot help feeling is not the same as it was twenty years ago. But, of course, there is a great deal more besides."

And, indeed, there was. For one thing, his great argument against the theories of the materialists, symbolized in the stones made bread, was started in the first issue of the *Diary*, published at the end of January 1876. "You understand, of course," he wrote, "that science is still in its infancy . . . but what if all knowledge—scientific discoveries which our sages don't even dream of—was suddenly disclosed to mankind? I ask, what would happen to men then? Why, at first they would all be beside themselves with delight. . . . They would feel they had been, as it were, showered with blessings; they would perhaps fly in the air over great distances, ten times faster than our railways; extract from the soil fabulous harvests, perhaps create new organisms by chemistry, and there would be enough meat to supply each man with three pounds a day, as our Russian socialists dream—in short, eat, drink and be merry. Ah, our philanthropists would then shout, now when man is fully provided for, he will show his true worth! There are no more material hardships, there is no more of the oppressive 'environment,' which was considered to be the cause of all evils, and now man will become just and righteous! There is no longer any need for continuous labor to earn the bare necessities of life, so now everyone will occupy himself with higher, more profound thoughts. . . . Now, only now the higher life has dawned! But I doubt if all these ecstasies would last for one generation of men. Men would suddenly realize that they have no life any more, no freedom of spirit, no freedom of will and personality, that somebody has stolen all that from them; that the image of man has vanished and in its place there has appeared the brutish image of the slave, and man would realize that he had become a brute. And mankind would rot away: men would be covered with festering wounds and would bite their tongues in torment whene they saw that life had been taken from them for bread, for 'stones made bread.' They would then realize that there could be no happiness in inactivity, that a mind that did not labor was doomed to decline, that it was impossible to love one's neighbor without giving something of one's labor to him, that it was infamous to get something for nothing and that *happiness does not lie in happiness but in its attainment.* People will become depressed and bored: everything has been done and there is nothing more left to do, everything is known and there is nothing more left to know. People will commit suicide in crowds and not, as now, in dark corners; people will gather in their thousands and destroy one another suddenly, in thousands, by some new method discovered by them with their other discoveries. And it would be then, perhaps, that those who survived would cry out to God: 'Thou art right, O Lord, man shall not live by bread alone!' "

That the central idea of his new "long novel"—The Legend of the Grand Inquisitor—had already taken shape in his mind at the beginning of 1876 became even more evident in the reply he wrote to V. A. Alexeyev, a member of the orchestra of the Marinsky Theater, who had asked him the meaning of his reference to "stones made into bread." "In the temptation of the devil," Dostoevsky wrote,[16] "these colossal world ideas have become merged and now eighteen centuries have passed and there are no ideas more difficult than these, nor can an answer be found to them as yet. 'The stones and the bread' stand for the present social question, the *environment.* It is not a prophecy, it has always been like that. 'Rather than go to the ravaged poor, who look more like beasts as a result of privations and oppressions, rather than go and preach to the hungry abstention from sins, meekness and chastity, would it not be better to *feed* them first? That would be humane. Before you, too, there were preachers, but, then, you are the Son of God, the whole world waited for you with impatience; then act as a being who possesses a higher mind and a greater sense of justice than the rest, give them food, give them *security,* give them a social organization that should provide them with bread and order—and make them responsible for their sins. If they should sin then, they would be ungrateful, but now they sin because of their hard life. It is sinful even to hold them responsible for it. You are the Son of God, you can do everything. Here are stones—see how many! All you have to do is to command and the stones will be turned into bread. Command, then, that henceforth the earth should produce without labor, teach man such a science or such an order as to make quite sure that their lives should henceforth be provided for. Don't you believe that the greatest vices and troubles of man have been caused by hunger, cold, poverty and a hard struggle for existence?'

"This," Dostoevsky continued, "is the first idea the evil spirit sug-

16 *Letters,* June 7, 1876.

gested to Christ. You must admit that it is difficult to deal with it. Present-day *socialism* in Europe, and in our country, too, eliminates Christ and is first of all concerned with *bread*, calls upon science and maintains that the cause of all men's troubles is *poverty*, struggle for existence, the obnoxious influence of the environment. To this Christ replies: man does not live by bread alone, that is to say, he propounds the axiom of the spiritual origin of man. The idea of the devil could only apply to man-brute. But Christ knew that you could not keep a man alive by bread alone. If man had no spiritual life, no ideal of Beauty, he would fall into a state of depression, he would die, he would become insane, he would commit suicide and indulge in pagan fantasies. But as Christ carried the ideal of beauty in Himself and in His word, he decided: rather put the ideal of beauty into men's souls, for then they will all become brothers to one another and, working for one another, they will be rich, while if given bread alone they will become enemies of one another out of boredom."

To the obvious question—why not give men Bread and Beauty together?—Dostoevsky replied that in that case man would be deprived of "the ideal of life," that is, of work, personality and the possibility of "sacrificing one's goods for one's neighbor. Incidentally," he added, "think of the present theories of Darwin and others about man's origin from apes. Without entering into a discussion of any theories, Christ simply declares that in addition to the animal world man also has a spiritual world. And, well, whatever man's origin, God *has breathed the breath of life* into him (though it is certainly bad that man may turn into a beast again by his sins)."

A great deal of the first issues of the *Writer's Diary* is devoted to the maltreatment of children (another prominent theme of *The Brothers Karamazov*). In December 1875, Dostoevsky often met in the street a seven-year-old boy who was sent out begging by his parents, which gave him the idea of his rather gruesome but moving fantasy—*A Boy at Christ's Christmas Party*, "a fictitious event, of course," he wrote in his *Writer's Diary*, "but showing that I am not exactly indifferent to the fate of our children." Indeed, he went specially to a children's Christmas party at the Petersburg Artists' Club to obtain a firsthand impression of the relations between parents and children, and on December 27, 1876, he visited a "colony" of delinquent children, while in another issue he dealt at length with the case of the maltreatment of a seven-year-old girl by her father.

In the same issue he pleaded for closer contact with the common people provided that the common people, that is, the peasants, agreed to accept "a great deal of what we have brought with us." He followed up his expression of faith in "the innate sense of justice" of the peasants by his story *The Peasant Marey*, a flashback to his childhood and his prison experiences, which, apart from its biographical interest, is hardly convincing proof of "the high degree of culture of our common people."

The whole of Dostoevsky's conception of the Russian peasant smacks of theory rather than fact. Unlike Tolstoy and Turgenev, he never really knew the Russian peasants, who do not figure in his novels except—and that really was the only experience he got out of prison—as thieves and murderers. In 1873, in one of his earlier issues of *A Writer's Diary*, he described the only time he came in contact with the "common people" in a Petersburg street. He saw a three-year-old girl stumble as she tried to pick up a pebble. He picked her up before her mother could come to her help and then asked the woman how old her daughter was. "The mother told me very affably but with reserve. I told her I also had a daughter of the same age, to which she replied: 'Maybe you are a good man, but what are you standing here for? You'd better be off.' The people around fell silent and seemed to think the same. I touched my hat and off I went." This incident does not show any particular understanding on Dostoevsky's part of how to talk to the "common people" and the curt injunction "to be off" certainly showed the peasant woman's "innate wisdom," but not in the sense Dostoevsky meant.

V

In the winter of 1875–1876 Dostoevsky's health showed little improvement. Vsevolod Solovyov, whom he continued to see frequently, records that he used to come to his place almost always after an epileptic fit. "Sometimes," Solovyov writes, "he was quite impossible after such an attack. He was so terribly irritable and behaved so oddly that he would not seem to be answerable for his actions. He would come in looking sullen and disgruntled, and seem to be searching for an excuse to say something nasty, and whatever one said to him he interpreted as a desire to offend and irritate him. Everything in my room seemed to him out of place or not as it should be: it was either too light or too dark to see anyone. If he was given strong tea which he liked, it was like beer, if he was given weak tea it was just hot water. If my wife and I tried to amuse him, he accused us of laughing at him."

In the middle of July he left for Ems again and stayed there till the middle of August. He stopped in Berlin, where he again went to the art gallery and then for the first time visited the zoo, where he admired all sorts of marvels, "such as huge crocodiles, snakes, tortoises, marine wonders, fishes, birds and, last but not least, a real live orangutan, which I saw for the first time in my life." The only other incident that he described at great length to Anna from Ems[17] happened at a railway station where the train had stopped for ten minutes. "Before that," he wrote, "the train had not stopped for a long time and we all naturally

[17] *Letters*, July 21, 1876.

rushed out to the place marked *pour hommes*. Just when it was full up with visitors all busily relieving themselves there *rushed in*—a beautifully dressed lady, by all signs an Englishwoman. She was obviously in great *need*, for she ran almost to the middle of the *convenience* before she noticed her mistake, that is, that she had gone in to *für Männer* instead of next door to *für Frauen*. She stopped dead as if thunderstruck with an air of the profoundest terror and surprise which lasted for no more than a second, then she uttered a piercing cry exactly as you do sometimes when you are frightened, threw up her hands a little over her head and struck them together producing a loud sound. I must say she saw everything, I mean, literally *everything*, for no one had any time to hide anything; on the contrary, they were all staring at her in similar stupefaction. Then she suddenly buried her face in her hands and slowly turned round (everything is ruined, everything is at an end, there is no need to hurry!) and, bending forward with her whole body, went out of the convenience without hurrying and not without majesty. I don't know whether she went to the *für Frauen;* if she was an Englishwoman I think she must have died on the spot for shame. But the remarkable thing was that there was no laughter. The Germans were all gloomily silent, while in Russia they would at once have started roaring with laughter from sheer delight."

Which, come to think of it, is the nicest thing Dostoevsky ever said about the Germans.

In Ems, the "cure" did not seem to be making any great progress this time. "I take walks, my appetite is not bad, but I sleep badly, three or four hours, because I keep perspiring, and when perspiring I get a bad, dry, cough," he wrote to Anna.[18] Five days later he wrote that he had had a terrible nightmare: he dreamed that he had lost her. "On the following night, that is, at 5 A.M., when I woke up and put my feet on the floor I felt so dizzy that I could not stand up and this went on for three minutes. I went to see the doctor and asked him whether I was not likely to have a stroke, but he told me there was not the slightest danger of that. . . ."

He was reading *Le Ventre de Paris* by Zola, "because," he wrote to Anna, "I have been terribly remiss during the last years in neglecting European literature, but I could hardly force myself to read it—it's such execrable stuff. And in Russia they are making a fuss over Zola as a literary celebrity, a luminary of realism. . . ." He met few people and made a point of avoiding meeting any Russians. He was annoyed at being unable to shake off a Russian journalist and his wife of left-wing tendencies. "They thrust themselves upon me," he wrote to Anna on August 11, "but at the same time treat me as though they were afraid to be soiled by my reactionary views. Vain and selfish creatures, especially the woman, a walking primer of liberal views: 'Oh, what is he

[18] *Letters*, July 27, 1876.

saying? Oh, what is he defending?' Those two think they can teach a man like me. . . . They just get on my nerves. . . ."

On his return to Petersburg, he resumed the publication of *A Writer's Diary*, which was turning out a really successful venture. Its first number sold 3,000 copies in four days, and two months later its sale increased to 6,000. In September he wrote to his brother Andrey: "Our time has flown like a dream. I know that my life cannot last very long, and yet far from wishing to die, I feel as though I were only just beginning to live. I don't feel tired at all, and yet I am already 55!"

In Ems he had gone to a service at which prayers had been offered for the success of the Montenegrin army, and on his return he threw himself passionately into the movement to send Russian volunteers to fight in the Serbian war against the Turks. He hailed these volunteers as "pioneers of the Russian political idea, the Russian desires and Russian will, which they announced before Europe. . . . It is reported," he wrote in a burst of ecstatic patriotism, "that a great many Russian officers have again been killed in the battles. The darlings!" He followed it up in the September issue by a scathing attack on Lord Beaconsfield ("*né* d'Israeli," he was careful to stress), the *piccola bestia*, whom he accused of being responsible for "the Bulgarian atrocities." But while eager for the liberation of the Slavs, for whom "Russia is their sun, their mother and protector and future liberator," Dostoevsky was far from pleased with the Slav and, particularly, Czech "intelligentsia," who, he was sorry to say, "are far from showing any interest in the success of our civic life, our internal organization, our reforms and our literature." But he hoped that at least those of the Slavs who shared the Orthodox faith with the Russians would seek their union with Russia. For, he wrote, "Russian Orthodox faith is the only thing the Russian people consider sacred; in it are their ideas and all truth and justice of life."

Soon, however, Dostoevsky was preoccupied with the fate of a twenty-year-old peasant woman who had thrown her six-year-old stepdaughter out of a window of a room on the fourth story of a tenement house. The child survived, but her stepmother was sentenced to two years and eight months of hard labor in a Siberian prison and then to lifelong deportation to Siberia. In the chapters of the October issue of his *Writer's Diary* Dostoevsky took up her case, insisting that she was not responsible for her action because she was pregnant at the time. At the end of October he paid a visit to the woman in prison. He pleaded her cause so eloquently that the court of appeal ordered a retrial. Dostoevsky was present at the second trial on April 22, 1877. The jury accepted the plea that her pregnancy had influenced her action and acquitted her in spite of the advice of the judge "not to be influenced by certain talented writers."

Two events that had an important literary sequel are commented on by Dostoevsky in the October issue of his journal: the suicides of

Herzen's seventeen-year-old daughter, who had chloroformed herself, and of a poor young seamstress, who had thrown herself out of a fourth-floor window, clutching an icon in her hands. "Some things," Dostoevsky wrote, "however *simple* they may seem, keep haunting you for a long time, just as though you were responsible for them. This gentle creature, who destroyed herself, involuntarily worries one. It was this death that reminded me of the suicide of a Russian *émigré*'s daughter, about which I had been informed last summer. How different those two human beings were, just as though they came from two different planets! And how different their deaths were! And which of the two had gone through greater torment on earth, if so idle a question may be considered proper and admissible?" The question was not an idle one: for in the November issue Dostoevsky provided an answer to it in one of his most profound and moving stories—*A Gentle Creature*.

These suicides, as well as the many letters with descriptions of other cases of suicide which Dostoevsky received during the winter of 1876, led him to assert in the December number of his journal that only a belief in immortality could have prevented them. "I declare," he wrote, "though I am not able to prove it, that love for mankind is quite incomprehensible and quite *impossible without belief in the immortality of a man's soul*. Those," he went on, "who deprive man of his belief in immortality and substitute for it 'love of mankind' as the highest aim in life, those, I say, merely raise their hands against themselves; for instead of love of mankind they plant in the heart of the man who has lost his faith only the germ of hatred of mankind. . . . Indeed, I assert that love of mankind *in general* is, as an *idea*, one of the most incomprehensible ideas for the mind of man. It can be justified only by feeling, but this feeling is only possible (again without adducing any proof) if it is accompanied by a conviction in the immortality of the soul." To the obvious question—if immortality exists, then why value life on earth so highly, he replied that "only by his belief in immortality does man attain his rational aim on earth," and he concluded with the rather doubtful syllogism: "If the belief in immortality is necessary for human existence, then it is a normal condition of man, and if it is a normal condition of man, then the immortality of the soul of man *undoubtedly exists*."

By the end of 1876 the success and popularity of *A Writer's Diary* had become the topic of conversation even in court circles, and on November 13 Dostoevsky received a letter from Pobedonostsev suggesting that he should send it to the heir to the throne; three days later Dostoevsky wrote a letter to the Tsarevich, couched in the usual servile language deemed appropriate in addressing royalty, asking for permission to send him the monthly issue of his journal.

"In 1877," Anna records in her reminiscences, "we continued to publish *A Writer's Diary* and although its success, both moral and financial, was growing steadily, the worries inseparable from the publication of a monthly journal also increased." In fact, but for the two issues published in August 1880 and in January 1881, the twelve issues of 1877 constitute Dostoevsky's last work as a journalist. It contains many ideas that found their way into *The Brothers Karamazov:* the idea of the twilight of the Catholic Church and his attempt to argue, as in his Legend of the Grand Inquisitor, that, as he wrote in the January 1877, issue, "socialism is simply a union of mankind brought about *by force*—an idea which derives from ancient Rome and which is entirely preserved in the Catholic Church"; the story of the Russian soldier martyred by Mohammedans in Central Asia; the devil's temptations of Christ in the desert; the maltreatment of children; Europe as "the country of holy miracles"; attacks on trial by jury; and many others.

The Russo-Turkish War, the declaration of which made Dostoevsky rush off to the Kazan Cathedral to offer up prayers for the victory of Russian arms, evoked a spate of articles in which war was hailed as a "salvation" rather than a "scourge" and the demand made for the annexation of Constantinople as "the spiritual center of the Eastern world, the head of which is Russia." This is rather arbitrarily linked with the Catholic Church and socialism. "The Eastern question," Dostoevsky wrote in the July-August number, "is essentially linked with the future of the Orthodox faith and the future of the Orthodox Church is closely linked with the destiny of Russia. What is the future of the Orthodox faith? The Roman Catholic faith, which long ago sold Christ for earthly possessions . . . and which for that reason had been the chief cause of materialism and atheism in Europe, quite naturally begot also socialism in Europe. For socialism aims at a solution of the problems facing mankind not in accordance with Christ's teachings but without God and without Christ, and it naturally had to arise in Europe in place of the Christian faith lost and distorted by the Catholic Church. The lost image of Christ has been preserved in all its pristine purity in the Orthodox faith. It is therefore from the East that the new word will spread across the world against the approach of socialism and it will again save European mankind. This is what the Eastern question means to Russia. I know," he added, realizing very well that when he let himself go like that he frightened even his best friends, "that many people would call such an opinion 'the ravings of a hysterical woman,' but they know what I am talking about. To realize such an aim Russia needs Constantinople, for it is the center of the Eastern world."

Dostoevsky, curiously enough, drew a line between the Orthodox faith and the Orthodox Church, or, rather, its priests. "The Russian clergy," he wrote in the same July–August number, "have long ago ceased answering the questions of the common people. With the exception of—alas!—a very few who still burn with zeal for Christ and who are mostly unknown just because they live for their flocks and not for themselves, if any question were to be put to some of them, they would answer it by denouncing the questioner to the police; others have so alienated their flocks by all sorts of extortions that no one would ever dream of coming to them with any questions." In *The Brothers Karamazov*, Zossima, the idealized holy man, is neither priest nor monk, but an "elder," a somewhat suspect figure in the Orthodox world, as is shown by the great pains Dostoevsky took to put him across as one of God's chosen spirits.

Dostoevsky also devotes a great deal of space in his *Writer's Diary* to Tolstoy's *Anna Karenina*, the last part of which Katkov refused to publish because of Tolstoy's scathing attack on some of the Russian "volunteers" for the Serbian war. He himself found that part, published by Tolstoy as a separate booklet, "far from innocent," but this did not prevent him from expressing his admiration for the novel as a whole; what struck him particularly was the fact that within recent years Europe had not produced anything comparable. This again led him to the rather astonishing assertion that "the gift of universality, the task of comprehending and uniting all the multifarious nationalities and removing their contradictions," has been granted only to Russian writers. Another much less paradoxical conclusion which he drew from Tolstoy's novel goes much further than Tolstoy's views on "men's guilt and criminal nature." It was abundantly clear from a study of *Anna Karenina*, Dostoevsky maintains, that "evil is hidden much deeper in man than is supposed by the socialist medicine men, that evil cannot be avoided whatever the organization of society, that man's soul will remain the same, that sin and abnormality spring from man's soul itself and that, finally, the laws of man's spirit are still so unknown, so unfamiliar to science, so vague and so mysterious, that there are not and cannot be either physicians or judges who can give their *final* decision, but that there is He who says: Vengeance is mine; I will repay. He alone knows *all* the mystery of the world and the final fate of man. Every human judge must know about himself that he is not a final judge, that he is a sinner himself, that the scales and measure in his hands will be absurdity, *if* he himself, holding in his hands the measure and scales, does not kneel before the law of the unsolved mystery and does not resort to the only way out—Mercy and Love." It is not so much in the scene of Anna Karenina's serious illness, when friend and foe "are suddenly transformed into higher beings, into brothers who forgive each other everything," that Dostoevsky sees the real solution of the human predicament; it is in its final scene, "in the somber and terrible picture of the collapse of the human spirit," which should make every judge of man "exclaim in fear and perplexity: No, it is not always that vengeance is mine and that I will repay." No one could be so inhuman as to blame the "bleakly fallen" criminal for having disregarded "the light that has for centuries been showing the way of salvation and for having *deliberately* rejected it. . . ."

The fact of the existence of so great a literary masterpiece as *Anna Karenina* led Dostoevsky to the further reflection that there was no reason why Russia should not "in good time" produce scientific works of equal magnitude. "It is surely impossible to accept the ridiculous idea," he observes, "that nature has endowed us only with literary abilities. The rest is merely a question of history, circumstances and time."

Dostoevsky's deep-seated propensity for the occult, which he was reluctant to stress in his writings, comes to light in the first chapter of the May–June issue of his *Writer's Diary*. In it he took quite seriously the "prognostications" of Johannes Lichtenberg published in 1528, especially the one about "a great eagle arising in the East which will make the Western islanders weep." He admitted that the "prophecy" was a little "obscure," but thought that "it seems to point to contemporary events." The phrase: "will make the inhabitants of the land of the virgin tremble . . . and will fly south to return what was lost" he believed pointed to England and the annexation of Constantinople by the Russians. The final phrase of the prophecy, "God will fire the Eastern eagle with the love of mercy and it will fly towards the difficult, flashing its two wings on the heights of Christendom," pointed, he was sure, to "Christ's mercy moving our people to undertake 'the difficult task' " that is to say, the fulfillment of Russia's political aspirations in the Near East.

This "prophecy" was sent to Dostoevsky by Vladimir Solovyov, who discovered it while studying mysticism and mystical philosophy at the Reading Room of the British Museum. Dostoevsky had always felt that, as he wrote to Strakhov,[19] he was "rather weak in philosophy, though," he added in a parenthesis, "not in my love for it, in my love for it I am strong." In Vladimir Solovyov, Dostoevsky found someone who could supply a philosophic basis for his beliefs. This he realized at once when, in 1873, he received from Vladimir Solovyov his M.A. thesis on *The Crisis of Western Philosophy*, in which Western philosophy was criticized for providing the answer to the question of *how* a man knows, but not of *what* he knows. Their identity of views on the Catholic Church and the role the Orthodox Church was destined to play in the world further cemented their friendship. How close this identity of view was can be gathered from a letter on the subject of resurrection that Dostoevsky wrote[20] to a disciple of Nikolai Fyodorov, another mystic philosopher. Fyodorov believed that men's power over nature would reach a point where they could "bring to life our ancestors, resurrect our dead fathers, by the active efforts of united mankind." Dostoevsky, told his correspondent that both he and Vladimir Solovyov, "the brilliant young philosopher," sympathized with this view, but, he went on, "you don't explain how you understand this resurrection of our ancestors and in

[19] *Letters*, June 9, 1870.
[20] *Letters*, March 24, 1878.

what form you imagine and believe it will come about. Do you understand it allegorically as Renan does? Renan understands it as the deepening of man's perception towards the end of humanity's span of life to such a degree as to make it absolutely clear to the mind of man in that remote future how much a certain ancestor has influenced mankind, how his influence has been exerted, etc. Thus the role of every man of a former age will be made perfectly clear, the reason for his actions be divined (by science, the powers of analogy) and we shall realize how much those ancestors have influenced us and in this way become reincarnated in us and hence also in the last people on earth, the harmonious beings who will know everything. Or: does your philosopher imagine literally and straightforwardly, as, indeed, religion hints at, that the resurrection will be real and personal, that the grief that separates us from the souls of our ancestors will be conquered by vanquished death and they will be resurrected not in our consciousness, not allegorically, but actually, personally, really in their bodies. (N.B. of course, not in their present bodies, for the very fact that when immortality comes there will be no more marriage and birth of children shows that the bodies in their first resurrection, which has been fixed to take place on earth, will be different from the present ones, that is, perhaps such as Christ's body after the resurrection and till His ascension.) There must be a reply to this question, for otherwise everything will be incomprehensible. I must warn you," he concluded significantly, "that we here, that is, Solovyov and I, at any rate, believe in real, literal, personal resurrection and that it will come to pass on earth."

It was a few months earlier that, at the suggestion of Vsevolod Solovyov, he visited a famous fortuneteller, whose predictions, Anna records dutifully, that great fame, as well as a family tragedy, awaited him, came true over two years later at the Pushkin celebrations in Moscow and a year later with the death of their younger son, Alexey.

The significant thing, however, in considering Dostoevsky's occult beliefs, is that, but for a few enigmatic references in Zossima's "discourses," Dostoevsky was very careful to keep them out of his novels. Even in his famous "philosophic" tale, *The Dream of a Ridiculous Man*, which he wrote in March 1877, the beatific creatures on the unknown planet who live in "the golden age" are free from all worries about survival after death or, indeed, about salvation: for they have no religion, and it is man, arriving among them with his doubts and atavistic fears, who shatters their happy lives.

It is quite true, of course, that had Dostoevsky revealed himself completely in his last novels, as he does with some circumspection in his *Writer's Diary*, he would, in his own phrase, have been "ruined," for he would have become the laughingstock of the great majority of his reading public. But that was not why he did not do it. It is rather because of the dichotomy in his own nature, the cleavage between the man and the creative artist, which appears most glaringly perhaps in his last and greatest novel. For in *The Brothers Karamazov* it is the characters and the ideas which, as a man, he considered to be evil that spring to life with quite overpowering force, while the ideas and characters he approved of are "made up" and in some cases, such as Alyosha's speech to the children at the end of the novel and the theme of the resurrection itself, show no characteristic touches of his genius and could, in fact, have been written by any third-rate novelist.

VI

In January 1877 Dostoevsky heard that Nekrasov was seriously ill, and he went to see him. Nekrasov spoke of their first meeting on that memorable night in May thirty-two years before, after Grigorovich and he had read *Poor People* and had come to congratulate him on having written a masterpiece. Dostoevsky was deeply touched at one of his subsequent visits when Nekrasov read some of his last poems to him and said about one of them: "I have written this about you." It described political prisoners and was entitled *The Unhappy*. Dostoevsky saw Nekrasov for the last time a month before his death. "He looked to me then almost like a corpse," he wrote in the December issue of his *Writer's Diary*, "and it even seemed strange to me to see a corpse like that speaking and moving his lips. And he not only spoke but also was in full possession of his faculties. I don't think he believed even then that he would be dead so soon. A week before he died the right side of his body was paralyzed and on the morning of December 28 I learned that he had died at eight o'clock on the previous night. I went to see him the same day. I was particularly struck by his terribly emaciated and distorted face. On returning home, I could not sit down to my work, took down the three volumes of his poems and began to read from the first page. I sat reading his poems till six o'clock in the morning and I seemed to live through those thirty years again. The first four poems in the first volume appeared in the *Petersburg Symposium* in which my first novel, too, was published. Then, as I went on reading the poems one after another, my whole life seemed to pass before me. I recognized and remembered those of his poems which I read in Siberia when, having served my four years' sentence, I was at last given the right to take a book in my hands. I also remembered my impression at the time. In short, that night I reread almost two-thirds of Nekrasov's writings and for the first time realized how much Nekrasov as a poet had meant in my life."

On December 30, Dostoevsky went to Nekrasov's funeral, walking bareheaded behind the coffin part of the way to the cemetery in spite of the bitter cold. Later he drove with Anna to the cemetery at the Devichy monastery. After spending half an hour in the overheated chapel at the funeral service, he went with his wife to look for Nekrasov's grave. "The silence of the cemetery," Anna writes, "had a calming effect on my husband and he said: When I die, Anna, bury me here or somewhere else, but not in the Writers' Corner in Volkov cemetery. I don't want to lie among my enemies. I have suffered enough from them while I was alive." At the graveside, Dostoevsky, too, made a speech in his "weak voice," in which he expressed the view that Nekrasov was an original poet who could be placed in that respect after Pushkin and Lermontov, a remark that, characteristically, provoked a few of the young radical students to protest loudly that Nekrasov was "higher" than Pushkin and Lermontov, who were merely "Byronists."

Of the correspondence Dostoevsky conducted with the readers of his *Writer's Diary* in 1877, mention should be made of the young Jewish girl, Sonia Lurye, whose domestic troubles he treated with understanding and tenderness, and of a Jewish writer and ex-convict, Avram Kovner, who sent him two of his manuscripts. Both protested against Dostoevsky's anti-Semitism. Kovner, in particular, pointed out that he did not seem to know anything about the frightful conditions among which the great mass of the Jewish population was condemned to live in the so-called "Pale." Dostoevsky's defense in his reply to Kovner and in the four articles he wrote on "the Jewish question" in the February number of his *Writer's Diary*, centered mainly on the *status in statu* (state within a state) argument of anti-Semites the world over. He finished, however, on a note of reconciliation, and expressed "in theory" full agreement with the demand of equal rights for Jews, though insisting that it was not the Russian who hated the Jew, but vice versa. Whenever pushed into a corner and forced to declare himself in public, Dostoevsky did his best to conceal his strong prejudices against persons or peoples, but he resented having to do so. In the case of his deep-seated anti-Jewish feelings, which went back to the dark, religious background of his childhood, this resentment expressed itself violently in a sentence at the beginning of *The Brothers Karamazov,* in which he concentrated all the venom of which his nature was capable, and two sentences of dialogue between Alyosha and Lisa, in which he seemed to lend credence to the medieval "blood libel" against the Jews.

In the spring of 1877 Dostoevsky acquired a house in Staraya Russa (it was actually bought by Anna's brother at her request and resold by him to Anna after Dostoevsky's death). At last, as he expressed it, he and his family had "a nest" of their own. They only spent the spring there, though. The summer months they spent at Maly Prikol, the estate of Anna's brother in the province of Kursk. At the end of June Dostoevsky had to go back to Petersburg for a short time to attend to his journal, while Anna and her two elder children went "on a pilgrimage" to Kiev. On his way back to Maly Prikol, Dostoevsky stopped for two days at his parental estate of Darovoye, owned by his sister Vera.

"His relatives told me afterwards," Anna writes in her reminiscences, "that my husband had visited the different places in the park and its surroundings, dear to him for the memories they recalled, and even walked to Chermoshnya, over a mile from Darovoye, a name which he later gave to the copse in *The Brothers Karamazov.* He also visited the cottages of the peasants, many of whom he remembered as being of the same age as he. The old men and women of the village as well as those who remembered him as a boy greeted him joyfully, invited him to their cottages and treated him to tea." So much for Anna's gushing version of the return of the prodigal to his ancestral home. In his own account of his visit to "the estate which once belonged to my parents," in the first chapter of the July–August number of his *Writer's Diary*, Dostoevsky makes no mention of any joyous demonstrations of the peasantry. He is, in fact, extremely reticent about the whole thing. "I have not been there for forty years," he writes, "though I wanted to visit it many times. I am afraid I could not manage to in spite of the fact that this small and in no way remarkable place left a most profound and powerful impression on my whole life." But he says nothing of his own impressions during the visit. He must have been well aware that some of the peasants he met knew of the murder of his father, if indeed they had not themselves taken part in it. The visit must have certainly revived memories of his father. In the same issue of his *Writer's Diary* he lets fall a few observations whose hidden meaning is not so difficult to divine. "Want and worries of their fathers," he writes, "leave a grim picture in the minds of children from the early days of their childhood. The children remember to their extreme old age the cowardliness of their fathers, their quarrels, arguments, accusations, bitter reproaches and even curses and, what is worse, they sometimes remember the despicable behavior of their fathers, their base actions in an attempt to obtain a better post or money, their disgusting intrigues and their vile obsequiousness." This "filth of memories," as he called it, was what Dostoevsky recalled about his own father. There was that idiot girl someone had raped and got with child. Who could it have been? What if . . . And so one of the themes of the plot of his greatest novel, in which the whole tragedy of mankind has been compressed within the narrow framework of one family, began to take shape in his mind. "There is," he wrote to his old friend Dr. Yanovsky,[21] "in my head and heart a novel that is asking to be born. . . ." He had other plans—he always had a great many ideas for novels jostling and crowding in his head. On December 24, 1877, he jotted down in one of his notebooks: "Memento: for the rest of my life: (1) write a Russian *Candide;* (2) write a book about Jesus Christ; (3) write my reminiscences; and (4) write a novel on *The Eighteen-Forties.*" Some of these were mere ideas, others already

[21] *Letters,* December 17, 1877.

existed in a rough draft (one of which, containing most of the elements of Dmitry Karamazov's story, he had already drafted in the autumn of 1874), but they were all eventually fused into *The Brothers Karamazov.*

In February 1875, Petersburg was full of rumors of what Dostoevsky described in a letter to Anna as "a colossal anecdote about certain persons known to us." It was a court scandal concerning the Grand Duke Nikolai Konstantinovich, a cousin of Alexander II, who had stolen a diamond from the icon in his mother's bedroom and pawned it for 3,000 rubles. He was certified insane and exiled to Tashkent. The Tsar's younger sons, it was felt, had to be guarded against similar *contretemps* and, generally, instructed about the facts of political life, and what person was more competent to do that than Dostoevsky? So one morning in January 1878 the tutor of the Grand Dukes came to see Dostoevsky and told him that the Tsar had expressed the wish that he should meet his younger sons and by his talks exercise "a beneficial influence" on them. The first meeting with the Grand Dukes did not take place till March since, according to their tutor, they happened to be occupied "with impressions of a different order." Their tutor took good care to instruct Dostoevsky about the subjects he had to discuss with them, and, according to Anna, those meetings, which took place at infrequent intervals during the next two or three years, made a "most favorable impression" on Dostoevsky. He found that though they knew how to stand up for their "sometimes immature" views, they did not show any disrespect for the opinions he himself expressed. In a letter to a woman correspondent on February 28, 1878, he wrote: "You think I am one of those who mend broken hearts, provide balm for lacerated souls, and specialize in banishing sorrow? Sometimes people write to me to that effect, but I know *for certain* that I'm much more likely to instill disappointment and disgust. I am no good at lulling people to sleep, though I sometimes have tried to do so. For, you see, all a great many people want is to be lulled to sleep." On the whole, it seems, the tutor of the Grand Dukes did well to have a private talk with Dostoevsky before letting him see his royal charges.

It was also in March 1878 that Dostoevsky took a hand in exposing a favorite trick of spiritualist mediums, of tying knots in a string both ends of which were attached with sealing wax to a piece of paper. Spiritualism was in great vogue in Russia at the time, but Dostoevsky's interest in the occult seems to go back entirely to his experiences of childhood in which demons, rather than ghosts, played a great role. At all events, it is clear from his letter to the daily *New Times*[22] that he did not believe in the "fourth" dimension of the spiritualists and was glad there was a perfectly rational explanation of the mysterious appearance of knots on the sealed string. He later accepted an invitation from the

22 *Letters,* March 28, 1878.

great scientist Dmitry Mendeleyev to be present at the meeting of a committee formed by him to investigate the claims of spiritualists, during which this particular claim was shown to be without foundation.

On March 30, 1878, Dostoevsky attended the trial of Vera Zasulich, accused of firing a shot at General Trepov, the governor of the Petersburg district, who had ordered a political prisoner to be flogged. She was acquitted by the jury and Dostoevsky witnessed the great ovation given her by a large crowd. This turned him against trial by jury, of which he had previously approved, and led him to treat it, in *The Brothers Karamazov*, as a farce.

Three days later a demonstration of Moscow students forced Dostoevsky to declare his political views more openly. The students had been set upon and mercilessly beaten by the butchers and other stallholders of a nearby market. The "common people," whom Dostoevsky held up as an example of all that was noble in the Russian character, ran amok in the streets and even besieged the university. Asked by five students of Moscow university to comment on this occurrence, Dostoevsky declared that in his view it was a reaction of the "common people" against the acquittal of Vera Zasulich and the ovation given her by people whom they assumed to have been "students." While careful to dissociate himself from the action of the Moscow "butchers," because "you can't prove anything with your fists," he tried to justify them on the ground that "things like that happened everywhere in the world. The English common people," he wrote, "often use their fists against their opponents at meetings and during the French Revolution the common people roared with delight and danced in front of the guillotine throughout its *activity*. All this is, of course, disgusting, but the fact remains that the common people (and not only the butchers) have turned against the younger generation which they associate with students, while the press, society and the younger generation have all combined in refusing to recognize the common people."

The students, Dostoevsky admitted, were not to blame, for they were merely "the children of a society which is a lie from every point of view," but if they really wished "to go to the people and remain with it," they should first stop despising it, "which is almost impossible for our upper classes in their relations with the common people." Another condition Dostoevsky laid down for a *rapprochement* with the common people "in which our salvation lies," was a belief in God which he thought was quite impossible "for our Europe-worshipers (though in Europe they do believe in God)."

A personal tragedy, the death of his little son Alexey, indirectly helped to advance Dostoevsky's work on *The Brothers Karamazov*, for it was followed by his visit to the Optina monastery,[23] which provided him

[23] The monastery, one of the oldest in Russia, is said to have been founded in the fourteenth century by Opta, a former brigand.

with the beginning of the novel, the part he always found most difficult.

Alexey died on May 16, 1878. "Yesterday," Dostoevsky wrote to his brother Nikolai on the same day, "our Alyosha was still happy, running about and singing, and today he is lying in his coffin. He had an epileptic fit at half past nine in the morning and at half past two he was already dead. The funeral will be on the eighteenth. Good-by, Kolya; have pity on Alyosha, you have often played with him (remember how you pretended to be drunk?). I've never been so sad." He even rushed off a letter to Pasha, his grief bringing back his old fondness for his stepson. "Spare a tear for my Alyosha, Pasha," he wrote. "May the Lord grant health to your children." And, indeed, the death of the child had greatly shaken Dostoevsky, who, Anna writes, loved the boy "with a special kind of love, as though anticipating that he would soon lose him, and what depressed him particularly was the fact that the child died of epilepsy, an illness he had inherited from his father. Judging by his appearance, though, my husband calmly and courageously bore the loss of our child, but I was very much afraid that by repressing his great grief he might injure still more his already bad health. I therefore asked Vladimir Solovyov to persuade my husband to accompany him to Optina monastery, which Solovyov intended to visit this summer."

Solovyov agreed to do so, and it was decided that by the middle of June Dostoevsky would go to Moscow to see Katkov about his new novel and then go with Solovyov to the ancient monastery where Father Amvrosy, famed for his Christian meekness and asceticism, was the "elder" at the time. Dostoevsky arrived in Moscow on June 19 and went to see Katkov next morning.

"Katkov," Dostoevsky wrote to Anna on June 20, "received me cordially, though rather *guardedly*. We began talking about general matters when, suddenly, a terrible thunderstorm broke. I thought if I talked to him about my business and the thunderstorm did not pass, I should have to sit there—rejected and humiliated—until the rain stopped. However, I had to broach the subject. I put it all *simply* and *frankly*. At my first words about my desire to contribute to his journal, his face brightened, but as soon as I said that I should like to get 300 rubles a folio page and a considerable advance, a change came over him. . . ." But two days later his proposal was accepted, and he was promised an advance of 2,000 rubles at once and another 2,000 rubles in October.

On July 23 he and Solovyov left for the Optina monastery. He spent two days in the monastery and saw Father Amvrosy (the prototype of Zossima) three times, once in a crowd of people (described in *The Brothers Karamazov*) and twice in his cell, where he talked to the "elder" in private. "When my husband told the elder about the misfortune that had befallen us and the stormy way in which I had expressed my grief," Anna writes, "the elder asked him if I was a believer and when my husband told him that I was, he sent me his blessing and he used the same words which the elder Zossima used to the bereaved mother in *The Brothers Karamazov*."

Now his work proceeded so quickly that by the end of December he had written 160 pages of the novel (published in the January issue of *The Russian Herald*). In November Dostoevsky was in Moscow again. He had brought with him the first chapters so as to be able to ask for the second installment of his advance, but he had to wait for a few days for Katkov to read them. Two days later, on November 9, he went to see Katkov again. At his office he met the Governor General of Moscow, in full-dress uniform, and this took him back to his early revolutionary days in Petersburg. "Suddenly," he wrote to Anna, "there entered Prince Dolgoruky, the Governor General *himself*, wearing four stars and the diamond order of St. Andrey. After greeting Katkov with great dignity in accordance with his high position (a little comically), he began shaking hands with the other visitors and first with me. Katkov hastened to introduce me and Dolgoruky was so good as to say: 'Why, of course, er–such–er–a famous man–er–er–er–' just like forty years ago in the good old days. . . ." Dostoevsky detested Russian officialdom, as, indeed, he made clear several times in his *Writer's Diary*, in which he even contrasted German officials favorably with their Russian counterparts.

In December 1878, and twice in March 1879, Dostoevsky took part in public readings, the two last with the participation of Turgenev. On March 9, 1879, he read "The Confessions of an Ardent Heart" from the third book of the first part of *The Brothers Karamazov* at a gathering in aid of the Russian Literary Fund. "Dostoevsky," writes Semyon Vengerov, the literary historian, who was present, "had no equal as a reader. He did not so much read as utter prophecies. In a high-pitched, clearly articulated and incredibly thrilling voice he read Mitya's account of how Katerina Ivanovna came to him for money to save her father, and never before have I observed such a dead silence in the hall, such an utter absorption of the spiritual life of a crowd of a thousand listeners in the words of one man. . . . When Dostoevsky read, his listener completely lost his own 'I' and was entirely in the power of this emaciated, unattractive old man, the piercing gaze of whose burning eyes seemed to be lost somewhere in the faraway distance."

Dostoevsky had sent off the entire first part to *The Russian Herald* at the end of January. "The third book," he wrote to Nikolai Lyubimov, the editor, "which I am sending you now *I do not consider at all bad*, on the contrary, I think it worked out *very well*."

It was at a dinner given shortly afterwards in honor of Turgenev that a clash occurred between the two old enemies. Turgenev made a speech in which he claimed that there was already some common ground on which the older and the younger generations could meet, for there was no reason why both should not agree to work together "to crown the edifice," a well-known euphemism for the introduction of a constitutional monarchy. After the applause had died down, Dostoevsky, whom even so die-hard a conservative as Prince Meshchersky considered to be "a fanatic supporter of Tsarist autocracy," saw at once what Turgenev was driving at and, jumping up from his seat, demanded that Turgenev should repeat what he had just said. "What do you want to foist on Russia?" he asked furiously. Turgenev, rising to his full height and towering over Dostoevsky, replied calmly that he was not going to reply to an *interrogation.* The ominous word quite clearly implied that Dostoevsky, who in *The Devils* had not hesitated to accuse Turgenev of associating with terrorists, was quite capable of turning police informer. This was so gross and, it must be added, so unjust an imputation that it took the wind out of Dostoevsky's sails, and he rushed out of the room.

What must have been even more galling to Dostoevsky was that he was still under police surveillance as a political suspect. In March 1879, he sent a request to the ministry of the interior for the removal of the police surveillance. "On hundreds of pages," he wrote, "I have been and still am expressing my political and religious views, which, I hope, are such as to give no cause to suspect my political propriety." His request was ignored by the ministry, and the police stopped opening his correspondence only a few months before his death, thanks to the intervention of a high official whom Dostoevsky approached during the Pushkin festivities in Moscow in June 1880.

But it was not only the police who suspected his views: Nikolai Lyubimov as well as so devoted a friend as Pobedonostsev, the future Procurator of the Holy Synod, seem to have been extremely upset by the views he expressed in the fifth book of the second part—the part containing "The Legend of the Grand Inquisitor." Indeed, even before he had sent that part in, Dostoevsky was afraid that Lyubimov and Katkov, two stalwarts of reaction, might refuse to publish it. "I put forward certain ideas and theses in my novel," Dostoevsky wrote to a friend from Staraya Russa, "which I feared they [that is, Lyubimov and Katkov] would greatly dislike, for until the very end of the novel one could really form a wrong impression of them. Now what I feared actually happened: they are finding fault with me. Lyubimov makes remarks and puts question marks in the margin of the proofs he sends me. So far I have been successful in persuading them not to tamper with my text, but now I am very much afraid that they may refuse to publish the chapter ["The Grand Inquistor"] I sent them a few days ago. That is why I have willy-nilly to be very tactful with them."

That was why Dostoevsky kept bombarding Lyubimov with letters in which he tried to prove that, contrary to what one might think, his intentions were good. On May 10, 1879, after declaring a little incautiously that "the fifth book of the second part, entitled 'Pro and

Contra,' is, in my opinion, the culminating point of my novel and must be written with special care," he hastened to add that "the ideas expressed in that part by Ivan Karamazov are the synthesis of modern Russian anarchism: a denial not of God but of the purport of His creation. The whole of socialism began with the denial of the purport of historic reality and reached the point of complete destruction and anarchy. My hero takes a theme which, *in my opinion*, is simply irrefutable: the senselessness of the suffering of children, and deduces from it the absurdity of the entire historic reality. . . . But," he added, a little too confidently, as it proved, "my hero's blasphemies will be solemnly refuted in the next book ["The Russian Monk"] on which I am now working with fear and trembling and reverence, considering my task (the defeat of anarchism) to be my civic duty."

The dichotomy in his nature, the cleavage between the creative artist and the embittered conservative politician, has never emerged so clearly as in these attempts to justify himself against the raised eyebrows of his reactionary friends. It is inconceivable that he should not have realized that Ivan Karamazov's views were a statement of mankind's tragic predicament rather than the "blasphemies" of an "anarchist." After he had sent off "The Legend of the Grand Inquisitor" he again wrote to Lyubimov to explain that "our modern *negationist* declares himself in favor of the devil's advice and maintains that it is more likely to bring happiness to man than Christ. For our Russian socialism, stupid but direful (for our youth is in it), it is a *warning* and I think a powerful one: the loaves of bread, the Tower of Babel (that is, the future reign of socialism) and the complete enslavement of the freedom of conscience—that is what the desperate negationist and atheist is driven to. The difference is that by refusing to admit that their ideal is the ideal of coercion over men's conscience and the reduction of mankind to the state of a herd of cattle our socialists are deliberate liars and Jesuits, while my socialist (Ivan Karamazov) is a sincere man who frankly admits that he agrees with the Grand Inquisitor's view of mankind that the religion of Christ has raised man higher than he really deserves. The question is put bluntly: 'Do you respect or despise mankind—you who claim to be its future saviors?' And all this they pretend to be in the name of love of man: 'Christ's law is hard and too unrealistic, weak men cannot possibly live up to it,' and instead of the law of Freedom and Enlightenment they take unto them the law of chains and enslavement by bread."

Considering that the Tsarist regime was not unacquainted with chains and enslavement, Dostoevsky's "explanation" must have seemed much more revolutionary to Lyubimov than the actual text of "The Grand Inquisitor" and, perhaps, removed any doubts he may have had about the wisdom of publishing it.

Pobedonostsev, Dostoevsky knew very well, would also have his doubts about Ivan Karamazov's "blasphemies." On May 19, 1879, he therefore dashed off a letter to the future Procurator of the Holy Synod in which he claimed that the views expressed in the first chapters of "Pro and Contra" were held by "almost the *entire* Russian upper-class society" and especially the younger generation, who, he declared, were no longer interested in the question of the existence of God, but denied "with all their might God's creation, God's world and its *purport*." But was he himself so sure of it? If he was, why the doubt in his mind about whether Katkov would agree to publish those chapters? "I have sent them off," he told Pobedonostsev, "but I cannot help feeling that for some reason they will suddenly decide not to publish them." To prove to Pobedonostsev that, in spite of it all, he was as convinced a Slavophile as ever, he added: "The trouble with us is that we have no native culture (something every other nation has), and that we have not got it is the fault of the nihilist Peter the Great, who tore it out by the roots. But since a man does not live by bread alone, our poor uncultured Russian cannot help inventing something utterly absurd and fantastic, something that is not like anything on earth (for though he has taken everything from European socialism, he has altered it so thoroughly that it is not like anything on earth)."

That Pobedonostsev was more than displeased with the first "Pro and Contra" chapters, feeling, no doubt, that Dostoevsky had turned devil's advocate, becomes apparent from his letter of June 9, 1879. "Alas," he wrote, "my dear Fyodor Mikhailovich, our life is so distorted, so encumbered and so entangled that it is difficult to find any simple human features in it. . . . We all wander about the world and torture ourselves with the question: what are we to do? This question leads us all astray and, quite naturally, a large number of our youth, grown up amid the miasmas of books, are enticed onto the road of lawlessness and lies. And not they alone—all of us, who regard ourselves as members of the intelligentsia, have lost our way and wander about as though a wood demon had cast a spell on us, and yet beside us lies the great Tsarist road of truth. . . ." Not a very enthusiastic reception of the intellectually most powerful part of Dostoevsky's novel. Dostoevsky did not reply to it for two months. It was only after he had sent off the sixth book of the second part ("The Russian Monk") that he wrote to Pobedonostsev from Ems,[24] drawing his attention to it and expressing the hope that he would let him know what he thought of it. "I am expecting the critics to abuse me for it," he declared. "As for myself, I realize that I have not done one tenth of what I had intended. I wrote this book *for a few* and," he concluded, repeating his statement to Lyubimov about the previous chapter, "consider it to be the culminating point of my work."

By the time Pobedonostsev received Dostoevsky's letter he had read the next installment of the novel, including the chapter on the Grand

[24] *Letters*, August 9, 1879.

Inquisitor. Sensing Dostoevsky's displeasure with his earlier comments on "Pro and Contra," he hastened to reassure him in his reply of August 16. "Your 'Grand Inquisitor,'" he wrote, "made a strong impression on me. I have not read anything so powerful for a long time. All I was waiting for was a rebuff, an objection and an explanation—but so far in vain." In his reply,[25] Dostoevsky repeated that his answer "to the whole of that *negative* side" would appear on August 31 in the sixth book of the second part. "That is why," he wrote, "I am so nervous about it, for I am not sure that it will be a *sufficient* answer. Particularly as the answer is not a direct one, not to the views expressed in 'The Grand Inquisitor' (and in the earlier chapters), point by point, but an indirect one. 'The Russian Monk' introduces something directly opposite to the outlook on life expressed in 'Pro and Contra'; but again, it is introduced not point by point, but, as it were, in an artistic picture. This is what worries me, I mean, shall I be understood, shall I attain even a little bit of what I am aiming at? In addition, there are my duties as an artist: I had to introduce a modest and majestic figure and yet life is full of comic elements and is only majestic in its inner meaning, so that because of the artistic requirements I was involuntarily forced to touch upon the rather vulgar aspects of my monk's biography so as not to impair artistic realism. Then there are some of the monk's sermons which will evoke violent protests that they are absurd because they are too enthusiastic. Of course, they are absurd in their ordinary meaning, but I can't help thinking that in a different, inner, meaning they are just."

In sending "The Russian Monk" to Lyubimov from Ems on August 19, Dostoevsky pointed out that many of Elder Zossima's sermons, or, rather, the way in which they were expressed, "belong to his person, that is to say, his artistic portrayal. So far as I am concerned, though I hold the same views as those he expressed, I should have expressed them in a different form and language. On the other hand, he *could not* express himself in a different language or in a different *spirit*. . . . Such, for instance, are the elder's discourses on *What is a monk* or *About masters and servants* or *Whether one can be a judge of one's fellow men*, etc. I took the face and figure from the ancient Russian monks and holy men: profound meekness combined with boundless, naïve hopes about Russia's moral and even political destiny. Have not St. Sergius and the archbishops Peter and Alexey regarded Russia in a similar way?"

On September 16, 1879, Dostoevsky sent off the beginning of the third part of his novel and, in his accompanying letter to Lyubimov, he implored him again not to cross out or alter anything. He was particularly anxious that the verb *to stink* used by the crazy monk, Ferapont, about Zossima's corpse should on no account be altered. "One little *nota bene*," he added in a postscript in this connection. "Don't for heaven's

[25] *Letters*, September 5, 1879.

sake think that in a work of mine I would presume to cast the slightest doubt on the miraculous powers of the relics of saints. It is merely a matter of the relics of the dead monk Zossima, and that is quite another matter."

By the end of 1879 less than two-thirds of *The Brothers Karamazov* had been published. The last installment appeared in 1880 in the October issue of *The Russian Herald.* But by the beginning of December 1879, Dostoevsky was sure of its great success. "My novel," he wrote to Lyubimov on December 8, "is being read everywhere; young people read it, people in high society read it, reviewers abuse and praise it, and, to judge by the impression it has created all around, I have never before had so great a success."

VII

The success of his novel made Dostoevsky a much-sought-after performer at all sorts of charitable functions. There can be no doubt that he tremendously enjoyed the deafening applause with which the audiences greeted his appearance on the platform and the numerous bows he had to take after his readings. Neither can there be any doubt that these readings had a disastrous effect on his health and, together with his heavy smoking, hastened his death.

In June 1879 he complained to several correspondents of the deterioration in his health. "My health," he wrote on June 15, "has not been at all satisfactory and I am thinking of going to Ems." On July 16 he wrote from Staraya Russa to another correspondent: "My health has become worse, and my children keep falling ill—first, my son had typhoid fever and then both of them had whooping cough, the weather is terrible, it is pouring with rain from morning till night, it is cold and damp, one is in constant danger of catching a chill, during the whole of the last month there were no more than three days without rain and perhaps only one sunny day. In such a state of mind and under such conditions I kept writing, working at night, listening to the wind howling and bringing down century-old trees."

The only solace he derived in this dismal situation was in the renewal of his friendship with Anna Korvin-Krukovsky. He had met her again with her husband, Charles Victor Jaclard, a French revolutionary leader who had played a prominent part in the Paris Commune, in Petersburg in 1874. "The summer of 1879 began very pleasantly," Anna records in her reminiscences: "A. V. Jaclard-Korvin arrived for the season in Russa with her family, which we liked very much. Almost every day my husband, on his way back from his walk, went to have a talk with this intelligent and kind woman who had played an important part in his life." But how greatly she really resented her husband's visits to the woman with whom he had been in love becomes clear from the catty way she tried to suggest in her letters to Dostoevsky that Jaclard was having an affair with the local doctor's wife.

"You seem to want to tell me something about Jaclard," Dostoevsky wrote to Anna from Ems four days after his arrival there on July 30. "Is he really running after her? Well, I suppose it's French taste, but what is his wife doing about it?" And two weeks later: "So it's true about Jaclard. Dear, oh dear! Well done, though. There's a real man for you, picking the flowers of pleasure, not like us, bullied and downtrodden."

However jocular the last sentence was meant to sound, there was more than a grain of truth in it, and Anna might have reacted quite strongly had she not been at the time engaged on a much more serious business.

In his letter to Anna from Ems,[26] Dostoevsky, in referring to the death of his late brother's wife, Emilia, tried once more to justify himself for his failure to make a success of *Epoch* by repeating his unconvincing argument that it was his brother's family that had been responsible for the loss of the 10,000 rubles he had received from his rich Moscow aunt. "I am always thinking of my death (thinking of it seriously here)," he went on, "and what I shall leave you and my children with. Now I am busy with the Karamazovs. I have to finish it well, give a jeweler's finish to it, but it is a difficult and a risky thing and it will take a great deal of my strength. It is also a fateful thing: it has to establish my name, otherwise there will be no more hope. After I finish my novel I shall have to open a subscription list for the *Writer's Diary* at the end of next year. On the money I hope to get from the subscriptions I shall buy an estate and until the next subscriptions come in shall have to live *somehow or other* on the sales of my books. Energetic measures must be taken, otherwise we shall never get anything. But enough of this. There will be plenty of time to discuss it with you, for I know you don't like the idea of a country estate while I am convinced (1) that land is capital which will treble in value by the time the children grow up and (2) that a man who owns land also takes an active part in the wielding of political power over the state." Four days later he reverted to the subject again. "I am still dreaming here of how to buy an estate," he wrote to Anna. "I have nearly gone mad on the idea. I am worried about the children and their future."

But while Dostoevsky was dreaming of taking "energetic measures," Anna was actually taking them without even consulting him. Would, one cannot help wondering, Dostoevsky have brought his action for the annulment of his aunt's will, and by doing so brought about a breach with his nearest relations, had not Anna spurred him on to take that step? In the end he won the action, the court ruling that a third of the estate should go to the four Dostoevsky brothers (the rest going to the

[26] *Letters,* August 25, 1879.

heirs of Alexandra Kumanin's half sisters), who had to compensate their sisters in cash for their share in the estate. Dostoevsky's share amounted to 1,600 acres, but as a great part of the estate consisted of marshland, Dostoevsky was willing to forego some of his share provided he got land of better quality. It took the heirs a long time to decide how the estate should be divided. In the summer of 1879 they at last agreed to meet in Moscow and, if an agreement were reached, to go to the estate and carry out the division on the spot. Anna said nothing about it to Dostoevsky. Knowing how anxious he was for the religious upbringing of his children, she told him that she was taking them on a "pilgrimage" to a monastery within eighty miles of Staraya Russa, but instead she took them to Moscow and from there to the estate where, she writes, "I was successful in obtaining for my husband's share 540 acres of timberland and 270 acres of arable land."

Timberland was, of course, a very valuable commodity, and Anna, no doubt, was very satisfied in having obtained so large a share of it, though she must have known how greatly Dostoevsky objected to the destruction of the Russian forests by the sale of timber. "With the destruction of our forests," Dostoevsky wrote to a correspondent,[27] anticipating the theme of a play by Chekhov ten years later, "the climate of Russia is definitely changing: there is nothing left to preserve moisture or to stop the winds." When it came to money, though, Anna was not worried by her husband's views. Still, before the 800 odd acres could be sold and an estate bought so that Dostoevsky's children, if not himself, could "wield political power over the state," a fantastic reason that could have occurred only to Dostoevsky, he had to come to an agreement with his sisters about paying them their compensation in cash. As Anna held the purse strings, it is not surprising that the question of compensation had not been settled before Dostoevsky's death in January 1881. However, it played a fateful part in hastening it.

VIII

Dostoevsky returned home from Ems at the beginning of September 1879, without any great improvement in his health. The doctor who had examined him on his arrival in Ems found, Dostoevsky wrote to his wife, that "some part of my lungs has changed its place the same as my heart which has also changed its place—all as a result of the emphysema," but he added as a consolation that "there is nothing at all wrong with my heart and that all these changes of position are not particularly dangerous." At the end of his stay he told his wife that his cure had not been particularly useful. "My cough is as bad now as when I arrived here," he wrote, "and the whole of the last week I have even felt a painful constriction in my chest as in my worst periods."

[27] *Letters*, June 15, 1879.

On his return to Petersburg he had himself examined by a doctor he trusted (a cousin of Anna's), who later told Anna that his illness had progressed so far as to become a threat to his life. It seems that the small blood vessels in the lungs had become so thin and brittle that they might burst at the slightest physical strain. The doctor advised Dostoevsky not to make any sudden movements or lift anything heavy and to try to avoid any excitements.

In Petersburg, however, he carried on with writing his novel and with his public readings. He was also beginning to be lionized in high society and was a frequent visitor at the Thursday at homes of the Countess Sofia Tolstoy, the widow of the dramatist Alexey Tolstoy. Describing such an at home in a letter to Leo Tolstoy on April 7, 1880, Strakhov wrote: "I found there Goncharov and Dostoevsky, who, I am told, do not miss a single Thursday, as well as Polonsky and Vladimir Solovyov. . . . The Countess is considered to be a woman of great intellect and she is extremely amiable, so that I felt a desire to follow the example of Goncharov and Dostoevsky. Only I am afraid I do not possess such a splendid cutaway coat as the ones they were wearing and which Solovyov considers absolutely shameless."

It was the Countess who presented Dostoevsky with a photograph of the Dresden Sistine Madonna, which Anna framed and hung over the sofa in Dostoevsky's study as a surprise for his birthday. "In the last year of his life," Anna writes, "I used to find my husband many times standing before this great picture, looking so deeply moved that he did not hear me come in and, not to disturb his devotional mood, I used to go out quietly."

On February 3, 1880, Dostoevsky was chosen vice-president of the Slav Philanthropic Society, and at an extraordinary meeting of the society on February 14 he read an address to the Tsar on the occasion of the twenty-fifth anniversary of his accession to the throne. On February 20 part of the Winter Palace was blown up in a third attempt to assassinate Alexander II. Alexey Suvorin, the publisher of *New Times*, who was a few years later to become one of Chekhov's closest friends, relates in his diary the following conversation he had with Dostoevsky a few days after the explosion in the Winter Palace: " 'Imagine,' Dostoevsky said, 'that you and I are standing at the windows of Daziaro's and looking at the pictures. Beside us stands a man who is pretending to be looking at the pictures. He is waiting for something and keeps looking round. Suddenly another man comes up to him hastily and says: "The Winter Palace will soon be blown up. I have set the fuse." We hear that. Imagine that we hear it, that the men are so excited that they do not lower their voices sufficiently. What would you and I have done? Would we have gone to the Winter Palace to warn them about the explosion or would we have gone to the police, or asked a policeman to arrest the man? Would you have gone?'

" 'No, I wouldn't.'

" 'Neither would I,' said Dostoevsky. 'Why not? It's horrible!' "

It may, indeed, have been horrible, but it also shows how obnoxious the role of informer had become to decent people and even to so fervent a supporter of the autocracy as Dostoevsky: he knew that a thing like that would have ruined his reputation forever.

In the same entry in his diary Suvorin reports Dostoevsky as telling him that the hero of his next novel would be Alyosha Karamazov, who would become a revolutionary, commit a political crime and be executed. Similar versions of Dostoevsky's proposed novel were left by Anna and Vladimir Solovyov. They all belong to the time when Dostoevsky himself hardly knew what the ending of *The Brothers Karamazov* would be. By the time he finished it, the idea that the Alyosha of the Epilogue could ever have become a revolutionary capable of committing a capital political crime must have seemed quite absurd even to those to whom Dostoevsky confided the plans of his next novel.

The next important event in Dostoevsky's life, an event that he came to regard as the crowning glory of his career, was the address he delivered in Moscow on June 8, 1880, on the occasion of the unveiling of the Pushkin Memorial. He went to Moscow as the delegate of the Slav Philanthropic Society. He wrote his speech before leaving for Moscow on May 22 "in the most *extremist* spirit of my convictions," he wrote to Pobedonostsev,[28] "and that is why I am expecting a certain amount of vilification. . . . I have already heard in Petersburg that there is a certain clique in Moscow which is trying to prevent certain things from being said at the unveiling, and that what they are afraid of are certain *reactionary* speeches which *some* people may make at the meeting of the Society of Lovers of Russian Literature, who have undertaken to organize the festivities. But I am not going to be put off and I am not afraid, for I am determined to serve our cause and I shall speak without fear. The professors are running after Turgenev, who seems to have become my enemy in good earnest. (He has spread a scandalous story about me in *The European Herald* about something that was supposed to have happened 35 years ago.) But I cannot glorify Pushkin and extol 'Verochka' at the same time."

The "scandalous story" for which Dostoevsky blamed Turgenev appeared in an extract from Annenkov's memoirs in which Dostoevsky was said to have insisted that his *Poor People* should be published with a "black border" round the pages. Dostoevsky violently denied the story and, indeed, no reliable evidence of its authenticity has been discovered. As for "Verochka," Dostoevsky was referring to Vera Zasulich, to whom Turgenev had dedicated *The Threshold*, one of his *Poems in Prose*, circulated in mimeographed copies, which Dostoevsky must have seen.

28 *Letters*, May 19, 1880.

Dostoevsky did not take Anna with him to Moscow, insisting that she should stay behind in Staraya Russa with the children, for which she "punished" him by not answering his letters and only scribbling a few words in pencil in reply, addressing him formally by his name and patronymic. It was only towards the end of the second week that she relented and began answering his letters.

In Moscow Dostoevsky arrived "exhausted and absolutely done in," as he wrote to Anna, but determined "to find out everything about the literary intrigues." He was, however, given a warm reception by his "enemies," who even gave a dinner in his honor on May 25. "The dinner," he wrote to Anna that night, "was indeed very splendid. A special hall was taken for the occasion. Fillets of sturgeon, two and a half feet long, a foot-long boiled sterlet, turtle soup, wild strawberries, quail, marvelous asparagus, ice cream, exquisite wines and champagne galore. Six speeches, some of them very long, were made in my honor. They spoke of my 'great' importance as an artist of 'universal sympathies,' a publicist and a Russian. Then followed innumerable toasts, everyone getting up to clink glasses with me. They were all wildly enthusiastic. I replied with a very successful speech which produced a great effect. . . ."

There was at first the danger that the celebrations might be postponed indefinitely because of the death of the Empress, but in the end permission was given to proceed with the unveiling of the Pushkin monument on June 6. In the meantime Dostoevsky basked in the glory of his fame. His most frequent visitors were Dmitry Grigorovich, his old fellow student at the Engineering College, with whom he had shared rooms and who had been responsible for taking the manuscript of *Poor People* to Nekrasov, and Professor Viskovatov, who was later to spread the discreditable story Strakhov was so eager to disclose in his letter to Tolstoy. On May 26 he was present at another dinner, when he was given "an enthusiastic welcome," again with "champagne galore and cigars at 75 rubles a hundred." On the same day, Grigorovich, he wrote to Anna,[29] "told me that Turgenev, who had come back from a visit to Tolstoy, was ill, and that Tolstoy [who had refused the invitation to take part in the Pushkin celebration and declared that the whole thing was a farce] had almost gone off his head or even perhaps completely gone off his head." On the following day he wrote to Anna that Katkov had confirmed that Tolstoy had gone mad. It had been suggested that he might go and see Tolstoy, for it was only a matter of two days' journey there and back, but, he declared, "I shan't go, though it would be very interesting." Describing the reception of the delegation by the Moscow Town Council on June 5, Dostoevsky wrote: "I saw (and even talked to) Pushkin's daughter. Ostrovsky—the local Jupiter—came up to me. Turgenev rushed up amiably. The others—the liberal

[29] *Letters*, May 27, 1880.

party, among them Pleshcheyev [to whom, by the way he had only just sent 200 rubles in repayment of part of the 1,000 rubles he had borrowed before his return from Siberia from the man who had stood beside him on the scaffold]—treats me with reserve and, as it were, haughtily: you are a reactionary, so to speak, and we are liberals."

On June 6 he laid a wreath at the memorial after its unveiling in the morning, then he went to the meeting at the university where, to his chagrin, the rector announced the election of Turgenev as "honorary member" of the university. "Then there followed," Dostoevsky wrote to Anna,[30] "a dinner with speeches. In the evening there was the reading at the Noblemen's Assembly with music. I read Pimen's soliloquy. In spite of the impossibility of the choice (for Pimen cannot be expected to shout so as to be heard all over the hall) and acoustically one of the worst halls, I am told that I read it superbly, though I could not be heard properly. I was given an excellent reception. For a long time I could not start for the applause, and after the reading I had to answer three calls. But Turgenev, who had read abominably,[31] received many more calls than I. . . . This morning Ivan Aksakov refused to read his speech after Turgenev (in which he spoke slightingly of Pushkin, refusing to acknowledge him as a national poet.) All the same, the reception I received [at the public meeting of the Society of Lovers of Russian Literature, at which Dostoevsky made only a short speech] was quite astonishing, although only the people in the stalls applauded me. Besides, men and women came in crowds behind the scene to shake hands with me. During the interval I walked through the hall and lots of people, young and old, rushed up to me, saying, You are our prophet, you have made us better men since we have read *The Brothers Karamazov*. (In short, I am convinced that the Karamazovs have had a tremendous influence.) The same thing happened when I left the meeting in the morning. . . . At last night's dinner two ladies brought me flowers. Today was a literary dinner. . . . I was forced to make a speech, but said only a few words—a roar of enthusiasm, literally, a roar. . . . When at half past nine I got up to go, a shout of hurrah was raised, in which even those who do not sympathize with my views had to join. Then the whole crowd of them rushed downstairs after me, ran out into the street without overcoats, helped me into a cab, and, suddenly, began kissing my hands, not only one, but dozens of them. . . ." But that was nothing to the reception he got after his speech next day.

"This morning," he wrote to Anna[32] at 8 o'clock in the evening, "I read my speech at the meeting of the Society of Lovers of Literature. The hall was packed. No, Anna, no, you cannot imagine the effect my speech

[30] *Letters*, June 7, 1880.

[31] Turgenev read Pushkin's poem *The Cloud*. At the third verse he dried up and he finished the poem together with the audience.

[32] *Letters*, June 8, 1880.

produced. My Petersburg successes are nothing, absolutely nothing, compared with it. When I came out, the hall resounded with applause and for a long, long time, they would not let me read my speech. I bowed, gestured to allow me to read–it was no use: excitement, enthusiasm (all because of the Karamazovs!). At last I began to read: I was interrupted at the end of every page and sometimes at every sentence by a thunder of applause. (This is a great victory for our ideas after 25 years of errors!) But when at the end I spoke about the *world-wide unity of man*, the hall seemed to be in hysterics, and when I finished–it was not just a roar, but a howl of enthusiasm: people I have never seen before cried, sobbed, embraced one another and *vowed to be better men and not to hate but love one another*. The meeting was in disorder: everyone rushed towards me onto the platform: society women, girl students, high civil servants, men students–they were all embracing and kissing me. All the members of our society on the platform embraced and kissed me, and literally wept with ecstasy. The calls went on for half an hour, people waved their handkerchiefs and, suddenly, for instance, two old men stopped me: 'We've been enemies for 20 years, did not talk to one another, and now we have embraced and made friends. It is you who reconciled us. You are our saint, you are our prophet!' 'Our prophet, our prophet!' people shouted in the crowd. Turgenev, about whom I put in a nice word in my speech, rushed up to embrace me with tears in his eyes. Annenkov ran up to me to shake hands with me and kiss me on the shoulder. 'You are a genius, you are more than a genius!' both said to me. Ivan Aksakov rushed onto the platform and announced that my speech *was not just a speech, but an historic event!* A dark cloud had covered the horizon and now Dostoevsky's speech, like the emerging sun, had dispersed everything and illuminated everything. From now on an era of brotherhood began and there would be no more misunderstandings. 'Yes! Yes!' they all shouted and again embraces and tears. The meeting was declared closed. I rushed behind the scenes to save myself, but everyone, particularly women, burst in after me. They kissed my hands, harassed me. One of them fell weeping at my feet in hysterics and fainted. Victory, complete victory! The chairman rang the bell and announced that the Society of Lovers of Russian Literature unanimously decided to elect me an honorary member. More shouts and screams. After an hour's break the meeting started again, but no one wanted to speak. Aksakov declared that he would not read his speech because the great speech of our genius Dostoevsky had said and solved everything. However, we made him read his speech. While the reading went on, a plot was being hatched. I felt so exhausted that I wanted to go home but they kept me there by force. During that hour they bought a huge laurel wreath, almost five feet in diameter, and at the end of the meeting over a hundred women rushed onto the platform and crowned me with the laurel wreath: 'For the Russian women about whom you have said so many good things.' All wept, more enthusiasm."

That night, after he had read Pushkin's poem *The Prophet* with similar success at another meeting, Dostoevsky laid the laurel wreath at the Pushkin memorial.

IX

The revivalist atmosphere of mass hysteria produced by Dostoevsky's "very clever, brilliant and cunningly skillful speech" (as Turgenev later described it) was only partly due to the growing excitement at the Pushkin celebrations; most of it was undoubtedly caused by the "electrifying magnetism," as one woman in his audience described it, of his husky voice and by what Vsevolod Solovyov characterized as his "passionate conviction and inspired and prophetic enthusiasm." In his speech Dostoevsky merely tried to father on Pushkin his own chauvinistic belief in the messianic destiny of the Russian people. "Had there been no Pushkin," he declared, "our faith in new Russian independence would never perhaps have been formed with such irresistible force, nor our now already conscious hope in our national strength, nor, finally, our belief in our independent destiny in the family of European nations." Even less convincing is his attempt to foist on Pushkin his own idea of submissiveness by interpreting Pushkin's early poem *The Gypsies* as expressing "the Russian solution of the question, the cursed question," in accordance with the common people's faith and its conception of justice: "Humble yourself, proud man, and first of all break down your pride. . . . When you conquer yourself, when you subdue yourself, you will be free as never before and you will begin the great work, and you will make others free and you will behold happiness, for your life will be full, and you will at last understand your people and its sacred truth."

No more convincing is Dostoevsky's idea, repeated many times before, that it is only the Russian people who possess the gift of what he called "universal responsiveness," that is to say, the ability to absorb the ideas of other nations, of "transmuting the Russian national spirit into the spirit of other nations"—a curious delusion, considering that he himself could never master a foreign language. "We have received the genius of other nations into our soul not with hostile but with friendly intent," he declared, "for we know by instinct, almost from the very first step, how to distinguish and remove contradictions, excuse and reconcile differences, and thereby have already shown our readiness and our propensity, which has only now revealed itself to ourselves, for a universal union with all the tribes of the great Aryan family. Yes, the destiny of the Russian is indubitably to become all-European and universal. To be a real Russian, to be fully Russian merely means (this has to be emphasized) to be the brother of all peoples, to be an *all-man*, if you like. . . . To a real Russian Europe and the destiny of the entire great Aryan tribe is as dear as Russia itself, as the destiny of his own native land. . . . Oh," he went on with ecstatic abandon, having by now reduced his audience to a state of limp acquiescence in any insane political doctrine that his inflamed imagination might conjure up, "Oh, the peoples of Europe do not realize how dear they are to us. And in future, I believe it, we, that is, of course, not we, but the future generations of Russians, will understand to a man that to be a real Russian can only mean to strive to bring about a final reconcilation of European contradictions, to point to a way out for the European heartsickness in the Russian soul, universal and all-uniting, to find a place in it with brotherly love for all our brothers, and, in the end, perhaps also to utter the final word of the great, general harmony, the final brotherly agreement of all tribes according to Christ's evangelical law! I know, I know perfectly well that my words may appear ecstatic, exaggerated and fantastic. Let them be so, but I am not sorry to have uttered them." And, still afraid that he had perhaps said more than was wise, he explained that he did not call for "economic glory, for the glory of the sword or science." He only meant "the brotherhood of men," which he claimed the "Russian heart" was perhaps more than any other nation destined to bring about, for he could descry its traces in the artistic genius of Pushkin. "Let our land be poor," he went on in his best prophetic vein, "but this poor land 'Christ has walked all over, blessing, in his guise of a slave.' Why, then, should we not be the receptacle of His last word? Was He not born in a manger himself?"

The logic of the last sentence is not very easy to follow, but it is not without significance that Dostoevsky should in his peroration have made use of the quotation from Tyutchev's poem as a statement of fact: Christ has become the "Russian Christ," for, as he was to explain in the August number of his *Writer's Diary*, the Russian peasants had long since become "enlightened" by accepting "the whole essence of Christ and his teaching," while Christianity no longer existed in Western Europe, Catholicism having turned it into idolatry, and Protestantism into "atheism."

A remarkable and characteristic omission in the speech is any mention of the Greek Orthodox Church, a fact that led Pobedonostsev to draw Dostoevsky's attention to an article on his speech in which the writer denounced him as "almost a heretic" and rebuked him for "ascribing to the Redeemer promises about 'universal brotherhood of peoples,' 'universal peace' and 'harmony' which He never made." Pobedonostsev's shrewd comment was: "If only you had a clear and firm hold of your idea yourself, if only it were grounded in faith and not in vacillation."

X

On June 11 Dostoevsky returned from Moscow to Staraya Russa, where he stayed for the rest of the summer and the beginning of autumn. There were still over 200 printed pages of *The Brothers Karamazov*, including five chapters of the eleventh book and the whole of the twelfth book and the Epilogue, to be written. In addition, he wanted to publish a special number of his *Writer's Diary* to reply to the attacks on his Pushkin speech which had begun to appear in both the liberal and the conservative press. The speech was published in *Moscow News* on June 13, but it seems that even Katkov, the arch-reactionary with whom Turgenev had refused to clink glasses at a banquet during the Pushkin festivities, got cold feet when he read it. "I see," Dostoevsky wrote to Countess Tolstoy,[33] "that they have left out from my speech literally all the essential points: (1) the universal responsiveness of Pushkin and his ability of complete re-embodiment into geniuses of other nations and (2) the fact that this ability stems entirely from our national spirit and that, therefore, Pushkin is our most national poet." It never occurred to Dostoevsky that within a comparatively short period after his death this process of "responsiveness" and "re-embodiment" would also be practiced by a great number of Western European and American writers so far as his own genius was concerned—without the advantage of the supposedly receptive Russian national spirit.

Between June 15 and October 1, he informed another correspondent, he wrote twenty printed folio pages of his novel and three more of the special number of his *Writer's Diary*, published on October 12, an amazing proof of his terrific vitality only a few months before his death. On October 1 he had a very severe epileptic attack which put him out of action for a week, and from October 10 (he had moved to his Petersburg flat on October 7) to October 30 he wrote another five printed folio pages, "that is," he explains in a letter to a correspondent,[34] "eighty of some of the most important pages of my novel." On November 8, he at last sent off the Epilogue. "Well," he wrote to Lyubimov, "so my novel is finished. I have worked three years on it—and this is a significant moment for me. I hope to publish a special edition of it before Christmas. But I am not saying good-by to you. You see, I intend to live and write for another 20 years."

But all the time his health was rapidly deteriorating. "My health is very bad," he wrote to a correspondent.[35] "My days are numbered." To his brother Andrey he wrote:[36] "I don't think I shall live long; it is

[33] *Letters*, June 13, 1880.
[34] *Letters*, October 18, 1880.
[35] *Letters*, October 15, 1880.
[36] *Letters*, November 28, 1880.

getting very difficult to last through the winter with my emphysema." Most of his work he was doing, as usual, at night. "It is night now," he wrote to a correspondent,[37] "six o'clock in the morning, the city is awakening, and I have not gone to bed yet. The doctor tells me that I must not do any work at night, that I ought to be asleep and not sit at my writing table for 10 or 12 hours. Why am I working at night? Why? Because as soon as I wake up at one o'clock in the afternoon the doorbell starts ringing: one man comes in to ask me to do one thing, another wants me to do something else, a third comes with some demand, a fourth insists that I should solve some insoluble 'cursed' question for him, for otherwise he threatens to kill himself. (And I have never seen him in my life before.) Then a deputation arrives from men students, from girl students, from secondary schools, from some charitable society—all anxious that I should read them something. So at what other time can I think, work, read, live? . . ."

One of these visitors was the fifteen-year-old D. S. Merezhkovsky, who read his poems to Dostoevsky and records him as saying: "To write well one must suffer, suffer!"

The requests for public readings were becoming the bane of his life, and yet he could not bring himself to refuse them: the critics had begun attacking him on all sides, and he felt that he had to keep in touch with his audiences. He loved the applause, too, the feeling that he held them in the hollow of his hand. "What an extraordinary thing," a woman friend of his wrote in her diary. "His life is hanging by a thread, thin, hollow-chested, can't speak above a whisper, and yet as soon as he starts reading, he seems to grow in stature and strength. Where, one wonders, does he get the strength, this masterful strength." Between October 14 and November 30, Dostoevsky gave four public readings. Writing to Ivan Aksakov,[38] while he was busy working on the January issue of his *Writer's Diary*, which he was planning to resume publishing during 1881, he complained of his constant "petty and stupid worries, such as public readings, etc., which cannot be avoided, and," he added, "my cruel ill-health . . . my emphysema is on the rampage again, I am terribly short-winded and, as a result, physically exhausted."

In spite of his general exhaustion, Dostoevsky took part in a reading at Countess Sofia Tolstoy's on January 19, 1881, taking the part of the hermit in Count Alexey Tolstoy's *Death of Ivan the Terrible*. A day or two later Orest Miller came to see him about another public reading on January 29. Dostoevsky, who was going through the proofs of his *Writer's Diary*, looked very agitated because he feared that the censorship would not pass a sentence or two in which he demanded that the government should "show confidence" in the peasants, for it was only from them that one would hear "the real truth." "If they don't pass it,"

[37] *Letters,* October 15, 1880.
[38] *Letters,* December 3, 1880.

he cried, "everything will be lost!" The moment was obviously not propitious for conducting negotiations, as Orest Miller learned when Dostoevsky rejected point-blank his suggestion that he should read a passage from *Eugene Onegin*, offering to read instead some of Pushkin's short poems.

A week before Dostoevsky's death, Anna recorded in a hitherto unpublished note: "On Friday, January 23, when he said he was worried about the state of my health, I said to him: 'Let me and the children go to Reval and you go to Ems. When you return, we shall spend the rest of the summer in Staraya Russa. After three weeks we shall have to go back to Petersburg because of the children.' 'All right, go if you like," he said, 'but I have other plans for the winter.' 'What plans?' 'These,' he replied. 'Now we have a little money and we shall get a little more from my *Writer's Diary* so that altogether we may have as much as 12 or 15 thousand rubles. Well, then, let's buy the estate near Moscow you've heard about. I shall then go to Ems and you'll look after the estate. We shall live there till the autumn, and then come back here. You and the children will look much better after a few months in the country.' " Dostoevsky, Anna adds, always dreamed of a country estate, but he invariably insisted that it should have woods. He did not care for pasture or arable land. A wood, even a small one, he regarded as constituting the natural wealth of an estate.

Two days later, on Sunday, January 25, Dostoevsky had a large number of visitors, including Maykov, Strakhov and Orest Miller. Anna records: "As soon as he got up on Sunday, Maykov arrived. They discussed the ending of the January issue of the *Writer's Diary* and the contents of the February issue. Then Orest Miller came and they talked about a change in the program [of the public reading on January 29]. Miller insisted that he ought to stick to the published program and read from *Eugene Onegin*, but in the end they agreed that he should choose something different. After his visitors had gone, he went out for a walk, namely to deliver the last page of the *Writer's Diary* to the printers, asking them to let him have the proofs the following day. He returned at half past six and in another half hour he had dinner. At dinner we kept talking about *Pickwick Papers*, the children remembering all sorts of incidents and telling him about them. After dinner he went to his study to have his coffee and then sat down to write a letter to Katkov and, having written it, called me in and read it to me. He had asked Katkov to send him the 4,000 rubles his journal still owed him for the Karamazovs, adding that it was his last request. In the evening he went for a walk."

The trouble started with a visit of his sister Vera Ivanov on January 26. According to Dostoevsky's daughter, Lyubov, who was almost twelve at the time and can be trusted to have remembered the events of that day, Vera had come to Petersburg specially for the purpose of persuading Dostoevsky to let his sisters have a part of his share of the Kumanin estate. There was, she records, a stormy scene between them, his sister bursting into tears and reproaching him for his callousness. Dostoevsky rushed back to his study. A short while later, he had his first hemorrhage. (Anna gives quite a different version of Dostoevsky's fatal illness, but she was obviously trying to conceal the circumstances of Vera's visit.) At half past four Dostoevsky's doctor arrived. During the auscultation Dostoevsky had another hemorrhage and lost consciousness. When he came to he at once sent for the priest to receive extreme unction. Before the arrival of the priest he took leave of his wife and children and gave them his blessing. "The loss of blood," records Suvorin, who was present in the patient's room, "greatly exhausted him, his head sank to his chest and his face darkened." After the administration of the Eucharist he felt much better, but his doctor insisted that two more doctors should be called in.

On Tuesday, January 27, he had no more hemorrhages. He seemed to have calmed down and become more cheerful. He asked to see the children and even said a few words to them in a whisper. In the afternoon he was getting worried about the *Diary*, but after Anna had made a few suggestions for cutting out seven superfluous lines, he calmed down. His condition on the day before he died Suvorin describes as follows: "One moment he expected to die shortly, issued instructions, worried about what was going to happen to his family, and another he was convinced that he was going to live, made plans of his future works, talked about how his children were going to grow up and the sort of education he was going to give them."

At 7 o'clock in the morning of Wednesday, January 28, Anna, who had spent all the night at Dostoevsky's bedside, woke up to find her husband staring at her.

"How do you feel, my dear?" she asked, bending over him.

"You know, Anna," he said in a whisper, "I have been awake for the last three hours, thinking all the time, and I have now realized clearly that I am going to die today."

Anna tried to comfort him, but he insisted that he was going to die that day.

"Light a candle, Anna," he whispered, "and give me my New Testament."

It was the New Testament the wives of the Decembrists had given him thirty years earlier in Tobolsk when he was on the way to his prison in Omsk. He had often told his fortune by opening it at random and reading the first sentence on the left-hand page. It was a bad Russian translation and often gave quite a wrong meaning to the words of the gospels—an ironic comment on the scene that followed.

He opened the book himself and asked Anna to read the first sentence on the left-hand page. Anna read: "But John restrained him and said,

I need to be baptized by you, and you come to me? But Jesus said to him in reply: do not restrain me, for this is how we have to fulfill all righteousness."

"Do you hear?" said Dostoevsky, closing the book. " 'Do not restrain me,' this means I am going to die."

In a footnote to this passage in her reminiscences Anna points out that in the most recent Russian translations of the gospels the words "do not restrain me" appear as "let it be so," but still goes on to assert that, "since the words of the gospels had such a profound significance in our lives," Dostoevsky would have recovered if the words of St. Matthew 3:14–15 had been different, though she goes on to say that he would probably not have survived the assassination of Alexander II on March 1.

At 9 o'clock Dostoevsky fell asleep, but woke up suddenly at 11. He had another hemorrhage and grew very weak. Later on many of his relations, including Pasha, came to see him, but no one was allowed to enter his room. Pasha, Anna records, insisted on going in to see his stepfather, but the doctor would not let him, and he kept peering in through the chink in the door. Dostoevsky, according to Anna, noticed it and, looking agitated, said to her: "Anna, don't let him in, he'll upset me." Poor Pasha had not a chance against Anna now. He kept demanding that a notary should be called in so that Dostoevsky could dispose of his possessions. But, as Anna dryly remarks, with the exception of the 4,000 rubles *The Russian Herald* still owed him for *The Brothers Karamazov*, which belonged to her and her children, Dostoevsky had no possessions to dispose of. As for the royalties on his books, he had made them over to her in 1873.

Among the many visitors that day was Maykov, who came in the morning and returned with his wife at half past six. Half an hour later Dostoevsky, "without any visible reason," as Anna expressed it, gave a shudder, raised himself a little on the sofa, and "a trickle of blood stained his face." He had another hemorrhage and lost consciousness. "My children and I knelt at the head of the bed," Anna writes, "trying with all our might not to burst into loud sobs, for the doctor warned us that the sense of hearing was the last thing that leaves a man and that a loud noise might prolong the agony and the suffering of the dying man. I held my husband's hand in mine and felt his pulse beating fainter and fainter."

A correspondent of a Moscow journal left the following account of his last minutes: "He lay dressed on a sofa with his head thrown back on the pillow. The light of the lamp and the candles on the small bedside table fell directly on his forehead and cheeks, white as paper, and on the bloodstain on his chin. The breath came with a kind of faint whistling sound from his throat and through the convulsively open lips.

His eyelids were half closed by the same kind of mechanically spasmodic process of his stricken organism. . . . He was in a coma."

Dostoevsky died at thirty-eight minutes past eight in the evening of January 28, 1881. He was fifty-nine years and three months old.

His body was taken to the chapel of the Alexander Nevsky monastery on the morning of January 31. Sixty-seven delegations, representing all sorts of societies and organizations, and thousands of people followed his hearse to the monastery along the streets that had been empty when, on Christmas Eve thirty-one years ago, he had been driven in chains to the snowy wastes of Siberia.

Throughout his life he may have been "vacillating," as Pobedonostsev put it, in religion and politics, but he never wavered in his aims as a writer. As a boy he wrote to his brother that he intended to devote his life "to the solution of the mystery of man," and a few months before his death, he wrote in his notebook that his aim as a writer had been "to find man in man while preserving the fullest possible realism. . . . People," he declared, "call me a psychologist. It is not true. I am only a realist in the highest meaning of the word, that is, I depict all the depths of the human soul."

BIBLIOGRAPHY

BIOGRAPHY AND BIOGRAPHICAL STUDIES

Annenkov, P. V., *Literaturnye vospominania* (Literary Reminiscences), Moscow, 1960

Belchikov, N. F., *Dostoevsky v protsesse petrashevtsev* (Dostoevsky at the Trial of the Members of the Petrashevsky Group), Moscow, 1936

Dolinin, A. S. (editor), *F. M. Dostoevsky, materialy i issledovanie* (F. M. Dostoevsky, Materials and Studies), Leningrad, 1935

Dostoevskaya, Anna, *Dnevnik* (Diary), Moscow, 1923

Dostoevskaya, Anna, *Vospominania* (Reminiscences), Moscow-Leningrad, 1925

Dostoevskaya, Lyubov, *Fyodor Dostoevsky: A Study*, London, 1921, New Haven, Conn., 1922

Dostoevsky, Andrey, *Vospominania* (Reminiscences), Leningrad, 1930

Glavek, I. I., *Prestuplenie i nakazanie: neizdannie materialy* (*Crime and Punishment:* Unpublished Materials), Moscow, 1931

Grigorovich, D. V., *Literaturnye vospominania* (Literary Reminiscences), Leningrad, 1928

Grossman, L. P., *Materialy, bibliographia i kommentarii* (Materials, Bibliography and Commentaries), Moscow, 1922

Gus, M., *Idei i obrazy F. M. Dostoevskovo* (The Ideas and Images of F. M. Dostoevsky), Moscow, 1962

Ignatyeva, N. I., and Konshina, E. N., *Zapisnie tetradi F. M. Dostoevskovo* (Dostoevsky's Notebooks), Moscow, 1935

Kovalevskaya, Sofia, *Vospominania detstva* (Reminiscences of Childhood), Moscow, 1960

Mackiewicz, Stanislaw, *Dostoevsky*, translated by N. Hart, London, 1948

Meshchersky, Prince Vladimir, *Moi vospominania* (My Reminiscences), Petersburg, 1898

Miller, Orest, *Materialy dlya zhizneopisania F. M. Dostoevskovo* (Materials for a Dostoevsky Biography), Petersburg, 1883

Milyukov, A. P. (and others: Pochinkovskaya, V. T.; Savelyev, A.; Solovyov, Vsevolod; Trutovsky, Konstantin; Yanovsky, S. D.), *Vospominania* (Reminiscences), Petersburg, 1912

Nechaeva, V. S. (and others), *Opissanie rukopissey F. M. Dostoevskovo* (Description of Dostoevsky's Manuscripts), Moscow, 1957

Panaev, I. I., *Literaturnye vospominania* (Literary Reminiscences), Leningrad, 1928

Pănaeva, Avdotya, *Vospominania* (Reminiscences), Moscow, 1956

Slonim, Mark L'vovich, *Three Loves of Dostoevsky*, New York, 1955, London, 1957

Strakhov, Nikolai, *Biographia, pisma i zametki is zapisnoi knizhki Dostoevskovo* (Biography, Letters and Notes from Dostoevsky's Notebook), Petersburg, 1883

Suslova, Apollinaria (Pauline), *Gody blizosti s Dostoevskim* (Years of Intimacy with Dostoevsky), Moscow, 1928

Troyat, Henri, *Firebrand: The Life of Dostoevsky*, translated by Norbert Guterman, New York, 1946, London, 1947

Volotskoy, *Kronika roda Dostoevskovo* (Dostoevsky's Family Tree), Moscow, 1933

Yarmolinsky, Avrahm, *Dostoevsky: A Life*, New York, 1934

Yermilov, V. V., *F. M. Dostoevsky*, Moscow, 1956

CRITICAL STUDIES

Abraham, Gerald, *Dostoevsky*, London, 1936

Belkin, A. A., *Dostoevsky v russkoy kritike* (Dostoevsky in Russian Criticism), Moscow, 1956

Berdyaev, Nikolai, *Dostoevsky: An Interpretation*, London, 1934, New York, 1936

Berdyaev, Nikolai, *Mirsozertsanie Dostoevskovo* (Dostoevsky's Outlook on Life), Prague, 1922

Brodsky, N. L. (editor), *Tvorcheski put' Dostoevskovo* (Dostoevsky's Creative Path), Leningrad, 1924

Carr, Edward H., *Dostoevsky*, New York and London, 1931

Chulkov, G. I., *Dostoevsky i pleyada Belinskovo* (Dostoevsky and Belinsky's Distinguished Following), Leningrad, 1926

Chulkov, G. I., *Dostoevsky i utopicheski sotsialism* (Dostoevsky and Utopian Socialism), Moscow, 1929

Curle, Richard, *Characters of Dostoevsky*, London, 1950

Freud, Sigmund, *Dostoevsky and Parricide*, London, 1929

Gide, André, *Dostoevsky*, New York and London, 1949

Gorky, Maxim, *Stati* (Articles), Vols. 24-26 of Collected Works, Moscow, 1955

Gourfinkel, Nina, *Dostoievski notre contemporain*, Paris, 1961

Grossman, L. P., *Put' Dostoevskovo* (Dostoevsky's Path), Leningrad, 1924

Grossman, L. P., *Tvorchestvo Dostoevskovo* (Dostoevsky's Creative Work), Odessa, 1921

Guralnik, U. A., *Dostoevsky v literaturno-esteticheskoi bor'be 60-kh godov* (Dostoevsky in the Literary and Aesthetic Struggles of the 1860's), Moscow, 1959

Ivanov, V., *Dostoevsky i roman tragedia* (Dostoevsky and Novel-tragedy), Moscow, 1916

Kashina-Evreinova, A. A., *Podpolye geniya* (A Psycho-analytical Study of Genius), Petrograd, 1923

Kirpotin, V. Y., *Dostoevsky: tvorchesky put'* (Dostoevsky: Creative Path), Moscow, 1960

Kirpotin, V. Y., *Zapiski iz myortvovo doma* (*tvorchestvo Dostoevskovo*) (*The House of the Dead:* Dostoevsky's Creative Work), Moscow, 1959

Lavrin, Janko, *Dostoevsky: A Study*, London, 1943, New York, 1947

Lloyd, J. A., *Fyodor Dostoevsky*, London, 1943, New York, 1947

Merezhkovsky, D. S., *Prorok russkoy revolutsii* (Prophet of Russian Revolution), Petersburg, 1906

Merezhkovsky, D. S., *Tolstoy i Dostoevsky* (Tolstoy and Dostoevsky), Petersburg, 1913

Murry, John Middleton, *Fyodor Dostoevsky: A Critical Study*, Boston and London, 1924

Pereverzev, V. F., *Tvorchestvo Dostoevskovo* (Dostoevsky's Creative Work), Moscow, 1912

Rozanov, V. V., *Legenda o velikom inkvizitore* (The Legend of the Grand Inquisitor), Petersburg, 1894

Shestov, L., *Dostoevsky i Nitsche* (Dostoevsky and Nietzsche), Petersburg, 1914

Shklovsky, Victor, *Za i protiv: Zametki o Dostoevskom* (For and Against: Notes on Dostoevsky), Moscow, 1957

Simmons, Ernest J., *Dostoevsky: The Making of a Novelist*, London, 1950

Steiner, George, *Tolstoy or Dostoevsky*, New York, 1959, London, 1960

Strochkov, Y. M., *Sovremyonoye sovetskoye literaturovedenie o Dostoevskom* (Contemporary Soviet Literary Criticism of Dostoevsky), Moscow, 1959

Zander, L. A., *Dostoevsky*, London, 1948

Zaslavsky, D. O., *Zametki o yumore i satire v proizvedeniakh Dostoevskovo* (Notes on Humor and Satire in Dostoevsky's Works), Moscow, 1959

Zhukov, L. A., *Kritika kapitalizma u Dostoevskovo* (Criticism of Capitalism in Dostoevsky's Works), Moscow, 1938

Zweig, Stefan, *Three Masters: Balzac, Dickens, Dostoevsky*, New York and London, 1930

LETTERS

Dostoevsky i Turgenev: perepiska (Dostoevsky and Turgenev: Letters), Leningrad, 1928

Perepiska L. N. Tolstovo i N. N. Strakhova (Letters of L. N. Tolstoy and N. N. Strakhov), Petersburg, 1914

Pisma, A. S. Donlinin, editor, Vols. I-IV, Moscow, 1928-1934-1959

WORKS

F. M. Dostoevsky: chetyre stati 1847 goda. S predisloviyem V. S. Nechaevoi (Four articles of 1847. With introduction by V. S. Nechaev)

F. M. Dostoevsky: sobraniye sochineni v desyati tomakh (F. M. Dostoevsky: Collected Edition of Works in Ten Volumes), Moscow, 1956-1958

Polnoye sobranie khudozhestvennykh proizvedeni F. M. Dostoevskovo (Complete Edition of Dostoevsky's Artistic Works), Moscow-Leningrad, 1926-1930

Polnoye sobranie sochineni F. M. Dostoevskovo (Complete Edition of Dostoevsky's Works), Petersburg, 1883

INDEX